MUSIC AT GERMAN COURT$

CHANGING ARTISTIC PRI

# Music at German Courts
# 1715–1760

## CHANGING ARTISTIC PRIORITIES

*edited by*

Samantha Owens, Barbara M. Reul, *and* Janice B. Stockigt

THE BOYDELL PRESS

First published 2011
The Boydell Press, Woodbridge
Paperback edition 2015

ISBN 978 1 84383 598 1 hardback
ISBN 978 1 78327 058 3 paperback

The Boydell Press is an imprint of Boydell & Brewer Ltd
PO Box 9, Woodbridge, Suffolk IP12 3DF, UK
and of Boydell & Brewer Inc.
668 Mt Hope Avenue, Rochester, NY 14620–2731, USA
website: www.boydellandbrewer.com

A CIP catalogue record for this book is available
from the British Library

The publisher has no responsibility for the continued existence or accuracy
of URLs for external or third-party internet websites referred to in this book,
and does not guarantee that any content on such websites is,
or will remain, accurate or appropriate

Designed and Typeset in Garamond Premier by
The Stingray Office, Chorlton-cum-Hardy, Manchester

# Contents

# List of Tables

# Foreword

*Michael Talbot*

To anyone who comes from one of Europe's older monarchies –
I am thinking here of such states as Spain and Denmark – it seems almost
axiomatic that there is only one court, a royal court, per realm. As if by
definition, the principal seat of this court is always in, or adjacent to, the capital
city. Such states, and the linguistic and cultural communities that they govern, can
be described as monocentric. All of them exhibit – even today, when some have
become republics – a clear-cut difference between metropolitan and provincial,
centre and periphery.

Two major European communities ran, and even today still run, counter to
this model: the Italian and the German (from which one should detach the Austrian, or Habsburg, realm, which in most respects belongs to the first type). Such
communities were, until well into the nineteenth century, polycentric: divided
into a number of different states governed in different ways by rulers of different
types and ranks, and always subject – through the vagaries of warfare, marriage,
or dynastic succession – to change of boundaries and allegiance. Here, one can
speak of a number of different courts of varying size and opulence, each occupying
a different principal location, which, in the case of Germany is termed a *Residenz*
or *Residenzstadt*. All the courts within a common language community to a great
extent share a lifestyle and protocol, even if, in the case of Germany, the availability
of alternative foreign models – principally, the French and the Italian – provide
the opportunity for significant local inflection and personal initiative on the part
of rulers.

What is the nature of the relationship between this plurality of courts, large,
small, and intermediate? Is it competitive or is it co-operative? The answer, as this
book shows, is that it is both at the same time. Each court, including its dependent
institutions, such as its *Hofkapelle* and in some cases its opera, seeks to outdo its
neighbours. But those whose admiration is to be earned and who are the ultimate
arbiters of a court's success are the competitors themselves, so these are not to be
permanently antagonized or belittled. What evolves in such a situation – and
I have seen a comparable process develop in an area with which I am more familiar,
that of the Venetian *ospedali* – is a tacit, but nonetheless efficacious, *system* wherein
co-operation and competition are finely balanced. Courts allow their musicians,

where this is not too inconvenient to themselves, to travel to other courts for specific purposes, especially ones connected with state festivities. Senior musicians at different courts lend one another music so that it can be copied and utilized elsewhere. Music-loving rulers exchange tips on the capacities and characters of singers and instrumentalists. *Hofkapellen* keep a close watch on each other to ensure that they stay up with the latest trends and tastes. Jokingly (or at least half so), one might liken this complex, many-sided relationship to that between modern British — and, I am sure, not only British — universities, where from one perspective a zero-sum game is being played (one university's failure is another's opportunity), but from another perspective all stand in mutual support against outsiders.

The present book, with its distinguished international cast of authors, provides a conspectus of music at selected German courts in the central decades of the eighteenth century. To some extent, it revisits territory familiar from Renate Brockpähler's celebrated and invaluable *Handbuch zur Geschichte der Barockoper in Deutschland* (1964), but its area of coverage is much wider, ranging over the full spectrum of music at court: sacred and secular, large-scale and intimate. By its very nature, it extends beyond music to describe courtly life in general. It reminds us that the history of musical institutions is no less important than that of the musicians themselves: indeed, we cannot understand a Pisendel, a Quantz, or a Fasch without first having a rounded picture of their places of work. It is also a celebration of Germany's reacquired unity, which has, paradoxically, brought fresh opportunities to study and assimilate intellectually the variety and significant contrasts within the German cultural and professional experience during the century before the one that witnessed the country's first unification.

# Preface

THIS VOLUME – first conceived in early April 2005, when the three editors presented papers at the conference held during the 9. Internationale Fasch-Festtage (Ninth International Fasch Festival) in Zerbst/Anhalt, Germany – is the outcome of a round table titled 'Changing Artistic Priorities of German *Hofkapellen*, 1715–1760', given during the Twelfth Biennial International Conference on Baroque Music in Warsaw (2006). Michael Talbot, chairperson of the session, suggested we publish and enlarge our findings, and in the months that followed the basic structure and contents of the book gradually emerged, as we approached potential authors and received their reactions to the project. John Spitzer and Neal Zaslaw's excellent book on *The Birth of the Orchestra* (Oxford University Press, 2004) had filled many previous gaps, but we wanted to provide English-speaking readers with a series of detailed case studies of German *Hofkapellen* based on a close reading of archival sources. The final selection, a mixture of fifteen Protestant and Catholic courts of varying sizes with different artistic priorities, was largely dependent upon the willingness of scholars to share the results of their archival research, and, of course, in the first instance on the existence of relevant primary source material.

This book would not have been published without the encouragement and advice of Michael Talbot, together with the support of Peter Holman and Wolfgang Ruf, especially during the planning and preparation stages. We are also grateful for the direct financial assistance received from the Faculty of Music, the University of Melbourne, Luther College, University of Regina, and Jane Hardie, on behalf of the Network for Early European Research, funded by the Australian Research Council. Many other individuals lent their expertise, most importantly Sandra Borzikowski, who proofread the tables; Piotr Szymczak, who translated the chapter on the Saxon court in Poland; Konstanze Musketa, who helped with numerous points of German translation; Szymon Paczkowski and Robert Curry, who checked diacritics for us in Chapters 2 and 3; and Jóhannes Ágústsson, who kindly clarified citation issues for primary sources held in Dresden. Thanks also go to John Griffiths (University of Melbourne), Christine Thomas (Abteilung Musikwissenschaft, Institut für Musik, Martin-Luther-Universität Halle-Wittenberg), Susan Lochran (School of Music) and Sarah Evans (Architecture and Music Library), both of the University of Queensland, and the Alexander von Humboldt-Stiftung, Bonn. The work of each contributor to this project is acknowledged with gratitude, and we thank the staff at Boydell & Brewer, especially Catherine Larner, Michael Middeke, and Caroline Palmer, who have been the most solicitous and helpful of editors. Finally, Jeffrey Dean deserves much praise for his attention to detail when copy-editing and typesetting the manuscript.

*Samantha Owens*
*Barbara M. Reul*
*Janice B. Stockigt*

*Dedicated to the memory*
*of*
*Andrew D. McCredie*

# Editorial notes

## ORIGINAL TEXTS

Original spelling has been maintained wherever possible; however, words entirely in uppercase letters have been regularized as appropriate and '/' signs indicating line breaks or commas (in *Fraktur* texts) have been modernized. In historical texts the equal sign has been replaced with a hyphen. Italics are used to represent roman type in a *Fraktur* context.

## TRANSLATIONS

The initial translation of Alina Żórawska-Witkowska's chapter (in Polish) on the Saxon court of the Kingdom of Poland was undertaken by Piotr Szymczak, while the chapters originally written in German (by Dieter Kirsch, Ursula Kramer, Michael Maul, Rashid-S. Pegah, Bärbel Pelker, Bert Siegmund, Wolfgang Ruf, and Rüdiger Thomsen-Fürst) were translated into English by Barbara M. Reul and Samantha Owens. The authors who wrote in English (Mary Oleskiewicz, Samantha Owens, Barbara M. Reul, Janice B. Stockigt, and Steven Zohn) provided their own translations of source material originally in foreign languages.

## ORTHOGRAPHY AND TERMINOLOGY

The first names and surnames of individuals which are spelt variously in the primary source documents cited by authors have been regularized throughout the book as appropriate. Commonly used alternative versions of names in brackets have been provided immediately after the first mention of the chosen standardized form. When only surnames are given, the first name or names are unknown. Single quotation marks have been used consistently to denote a direct quotation (or translation, especially in the tables) from an original source. With regard to instruments, the terms kettledrums and timpani are used interchangeably throughout this volume.

## PITCH

The Helmholtz pitch notation system, which designates middle C as *c'*, is used.

## LIBRARY SIGLA AND ABBREVIATIONS

For reasons of consistency and ease for our largely English-speaking readership, we have adopted the RISM system of sigla (see also *Grove Music Online* <www.oxfordmusiconline. com>). All sigla used in this volume — some of which were newly devised — can be found in the List of Abbreviations, on pp. xviii–xix. For our German readers, we have occasionally also provided the German equivalent at the initial listing in the relevant chapter (for example, 'D-DSsa; in German sources usually HStAD').

## TABLES

All tables are given at the end of the chapter to which they pertain. Sources are given in the notes following each table, followed by specific endnotes; these may recur within a table.

The information provided by authors in the tables that detail membership of individual court music establishments is typically drawn from a number of primary or secondary sources and, therefore, should not be understood as strict transcriptions. The generic designation 'Court Music Establishment' was chosen to emphasize the contributions made by individuals and groups of performers who were active as musicians at the court but not regular members of the *Hofkapelle*. These included, for example, trumpeters, kettledrummers, and *Hautboisten* as well as persons who carried out musical duties while holding other appointments. The category 'Additional personnel' draws attention to individuals who provided general and specific support to various aspects of courtly musical life, including copyists, *Calcanten*, poets, and *Tanzmeister*.

In the numeric overview, every person listed in a specific column is counted only once; if he or she was skilled on more than one instrument, or both sang and played, references such as '*See* Violin *and* Oboe' denote their other area(s) of expertise. Within individual categories (for example, 'Violins' or 'Flutes'), the musicians have been listed in order of hierarchy wherever possible. In the case of individuals who served over extended periods of time and thus appear more than once in a table, this means that they are not necessarily listed in the same row across columns. Specific salaries have only been included in the tables for Chapters 2, 3, and 4; otherwise, readers are referred to the individual chapters for relevant information on this topic.

# Contributors

**Dieter Kirsch** studied German literature, history, and musicology in Munich prior to finishing a graduate performance degree in lute in Cologne. From 1968 to 2004, he was a faculty member at the Hochschule für Musik Würzburg, which he directed from 1995 to 2003. His scholarly work has focused on the history of music in Mainfranken as well as instruments of the lute family and their literature. Recent publications include the *Lexikon Würzburger Hofmusiker* (Würzburg: Echter, 2002), a classification of the mandora, and editions of works for lute by Santino Garsi da Parma (1542–1604?) and Sylvius Leopold Weiss (1686?–1750).

**Ursula Kramer** is a graduate of the Johannes Gutenberg-Universität Mainz. Her doctoral dissertation (1992) focused on the function of the opera orchestra in the nineteenth century, while her *Habilitationsschrift* (2001) was published as *Schauspielmusik am Hoftheater in Darmstadt, 1810–1918* (Mainz: Schott, 2008). Between 2001 and 2004, Kramer taught in Mainz as a university lecturer and subsequently held a temporary professorship at the Universität Göttingen. She returned to Mainz in 2007, where she was promoted to 'Ausserplanmässiger Professor' and elected president of the Christoph-Graupner-Gesellschaft (Christoph Graupner Society), Darmstadt.

**Michael Maul** studied musicology, journalism, and business administration in Leipzig between 1997 and 2002. From 2003 until 2006, he undertook a doctoral dissertation on baroque opera in Leipzig (1693–1720), supervised by Christoph Wolff at the Albert-Ludwigs-Universität Freiburg, which has recently been published by Rombach (2 vols., Freiburg im Breisgau, 2009). Since 2002, under the auspices of the Bach-Archiv Leipzig and the Ständige Konferenz Mitteldeutsche Barockmusik, he has systematically investigated the extant archival sources of central Germany, revealing much musicologically relevant material, including important Bach documents. He has worked on the staff of the Bach-Archiv Leipzig since 2004.

**Mary Oleskiewicz**, Associate Professor at the University of Massachusetts Boston, specializes in music and performance practice at the eighteenth-century Dresden and Berlin courts, the works of the Bach family, and the history of the flute. She is also an internationally acclaimed performer on historical flutes. As a Fellow of the Alexander von Humboldt-Stiftung, she resided in Berlin as Visiting Professor at the Universität der Künste from 2006 to 2008, while researching monographs on Quantz and music at the court of Frederick 'the Great'. Her publications include numerous scholarly essays, articles, and critical editions of music by Quantz for A-R Editions and Steglein Publishing, and music by Emanuel Bach for *Carl Philipp Emanuel Bach: The Complete Works* (Los Altos, Calif.: Packard Humanities Institute); her recordings of Baroque music appear on Naxos and Hungaroton Classic.

**Samantha Owens** graduated in 1996 with a PhD from Victoria University of Wellington (New Zealand) and currently holds a senior lectureship at the University of Queensland (Brisbane, Australia). In 2009/10 she was a Fellow of the Alexander von Humboldt-Stiftung based at the Institut für Musik, Martin-Luther-Universität Halle-Wittenberg, and from 2011 to 2017 is an Associate Investigator with the Australian Research Council Centre of Excellence for the History of Emotions. Her research focuses on early-eighteenth-century German court music, seventeenth-century *Singballett*, and the life and works of Johann Sigismund Cousser (1660–1727) and has appeared in a variety of publications, including *Early Music, Music & Letters, Eighteenth-Century Music*, and *Grove Music Online*. A-R Editions (Middleton, Wisc.) published her critical edition of *Adonis*, a German-language opera probably by Cousser, in 2009.

**Rashid-S. Pegah** has worked extensively in the field of early music in radio and as a freelance researcher. His numerous publications include articles on a variety of topics, including the operas of Georg Philipp Telemann and musical life at the courts of Sophie Charlotte of Brandenburg-Prussia and Christian Ernst of Brandenburg-Culmbach-Bayreuth. He was co-author of the entry on Ruggiero Fedeli in *Die Musik in Geschichte und Gegenwart* (2nd edn) and in 1999 acted as co-curator for an exhibition on Sophie Charlotte for the Stiftung Preußische Schlösser und Gärten Berlin-Brandenburg. Currently, he is undertaking study in history and philology at the Julius-Maximilians-Universität Würzburg.

**Bärbel Pelker** joined the Forschungsstelle Mannheimer Hofkapelle in 1990 after finishing her doctoral thesis, which focused on the German concert-overture in the nineteenth century, and since 2006 has worked at the Forschungsstelle Südwestdeutsche Hofmusik, both hosted by the Heidelberger Akademie der Wissenschaft (Heidelberg Academy of Sciences and Humanities). Her scholarly activity includes numerous contributions to the series Quellen und Studien zur Geschichte der Mannheimer Hofkapelle and Musik der Mannheimer Hofkapelle, while her facsimile edition of *Günther von Schwarzburg*, a *Singspiel* by Ignaz Holzbauer, appeared as the first volume of Quellen zur Musikgeschichte in Baden-Württemberg in 2000. She was the specialist adviser for music in southern Germany during the eighteenth century for *Die Musik in Geschichte und Gegenwart* (2nd edn).

**Barbara M. Reul** is Associate Professor of Musicology at Luther College, University of Regina (Canada). She is the recipient of the 2005 Fasch Prize of the City of Zerbst, has served as president of the Internationale Fasch-Gesellschaft (International Fasch Society), Zerbst since 2008, and maintains the Society's bilingual website, <www.fasch.net>. Recent publications include *Musik an der Zerbster Residenz*, Fasch-Studien, 10 (co-edited with Konstanze Musketa; Beeskow: Ortus, 2008), *The Unknown Schubert* (co-edited with Lorraine Byrne Bodley; Aldershot: Ashgate, 2008), and an article on employment practices at the court of Anhalt-Zerbst during the eighteenth century (forthcoming in a volume edited by Sterling Murray; Ann Arbor, Mich.: Steglein, 2010).

**Wolfgang Ruf** studied musicology in Freiburg im Breisgau under Hans Heinrich Eggebrecht and Rolf Dammann, graduating in 1974 with a doctoral thesis on the contemporary reception of Mozart's *The Marriage of Figaro*. Between 1974–83, he was an academic assistant at the Universität Freiburg's Institute of Musicology and in 1983–85 directed the project *Handwörterbuch der musikalischen Terminologie*. He completed his *Habilitationsschrift* on *Modernes Musiktheater: Studien zu seiner Geschichte und Typologie* in 1984 and subsequently held posts as Professor of Musicology at the Universität Mainz (1985–94) and the Martin-Luther-Universität Halle-Wittenberg (1994–2007). From 1998 until 2007, Ruf served as editorial director of the *Hallische Händel-Ausgabe* (with Terence Best).

**Bert Siegmund** studied musicology at the Martin-Luther-Universität Halle-Wittenberg with Bernd Baselt and Günter Fleischhauer, graduating in 1990 with a *Diplomarbeit* (MA thesis) focusing on the instrumental works of Gottfried Heinrich Stölzel. At present he is working as a musicologist for the Stiftung Kloster Michaelstein, preparing a thematic catalogue of Stölzel's works, carrying out regional musicological research, and preparing performing editions.

**Janice B. Stockigt** is a Principal Fellow of the University of Melbourne, where her PhD was awarded the inaugural Chancellor's Prize (1994). Since then she has held two research grants from the Australian Research Council. Her monograph *Jan Dismas Zelenka (1679–1745): A Bohemian Musician at the Court of Dresden* (Oxford University Press, 2000) was awarded the Derek Allen Prize for Musicology of the British Academy and the Woodward Medal of the University of Melbourne. Her continuing investigations into the musical life of Dresden during the first half of the eighteenth century have led to several publications.

**Rüdiger Thomsen-Fürst** holds an MA degree from the Universität Hamburg in historical and systematic musicology, as well as modern German literature. His doctoral dissertation examined the musical life of Rastatt during the eighteenth century. In 1996, he joined the Forschungsstelle Mannheimer Hofkapelle and since 2006 has worked at the Forschungs-stelle Südwestdeutsche Hofmusik, both hosted by the Heidelberger Akademie der Wissenschaft (Heidelberg Academy of Sciences and Humanities). His research focuses on *Hofkapellen* in southwestern Germany during the eighteenth century.

**Michael Talbot** is Emeritus Professor of Music at the University of Liverpool and a Fellow of the British Academy. He has published extensively on Italian music of the first half of the eighteenth century and takes a special interest in the life and music of Vivaldi. He has edited several of Vivaldi's instrumental and sacred vocal works for the new critical edition published by Ricordi.

**Alina Żórawska-Witkowska** studied musicology at the Uniwersytet Warszawski (University of Warsaw) between 1967 and 1972 under Zofia Lissa, completing a doctoral dissertation on music at the court of Stanisław August Poniatowski in 1985 and, in 1998, a postdoctoral dissertation on music at the Polish court of August the Strong. She is currently a professor at Warsaw University's Musicological Institute, where she directs the general music history department. In 1984/85, she held a residential scholarship from the Italian government at the Università degli Studi di Bologna. Her research focuses on baroque and classical music history, in particular the musical culture of Poland and the dissemination of Italian opera, and she has undertaken extensive archival work in Dresden.

**Steven Zohn** is Associate Professor of Music History at Temple University (Philadelphia) and a noted performer on historical flutes. He is the author of *Music for a Mixed Taste: Style, Genre, and Meaning in Telemann's Instrumental Works* (Oxford University Press, 2008), and of numerous studies focusing on music of the German late baroque. Among his most recent publications is an edition of C. P. E. Bach's flute and keyboard duos for *Carl Philipp Emanuel Bach: The Complete Works*.

# List of Abbreviations

## INSTRUMENTS

| | | | |
|---|---|---|---|
| bn | bassoon | rec | recorder |
| cb | contrabass | timp | timpani (kettledrums) |
| cl | clarinet | tpt | trumpet |
| fl | flute | va | viola |
| hn | *Waldhorn* | va d'am | viola d'amore |
| hpd | harpsichord | vc | violoncello |
| kbd | keyboard | vdg | viola da gamba |
| ob | oboe | vn | violin |
| org | organ | | |

## LIBRARIES AND ARCHIVES

| | |
|---|---|
| D-AN | Ansbach, Staatliche Bibliothek (Schloßbibliothek) |
| D-B | Berlin, Staatsbibliothek zu Berlin – Preußischer Kulturbesitz |
| D-Bga | Berlin, Stiftung Preußischer Kulturbesitz, Geheimes Staatsarchiv |
| D-BAa | Bamberg, Bayerisches Staatsarchiv |
| D-BHa | Bayreuth, Stadtarchiv |
| D-BHu | Bayreuth, Universitätsbibliothek |
| D-Ddpa | Dresden, Dompfarramt |
| D-Dl | Dresden, Sächsische Landesbibliothek – Staats- und Universitätsbibliothek |
| D-Dla | Dresden, Sächsisches Hauptstaatsarchiv |
| D-DEla | Dessau, Landeshauptarchiv Sachsen-Anhalt, Abteilung Dessau |
| D-DS | Darmstadt, Universitäts- und Landesbibliothek |
| D-DSa | Darmstadt, Stadtarchiv |
| D-DSsa | Darmstadt, Hessisches Staatsarchiv |
| D-DÜha | Düsseldorf, Nordrhein-Westfälisches Hauptstaatsarchiv |
| D-ERu | Erlangen, Universitätsbibliothek |
| D-FRu | Freiburg im Breisgau, Universitätsbibliothek |

| | |
|---|---|
| D-Gs | Göttingen, Niedersächsische Staats- und Universitätsbibliothek |
| D-GOl | Gotha, Forschungs- und Landesbibliothek, Musiksammlung |
| D-GOtsa | Gotha, Thüringisches Staatsarchiv |
| D-HAf | Halle an der Saale, Hauptbibliothek und Archiv der Franckeschen Stiftungen |
| D-HAu | Halle an der Saale, Martin-Luther-Universität, Universitäts- und Landesbibliothek Sachsen-Anhalt |
| D-HEu | Heidelberg, Ruprecht-Karls-Universität, Universitätsbibliothek |
| D-KA | Karlsruhe, Badische Landesbibliothek |
| D-KAg | Karlsruhe, Generallandesarchiv |
| D-Mbs | Munich, Bayerische Staatsbibliothek |
| D-Mhsa | Munich, Bayerisches Hauptstaatsarchiv |
| D-MGs | Marburg, Hessisches Staatsarchiv Marburg |
| D-MHrm | Mannheim, Reiss-Engelhorn-Museen, Theater- und Musikgeschichtliche Sammlungen |
| D-MHsa | Mannheim, Stadtarchiv |
| D-MHu | Mannheim, Universitätsbibliothek |
| D-RT | Rastatt, Bibliothek des Friedrich-Wilhelm-Gymnasiums |
| D-RUhb | Rudolstadt, Historische Bibliothek |
| D-RUkb | Rudolstadt, Stadtbibliothek |
| D-RUl | Rudolstadt, Thüringisches Staatsarchiv |
| D-Sha | Stuttgart, Hauptstaatsarchiv |
| D-Sl | Stuttgart, Württembergische Landesbibliothek |
| D-SHm | Sondershausen, Schloßmuseum |
| D-SHs | Sondershausen, Stadt- und Kreisbibliothek 'Johann Karl Wezel' (in D-SHm) |
| D-SHst | Sondershausen, Evangelisch-lutherisches Pfarramt St Trinitatis, Bibliothek |
| D-W | Wolfenbüttel, Herzog-August-Bibliothek |
| D-Wa | Wolfenbüttel, Niedersächsisches Staatsarchiv |
| D-WERa | Wernigerode, Landeshauptarchiv Sachsen-Anhalt, Zweigstelle Wernigerode |
| D-WÜd | Würzburg, Diözesanarchiv |
| D-WÜsa | Würzburg, Stadtarchiv |
| D-WÜst | Würzburg, Staatsarchiv |
| D-ZEo | Zerbst, Gymnasium Francisceum, Historische Bibliothek |
| D-ZEsb | Zerbst, Evangelisches Pfarramt St Bartholomäi, Bibliothek |
| I-Bc | Bologna, Museo Internazionale e Biblioteca della Musica (before 2004, Civico Museo Bibliografico Musicale) |
| I-Rar | Rome, Archivum Romanum Societatis Iesu |
| PL-Kc | Cracow, Muzeum Narodowe w Krakowie, Biblioteka Książąt Czartoryskich |

| PL-Kj | Cracow, Biblioteka Jagiellońska |
| PL-KO | Kórnik, Biblioteka Kórnicka Polskiej Akademii Nauk |
| PL-Wagad | Warsaw, Archiwum Główne Akt Dawnych |
| US-Wc | Washington, D.C., Library of Congress |

# 1

# 'Das gantze *Corpus* derer *musici*renden Personen': An Introduction to German *Hofkapellen*

## *Samantha Owens and Barbara M. Reul*

WHAT WAS MUSICAL LIFE at German courts really like during the first six decades of the eighteenth century? Securing a permanent post in a court music establishment could mean job security, as well as a steady income and a host of other benefits — such as Johann Sebastian Bach and Georg Philipp Telemann had enjoyed in Weimar and Köthen and in Eisenach respectively prior to their appointments in the *Freie Reichstädte* (Imperial Free Cities) of Leipzig and Hamburg. And yet despite the fact that the political landscape of what we now call Germany featured countless small-to-medium-sized courts similar to those experienced first-hand by Bach and Telemann, general music histories tend to focus on the *Hofkapellen* of Berlin and Dresden, primarily because of an interesting connection to the *Thomaskantor* and his oeuvre.[1]

In his pioneering study of court society during the early modern period, the so-

---

[1] Recent case studies which have focused on music at German courts during this period but are not covered in this volume include, for example: Christiane Engelbrecht, 'Die Hofkapelle des Landgrafen von Hessen-Kassel', *Zeitschrift des Vereins für Hessische Geschichte und Landeskunde*, 68 (1957), 141–73; Gustav Bereths, *Die Musikpflege am kurtrierischen Hofe zu Koblenz-Ehrenbreitstein* (Mainz: Schott, 1964); Robert Münster, 'Die Musik am Hofe Max Emanuels', in *Kurfürst Max Emanuel, Bayern und Europa um 1700*, ed. Hubert Glaser (Munich: Hirmer, 1976), 1: 295–316; Klaus Häfner, 'Johann Caspar Ferdinand Fischer und die Rastatter Hofkapelle: Ein Kapitel südwestdeutscher Musikgeschichte im Zeitalter des Barock', in *J. C. F. Fischer in seiner Zeit: Tagungsbericht Rastatt 1988*, ed. Ludwig Finscher, Quellen und Studien zur Geschichte der Mannheimer Hofkapelle, 3 (Frankfurt am Main: Peter Lang, 1994), 137–79; Ute Omonsky, *Musik am Rudolstädter Hof: Die Entwicklung der Hofkapelle vom 17. Jahrhundert bis zum Beginn des 20. Jahrhunderts* (Rudolstadt: Thüringer Landesmuseum Heidecksburg, 1997); Christofer Schweisthal, *Die Eichstätter Hofkapelle bis zu ihrer Auflösung 1802: Ein Beitrag zur Geschichte der Hofmusik an süddeutschen Residenzen* (Tutzing: Schneider, 1997); Claudia Valder-Knechtges, 'Die kurfürstliche Hofmusik im 18. Jahrhundert', in *Der Riss im Himmel: Clemens August und seine Epoche*, ed. Frank Günter Zehnder (Cologne: DuMont, 2000), 151–70; Juliane Riepe, '"Essential to the reputation and magnificence of such a high-ranking prince": Ceremonial and Italian Opera at the Court of Clemens August of Cologne and Other German Courts', in *Italian Opera in Central Europe*, 1: *Institutions and Ceremonies*, ed. Melania Bucciarelli, Norbert Dubowy, and Reinhard Strohm (Berlin: Berliner Wissenschafts-Verlag,

ciologist Norbert Elias noted that the term 'court' changed its meaning depending on the period.[2] Different types of court emerged in the German-speaking lands of the Holy Roman Empire during the seventeenth and early eighteenth centuries; the historian Volker Bauer has categorized these as the 'zeremonieller Hof' (ceremonial court), the 'geselliger Hof' (sociable court), the 'Musenhof' (court of muses), the 'Kaiserhof'' (imperial court), and the 'hausväterlicher Hof'.[3] Similarly, John Spitzer and Neal Zaslaw have concluded that 'orchestras . . . meant many things to many people, and their meanings changed over time'. It is, therefore, no surprise that the birth of the orchestra was 'not an event, but a process' — the practical, day-to-day aspects of which took varied forms, as can be seen in this volume.[4]

At first glance it might seem that musical ensembles at German courts were as diverse as the Empire's kaleidoscopic political landscape; however, set against this complex backdrop, there were certain commonalities between the music establishments employed at individual courts, as well as differences. A brief description of how *Hofkapellen* generally functioned in the German-speaking lands during the first half of the eighteenth century, touching upon key terminology used in the volume, will also expose a number of popular misconceptions that surround the nature of musical life at German courts.[5]

Although the term 'Kapelle', like its parent word in Italian, 'cappella', was used in a variety of senses in the context of German court music throughout the seventeenth and eighteenth centuries, with or without the prefix 'Hof' (court) it

2006), 147–75; and Maik Richter, *Die Hofmusik in Köthen: Von den Anfängen (um 1690) bis zum Tod Fürst Leopolds von Anhalt-Köthen (1728)* (Saarbrücken: Müller, 2008).

[2] Norbert Elias, *The Court Society*, trans. Edmund Jephcott (New York: Pantheon, 1983), 36 n. 2 [German original, *Die höfische Gesellschaft: Untersuchungen zur Soziologie des Königtums und der höfischen Aristokratie* (Neuwied: Luchterhand, 1969)]. For a critique of Elias's theories, see Jeroen Duindam, *Myths of Power: Norbert Elias and the Early Modern European Court* (Amsterdam: Amsterdam University Press, 1995), and the same author's 'Norbert Elias und der frühneuzeitliche Hof: Versuch einer Kritik und Weiterführung', *Historische Anthropologie*, 6 (1998), 370–87.

[3] Volker Bauer, *Die höfische Gesellschaft in Deutschland von der Mitte des 17. bis zum Ausgang des 18. Jahrhunderts: Versuch einer Typologie* (Tübingen: Niemeyer, 1983), 55–80. The term 'hausväterlich' generally denotes a court characterized by prudent expenditure, in which the ruler assumes the role of a responsible patriarch, with his household acting as a model for both his courtiers and his subjects more generally; see Bauer, *Die höfische Gesellschaft*, 66 ff.

[4] John Spitzer and Neal Zaslaw, *The Birth of the Orchestra: History of an Institution, 1650–1815* (Oxford: Oxford University Press, 2004), 530–31. Their volume was preceded by only one other specialized study in English, Adam Carse's *The Orchestra in the XVIIIth Century* (Cambridge: Heffer, 1940).

[5] The decision to focus this volume on German courts to the exclusion of music establishments elsewhere in the Holy Roman Empire was determined by the present authors' own areas of expertise. Readers interested in the imperial *Hofkapelle* in Vienna are referred to Ludwig von Köchel, *Die kaiserliche Hof-Musikkapelle in Wien von 1543 bis 1867* (Vienna, 1869); Friedrich W. Riedel, *Kirchenmusik am Hof Karls VI. (1711–40): Untersuchungen zum Verhältnis von Zeremoniell und musikalischen Stil im Barockzeitalter* (Munich: Katzbichler, 1977) [Diss., Universität Mainz, 1971]; and Eleanor Selfridge-Field, 'The Viennese Court Orchestra in the Time of Caldara', in *Antonio Caldara: Essays on his Life and Times*, ed. Brian W. Pritchard (Aldershot: Scolar Press, 1987), 115–51.

first and foremost referred to a musical venue – the chapel – rather than to an ensemble. As Julius Bernhard von Rohr explained in 1733 (perhaps partly tongue-in-cheek),

> Die Hof-Capellen sind von vielen Jahren her an den allermeisten Orten also erbauet, daß Fürstliche Personen aus ihren Gemächern sich trockenes Fusses in die Kirche begeben, und dem Wort Gottes daselbst zuhören können.

> *Hofkapellen* [court chapels] have for many years and in most places been built in a way that allows princely persons to proceed from their apartments to church without getting their feet wet, and listen to the Word of God there.[6]

Over time, however, 'Kapelle' came also to denote the musicians who commonly performed in that space, in much the same way that the orchestra derived its name. Thus the opening of the entry 'Capelle' in Johann Heinrich Zedler's *Universal-Lexicon* (1731–54) reads: 'Capelle, bedeutet 1. In grosser Herren Hof Kirchen den Ort wo man *musici*ret[;] 2. Das gantze *Corpus* derer daselbst *musici*renden Personen' (*Kapelle*, means 1. In the court churches of grand lords, the place where one performs music; 2. The entire body of people performing music in that said place).[7] The nomenclature used to describe the musicians in a collective sense could, and did, differ widely from court to court, but *Hofkapelle* and *Kapelle* were among the most commonly used labels.[8] The phrase 'Hof-Music' or 'Hof-Musique', often rendered at the time (and in modern German) as *Hofmusik*, could also refer to this same group of vocalists and instrumentalists. It was, however, sometimes used in a slightly broader sense to include the *Hoftrompeter und Hofpaucker* (court trumpeters and kettledrummers) and other musicians at court as well, where these were not considered official members of the *Hofkapelle*. But, as Martin Ruhnke has pointed out, there were simply no clear-cut definitions of these terms.[9]

Members of a *Hofkapelle* were appointed, officially at least, by the ruler of a court, whether *König* (king), *Kurfürst* (elector), *Herzog* (duke), *Fürst* (prince),

[6] Julius Bernhard von Rohr, *Einleitung zur Ceremoniel-Wissenschafft der grossen Herren*, 2nd edn (Berlin, 1733), 72, §22.

[7] Johann Heinrich Zedler, *Grosses vollständiges Universal-Lexicon aller Wissenschaften und Künste* (Halle and Leipzig, 1731–54), 64 vols., 'Capelle', v (1733): 623. This source contains numerous articles that had previously appeared in specialized lexicons.

[8] The early 'Kapelle' had its roots in the 'gemischte Kantorei' (an ensemble that comprised singers and instrumentalists), see Erich Reimer, *Die Hofmusik in Deutschland 1500–1800: Wandlungen einer Institution*, Taschenbücher zur Musikwissenschaft, 112 (Wilhelmshaven: Noetzel, 1991), 22–9.

[9] For a brief overview of the various terms used in this context, see Martin Ruhnke, 'Kapelle', III: 'Von der *Kapelle* zum Orchester', in *Die Musik in Geschichte und Gegenwart: allgemeine Enzyklopädie der Musik*, 2nd rev. edn (Kassel: Bärenreiter, 1994–2008), Sachteil, v: 1788–97, at 1794. As time went on, in Germany the term *Kapelle* 'was applied to any organized musical group, of voices or of instruments, in the church, the concert hall, or the opera house' (Alex Lingas, 'Chapel', *The Oxford Dictionary of Music Online*, <www.oxfordmusic.com>), and by the nineteenth century 'denoted a small dance band or brass ensemble' (Adele Poindexter and Barbara H. Haggh, 'Chapel', *Grove Music Online*, <www.oxfordmusic.com> accessed 8 October 2009).

*Fürstbischof* (prince-bishop), *Landgraf* (landgrave), or *Markgraf* (margrave). Lesser noblemen often also occasionally employed their own *Kapellen*, albeit on a smaller scale, as was the case with both the Saxon prime minister Count Heinrich von Brühl and field marshal Count Jakob Heinrich von Flemming, to name but two examples.[10] While the latter ensembles were clearly of a superior quality and at times even served to reinforce music performed at the Dresden court, according to Johann Mattheson in 1725,

> fast jeder *Grand Seigneur en diminutif,* und jeder Dorff-Herrscher gleich ein Paar *Violons, Hautbois, Cors de chasse &c.* zur Aufwartung um sich haben will, doch so, daß sie zugleich eine voll-jährige Liverey tragen, Schuputzen, Perüken pudern, hinter der Kutsche stehen, und Laquaien Besoldung so wohl, als Bewirthung, geniessen; dabey beßere Musicanten agiren sollen, als alle Kunst-Pfeiffer. Da betrachte mir ein Mensch, ob solche Bediente wohl was rechtes wissen können?

> almost every *Grand Seigneur en diminutif* and every village chieftain wants to have at his service a pair of violins, oboes, hunting horns, and so on, but at the same time requires that they wear an all-season uniform, polish shoes, powder wigs, stand behind the coach, and enjoy a lackey's salary as well as board; and yet, better musicians should be doing this, rather than all these *Kunstpfeifer.* That makes one wonder whether such servants really have the proper qualifications?[11]

The majority of musicians employed at the larger *Hofkapellen* discussed in this volume were clearly of a considerably higher standard than those dismissed by Mattheson as glorified lackeys. Although the terminology used to describe them differed from court to court, among the main body of musicians the highest level of musical proficiency was expected from a *Cammermusicus* (chamber musician), a singer or instrumentalist whose rank allowed him (or her) to gain entrance to, and thus perform in, the private chambers of their patron. Lesser-ranked musicians were generally not permitted in these quarters, although there were undoubtedly exceptions to the rule. Lower down in the hierarchy were the regular *Hofmusici* (ordinary court musicians), followed by trainees and apprentices of various kinds (such as *Kapellknaben,* 'Accessisten', or 'Scholaren'), as well as others who augmented the *Kapelle* from time to time. The latter could include unpaid volunteers,

---

[10] See Ulrike Kollmar, *Gottlob Harrer (1703–55), Kapellmeister des Grafen Heinrich von Brühl am sächsisch-polnischen Hof und Thomaskantor in Leipzig,* ed. Wolfgang Ruf, Schriften zur mitteldeutschen Musikgeschichte, 12 (Beeskow: Ortus, 2006), and Szymon Paczkowski, 'Muzyka na dworze marszałka Jakuba Henryka Flemminga (1667–1728)' [Music at the Court of Marshal Jacob Heinrich Flemming], *Środowiska kulturotwórcze i kontakty kulturalne Wielkiego Księstwa Litewskiego od XV do XIX wieku* [The Circles of Cultural Creativity in the Grand Duchy of Lithuania from the Sixteenth until the Nineteenth Century], ed. Urszula Augustyniak (Warsaw: Wydawnictwo Neriton, 2009), 67–82.

[11] Johann Mattheson, *Critica musica* (Hamburg, 1725), II: 169–70 n. a. A *Kunstpfeifer* was a civic musician required to be proficient on a wide selection of instruments, both wind and strings.

generally students instructed in music by the salaried court musicians, whose tuition fees were often subsidized by the court as a 'Lehrgeld'. Other individuals supporting the *Hofkapelle* on a regular basis (and integral to their continuing success) were music copyists (*Notisten*), instrument makers and tuners, *Kapelldiener* (general servants associated with the ensemble), the *Hofkirchner* (caretaker), and the lowly *Calcant* who operated the organ bellows.[12] Some of these employees may have occasionally performed with the *Kapelle*, as was also the case with the court *Tanzmeister*, who was sometimes called upon to serve as a violinist.[13]

Not all courts divided their principal musicians into *Cammermusici* and *Hofmusici*.[14] One example of this approach is provided by an extant 'Hof-Ordnung' of the Elector-Archbishop of Cologne, Joseph Clemens (1671–1723), which details the ceremonial associated with, and the members of, his courtly household in Bonn for the year 1717.[15] Recorded under the heading 'Die Churfürstl. Hof-*Musicanten*' (the electoral court musicians) are the names of ten to twelve '*Vocalisten*' (vocalists) and sixteen '*Instrumentalisten*' (instrumentalists), clearly not divided by rank, at least on the face of this evidence. This list, reproduced in Johann Christian Lünig's *Theatrum ceremoniale historico-politicum* (Leipzig, 1719–20), provides, in effect, a typical example of a German *Hofkapelle* in the early eighteenth century, albeit one in miniature. Two further categories of musicians employed at the court follow the 'Hof-*Musicant*en': one 'Ober-Trompeter' (chief trumpeter), six trumpeters, and a 'Paucker' (kettledrummer); plus six 'Hof-*Hautbois*' (court *Hautboisten*, see below). Then, almost at the very end of this hierarchy, comes the '*Calcant* von der Hof-*Musique*'.[16]

To give an approximate indication of the overall status of these musicians, a summary of the 'Chur-Cöllnische Hof-Aufwartungs-*Instruction*' outlines the strict regulations regarding the extent to which individual courtiers (as well as

---

[12] Regarding the latter position, see Walter Salmen, *Calcanten und Orgelzieherinnen: Geschichte eines 'niederen' Dienstes* (Hildesheim: Olms, 2007).

[13] Generally not considered part of the *Hofkapelle*, the *Tanzmeister* nevertheless frequently worked in close proximity to the musicians; at the Württemberg court in 1711, for example, the dancing master's contract required his attendance at court balls in order to ensure the orchestra adhered to the proper tempos for each dance. See Samantha Owens, 'Not Always the Same Minuets': Dance at the Württemberg Court, 1662–1711', *The Court Historian*, 15.2 (2010), 133–44. See also Monika Fink, 'Die Bedeutung der Tanzmeister im 18. Jahrhundert', in *Tanz und Musik im ausgehenden 17. und im 18. Jahrhundert* (Blankenburg am Harz: Kultur- und Forschungsstätte Michaelstein, 1993), 31–44, and Walter Salmen, *Der Tanzmeister: Geschichte und Profile eines Berufes vom 14. bis zum 19. Jahrhundert* (Hildesheim: Olms, 1997).

[14] See, for example, the discussions of the *Hofkapellen* of Saxony-Dresden and Hesse-Darmstadt in Chapters 2 and 12 respectively.

[15] For a general discussion for the role of music in court ceremonial, see Juliane Riepe, 'Hofmusik in der Zeremonialwissenschaft des 18. Jahrhunderts', *Händel-Jahrbuch*, 49 (2003), 27–52.

[16] Johann Christian Lünig, *Theatrum ceremoniale historico-politicum, oder Historisch- und politischer Schau-Platz*, 2 vols. (Leipzig, 1719–20), II, 'Churfürst Joseph Clementis zu Cölln Hof-Ordnung zu Bonn de Anno 1717', 1512–21, under 'Verzeichnuß Der von Ihr. Churfürstl. Durchl. zu Cölln, u. Unsers gnädigsten Herrns Hof-*Suite*', at 1520–21. The exact number of vocalists is unclear, on account of the possible omission of two commas; see n. 25 below.

visitors) were permitted, according to rank, to venture within the palace.[17] The six locations where members of the court were to wait upon the elector were:

1. Unter der Stiegen das *Vestibule*, oder Vorplatz des Haupt-Aufgangs.
2. Der Obere Vor-Saal vor dem Haupt-Saal oder Stiege.
3. Der *Guarde*-Saal.
4. Die Churfürstl. Ritter-Stube.
5. Die Churfürstl. *Antichambre*.
6. Das Churfürstl. *Retirade*-Zimmer.

1. Under the staircase [of] the vestibule, or forecourt of the main entrance.
2. The upper anteroom before the main hall or staircase.
3. The Guards' Hall.
4. The electoral Knights' Hall.
5. The electoral antechamber.
6. The electoral 'retiring' room.[18]

Among those given permission to wait in the *Ritterstube* were 'alle Churfürstl. Hof-*Musicant*en, Trompeter und Paucker' (all of the electoral court musicians, trumpeters and kettledrummers).[19] This indicates that they held an intermediate-to-high ranking within the court hierarchy as a whole.[20]

As was the case with the *Hofkapelle* in Bonn, the majority of German *Hofka-pellen* employed vocalists, the number and nature of which were dependent upon numerous factors. These included the court's adherence to tradition, religious denomination (whether Lutheran, Catholic, or Calvinist) and level of religious observance, budgetary constraints, and — perhaps above all — the artistic priorities of the ruler in question, which in some cases displayed a sharp inclination towards

[17] Lünig, *Theatrum ceremoniale*, 1513. On this topic, see also John Samuel Klingensmith, *The Utility of Splendor: Ceremony, Social Life, and Architecture at the Court of Bavaria, 1600–1800* (Chicago and London: The University of Chicago Press, 1993).

[18] Lünig, *Theatrum ceremoniale*, 1513. The '*Retirade*-Zimmer' appears to have been the private room of the elector-archbishop, although this sixth level is later also referred to in the 'Hof-Ordnung' as the 'Churfürstl. Stuhl-Zimmer, wo der Churfürstl. Thron oder *Baldachin* ist' (Electoral throne room, where the electoral throne or baldachin [canopy of state] is [located]), 1515. See also Christoph Brandhuber, '"Recreatio Principis": Fürsterzbischof Franz Anton Fürst von Harrach [r. 1709–27] und seine *Retirade*', *Österreichische Zeitschrift für Kunst und Denkmalpflege*, 63.1/2 (2009), 118–25.

[19] Lünig, *Theatrum ceremoniale*, 1514. Interestingly, this document also lists 22 November (St Cecilia's Day) as 'Der Hof-*Musicant*en-Fest[tag]' (the court musicians' feast day), which ranked as one of the nine church feast days among the fifth level of 'Churfürstliche Hof-Capellen-Täge' (electoral court chapel days), the sixth being the lowest level (1512–13).

[20] For a discussion of the social status of German court musicians around this time, see Christoph-Hellmut Mahling, 'The Origin and Social Status of the Court Orchestral Musician in the Eighteenth and Early Nineteenth Century in Germany', in *The Social Status of the Pro-fessional Musician from the Middle Ages to the 19th Century*, ed. Walter Salmen, trans. Herbert Kaufman and Barbara Reisner (New York: Pendragon Press, 1983), 219–64 [German original, 'Herkunft und Sozialstatus des höfischen Orchestermusikers im 18. und frühen 19. Jahrhundert in Deutschland', in *Der Sozialstatus des Berufsmusikers vom 17. bis 19. Jahrhundert* (Kassel: Bärenreiter, 1971)].

either sacred or secular vocal music. It is clearly impossible to describe the 'typical' make up of the forces employed for sacred repertoire at German courts during the first six decades of the eighteenth century. Music presented in the *Hofkirche* could be performed by adult vocalists (at some courts a mixture of females and males, sometimes including falsettists and castratos) or young boys.[21] The latter were generally labelled either *Choralknaben* or, more usually, *Kapellknaben*, and were sometimes expected not only to sing but also to perform on instruments when required. In certain locations, including, for example, the Catholic court of Dresden, *Kapellknaben* were primarily vocalists who were also taught instruments, and served as altar boys.[22] Yet at a number of other German courts *Kapellknaben* were trained and employed first and foremost as instrumentalists. For this reason we have avoided the common English translation of the term *Kapellknaben* as 'choirboys' throughout the volume. At least one court, that of Württemberg-Stuttgart, also employed young women as trainee vocalists, generally referred to by the title 'Lehr-Discantistinnen', but occasionally also as *Kapellknaben*. At Lutheran courts, one male vocalist usually held the position of *Hofkantor*.[23] The post of *Hoforganist* was also traditionally (but not exclusively) linked to service in the court chapel.[24]

Among the various secular vocal genres in vogue at German courts during this time, opera and the serenata were particularly popular genres for the celebration of festive events such as princely birthdays and name-day celebrations, or *Heimführungen* (marking the arrival of a bride at her new court). It was on such occasions that vocalists and instrumentalists joined forces to present especially lavish performances of both sacred and secular music – although these two groups of musicians frequently performed together in the day-to-day life of the court as well, to varying degrees at different courts. As is the case with the 1717 listing of the Bonn *Hofkapelle* referred to above, which provides only the musicians' surnames for the main body of vocalists and instrumentalists, extant primary sources frequently record the names of *Hofkapelle* members, but fail to specify their duties or name the instrument(s) they played.[25] Yet, as demonstrated by those more detailed documents which do survive, many musicians were proficient on at least two or

[21] For further details, see the information regarding membership of court music establishments provided in the tables that accompany individual chapters in this volume.

[22] See Janice B. Stockigt, 'The *Kapellknaben* of the Catholic Court Church in Dresden, 1722–33', *Studies in Music*, 29 (1989), 13–24.

[23] More research needs to be carried out in order to clarify the role of *Kantoren* at German courts. In 2007, a scholarly conference held in Erfurt, Germany, focused on 'Der mitteldeutsche Kantor' (The *Kantor* in Central Germany), with emphasis on the dual nature (musician/educator) of the position.

[24] On the role of the *Hoforganist*, see Siegbert Rampe, 'Sozialstatus und Wirkungsbereich mitteldeutscher Hoforganisten des 17. und 18. Jahrhunderts', in *Mitteldeutschland im musikalischen Glanz seiner Residenzen: Sachsen, Böhmen und Schlesien als Musiklandschaften im 16. und 17. Jahrhundert*, ed. Peter Wollny (Beeskow: Ortus, 2005), 171–82.

[25] Lünig, *Theatrum ceremoniale*, 1520: '*Vocalist*en. Herren *Flaymanni, Kircher, Dhelphi Court* [sic], *Castelino, Ambrosini, Marquiero, Du Croux, Rissack, le Long Kamter* [sic] *& Schwöller*' and '*Instrumentalist*en. Herren *Havec, Deridder, Canta, Maximilien Augarthe, le Cerf, Van der Huque, Corniller, Thireur, Franz Augarthe, Graeb, Rubini, Sommerini,* Stumpff der Aeltere, Stumpff der Jüngere, *Maurice* der Aeltere, *Maurice* der Jüngere.'

three instruments, or were both skilled singers and players, their various talents in this respect being utilized by court *Kapellmeister* when considering repertoire for performance at court. It is equally essential that this be taken into account when considering the overall constitution of a *Hofkapelle*. Depending upon the nature of surviving source material, the tables which accompany each chapter listing membership of court music establishments provide much or little information in this respect.

Further complicating this already complex situation is the existence of two additional, distinct groups of musicians at most German courts, referred to in Bonn as the 'Trompeter und Paucker' and the 'Hof-*Hautbois*'. The chief responsibility of the trumpet and kettledrum ensemble, which generally comprised around six to eight musicians, was to provide fanfares on a daily basis at court, as described by J. B. von Rohr in his chapter on 'Tafel-*Ceremoniel*':

> Bevor man zu den Fürstlichen Tafeln anrichtet, wird gemeiniglich mit Trompeten und Paucken angekündiget, daß diejenigen, die die Speisen aufsetzen sollen, sich vor der Küche versammlen. Man findet in vielen Fürstlichen Hof-Ordnungen *disponirt*: Wenn zur Tafel geblasen wird, sollen sich so bald die *Pagen* und *Laqueyen* vor die Küche einfinden, dabey gebührlich verhalten und die Speisen vorsichtig auftragen, damit nichts verschüttet werde . . . Zuweilen lassen sich bey iedem Gange, der aufgetragen wird, Trompeten und Paucken hören.

> Prior to serving [a meal] at the princely table, trumpets and kettledrums commonly herald that those who are to set out the dishes are to assemble before the kitchen. Many princely court regulations recommend: When the call 'to table' is sounded, the pages and lackeys must quickly gather in front of the kitchen, behave themselves properly, and take care when serving the dishes in order to avoid spills . . . On occasion, trumpets and kettledrums can be heard performing during every single course that is being served.[26]

The rights of trumpeters and kettledrummers were protected by imperial privilege, which also stipulated that they serve exclusively 'Fürsten, Grafen und rittermäßigen Personen' (princes, counts, and persons of knightly rank).[27] Although all were required to participate in at least one military campaign before legally qualified to train an apprentice ('Lehr-Junge'), according to Zedler's *Universal-Lexicon* the trumpeters were divided into three main types: 'Hof-Trompeter, die an Fürstlichen Höfen ihre Kunst exerciren' (Court trumpeters, who exercise their art at princely courts); 'Feld-Trompeter, die unter der Militz sind' (Field trumpeters, who are [in service] with the military); and 'Schiff-Trompeter, die sich auf den Schiffen und bey den Flotten hören lassen' (Ship trumpeters, who can be heard on ships and with the navy). Of these, the entry on 'Trompeter' went on to explain,

alle . . . sind entweder musicalisch, die die Music zugleich mit verstehen,

---

[26] Rohr, *Einleitung zur Ceremoniel-Wissenschafft*, 93, §10.
[27] Zedler, *Universal-Lexicon*, 'Trompeter', XLV (1745): 1119–20.

und nach den Noten zu blasen wissen, oder nicht musicalisch, die nur so die Trompeter- und Feld-Stückgen erlernet. Die musicalischen Trompeter sind bey Hofe die angenehmsten[;] sie müssen zur Tafel blasen, in der Capelle mit aufwarten, wenn bey Solennitäten das Te Deum laudamus angestimmt wird.

all . . . are either 'musical', in that they understand music and can play from notes [that is, are capable of reading music], or they are 'not musical', and have only learnt [to play] trumpeter and field pieces [that is, by ear]. The 'musical' trumpeters at court are the most pleasant [to listen to]; they have to sound the call to table, [and] serve in the *Kapelle* [chapel], when the *Te Deum laudamus* is performed on solemn occasions. [28]

Thus, although they were invariably operating as a separate unit that was almost completely detached from the *Hofkapelle* in administrative and practical terms, the trumpeters were sometimes considered part of a larger *Hofmusik*.[29]

A further group of musicians who made an important contribution to the musical life at German courts during this period were the *Hautboisten*. Generally members of a court or military *Hautboistenbande* (oboe band), these men were either under the direct authority of the court or associated with it in some capacity, as, for example, was often the case with regimental bands. Led by a 'Premier Hautboist', the number of musicians in such ensembles differed from place to place, with an average of between six to nine members.[30] In 1704, Johann Philipp Krieger's *Lustige Feld-Music*, scored for 'Premier Dessus', 'Second Dessus', 'Taille', and 'Basson', included three copies each of the first oboe and the bassoon parts respectively, with two copies of the second oboe part.[31] Over two decades later, in 1726, Hans Friedrich von Fleming specified that 'hat man jeztund sechs *Hautboi*sten . . . zwey *Discante*, zwey *la Taillen*, und zwey *Bassons*' (these days one has six *Hautboisten* [in a regimental band] . . . two trebles, two tenor oboes, and two bassoons).[32] But these instrumentalists were not solely professional oboe or bassoon players; indeed, *Hautboisten* were routinely expected to be able to perform on a variety of different instruments, both wind and strings. Thus, to translate the term *Hautboist* (as used in German sources of this period) as 'oboist' would be misleading. In addition to

---

[28] Ibid., 1120.

[29] See also Andreas Lindner, *Die kaiserlichen Hoftrompeter und Hofpauker im 18. und 19. Jahrhundert* (Tutzing: Schneider, 1999), and Don L. Smithers, *The Music and History of the Baroque Trumpet before 1721* (Carbondale: Southern Illinois University Press, 1988).

[30] Regarding the number of personnel employed in *Hautboistenbanden*, cf. Achim Hofer, 'Geburtsmomente der Harmoniemusik: Beispiele – Perspektiven', in *Zur Geschichte und Aufführungspraxis der Harmoniemusik*, ed. Boje E. Hans Schmuhl and Ute Omonsky (Blankenburg am Harz: Kultur- und Forschungsstätte Michaelstein, 2006), 37–52, at 43–4, 47.

[31] Robert Eitner, ed., 'Johann Philipp Krieger: Eine Sammlung von Kantaten, einer Weihnachts-Andacht, einer Begräbnis-Andacht, Arien und Duette aus seinen Singspielen, zwei Sonaten für Violine, Viola da Gamba und Bassus continuus und zwei Partien aus der Lustigen Feldmusik zu 4 Instrumenten', *Beilage zu den Monatsheften für Musikgeschichte*, 29 (1897/8), 95–128.

[32] Hans Friedrich von Fleming, *Der vollkommene teutsche Soldat, welcher die gantze Kriegs-Wissenschafft, insonderheit was bey der Infanterie vorkommt . . .* (Leipzig, 1726), 181, §2.

performing as a unit in oboe-band formation (at court balls, military parades, or firework displays, to name but three examples), the versatility of individuals in the group meant that they substituted for, or performed alongside, the court musicians from time to time.[33] Their inferior rank carried with it the added advantage (at least in some eyes of some rulers and court officials) of being less costly in salary terms, but occasionally also led to noticeably lower standards of musical performance.[34]

A pair of *Waldhornisten* (horn players) frequently performed with *Hautboisten-banden* at court and indeed was sometimes specifically employed as part of those ensembles. At many courts horn players were initially attached to the *Jagd* (hunt), but during the early decades of the eighteenth century they were increasingly required to perform alongside the court musicians.[35] Before long, the fashion for horns had spread beyond the courtly environment, with Lady Mary Wortley Montagu commenting on public balls held in Vienna in 1717, 'They are magnificently furnished, and the music good, if they had not that detestable custom of mixing hunting horns with it, that almost deafen the company. But that noise is so agreeable here, they never make a concert without them.'[36] By the second half of the eighteenth century, if not before, horn players were considered an indispensable component of the orchestra.[37]

The overall leadership of the *Hofkapelle*, as well as of the *Hoftrompeter und Paucker* ensemble and the *Hautboistenbande* (at least when individuals from these two groups were performing with *Hofmusici* and *Cammermusici*), was undertaken by the court *Kapellmeister*. As outlined in his employment contract, he was generally in charge of selecting music and rehearsing the musicians, and was expected not only to compose but also to carry out a host of other additional tasks, supported by deputies. As is evident from the tables in this volume listing membership of court music establishments, the responsibilities and titles of these executive members differed widely from place to place, with such designations as *Oberkapellmeister* (chief *Kapellmeister*), *Vicekapellmeister*, *Kapelldirector*, and, of course, concertmaster. The latter position, referred to in archival sources as, for example, 'Concertmeister',

---

[33] See also Renate Hildebrand, 'Das Oboenensemble in der Deutschen Regimentsmusik und in den Stadtpfeifereien bis 1720', *Tibia*, 1 (1978), 7–12, and Samantha Owens, 'Regimental & Courtly Oboe Bands in Early Eighteenth-Century Württemberg', *ABA Journal of Band Research*, 34 (1999), 1–18.

[34] On the status of *Hautboisten*, see Werner Braun, 'The "Hautboist": An Outline of Evolving Careers and Functions', in *The Social Status of the Professional Musician*, 123–58 [German original, 'Entwurf für eine Typologie der "Hautboisten"', in *Der Sozialstatus des Berufsmusikers*]. For a specific example of a complaint regarding the performance standards of *Hautboisten*, see Chapter 6, 'The Court of Württemberg-Stuttgart', pp. 165–95 below.

[35] Zedler, *Universal-Lexicon*, 'Waldhorn', LII (1747): 1366, notes that the horn was 'ehemahls gantz allein auf der Jagd gebrauchet worden' (formerly used exclusively for the hunt).

[36] *The Letters and Works of Lady Mary Wortley Montagu*, ed. Lord Wharncliffe, 3rd edn (London, 1861), I: 263.

[37] For further information, see also the relevant sections of Horace Fitzpatrick, *The Horn and Horn-Playing and the Austro-Bohemian Tradition from 1680 to 1830* (London: Oxford University Press, 1970), and *Jagd- und Waldhörner: Geschichte und musikalische Nutzung*, ed. Boje E. Hans Schmuhl with Monika Lustig (Blankenburg am Harz: Kultur- und Forschungsstätte Michaelstein, 2006).

*Maître de concerts*, or 'premier de l'orguestre', was by no means restricted to violinists: gamba players, cellists, and even woodwind specialists were represented in this role as well. This should perhaps come as no surprise, since, as noted by Johann Joachim Quantz, an instrumental ensemble could in principle be led by any of its members; however, the best choice was a violinist.[38] At larger courts, a higher level of artistic leadership above even the *Kapellmeister* often took the form of an aristocrat specially appointed to take responsibility for musical matters, sometimes also for theatrical performances or festivities more generally. Examples include the *Directeur des plaisirs* in Dresden, the *Intendant* at Mannheim, the 'Ober-Music-Director' at the Württemberg court, and the 'Director der Hofmusik' in Würzburg. The degree to which these men actually involved themselves in artistic decision-making undoubtedly varied from court to court.

For the ordinary court and chamber musicians on the ground, differences in capability, but not necessarily in seniority, typically translated into higher wages. These generally featured a component of payments in kind in addition to money, including food, beverages, firewood, grain, candles, and similar items. Other much sought-after benefits involved the permission to travel and the possibility of a pension in retirement. Regardless of the size of the court where they were employed, musicians were often forced to supplement their incomes as clerks, secretaries, valets, and lackeys, while others took on music-related duties such as the copying of music or the writing of poetry to be set to music (although many courts also retained their own court poets, some specifically employed within the *Hofkapelle*). In addition to the official court composers (particularly common at the larger courts such as Dresden or Berlin), selected *Hofkapelle* members besides the *Kapellmeister* were also accomplished in this field and could sometimes earn bonuses for their efforts. Even the *Kapellmeister* could seize the opportunity to augment his salary by providing another court with his compositions as 'Kapellmeister von Haus aus' (*Kapellmeister* by proxy), although some locations had strict regulations – at least in theory – regarding the dissemination of music beyond the confines of their own court.[39]

Otherwise, the *Kapellmeister* usually relied on the financial support of his employer to purchase new music or exchange his own works, as is illustrated by extant inventories of court music libraries. Naturally, it is not always possible to determine how and where this music was acquired, how and by whom it was transported, or what percentage was actually performed once the music arrived.[40] Many musicians maintained their own personal music collections, the importance of which cannot be overestimated: these collections represented a source of valuable

[38] Johann Joachim Quantz, *Versuch einer Anweisung die Flöte traversiere zu spielen* (Berlin, 1752), 178–9, 'Hauptstück XVII', '1. Abschnitt: Von den Eigenschaften eines Anführers der Musik', §3.

[39] Samantha Owens, '"zum Fürstl: Hoff Staat gehörige Musicalien": The Ownership and Dissemination of German Court Music, 1665–c. 1750', in *Musik an der Zerbster Residenz*, ed. Konstanze Musketa and Barbara M. Reul, Fasch-Studien, 10 (Beeskow: Ortus, 2008), 103–15.

[40] Unfortunately, consideration of surviving court music collections (which sometimes include sets of vocal or instrumental parts) was largely beyond the scope of the present volume.

capital (both musical and financial) in times of difficulty, particularly when rulers changed and musicians were unexpectedly released. Those musicians lucky enough to gain permission to travel — many of whom were virtuosos who enjoyed great success abroad — on occasion became recruitment agents on their employer's behalf. Yet others, although not acting in this capacity officially, would have certainly (even if unwittingly) served as ambassadors for the reputation of their court and its working conditions. Records such as court account books, published calendars, and appointment decrees, indicate that musicians were recruited not only from throughout the German-speaking lands (from the surrounding region and often locally, with successive generations of the same musical family being a common occurrence) and across Europe, but, above all, from Italy, France, and Bohemia.[41]

Networks between individual musicians (some dating back to their school days) as well as dynastic links between ruling families were undoubtedly critical. That musicians frequently moved from one court to another, either permanently or as visitors (sometimes even 'on loan' from another court for extended periods), can be seen throughout the present volume. Significant court events, such as weddings or baptisms, were of particular importance in this regard. Not only did they provide an opportunity for the members of ruling families from different courts to mix socially and engage in politics of various kinds, but travelling in their retinues were often sizeable numbers of musicians. For the latter, these occasions offered the chance to meet colleagues from other locations, exchange music, hear one another perform, participate alongside one another in large-scale productions, and (presumably) take lessons from established masters. These myriad complex networks thus existed on numerous levels. But the nature and quality of music performed at any one court was first and foremost determined by the interaction between the musicians (regardless of rank) and the rulers, whose budgets varied as much as their respective attitudes towards cultural competition and regard for tradition, and their personal musical tastes. Naturally, both groups were also directly affected by circumstances largely beyond their control, above all the advent of war. In particular, the conflicts fought over the Spanish succession (1701–14) and the Polish succession (1733–38), as well as the Seven Years' War (1756–63), were to have a hugely negative impact upon German *Hofkapellen* during this period.

Through a series of individual case studies, this volume investigates the realities of musical life at fifteen German courts of varied size, religious denomination, and geographical location during the first six decades of the eighteenth century. In order to detail and at the same time map (in the form of tables) the significant shifts that occurred in the artistic priorities of each court, particular reference has been made to series of 'snapshots', or in effect 'core sample' years. Although the initial intention was to choose four evenly-spaced points in time, namely 1715, 1730, 1745, and 1760, the extent to which archival material survives has, in fact,

---

[41] On this topic, see also Mahling, 'The Origin and Social Status of the Court Orchestral Musician', 224–6, and Norbert Dubowy, 'Italienische Instrumentalisten in deutschen Hofkapellen', in *The Eighteenth-Century Diaspora of Italian Music and Musicians*, ed. Reinhard Strohm, Speculum Musicae, 8 (Turnhout: Brepols, 2001), 61–120.

dictated a rather more diverse selection of dates.⁴² In any event, placing a variety of *Hofkapellen* under the microscope in respect of particular years serves to highlight both individual and shared patterns of development and decline. These institutions range from the relatively small Central German *Hofkapellen* of the duchy of Saxony-Gotha-Altenburg (Chapter 7), the three secundogeniture duchies of Saxony-Weißenfels, Saxony-Merseburg, and Saxony-Zeitz (Chapter 8), and the principality of Sondershausen (Chapter 10) to the more widely celebrated, large-scale music establishments of the kingdoms and electorates of Brandenburg-Prussia (Chapter 4) and Saxony-Dresden (Chapter 2), and of the electoral Palatinate in Mannheim (Chapter 5). A separate chapter deals with the Polish *Kapelle*, the travelling orchestra associated with the Saxon rulers of the kingdom of Poland (Chapter 3).

Four South German courts can be taken to represent medium-sized *Hofkapellen*, comprising the closely linked courts of the duchy of Württemberg-Stuttgart (Chapter 6), the landgraviate of Hesse-Darmstadt (Chapter 12), and the margraviate of Baden-Durlach in Karlsruhe (Chapter 13), together with that of the Catholic prince-bishopric of Würzburg (Chapter 11), which provides a telling example of how a series of elected regents (in contrast to one of hereditary rulers) could affect the long-term development of a *Hofmusik*. And last, but certainly not least, the principality of Anhalt-Zerbst (Chapter 9) and the margraviate of Brandenburg-Culmbach-Bayreuth (Chapter 14) demonstrate just how disparate the fortunes of German court music establishments could be even within the same year (1760) as a result of the ravages of war.

By way of conclusion, the final chapter in the volume tells the story from the perspective of the musicians themselves, drawing upon the writings of six prominent figures, each of whom had experienced the musical life of German courts at first hand. Their commentary provides an important counterbalance to the 'official view' represented by the primarily administrative archival documents upon which the volume is largely focused. For, as Jeroen Duindam has pointed out, 'the basis for any analysis of the court remains thin, as concrete data regarding numbers, costs, hierarchies, and routines are sorely lacking. Indeed, the early modern European court in many respects remains a world unknown to us.'⁴³ What emerges from

⁴² See the List of Tables, pp. vii–viii above. Occasionally, in addition to consulting primary sources, it has been necessary to draw upon the ground-breaking work undertaken by earlier scholars, including Moritz Fürstenau, Curt Sachs, Josef Sittard, Friedrich Walter, and Arno Werner. For a number of German court music establishments, such volumes remain the fundamental studies to this day, as, for example, Clemens Meyer, *Geschichte der Mecklenburg-Schweriner Hofkapelle* (Schwerin: Davids, 1913), and Gustav Friedrich Schmidt, *Neue Beiträge zur Geschichte der Musik und des Theaters am herzoglichen Hofe zu Braunschweig-Wolfenbüttel* (Munich: Berntheisel, 1929).

⁴³ Jeroen Duindam, 'Norbert Elias and the History of the Court: Old Questions, New Perspectives', *Hof und Theorie: Annäherungen an ein historisches Phänomen*, ed. Reinhardt Butz, Jan Hirschbiegel, and Dietmar Willoweit (Cologne: Böhlau, 2004), 91–104, at 94. Duindam's desire to redress the situation led to his own in-depth archival research, resulting in his study *Vienna & Versailles: The Courts of Europe's Dynastic Rivals, 1550–1780* (Cambridge and New York: Cambridge University Press, 2003).

the wealth of primary source material examined in this volume is not only an in-depth picture of music making within the daily life of individual courts — *Music at German Courts, 1715–1760: Changing Artistic Priorities* also serves to illustrate the extraordinary diversity of eighteenth-century German court music establishments without losing sight of what these *Kapellen* had in common.

# KINGDOMS AND ELECTORATES

# 2

# The Court of Saxony-Dresden

## Janice B. Stockigt

D RESDEN – SEAT OF TWO SUCCESSIVE Saxon electors from the house of Wettin and elected kings of Poland – exemplifies a brilliant European court whose cultural climate and musical excellence was, by the mid-eighteenth century, equal to the best then offered. Developments of this era owed much to the personalities, tastes, and change of confession of the rulers whose leadership covered the years of the snapshots.[1] For more than fifty years the music of Dresden reflected first the preference for French culture of Saxon Elector Friedrich August I (1670–1733; as king of Poland titled August II 'the Strong'). On the other hand the highly developed musical tastes of his son and successor, Electoral Prince Friedrich August II (1696–1763), and his eldest surviving son and heir, Electoral Prince Friedrich Christian (1722–1763), veered towards Italy.[2] After election as king of Poland in October 1733 and coronation in January 1734, Friedrich August II – now titled August III – and his Habsburg-born consort Maria Josepha (1699–1757) provided powerful musical patronage in Dresden. They and family members often determined the selection of musicians and repertoire for Dresden, whose court witnessed musical advances that came to have far-reaching effects upon contemporary developments, musical standards, and continuing musical institutions.

The sons and daughters of August III and Maria Josepha contributed to this enlightened musical patronage, with strong musical connections established through marriages between Dresden and the courts of Naples, Munich, and Versailles.[3]

In the preparation of this chapter I am indebted to Samantha Owens, Barbara M. Reul, and Jóhannes Ágústsson for their expert advice and generous help. I acknowledge with gratitude the assistance of the archivists and librarians of the Sächsisches Hauptstaatsarchiv (D-Dla) and the Sächsische Landesbibliothek – Staats- und Universitätsbibliothek (D-Dl) in Dresden.

[1] The conversion to Catholicism by Saxon Elector Friedrich August I in 1697 was followed in 1712 by the conversion of his son and heir, Electoral Prince Friedrich August. Neither ruler enforced the canon (established at the Peace of Westphalia, 1648) 'Cuius regio, eius religio' (whose realm, his religion).

[2] Important musical observations made by Electoral Prince Friedrich Christian during his *Kavaliersreise* to Italy (1738–40) are documented by Alina Żórawska-Witkowska, 'Federico Cristiano in Italia: Esperienze musicali di un principe reale polacco', *Musica e storia*, 4 (1996), 277–323.

[3] In 1738 Maria Amalia (1724–1760) married Charles VII, king of the Two Sicilies (king of

Electoral Prince Friedrich Christian's wife (and cousin) Maria Antonia Walpurgis of Bavaria (1724–1780) was a notable musician in her own right, and catalogues of her music library (which later included her husband's collection), as well as other royal music collections, testify to her intense interest in the art. If the royal music holdings catalogued in Dresden are a guide, then the exchange of scores between members of this family must have enriched libraries of major European courts.[4]

Bird's-eye views of the most important Dresden music organizations during these snapshot years are given in the *Königl. Polnischer und Churfürstl. Sächsischer Hof- und Staats-Calender* (hereafter *Hof- und Staats-Calender*), published in Leipzig almost annually from 1728 until 1757, resuming in 1764 following the Peace (or Treaty) of Hubertusburg that marked the end of the Seven Years' War.[5] These published lists do not reveal the complex situations of multitudes of musicians maintained by the Dresden court and by powerful court members.[6] Despite compilation towards the end of the year prior to publication (and remembering that the number of musicians available did not always correlate with court records), these publications present the most consistent record of the Dresden court's musical establishments. A multitude of references to the numerous musicians who functioned in Dresden during this era are found today in the copious court records housed in the Sächsisches Hauptstaatsarchiv in Dresden.

Throughout the years of this study the Dresden court was served by several ensembles, each with its own status, function, and internal hierarchy: all components were vital to the smooth functioning of a great musical machine. The most

Spain from 1759); in 1747 a double marriage saw Electoral Prince Friedrich Christian and his sister Maria Anna (1728–1797) wed their Bavarian cousins Maria Antonia and Maximilian III Joseph, elector of Bavaria (1727–1777); and in 1747 Maria Josepha ('Marie-Josèphe de Saxe', 1731–1767) married the widowed dauphin of France, Louis-Ferdinand (1729–1765).

[4] Catalogues of the music libraries of Dresden court members include an incomplete and untitled volume (possibly of Maria Josepha's music collection), D-Dl, Bibl.-Arch. III Hb 787ᶜ; a catalogue of the music collection of August III ('Catalogo della Musica e de Libretti di S. M. Augusto III . . .', into which is bound the final catalogue of the music collection of Maria Antonia), D-Dl, Bibl. Arch. III Hb 787ʰ; and the catalogue of the collection of Friedrich August III [King August I of Saxony, d. 1827] ('Catalogo della Musica, e de' Libretti de S. M. Augusto III. la quale si trova nella Biblioteca Musicale'), D-Dl, Bibl.-Arch. III Hb 787ⁱ.

[5] Editions of the *Hof- und Staats-Calender* used for this chapter are kept in D-Dl, Hist. Sax., I 179. Because liturgical calendars and reports of court activities are mainly published without pagination, recent folio numbering is given in square brackets. From 1738, those pages that name *Hofkapelle* members are paginated.

[6] The *Kapelle* of Saxon Prime Minister Count von Brühl has been examined by Ulrike Kollmar in *Gottlob Harrer (1703–55), Kapellmeister des Grafen Heinrich von Brühl am sächsisch-polnischen Hof und Thomaskantor in Leipzig*, ed. Wolfgang Ruf, Schriften zur mitteldeutschen Musikgeschichte, 12 (Beeskow: Ortus, 2006). On the *Kapelle* of Count Jakob Heinrich von Flemming, see Szymon Paczkowski, 'Muzyka na dworze marszałka Jakuba Henryka Flemminga (1667–1728)' [Music at the Court of Marshal Jacob Heinrich Flemming], in *Środowiska kulturotwórcze i kontakty kulturalne Wielkiego Księstwa Litewskiego od XV do XIX wieku* [The Circles of Cultural Creativity in the Grand Duchy of Lithuania from the Sixteenth until the Nineteenth Century], ed. Urszula Augustyniak (Warsaw: Wydawnictwo Neriton, 2009), 67–82. Other Dresden court members (Count Sułkowski, for example) also maintained music ensembles and regimental bands.

prestigious group was 'Die Königliche Capell- und Cammer Musique' or 'Orchestre' (*Hofkapelle*) under the authority of a *Directeur des plaisirs*. It comprised a *Kapellmeister*, a court poet (first listed with the *Hofkapelle* in the *Hof- und Staats-Calender* of 1735), singers, instrumentalists, and support staff. A list of musicians dated 'Decembris 1711' refers to the ensemble as the 'Königl: Poln: und Churfürstl: Sächß: *Music* und *Orchestra*',[7] and although another list of brief autobiographies of the musicians from 1717–18 divides them into '*Hoff* und Cammer *Musici*',[8] this distinction is not observed in later documents: the ensemble was generally titled 'Orchestra' (or 'Orchestre') with hierarchical structures within each section, as demonstrated by salaries (see Table 2.1, pp. 38–40 below). In 1728 the musicians were listed in the first edition of the *Hof- und Staats-Calender* under the heading 'Hof Capelle'; from 1729 until 1756 the heading was 'Die Königl. Capelle und Cammer-*Musique*'. From 1730, the Jesuits from the province of Bohemia who staffed the royal chapel often referred to royal singers and instrumentalists as 'virtuosi'. After the Seven Years' War the group was named simply the 'Capell- und Cammer Musique'. Royal musicians were directed in the opera, church, and chamber by three outstanding *Kapellmeister*, Johann Christoph Schmidt (1664–1728), Johann David Heinichen (1683–1729), and Johann Adolf Hasse (1699–1783), and by the court and church composers Jan Dismas Zelenka (1679–1745), Giovanni Alberto Ristori (1692–1753, son of Tommaso Ristori), Father Johann Michael Breunich SJ (1699–1755; a former chaplain in the entourage of Maria Josepha), Tobias Butz (d. 1760), and Johann Georg Schürer (*c*.1720–86). Instrument inspectors and repairers, valets, porters, organ builders and attendants, and tuners as well as so-called *Aufwärter* (expectants) supported the royal musicians.

Attached to the *Hofkapelle* were music scribes, whose meticulous copy of performance materials and arrangements of woodwind parts ensured smooth and error-free performances.[9] Moreover, their responsibility extended to the compilation of new musical scores of compositions acquired for Dresden that then became the working documents into which composers noted their alterations and additions (especially of a viola part if none had existed, and the addition of parts for ripieno oboes and bassoons). From the revised score new parts were drawn, and these might be further modified by copyists, whose abilities to sort out inconsistencies and problems of range contributed to the performance brilliance of Dresden. Members of the *Hofkapelle* taught younger players. The most noteworthy student of the court flautist Pierre-Gabriel Buffardin (*c*.1689–1768) was Johann

---

[7] D-Dla, 10026 Geheimes Kabinett, Loc. 910/1, 'Acta. Das Churfürstl: *Orchestre* und deßen Unterhaltung ingleichen das grosse Opern-Haus und andere zum *Departement* des *Directeur des Plaisirs* gehörige Angelegenheiten betr. Anno [1711, 1717], 1764, 65, 66, 67, 68': 'Die Königl: Poln: und Churfürstl: Sächß: *Music* und *Orchestra* . . . 1. Decembris 1711', fols. 1ʳ–2ʳ.

[8] D-Dla, 10006 Oberhofmarschallamt, K 11, No. 5, 'Königl: Poln: und Churfürstl. Sächs: Hof-Buch von 1717 bis 1720': 'Derer Königl Pohl und Churfl: Sächs. Hoff und Cammer Musici, wie alt Einjeder, wo er her ist, u: wie lang beÿ Hoffe alß . . .', pp. 90 ff.

[9] Rousseau expected a good copyist to draw out from the violin part an oboe part suited to the instrument. See Jean-Jacques Rousseau, *Dictionnaire de musique* (Paris, 1768), 130–31. Examples of Dresden practices are given in Janice B. Stockigt, *Jan Dismas Zelenka (1679–1745): A Bohemian Musician at the Court of Dresden* (Oxford: Oxford University Press, 2000), 241–6.

Joachim Quantz (1697–1773); Zelenka instructed aspiring composers, including Gottlob Harrer (1703–1755), one-time *Kapellmeister* to the Saxon prime minister Count Heinrich von Brühl, who was appointed by the Leipzig town council to succeed Johann Sebastian Bach on 8 August 1750.[10]

Twelve trumpeters and two kettledrummers (*Hoftrompeter und Paucker*) served the court. They were sorted into 'field' and 'musical' players who performed with the *Hofkapelle* in the church and opera and were in constant attendance on formal occasions.[11] From this group were drawn players of the *Intraden* performed during processions of royal and electoral family members within the Catholic court church.[12] This *Hoftrompeter und Paucker* ensemble played for the ceremonial *Fackeltanz* (torch dance) on state occasions when the king led the polonaise (the principal Dresden court dance), and they were heard at outdoor entertainments, such as *Carousels* (tournaments). Numerous reports are given of court banquets being announced by trumpets and timpani, and of their playing during toasts. The presentation of various courses to the royal table during ceremonial dinners was 'carefully orchestrated using kettle drums and trumpets as a means of delivering instructions and prompts to the guests and staff in other rooms'.[13] *Hof- und Staats-Calender* entries and salary lists name trumpet and timpani *Scholaren* (apprentices) attached to this group.[14]

The Dresden court also kept ensembles of *Bock-* and *Jagd-Pfeifer*. If the *Bock-pfeifer* ensemble of the Dresden court resembled the type employed at the court of Württemberg, it would have comprised Polish bagpipes (*Polnische Böcke*) and violins of various sizes.[15] This would account for their music usually being heard out-

[10] See *The New Bach Reader: A Life of Johann Sebastian Bach in Letters and Documents*, ed. Hans T. David and Arthur Mendel, rev. and enlarged by Christoph Wolff (New York: Norton, 1998), 245–8, documents 274–5.

[11] See Ortrun Landmann, 'The Dresden Hofkapelle during the Lifetime of Johann Sebastian Bach', *Early Music*, 17 (1989), 17–30, at 23, who notes that the Saxon elector held the title of Grand Marshal ('Erz-Marschall'), retaining trumpeters and timpanists as insignia of his rank, thus making the Saxon court trumpeters 'the highest ranking group of their kind in the Holy Roman Empire'.

[12] Six fanfares attributed to Zelenka (zwv 212) are held in D-Dl, Mus. 2358-N-1. Perhaps these are the '6 Marcie per la Cavalleria' for four trumpets and timpani entered into the 'Catalogo della Musica, e de' Libretti de S. M. Augusto III', D-Dl, Bibl.-Arch. III Hb 787[i].

[13] Maureen Cassidy-Geiger, 'Innovations and the Ceremonial Table in Saxony, 1719–47', in *Zeichen und Raum: Ausstattungen und höfisches Zeremoniell in den deutschen Schlössern der frühen Neuzeit*, ed. Peter-Michael Hahn and Ulrich Schütte, Rudolstädter Forschungen zur Residenzkultur, 3 (Munich and Berlin: Deutscher Kunstverlag, 2006), 135–66, esp. 135.

[14] Under the heading 'Hof-Trompeter und Paucker auch Scholaren' in the *Hof- und Staats-Calender* (1745), 8, for example, two 'Trompeter-Scholaren' are listed. See also D-Dla, 10006 Oberhofmarschallamt, K 11, No. 6, 'Königl. Pohlnisches und Churfürstl. Sächsisches Hoff-Buch von 1721 usq. 1725', p. 40, where two 'Paucker Junge[n]' and two 'Trompeter Junge[n]' were listed during those years.

[15] See Samantha Owens, '"Gedancken für ein Gantzes Leben": *Polnischer Bock* Music at the Württemberg Court c.1730', *The Consort: European Journal of Early Music*, 54 (1998), 43–56. Although Fürstenau states that from 1748 this group was named 'Hofpfeifer', this title was not used in the *Hof- und Staats-Calender* until the edition of 1756. See Moritz Fürstenau, *Zur Ge-*

doors at shooting competitions and in association with the hunt.[16] But although the *Jagdpfeifer* provided outdoor music, they also played indoors. Following the performance of Hasse's opera *Demofoonte* (Carnival, 1748), for example, music for dancing in the parade hall of the Dresden palace was played by the *Cadets- und Jagd-Pfeifer*, while the *Hautboisten* of the Swiss and Grenadier Guards played in another room.[17]

The few references to military ensembles in the *Hof- und Staats-Calender* present the tip of an iceberg, since countless unnamed wind and percussion players were active in and around Dresden, especially from the late 1720s. The calendars list a few of these, but a multitude of musicians from – among others – the *Garde du Corps*, the Dragoons, the *Grand Musquetairs*, and the Janissary Company was available in Dresden and its surrounds. The services of the *Jagdpfeifer* ensemble along with the *Janitscharen-Musicanten* (Janissary musicians) were called upon to provide *Tafelmusik* at Pilnitz when court members went there on a sleigh ride in January 1731.[18] An example of a march (titled 'Aufzug, so die Hautboisten bey dem Carousel 1738 geblasen') composed in three parts for 'Hautbois' 1 and 2 and 'Basso.' (the latter possibly an abbreviation for *basson*) to be played while jurors made assessments at a *Carousel* held on 10 May 1738 in the Zwinger – that complex of open spaces, pavilions, and galleries adjacent to the Dresden court – gives an idea of the music played by military musicians.[19] Great stability and numerous family connections are to be observed in each of the Dresden court ensembles throughout these years. For example, three generations of string players named Lehneis (or Lehneiß) are seen throughout Table 2.2 (pp. 40–49 below). Movement from one musical institution to another was possible: the rise of Quantz from the Polish *Kapelle* to the *Hofkapelle* is the prime example (see Chapter 3, 'The Saxon Court of the Kingdom of Poland'). A musician might move from one instrument to another in the *Hofkapelle*, as seen with the horn player Johann Georg Knechtel, who became a member of the violoncello section. An example of a musician who had been trained as a *Jagdpfeifer* and then had a dual role in the Polish *Kapelle* and the *Hofkapelle* was the bassoonist Franz Adolph Christlieb (see Table 2.2). As a musician aged, the *Hofkapelle* could retain his expertise by allowing the player to take on different tasks: by 1764 Augustin Uhlig, a long-serving violinist of the *Hofkapelle*, was also listed as an instrument inspector.

In the Catholic court church (located in the renovated theatre of the Dresden

---

*schichte der Musik und des Theaters am Hofe der Kurfürsten von Sachsen und Könige von Polen*, 2 vols. (Dresden, 1861–2), II (reprint with commentary and indexes by Wolfgang Reich, Leipzig: Peters, 1979), 67 n. *.

[16] See, for example, *Hof- und Staats-Calender* (1738), [fol. 3ʳ col. 2]; Fürstenau noted that this ensemble comprised sixteen players (*Zur Geschichte der Musik und des Theaters*, II: 67), a number confirmed in lists published in the *Hof- und Staats-Calender* after 1731.

[17] *Hof- und Staats-Calender* (1749), [fol. 7ʳ (p. 13) col. 2].

[18] *Hof- und Staats-Calender* (1732), [fol. 19ᵛ col. 2].

[19] The music, composed by 'Capell Musicus Wilhelm' (Hugo), is kept in D-Dla, 10006 Oberhofmarschallamt, B 28 A 'Königl: Sicilianische Vermählung 1738, Vol. 1' (indexed as '*Musique der Hautboisten*'), fol. 199ʳ.

palace) magnificent music was heard on Sundays and feast days.[20] Foundation documents specified the duties of the mainly Bohemian *Kapellknaben* who were to play a vital musical role in this church.[21] Initially the group was to consist of six choristers (named *clercs*), four instrumentalists, a choral director, and organist. This was the approximate number maintained until 1727, when a decision was taken to expand this ensemble.[22] The musical training received by these boys and young men led many to become members of the Dresden *Hofkapelle*. The former *Kapellknaben* Johann Georg Schürer and Joseph Schuster became Dresden court musicians, while the organist to the choristers during the 1720s, Augustin Uhlig, became a violinist of the *Hofkapelle*.[23] The eminent violinist František (Franz) Benda (appointed to the *Kapelle* of Prussian Crown Prince Friedrich in 1733) was a former *Kapellknabe* of this church.[24] Although a small music ensemble was retained for the Lutheran chapel of the Dresden palace (the 'Hof-Kirchen-Capelle'), in 1737 it moved to the Sophienkirche.

During these years French and Italian companies of musicians, actors, and dancers entertained the two elector-kings and their courts, whilst illustrious visiting performers – including those of touring operatic troupes such as the company of Pietro Mingotti – were welcomed in Dresden.[25] Throughout the reigns of August II and August III, the whole or part of the Dresden musical apparatus was required to follow the court to the Saxon palaces of Moritzburg, Pilnitz, and the hunting palace of Hubertusburg at Wermsdorf. In 1716 August II established the Polish *Kapelle* to accompany him to his kingdom (see Chap. 3, 'The Saxon Court of the Kingdom of Poland'). This present chapter is concerned with the distinguished Dresden *Hofkapelle* around the years of the snapshots.

[20] Fürstenau, *Zur Geschichte der Musik und des Theaters*, II: 39, citing Iccander (Johann Christian Crell, 1723).

[21] A copy of the 'Reglements [*sic*] du Roy pour l'Eglise et Chapelle Royale, ouverte aux Catholiques', each set signed 'Augustus Rex', is kept in I-Rar (ARSI), Fondo Vecchia Compagnia, Provinciae Bohemiae (hereafter Boh.) 205/1. See Stockigt, *Jan Dismas Zelenka*, 26–9.

[22] I-Rar, Fondo Vecchia Compagnia, Boh. 143, p. 19.

[23] Schürer, a 'discantista' (treble), is first mentioned in the 'Diarium Missionis Societatis Jesu Dresdae' as arriving to the Jesuit house from Bohemia on 16 May 1732; Joseph Schuster ('altista et organista', father of the composer of the same name), arrived on 3 June 1735. The Jesuit 'Diarium' is held in D-Ddpa, with extracts from 1712–38 published by Wolfgang Reich, *Zelenka-Studien II: Referate und Materialien der 2. Internationalen Fachkonferenz Jan Dismas Zelenka (Dresden und Prag 1995)*, ed. Wolfgang Reich and Günter Gatterman, Deutsche Musik im Osten, 12 (Sankt Augustin: Academia-Verlag, 1997), 315–75; excerpts from 1739–42 are published by Gerhard Poppe, 'Ein weiterer Faszikel aus dem *Diarium Missionis Societatis Jesu Dresdae* wiederaufgefunden', in *Die Oberlausitz: Eine Grenzregion der mitteldeutschen Barockmusik*, ed. Peter Wollny, Jahrbuch der Ständigen Konferenz Mitteldeutsche Barockmusik 2006 (Beeskow: Ortus, 2007), 193–204.

[24] Benda left Dresden for Prague on 5 May 1723; see D-Ddpa, 'Diarium'.

[25] Fürstenau, *Zur Geschichte der Musik und des Theaters*, II: 242–3.

## 1715: THE REIGN OF AUGUST II

In the first third of the eighteenth century the court music of Dresden reflected the French taste of August II, a predilection to be expected since part of his *Kavaliersreise* was spent in France (1687 and 1688) where he attended the French opera, the Comédie Française, and the Comédie Italienne in Parisian theatres, and plays at Saint-Cloud. Soon after his succession as elector of Saxony (1694), August employed a French oboe band ('Bande Hautboisten oder Kammerpfeifer'), the most up-to-date type of ensemble of woodwind instruments, which had recently undergone radical development within the French court orchestra.[26] Although all musicians of the Dresden court were dismissed at Easter 1707, most of the instrumentalists were re-employed, and certain members of the *Hautboisten Bande* became royal musicians. From 1708 an ensemble of French dancers, actors, and musicians was employed: in 1711 the musicians from this group performed Zelenka's *Missa Sanctae Caeciliae* in the Catholic court church.[27] An ensemble of actors and singers skilled in the performance of the *commedia dell'arte* arrived in 1716 from Venice, headed by Tommaso Ristori.

Dresden *Hofkapelle* lists drawn up between 1711 and 1717 give a blueprint of an orchestra of thirty or more instrumentalists, for which coming generations of composers of symphonies wrote. The real beginning of the Dresden *Hofkapelle*, however, is seen around the year 1717. At least two orchestral lists were drawn up in that year; one is dated,[28] and the other is undated but signed by the king ('Augustus Rex').[29] Brief autobiographies provided in late 1717 and early 1718 by thirty-one members of the *Hofkapelle* demonstrate a fascinating cultural mix of German, Italian, and French-trained instrumentalists, with a sprinkling of players born in Austria, Bohemia, Brabant, Luxembourg, Poland, and Spain (see Table 2.1).[30] A strong Venetian element was introduced to Dresden as the result of Electoral Prince Friedrich August's *Kavaliersreise*. Following visits to Venice during 1712, and again in 1713, this prince was stationed in Venice from 1716 until 1717, when he appointed Heinichen as his personal *Kapellmeister*, engaged the violinist Francesco Maria Veracini (1690–1768), and hired an entire Italian operatic troupe under the direction of Antonio Lotti — a project that had been developing in Dresden and Warsaw for some time, and one requiring much fine-tuning.[31] Not only do these engagements

---

[26] Ibid., 12.

[27] D-Dpa, 'Diarium', 22 November 1711.

[28] D-Dla, 10026 Geheimes Kabinett, Loc. 383/4, 'Die *Bande* Französischer *Comoedianten* und *Orchestra* betr. *ao* 1702 . . . [17]20': 'Die Königl. Pohl: und Churfürstl.-Sächß. *Music* und Orchestra . . . 1. Aug. 1717', fol. 182r-v.

[29] D-Dla, 10026 Geheimes Kabinett, Loc. 910/1, 'No: 1 Verzeichnüß derer *Musicorum* so in der Königl. *Orchestra* sich befinden, alß . . .' (c.1717), fol. 5r-v.

[30] D-Dla, 10006 Oberhofmarschallamt, K II, No. 5, fols. 90 ff.

[31] John Walter Hill, 'The Life and Works of Francesco Maria Veracini', 2 vols. (PhD diss., Harvard University, 1972), I: 59–62 and 75–8; and Alina Żórawska-Witkowska, 'Das Ensemble der italienischen Oper von Antonio Lotti am Hof des Königs von Polen und Kurfürsten von Sachsen August II. des Starken (1717–20)', in *IX International Musicological Congress 'Musica*

reveal the highly developed musical taste of this young prince: they demonstrate early planning of celebrations to mark his return to Dresden with a bride from the imperial family – an alliance desired and plotted for by August II. Full-scale operas composed by Lotti leading up to this homecoming included *Giove in Argo* (1717) and *Ascanio* (1718). Following the arrival of the electoral prince and Maria Josepha, Lotti's *Teofane* was given on 13 September 1719 in the newly built opera house, whose orchestra pit was capable of holding thirty-eight to forty-one musicians.[32] A salary list of those who came from Venice in 1717 (the undated document signed 'Augustus Rex') shows annual payments to Lotti's musicians that must have caused resentment among *Hofkapelle* members. Lotti and his wife received 10,500 *Thaler*, salaries of singers ranged between 3,000 and 7,000 *Thaler*, the bass players Gerolamo Personelli and Angelo Gaggi (Gagi) received 1,000 and 400 *Thaler* respectively, while the *souffleur* (prompter) Felicetti (Giovanni Felice Maria Picinetti) received 200.[33]

Between 1709 and 1728, the Dresden *Hofkapelle* was led by the Spanish-born concertmaster Jean-Baptiste Volumier (Woulmier or Woulmyer, 1670–1728), who had been educated at the French court, entering royal service in Dresden in 1709.[34] Under his direction, French performance techniques were introduced into the Dresden *Hofkapelle*. Documents report that in 1715 Volumier travelled to Cremona to take delivery from Antonio Stradivari of six violins, three violas, and three violoncellos,[35] a move probably designed to give the Dresden *Hofkapelle* a homogeneous string sound.[36] By the end of 1717 the string section comprised six violins (including Volumier), six or seven violas, four violoncellists, and one 'Contrebass' player – Zelenka, who in 1716 and *c.*1716–*c.*1719 was stationed in Vienna. Perhaps it was because of his absence that the Saxon prince, at Lotti's insistence, hired for Dresden Italian players of the 'grand violon', Personelli and Gaggi. Such players were considered necessary to accompany the voices (surviving parts from Dresden-based composers show that the violoncello usually accompanied recitatives and

*Antiqua Europae Orientalis': Bydgoszcz, September 5th–19th, 1991*, ed. Eleonora Harendarşka, Musica Antiqua: Acta Musicologica, 9/1 (Bydgoszcz: Filharmonia Pomorska im. Ignacego Paderewskiego, 1991), 477–504.

[32] Ortrun Landmann, 'Topographische und aufführungspraktische Anmerkungen zu Hasses Dresdner Wirken', in *Johann Adolf Hasse in seiner Zeit*, ed. Reinhard Wiesend (Stuttgart: Carus, 2006), 317–42, at 321: 'Die Pöppelmann-Oper am Zwinger.'

[33] D-Dla, 10026 Geheimes Kabinett, Loc. 910/1, 'No: 2 Besoldung der Italienischen Operisten', fol. 10r.

[34] D-Dla, 10006 Oberhofmarschallamt, K II, No. 5, fol. 91r: 'Entré au Service de sa Majestá L'année 1709; Natif Espagnol. Elevé a [*sic*] la Cour de France.'

[35] See Kai Köpp, *Johann Georg Pisendel (1687–1755) und die Anfänge der neuzeitlichen Orchesterleitung* (Tutzing: Schneider, 2005), 280. Four letters held in a private collection in Warsaw (yet to be authenticated) signed by Don Alfonso Costanzi and dated between December 1714 and June 1715 (the first on behalf of Jean-Baptiste Volumier; the last on behalf of August II) document this order and purchase, and are described by Zbigniew Zawadzki, 'Korespondencja dworu Króla Augusta II Sasa z Mistrzem Antonio Stradivari', *Ruch muzyczny*, 7/20 (1963), 12. I am very grateful to Alina Żórawska-Witkowska for bringing these sources to my attention.

[36] Suggested by Brian Clark in his review of Köpp, *Johann Georg Pisendel* in *Early Music*, 34 (2006), 146–8.

vocal solos, with the violone or contrabass entering during ritornellos) and to provide both a harmonic foundation and rhythmic momentum for the orchestra.[37] An account dated 'di 16 Maggio 1719' shows a Venetian order signed by Alessandro Fedeli for two matching 'Violoni' and two matching 'Violette', cases (one case only for the two 'Violette'), as well as bows and strings for the 'Violoni'.[38] Personelli entered Dresden court employment in 1718,[39] while the name of the Venetian *souffleur* (and cellist) Felice Picinetti already had appeared on a payment list of the *Hofkapelle* dated 1 August 1717 as 'Felicetti, vom 1 May 1717'.[40]

The wind section of 1717 included two or three flautists, four oboists, three or four bassoonists, and two horn players who, after the purchase in Vienna in 1718 of two *Waldhörner* with silver mouthpieces and two sets of six crooks, would be capable of playing in a minimum of six different keys.[41] Although the term *Cammermusicus* was used in earlier years by certain musicians, this distinction evolved to denote a particularly special rank. Tables 2.1 and 2.2 reveal a small sub-section of instrumentalists with the title 'Cam[m]er Musicus' who, together with the *Kapellmeister*, concertmaster, and composers, constituted an elite musical core.[42] Table 2.1 shows most of the musicians heard during the magnificent and widely reported celebrations surrounding the return to Dresden from Vienna of the recently-married electoral prince and Maria Josepha, a young woman who was to become a powerful patron of the court music, especially the music of the Catholic court church. The festivities planned by August 11 drew numerous visitors, among them Georg Philipp Telemann, George Frideric Handel, and Gottfried Heinrich Stölzel (1690–1749).

[37] D-Dla, 10026 Geheimes Kabinett, Loc 383/2, 'Acta. Die Engagements einiger zum Theater gehöriger Personen u.s.w. betr. 1699 sq. ao 1747–1770 [dates crossed out]': 'Specification des pensione accordées par Monsieur Le Prince Royal aux Musiciens et autres gens actuellement engages pour L'Opera . . .', fol. 53ᵛ: 'Comme un homme qui joue du grand violon, et qui a la pratique pour accompagner les voix, et donne le mouvemᵗ, à tout L'Orguestre, est absolument necessaire, Monseigʳ, Le Prince à l'instance du Maitre [*sic*] Lotti a engagé un habil homme Girolamo Personelli . . .'. See Shelley Hogan, 'The Bass Ripieno Section of the Dresden *Hofkapelle* during the First Half of the Eighteenth Century' (PhD diss., University of Melbourne, in progress). Personelli (also named Momolo Personé) remained in Dresden until his death in 1728.

[38] D-Dla, 10026 Geheimes Kabinett, Loc. 907/3, 'Die Operisten, Musicos, Sänger und andere zur Opera gehörige Personen betr: ao 1717, 18, 19, [17]20', fol. 124ʳ; this document to be reproduced by Hogan, 'The Bass Ripieno Section of the Dresden *Hofkapelle*'.

[39] D-Dla, 10006 Oberhofmarschallamt, K 11, No. 6: salary lists, fols. 3ᵛ–4ʳ.

[40] D-Dla, 10026 Geheimes Kabinett, Loc. 383/4, fol. 182, and confirmed in D-Dla, 10006 Oberhofmarschallamt, K 11, No. 5, fol. 92ᵛ.

[41] See Fürstenau, *Zur Geschichte der Musik und des Theaters*, 11: 58, and Thomas Hiebert, 'The Horn in Early Eighteenth-Century Dresden: The Players and Their Repertory' (DMA diss., University of Wisconsin-Madison, 1989), 53–4, where it is suggested that these horns were ordered from the Leichnambschneider brothers by the electoral prince when in Vienna (1717–19).

[42] Fürstenau, *Zur Geschichte der Musik und des Theaters*, 11: 91 n. *, noted that, until the mid-eighteenth century, the title *Cammermusicus* was bestowed as a special recognition upon certain Dresden court musicians. Yet many Dresden court musicians appear to have titled themselves *Cammermusicus*, as seen in their autobiographies of *c*.1717; see D-Dla, 10006 Oberhofmarschallamt, K 11, No. 5, fols. 90 ff.

The Dresden opera came to a halt in 1720. After the return to Venice of Lotti and various members of his company in the latter part of 1719, the remaining singers — including the castratos Berselli and Senesino — caused a major disruption to a rehearsal of Heinichen's opera *Flavio Crispo.* This scandal led to the closure of the opera, and serious attention then turned to the music of the Catholic court church.[43] At the time of its foundation instruments purchased for this church included a large string bass, two violins with cases, four recorders with bassoon (possibly a *Chorist-Fagott*), and a viola; a small organ was built by Johann Heinrich Gräbner.[44] In 1712 a positive organ was acquired.[45]

Although surviving sets of printed part books containing motets by French and French-based Italian composers hint at the style of sacred music considered most suited for a Catholic monarch during the early days,[46] this began to change after the arrival of Lotti's troupe, whose members occasionally performed in the Catholic chapel. On 27 November 1717, for example, the Jesuit 'Diarium' reported that the 'Musici Regii Itali' (the king's Italian musicians) had a solemn mass celebrated in honour of St Cecilia.[47] The mass was not performed on the day of the feast (22 November) because the organ was 'discordant' ('discordatum organum'), which suggests either that the principal instrument was out of tune with itself or that its pitch was at variance with the pitch at which the *Hofkapelle* then played. The organ was gradually brought into agreement with the *Cammerton* tuning used by the woodwind players. In 1722 Zelenka insisted that the organ be modified to *Cammerton* ('Cammer-Thon ut vocant'), an alteration paid for by Maria Josepha.[48] The tuning fork used for the Dresden *Kapelle* during Hasse's directorship sounded at $a' = 417$ Hz.[49]

The discipline and execution of the Dresden *Hofkapelle* made a deep impression upon the young Quantz, who noted that when he first visited Dresden in 1716 he perceived that musical performance was much more than the mere playing of written notes.[50] Dresden musicians were given opportunities for development during court-ordered visits: between 1714 and 1718 Johann Georg Pisendel (1687–1755) travelled to France, Italy, Berlin, and Vienna, visits that must have presented the

[43] This era of music in the Dresden Catholic court church is documented by Wolfgang Horn, *Die Dresdner Hofkirchenmusik 1720–45: Studien zu ihren Voraussetzungen und ihrem Repertoire* (Kassel: Bärenreiter; Stuttgart: Carus, 1987).

[44] Fürstenau, *Zur Geschichte der Musik und des Theaters*, II: 37, wrote: 'In der Rechnung von 1709 findet sich . . . einer [*sic*] großen Baßgeige (16. Thlr.), 2 guten Violinen mit Futteral (14. Thlr.), 4 Flauten mit Fagott (6. Thlr.), und 1 braggia (3. Thlr.).'

[45] The acquisition of the positive and its placement in the chapel is reported in the 'Diarium' (D-Dpa) on 13, 29, and 30 September 1712.

[46] The French prints held in D-Dl are of motets by André Campra, 1700 (Mus. 2124-E-1); Paolo Lorenzani, 1693 (Mus. 2021-E-1); Jean-Baptiste Lully, 1684 (originals missing; nineteenth-century copies held: Mus. 1827-D-1); and Pierre Robert, 1684 (Mus. 1718-E-1).

[47] D-Dpa, 'Diarium', 27 November 1717.

[48] Ibid., 24 March 1722.

[49] Fürstenau, *Zur Geschichte der Musik und des Theaters*, II: 289–90.

[50] Johann Adam Hiller, 'Quanz [*sic*] (Johann Joachim)', *Lebensbeschreibungen berühmter Musikgelehrten* (Leipzig, 1784; facs. repr. Leipzig: Edition Peters, 1979), 200–231, at 208–9.

future Dresden concertmaster with outstanding opportunities to create networks, to develop his technique and style, and to assemble a music collection. During his visit to Venice in 1716, for example, Pisendel became Antonio Vivaldi's student. There, he amassed a number of his teacher's violin sonatas and concertos (making Dresden the most important repository of Vivaldi's music in the German-speaking lands) and collected violin compositions by Tomaso Albinoni.[51] Zelenka's studies with the imperial *Kapellmeister* Johann Joseph Fux and his access to Viennese musical sources presents another example of connections made by Dresden musicians.[52] His acquisition of six part books in Vienna of trios from Lully's operas (*Les Trio des opera de Monsieur de Lully*, Amsterdam, 1690–91),[53] and copies of church music (including masses of Palestrina) must be viewed within the context of the taste for secular music of August II, and the style of sacred music regarded as appropriate for a Catholic monarch – especially a monarch whose son was about to visit Vienna in order to court an Austrian archduchess. In 1712, Zelenka had petitioned the king asking for a year of travel to Italy to perfect himself in the solid church style ('soliden Kirchen Stylo'), and to France to acquire good taste ('bon goust').[54]

Two sets of manuscript parts of instrumental music from this era demonstrate the adaptability of Dresden's musicians to be organized to perform in the French manner and the Italian style. A set of eleven plus three parts for an ouverture with accompanying pieces from Lully's *Acis et Galatée* (LWV 73) – one of many sets of parts of Lully's incidental music kept in Dresden – comprises

'Premier Dessus De Violon' ('M^r Woulumier')
'Second Dessus De Violon'
'3^me Violon: Ripieno'
'Haute Contre De Violon'
'Taille De Violon'
'Basse et Basson' (two copies)
'Basse Continüe' (two copies; unfigured)
'1^r hautbois et fluttes'
'2^me hautbois et fluttes'

Prache de Tilloy, cellist and copyist of the *Hofkapelle*, prepared eleven of the fourteen parts (his name is given on the part for 'Premier Dessus De Violon': 'M^r Woulumier'). Three additional parts in the hand of another scribe are for 'Violon

[51] On the Vivaldi and Albinoni sources in Dresden, see Michael Talbot, *Vivaldi* (London: Dent, 1993), 46–7, and Talbot, *Tomaso Albinoni: The Venetian Composer and His World* (Oxford: Clarendon Press, 1990), 168–75, respectively. Concerning Pisendel's travels to Venice see Köpp, *Johann Georg Pisendel*, 81–105. On Pisendel's collection of instrumental music, finally acquired by the Dresden court in December 1765, see Manfred Fechner, *Studien zur Dresdner Überlieferung von Instrumentalkonzerten deutscher Komponisten des 18. Jahrhunderts*, Dresdner Studien zur Musikwissenschaft, 2 (Laaber: Laaber-Verlag, 1998), 12.

[52] An overview of Zelenka's manuscript collection copied in Vienna ('Collectaneorum Musicorum', D-Dl, Mus. 1-B-98) is given in *Zelenka-Dokumentation: Quellen und Materialien*, 2 vols., ed. Wolfgang Horn et al. (Wiesbaden: Breitkopf & Härtel, 1989), 1: 69–86.

[53] D-Dl, Mus. 1827-F-27, 1–2.

[54] Horn et al., *Zelenka-Dokumentation*, 1: 103, document 2.

Ripieno', 'Bass de Viole', and 'Basse Continu'.[55] Despite the listing of 'Corni' on the catalogue label attached to the wrapper for these parts (and on covers to most Dresden sets of parts to Lully's suites), horn parts are not kept with these performance materials.

Seventeen performance parts for Telemann's concerto for two solo violins (TWV 52:e 4) with four-part string accompaniment (which became the norm in Dresden) are still held.[56] Each part bears the name of the musician who once played this work, which was copied – if not performed – after Volumier's appointment in 1709 and before the loss to the *Hofkapelle* in 1711 of violinist Carlo Fiorelli.[57] The parts are for:

'Violino 1 Concertino' (originally 'Concertato') – 'Sig$^r$ Voloumier'
'Violino Pzio Concertino' – 'del Sig$^r$ Fiorelli'
'Violino 1 in Ripieno' – 'Mons: Lotti'[58]
'Violino 1 in Ripieno' – 'Mons: Rybitzky'
'Violino 1 in Ripieno' – 'Mons: D'Uc [edge of page cropped]'[59]
'Violino 1 in Ripieno' – 'Mons: Le Gros'
'Violino 2$^{do}$ in Ripieno' – 'Mons: [Gottfried] Heering'
'Violino 2$^{do}$ in Ripieno' – 'Mons: Lehneis'
[alto] 'Viola' – 'Mons: [Johann Heinrich] Praetorius'
'Viola' – player not named
'Violono in Ripieno' – 'Mons: la France'[60]
'Violono [or Violone] in Ripieno' – 'Mons: Hennig'[61]
'Violono in Ripieno' – 'Mons: Hennig'
'Hautbois 2' – player not named (N.B. Hautbois 1 part missing)
'Basso Continuo' (figured) – 'Mons: Selencka' [Zelenka]
'Basso Continuo' (figured) – player not named
'Basso Continuo' (figured) – 'Mons: [Christian] Pezold'

Except for Zelenka, each named player is identified in an undated salary list

[55] D-Dl, Mus. 1827-F-31.

[56] D-Dl, Mus. 2392-O-56; discussed by Fechner, *Studien zur Dresdner Überlieferung von Instrumentalkonzerten*, 236–8.

[57] Köpp, *Johann Georg Pisendel*, 310 n. 11, where it is noted that Pisendel was appointed from 1 January 1712 to fill Fiorelli's place.

[58] Johann Friedrich Lotti, born c.1669 in Hanover (D-Dla, 10006 Oberhofmarschallamt, K 11, No. 5, fol. 92$^v$), where Matteo Lotti, Antonio Lotti's father, was *Kapellmeister*.

[59] Possibly Jean Baptiste D'Ucé, listed in 1711 as a player of the 'Flute Allemande'; see D-Dla, 10026 Geheimes Kabinett, Loc. 910/1, fol. 1$^r$. He was dismissed from Dresden in 1713. See Mary Oleskiewicz, '"For the Church as Well as For the *Orchestra*": J. S. Bach, the *Missa*, and the Dresden Court, 1700–50', *Bach: Journal of the Riemenschneider Bach Institute*, 38/2 (2007), 1–38, at 4–5.

[60] Either Jean Baptiste du Houlondel ('Le France le Fils') or Robert du Houlondel ('Le France le Pere'), violoncellists with the Dresden *Hofkapelle*; see D-Dla, Oberhofmarschallamt, K 11, No. 5, fols. 91$^v$ and 92$^v$.

[61] In 1711, Gottfried Heering was listed as a 'Braccist', and Daniel Hennig as a player of the 'Basson'; see D-Dla, 10026 Geheimes Kabinett, Loc. 910/1, fol. 1$^v$.

(*c*.1710),[62] while apart from Fiorelli, each player was named in the salary list dated '1. Decembris 1711'.[63]

From 1717 the Dresden *Hofkapelle* continued to develop under the general directorship of *Kapellmeister* (soon to become *Oberkapellmeister*) Schmidt and *Kapellmeister* Heinichen, and the leadership of Volumier. With the deaths in 1728 of Volumier and Schmidt, followed by the passing of Heinichen in 1729, this era ended. Wolfgang Horn terms the years between 1729 and 1734 as the 'Interregnum'.[64]

## 1730: THE END OF THE ERA OF AUGUST II

When August II died in Warsaw on 1 February 1733, Dresden had been elevated from a German city to a European centre.[65] The beginnings of a new musical regime, however, were evident in 1730 when the court witnessed the first fruits of a plan to re-establish opera seria in Dresden. In the mid-1720s, a project was put in place in which young singers were recruited and trained in Italy at the expense of the Dresden court.[66] Five members of this group were first heard in Dresden on 6 June 1730.[67] These singers were almost certainly among those who, accompanied by virtuosos and the entire *Kapelle*, performed Ristori's now-missing cantata *Egloga al Campo di Radewitz* on the river Elbe from Maria Josepha's replica of the Venetian state gondola, the *Bucantaurus*. This performance, given during military exercises organized by August II held at Zeithain, was preceded by an astonishing flotilla of numerous sloops, brigantines, frigates, and gondolas.[68] From each second vessel, military musicians played regimental marches. Among those listening from the riverbank was Crown Prince Friedrich – from 1740, Friedrich II, king in Prussia.

In July 1731 Hasse and his wife, the celebrated mezzo-soprano Faustina Bordoni-Hasse, first arrived in Dresden. The male alto Antonio Gualandi (known as Campioli), who had been involved in training the singers in Venice, also came to

---

[62] Ibid., fol. 7$^{r-v}$.

[63] Ibid., fols. 1$^r$–2$^r$.

[64] Horn, *Die Dresdner Hofkirchenmusik*, 88–92.

[65] Observed by Helen Watanabe O'Kelly, *Court Culture in Dresden from Renaissance to Baroque* (Basingstoke: Palgrave, 2002), 237.

[66] See Alina Żórawska-Witkowska, 'Beitrag zur Bildungsgeschichte der italienischen Opernsänger: I Virtuosi di S. M. Il Re di Polonia, Elettore di Sassonia, 1724–30', in *10th International Musicological Congress 'Musica Antiqua Europae Orientalis': Bydgoszcz, September 7th–11th, 1994*, ed. Eleonora Harendarżka, Musica Antiqua: Acta Musicologica, 10/1 (Bydgoszcz: Filharmonia Pomorska im. Ignacego Paderewskiego, 1994), 401–11.

[67] *Hof- und Staats-Calender* (1731), [fol. 30$^v$ col. 2]; in this edition, sopranos Anna and Maria Rosa Negri, male sopranos Ventura Rochetti and Giovanni Bindi, and male alto Domenico Annibali are listed as members of 'Die Königl. Capelle und Cammer-Musique'. Fürstenau, however, stated that the soprano Maria Santina Cattaneo (sister of the Dresden *Cammermusicus* violinist Francesco Maria Cattaneo) and alto Casimiro Pignotti also arrived in 1730; see *Zur Geschichte der Musik und des Theaters*, II: 166. Maria Santina Cattaneo is first listed in the *Hof- und Staats-Calender* (1732), [fol. 30$^r$ col. 1].

[68] Reported in the *Hof- und Staats-Calender* (1731), [fols. 36$^v$ col. 2 – 37$^r$ col. 1].

Dresden that year. The solo vocal strength available for the Dresden opera of 1730 is seen in Table 2.2. Beginning with the production in 1731 of Hasse's *Cleofide*, a steady stream of operatic performances placed Dresden in a pre-eminent musical position.[69] These were enhanced by intermezzos and ballets performed by an expanding ensemble of French dancers with music composed by Louis André (1682–1739). Although not formally appointed until 1 February 1730, Pisendel's authoritative leadership (his initials are often seen on violin parts of this era) began to be asserted after the death of Volumier.[70] Table 2.1 shows that by 1717 the practice of Dresden court musicians playing two or more instruments had almost died out – a fact noted in 1730 by Johann Sebastian Bach in his memorandum to the Leipzig town council. There, he observed that one only needed to visit Dresden to see how the musicians were paid, free from 'chagrin', and required to excel on one instrument alone.[71] The highly successful musical association between Hasse – whose appointment as *Kapellmeister* was formalized by 1734 – and Pisendel led to great advances in orchestral discipline and performance style in Dresden. Hiller's biography of Pisendel claimed that Hasse discussed all details of his compositions with the concertmaster, who would then look through the parts prepared by court copyists and mark up performance details.[72] Within this cosmopolitan ensemble Pisendel developed a style that fused French and Italian musical mannerisms and performance practices. Years later Quantz would term this the 'vermischter Geschmack' (mixed taste), a style embracing both performance and composition that Germans could claim as being their own.[73] Moreover, the continuing pan-European membership of the *Hofkapelle* is evident from the names of the players: of the close to thirty instrumentalists under Pisendel's direction in 1730 (see Table 2.2), seventeen were Germans, whose names were printed in *Fraktur* (Gothic) type while the names of the remaining non-German members were printed in a roman typeface.[74] On the other hand, by 1730 almost all, if not all, singers of the *Hofkapelle* were Italian.[75] From Harrer's autobiography it is known that in addition to vocalists of the *Hofkapelle* August II had kept a 'musicus chorus' of unnamed singers.[76]

[69] Operas performed in Dresden and Warsaw (between 1627 and 1763) are listed in Fürstenau, *Zur Geschichte der Musik und des Theaters*, II, 'Sachregister', pp. xlvi–il.

[70] Köpp, *Johann Georg Pisendel*, 448–9.

[71] David et al., *The New Bach Reader*, 145–51, document 151.

[72] 'Pisendel (Johann Georg): Königl. Polnischer und Churfürstl. Sächsischer Concertmeister', in Hiller, *Lebensbeschreibungen berühmter Musikgelehrten*, 192–3; Pisendel's hand is seen in many manuscripts kept in D-Dl.

[73] Johann Joachim Quantz, *Versuch einer Anweisung die Flöte traversiere zu spielen*, 3rd edn (Breslau, 1789; repr. Kassel and Basel: Bärenreiter, 1953), 332, 'Hauptstück XVIII', §87. See also Steven Zohn, *Music for a Mixed Taste: Style, Genre and Meaning in Telemann's Instrumental Works* (New York: Oxford University Press, 2008), 3–5.

[74] This differentiation ceased in the 1739 edition of the *Hof- und Staats-Calender*. Music composed for Dresden during this era shows French instrumental names either being replaced with Italian terms, or else used concurrently, for example: *hautbois/oboé, corne de chasse / corno da caccia* (or *Waldhorn*), and *basson/fagotto*.

[75] *Hof- und Staats-Calender* (1731), [fol. 49ʳ col. 2 – 49ᵛ col. 1].

[76] See Wolfgang Reich, 'Jan Dismas Zelenka und seine Dresdner Kopisten', in *Zelenka-*

The repertoires gathered by Volumier and Pisendel, among others, illustrate the type of instrumental music performed during the concerts given at Dresden court functions. These collections, which later came to be housed in the *Hofkirche*, are so vast that discussion is beyond the scope of this chapter. Concertos by Telemann, Heinichen, Pisendel, Johann Friedrich Fasch (1688–1758), Gottfried Heinrich Stölzel, Quantz, and Johann Gottlieb Graun (1702/3–1771) are among the many still held in Dresden.[77] Resounding at Dresden court entertainments were countless instrumental solo, trio, and quadro sonatas by composers such as Tomaso Albinoni, Francesco Maria Veracini, and Antonio Vivaldi, with some items becoming larger-scale pieces when *Dubletten* (extra parts) were prepared.

Following the death of August II, a reorganization of Dresden's court music affected the *Kapellknaben* institute of the Catholic church. This now considerable body of young musicians (by 1731, seventeen so-called *Juvenes* lived in the Jesuit house[78]) was reduced to six, who were to serve at the altar and assist the Jesuit fathers. The music of the church was to be sung by male members of the *Hofkapelle* (named the *Majores*), an arrangement that was less than successful owing to the non-co-operation of the castratos.[79] It is acknowledged, however, that late in 1733 these singers were seriously overworked: in addition to their duties in the church they sang a 'Pastorale' in the Dresden palace on 7, 8, and 12 October, while performances of Italian opera were given on 17, 19, 24, and 26 November.[80] A 'Diarium' entry of 21 January 1737 noted that a keyboard instrument ('cymbalum') and either flutes or recorders ('par flautarum') were loaned from the 'repositorio Regis instrumentorum' (royal instrument collection) to the *Juvenes*, an indication that not only did their musical education continue, but loans could be made to them from the court's instrument collection.[81] While the music of the Catholic court church flourished, the Lutheran court church and its music – already weakened owing to decisions taken at the end of the seventeenth century – diminished to the point where this Protestant chapel (to which Wilhelm Friedemann Bach was organist between 1733 and 1746) was closed and moved to the Sophienkirche. In 1737 it was decided to replace the original Catholic court church with a much larger building.

Although numerous performance materials of sacred music once kept in the Dresden Catholic court presumably were shifted to the Soviet Union in 1946 (at

---

*Studien I: Referate der Internationalen Fachkonferenz J. D. Zelenka, Marburg, J.-G.-Herder-Institut, 16.–20. November 1991*, ed. Thomas Kohlhase, Musik des Ostens, 14 (Bärenreiter: Kassel, 1993), 109–40, at 111–13.

[77] Fechner investigated concertos by these composers in *Studien zur Dresdner Überlieferung von Instrumentalkonzerten*. For details of a research project currently being undertaken at D-Dl involving this repertory, see the website <www.slub-dresden.de>.

[78] I-Rar, Fondo Vecchia Compagnia, Boh. 148, p. 29.

[79] I-Rar, Fondo Vecchia Compagnia, Boh. 150, p. 34; see also Stockigt, *Jan Dismas Zelenka*, 201–2.

[80] D-Dla, 10006 Oberhofmarschallamt, O I, No. 3, 'Journal 1733', fols. 69ʳ–80ʳ.

[81] The instrument collection was housed in the 'Instrument Cammer' (instrument room) of the *Prinzenpalais* (princes' palace), home to the younger members of the royal and electoral family on Pirnaischer Gasse, Dresden. It was destroyed by fire during the siege of Dresden in 1760; see Fürstenau, *Zur Geschichte der Musik und des Theaters*, II: 360.

least twenty-one items have been viewed in Moscow[82]), a few examples survive in Dresden today. Three items from *c.*1730 composed by Johann Antonín Reichenauer, Františeck Ludvík Poppe, and Benedict Anton Aufschnaiter were performed at least once in the original church by members of the *Hofkapelle* led by Pisendel and directed by Zelenka, who became responsible for the court church music during the 'Interregnum'.[83] These parts show that a minimum of four solo and four ripieno singers (SATB and SATB) were accompanied in the church by a minimum of three first and either two or three second violins, one or two violas, one violoncello, one string bass instrument (which might be titled 'Violone', 'Contrabass', or 'Basso'), one first and one second oboe, organ, and, in one case, theorbo. The writing seen in the parts reveals that, as a general rule, the accompaniment of instrumental or vocal soloists was provided by three- or four-part strings (violin 1, violin 2, viola, and violoncello), while the full orchestra (including oboes, bassoons, and the string basses) played the ritornellos and supported the chorus in concerted vocal writing.

During the reign of August III as king of Poland, when Dresden was becoming a major centre of European diplomacy, the *Hofkapelle* underwent considerable expansion. This ensemble and its repertoire represent the aural equivalent of the fabulous collections of art, porcelain, and *objets d'art* for which Dresden was so admired.

### 1745: THE REIGN OF AUGUST III

The quality of musical patronage exercised by August III and the fruits of this benefaction – performances of the Dresden *virtuosi* in the opera house, the church, and in the palace – were celebrated in a panegyric written by the Dresden writer Johann Gottlob Kittel (pseudonym Micrander), published in 1740.[84] The poem, which presents a contemporary view of outstanding *Hofkapelle* members, gives an account of Kittel's imaginary dream in which Apollo called the 'Virtuosen' of London, Vienna, Paris, Rome, Naples, Madrid, and Dresden to Parnassus for a musical competition. Kittel's poem pays warm tribute to the principal Dresden court musicians, who are presented in the approximate order in which they were listed in the *Hof- und Staats-Calender* of 1741. *Kapellmeister* Hasse (whose compositions and keyboard playing are especially noted) and Faustina head the stellar cast, followed by the most highly regarded, 'vollkommner Virtuos' (perfect virtuoso),

[82] Karl Wilhelm Geck, 'Dresdner Musikmanuskripte in Moskau', *SLUB Kurier: Aus der Arbeit der Sächsischen Landesbibliothek – Staats- und Universitätsbibliothek Dresden*, 20/3 (2006), 6–8.

[83] All in D-Dl: Reichenauer, *Litaniae Lauretanae* (Mus. 2494-D-3); Poppe, *Litaniae Lauretanae* (Mus. 3610-E-2a); Aufschnaiter, *Ave Regina* (Mus. 2005-E-2a).

[84] Johann Gottlob Kittel, *Denen Bey Ihro Königl. Majest. in Pohlen und Churfürstl. Durchl. zu Sachsen, Welt-gepriesenen Hof-Capelle Befindlichen Virtuosen . . . folgendes Lob-Gedichte Im Monath Junio 1740* (Dresden, [1740]), D-HAu, Bibliotheca Ponickaviana (the former collection of Count Ponickau), K. 33 F [D-HAu shelfmark: Pon Ya 4004, FK]. This poem was discovered by Szymon Paczkowski, who kindly brought it to my attention; a facsimile, with epilogue by Gerhard Poppe, is published (Beeskow: Ortus, 2008).

the church composer Zelenka, whose music was thought to provide a foretaste of heavenly pleasure,[85] while the soprano castratos Venturini (Ventura Rochetti) and Bindi and alto castratos Annibali and Pozzi represent the heavenly chorus. The lines devoted to Pisendel suggest that the lyre of Orpheus in the heavenly firmament should be replaced with Pisendel's violin. Kittel predicts that the music of the little-known church composer Tobias Butz, listed in the *Hof- und Staats-Calender* between church composers Zelenka and Bach,[86] would one day place him alongside his teacher, Zelenka – an unfulfilled prophecy since Butz died in January 1760, a year of chaos when Dresden was besieged by Austrian and Prussian forces and the court members were in exile in Warsaw or taking refuge in Munich.[87] The playing of the violinist Francesco Maria Cattaneo is extolled. The principal woodwind players, oboist Johann Christian Richter, flautists Buffardin and Quantz, and chalumeau player Johann Wilhelm Hugo[88] are described as being an incomparable 'vierfach[es] Kleeblatt' (four-leafed clover). The main members of the bass section, bassoonist Johann Gottfried Böhme, and 'Contre-Baß' player Georg Friedrich Kästner (Personelli's successor), whose resonant tone brought the music to life by providing the foundation ('Fundament') and right strength ('Force') are lauded, whereas three cellists (their instruments are named 'Bassets') – Picinetti, Agostino Angelo de Rossi, and Angelo (Arcangelo Califano) – are especially mentioned because their playing gave such amusement. (Did they launch into improvised obbligato bass passages or display exceptional double-stopping?)[89] Kittel extolled the sound of the pantaleon, the large dulcimer developed by Pantaleon Hebenstreit, and praised with affection the magical tone of Sylvius Leopold Weiss's lute. Finally, the players of the *Waldhorn* and the 'helles Hifft'[90] – Johann Georg Knechtel and Anton Hampel (to whom the technique of hand-stopping is attributed[91]) – are admired because at times they might sound like a trumpet ('Bald auf Trompeten-Art'), and at others, like the recorder ('bald im Fleut-doucen-Thon'). Apollo's final

[85] Kittel, *Lob-Gedichte*, unpaginated: 'Du kanst zu Gottes Ehr, die Seelen zu ergötzen, Auf das beweglichste die Kirchen-Stücken setzen, Die also rührend sind, daß die andächtge Brust[,] Den Vor[ge]schmack schon empfindt von jener Himmels-Lust' (To delight the soul in God's honour, you are able to write church music in the most stimulating manner, which is so touching that the reverent breast receives a foretaste of those heavenly pleasures).

[86] Bach's name first appeared as a titular member of the court in the *Hof- und Staats-Calender* (1738), 14.

[87] The only known work of Tobias Butz to survive in Dresden is a mass setting (D-Dl, Mus. 2834-D-1) dedicated to 'Son Altesse Roial et Electoral de Saxe' (later August III).

[88] According to Kittel, Hugo (also 'Hucho'), crafted his own chalumeaux. He was listed as an oboist in the *Hof- und Staats-Calender* from 1733. Experimentation with instrument making engaged certain members of the *Hofkapelle*, the most famous being Quantz. The playing and activities of the Dresden court woodwind players might have caused the move in 1739 of an apprentice instrument maker, (Carl) August[in] Grenser, from Leipzig to Dresden.

[89] Zohn, *Music for a Mixed Taste*, 240–57, gives examples of obbligato bass parts (including specimens from Dresden-based composers) with virtuosic bass-line divisions, some of which are 'so elaborate as to resemble diminution exercises, and it is tempting to view them as "frozen" improvisations of bassoonists or cellists' (p. 244).

[90] The 'helles Hifft' is a small signal horn, originally an animal horn, later made of metal.

[91] Hiebert, 'The Horn in Early Eighteenth-Century Dresden', 193.

praise, however, is reserved for the patron of these musicians, August III, because this 'Herr von Wunder-hohen Gaben' (lord of miraculous gifts) ruled and governed in a manner that brought perfect harmony to his subjects. A notable omission from the list is Ristori, who travelled to Naples in 1738. After this absence his name next appears in the 'Diarium' on 24 March 1741. The Dresden viola players rate no mention at all.

Although 1745 represented the midpoint of this splendid era of Dresden's musical achievements, the disasters awaiting Saxony were adumbrated when, in December, the victorious Prussian Friedrich II entered Dresden at the conclusion of the Second Silesian War. Table 2.2 shows that in that year the Dresden *Hofkapelle* could provide the five different-sized instrumental ensembles with ratios suggested by Quantz (in 1752), who specified for the smallest ensemble of four violins the use of one viola, one cello, and a string bass ('Contraviolon') of medium size were needed; to which for six violins a bassoon should be added; eight violins required two violas, two violoncellos and a second 'Contraviolon', to be larger than the first; for ten violins an additional violoncello was necessary, whereas for the largest ensemble of twelve violins, it was recommended that three violas, four violoncellos, two 'Contraviolone', four flutes, four oboes, three bassoons and, in the pit, another keyboard and theorbo should be used.[92] Caution is required, however, when attempting to arrive at strict formulae for the composition of instrumental groups in Dresden. The *Hofkapelle* had to be flexible enough to adapt to a variety of performance venues (church, chamber, and theatre) both in and outside of the city. For example, in November 1739 the composer Zelenka travelled with a group of nineteen *Hofkapelle* members to perform the high mass ('Hoch-Amt') that followed the churching of Maria Josepha in the chapel of the hunting castle Hubertusburg. Accompanying the five male singers (SAATB: Venturini, Annibali, Nicolini, Johann Joseph Götzel, and Johann David Bahn) was an ensemble of four violins (Pisendel, Carl Matthias Lehneis, Joseph Titerle, and Johann Georg Fickler), two violas (Johann Gottlieb Morgenstern and Johann Adam), pairs of flutes (Buffardin and Quantz) and oboes (Richter and Hugo), and a basso continuo section comprising bassoon (Carl Morasch), violoncello (Rossi), violone (Kästner), and organ (the violinist Augustin Uhlig). Presumably, Zelenka directed the music.[93]

Royal music catalogues demonstrate the extent of collections of operas, arias, cantatas, serenatas, pastorales, and intermezzos — many either composed for specific celebrations, or dedicated to members of the Dresden court. For example, Francesco Bartolomeo Conti's cantata *L'Istro* (libretto by Apostolo Zeno), sung at the marriage ceremonies in Vienna of the Saxon electoral prince and Maria Josepha in 1719,[94] is listed in the 'Catalogo . . . S. M. Augusto III'. The 'Concerti

[92] On these ratios and Quantz's plans for the placement of the instrumentalists in both the pit and chamber, see *Versuch einer Anweisung*, 185, 'Hauptstück XVII', 'Abschnitt I', §16.

[93] A positive was brought from Dresden and played by Augustin Uhlig. D-Dla, 10006 Oberhofmarschallamt, I 66b, 'Königl. Herbst Reise von Dresden nach Hubertusburg 1739', vol. II, fol. 139ʳ.

[94] D-Dl, Mus. 2190-I-1.

con molti Stromenti' by Vivaldi, listed in a music catalogue of Maria Antonia,[95] represent works performed for and presented to Electoral Prince Friedrich Christian when he visited the Venetian Ospedale della Pietà during his *Kavaliersreise* in March 1740.[96]

Guest soloists were admitted as *virtuosi* to the court ensemble, or else they might be appointed to honorary positions. Following receipt of his court title in 1736, Bach gave a recital to a large and distinguished audience on the Silbermann organ of the Frauenkirche.[97] Apart from performances for the opera and church, members of the Dresden *Hofkapelle* were heard at intimate court gatherings, where music was listened to with critical attention. On 5 August 1744, Count Wackerbarth reported that Electoral Prince Friedrich Christian and his guests (including brothers and sisters) were entertained with a concert in the palace.[98] It was given by the sopranos Maria Rosa Negri and Wilhelmine (Guglielma) Denner, contralto Margherita Ermini, followed by 'Besuzzi' (the oboist Antonio Besozzi), 'Weiss' (Sylvius Leopold Weiss), and an unnamed 'Virtuoso de Viole di Gamba' – probably Carl Friedrich Abel.[99]

Occasional *Hof- und Staats-Calender* items report performances of Saxon princes and princesses: the fourteen-year-old Princess Maria Josepha (from 1747 dauphine of France), for example, accompanied the castrato Giovanni Bindi on the 'clavecin' during the Gala held on her name day, 17 March 1746.[100] A plan of the Dresden palace drawn that year shows that a 'chambre du concert' of eighty square metres had been established on the second floor of the palace in the northeast corner.[101] Here, concerts were given and final rehearsals of opera and oratorio took place in the presence of Maria Josepha. Already she had arranged the purchases of the musical estates of the deceased Dresden composers Schmidt and Heinichen, and the collection of the concertmaster Volumier. After the deaths of Zelenka (in 1745), Ristori (1753), and Pisendel (1755), their music libraries were also acquired for the Dresden court, all of which seem to have been housed in the queen's

[95] This catalogue, which incorporates the music collection of Maria Antonia's late husband, Prince Friedrich Christian, is bound in with the catalogue of August III (D-Dl, Bibl. Arch. III Hb 787ʰ). Talbot, *Vivaldi*, 68, identifies Vivaldi's sinfonia and concertos as RV 149, 540, 552, and 558 (D-Dl, Mus. 2389-O-4, 1/2).

[96] Prince Friedrich Christian's journal entry of 21 March 1740 notes, 'Le dernier concert des deux violons a été fort joli'; see Żórawska-Witkowska, 'Federico Cristiano in Italia', appendix 1, p. 314.

[97] David et al., *The New Bach Reader*, 188–9, document 191.

[98] D-Dla, 10026 Geheimes Kabinett, Loc. 666/9, 'Correspondance du Comte de Wackerbarth d. du Rev: P. Guarini d. l'an 1744 d. 1745. 1746', unfoliated. Information kindly supplied by Jóhannes Águstsson.

[99] Guglielma (Wilhelmine) Denner and Besozzi (as 'Antonio Pezoti') were first listed as *Hofkapelle* members in the *Hof- und Staats-Calender* of 1748 (p. 18) and 1741 (p. 15), respectively; and although Carl Friedrich Abel was listed as a 'Violgambist' in the *Hof- und Staats-Calender* (1745), 17, this is an early reference to him in Dresden records.

[100] *Hof- und Staats-Calender* (1747), [fol. 14ʳ col. 2].

[101] Landmann, 'Topographische und aufführungspraktische Anmerkungen', 322, illus. 9–10.

apartments until after the Seven Years' War.[102] Although in 1745 more than ten years of the golden musical age were ahead for the Dresden *Hofkapelle* under the direction and leadership of Hasse and Pisendel, Dresden was to experience even greater suffering and humiliation when Friedrich II, king in Prussia, would return.

## 1756–63: THE SEVEN YEARS' WAR

The years leading up to the last of the Silesian Wars (the Seven Years' War, 1756–63) saw the continuing flourishing of opera (six different productions in 1754; eight in 1755; and five in 1756),[103] a greatly expanded vocal component of about twenty-three singers (mainly Italian), and an orchestra of approximately forty-seven members led by Pisendel's successor, the former 'Cammer-Violinist' Francesco Maria Cattaneo (see Table 2.2). Ratios within the orchestra had altered so that the full ensemble had powerful outer lines of upper and lower strings and woodwinds with reduced inner instrumental voices. Although the membership of the Dresden *Hofkapelle* remained cosmopolitan, in a letter to Telemann dated 3 June 1752 Pisendel revealed that he had asked Hasse not to employ more Italians because they tended to be self-directed, playing without listening to others.[104] This hints at the orchestral discipline that developed under Pisendel's leadership: individual virtuosity was subject to the unity of the whole. Of the Dresden orchestra at its zenith in the 1750s, the French encyclopaedist Jean-Jacques Rousseau wrote glowingly of its arrangement and perfection of ensemble. He stated that while the best orchestra in Europe – from the point of view of size and understanding of its players – was that of Naples (where Maria Amalia – eldest daughter of August III and Maria Josepha – was now queen of the Two Sicilies), the best arrangement and ensemble was the opera orchestra of Dresden conducted by Hasse.[105] After Burney's visit to the Dresden opera house in 1772 (the pit could hold up to one hundred players following remodelling in 1748), he reported, '. . . I was extremely curious to see this celebrated scene of action, where general Hasse, and his well disciplined troops, had made so many glorious campaigns, and acquired such laurels'.[106]

Following its dedication in 1751, the much larger *Hofkirche* (today, the Catholic Cathedral of the diocese of Dresden-Meissen) replaced the original royal chapel. The new acoustical environment of this building led to changes in the musical repertoire. The type of revision that took place is to be seen in reworkings of several

[102] Regarding the acquisition of these music collections, see Fürstenau, *Zur Geschichte der Musik und des Theaters*, II: 181.

[103] Ibid., II, 'Sachregister', p. xlviii.

[104] Hans Grosse and Hans Rudolf Jung, eds., *Georg Philipp Telemann: Briefwechsel* (Leipzig: VEB Deutscher Verlag für Musik, 1972), 360–63, at 361–2, No. 120: letter of Johann Georg Pisendel to Telemann.

[105] Rousseau, *Dictionnaire de musique*, 354. Rousseau provided a diagram of the seating arrangements of the orchestra, reproduced in Fürstenau, *Zur Geschichte der Musik und des Theaters*, II: 291.

[106] Charles Burney, *The Present State of Music in Germany, The Netherlands and United Provinces*, 2nd edn (London, 1775; facs. repr. New York: Broude Brothers, 1969), II: 50–52.

Vespers psalms by Paolo Bellinzani, repertoire once sung by the *Kapellknaben* in the original church.[107] For example, to supplement a setting of *Lauda Jerusalem* (Psalm 147) in a set of twelve part books, at least eleven vocal and seventeen instrumental parts were prepared.[108] The organ of this church, the last to be built by Gottfried Silbermann, was consecrated on 2 February 1754.[109] By 1765, more than 1,000 items of sacred music were catalogued and housed in the *Hofkirche*.[110] These ranged from *a cappella* works of Palestrina (surviving parts show that instruments doubled the voices) to a large collection of liturgical works attributed to Baldassare Galuppi (1706–1785) provided by the Venetian copying house of Iseppo Baldan.

On 1 October 1756, at the beginning of the Seven Years' War, Saxon troops were defeated by the Prussians at the Battle of Lobositz. August III then departed for Poland, leaving Maria Josepha in Dresden at her wish. There she died on 17 November 1757. Musical development came to a halt in Saxony. Following his return from exile in Poland, August III died on 5 October 1763. His eldest surviving son and heir, Friedrich Christian, succeeded as elector of Saxony, but within two months he also passed away. Hasse composed the Requiem masses for the funerals held in the *Hofkirche*,[111] and in February 1764, he and Faustina permanently left Dresden.

Finally, although the *Hof- und Staats-Calender* and court records indicate a continuation of the famous musical institutions of Dresden, the Seven Years' War left Saxony in financial ruin. Many singers and instrumentalists of the *Hofkapelle* were about to become pensioned off, and others had moved away. When, in 1772, Charles Burney visited Dresden he noted that, during the reign of August III,

> this city was regarded by the rest of Europe, as the Athens of modern times; all the arts, but particularly, those of music, poetry, and painting, were loved and cherished by [the king] with a zeal and munificence, greater than could be found in the brightest period of ancient history.[112]

Burney then wondered whether the distresses inflicted upon Saxony resulted from the excesses of its rulers. Be that as it may, the patronage and taste of members of the Wettin family – August III and Maria Josepha in particular – left Dresden a legacy that today places it among the great cultural centres of the world.

---

[107] D-Dl, Mus. 2431-E-1.

[108] D-Dl, Mus. 2-E-736. Listed as an anonymous work in the 'Catalogo' of sacred music kept in the Dresden *Hofkirche* (compiled in 1765 under Schürer's direction; see D-B, Mus. ms. theor. Kat. 186). These parts must have been copied after 1758, when Carl Matthias Lehneis, successor to concertmaster Cattaneo (d. 1758), led the orchestra: the initials 'S. L.' (Signor Lehneis) are written on a 'Violino 1' part.

[109] In 1869, Julius Reitz reported the tuning to be 'chorus-tone [i.e. *Chor-Ton*] . . . representing for A 855 vibrations [$a' = 427.5$ Hz]'; see Royal Society of Arts (Great Britain), *Information Collected by the Society of Arts in Relation to Musical Pitch in Continental Cities* (London, 1869), 2.

[110] As seen in the 'Catalogo' of 1765 (D-B, Mus. ms. theor. Kat. 186).

[111] D-Dl, Mus. 2477-D-4a (for which 118 parts were once held in Dresden), and D-Dl, Mus. 2477-D-5a.

[112] Burney, *The Present State of Music* (1775), II: 59–60.

TABLE 2.1. Select Information on the Musicians of the Royal Polish and Electoral Saxon Orchestra, c.1717

| No. | Name of Musician | Salary in Thaler | Birthplace | Year entered Electoral/ Royal Service |
|---|---|---|---|---|
| 1. | Johann Christoph Schmidt (*Oberkapellmeister*) | 1,200 | Hohenstein [Hohnstein] in [the district of] Meissen [Saxony]^a | 1676 |
| 2. | Johann David Heinichen (*Kapellmeister*) | 1,200 | Krössuln [near Weißenfels]* | 1717/1718 |
| 3. | Jean-Baptiste Volumier ('Maitre de Concert') | 1,200 | Spain | 1709 |
| 4. | Francesco Maria Veracini ('Compositeur de la Chambre') | 1,200 | [Florence]* | [1717] |
| 5. | Pantaleon Hebenstreit (pantaleonist) | 1,200 | Thuringia | 1714 |
| 6. | Christian Petzold ('Cammer Componist und Organist') | 450 | Königstein | 1709 |
| 7. | Agostino Antonio de Rossi (vc; *Cammermusicus*) | 500 | Rome | 1709 |
| 8. | Gottfried Bentley (theorbo; *Cammermusicus*) | 400 | Dresden | 1709 |
| 9. | Francesco Arigoni (theorbo) | 400 | Rome | 1697 |
| 10. | Johann Georg Pisendel (vn; *Cammermusicus*) | 500 | Cadolzburg ([margraviate of Brandenburg-Ansbach) | 1712 |
| 11. | Johann Christian Richter (ob) | 480 | Dresden | 1709 |
| 12. | Pierre-Gabriel Buffardin (fl) | 500 | Provence | 1716^b |
| 13. | Simon le Gros (vn) | 500 | Paris* | 1700 |
| 14. | Francesco Hunt (vn) | 400 | Florence | 1710 |
| 15. | Adam Rybitzky (vn) | 300^c | Kierkrz (Greater Poland [Wielkopolska]) | 1698 |
| 16. | Johann Friedrich Lotti (vn) | 400 | Hanover | 1709 |
| 17. | Felicetti (Giovanni Felice Maria Picinetti) (vc) | 500 | Venice | 1717 |
| 18. | Jan Dismas Zelenka ('Contre Basse') | 400 | Louňovice (Bohemia)* | 1711 |
| 19. | Jean Cadet (fl and bn) | 400 | Aizelles (Picardy) | 1711 |
| 20. | Charles Henrion (ob) | 300 | Luxembourg | 1696/1709 |
| 21. | Johann Georg Lehneis (va) | 300 | Regenstauf (in [Upper] Palatinate) | 1697 |
| 22. | Jean Baptiste Prache de Tilloy (vc and copyist) | 300 | Paris | 1699 |
| 23. | Martin Golde (va) | 240 | Dresden | 1709 |

| | Name | Place | | Year |
|---|---|---|---|---|
| 24. | Johann Wolfgang Schmidt (org and copyist) | Hohnstein [Saxony][a] | 300 | 1709 |
| 25. | Michael Petzschmann (va) | Leipzig | 220 | 1699 |
| 26. | Jean Baptiste du Houlondel ('Le France le Fils') (vc) | Brussels | 250 | 1709 |
| 27. | Johann Martin Blockwitz (Blochwitz) (ob) | Geithain [near Leipzig] | 280 | 1711 |
| 28. | Johann Adalbert Fischer (hn) | Pressnitz (Bohemia) | 300 | 1710 |
| 29. | Adam Franz Saum (Samm) (hn) | Arnstein ([Lower] Franconia) | 300 | 1710 |
| 30. | Christian [David] Weigelt (fl, later ob) | Eibenstock [in the *Erzgebirge* (Ore Mountains)]* | 200 | 1711 |
| 31. | Carl Joseph Rhein (va) | Vienna | 280 | 1712 |
| 32. | Caspar Ernst Quatz (bn) | Berlin | 240 | 1709 |
| 33. | Martin Seyffert (ob) | Neubrandenburg [Mecklenburg-Vorpommern] | 220 | 1713 |
| 34. | Johann Christoph Reichel (va) | Burkhardswalde (near Wesenstein [Saxony]) | 200 | 1712 |
| 35. | Johann Gottfried Böhme (bn) | Lützschena [near Leipzig] | 300 | 1715 |
| 36. | Georg Friedrich Kästner (va) | Prettin [near Wittenberg] | 200 | 1715 |
| | Additional members:[d] | | | |
| | Georg August Kümmelmann (instrument inspector) | Nuremberg | 100[e] | 1693 |
| | Johann Jacob Lindner (copyist) | Königstein | 50 | 1677 |
| | Johann Heinrich Gräbner (organ builder/tuner) | Dresden | 150 | 1702 |
| | Gottlob Werner (servant) | Dresden | 100 | 1709 |
| | | [Total] | 17,050[f] | |

*Sources*

This information is chiefly taken from D-Dla, 1oo26 Geheimes Kabinett, Loc. 910/1, fol. 5[r-v]. This list must date after the order dated '2o Novembr. 1717' to place Veracini on the payroll of the Dresden court from 1 August 1717 (see Hill, 'The Life and Works of Francesco Maria Veracini', I: 76–7, II: 902–3).

Source for places of birth and dates of entry into royal service (Dresden) is D-Dla, 1oo6 Oberhofmarschallamt, K II, No. 5, fols. 9off.

* Information on those musicians whose names are marked with an asterisk comes from D-Dla, 1oo6 Oberhofmarschallamt K II, No. 6, pp. 3–4, 72–8.

[a] 'Hohenstein' is the spelling given in this document by Johann Christoph and Johann Wolfgang Schmidt; however, according to Michael Maul (personal communication to author), on the basis of early documentation pertaining to Johann Christoph Schmidt (including matriculation records of the University of Leipzig and the *Kreuzschule* in Dresden, among others), he was born at Hohnstein (near Pirna, in the Sächsische Schweiz [Saxon Switzerland] region).

[notes to table cont. overleaf]

[*notes to Table 2.1 (cont.)*]

b  The year of Buffardin's entry into the Dresden *Hofkapelle* is usually given as 1715, which might be, in fact, the year of his arrival in Dresden.

c  Rybitzky was also paid an extra 50 *Thaler* 'wegen *repetition der Ballette*' (for rehearsals of the ballets).

d  'Hier zu gehören noch Ferner.'

e  Kümmelmann was also paid an extra 40 *Thaler* for instrument repair ('zur Reparatur der Instrument Cammer').

f  Following the list given above (D-Dla, 10026, Geheimes Kabinett, Loc. 910/1, fol. 6), this remark is written: 'dieses *capitel* steiget mit 1000 vor den Lautenisten Veis' (this amount increases by 1,000 for the lutenist Veis). According to Fürstenau, Sylvius Leopold Weiss was formally appointed to the Dresden *Hofkapelle* on 23 August 1718; see *Zur Geschichte der Musik und des Theaters*, II: 126.

TABLE 2.2. Membership of the Royal Polish and Electoral Saxon Court Music Establishment in *c.*1717, 1730, 1745, 1756, and 1764

| *Year* | *c.1717* | *1730* | *1745* | *1756* | *1764* |
|---|---|---|---|---|---|
| Ruler | Elector Friedrich August I (r. 1694–1733) (as August II, King of Poland, r. 1697–1706 & 1709–33) | | Elector Friedrich August II (r. 1733–63) (as August III, King of Poland, r. 1733–63) | | Prince Franz Xavier, Regent of Saxony (r. 1763–68) |
| Numeric Overview | 2 *Kapellmeister* 1 concertmaster 32 instrumentalists 4 additional personnel | 1 concertmaster 33 instrumentalists 10 vocalists 4 additional personnel | 1 *Kapellmeister* 1 concertmaster 44 instrumentalists 16 vocalists 6 additional personnel | 1 *Kapellmeister* 1 concertmaster 48 instrumentalists 24 vocalists 10 additional personnel | 1 concertmaster 44 instrumentalists 15 vocalists 9 additional personnel |

| | Baron Woldemar von Löwendahl | Heinrich August von Breitenbauch | Carl Heinrich von Dieskau | Friedrich August von König |
|---|---|---|---|---|
| *Directeur des plaisirs* | [Baron Johann Siegmund von Mordaxt] | | | |
| *Oberkapellmeister* | Johann Christoph Schmidt | | Johann Adolf Hasse | Vacant[a] |
| *Kapellmeister* | Johann David Heinichen | Johann Adolf Hasse | | |
| *Vicekapellmeister* | | | Vacant | |
| *Kirchen-Compositeur* (church composer)[b] | | Jan Dismas Zelenka<br>Tobias Butz<br>Johann Sebastian Bach (titular position) | Tobias Butz<br>Nicola Porpora (titular position)<br>Johann Georg Schürer[c] | Johann Georg Schürer |
| *Compositeur de la chambre* (chamber composer) | Francesco Maria Veracini | | | |
| *Maître de concerts* (concertmaster) | Jean-Baptiste Volumier (Woulmyer) | Johann Georg Pisendel | Francesco Maria Cattaneo | Carl Matthias Lehneis |
| Instrumentalists | | | | |
| Violin | Johann Georg Pisendel<br>Simon le Gros<br>Francesco Hunt | Francesco Maria Cattaneo, 'Cammer-Violinist'<br>Carl Joseph Rhein<br>Simon le Gros<br>Johann Friedrich Lotti | Carl Matthias Lehneis<br>Lorenzo Carazzi<br>Augustin Uhlig | Lorenzo Carazzi<br>Augustin Uhlig (also instrument inspector)<br>Johann Georg Fickler |

| Year | c.1717 | 1730 | 1745 | 1756 | 1764 |
|---|---|---|---|---|---|
| Violin (cont.) | Adam Rybitzky | Francesco Hunt | Carl Matthias Lehneis | *Johann Franz Hancke | Franz Zich |
| | Johann Friedrich Lotti | Adam Rybitzky | Lorenzo Carazzi | *Joseph Titerle | François de Francini |
| | | Carl Matthias Lehneis^d | Augustin Uhlig | Christoph Wilhelm Taschenberg | Franz Nikolaus Hunt |
| | | | Johann Franz Hancke | Johann Georg Fickler | Johann Baptist Georg Neruda |
| | | | Joseph Titerle | Franz Zich | Felice Picinetti |
| | | | Christoph Wilhelm Taschenberg | François de Francini | Friedrich Gottlob Haller |
| | | | Johann Georg Fickler | Francesco Hunt | Franz Fiedler |
| | | | Franz Zich | Johann Baptist Georg Neruda | Johann Baptista Hunt |
| | | | François de Francini | Felice Picinetti^e | Johann Eiselt |
| | | | Francesco Hunt | Gottfried Friedrich Göricke | Joseph Dietze |
| | | | Felice Picinetti | Friedrich Gottlob Haller | Simon Uhlig |
| | | | | Franz Fiedler | Anton Lehneis |
| | | | | Johann Baptista Hunt | Ludovicus Neruda |
| | | | | Johann Eiselt | |
| Viola | Johann Georg Lehneis | Martin Golde | Johann Christoph Reichel | *Johann Gottlieb Morgenstern | Johann Adam (also 'Ballet-Compositeur') |
| | Martin Golde | Johann Christoph Reichel | Johann Gottlieb Morgenstern | Johann Adam | Johann Huber |

| | | | | | |
|---|---|---|---|---|---|
| | Johann Gottfried Röhr<br>Johann David Lange | Johann Huber<br>Johann Gottfried Röhr<br>Johann David Lange | Johann Adam[f]<br>Johann Huber | Johann Gottlieb Morgenstern | Michael Petzschmann<br>Carl Joseph Rhein<br>Johann Christoph Reichel<br>Georg Friedrich Kästner |
| Violoncello | Joseph Zicka (Zyka)<br>Joseph Franz Hofmann<br>Antonio Picinetti<br>Johann Georg Knechtel<br>Friedrich Joseph Zicka | Joseph Zicka (Zyka)<br>Joseph [Franz?] Hofmann<br>Antonio Picinetti<br>Johann Georg Knechtel | Agostino Antonio de Rossi<br>Giovanni Felice Maria Picinetti ('Felicetti')<br>Arcangelo Califano<br>Joseph Zicka (Zyka)<br>Carl Friedrich Abel (vdg) | Giovanni Felice Maria Picinetti ('Felicetti')<br>Agostino Antonio de Rossi<br>Jean Baptiste Prache de Tilloy | Agostino Antonio de Rossi<br>Giovanni Felice Maria Picinetti ('Felicetti')<br>Jean Baptiste Prache de Tilloy (also copyist) |
| Violone/Contrabass | Johann Caspar Horn<br>George Christoph Balch<br>Anton Dietrich | Georg Friedrich Kästner (also instrument inspector)<br>Johann Caspar Horn | Georg Friedrich Kästner<br>Johann Samuel Kayser | Robert du Houlondel ('le Pere')<br>Jean Baptiste du Houlondel ('le Fils')<br>Jan Dismas Zelenka, 'Contra-Basso & Compositeur'<br>Georg Friedrich Kästner | Jean Baptiste du Houlondel ('le Fils')<br>[Jan Dismas Zelenka, 'Contre Basse'[g]] |

| Year | c.1717 | 1730 | 1745 | 1756 | 1764 |
|---|---|---|---|---|---|
| Flute | Pierre-Gabriel Buffardin | Pierre-Gabriel Buffardin | Pierre-Gabriel Buffardin | Wenzel Gottfried Dewerdeck | Franz Joseph Götzel |
|  | Jean Cadet (also bn) | Johann Joachim Quantz | Wenzel Gottfried Dewerdeck | Franz Joseph Götzel | Antoine François Derablé |
|  | Christian [or David] Weigelt | Johann Martin Blockwitz (Blochwitz) | Franz Joseph Götzel | Pietro Grassi Florio | Johann Adam Schmidt |
| Oboe | Johann Christian Richter | François (Franciscus) le Riche, 'Hautbois de la Chambre'[h] | [Johann Christian Richter][j] | Antonio Besozzi | Antonio Besozzi |
|  | Charles Henrion | Johann Christian Richter | Antonio Besozzi | Carlo Besozzi | Carlo Besozzi |
|  | Johann Martin Blockwitz (Blochwitz) | Charles Henrion | Johann Wilhelm Hugo | *Johann Wilhelm Hugo | Johann Christian Fischer[i] |
|  | Martin Seyffert | Martin Seyffert | Gottlieb Benjamin Lachmann | Franz Ziencken | Johann Franz Zinke |
|  |  | Christian [or David] Weigelt] | Franz Ziencken | Christian Wopst |  |
|  |  |  | Christian Wopst | Johann Christian Taube |  |
| Bassoon | Caspar Ernst Quatz | Johann Gottfried Böhme | Johann Gottfried Böhme | *Johann Casimir Lincke | Christian Friedrich Mattstädt |
|  | Johann Gottfried Böhme | Jean Cadet | Caspar Ernst Quatz | Carl Morasch | Carl Christian Ritter |
|  | *See* Flute | Caspar Ernst Quatz | Johann Casimir Lincke | Christian Friedrich Mattstädt | Franz Adolph Christlieb |

| | | | | | |
|---|---|---|---|---|---|
| | | | Carl Morasch, Christian Friedrich Mattstädt | Johann Ritter, Samuel Fritzsche, Franz Adolph Christlieb (also music copyist) | Johann Gabriel Zeisig |
| *Waldhorn* | Johann Adalbert Fischer, Adam Franz Saum (Samm) | Johann Adam Schindler, Andreas Schindler | Johann Georg Knechtel, Anton Joseph Hampel | Anton Joseph Hampel, Carl Haudeck | Carl Haudeck, Anton Joseph Hampel, Johann Adolph Faustinus Weiss |
| Theorbo | Gottfried Bentley, Francesco Arigoni | | | | |
| Lute | Sylvius Leopold Weiss, 'Cammer-Lautenist' | Sylvius Leopold Weiss, 'Cammer-Lautenist' | Sylvius Leopold Weiss, 'Cammer-Lautenist' | | |
| Pantaleon | Pantaleon Hebenstreit | Pantaleon Hebenstreit | Pantaleon Hebenstreit[k] | Christlieb Siegmund Binder | |
| Organist | Christian Petzold, 'Cammer-Componist und Organist'; Johann Wolfgang Schmidt (also music copyist) | Christian Petzold, 'Componist und Organist'; Johann Wolfgang Schmidt (also 'Clavecin') | Giovanni Alberto Ristori, 'Cammer-Organist'; Peter August | Peter August; Constantin Joseph Weber | Peter August; Christian Gottlob Binder |
| Vocalists[1] Soprano | Andrea Ruota | Faustina Bordoni-Hasse (mezzo) | Faustina Bordoni-Hasse (mezzo) | Faustina Bordoni-Hasse (mezzo) | Wilhelmine Denner |

# JANICE B. STOCKIGT

| Year | c.1717 | 1730 | 1745 | 1756 | 1764 |
|---|---|---|---|---|---|
| Soprano (cont.) | | Anna Negri | Maria Rosa Negri | Maria Rosa Negri-Pavona | Maria Elisabeth Denner |
| | | Maria Rosa Negri | Ventura Rochetti ('Venturini') | Teresa Albuzzi-Todeschini | Salvatore Pacifico |
| | | Ventura Rochetti ('Venturini') | Giovanni Bindi | Wilhelmine (Guglielma) Denner | Nicolaus Spindler |
| | | Giovanni Bindi | Salvatore Pacifico | Caterina Pilaja | |
| | | Lodovica Seyfried | | Angelo Maria Monticelli | |
| | | | | Ventura Rochetti ('Venturini') | |
| | | | | Salvatore Pacifico | |
| | | | | Bartolomeo Putini | |
| | | | | Giovanni (Giuseppe) Belli | |
| | | | | Nicolaus Spindler | |
| Alto | | Nicola Pozzi ('Nicolini') | Margherita Ermini | Sophie Pestel (née Denner) | Domenico Annibali |
| | | Margherita Ermini | Sophie Pestel (née Denner) | Nicola Pozzi ('Nicolini') | Giuseppe Perini |
| | | Domenico Annibali | Nicola Pozzi ('Nicolini') | Domenico Annibali | |
| | | | Domenico Annibali | Pasquale Bruscolini ('Pasqualino') | |
| Tenor | | Matteo Lucchini | Angelo Amorevoli | Angelo Amorevoli | Angelo Amorevoli |

| | | | | |
|---|---|---|---|---|
| **Bass** | Ludwig Cornelius<br>Franz Ignatius Seydelmann<br>Johann David Bahn<br>Joseph Schuster<br>Joseph Brandler<br>Gabriel Joseph Führig<br>Thadeus Butz<br>Johann Ernst Tittel | Johann Joseph Götzel<br>Ludwig Cornelius<br>Johann David Bahn<br>Biaggio Campagnari<br>Joseph Schuster<br>Joseph Brandler | Johann Joseph Götzel<br>Ludwig Cornelius<br>Johann David Bahn<br>Biaggio Campagnari<br>Joseph Schuster<br>Anton(ius) Führich | Cosimo Ermini |
| **Additional Personnel** | | | | |
| **Poet** | Giannambrogio Migliavacca | Giannambrogio Migliavacca | Giovanni Claudio Pasquini | |
| **Copyists** | Johann Gottfried Grundig<br>Johann George Kremmler<br>Matthias Schlettner<br>Carl Gottlieb Uhle | Johann George Kremmler<br>Johann Gottfried Grundig<br>George Christoph Balch<br>Matthias Schlettner<br>Leonhard Butz<br>*See* Bassoon | Johann George Kremmler<br>Johann Gottfried Grundig<br>Johann Jacob Lindner | Johann Jacob Lindner<br>*See* Violoncello *and* Organist |
| **Orgelmacher** | Johann Daniel Silbermann (listed as 'Orgelbauer') | Johann Heinrich Gräbner (jun.)<br>Johann Gottfried Gräbner<br>Johann Daniel Silbermann | Johann Heinrich Gräbner (jun.)<br>Johann Gottfried Gräbner | Johann Heinrich Gräbner (sen.) (listed as 'Orgelbauer') |

| Year | c.1717 | 1730 | 1745 | 1756 | 1764 |
|---|---|---|---|---|---|
| 'Stimmer' (tuner) | | | | | Johann Gottfried Gräbner / Johann Heinrich Gräbner (jun.) |
| Instrument inspector | Georg August Kümmelmann | Georg August Kümmelmann | Vacant | *See* Violone/Contrabass | *See* Violin |
| Servant | Johann Gottlob Werner | Johann Gottlob Werner | Johann Gottlob Werner | Johann Gottfried Werner | Johann Gottfried Werner |

*Sources*

*c.1717*: D-Dla, 10026 Geheimes Kabinett, Loc. 910/1, fol. 5r-v: 'No: 1 Verzeichnüß derer *Musicorum* so in der Königl. *Orchestra* sich befinden, alß', *c.*1717. This list must date after the order dated 20 November 1717 to place Veracini on the payroll of the Dresden court from 1 August 1717. See Hill, 'The Life and Works of Francesco Maria Veracini', I: 75–8, II: 902–3. Two vocalists of the *Hofkapelle*, 'Mr. Diart' and 'Mr. Beaureguard' (Boucard or Bourgard), named in both earlier and later documents are missing from this list.

*1730*: 'Die Königl. *Capelle* und Cammer-*Musique*': list based on information in *Hof- und Staats-Calender* (1731), fol. 49r-v (recent pagination). This list also includes the 'Musiciens vocals François': five singers and the 'compositeur' Louis André.

*1745*: 'Die Königliche Capell- und Cammer-Musique': list based on information in *Hof- und Staats-Calender* (1746), 17. This list continues on p. 18 with names of twenty-nine members of the 'Danse' and one 'Valet'; five 'Autres Personnes employées au Theatre'; two 'Souffleurs de l'Opera'; eleven members of the 'Italiänische Comödianten'; and six 'Pensionaires'.

*1756*: 'Königliche Capell- und Cammer-Music': list based on information provided in *Hof- und Staats-Calender* (1757), 25–6, with information given in Fürstenau, *Zur Geschichte der Musik und des Theaters*, II: 294–5. Differences between the published list and one provided by Fürstenau are: Father Michael Breunich (not Porpora) was named as one of three *Kirchen-Compositeurs*. Differences in numbers of instrumentalists are: four (not five) viola players (unnamed), three (not four) cellists ('2 Italiener und 1 Deutscher, Zyka'), and six (not five) bassoonists. Constantin Joseph Weber (organist) is missing from Fürstenau's list, which also shows that four (not five) copyists were employed in 1756.

* According to information published by Marpurg titled 'vi. Die Koenigl. Capell- und Cammer-Music zu Dresden, 1756', those players whose names are marked above with an asterisk were now 'Pensionairs'; see Friedrich Wilhelm Marpurg, *Historisch-kritische Beyträge zur Aufnahme der Musik*, II, 'Fünftes Stück' (Berlin, 1756), 475–7.

*1764*: Based on the payment list dated 1 January 1764, in D-Dla, 10026 Geheimes Kabinett, Loc. 910/1, fol. 23r.

a Hasse and Faustina finally left Dresden on 20 February 1764. The sum of 1,000 *Thaler* was set aside for the position of *Kapellmeister*; see 'Extract' dated 1 January 1764, in D-Dla, 10026 Geheimes Kabinett, Loc. 910/1, fol. 23r.

b  The Dresden court composers (for both church and chamber) stood apart from the instrumentalists at this time: their duties were to supply repertoire and rework newly collected works; thus, they are not included in the numeric overview.

c  Schürer's name is given as 'Adam Schierer'.

d  Carl Matthias Lehneis (born in Vienna) entered the Dresden Hofkapelle in 1720 as a 'Violinist Schola[r]'; see D-Dla, 10006 Oberhofmarschallamt, K 11, No. 7, 'Königl. Pohlnische und Churfürstl. Sächß. Hoff Bediente 1726 bis 1729', without foliation.

e  Felice and Antonio Picinetti (see Violoncello) were brothers, according to Marpurg, Historisch-kritische Beyträge, II: 476–7; they were the sons of Giovanni Felice Maria Picinetti ('Felicetti'; see Violoncello, c.1717, 1730, and 1745; he died in 1754).

f  Although listed with the viola section, Johann Adam was also the composer of ballet music for the opera; see Fürstenau, Zur Geschichte der Musik und des Theaters, II: 226–7.

g  Zelenka was absent from Dresden and living in Vienna in 1717.

h  Despite this listing, François Le Riche acted as an agent of the Dresden court, purchasing jewellery, foreign wares, and horses; see Fürstenau, Zur Geschichte der Musik und des Theaters, II: 66–7. In a brief autobiography provided in c.1717 (D-Dla, 10006 Oberhofmarschallamt, K 11, No. 5, fol. 90ʳ) Le Riche described himself as a 'Musicien de la chambre'.

i  Although listed here, oboist Johann Christian Richter died in 1744.

j  Johann Christian Fischer was also listed as a 'Cammer-Musicus' to Prince Carl; see the Hof- und Staats-Calender (1765), 78.

k  Also listed in the Hof- und Staats-Calender (1746), 16, as 'Capell-Director' of the Dresden court Protestant church music (under the heading 'Hof-Kirchen-Capell-Bediente').

l  The vocalists of Antonio Lotti's operatic company (employed at the court from September 1717) appear to have been paid from a separate budget and thus were not official members of the Hofkapelle.

# 3

# The Saxon Court of the Kingdom of Poland

*Alina Żórawska-Witkowska*

FROM 1573 ONWARDS, the rulers of the Polish–Lithuanian real union (the kingdom of Poland and the grand duchy of Lithuania) were appointed in elections. Each monarch's court would become dissolved upon the king's death, and the royal collections of art, books, and music were handed down to the king's heirs. As a result, a new monarch had to organize a new court and accumulate new collections; on the other hand, he would typically inherit from his predecessor some of the personnel, including musicians. This was the case with the two Saxon electors, Friedrich August I (also known as August the Strong) and his son, Friedrich August II. Both became kings of Poland and grand dukes of Lithuania, and as such they were known as August II (1697–1706 and 1709–33) and August III (1733–63), respectively.[1] After their respective deaths, most of the records and all of their music collections previously held in Warsaw were removed to Dresden and incorporated into its collections.[2] It is therefore difficult to neatly pinpoint those works composed for, or performed at, the Polish court among the many music scores in the Dresden royal-electoral collections.

In any case, the situation that resulted from the Polish(/Lithuanian)–Saxon personal union was rather peculiar. Each of the two Augusts had to simultaneously retain two separate state structures that were markedly different in terms of size, ethnic composition, religion, political system, economic development, and culture. Saxony and the Polish-Lithuanian Commonwealth had to compete for royal attention, a rivalry in which the native Saxony of both August II and August III was an outright winner over the alien lands of Poland-Lithuania. In a reign that spanned about thirty years, August II made twenty-six trips to Poland, spending a little more than eleven years in Warsaw. The travel log of August III was similar:

The author carried out research in the Sächsisches Hauptstaatsarchiv in Dresden (D-Dla) prior to a recent internal reorganization of parts of the archive and therefore, where applicable, citations refer to the earlier cataloguing system.

[1] August II was restored to the Polish throne in 1709, although it was not until February 1710 that he returned to Warsaw. August III was elected King of Poland in October 1733 and crowned in 1734.

[2] The documentation relating to the court is now held in D-Dla, with music-related material in D-Dl.

over the course of thirty years he made only ten trips amounting to twelve years in Warsaw. Furthermore, of those twelve, six and a half years were spent there in exile, necessitated by the Seven Years' War, which raged in Saxony between 1756 and 1763.[3] Obviously, this shows that the two kings considered their electoral responsibilities in Saxony and the splendour of their Saxon court to be a higher priority than Warsaw. Their most important music ensembles were based in Dresden. These included the royal *Hofkapelle*, which despite its description as 'royal' (referring to the kingdom of Poland) primarily performed at the electoral court in Saxony, an Italian opera troupe, and a French comedy and dance troupe. There were also various other companies such as the *comici italiani* and ballet dancers, as well as court trumpeters and kettledrum players, and *Jagdpfeifer* and *Bockpfeifer* ensembles. In contrast, the court in Warsaw only supported a Polish ensemble, the 'Pohlnische Capelle' (1715–33, that is during the reign of August II, and 1734–63, during August III's reign), and a Janissary ensemble (1717–33). When the court travelled to the royal residences in Poland, however, it was accompanied by artists seconded from the various Dresden ensembles to meet the specific needs of the monarch.

Written sources relating to the Polish ensembles of both Saxon kings mainly comprise financial documents, in which economic issues take precedence. Most of the documents are in German, which at that time lacked a uniform or consistent terminology for musical instruments. As a result, the material contains borrowed terms from French and Italian, many of them corrupted, thus resulting in problems of interpretation. To varying degrees, the information provided on the constitution of those ensembles must be regarded as an approximation. It is important to note that the actual number of musicians working at any given time tended to be much higher than that reflected in the financial records. The body of officially engaged and salaried musicians as listed in payrolls was supplemented by additional diverse personnel, such as supernumeraries, expectants (who volunteered their services), members of other ensembles retained by individual aristocrats or churches, and visiting artists. Despite their seeming objectivity, these financial records shed no light on the important role played by these undocumented musicians.

[3] Cf. the chronological tables of court visits to Poland edited (and co-edited) by Alina Żórawska-Witkowska in *Pod jedną koroną: Kultura i sztuka w czasach unii polsko-saskiej* [Under a Single Crown: Culture and Art in the Times of the Polish-Saxon Union], ed. Marta Męclewska and Barbara Grątkowska-Ratyńska (Warsaw: Zamek Królewski w Warszawie, 1997), 57–61 [published in German as *Unter einer Krone: Kunst und Kultur der sächsisch-polnischen Union*, ed. Werner Schmidt (Leipzig: Edition Leipzig, 1997), 49–53, 58–63]; and Żórawska-Witkowska, 'Between Dresden and Warsaw: The Travels of the Court of August III of Poland (Friedrich August II of Saxony)', in *Polish Studies on Baroque Music*, ed. Szymon Paczkowski and Anna Ryszka-Komarnicka, *Musicology Today*, 6 (2009), 7–24.

## THE REIGN OF KING AUGUST II

The history of August II's Polish ensemble was shaped by two main phases within the king's reign in Poland-Lithuania, which were demarcated by major political events. The reign of August II was inaugurated with great momentum. Initially, he focused his energies on his new kingdom and vigorously pursued his artistic ambitions in Warsaw. There, in 1697, the king organized the 'Königlich Pohlnische Capelle', a shared artistic project for his Polish and Saxon courts. In 1699, he invited to Warsaw the Italian comedy troupe of Gennaro Sacco (February–May), the French comedy troupes of Denis Nanteuil (May–August?) and Jean Fonpré (May 1700–1703/4?), and, above all, the French operatic ensemble of Louis Deseschaliers (June 1700–1703/4).[4]

### *The 'Königlich Pohlnische Capelle', 1697–1707 (1702)*

August II began to organize his royal ensemble soon after his coronation, which was held in Cracow. The amount of money earmarked for the musicians' upkeep – '5270 Thlr. 20 gr.[:] denen sämtl. Musicis auf 9. Monathe als vom 1. Oct. 1697 bis mit Ult: Junij 1698' (5,270 *Thaler*, 20 *Groschen* for all the musicians for nine months from 1 October 1697 until the end of June 1698)[5] – would suggest that the initial number of musicians was somewhere between twelve and twenty. It was not until the latter half of 1698 that the total number rose to forty-one and the upkeep costs increased to 12,000 *Thaler* per annum. The list of members drafted in the spring of 1699 included two *Kapellmeister* (Johann Christoph Schmidt and Jacek Różycki); a poet (Pietro Francesco de Silva); eight singers, including two castrato sopranos (Michele Angelo Stella and Francesco Michaeli); two castrato altos (Filippo Antonio Scandalibene (Scandalibeni) and Pietro Benedetti); two tenors (Viviano Agostini and Daniel Fierszewicz, who were also composers); two basses (Giovanni Battista Benedetti and Makowski[6]); two organists (François de Tilly and Piotr Kosmowski [Pietro Cosmorsky]); a theorbo player (Francesco Arigoni); and six violinists, including the concertmaster Georg Gottfried Backstroh. Other instruments listed include three violas, one *basse de violon*, six oboes, four bassoons, four trumpets, one kettledrum player, and a copyist and a servant.[7]

The ensemble comprised artists from various locations and of different

---

[4] See Alina Żórawska-Witkowska, *Muzyka na dworze Augusta II w Warszawie* [Music at the Court of August II in Warsaw] (Warsaw: Zamek Królewski w Warszawie, 1997).

[5] D-Dla, 10026 Geheimes Kabinett, Loc. 32623, 'Der Königl. Pohln. Capelle von Musicis Besoldungs Rückstände . . .', fol. 4.

[6] Makowski's first name is unknown.

[7] For a full list of names, see Żórawska-Witkowska, *Muzyka na dworze Augusta II*, 77–8 (list based on D-Dla, 10026 Geheimes Kabinett, Loc. 32623, 'Der Königl. Pohln. Capelle von Musicis Besoldungs Rückstände . . .', fols. 4–33; Loc. 383, vol. 1: 'Die Bande Französischen Comoedianten und Orchestra . . .', fol. 110; Loc. 910, vol. 1: 'Acta das Chur-Fürstl. Orchestre und deßen Unterhaltung . . .', fol. 1).

nationalities. Nineteen instrumentalists with German names presumably came from Dresden: several had been members of the *Kapelle* of Johann Georg III, elector of Saxony (d. 1691). The Polish and Italian contingent, which numbered fourteen, probably included former members of the royal ensemble of King Jan III Sobieski of Poland. The poet De Silva had been secretary to Cardinal Michał Radziejowski, primate of Poland and Lithuania. Four of the oboe players, including two Frenchmen, Jean-Baptiste Henrion and Charles Henrion, had come from Vienna.

The above demonstrates that the royal ensemble was intended as a highly ambitious project, with its musicians capable of serving a variety of functions. The instrumental section was based on the French model because it was intended for accompanying French operatic and comedy performances. Italian and Polish singers were required for performances of Italian theatre pieces, of which they had gained first-hand experience at the court of Jan III Sobieski. They were also familiar with a repertoire of Catholic sacred music – a much-needed element of expertise that was missing among the Protestant members of the Saxon contingent.

The bright prospects for Warsaw's musical life were nipped in the bud by the Great Northern War begun by August II in 1700. When he fled the city in May 1702, Warsaw was overrun by Swedish forces; in the autumn the majority of the royal ensemble followed the king to Saxony. Charles XII of Sweden had exerted pressure to have Stanisław Leszczyński installed as the new king of Poland, an event that occurred on 12 July 1704. August II abdicated on 24 September 1706. On 12 April 1707, his joint Polish-Saxon 'Königlich Pohlnische Capelle' was dissolved. In its place, August set up a new ensemble in Dresden – a purely instrumental body consistently referred to in the sources as the 'Orchestra'. It included several members of the former Polish ensemble, such as *Kapellmeister* Schmidt, Arigoni, Kosmowski, Daniel Hennig, the Rybicki (Rybitzky) brothers, and the Henrion brothers.[8]

In the end, August II finally returned to Poland-Lithuania as its monarch in 1709, but did not regain actual power until 1716. As a result, Warsaw had no royal music ensemble between May 1702 and the early months of 1716, and the political turmoil (which unfortunately had coincided with various natural disasters) effectively wiped out all cultural life at the Polish court. In military matters at least, this combination of calamitous circumstances was of August's own doing, but it effectively cooled the king's affection for Poland and caused him relocate his artistic patronage to Dresden.

---

[8] The roster of this orchestra is not known before 1709 (D-Dla, 10026 Geheimes Kabinett, Loc. 383, vol. I, fol. 110), as published by Moritz Fürstenau, *Zur Geschichte der Musik und des Theaters am Hofe der Kurfürsten von Sachsen und Könige von Polen*, 2 vols. (Dresden, 1861–2), II (repr. with commentary and indexes by Wolfgang Reich, Leipzig: Peters, 1979), 49–50.

## The 'Pohlnische Capelle', 1716–33

The second phase of August II's reign in Poland-Lithuania coincided with the activity of his 'Pohlnische Capelle' (also known as the 'Pohlnische Capell-Musique', 'Pohlnisches Orgester', and 'Notre Orchestre de Pologne') during a period of political stabilization. Now, the king's Polish ensemble, which numbered about a dozen players, was mainly intended to meet the artistic requirements in Warsaw, although on occasion it also had to perform in Saxony. The name of the ensemble related purely to its geographical location since it never included Polish musicians.

## The Development of the Polish Hofkapelle from 1715 until 1719

An annual salary of 400 *Thaler* was disbursed from the coffers of the Polish court to the organist Piotr Kosmowski beginning in September 1715, although this position was not actually part of the Polish ensemble.[9] August II did not begin to organize the ensemble until late 1715, when he requested all the musicians from his Royal Infantry Guard Corps ('sämtl. bey dem Corps unserer Fuß-Trabantem befindl. Musicis') follow him to Poland.[10] When the king arrived in Warsaw from Saxony in mid-February 1716, he was accompanied by twelve musicians.[11] For many years four of them formed the core of August II's Polish ensemble: violinists Heinrich Schulze (Schulz) and Christian Friedrich Friese, the bass player Daniel Hasse, and the horn player Gottfried Grossmann.[12]

The arrival at Warsaw of Tommaso Ristori's troupe of *comici italiani* in February 1716 was the reason for summoning those musicians. Their performances (of *commedie dell'arte*, intermezzos, and presumably also minor operatic pieces[13]) required the assistance of an orchestra, if only a small one. In the records from 1716 to 1717, the orchestra is still referred to in descriptive terms that state its provenance and function.[14] In setting up his Warsaw ensemble, August II chose not to

---

[9] Among others, D-Dla, 10026 Geheimes Kabinett, Loc. 3521, 'Pohlnische General-Cassa Sachen', vol. I, fols. 74–5; Loc. 3521, vol. VII, 'Königliche Pohlnische General-Cassa Rechnung von ultimo Decembris Anno 1716 bis ultimo Decembris 1717', fol. 33.

[10] D-Dla, 10026 Geheimes Kabinett, Loc. 907, vol. I, 'Die Italiaenische Comoedianten . . .', fol. 36.

[11] D-Dla, 10006 Oberhofmarschallamt, I, No. 24, fol. 454.

[12] Although Daniel Hasse is described repeatedly in court records under the rubric 'Contra-Basson', it seems that he was also (or perhaps even solely) a string bass player (contrabass or violoncello). Iconographic evidence does, however, suggest that a contra-bassoon was available to royal ensembles, including the Polish *Kapelle*; see Ortrun Landmann, 'The Dresden *Hofkapelle* during the Lifetime of Johann Sebastian Bach', *Early Music*, 17 (1989), 17–30, especially the drawing (after Pöppelmann) of the forty-ninth birthday celebrations for August the Strong reproduced over pp. 18–19.

[13] Żórawska-Witkowska, *Muzyka na dworze Augusta II*, 290 ff.; Żórawska-Witkowska, 'Il teatro musicale italiano a Varsavia al tempo di Augusto II il Forte (1697–1733): Un tentativo di ricostruzione del repertorio', in *Il teatro musicale italiano nel Sacro Romano Impero nei secoli XVII e XVIII*, ed. Alberto Colzani, Norbert Dubowy, Andrea Luppi, and Maurizio Padoan (Como: A.M.I.S., 1999).

[14] D-Dla, 10026 Geheimes Kabinett, Loc. 907, vol. I, fols. 34–35, 37–38; Loc. 3522, 'General-

draw upon the membership of his Dresden ensemble and contented himself with musicians of a lesser status at that time (as can be inferred from their relatively low wages and origins as military musicians).

We do not know which instruments the twelve members of this ensemble played; it was later referred to as the 'Pohlnisches Orgester'.[15] It must have replicated the Italian theatre orchestra model and included first and second violins, a viola, a basso continuo section, pairs of flutes or oboes, and horns. Giovanni Alberto Ristori, son of Tommaso, who had arrived in Warsaw with the troupe of *comici italiani*, assisted with the orchestra. A harpsichord player and an opera composer with an established reputation in Italy, Ristori was not formally retained at the Polish-Saxon court until 1 January 1717. After that date, as a composer of Italian music he drew an annual salary of 600 *Thaler* from the Polish coffers until 1733.[16] Musical scores of his intermezzos, presumably performed in Warsaw, include only the violin and the basso continuo parts, occasionally supplemented by a viola and, in one case, a colascione (a member of the lute family).[17] The vocal parts were performed by singers from the *comici italiani* troupe, the soprano Orsola Costa, the alto Rosalia Del Fantasia, the tenor(?) Giovanni Micheli, and the bass Carlo Malucelli.[18]

From 1 September 1717 onwards, the maintenance costs of the ensemble were borne by the monarch's Polish court. Presumably, the bills had formerly been met by Dresden under a pre-existing arrangement, with the Polish court only reimbursing the difference in exchange rates between the Polish and the Saxon currencies. The annual amount divided among the twelve musicians was 2,116 *Thaler*, includ-

---

Casse de Anno 1720/1721', without foliation: 'die vormahls bey hiesigen Trabanten gestandenen, nunmehro aber sich in Warschau befindliche Musicanten'; 'die zu Warschau befindliche Musikanten'; 'Musici bey der Ital: Comoedie'; 'Musici von der Ital. Comoedie' (the musicians who had previously accompanied the local bodyguards, but who are now present in Warsaw; the musicians now present at Warsaw; musicians performing with the Italian *Comoedie*; the musicians of the Italian *Comoedie*).

[15] For example, D-Dla, 10026 Geheimes Kabinett, Loc. 383, vol. 11: 'Französische Comoedianten und Orchestra betr. Ao 1721–33', fol. 186; Loc. 907, vol. 1, fol. 50; Loc. 1386, 'Ordres du Roi à Volmar 1720–28', fol. 9; 10006 Oberhofmarschallamt, O IV, No. 101, records dated 15 and 18 February 1720. Other labels used included 'Pohlnische Capelle', 'Unsere Pohlnische Capelle', 'Notre Orchestre de Pologne', and 'Pohlnische Capellmusique'. For a list of names of players, see Żórawska-Witkowska, *Muzyka na dworze Augusta II*, 86.

[16] D-Dla, 10026 Geheimes Kabinett, Loc. 907, vol. 1, fol. 40. Ristori's handwritten acknowledgements of receipt of his salary received in Warsaw from the period 1725–6 are in PL-Wagad, AK 1/43, AK 1/44, AK 1/46a, and AK 1/46b. Contrary to the assertions of Fürstenau, *Zur Geschichte der Musik und des Theaters*, II: 120, and Carl Rudolf Mendelberg, *Giovanni Alberto Ristori: Ein Beitrag zur Geschichte italienischer Kunstherrschaft in Deutschland im 18. Jahrhundert* (Leipzig: Breitkopf & Härtel, 1916), 3–4, these documents do not confirm Ristori's position as director or *Kapellmeister* of August II's Polish ensemble.

[17] Giovanni Alberto Ristori, *Delbo e Dorina* (D-Dl, Mus. 2455-F-11); *Despina, Simona e Trespone* (Mus. 2455-F-14); *Fidalba e Artabano* (Mus. 2455-F-12); *Lisetta e Castagnacco* (Mus. 2455-F-13); *Serpilla e Serpello* (Mus. 2455-F-15).

[18] Żórawska-Witkowska, *Muzyka na dworze Augusta II*, 185 ff.

ing a livery allowance of 300 *Thaler* (that is 25 *Thaler* per person).[19] The first extant list of salaries referring to specific individuals dates to 1718.[20] In most cases, their musical specializations can be traced using later records. Of the twelve musicians who had arrived in Warsaw late in 1715, only four were still remaining in 1718. Those included the violinists Schulze and Friese, the bass player Daniel Hasse, and the horn player Grossmann. The instrumentalists presumably included four violinists, one viola player (?), one bass player, one lute player, one bassoonist, two flautists/oboists, and two horn players. If required, the ensemble could be augmented by the organist Kosmowski and the harpsichordist Ristori. Until 1733, the violinist and composer Schulze was the concertmaster.[21] The ensemble did not have its own *Kapellmeister*. Presumably, at the artistic helm were the successive leaders of the Dresden ensemble, including Johann Christoph Schmidt, Johann David Heinichen, and Johann Adolf Hasse.

The levels of payment received by the musicians in the Polish *Kapelle* were obviously low: four of the highest-paid members (Schulze, Daniel Hasse, and the two Friese brothers, all hired in 1715) received 200 *Thaler* per annum each; two horn players were each paid 130 *Thaler* a year; and the other six musicians had to make do with 126 *Thaler* per annum per person. Compared to the remuneration received by the Dresden ensemble, those sums were modest indeed. Another example of the ensemble's financial difficulties is documented in a letter written by its administrative director, Baron Adolph von Seyffertitz.[22] He approached the king requesting funding to cover basic needs such as the purchase of new works by famous masters, stationery for the composers, instruments and strings, and maintenance costs, especially those of the harpsichords.

Late in February 1718, the *comici italiani*, Giovanni Alberto Ristori, and the Polish ensemble all travelled to Dresden.[23] The ensemble presumably took part in the premiere of Ristori's *dramma per musica* entitled *Cleonice* (Moritzburg, 15 August 1718).[24] The musicians also contributed to the splendour of several royal feasts, for example the name day of August 11 on 3 August in Dresden, and also on 14 August at Moritzburg.[25] At that point, a member was replaced by the oboist

[19] For example, D-Dla, 10026 Geheimes Kabinett, Loc. 3521, 'Pohlnische General-Cassa Sachen . . .', vol. III, fols. 10, 16.

[20] See Table 3.1 (pp. 74–6 below): Giovanni Alberto Ristori received 600 *Thaler*; Heinrich Schulze and Christian Friedrich Friese, 200 *Thaler* each; Matthias Siegmund Köhler, Carl Anton Schauer, Michael Simon, Daniel Hasse, and Johann Blume, 126 *Thaler* each.

[21] Schulze was also referred to as 'Premier Musicus', 'Direktor', 'premier de l'orguestre', and 'prefectus'. The D-Dl holdings include two violin concertos bearing his name: Mus. 2809-O-1 and Mus. 2809-O-2.

[22] D-Dla, 10026 Geheimes Kabinett, Loc. 907, vol. I, fol. 38; Loc. 383, vol. II, fol. 187.

[23] D-Dla, 10006 Oberhofmarschallamt, O IV, No. 99, record dated 1 March 1718.

[24] Friedrich August Freiherr ô Byrn, 'Giovanna Casanova und die Comici italiani am polnisch-sächsischen Hofe', *Neues Archiv für Sächsische Geschichte und Alterthumskunde*, 1/4 (1880), 289–314, at 294.

[25] D-Dla, 10006 Oberhofmarschallamt, O IV, No. 99, record dated 3 August 1718; G, No. 17, record dated 14 August 1718.

Johann Joachim Quantz.[26] In his biography published in 1755, Quantz mentions that he was assessed by Baron von Seyffertitz, and received a salary of 150 *Thaler* per annum in addition to free lodgings in Poland.[27] For the 21-year-old *Kunstpfeifer* from Dresden, a position in the Polish ensemble was a major career opportunity; Quantz now advanced into the circle of the royal-electoral court.

The Polish *Kapelle* spent the second half of 1718 in Poland, but early in 1719 travelled to Dresden again in order to join in the preparations for the wedding celebrations of Friedrich August (the future August III) and Archduchess Maria Josepha, scheduled for September. Between 24 June and 20 July 1719, records show that the Polish ensemble played in the Zwinger at numerous royal *assemblées*, which often involved dancing.[28] As part of the festivities, the ensemble took centre stage on 17 September during the so-called 'Turkish feast' organized in the Turkish palace (now the Taschenberg Palais). In common with all the servants, the members of the Polish ensemble were dressed in Turkish costumes. They played during the meal and later provided music for dancing.[29] Despite all the additional work — from 6 to 12 October, the ensemble also accompanied the court to Moritzburg[30] — they were compensated with a meagre bonus of 80 *Thaler*.[31]

In the 1720s, the ensemble travelled back and forth between Poland and Saxony at regular intervals. From February 1720 until December 1724, the musicians stayed in Warsaw to accompany the performances of the royal French comedy and dance troupe.[32] This must have presented a major challenge for the ensemble, as members had to change their specialisation and playing style from that of Italian performances (*comici italiani* style) to that of the French theatre, which was entirely new to them (and included *opéra-ballet*, *ballet*, *comédie-ballet*, *comédie-lyrique*, *divertissement*, *fragments*, and *pièce d'agrément*). August II ordered Ristori to stay in Dresden, stating that another musician had been found in Warsaw who would be able to direct the orchestra under the new performance conditions.[33] The new musician was Louis André, previously connected with the Académie de Musique in Brussels. On 1 April 1720, he was hired by the Polish-Saxon court to

---

[26] D-Dla, 10026 Geheimes Kabinett, Loc. 3530, 'Dreßdner Brieff-Copier-Buch . . .', fol. 608; ackowledgements of receipt by Johann Joachim Quantz in PL-Wagad, AK I/43, AK I/44, AK I/46a, AK I/46b.

[27] Johann Joachim Quantz, 'Lebenslauf, von ihm selbst entworfen', in Friedrich Wilhelm Marpurg, *Historisch-kritische Beyträge zur Aufnahme der Musik* (Berlin, 1754–78; repr. Hildesheim/New York: Georg Olms, 1970), I, 'Drittes Stück' (1755), 208 ff.

[28] D-Dla, 10006 Oberhofmarschallamt, G, No. 19, record dated 24 June 1719; O IV, No. 100, records dated 1, 8, 11, and 15 July 1719.

[29] D-Dla, 10006 Oberhofmarschallamt, B, No. 20b, fols. 719–20: 'Bey der Tafel ließen sich die Pohlnische Capelle hören.' This scene was recorded for posterity by Matthäus Daniel Pöppelmann in an engraving currently in the Archiv für Kunst und Geschichte, Berlin.

[30] D-Dla, 10006 Oberhofmarschallamt, G, No. 18, fol. 11.

[31] D-Dla, 10026 Geheimes Kabinett, Loc. 383, vol. IV: 'Acta. Die Engagements einiger zum Theater gehörigen Personen . . .', fol. 169.

[32] D-Dla, 10026 Geheimes Kabinett, Loc. 383, vol. II, fol. 255; 10006 Oberhofmarschallamt, O IV, No. 101, record dated 15 February 1720.

[33] D-Dla, 10026 Geheimes Kabinett, Loc. 2094, vol. CLXXXI, fol. 19; Loc. 2095, vol. CCVI, fol. 41.

compose French music and manage theatrical sets (as 'compositeur de musique et machiniste'). His salary was 1,200 *Thaler* paid from the Saxon coffers, with the Polish court providing merely 72 *Thaler* to cover the cost of lodging in Warsaw.[34] Beginning in 1721, André is described in the documents as *Maître de chapelle*, a title he also used to describe himself in his music manual published in Warsaw in 1721.[35]

From 1720 to 1724, the Polish ensemble was supplemented by two additional musicians seconded from the Dresden ensemble, the violinist Carl Joseph Rhein and the organist and copyist Johann Wolfgang Schmidt, a brother of the *Ober-kapellmeister* Johann Christoph Schmidt. Rhein's responsibility was to provide music for dance rehearsals; Schmidt played the harpsichord and maintained the keyboard instruments.[36] In 1724 the ensemble was given a servant who was paid 40 *Thaler* annually. His duties included the transport of instruments to various performing venues.[37] Also assisting the ensemble between 1722 and 1726 was Jacques Guenin, a copyist of French music, who was remunerated on a pro rata basis.[38]

In the autumn of 1720, the members of the Polish *Kapelle* submitted a petition to the king complaining about their insufficient remuneration. The appeal was successful, and the musicians received an increase in pay, effective from 1 January 1721. The highest-paid members of the ensemble (Schulze, Daniel Hasse, and the Friese brothers) now each received 240 *Thaler* per annum, and the remaining members each received 216 *Thaler*. As a result, the annual cost of maintaining the Polish *Kapelle* rose to 2,688 *Thaler*.[39] However, these salaries remained at the level of the lowest-paid members of the Saxon *Kapelle*.

Discouraged by his meagre salary and by the cultural stagnation that descended on Warsaw whenever the court returned to Saxony, the enterprising Quantz made a spirited effort to lift his career out of the doldrums: in the spring of 1724 he set out for Italy. Later that year, the king ordered all Warsaw-based musicians and theatrical personnel to Dresden.[40] This was presumably connected with a *divertissement* to be produced in Dresden on 12 February 1725: *Le triomphe de l'Amour*, set to music by Louis André, who was still unknown in Saxony at that time. The Polish ensemble returned to Warsaw in May 1725, with the *comici italiani* following in October. In November, they were joined by a troupe of ten French dancers who

[34] D-Dla, 10026 Geheimes Kabinett, Loc. 383, vol. I, fol. 276.

[35] D-Dla, 10026 Geheimes Kabinett, Loc. 3522, 'General-Casse de Anno 1720/1721', record dated June 1721; Loc. 3522, 'Königl. Pohln. General-Cassa-Buch . . .', records dated April and November 1723; I-Bc, E.101, 'Essay de Principes de Musique . . . par Monsieur André, Maitre de Chapelle de Sa Majesté le Roy de Pologne, et Electeur de Saxe, a Varsovie 1721.'

[36] D-Dla, 10026 Geheimes Kabinett, Loc. 383, vol. II, fols. 255ff.; Loc. 907, vol. II: 'Die Operisten, Musicos, Sänger und andere zur Opera gehörige Personen . . .', fol. 206; Loc. 1386, 'Ordres du Roi à Volmar 1720–28', fols. 9, 91; PL-Wagad, AK 1/43, AK 1/44, AK 1/46a, AK 1/46b.

[37] D-Dla, 10026 Geheimes Kabinett, Loc. 1386, 'Ordres du Roi à Volmar 1720–28', fol. 91.

[38] See, for example, D-Dla, 10026 Geheimes Kabinett, Loc. 3522, 'Königl. Pohln. General-Cassa-Buch . . .', record dated 19 January 1723; Loc. 1386, 'Ordres du Roi à Volmar 1720–28', records dated 1722–7.

[39] D-Dla, 10026 Geheimes Kabinett, Loc. 1386, 'Ordres du Roi à Volmar 1720–28', fol. 9.

[40] Ibid., fols. 111–12, 137; PL-Wagad, AK 1/43, AK 1/52.

belonged to the royal ensemble headed by Louis Dupré and Louise de Vaurinville. The theatrical troupes were accompanied by Giovanni Alberto Ristori and André, composers of Italian and French music, respectively. In October (or possibly November) the concertmaster of the Dresden ensemble, Jean-Baptiste Volumier (Woulmier) followed; his composing skills presumably boosted the standards of ballet performances until September 1726.[41] At the same time, the Polish ensemble was also supplemented by the violinist Francesco Maria Cattaneo, then in the service of Field Marshal Jakob Heinrich von Flemming,[42] and with Louise Dimanche, a female singer and dancer hired for royal service in Warsaw, who took her husband's name of de Mouchy.[43] This increased activity was undoubtedly connected with the Saxon-Electoral Prince Friedrich August's first visit to Warsaw. He stayed in the city from December 1725 until September 1726, during which time Italian comedies and French ballets were staged three times a week, including penitential days. Concerts at court were also organized for the prince's entertainment three times a week.[44] Dimanche sang French cantatas; Cattaneo played instrumental music which must have been so accomplished that he later entered the service of the prince.

Concerning the repertoire, fortunately, a list of works copied for the Polish court by Jacques Guenin between November 1725 and April 1725 exists.[45] The list is not very specific, but it yields information regarding the types of pieces performed, such as various ballet *divertissements* from French operas and comedies (including *Les Fêtes vénitiennes* by André Campra). The document also reveals that the ballerina Louise de Vaurinville performed the choreographically innovative *symphonie de la danse* by Jean-Ferry Rebel entitled *Les Caractères de la danse*. In addition, Dimanche sang cantatas by Campra and Jean-Baptiste Stuck. It is highly likely that Italian theatrical music, German instrumental music, Latin church music, and various Polish dances (polonaises, *mazurs* (mazurkas), and *kozaks*) – very popular at balls – were also performed. In this sense, Warsaw participated in the fusion of the Italian, French, German, and apparently also Polish musical styles, later described by Quantz described as the 'vermischter Geschmack' (mixed taste).[46]

Another interesting memo was drafted during the Polish ensemble's next visit to Dresden in July 1728. Its author (perhaps the violinist Heinrich Schulze) listed

---

[41] D-Dla, 10026 Geheimes Kabinett, Loc. 1386, 'Ordres du Roi à Volmar 1720–28', fol. 216; PL-Wagad, AK 1/43, AK 1/44, AK 1/46a, AK 1/46b.

[42] Karl Biedermann, 'Aus der Glanzzeit des sächsisch-polnischen Hofes', *Zeitschrift für Deutsche Kulturgeschichte*, 3rd ser. 1 (1891), 214–18; Irena Bieńkowska, 'Notatki o muzykach Jakuba Henryka Fleminga' [Notes on Jakob Heinrich von Flemming's Musicians], *Barok: Historia-Literatura-Sztuka*, 3/2 (1996), 155–67.

[43] D-Dla, 10026 Geheimes Kabinett, Loc. 383, vol. 1, fols. 141–2; PL-Wagad, AK 1/41, AK 1/50, AK 1/51.

[44] PL-Wagad, AK 1/50, fols. 16–41; PL-Kc, MS 2748, cited in Jerzy Jackl, 'Z badań nad teatrem czasów saskich' [Research on Theatre in the Saxon Period], *Pamiętnik Teatralny*, 1 (1960), 100.

[45] PL-Wagad, AK 1/50; a copy of the list is available in Żórawska-Witkowska, *Muzyka na dworze Augusta II*, 93–5.

[46] On the 'vermischter Geschmack', see Chapter 2, 'The Court of Saxony', p. 30 n. 73 above.

a number of problems plaguing the ensemble, pointing out, among other things, that the musicians were underpaid and that their living conditions in Warsaw were poor.[47] As a matter of fact, the list of members published in the first official court calendar (compiled late in 1727) included ten musicians and one servant.[48] By 1728 the number had risen to twelve: a financial document records the salary of Friedrich Töppert (Döbbert), a new oboe player, and that of Quantz, although he was no longer with the Polish ensemble.[49]

In 1729, a new member, the bassoonist Carl Morasch, was appointed at a salary of 216 *Thaler* per year; the violinist Friese and the horn player Grossmann were replaced by the Czech Balthazar Villicus, a violinist formerly active at the court of Stanisław Cetnar, vice-chancellor of Lithuania, and Joseph Carl Lindemann, a horn player.[50]

### *The Development of the Polish Hofkapelle from 1729 until 1733*

After an absence of two years, August II returned to Warsaw in May 1729, remaining until September. He ordered his *comici italiani* and the Polish *Kapelle* to follow him from Dresden to Poland. Late in November 1729, the ensemble went back to Saxony, presumably in connection with the visit of Friedrich Wilhelm I, king in Prussia, scheduled for June 1730.[51] They returned to Poland while the guest of honour was still at Radewitz, and on 30 June they played at a ball hosted by the Russian envoy Piotr Bestuzhev to celebrate the coronation of Russia's new empress, Anna Ivanovna.[52] The cost of the ensemble's travel to Poland came to 615 *Thaler*, paid from the Polish court coffers.[53] The musicians arrived two months before the monarch and his *comici italiani*. Late in autumn 1730, the ensemble yet again took part in Italian theatre performances in Warsaw.

In that year the Polish *Kapelle* remained at twelve musicians headed by Heinrich Schulze, now titled 'premier de l'orguestre'.[54] The ensemble comprised four violinists, who probably also included a viola player, one oboist, two horn players, and four members of the bass section — a bassoonist, a lutenist, a violoncellist,

[47] D-Dla, 10026 Geheimes Kabinett, Loc. 383, vol. I, fols. 186–7.

[48] *Königl. Polnischer und Churfürstl. Sächsischer Hoff- und Staats Calender auf das Jahr 1728*, without pagination. These publications are referred to hereafter as *Hof- und Staats-Calender* (year).

[49] See, among others, D-Dla, 10026 Geheimes Kabinett, Loc. 3521, 'Pohlnische General-Casse-Sachen . . .', vol. IV, without foliation.

[50] D-Dla, 10026 Geheimes Kabinett, Loc. 3521, 'Pohlnische General-Casse-Sachen . . .', vol. IV, without foliation; Loc. 1374, 'Concepte de Anno 1729. Die Pohln. General Casse betr.', without foliation; and PL-Wagad, Archiwum Publiczne Potockich, MS 163a, vol. IV, list dated 19 May 1729.

[51] D-Dla, 10026 Geheimes Kabinett, Loc. 1374, 'Concepte de Anno 1729', without foliation, order dated Warsaw, 24 August 1730.

[52] *Kurier Polski*, No. 28, 1730.

[53] D-Dla, 10026 Geheimes Kabinett, Loc. 3522, 'Die polnische General Kasse betr. 1729–32', without foliation.

[54] *Hof- und Staats-Calender* (1731), without pagination.

and a player of the 'Contra-Basson'. Late in 1730, two Venetian musicians visited Warsaw, who undoubtedly performed with the Polish *Kapelle*. They were Casparo (Gasparo) Janeschi, a viola da gamba player and cellist, and Giovanni Verocai, a composer and violinist, formerly the concertmaster and opera director in Breslau (now Wrocław). On 30 December 1730, at the invitation of Empress Anna of Russia the royal *comici italiani* under Tommaso Ristori, joined by Janeschi, Verocai, Giovanni Alberto Ristori, two horn players, and one bassoonist, set out from Warsaw for the exotic destination of Moscow.[55]

After that trip, the Polish *Kapelle* remained in Warsaw until the end of August II's reign, its activity being limited to performing in various types of worship, for concerts, and at balls. In 1731, the Polish newspaper *Kurier Polski* recorded on several occasions the ensemble took part in events organized by powerful aristocrats. This practice may have developed earlier in order to provide the musicians with a source of additional income.

In December 1731, Villicus died.[56] He was replaced by the Czech violinist František (Franz) Benda, who had been in Poland since the middle of 1728 as *Kapellmeister* and concertmaster of an ensemble comprising nine members maintained by Fabian Szaniawski, the *starosta* (chief alderman) of Sochaczew.[57]

In 1732, August II's Polish *Kapelle* was given its second and final pay rise: Schulze received 280 *Thaler* a year; 250 *Thaler* were given to each of the violinists Matthias Siegmund Köhler and Benda, and the bass player Hasse; the remaining members were allocated 230 *Thaler* each. The number of musicians remained at twelve, with the total annual salary amounting to 2,870 *Thaler*.[58] Late in 1732, the Polish *Kapelle* was augmented by three additional appointments: the Czech violinist Jiří (Georg) Čart (Zarth or Czarth), the oboist Johann Caspar Grund, and a certain Franz Lutter, a musician of unknown specialization. The expanded ensemble of fifteen now consisted of six violinists (presumably including one or two viola players); two oboists/flautists; two horn players; four members of the bass section (a bassoonist, a lutenist, a violoncellist, and a 'Contra-Basson' player); and one unknown instrumentalist (perhaps a viola player). A second servant was now hired to handle the increased demands of the enlarged ensemble (see Table 3.1, pp. 74–6 below).[59] Several months later, on 1 February 1733, August II died in Warsaw. His Polish court was dissolved, and all moveable effects in his Warsaw

[55] D-Dla, 10026 Geheimes Kabinett, Loc. 383, vol. IV, fol. 191; Loc. 3309, 'Briefe von Thiolly aus Dresden und Warschau an den Grafen von Lagnasco . . .', letter from Moscow, 19 February 1731; Robert-Aloys Mooser, *Annales de la musique et des musiciens en Russie au XVIIIe siècle*, I (Geneva: Mont Blanc, 1948); Jaroslav Bužga, 'Moskauer Gastspiel Dresdner Musiker und Schauspieler im Jahre 1731', *Beiträge zur Musikwissenschaft*, 2 (1984), 129–39.

[56] D-Dla, 10006 Oberhofmarschallamt, G, No. 32, fol. 54.

[57] *Hof- und Staats-Calender* (1733), without pagination; the autobiography of Franz Benda published in the *Neue Berliner Musikzeitung*, 10 (1856), Nos. 32–5, a Czech translation of which was published by Jaroslav Čeleda as *Vlastní životopis Františka Bendy* (Prague: Topičova Edice, 1939).

[58] D-Dla, 10026 Geheimes Kabinett, Loc. 3522, 'Die polnische General Kasse betr. 1729–32', without foliation.

[59] *Hof- und Staats-Calender* (1733), without foliation.

residences (the royal palace and the so-called Saxon palace) were taken to Saxony. His only legitimate son, Prince Friedrich August, commenced a long and arduous campaign to ascend to the Polish throne.

Any comparison between the Polish *Kapelle* and its Dresden counterpart will invariably favour the latter. Indeed, the Dresden 'Königliche Capelle und Cammer-Musique' compared favourably with orchestras across Europe. As a result of August II's decision in 1715 to establish the Polish *Kapelle* as an itinerant ensemble, musical life at the Polish court was inferior to that in Dresden. But the Polish ensemble was undoubtedly a skilled group of performers, providing solid training that could act as a springboard for future career possibilities: Quantz, Benda, and Čart later found employment in respected European ensembles; Ristori and Morasch were subsequently promoted to the Dresden *Kapelle*, while Johann Blume, Daniel Hasse, Matthias Siegmund Köhler, Joseph Carl Lindemann, Sebastian Reimel, Carl Anton Schauer, and Philipp Bernard Troyer became members of the Polish *Kapelle* of August III – an exacting music lover and patron.

### THE REIGN OF AUGUST III

Like the reign of his father, the rule of August III divided into two unequal parts marked by a dramatic turning point. He enjoyed more than twenty years of peace, followed by close to seven years of war, beginning on 29 August 1756 and ending with the Peace of Hubertusburg on 15 February 1763. The ailing king, increasingly feeble and depressed by Saxony's military setbacks, was forced against his will to spend the war years in Warsaw. However, the continuing presence of his court enabled that city to compete at last with Dresden in musical matters. The final years in the life of August III were marked by a boom in the city's cultural life and, consequently, in Poland at large.

### *The Development of the Polish Hofkapelle from 1734 until 1756*

On 5 October 1733, August III, with the support provided by Empress Anna of Russia, was elected as pretender to the Polish throne, his rival being Stanisław Leszczyński, who was backed by France. A hasty, modest coronation for August III and his wife Maria Josepha was held in Cracow on 17 January 1734.

Although no document has survived that specifically confirms the dissolution of August II's Polish *Kapelle*, as described by Moritz Fürstenau it is evident that some of its members formed the basis of August III's Polish *Kapelle*.[60] In the relevant records, the 'Pohlnische Reise Cammer Casse', the ensemble is generally not referred to by its proper name, its members being listed under the administrative headings 'Comedie und Musique' or 'Königl[iche] Capell- und andere Musique'.[61]

---

[60] Fürstenau, *Zur Geschichte der Musik und des Theaters*, II: 202–4.

[61] Other, less common, labels include 'das Orchester in Warschau', 'pohlnisches Orchester', or 'Unsere Pohlnische Capelle', see D-Dla, 10026 Geheimes Kabinett, Loc. 3524, vol.

The first list of members of this ensemble was drafted on 2 March 1734, while August III was staying in Cracow. Only six names are listed, with the total annual salaries of the musicians (payable as of 1 January) amounting to 1,400 *Thaler*. All the musicians – Daniel Hasse, Lindemann, Reimel, Blume, Schauer, and Troyer – were former members of August II's Polish *Kapelle*, and their wages remained at the same level as in 1733.[62] The ensemble's instrumentalists comprised two violinists, one horn player, and three 'Bassisten'; they formed the core of the regular group and were undoubtedly complemented by other musicians. The latter were drawn from at least three different ensembles: that of St John's Collegiate Church in Warsaw, the recently formed Warsaw ensemble of cabinet minister Heinrich von Brühl, and the Dresden *Kapelle*.[63]

As many as thirteen members of the latter ensemble arrived in Warsaw on 3 December 1735. These included four singers, a soprano, Giovanni Bindi; two altos, Domenico Annibali and Nicola Pozzi; and a tenor, Johann Joseph Götzel. The nine *Cammermusici* comprised the concertmaster Johann Georg Pisendel, the flautist Pierre-Gabriel Buffardin (Bouffardin), violinists Carl Matthias Lehneis, Augustin Uhlich (Uhlig), Joseph Titerle, and Johann Georg Fickler, the cellist Arcangelo Califano, the bassoonist Carl Morasch, and the horn player Johann Georg Knechtel.[64] Two others must have been present in Warsaw at the time, namely Giovanni Alberto Ristori (then organist of the Dresden *Hofkapelle*) and Stefano Benedetto Pallavicino, a poet at the royal-electoral court. Because of these and other new arrivals, the royal court in Warsaw now boasted a strong and excellent ensemble with at least twenty-six talented members, including five singers joined on occasion by a bass from the Collegiate Church ensemble, presumably Józef Sękowski (Senkowski), the 'Bassist' who was later hired by the Polish *Kapelle*. The instrumental forces numbered nine violinists, six bass players, including two violoncellists, a double bassist, a bassoonist, two lutenists, two flautists/oboists, two horn players, and two keyboard players (harpsichord/organ). On special occasions, the various ensembles – the Polish and Dresden *Kapellen*, Brühl's ensemble, as well as musicians from the Collegiate Church and possibly also from other Warsaw churches – were combined. They were reinforced by selected musicians drawn from the royal ensembles of court trumpeters and kettledrum players and *Bockpfeifer*.

VIII: 'Pohlnische Reise-Cammer-Cassa Sachen Ao 1739', fols. 79, 104; Loc. 3525, vol. XIII: 'Pohlnische Reise-Cammer-Casse-Sachen betr. Anno 1747. seq. . . .', fol. 210. See also Alina Żórawska-Witkowska, 'Noch einmal zum Thema der "Pohlnischen Capelle" August III', in *Johann Georg Pisendel: Studien zu Leben und Werk*, ed. Ortrun Landmann, Hans-Günter Ottenberg, and Wolfgang Mende, Dresdner Beiträge zur Musikforschung, 3 (Hildesheim, Zurich, and New York: Georg Olms, 2010), 615–34.

[62] D-Dla, 10026 Geheimes Kabinett, Loc. 464, 'Die Sächsische Reise-Cammer-Casse 1734–55', fol. 26.

[63] D-Dla, 10026 Geheimes Kabinett, Loc. 3524, vol. IV: 'Pohlnische Reise-Cammer-Casse Sachen Ao 1736 . . .', fol. 83; Ulrike Kollmar, *Gottlob Harrer (1703–55), Kapellmeister des Grafen Heinrich von Brühl am sächsisch-polnischen Hof und Thomaskantor in Leipzig*, ed. Wolfgang Ruf, Schriften zur mitteldeutschen Musikgeschichte, 12 (Beeskow: Ortus, 2006), 53 ff.

[64] D-Dla, 10006 Oberhofmarschallamt, I, No. 74, fols. 149–50; O II, No. 1, record dated 3 December 1735.

Between 1735 and 1736, serenatas by Ristori with texts by Pallavicino were performed, adding splendour to many festivities at the Polish court. In the absence of a suitable theatrical venue, the serenatas were used as a substitute for the *dramma per musica*, August III's favourite genre.[65] The scores and the incomplete instrumental vocal parts of Ristori's Warsaw serenatas include parts for four vocalists (SAAT), violins 1 and 2, 'viola' or 'violetta' (occasionally *divisi*), violoncellos, contrabasses, bassoons, harpsichord, pairs of flutes/oboes ('flauto traverso ô oboe'), horns ('corni da caccia'), and occasionally also a chalumeau. The first violin parts are signed with the monogram or the full name of the person who used them, Pisendel.[66]

As reflected in the financial documents of the court for the period 1734 to 1736, the king's needs were met in full, despite the ensemble's rather modest size. The first significant expansion of the Polish *Kapelle* took place in 1738, when its number rose to thirteen people, undoubtedly in connection with the Warsaw season of the new royal troupe of the *comici italiani* of Andrea Bertoldi. In addition to *commedie dell'arte,* their repertoire included a *dramma ridicolo per musica* (a parody of opera seria) entitled *Il Costantino,* performed on 10 February 1739. The composer was Giovanni Verocai, who probably also directed the Warsaw performance on his return from St Petersburg to Braunschweig.[67]

While the Polish *Kapelle* expanded, it continued to rely on external recruits from ensembles mentioned above as well as musicians employed by various Polish and Lithuanian aristocrats. The foreigners in the *Kapelle* were drawn from different sources, depending on August III's political situation as well as the length and nature of the special occasions that occurred while the court was resident in Warsaw. These included carnival, Advent, and birthdays and name days of the ruler or his consort, to name but a few; all entailed different artistic formats. Moreover, various royal-electoral artists were summoned specifically from Dresden (see Table 3.2, p. 77 below). The *comici italiani* came in 1738/9, 1740, 1748/9, and 1754,[68] while dancers arrived in 1748/9, and 1754.[69]

A number of composers were also ordered to Poland: in 1748/9 Giovanni

---

[65]  Alina Żórawska-Witkowska, 'Giovanni Alberto Ristori and his Serenate at the Polish Court of Augustus III, 1735–46', *Music as Social and Cultural Practice: Essays in Honour of Reinhard Strohm*, ed. Melania Bucciarelli and Berta Joncus (Woodbridge: Boydell and Brewer, 2007), 139–58.

[66]  D-Dl, Mus 2455-L-1 and Mus. 2455-L-1a, *Cantata à 4 Voc: per il Giorno natalizio di S. M. la Regina l'Anno 1735 . . .* ; Mus. 2455-L-2 and Mus. 2455-L-2a, *Componimento per musica da cantarsi in Varsavia il felicissimo Giorno del Nome della Maestà del Rè . . .*, 1736; Mus. 2455-G-1 and Mus. 2455-G-1a, *Versi cantati in Varsavia nel celebrarsi per Ordine Reggio il Giorno della Coronazione della Maestà d'Anna Imperadrice [sic] delle Russie 1736 . . . .*

[67]  Alina Żórawska-Witkowska, 'Parodies of Dramma per Musica at the Warsaw Theatre of August III', in *Italian Opera in Central Europe, 1614–1780, III: Opera Subjects and European Relationships*, ed. Norbert Dubowy, Corinna Herr, and Alina Żórawska-Witkowska (Berlin: Berliner Wissenschafts-Verlag, 2007), 125–45.

[68]  Alina Żórawska-Witkowska, 'The Comici Italiani Ensemble at the Warsaw Court of Augustus III', *Musicology Today*, 2 (2005), 72–105.

[69]  Alina Żórawska-Witkowska, 'Tancerze na polskim dworze Augusta III' [Dancers at the Polish Court of August III], *W stronę Francji . . . : Z problemów literatury i kultury polskiego Oświecenia* [Towards France . . . : Literary and Cultural Issues of the Polish Enlightenment], ed.

Alberto Ristori was seconded to Warsaw presumably in connection with an exceptionally busy artistic schedule of the *comici italiani*, and is referred to in the relevant records as *Kapellmeister*. Johann Michael Breunich (with personal copyist Johann Gottlieb Haußstädler) came in 1744/5, 1746, 1748/9, 1750, 1752, and 1754. His occasional serenatas were performed principally for Queen Maria Josepha's birthday and name day (8 December). Johann Adam, viola player and composer of ballet music, was summoned in 1748/9 and 1754. It is also possible that *Oberkapellmeister* Hasse came in 1754; he certainly returned in 1759, 1760, 1761, and 1762/3.[70]

Thus, the Polish *Kapelle* grew steadily, and over time came to comprise not only instrumentalists and singers, but also a servant (from 1739), three dancers (from 1749),[71] a theatre inspector (from 1753), and a tailor specializing in costumes for male opera singers (from 1762 at the latest). Consequently, in 1739 the ensemble comprised thirteen musicians with an annual budget of 2,871 *Thaler*, 10 *Groschen*.[72] By 1754, the number had risen to twenty-seven members with an annual budget of 6,589 *Thaler*, 14 *Groschen*.[73] Between 1736 and 1754, the highest-paid instrumentalist, the violinist Köhler, received 280 *Thaler* per year and had apparently taken over Schulze's duties as concertmaster, despite the fact that he was never identified as such in the extant records.

Also noteworthy is the appearance of Polish musicians in listings of the ensemble from 1736 onwards. The organist Józef Czanczik was hired with a comparatively high annual salary of 273 *Thaler*, 10 *Groschen*; his duties also included

Elżbieta Z. Wichrowska (Warsaw: Wydział Polonistyki Uniwersytetu Warszawskiego, 2007), 201–25.

[70] The sources attesting to the activity of those many artists — too numerous to be listed here — will be contained in the forthcoming book by the present author, *Muzyka na polskim dworze Augusta III* [Music at the Polish Court of August III]. The Warsaw sojourn of Hasse has been described in Alina Żórawska-Witkowska, 'Johann Adolf Hasse, Oberkapellmeister króla polskiego i elektora saskiego: sława – zapomnienie – przywracanie sławy' [Johann Adolf Hasse, the *Oberkapellmeister* of the King of Poland and Elector of Saxony: Fame – Oblivion – Revival], in *Sława i zapomnienie* [Fame and Oblivion], ed. Dariusz Konstantynów (Warsaw: Instytut Sztuki Polskiej Akademii Nauk, 2008), 23–40.

[71] These dancers were Marie Blanchard and Angelica Zabati (Angelique Sabati), who each earned 200 *Thaler*, and Nicolas Nayreau Mondonville (100 *Thaler*); the sums paid from the Polish court's coffers were only a source of additional income ('Besoldungs-Zulage') on top of their regular Saxon salaries (400 *Thaler* each); see D-Dla, 10026 Geheimes Kabinett, Loc. 3525, vol. XIII, fol. 284.

[72] D-Dla, 10026 Geheimes Kabinett, Loc. 3524, vol. VIII, fols. 56, 79.

[73] D-Dla, 10026 Geheimes Kabinett, Loc. 3526, 'Die Reise Kammer Kasse betr. 1737–63', fol. 39. In comparison, in 1741 the ensemble comprised sixteen musicians with a budget of 3,571 *Thaler*, 10 *Groschen*; see Loc. 3524, vol. X: 'Pohlnische Reise Cammer-Casse Sachen Ao 1741', fol. 58. In 1743, there were twenty-one musicians costing a total of 4,671 *Thaler*, 10 *Groschen*; see Loc. 3524, vol. XI: 'Pohlnische Reise-Cammer-Casse Sachen Anno 1742/43/44', fol. 154. In 1747, this number had increased to twenty-five, at a cost of 5,523 *Thaler*, 10 *Groschen*; see Loc. 3527, 'Jahres Rechnung . . . 1747', fols. 183–95. By 1751, twenty-six musicians were in service, with an annual budget of 6,463 *Thaler*, 10 *Groschen*; see Loc. 3525, vol. XIII, fols. 602–3. By 1753, only the salaries went up by 100 *Thaler* to 6,563 *Thaler*, 10 *Groschen*; see Loc. 3525, vol. XIV: 'Pohlnische Reise-Cammer-Casse-Sachen 175[3] seq.', fols. 61–79.

the maintenance of keyboard instruments.[74] Moreover, the elderly organist Kos-mowski, who had been active at the court for at least fifty-six years, was formally engaged by the Polish *Kapelle* with an annual salary of 126 *Thaler*, 20 *Groschen*, presumably a type of pension.[75] In 1739, the 'Bassist' Józef Sękowski was hired with a salary of 133 *Thaler*, 10 *Groschen*, which was paid from the Polish court coffers.[76] This must have supplemented his regular salary drawn from his work with the en-semble of the Collegiate Church. The singer Stefan Jaroszewicz, a rare example of a Polish castrato, joined the *Kapelle* in 1740.[77] Three years later, Dominik Jaziomski (Jeziomski) was hired as an oboist; over time, his responsibilities grew to also in-clude administrative duties and conducting.[78] In 1754, Köhler was replaced by the violinist Antoni Kossołowski (Kozłowski), concertmaster in the ensemble of the military commander Grand Crown Hetman Jan Klemens Branicki in Białystok. The royal treasury paid Kossołowski an annual salary of 200 *Thaler* in addition to his main salary paid by Branicki.[79] The position of concertmaster in the Polish *Ka-pelle* of August III, first mentioned specifically in 1755, went to Christian Friedrich Horn, the concertmaster of the powerful courtier Heinrich von Brühl. The Polish court treasury paid Horn only 100 *Thaler* per year; his principal source of income must therefore have come from von Brühl's coffers when he was prime minister.[80]

Transactions of this kind were both artistically and economically beneficial to the Polish court and also occurred between the two royal ensembles. In 1738, a Saxon *Cammermusicus*, a violinist named Johann Franz Hantke (Hancke), was seconded to Warsaw; from 1740 onward he drew from the Polish coffers 180 *Thaler* a year to supplement his main salary in Dresden.[81] On occasion, musicians from the Polish *Kapelle* were also listed as members of the Dresden ensemble, for example, the bassoonist Christian Friedrich Mattstädt. He was hired by the Polish

---

[74] D-Dla, 10026 Geheimes Kabinett, Loc. 3524, vol. V: 'Pohlnische Reise-Cammer-Casse Sachen Ao 1736 . . .', fol. 154; Loc. 3525, 'Copie der Königl. Pohln. Churfürstl. Sachs. Reise-Cammer-Casse-Geld-Rechnung . . .', fol. 243.

[75] D-Dla, 10026 Geheimes Kabinett, Loc.. 3525, 'Copie der Königl. Pohln. Churfürstl. Sachs. Reise-Cammer-Casse-Geld-Rechnung . . .', fol. 239.

[76] D-Dla, 10026 Geheimes Kabinett, Loc. 3524, vol. VIII, fol. 56.

[77] D-Dla, 10026 Geheimes Kabinett, Loc. 3524, vol. IX: 'Pohlnische Reise-Cammer-Casse Sachen Ao 1740', fol. 104. See also Alina Żórawska-Witkowska, 'Federico Cristiano in Italia: Esperienze musicali di un principe reale polacco', *Musica e storia*, 4 (1996), 277–323.

[78] *Kurier Polski*, No. 89, 1755; PL-Wagad, Archiwum Skarbu Koronnego, 'Rachunki i kwity', No. 16, section 5.

[79] Marpurg, *Historisch-kritische Beyträge*, I, 'Fünftes Stück' (1755), 447–8; Alina Żórawska-Witkowska, 'Muzyka na dworze Jana Klemensa Branickiego' [Music at the Court of Jan Klemens Branicki], in *Dwory magnackie w XVIII wieku: Rola i znaczenie kulturowe* [Eighteenth-Century Aristocratic Courts: Role and Cultural Significance], ed. Teresa Kostkie-wiczowa and Agata Roćko (Warsaw: DiG, 2005), 221–44.

[80] D-Dla, 10026 Geheimes Kabinett, Loc. 3526, 'Die Reise Kammer Kasse betr. 1737–63', fol. 53. See also Kollmar, *Gottlob Harrer*.

[81] Including among others: D-Dla, 10026 Geheimes Kabinett, Loc. 3524, vol. X, fol. 58; Loc. 585, 'Reglement der Reise-Cammer-Casse v. d. J. 1753–63', fol. 459; Loc. 3527, 'Königlich-Pohlnische Reise Cammer-Cassa Haupt-Geld-Rechnung auf das Jahr 1757', fol. 208.

*Kapelle* in 1744 and was listed as a member of its Dresden counterpart as of 1745.[82] Particularly strong ties existed between the Polish ensemble of August III and that of Prime Minister von Brühl. The latter's group appears to have functioned in practical terms as a supplement to the royal Polish *Kapelle*, with an inextricable bond existing between the two, especially during the Seven Years' War.

The ensemble grew to twenty-five members as a result of the court's unusually long stay in Warsaw from June 1748 to February 1749, a sojourn that also included the opening of a new theatre in the city, inaugurated on 3 August 1748. This venue was suited for *dramma per musica* productions, but the season of 1748/9 was filled with performances by the *comici italiani,* alongside ballets performed by a group of sixteen dancers selected from the twenty-four members of the king's ballet troupe. Among the many *commedie dell'arte* and comedies (including, among others, several by Carlo Goldoni), there appeared on 4 November 1748 yet another parody of opera seria, a *dramma per musica* entitled *Le contese di Mestre e Malghera per il trono.* The libretto by Antonio Gori had been adapted by Giovanna Casanova and the music composed by Salvatore Apollini.[83] In keeping with the general practices of Italian comedy, the score employs modest forces, comprising only first and second violins and a basso continuo section, occasionally augmented with a trumpet and horns. At the time, the Polish *Kapelle* numbered twenty-four members, including two or three singers (the castrato Stefan Jaroszewicz, the bass Sękowski, and the tenor Franz Ignaz Seydelmann); the organist Czanczik; seven or more violinists; at least three bass players performing on lute, double bass, and bassoon; one flautist, two oboists, four (!) horn players, and three unspecified musicians who might have included a viola player, another flautist, and a bassoonist (see Table 3.1).[84] In October 1750, a 'Besoldungs-Zulage' (salary supplement) of 200 *Thaler* was disbursed to a Saxon singer, the alto Nicola Pozzi, whose annual wage in Dresden was 1,000 *Thaler.*[85]

In 1754, an important event in the musical life of Warsaw, and presumably a milestone in the history of the Polish *Kapelle*, was the performance of the first *dramma per musica* presented in the Polish capital under the auspices of the Saxon kings. The piece in question was *L'eroe cinese*, premiered on 7 October 1754, with a libretto by Pietro Metastasio and music by Johann Adolf Hasse, who possibly directed the premiere.[86] The opera parts were given to singers from the Dresden ensemble, Bartolomeo Putini and Giovanni (Giuseppe) Belli (sopranos), Teresa

[82] D-Dla, 10026 Geheimes Kabinett, Loc. 3524, vol. XII: 'Pohlnische Reise-Cammer-Casse Sachen Anno 1745/46', fols. 1, 322. See also Kollmar, *Gottlob Harrer.*

[83] Score in D-Dl, Mus. 2429-F-1, ed. Maria Giovanna Miggiani and Piermario Vescovo, in *Problemi di critica Goldoniana*, 10–11 (2004), 77–352. See also Żórawska-Witkowska, 'Parodies of Dramma per Musica'.

[84] D-Dla, 10026 Geheimes Kabinett, Loc. 3525, vol. XIII, fols. 112, 211–12.

[85] D-Dla, 10026 Geheimes Kabinett, Loc. 3525, vol. XIII, fol. 381 (583).

[86] The singers are listed in the libretto printed in Warsaw in 1754. As for Hasse's participation, it would seem that a performance of a work representing a genre not seen at Warsaw for decades and simultaneously offering the first taste of Hasse's operatic talent on the local scene was reason enough for the composer to visit Poland. The available biographical accounts are silent regarding Hasse's potential activity elsewhere in the same period.

Albuzzi-Todeschini and Pasquale ('Pasqualino') Bruscolini (altos), and Ludwig Cornelius (tenor). Eight performances were given, interspersed with thirteen Italian comedies. All of these performances – operas and comedies alike – included three ballets, with music probably composed by Johann Adam. The newly created position of theatre inspector was held by Francesco Torri with a salary of 100 *Thaler*.[87] In autumn of 1754, the royal ensemble's range of duties also included participating in royal devotions and concerts, and possibly also in the concerts hosted by Prime Minister von Brühl, whose musicians performed alongside members of the *Hofkapelle*.

## The Seven Years' War, 1756–63

The Seven Years' War brought with it a radical shift in relations between Dresden and Warsaw. Faced with the victorious military advance of Friedrich II (king in Prussia) in Saxony, August III and Prime Minister von Brühl were forced to leave and flee to Warsaw, where they spent the period from 27 October 1756 to 25 April 1763 'in exile'. In these circumstances the Dresden artists took different courses of action: some sought employment elsewhere in Europe; others remained in Saxony awaiting the re-establishment of the court; and others decided to take up employment in Warsaw. On 20 December 1756, the *Oberkapellmeister* of the Dresden court, Johann Adolf Hasse, left for Venice and Naples, and later settled in Vienna. During these years, he completed various commissions for the Polish court, and even made several trips to Warsaw in order to personally oversee some of the local premieres of his *drammi per musica*.[88]

The Polish *Kapelle* of August III, which had previously ranked so low in the Dresden-Warsaw hierarchy that it was not acknowledged in the printed court calendars, were now burdened with the major task of providing music for August III. They were assisted by those artists who were gradually returning to service at the royal-electoral court and by newly hired musicians arriving in Warsaw. The onset of the war also caused considerable confusion within the *Kapelle*, which was mostly made up of Saxons. Some of the musicians decided to remain in Dresden, and others relocated from Saxony to Poland, beginning in autumn of 1756. Also present in Warsaw were members of von Brühl's ensemble, whose passports issued for the journey identified each as a musician from the Polish *Kapelle* ('Musicus in der Königl. Poln. Capelle'). These included the oboists Johann Christian Fischer and Johann Gottlieb Matthau, the violinist Johann August Spangenberg, and the lutenist Johann Kropfgans.[89] Presumably, this was a formality, as von Brühl made his artists available to the king on an all but exclusive basis. In Warsaw the boundaries between the Polish *Kapelle* of August III and the private ensemble of his prime

---

[87] D-Dla, 10026 Geheimes Kabinett, Loc. 3526, 'Die Reise Kammer Kasse betr. 1737–63', fol. 39.

[88] The operas performed in Warsaw that Hasse could have overseen personally were: *Nitteti* (3 August 1759), *Demofoonte* (7 October 1759), *Artaserse* (3 August 1760), *Semiramide riconosciuta* (7 October 1760), *Zenobia* (7 October 1761), and *Il re pastore* (7 October 1762).

[89] D-Dla, 10006 Oberhofmarschallamt, I, No. 154; I, No. 162 b, fol. 50.

minister had long been blurred, and this approach was now applied in Saxony. Prime Minister von Brühl also oversaw all theatrical events at the royal court.

Although the numbers and types of positions in the Polish *Kapelle* between 1757 and 1759 were not markedly different from those recorded in 1754, there was the inevitable turnover of personnel. In 1757, the deceased Jaroszewicz, who had received a salary of 400 *Thaler*, was replaced by Pasquale Bruscolini. This alto from the Dresden ensemble had earned 2,000 *Thaler* in 1756.[90] After the death of the castrato Pozzi in Dresden in May 1758, the alto Giuseppe Perini was hired on an annual salary of 300 *Thaler*.[91] The following year, Lucia Torri, widow of Francesco Torri, inherited his duties as theatre inspector, and received a higher wage of 250 *Thaler*, presumably in connection with the theatre's increased operatic activity.[92]

The last known roster, drafted in 1762, listed thirty-five positions including twenty-nine musicians, one servant, three dancers, a theatre inspector, and an opera tailor.[93] Specifically, the *Kapelle* included four singers (Bruscolini, Perini, Seydelmann, and Sękowski); the organist Czanczik; at least seven violinists, who included concertmasters Christian Friedrich Horn (also employed by von Brühl) and Antoni Kossołowski (who doubled as a musician of Hetman Branicki); four 'Bassisten' (bass players), among them violoncellist Heinrich Megelin, also part of von Brühl's ensemble;[94] two bassoonists, one flautist, two (?) oboists, two horn players; nine undesignated musicians; three dancers; the theatre inspector, one servant, and an opera tailor. Their salaries totalled 6,526 *Thaler*.[95] At that time, the Warsaw court retained Carl Gottlob Uhle as a copyist, aided by two unnamed 'Schreibschüler' (presumably copyists in training), and two musicians, most probably members of the royal ensemble.[96]

The Polish *Kapelle* was augmented with singers from Dresden, who returned in increasing numbers to serve at the court of August III: sopranos Bartolomeo Putini (1760–61)[97] and Caterina Pilaja (1761–3),[98] and the tenor Angelo Amorevoli

---

[90] D-Dla, 10026 Geheimes Kabinett, Loc. 3527, 'Königlich-Pohlnische Reise Cammer-Cassa Haupt-Geld-Rechnung auf das Jahr 1757', fol. 200.

[91] Perini was a former member of the troupe of Angelo and Pietro Mingotti; see D-Dla, 10026 Geheimes Kabinett, Loc. 3526, 'Die Reise Kammer Kasse betr. 1737–63', fol. 53.

[92] Ibid.

[93] D-Dla, 10026 Geheimes Kabinett, Loc. 3528, 'Summarischer Extract der Königlichen Reise-Cammer-Cassen-Rechnung auf das Jahr 1762', fols. 212–32.

[94] Beginning in 1759, the Polish treasury disbursed to him only 60 *Thaler* per annum; see D-Dla, 10026 Geheimes Kabinett, Loc. 3526, 'Die Reise Kammer Kasse betr. 1737–63', fol. 53.

[95] D-Dla, 10026 Geheimes Kabinett, Loc. 3528, 'Summarischer Extract der Königlichen Reise-Cammer-Cassen-Rechnung auf das Jahr 1762', fols. 275–80.

[96] D-Dla, 10026 Geheimes Kabinett, Loc. 907, vol. III: 'Die Italiänische Sänger und Sängerinnen, das Orchestre . . . 1740–64', fol. 310; and RISM-Arbeitsgruppe Deutschland, ed. (with description and commentary by Ortrun Landmann), *Katalog der Dresdener Hasse-Musikhandschriften*, CD-ROM (Munich: Saur, 1999), companion vol., 28, 31.

[97] Including, among others, D-Dla, 12528 Fürstennachlass Maria Antonia, No. 70 G, letter of Heinrich von Brühl, 1 March 1760; No. 10 K, letters by the same dated 1 February and 10 October 1761.

[98] Including, among others, D-Dla, 10026 Geheimes Kabinett, Loc. 907, vol. III, fol. 328;

(1762–3).[99] Additional new singers — the sopranos Antonio Mariottini (1760–83), Giuseppe Galieni (1761–3), and Elisabeth Teuber (Teyber) (1762–3), the castrato Luca Fabris (1762–3), and the tenor Michele Caselli (1758–63) — were hired in Warsaw and later also sang in Dresden.[100] Moreover, certain excellent new artists were hired in Warsaw, including Johann Christian Fischer, probably identical with the virtuoso oboist later famous throughout Europe,[101] as well as the violoncellist Heinrich Megelin and the violinist Cajetanus Meyer.[102] The latter, also known as Gaitano or Gaetani, would later become the most influential musician in the court ensemble of King Stanisław August Poniatowski, for whom he worked as concert-master, *Kapellmeister*, music director, and composer until 1792.[103]

The Polish court also continued to use singers from different private aristo-cratic ensembles as required. For instance, in 1759 three castratos were borrowed: Antonio Francia, called Perelli, from the ensemble of Wacław Rzewuski, *voivod* (governor) of Podole, an unidentified young singer from the ensemble of Fran-ciszek Salezy Potocki, *voivod* of Kiev, and a certain Giorgi, recently hired by von Brühl.[104] Obviously, those were not the only ensembles available to the king to draw from. As noted by Jędrzej Kitowicz, a contemporary eighteenth-century Polish diarist, in the final years of his reign, the king 'dobierał sobie . . . na opery kapele różnych panów, mianowicie [Michała] Wielhorskiego, kuchmistrza lite-wskiego i księcia [Fryderyka Michała] Czartoryskiego, kanclerza wielkiego lite-wskiego, tak, że liczba muzykantów grających opery przenosiła sto osób' (would select . . . for his operas [members from] the ensembles of different nobles, such as [Michał] Wielhorski, master of the Lithuanian kitchens, and Prince [Fryderyk Michał] Czartoryski, grand chancellor of Lithuania, so that the number of musi-cians playing in operas would exceed one hundred people).[105] A musician who certainly co-operated closely with the royal court was Mattia Gerardi (Gherardi), the *Kapellmeister* of the *voivod* of Kiev in 1760, later hired in that capacity by King Stanisław August Poniatowski.[106]

10006 Oberhofmarschallamt, O 11, No. 4, record dated 4 October 1761; 12527 Fürstennachlass Friedrich Christian, No. 2 C, letter by August III dated 16 September 1761.

[99] Including, among others, D-Dla, 10006 Oberhofmarschallamt, I, No. 154, record dated 25 August 1762; I, No. 162a, fol. 193.

[100] See Alina Żórawska-Witkowska, 'I drammi per musica di Johann Adolf Hasse rappre-sentati a Varsavia negli anni 1754–63', in *Johann Adolf Hasse und Polen*, ed. Irena Poniatowska and Alina Żórawska-Witkowska (Warsaw: Instytut Muzykologii Uniwersytetu Warszawsk-iego, 1995), 123–48.

[101] D-Dla, 10006 Oberhofmarschallamt, I, No. 154, record dated 29 November 1756; I, No. 162 b, fols. 23, 50, 68.

[102] D-Dla, 10006 Oberhofmarschallamt, I, No. 154, record dated 25 March 1758.

[103] Alina Żórawska-Witkowska, *Muzyka na dworze i w teatrze Stanisława Augusta* [Music at the Court and Theatre of King Stanisław August] (Warsaw: Zamek Królewski w Warszawie, 1995).

[104] Żórawska-Witkowska, 'I drammi per musica'.

[105] Jędrzej Kitowicz, *Pamiętniki czyli Historia polska*, ed. Przemysława Matuszewska and Zofia Lewinówna (Warsaw: Państwowy Instytut Wydawniczy, 1971), 118.

[106] See Żórawska-Witkowska, *Muzyka na dworze i w teatrze Stanisława Augusta*.

Eleven *drammi per musica* by Hasse were premiered at the Warsaw opera house at that time, numbering 116 performances in total. Between 1761 and 1762, the royal court was also visited by the commercial French troupe of Giovanni Francesco Albani, whose performances required musical accompaniment, presumably provided by musicians from the royal Polish *Kapelle*.[107] Hasse's oratorios were also performed by court artists in Warsaw churches during Holy Week. Professional musicians performed in numerous concerts held at the royal court, including an Italian cellist, most likely Giuseppe dall'Oglio, who performed in September 1758,[108] as did noble *dilettanti*. For instance, in December 1758, and in January 1759, the Saxon Prince Carl, who had recently received the title of prince of Courland (in German, Kurland), displayed his flute-playing skills, while the aristocrat Michał Wielhorski performed on the lute and the violin.[109] It is possible that Johann Adolf Hasse took part in these concerts as well.

This situation, highly interesting in terms of musical activity, changed rapidly when the news of the Peace of Hubertusburg, signed on 15 February 1763, reached Warsaw. In March, the court and its entourage of artists, envoys, and ministers began their exodus to Dresden. The king followed, leaving Warsaw on 25 April. Only the royal Polish *Kapelle* (or a sizeable portion thereof) remained in the city. In the autumn 1763, the ensemble carried out its final duty, performing during the exequies that followed August III's death in Dresden.[110] In late October, Baron Wilhelm August Goltz, representative of the court in Warsaw, received official instructions from Dresden to 'kapeli nadwornej królewskiej podziękował za . . . służbę' (thank . . . the royal court ensemble for its service).[111]

The *Kapelle* was then dissolved (the exact date is unknown). Certain members were transferred to the Dresden ensemble (Perini, Seydelmann, Göricke, Huber, Johann Caspar (?) Horn, Mattstädt, and Christlieb). Others found employment in the Collegiate Church in Warsaw (Czanczik and Jaziomski, and initially also Gerardi). But most were hired by Poland's new king, Stanisław August Poniatowski, for his orchestra (Matteo Roiz (Ronzo), Carl Hübner, Christian Friedrich Horn, Gaitano, Johann Trax, J. Oszewski (Oschetski), Johann Christian Horn, Wacław Czermak, Franz Joseph Glöckner, Heinrich Megelin, Mattia Gerardi, and possibly others). The age-old tradition of maintaining continuity in personnel in the successive Polish royal ensembles was retained: the first ensemble of August II had included musicians from that of his predecessor, Jan III Sobieski; the basis of the Polish *Kapelle* of August III comprised his father's former musicians; and the core of the orchestra established by the last king of Poland, Stanisław August Poniatowski, used artists in the employ of his Saxon predecessor.

[107] Alina Żórawska-Witkowska, 'Die Oper in Warschau in der zweiten Hälfte des 18. Jahrhunderts: Vom Hoftheater Augusts III. zum öffentlichen Theater von Stanisław August Poniatowski', *Musikgeschichte in Mittel- und Osteuropa*, 3 (1998), 78–93.
[108] D-Dla, 10006 Oberhofmarschallamt, O 11, No. 4, record dated 3 September 1758.
[109] For example, D-Dla, 12527 Fürstennachlass Friedrich Christian, No. 240, letters dated 23 December 1758 and 31 January 1759.
[110] PL-Wagad, Archiwum Skarbu Koronnego, 'Rachunki i kwity', No. 16, section 5.
[111] PL-KO, MS 447, fol. 71.

Between 1734 and 1762, the number of positions in the Polish *Kapelle* rose
from six to thirty-five, with the budget increasing from 1,400 to over 6,526 *Thaler*.
Financial records, no matter how detailed, cannot reflect the richness of artistic
realities, which were determined as much by pragmatic economic calculations as
by political considerations. These included connections with private ensembles, resulting from factional rivalries between powerful aristocrats. Whilst the picture of
the Polish *Kapelle* presented here — based upon extant court records — may convey
the impression of considerable confusion and *ad hoc* decisions, this apparent chaos
was, in fact, closely controlled by Saxon court officials.

The Polish ensemble of August III maintained closer links to Warsaw than
its predecessor; however, the *Kapelle* does not seem to have been used as a unit
for performances in Dresden, even though a number of the musicians appear to
have had homes and families in the Saxon capital. With regard to nationalities,
Germans dominated among the instrumentalists, but there were also Italians, Bo-
hemians, and Poles. The basic idea behind the composition of the Polish *Kapelle*
of August III was primarily to meet the requirements of church ritual, as the king
and, to an even greater extent his wife Maria Josepha, were great lovers of religious
solemnities. For this reason, vocalists such as Jaroszewicz, Perini, Seydelmann, and
Sękowski (SATB), who did not take part in *drammi per musica*, were primarily employed for the performance of sacred music. The repertoire at the Polish court of
August III represented not only a variety of genres and a diversity of musical styles.
These included Latin church music modelled both on Palestrina and Italian opera,
Italian *drammi per musica*, *commedie dell'arte*, and comedies, as well as French bal-
lets, chamber music by German, Austrian, and probably also Polish composers, and
dance music, which in Poland was dominated by polonaises and *mazurs*.

TABLE 3.1. Membership of the Polish *Kapelle* in 1718, 1732, and 1748

| *Year* | *1718* | *1732* | *1748* |
|---|---|---|---|
| Ruler | King August II (r. 1697–1706 & 1709–33) | | King August III (r. 1733–63) |
| Numeric Overview | 1 *Compositeur*<br>12 instrumentalists | 1 *Compositeur*<br>15 instrumentalists<br>2 additional personnel | 22 instrumentalists<br>3 vocalists<br>1 additional person |
| *Compositeur* | Giovanni Alberto Ristori (600 *Thaler*) | Giovanni Alberto Ristori (600 *Thaler*) | |
| Instrumentalists | | | |
| *Director* ('premier de l'orguestre' [concertmaster]) | Heinrich Schulze (vn; 200 *Thaler*) | Heinrich Schulze (vn; 200 *Thaler*) | |
| Violin | Christian Friedrich Friese (200 *Thaler*) | Matthias Siegmund Köhler (250 *Thaler*) | Matthias Siegmund Köhler (280 *Thaler*) |
| | Matthias Siegmund Köhler (126 *Thaler*) | František (Franz) Benda (250 *Thaler*) | George Elias Müller (200 *Thaler*) |
| | Carl Anton Schauer (126 *Thaler*) | Carl Anton Schauer (230 *Thaler*) | Gottfried Friedrich Göricke (200 *Thaler*) |
| | Michael Simon (va?; 126 *Thaler*) | Philipp Bernard Troyer (230 *Thaler*) | Carl Hübner (200 *Thaler*) |
| | | Jiří (Georg) Čart (Zarth or Czarth) (salary not listed) | Matteo Roiz (Ronzo) (vn?; 200 *Thaler*) |
| | See Director | See Director | Johann Trax (200 *Thaler*) |
| | | | Johann Franz Hantke (Hancke) (180 *Thaler*) |

| | | | |
|---|---|---|---|
| Bass players | Daniel Hasse (cb or vc and bn; 200 *Thaler*)<br>Johann Blume (lute?; 126 *Thaler*) | Daniel Hasse ('Contra-Basson',[a] 250 *Thaler*)<br>Johann Blume (lute?, 'Bassist'; 230 *Thaler*)<br>Sebastian Reimel (vc?, 'Bassist'; 230 *Thaler*)<br>Carl Morasch (bn?, 'Contra-Basson'; 230 *Thaler*) | Johann Blume (lute?; 230 *Thaler*)<br>Johann Caspar Horn (cb; 200 *Thaler*) |
| Flute | Johann Nicolas Friese (also ob; 200 *Thaler*) | Friedrich Töppert (Döbbert; 230 *Thaler*) | Johann Michael Huttmann? (200 *Thaler*) |
| Oboe | *See* Flute<br>Christian Paschek (or bn; 126 *Thaler*)<br>Christian Seydel (or bn; 126 *Thaler*) | Johann Caspar Grund (230 *Thaler*) | Dominik Jaziomski (300 *Thaler*) |
| Bassoon | *See* Oboe *and* Bass players | *See* Bass players | Johann George Bencker (252 *Thaler*)<br>Christian Friedrich Mattstädt (200 *Thaler*) |
| *Waldhorn* | Gottfried Grossmann (130 *Thaler*)<br>Johann Küntzel (130 *Thaler*) | Johann Georg Kurzweil (230 *Thaler*)<br>Joseph Carl Lindemann (230 *Thaler*) | Jan (Johann) Czermak (240 *Thaler*)<br>Václav (Wenzel or Wacław) Czermak (240 *Thaler*)<br>Joseph Carl Lindemann (230 *Thaler*)<br>Christoph Stephan Scheinhardt (200 *Thaler*) |
| Lute | *See* Bass players | *See* Bass players | |
| Organ | | | Józef Czanczik (400 *Thaler*) |
| Instrument(s) not specified | | Franz Lutter (salary not listed) | Christoph Ehrenfried Riedel (200 *Thaler*) |

| Year | 1718 | 1732 | 1748 |
|---|---|---|---|
| Instrument(s) not specified (*cont.*) | | | Friedrich Treptau (200 *Thaler*) |
| | | | Antonio Stephan (200 *Thaler*) |
| | | | Johann Caspar Knoth (for half of the year; 200 *Thaler*) |
| **Vocalists** | | | |
| Castrato | | | Stefan Jaroszewicz (400 *Thaler*) |
| Tenor | | | Franz Ignaz Seydelmann (242 *Thaler*) |
| Bass | | | Józef Sękowski (Senkowski) (133 *Thaler*, 10 *Groschen*) |
| **Additional Personnel** | | | |
| *Instrumenten-Diener* (servant) | | Johann Georg Müller (50 *Thaler*) | Jan Tokarski (36 *Thaler*) |
| | | Johann Georg Nöller (salary not listed) | |

*Sources*

1718: Based on information in D-Dla, 10026 Geheimes Kabinett, Loc. 3521, 'Pohlnische General-Cassa Sachen . . .', vol. III, fol. 10; none of the musicians are identified by instrument type in this document.

1732: Based on information in the *Hof- und Staats-Calender* (1733), without pagination; and D-Dla, 10026 Geheimes Kabinett, Loc. 3522, 'Die polnische General Kasse betr. 1729–32', without foliation.

1748: Based on information in D-Dla, 10026 Geheimes Kabinett, Loc. 3525, vol. XIII, fol. 211; none of the musicians are identified by instrument or voice type in this document.

a See p. 55 n. 12 above.

TABLE 3.2. Royal-Electoral Artists Summoned to Poland from Dresden between 1740 and 1754

| Date | Singers | Instrumentalists |
|---|---|---|
| 1740/41 | Margherita Delfini-Ermini (buffo alto) | |
| | Cosimo Ermini (buffo bass) | |
| 1744/5 | Domenico Annibali (alto) | |
| | Giovanni Bindi (soprano) | |
| | Anton Führig (Führich) (bass) | |
| 1746 | Domenico Annibali (alto) | |
| | Ventura Rochetti (soprano) | |
| | Joseph Schuster (bass) | |
| 1748/9 | Domenico Annibali (alto) | François de Francini (violinist, specializing in ballet music) |
| | Ludwig Cornelius (tenor) | Joseph Zyka (Zicka or Syka) (cellist) |
| | Joseph Schuster (bass) | Peter August (organist) |
| 1750 | Ventura Rochetti | |
| | Nicola Pozzi (alto) | |
| | Ludwig Cornelius (tenor) | |
| | Anton Führig (bass) | |
| 1754 | Teresa Albuzzi-Todeschini (soprano) | Wenzel Gottfried Dewerdeck (flautist) |
| | Wilhelmine Denner (soprano) | |
| | Bartolomeo Putini (soprano) | |
| | Giovanni (Giuseppe) Belli (soprano) | |
| | Pasquale Bruscolini (alto) | |
| | Domenico Annibali (alto) | |

# 4

# The Court of Brandenburg-Prussia

## *Mary Oleskiewicz*

THE PRUSSIAN HOHENZOLLERN KINGS were descendants of the 'Great Elector' Friedrich Wilhelm I of Brandenburg (r. 1640–88) and his first wife, Luise Henriette of Orange (1627–1667). Under Elector Friedrich III – crowned as Prussian King Friedrich I in 1701 – and his second wife, Sophie Charlotte (d. 1705), music rose to a central place in Hohenzollern court life.

Under Friedrich Wilhelm I (r. 1713–40), music was all but exiled to the military. Yet chamber music continued to be fostered by Queen Sophie Dorothea (1687–1757), daughter of King George I of England, who supported her children's musical education. Crown Prince Friedrich (1712–1786) and Princesses Wilhelmine (1709–1758), Luise Ulrike (1720–1782), and Anna Amalie (1723–1787) became accomplished musicians and significant patrons of the arts. During the 1730s Friedrich and his sister Wilhelmine (Margravine of Brandenburg-Bayreuth from 1735) would establish significant *Hofkapellen* of their own.

Under Friedrich II (king from 1740), Prussia became a major European power with a corresponding cultural agenda. The court orchestra flourished until the outbreak of the Seven Years' War in 1756, and the capital became a centre for public and private music making. Friedrich's younger brothers, Princes August Wilhelm, Ferdinand, and Heinrich, also established *Hofkapellen*, and his youngest sister Princess Amalie played several instruments, composed, and developed a keen interest in contrapuntal music, collecting scores that served as a foundation for the cultivation of music by Handel and members of the Bach family. Several members of a secondary Hohenzollern line, the margraves of Brandenburg-Schwedt, also established significant *Hofkapellen* and are treated below in an excursus.

## COURT MUSIC BEFORE 1740

During the eighteenth century the court resided alternatively in palaces in Berlin, Charlottenburg, and Potsdam, as well as in neighbouring Schönhausen,

I am grateful for a generous research fellowship from the Alexander von Humboldt-Stiftung, which enabled me to carry out extensive archival research into the Prussian court's music.

Oranienburg, Rheinsberg, Wusterhausen, after 1741 Breslau, and, during the Seven Years' War, Magdeburg. The first Prussian queen, Sophie Charlotte, held court in Lietzenburg (today Charlottenburg) until her death in 1705. An accomplished harpsichordist, Sophie Charlotte composed and cultivated Italian chamber music and opera, hosting Italian artists such as Giuseppe Torelli, Attilio Ariosti, and Giovanni Bononcini; Corelli dedicated his Opus 5 violin sonatas (Rome, 1700) to her.[1] She also assembled a large library of Italian operas and instrumental music. The *Hofinstrumentenmacher*, Michael Mietke, built two harpsichords for the court (one for her private use); both remain in Charlottenburg palace today.

King Friedrich I, who played the flute, transformed the *Hofkapelle* into a modern orchestra, replacing players of the viola da gamba and obsolete wind instruments with violinists. At his death in 1713, the *Hofkapelle* numbered twenty-nine musicians of mostly German origin (see Table 4.1, pp. 111–17 below): eleven or twelve violinists, two viola players, five cellists (one of whom played lute and gamba), four oboists, three bassoonists (one of whom also played trumpet), and four singers. Some of the oboists doubled on flute, while two *Jagdmusiker* (musicians of the hunt) played horn as needed. One cellist probably also played contrabass. The organist Gottlieb Hayne (1683–1757), listed as a court cellist in the Berlin *Adreß-Kalender*, may in fact have played keyboard. Most prominent in 1713 were the singer and composer Augustin Reinhard Stricker (dedicatee of Mattheson's *Beschütztes Orchestre*, 1717) and the oboist Peter Glösch, to whom Telemann dedicated his *Kleine Cammer-Music* (1716); the violinist and dancing master Jean-Baptiste Volumier, who had served as concertmaster until 1709, was by this date concertmaster of the Dresden *Hofkapelle*. The duties of the Berlin *Hofkapelle* included performing for court spectacles and the occasional opera, as well as for *Tafelmusik* twice daily, in the afternoon and evening.[2] The *Hofkapelle* performed for the last time for the king's burial in May 1713.

Upon his accession, the 'Soldier-King' Friedrich Wilhelm I (r. 1713–40) disbanded the *Hofkapelle*, retaining, however, one chamber trumpeter and the violinist Heinrich Gottfried Pepusch, reputedly because of his great height.[3] Pepusch led the military musicians for the king's famous *Leibgarde* (life guard) of tall soldiers, directing functional music involving four to six players for balls and other festivi-

---

[1] Anecdotal reports of a visit by Handel cannot be confirmed. For an overview of the court's musical life from this period, see Curt Sachs, *Musik und Oper am kurbrandenburgischen Hof* (Berlin: Julius Bard, 1910; repr. Hildesheim and New York: Georg Olms, 1977), and Günther Wagner, 'Sophie Charlotte und die Musik', in *Barockmusik in Berlin: Sophie Charlotte und ihre Favoriten* (Berlin: Großmann, 1987), 9–15; on the Prussian court's instruments and instrument makers, see Herbert Heyde, *Musikinstrumentenbau in Preußen* (Tutzing: Hans Schneider, 1994).

[2] Sachs, *Musik und Oper*, 67.

[3] In addition to the trumpeter Beyersdorff (one of the previous twenty-four *Hoftrompeter*), Friedrich Wilhelm I also retained the *Domkantor* Petraeo, the *Pulsanten* (bell-ringers), and the organ builder, Arp Schnitger, though from now on he was paid only for tuning. The court instrument maker Mietke was dismissed. See D-Bga, I. HA Rep. 36 No. 339 'Königliche Preußische Hoff Staats Cassen Rechnung von Trinitatis 1712 bis Trinitatis 1713' and similarly entitled documents for subsequent years.

ties. The court would not cultivate opera or 'grosse Hofkonzerte' (grand court concerts) for another twenty-seven years.

An *Hautboistenschule*, established by 1729 in the military orphanage at Potsdam, provided the army with musicians. Pepusch was its director (see Table 4.1), paid from the royal *Hofstaatskasse* (court budget). His duties were taken over in 1738 by the 'Cammer Musicant' Sydow, who was retained by Friedrich II; he was succeeded in 1754 by the court oboist Friedrich Wilhelm Pauly.[4] The position became vacant during the Seven Years' War, being filled only in 1768, when Johann Joachim Quantz recommended Johann Christian Jacobi, an oboist from the *Hofkapelle* of Margrave Karl of Schwedt (see Table 4.4, pp. 129–30 below).

Following Friedrich Wilhelm's dissolution of the royal *Hofkapelle,* many musicians found employment at other German courts. The majority went to that of Prince Leopold of Anhalt-Köthen (1694–1728): Stricker, as *Kapellmeister*; the violinists Joseph Spieß and Martin Friedrich Marcus (Marcks); the oboist Ludwig Rose and the bassoonist Christoph Torbey (Torley); the singer Christian Frohböse (Frobese) and the copyist Johann Kreyser.[5] The cellist Christian Bernhard Linicke joined the *Hofkapelle* of the Margrave Christian Ludwig of Brandenburg-Schwedt in Berlin, leaving for Köthen in 1716. The violinist Johann Georg Linicke became concertmaster at Weißenfels, joining Anton Balthasar König, who had left Prussian service in 1708. The vocalist Campioli (Antonio Gualandi) would train singers for the Dresden opera, eventually performing the role of Poro in the premiere there of Johann Adolf Hasse's *Cleofide* in 1731. The cellist Gottfried Dümler was organist at Berlin's Georgenkirche from 1718 until 1722. A few remained in Berlin as private teachers, among them Glösch, who later trained young oboists for the royal *Kapelle* of Friedrich II. Gottlieb Hayne became *Domorganist* (cathedral organist) in Berlin, but remained in the employ of Queen Sophie Dorothea as music teacher to her children.[6]

Sophie Dorothea performed chamber music in Schloß Lietzenburg with both amateurs and visiting artists. It is reported that she maintained a small *Hofkapelle,* but the only surviving records of her *Hofstaat* are receipts from 1752/3, when Hayne, one of three or four musicians paid, received 300 *Thaler.*[7] From 1740 until 1742 he served Princess Amalie for a salary of 400 *Thaler.*[8] Also receiving 300 *Thaler* from the queen's *Hofstaat* were Johann Caspar Richter and Charles du Bois,

---

[4] On Sydow, see D-Bga, Brandenburg-Preußisches Hausarchiv, Rep. 36 No. 359, 'Königlich Preußische Hoff Staats Cassen Rechnung von Trinitatis 1729 bis Trinitatis 1730', p. 32, and the similarly entitled accounts for 1738/9 and 1739/40 (No. 369, p. 33; No. 370, p. 35).

[5] Friedrich Smend, *Bach in Köthen* (Berlin: Christlicher Zeitschriftenverlag, 1951), trans. John Page and ed. Stephen Daw (St. Louis: Concordia, 1985), 37–8; and Ernst König, 'Die Hofkapelle des Fürsten Leopold zu Anhalt-Köthen', *Bach-Jahrbuch,* 46 (1959), 160–67.

[6] Sachs, *Musik und Oper,* 177.

[7] D-Bga, Brandenburg-Preußisches Hausarchiv, Rep. 46 N No. 20a, 'Belege zur Hofstaatskasse von Königin Mutter Sophia Dorothea für das Jahr 1752/53.' The receipts in question are on fols. 79–83; Hayne signed the receipt on fol. 80.

[8] Curt Sachs, 'Prinzessin Amalie von Preußen als Musikerin', in *Sonder-Abdruck aus dem Hohenzollern Jahrbuch,* ed. Paul Seidel (Berlin: Giesecke & Devrient, 1910), 181–91, at 183.

while the 'Vorsänger' (*Kantor*) Hen. Wilh[elm] Conrad, who may have served in the chapel at Lietzenburg, received 50 *Thaler*.[9]

In 1715, several Dresden chamber virtuosos, including violinist Johann Georg Pisendel, travelled to the Prussian court, where Pisendel performed for the king at a supper hosted by Count Jakob Heinrich von Flemming, then in Berlin.[10] Pisendel would visit the court again in 1728, and at the invitation of Crown Prince Friedrich in 1734 and (as king) in 1744.

## The 'Hochfürstliche Kammer- und Capellmusik' (1732–40): Nauen, Ruppin, and Rheinsberg

The most important events for the future of music at the Prussian court were the state visit of Friedrich Wilhelm I to Dresden from 12 January to 11 February 1728 and the return visit of August II, elector of Saxony and king of Poland, to Berlin in May. These visits exposed the sixteen-year-old Prussian Crown Prince Friedrich to a new world of artistic extravagance that included theatre, opera, and virtuoso instrumentalists, forever altering his taste and his cultural agenda. Unpublished Dresden court journals, which describe the Berlin court's visit to Dresden, note that on 26 January,

> Le Prince Royal de Prusse, après s'etre amusé le matin à entendre des concerts de Musique, et à expedier quelques lettres pour Berlin, dina chez son Exc. le Feldm., vit la comedie, et soupa comme il avoit diné, c'est à dire chez le Feldm., où il y eut en même têms bal, tant avant qu'a près souper.

> The royal Prince of Prussia, having amused himself in the morning with a concert of music, sent some letters to Berlin, dined with his excellency the *Feldmarschall* [Field Marshal Count Jakob Heinrich von Flemming], saw a comedy, and supped as he had dined, that is to say with the *Feldmarschall*, where a ball was held before and after the meal.[11]

One of the above-mentioned letters to Berlin was sent to his sister Wilhelmine. Dated Dresden, 26 January 1728, it describes the concert in which Friedrich

---

[9] Richter is probably the Johann Friedrich Richter named in 1754 by Friedrich Wilhelm Marpurg as bassoonist in the *Hofkapelle* of Margrave Karl of Brandenburg-Schwedt (see Table 4.4). Marpurg notes that this Richter formerly belonged to the *Hofkapelle* of the queen, from whom he was still receiving a pension. See Marpurg, *Historisch-kritische Beyträge zur Aufnahme der Musik* (Berlin, 1754–78), I, 'Zweytes Stück' (1754), 159. Du Bois is the only other member of the queen's *Hofstaat* to receive this comparatively high salary and thus is probably also a musician.

[10] As reported by Johann Adam Hiller, ed., *Wöchentliche Nachrichten und Anmerkungen die Musik betreffend* (Leipzig, 1766–70), I, '36. Stück' (3 March 1767), 280–81: 'Lebenslauf: Des ehemaligen königl. Pohlnischen und Churfürstl. Sächsischen Concertmeisters: Herrn Johann Georg Pisendel'.

[11] D-Dla, 10026 Geheimes Kabinett, Loc. 3497/3, *Varia, journeaux de Varsovie, de Dresde et de Berlin*, especially 'Journal du 26. Janv. 1728 de Dresde', no pagination. Translations are the present author's, unless otherwise stated. I wish to thank Claire Fontijn and David Schulenberg for helpful suggestions on rendering period French.

himself performed, probably as harpsichordist: 'j'ai eu musique ou je me suis fait entendre. Ricter[,] Bufardain[,] Kuans[,] Bishendel[,] et Weis ont joué avec[.] je les admire car se sont les plus abiles maitres d'ici' (I have had music in which I allowed myself to be heard. [Johann Christian] Richter, [Pierre-Gabriel] Buffardin, Quantz, Pisendel, and [Sylvius Leopold] Weiss have played with [me]. I marvel at them, for they are the most capable masters here).[12]

This encounter was the beginning of Friedrich's long relationship with musicians in Dresden, some of whom would form the core of the future royal Prussian *Hofkapelle*. Significantly, the Dresden court was the first in Germany to cultivate the French transverse flute as a virtuoso instrument. After dining with Count Flemming – a powerful political figure and Saxon envoy to Berlin – Friedrich mentioned his interest in learning the flute to Flemming's daughter; Buffardin subsequently conveyed to him his first flute, a gift from the Polish king.[13]

In May the Dresden court travelled to Berlin via the Elbe, more than three hundred persons in all, including Quantz, Buffardin, Pisendel, and Weiss, whom Friedrich had admired, and whose presence was explicitly requested by the queen of Prussia.[14] Quantz, who remained for several months, appeared several times before the queen, who offered to engage him at a salary of 800 *Thaler*. The Polish king would not part with him, but Count Flemming arranged for Quantz to visit Prussia twice a year to instruct the crown prince on the flute.[15] The arrangement continued until 1742, when Quantz entered the Prussian *Hofkapelle* under the new king.

During the same state visit, the violinists Pietro Locatelli and Johann Gottlieb Graun also performed before the queen. An eyewitness account by Wilhelm Stratemann, envoy from Braunschweig to the Berlin court, reports:

> Vorgestern, den 27. haben Ihro Majestät die Königin die hier anwesende[n] berühmte[n] beyde[n] Violinisten vor Sich in Mon-Bijou spielen laßen, wobey zugleich die älteste Prinzeßinn fast 2 Stunden lang auf den Flügel accompagniret hat; von denen beyden Virtuosen soll aber vor das mahl der Merseburgsche Capell-Meister Graum vor dem Italiäner Locotelli [*sic*] approbation gefunden haben. und wolle die Königin ihn auch daher zu Ihrem Hof Musicum machen.
>
> Her Majesty the Queen had the two famous violinists here in attendance perform before her the day before yesterday, the 27th [May 1728], in Mon-bijou palace. The oldest princess accompanied them for almost two hours at the keyboard. Of the two violinists, the Merseburg *Kapellmeister* Graun

---

[12] D-Bga, Brandenburg-Preußisches Hausarchiv, Rep. 47 No. 305, vol. I, fol. 1ᵛ.

[13] Mary Oleskiewicz, 'The Flute at Dresden: Ramifications for Eighteenth-Century Woodwind Performance', in *From Renaissance to Baroque: Change in Instruments and Instrumental Music in the Seventeenth Century*, ed. Jonathan Wainwright and Peter Holman (Aldershot: Ashgate, 2005), 145–65; Friedrich Förster, *Leben und Thaten Friedrichs des Großen, Königs von Preußen*, v (Meissen, 1840), 1040–41.

[14] Quantz's autobiography of 1762, reproduced in Horst Augsbach, *Johann Joachim Quantz: Thematisch-systematisches Werkverzeichnis (QV)* (Stuttgart: Carus, 1997), 266–7, reports their presence at the queen's request.

[15] Förster, *Leben und Thaten Friedrichs des Großen*, 1041.

especially found approbation over the Italian Locatelli, so much that the queen wanted him to enter her service.[16]

Hence the queen also tried to engage Graun, who, like Quantz, would later serve the crown prince. The princess must have been Wilhelmine, who would later prefer Graun's violin playing over that of all Italian violinists, including Giuseppe Tartini.

The assembly of Crown Prince Friedrich's *Hofkapelle* at Ruppin and Rheinsberg, which hitherto has received less attention than the history of his royal *Hofkapelle* after 1740, will receive special emphasis here. In 1732 the crown prince received his first military command, in Ruppin, and his first private residence. After living first in Nauen, he soon moved to quarters in Ruppin. His marriage on 12 June 1733 to Princess Elisabeth Christine of Braunschweig-Wolfenbüttel-Bevern occasioned the purchase of a new palace in Rheinsberg, which became habitable in 1736. His new independence allowed Friedrich to begin building a *Hofkapelle*. By 1737 the ensemble was similar in size and proportions to other princely *Kapellen* in Berlin, comprising four first and three second violins ( J. G. Graun, Franz Benda, Georg Czarth [Čart or Zarth], and Ehmes [Ems or Emis]; Joseph Blume, Johann Caspar Grundke, and Christiani), two violas (Johann Georg Benda and Reich), cello (Antonius Hock), contrabass (Johann Gottlieb Janitsch), one or two flutes (Quantz and Buffardin, as visiting musicians), two horns (Johann Ignatius Horzitzky and Görbich), bassoon (Kottowsky), theorbo (Ernst Gottlieb Baron), harp (Petrini), and a vocalist (Carl Heinrich Graun).[17]

Friedrich's strained relations with his father are well known. From 1732 until 1740, he assembled musicians with the clandestine support of his mother, and relied on musicians borrowed from other courts, some of whom visited for weeks or months at a time.[18] He also shared musicians with his sister in Bayreuth, who was simultaneously building a *Hofkapelle* on limited means. In addition to playing and composing flute music, the crown prince had broader musical ambitions, seeking the best singers and violinists. Lacking the means as yet to sponsor operas, he cultivated vocal and instrumental chamber music.

Music performed at Friedrich's princely court included works that he composed or commissioned for himself, his sister Wilhelmine, and her spouse, Margrave

---

[16] The original German text is cited from Albert Dunning, *Pietro Antonio Locatelli: Der Virtuose und seine Welt*, I (Buren: Frits Knuf, 1981), 112; on p. 114 Dunning misunderstands the expression 'vor das mahl' (especially) to mean 'vor dem Essen' (that is, before the meal).

[17] Information for the Rheinsberg *Hofkapelle* derives mainly from Crown Prince Friedrich's correspondence with his sister Wilhelmine, some of it unpublished; composer biographies published by Marpurg, *Historisch-kritische Beyträge*; Hiller, *Wöchentliche Nachrichten*, and also his *Lebensbeschreibungen berühmter Musikgelehrten und Tonkünstler neuerer Zeit* (Leipzig, 1784); and various dictionaries, including Johann Gottfried Walther, *Musicalisches Lexicon oder musicalische Bibliothec* (1732), ed. Friedericke Ramm (Kassel: Bärenreiter, 2001), and Carl von Ledebur, *Tonkünstler-Lexicon Berlin's von den ältesten Zeiten bis auf die Gegenwart* (Berlin, 1861).

[18] Quantz reported that it was the 'queen mother who encouraged the prince in his favourite amusement and . . . engaged musicians for his service' through secret negotiations, placing the musicians in considerable danger. See Charles Burney, *The Present State of Music in Germany, the Netherlands, and the United Provinces* (London, 1773), II: 138.

Friedrich, including chamber works by Franz Benda, J. G. Graun, Quantz, and Hasse, as well as cantatas by C. H. Graun. Manuscripts of these works — especially those of Quantz, Christoph Schaffrath, and the Grauns — were exchanged between the courts of Berlin, Bayreuth, and Dresden well into the 1750s. Friedrich's princely court was particularly important as an early centre for the development of the solo concerto, Quantz providing many such works for flute, Schaffrath for keyboard. Between 1732 and 1756 Friedrich composed arias, sinfonias, concertos, and 121 flute sonatas.[19] Wilhelmine also composed, and she commissioned works from her court composers, some of which she sent to her brother.[20]

Visiting artists were a staple of Friedrich's princely *Hofkapelle*. Before his permanent engagement in 1732, the violinist J. G. Graun was a frequent guest. According to a letter of Friedrich to his sister Wilhelmine, written on 24 October 1732, Graun performed in Ruppin before the margrave, her husband; the latter, however, preferred the 'petit Violon' (little violinist) Hoffmann, a musician in the *Kapelle* at Bayreuth. After dinner a castrato performed, whom Friedrich described as 'un ecoillér de la Faustina' (a student of Faustina (Bordoni-Hasse, 1693–1781)). A letter of 15 December describes daily chamber concerts at Ruppin from four o'clock until seven o'clock in the evening, in which Friedrich played flute and viola accompanied by Graun on violin and the queen's musician Hayne on harpsichord.[21]

In Graun's absence the Weimar court violinist Johann Pfeiffer filled in at Nauen in April and May of 1732. Pfeiffer was one of Wilhelmine's guest musicians; though he would later become her *Kapellmeister*, he did not meet Friedrich's standards:

> Nous egsersons ici de la belle magniere, mais les muses, vienent de teims en teims nous de lasér des fatiges de Mars[.] Pfeifer qui est un de leurs nouriçons, à eté yci, et à joué aveque moi. il à une grande vitesse, mais il n'a pas le coup d'arché de Grauen, et ces adajios ne sont pas asséz touchents[.]

> We carry out fine manoeuvres here, but the muses come from time to time to lighten the efforts of Mars. Pfeiffer, who is one of their offspring, has been here and has played with me. He has great speed, but he lacks Graun's bow stroke, and his adagios are not sufficiently expressive.[22]

Graun, the future concertmaster of the Prussian *Hofoper*, was already the model against which Friedrich measured all other violinists. A pupil of Tartini, Graun had also studied with Pisendel in Dresden. With Quantz, Graun ensured that the Dresden style would prevail at the Prussian court. Other violinists were required to study with Graun to learn his style and bow stroke. In 1732, at Graun's invitation,

---

[19] Mary Oleskiewicz, 'Friedrich der Grosse', in *Lexikon der Flöte*, ed. András Adorján and Lenz Meierott (Laaber: Laaber-Verlag, 2009), 314–17.

[20] On Wilhelmine as a composer, see also Chapter 14, 'The Court of Brandenburg-Culmbach-Bayreuth', pp. 402–3 below.

[21] D-Bga, Brandenburg-Preußisches Hausarchiv, Rep. 47 No. 305, vol. 1, fol. 175ʳ, Ruppin, 24 October 1732; fol. 191ʳ, Ruppin, 15 December 1732.

[22] D-Bga, Brandenburg-Preußisches Hausarchiv, Rep. 47 No. 305, vol. 1, fol. 95ᵛ, Nauen, 2 May 1732.

the violinist and gambist Johann Christian Hertel also visited Ruppin and had the honour of performing numerous times at court.[23]

The next additions to the crown prince's *Kapelle*, engaged following the death (on 1 February 1733) of August II, had been members of the latter's so-called Polish *Kapelle*.[24] Franz Benda, the first of these, arrived in Ruppin on 12 April 1733. He possessed a beautiful tenor voice and was required to sing arias almost every evening.[25] The violinist and flautist Georg Czarth was in Ruppin by 29 December 1733.[26] Christoph Schaffrath, who had also served the King of Poland, was engaged at about the same time.[27] On March 16, Wilhelmine acknowledged receiving copies of difficult keyboard concertos by Schaffrath, 'a new virtuoso' about to enter Friedrich's *Hofkapelle*:

> Bendo ma porté deux Concerts pour le Cembalo d'un nouveau vertuoso que vous allez prendre en service qui sont trés beaux mais qui m'ont bien rompu la Tête[.] il faut qu'il soit bien habile et fort dans la composition.

> Benda brought me two harpsichord concertos by a new virtuoso whom you are going to take into service. They are very beautiful but they really wracked my brains[.][?] He must be very skilled and strong in composition.[28]

On 28 March, Friedrich replied from Ruppin, promising Wilhelmine

> je ne manquerai pas de comendér nouveaux conserts chéz Schafrot, qui ce trouvera fort heureux de les savoirs aprouvéz dé La Deessé de la musique et de nostre Souvreine protectrisse.

> I will not forget to order new concertos [from] Schaffrath, who will be very

---

[23] Marpurg, 'Leben Johann Christian Hertels', *Historisch-kritische Beyträge*, III, 'Erstes Stück' (1757), 46–64, at 46.

[24] See Chapter 3, 'The Saxon Court of the Kingdom of Poland', pp. 51–77 above.

[25] Hiller, 'Lebenslauf des Herrn Franz Benda, königlichen Preußischen Kammermusikus', *Wöchentliche Nachrichten*, I, '26. Stück' (23 December 1766), 199. Once the singer C. H. Graun was permanently engaged, Benda ceased singing at court on account of headaches but continued to offer voice instruction.

[26] On 29 December 1733 Friedrich told Wilhelmine that his daily music 's'etent ogmenti du chanteur Grauen, et d'un Violon, qui est encore meillieur que Benda' (is being augmented by the singer Graun and a violinist better than Benda); on 11 January 1734 he repeated that he had engaged another violinist who was 'asséz bon' (very good); see D-Bga, Brandenburg-Preußisches Hausarchiv, Rep. 47 No. 305, vol. I, fol. 91r; vol. II, fol. 6v. Horst Richter supposed that this new violinist was Joseph Blume, but Blume had been hired earlier in 1733; see Richter, 'Ich bin Komponist: Friedrich II. von Preußen in seinen musikalisch-schöpferischen Kronprinzenjahren in Ruppin und Rheinsberg', in *Die Rheinsberger Hofkapelle von Friedrich II.: Musiker auf dem Weg zum Berliner 'Capell-Bedienten'*, ed. Ulrike Liedke (Rheinsberg: Musikakademie Rheinsberg, 2005), 11–46, at 26.

[27] Hartmut Grosch, 'Christoph Schaffrath: Komponist – Cembalist – Lehrmeister', in *Die Rheinsberger Hofkapelle*, 204–23, at 205, transcribes Schaffrath's petition for the organist position at the Dresden Sophienkirche, dated 2 June 1733, in which he states that he had served August II as 'Clavicembalist' for three years.

[28] D-Bga, Brandenburg-Preußisches Hausarchiv, Rep. 46 W No. 17, vol. I, 2, fol. 22v, Bayreuth, 16 March 1734.

glad to know that the goddess of music and our Sovereign Protectress has approved of them.[29]

Such commissions continued in subsequent years. On 19 March 1734, in anticipation of his impending departure to campaign in the War of the Polish Succession, Friedrich offered to send Wilhelmine 'les deux Grauens Schart Schafrot, et toute la bande' (both Grauns, Czarth, Schaffrath, and the whole band).[30]

Friedrich engaged Graun's brother, Carl Heinrich, on a visiting basis from November 1733 until his permanent appointment as a vocalist in the *Hofkapelle* in 1735. According to Hiller, it was Graun's

> vornehmste Beschäftigung, sich mit Singen vor dem Prinzen hören zu lassen. Er setzte also viele italiänische Cantaten in Musik, deren Worte theils aus den Singgedichten des Paolo Rolli genommen, theils vom Prinzen selbst, in französischer Sprache, entworfen, und von dem damaligen italiänischen Poeten Bottarelli in Berlin, ins Italiänische übersetzt sind.

> foremost duty to sing before the prince. He therefore composed many Italian cantatas to song texts by Paolo Rolli or those drafted in French by the prince himself, which were translated into Italian by the Italian poet [Giovanni Gualberto] Bottarelli, then in Berlin.[31]

In 1734 Graun accompanied Benda to Bayreuth, where the two sang duets.[32]

Joseph Blume, a violinist from Munich, arrived in Ruppin in 1733.[33] His appointment followed that of Franz Benda, and he would join Friedrich's select chamber ensemble after 1740. Johann Georg Benda arrived from Dresden on or after 8 April 1734 and was immediately engaged as viola player; after 1740 he would play violin in the royal *Hofkapelle*. On 27 December 1734, Friedrich wrote to Wilhelmine, 'J'ai resseux[?] trois nouveaux viollons dont il y en à un qui est aussi fort que Benda, le segond comme Ems, et le troissieme bon pour le Ripino' (I've received three new violinists; one of them is as good as Benda, the second like Ems [*recte* Ehmes], and the third good for the ripieno).[34] These players must have included J. G. Benda

---

[29] D-Bga, Brandenburg-Preußisches Hausarchiv, Rep. 47 No. 305, vol. II, fol. 34ʳ.

[30] Ibid., fol. 33ʳ; the offer is repeated in a letter of 24 May (fol. 56ʳ). Hans D. Hoch, 'Georg Czarth: Geiger und Komponist aus Böhmen', *Die Rheinsberger Hofkapelle*, 136–46, at 140, supposes that Czarth was still in Dresden, citing a payment to him dated June 1734. But Marpurg, 'Lebensnachrichten von einigen Gliedern des königl. Preußischen Capelle ... [Georg Czarth]', *Historisch-kritische Beyträge*, I, 'Sechstes Stück' (1755), 547–8, at 548, confirms that Czarth's transfer from the Polish *Kapelle* to the Dresden *Hofkapelle* in 1733 lasted only one year, and that in 1734 he entered service in Ruppin. Nevertheless, the *Königl. Polnischer und Churfürstl. Sächsischer Hof- und Staats-Calender* continued to list him as a member of the Dresden *Hofkapelle* in 1735 and 1736.

[31] Hiller, 'Graun (Carl Heinrich)', *Lebensbeschreibungen*, 76–98, at 88. Graun did not receive the title *Kapellmeister* until 1740, when he became director of the *Hofoper*.

[32] Hiller, 'Benda', *Wöchentliche Nachrichten*, I, '25. Stück' (16 December 1766), 192.

[33] Concerning Blume's arrival, see Marpurg, 'Lebensnachrichten [Joseph Blume]', *Historisch-kritische Beyträge*, I, 'Sechstes Stück' (1755), 546–7, at 546.

[34] D-Bga, Brandenburg-Preußisches Hausarchiv, Rep. 47 No. 305, vol. II, fol. 174ʳ, Ruppin,

and Johann Caspar Grundke, who played violin in the *Hofkapelle* and, from 1740, oboe. Grundke is probably identical to the 'Johann Caspar Grund' listed as oboist in the Polish *Kapelle* in 1733.[35] The player 'good for the ripieno' may well be Christiani, who in 1740 was paid 300 *Thaler* like other second violinists (see Table 4.2, pp. 118–26 below). Replaced in September 1742 by the violinist Georg Benda, he is possibly the Georg Gustav Christiani who played violin in the *Hofkapelle* of the king's brother Prince Ferdinand by 1755. Ehmes was Friedrich's fourth violinist, as a letter of 1736 to Wilhelmine reveals:

> Selon Vos ordres je Vous envoye Ems qui est mon 4trieme Viollon et qui je crois reponcdra mieuxs à L'usaje du Ripino que Vous en Vouléz faire que Blum[.] il peut aussi jouér Sollo quoi que ce ne foit pas avec toute La finesse quil faut . . .

> Following your orders I send you Ems [*recte* Ehmes], who is my fourth violin and who, I believe, will serve better as a ripienist, which you want to make of him, than Blume. He can also play solo, although he doesn't do this with all the finesse that is necessary . . .[36]

Ehmes was one of two musicians obtained in 1734, just a few months after the dissolution of the *Hofkapelle* of Margrave Christian Ludwig of Brandenburg-Schwedt (see Table. 4.4). The second was Kottowsky, whose instrument has not been previously identified: Walther's *Musicalisches Lexicon* (1732) describes 'Kuddoffsky' as a 'berühmter Fagottist' (famous bassoonist) who served in Christian Ludwig's *Hofkapelle* in Berlin.[37]

The harpist Petrini must have joined the *Kapelle* no later than 1736, for in a letter to Wilhelmine dated 2 September Friedrich mentions 'le joueur D' Harppe' (the harp player) and the bassoonist Kottowsky.[38] The contrabassist Johann Gottlieb Janitsch entered the *Hofkapelle* in the same year. He founded a musical academy at Rheinsberg that met on Fridays, a venture he and other members of the *Kapelle* would continue in Berlin. 1737 marked the arrival of the theorbist Ernst Gottlieb Baron, who was immediately sent to Dresden to obtain an instrument and instruction from Weiss.[39] Between 1736 and the end of the Rheinsberg period, several other musicians joined the *Hofkapelle*. Their dates of entry are uncertain:

27 December 1734. Czarth, already in Ruppin and known to Wilhelmine, cannot have been among them.

[35] *Königl. Polnischer und Churfürstl. Sächsischer Hof- und Staats-Calender* (1733).

[36] D-Bga, Brandenburg-Preußisches Hausarchiv, Rep. 47 No. 305, vol. III, fol. 28ʳ, 'Remusberg' (Rheinsberg), 22 October 1736.

[37] Walther, *Musicalisches Lexicon*, 314. Richter, 'Ich bin Komponist', 42, confuses Kottowsky (first name is unknown) with the flautist Georg Wilhelm Kottowsky (Kodowsky) (b. 1735), who entered Prussian service in April 1750; see D-Bga, I. HA Rep. 36 No. 2447.

[38] D-Bga, Brandenburg-Preußisches Hausarchiv, Rep. 47 No. 305, vol. III, fol. 34ʳ.

[39] Marpurg, 'Lebensnachrichten [Gottlieb Baron]', *Historisch-kritische Beyträge*, I, 'Sechstes Stück' (1755), 545–6. Ledebur, *Tonkünstler-Lexicon Berlin's*, 32, gives the date as 1734.

the viola player Reich or Richter, the cellist Antonius Hock, and the horn players Johann Ignatius Horzitzky and Görbich.[40]

Friedrich received numerous guest virtuosos as crown prince. Previous literature about the *Hofkapelle* has overlooked much of this activity, which permitted a more varied repertoire than has been thought possible. One hitherto unnoticed visit, by Pisendel and a castrato from Dresden, was expected early in 1734. On 11 January, Friedrich wrote to his sister from Potsdam:

> le Chanteur Grauen est deveneux beaucoup meilleur quil n'etoit outre lui[.] j'ai engaje encore un Viollon qui est asséz bon, bishendel et un Chanteur de Dresden viendront ici, j'atens Vos ordres pour Vous envoyér Benda

> The singer Graun has become much better than he was; besides him I have engaged another violin who is very good. Pisendel and a singer from Dresden will come here; I await your orders to send Benda.[41]

The male singer is not identified. Later that year Friedrich received the Dresden virtuoso lutenist Sylvius Leopold Weiss while camped at Heidelberg. Weiss accompanied Friedrich on the flute, and Weiss's daughter also performed:

> Weis à joué hiér dens ma Tente, il joue tres bien et acompagne ferme, il à une petite fille qui est de 12 an et que joue deja tres jolliment[.] j'ai atendeur tout les Violons d'ici qui passent pour tout ceux de Majenu de Darmstat et de Manehim, mais il n'y en à pas un qui aproche de Benda . . .

> Weiss played here in my tent; he plays very well and accompanies strongly. He has a little twelve-year-old daughter who already plays very well. I have heard all the violinists who are passing from Mainz, Darmstadt, and Mannheim, but not one of them approaches Benda. . . .[42]

Carl Philipp Emanuel Bach was in Berlin during 1738, when he received an 'unexpected call' to the court in Ruppin. From this date he must have informally served Crown Prince Friedrich on a visiting basis, much as the Grauns and others had done before obtaining permanent appointments.[43] As Schaffrath had been engaged since 1734, it was not possible to offer Bach a permanent position. Friedrich's

---

[40]  See Carl Wilhelm Hennert, *Beschreibung des Lustschloßes und Gartens . . . zu Reinsberg* [*sic*] (Berlin, 1778), 21, and the Rheinsberg *Kapelle* members listed in D-Bga, I. HA Rep. 36 No. 372 (1740/41). Hennert mentions Reich as a player of 'Bratsche' (viola), but the *Hofstaat* of 1740 names only Richter, without instrument designation. See Table 4.2.

[41]  Letter to Wilhelmine, 11 January 1734, D-Bga, Brandenburg-Preußisches Hausarchiv, Rep. 47 No. 305, vol. 11, fol. 6ᵛ.

[42]  D-Bga, Brandenburg-Preußisches Hausarchiv, Rep. 47 No. 305, vol. 11, fol. 108ʳ, dated 22 August 1734, 'aux Campe de Heidelberg'. Gustav Berthold Volz, *Friedrich der Große und Wilhelmine von Baireuth: Briefe*, 1 (Leipzig: Koehler, 1924), 235, translates the passage incorrectly, stating that the daughter played the flute. In August 1739, Weiss was at the Bayreuth court; see Wilhelmine's letter in Rep. 47 W, vol. 1, 4, fol. 87ʳ (7 August 1739).

[43]  Mary Oleskiewicz, 'Like Father, Like Son? Emanuel Bach and the Writing of Biography', in *Music and Its Questions: Essays in Honor of Peter Williams*, ed. Thomas Donahue (Richmond, Va.: Organ Historical Society Press, 2007), 253–79.

correspondence with Wilhelmine in 1735 mentions, however, that 'un *fils de Back*' (a son of Bach) had already played for him at the 'Clavessin' (keyboard) in Berlin,[44] presumably in the *Stadtschloß* – where Sebastian Bach had performed before the Margrave Christian Ludwig of Brandenburg-Schwedt in 1719. Emanuel Bach's autobiography fails to mention an earlier call to court, and thus the possibility cannot be ruled out that the unnamed son of Bach was his elder brother Wilhelm Friedemann. In any case, the letter reveals Friedrich's awareness of the Leipzig *Kantor*, who would visit Potsdam in 1747.

A previously unknown letter of 1737 documents a visit to Rheinsberg by Pierre-Gabriel Buffardin, principal flautist in Dresden, who was expected to arrive in Rheinsberg in the company of C. H. Graun. On March 15, Friedrich writes to Wilhelmine:

> Nous gardons nostre petit coin ici comme si nous y etions enracinés tantôt nous avons bonne compagnie tantôt nous sommes fort solitaires; c'est le sort des compagniards, quoi que cette diversité ne laise pas aussi d'avoir ses agremens; j'atans tout les jours Grauen qui amenera Bufardein avec lui.

> We stay in our little place here as if we were rooted in it: sometimes we have good company, sometimes we are quite alone. It is the fate of country folk, although this variety does not have so much charm; every day I wait for Graun, who is bringing Buffardin with him.[45]

C. H. Graun had gone to Dresden for Carnival. Buffardin also had close connections to Friedrich's musicians through his Dresden colleague and former pupil Quantz. Reports of a visit in 1738 by another flautist, Michel Blavet, whom Quantz had befriended in Paris in 1726, cannot be confirmed.[46]

Correspondence between Friedrich and Wilhelmine during 1732–41 shows that Quantz's trips to Ruppin and Rheinsberg were usually followed by a stay in Bayreuth, where he performed chamber music and instructed the margrave in flute. The visits normally took place in summer or early autumn and again in winter. In July 1732 Quantz spent at least four weeks in Ruppin, followed by visits of similar length to Ruppin in November and Bayreuth in December. He returned to Prussia early in January 1733, staying possibly until mid-March or later and commuting between Rheinsberg and Berlin, where Wilhelmine was residing. In Berlin Quantz served her, the queen, and the crown prince in turn, according to the queen's orders. Wilhelmine's violinist Hoffmann and her lutenist, presumably Adam Falckenhagen, accompanied her to Berlin.[47]

Following the death of Quantz's employer August II, a serious dispute erupted

[44] D-Bga, Brandenburg-Preußisches Hausarchiv, Rep. 47 No. 305, vol. II, fol. 224ʳ, letter dated Berlin, 8 June 1735.

[45] Ibid., vol. III, fol. 161ʳ, 'Remusberg' (Rheinsberg), 15 March 1737.

[46] Louis Vaissier, 'Michael Blavet, 1700–68: Essai de biographie', *Recherches sur la musique française classique*, 22 (1984), 131–59, at 138.

[47] D-Bga, Brandenburg-Preußisches Hausarchiv, Rep. 46 W No. 17, vol. I, 1, fol. 38ᵛ, Bayreuth, 18 October 1732.

after Quantz rejected Friedrich's offer of a permanent engagement at Rheinsberg. Quantz ceased his visits to both Friedrich and Bayreuth for almost two years and when, during this period, he published six flute sonatas (Op. 1) in 1734, Wilhelmine's angry response foreshadowed Friedrich's policy as king to prohibit dissemination of compositions by his employees:

> Bendo fait merveille[.] je crois qu'il deviendera avec le tems plus fort que Graun et avec cella fort traitable ce qui est assez Rare ces habiles M[on]rs la etant dans cella a l'ordinaire capricieux come la mule du Pape[.] je suis fort en colere contre Quantz ayant fait imprimer 6 de ces Solos[.] je crains que les concerts suivront aussi[.]

> Benda is doing marvellously. I believe that, with time, he will be better than Graun and with that, very amenable — which is quite rare in these clever men, who, in this way, are ordinarily more capricious than the pope's mule. I am very angry at Quantz, who has published six of his solos. I fear that the concertos will also follow.[48]

Quantz resumed his visits to Rheinsberg at the end of November 1735, staying at least eight weeks and proceeding via Dresden to Bayreuth, where he arrived about 29 January 1736 and remained for more than four weeks. Further visits can be documented during 1738 to Rheinsberg (October/November) and Bayreuth (December/January), and in 1739 to Rheinsberg (September/October) and Bayreuth (January). Quantz also visited Bayreuth during May 1741, while Friedrich was fighting the First Silesian War.

## THE ROYAL *KAPELLE* OF FRIEDRICH II 'THE GREAT' BETWEEN 1740 AND THE 1760S

The best known musical activities of the Prussian court under King Friedrich are the royal opera and the private chamber concerts in which he himself participated. But there were also various concerts of other sorts and music for plays, ballets, and court balls. Also worthy of consideration here are a number of special musical visits to the court, as well as the teaching activities of several court musicians. The king continued his musical activity even when at war, and this too merits discussion. Given the immense scope of activity at this court, however, it will only be possible to treat a few aspects of the *Hofkapelle* in any detail.

Considerable mythology today envelops Friedrich and his musicians. As king, Friedrich took personal responsibility for running the court's business. He eliminated offices that interfered with his oversight of finance and state affairs and organized the court's accounts in such a way that he alone had a complete view of the state's resources, relying on a few trusted servants to carry out his orders. His intervention in court affairs was particularly unusual at the creative level: in

---

[48] Ibid., vol. 1, 2, fols. 29$^v$–30$^r$ (27 March 1734).

addition to sketching and overseeing the implementation of architectural designs and decoration for his palaces, gardens, and the like, he hired, and fired musicians and theatre personnel, negotiated salaries, attended rehearsals, and coached singers. He also chose and even drafted librettos for the opera, composing arias as well as ornamentation and cadenzas for singers. Although he participated in court ritual, he preferred a solitary existence, maintaining a small chamber ensemble for private concerts in which he participated as flautist and composer.

The secondary literature about the king's musical taste, his relationships with his musicians, and their duties and pay has relied heavily on anecdotal literature and nineteenth-century accounts, overlooking archival evidence. The writings of Charles Burney in particular, which do not reflect the period before the Seven Years' War, have been granted excessive authority. Despite heavy archival losses during World War II, a wealth of primary information survives that permits a more accurate evaluation of the court's music for the period from 1741.

Although Friedrich hired exclusively Italian opera singers up to 1760, his instrumentalists were, with few exceptions, of German and Bohemian origin. In 1739 he and his sister Wilhelmine exchanged views on the merits of Italian and German musicians, initiated by a letter from Wilhelmine:

> quand on a une fois entendu une bonne voix Italliene[,] les Allemandes ne plaisent plus tant[.] cette Nation a quelque chose dans le Gozier qui leur est Unique et qu'il est difficile d'imiter quand on n'a pas été des sa tendre jeunesse ellevé en Italie[.] A dailleurs La Force de L'expretion qui fait une des plus Belle partie de La voix n'est pas donnée aux Allemands[.] en revange[,] je ne chercherai j'amais les Instruments en Itallie et malgré tout le cas qu'ils font de Leur Dardini[.] je suis persuadée que Graun et Bendo les surpasse de Beaucoup pour l'agrement[.]

> Once one has heard a good Italian voice, the German ones don't please so much; there is something in the throat that is unique to them and that takes too long to learn if one has not been raised in Italy from one's earliest youth. Moreover, the power of expression that constitutes one of the most beautiful parts of the voice is not possessed by the Germans. On the other hand, I would never seek instrument[alist]s in Italy despite all the fuss they make about their Tartini. I am convinced that Graun and Benda much surpass them in appeal.[49]

Wilhelmine had accompanied Locatelli in Berlin in 1728; whether she ever heard Tartini is uncertain. Friedrich responded: 'Certainly the Italians have much purer tone and better diction than the Germans, which is called "Granito" in Italian. Moreover, our musicians are more learned and much better versed in music theory than the people on the other side of the Alps. Every nation has its strengths, but none of them are perfect.'[50] In 1749 Friedrich declined an opportunity to hire

---

49 Ibid., vol. 1, 4, fol. 108ᵛ (29 November 1739).
50 See Volz, *Friedrich der Große und Wilhelmine von Baireuth: Briefe*, 1: 430, dated Berlin,

one of Tartini's best students, Pasquale Bini, although the latter was strongly recommended by Friedrich's friend and adviser Francesco Algarotti.[51]

Upon his accession in May 1740, Friedrich began to reorganize his *Hofkapelle*
in order to establish a *Hofoper*. He immediately gave orders to erect an opera house
and had new contracts drawn up with his musicians. Their payments are recorded
in annual accounts called 'Capelletats', each of which lists disbursements for a fiscal
year beginning on 1 June and divided into four quarters (some payments for less
than a quarter are listed on a monthly basis). During the first years of his reign,
the 'Capelletats' designate those musicians retained from Rheinsberg as the 'erste
Capelle' (first *Kapelle*).[52] Friedrich expanded the *Hofkapelle* by issuing contracts
to a second group, including those who had been providing services on a visiting
basis, such as Emanuel Bach, as well as new players. This second group appears in
the 'Capelletats' as 'die *Capell* so anno 1741 dazugekommen' ([members of] the
*Kapelle* who arrived in 1741). Some came directly from other local *Hofkapellen*,
such as the violinist Johann Gabriel Seyffarth, from the *Hofkapelle* of the Margrave
Friedrich Heinrich of Brandenburg-Schwedt, and the cellist Christian Friedrich
Schale, who had served Margrave Karl since 1735.[53] Others in this group included
the viola players Johann Samuel Encke, Georg Heinrich Gebhardt, and Christian
Carl Rolle, the gambist Christian Ludwig Hesse, the oboists Schück and Michae-
lis, the 'Contra Violon' player Johann Christoph Richter, Kindt (whose instru-
ment is not designated), and the Russian violinist Ivan (Iwan) Böhme (a pupil of
J. G. Graun). Among the vocalists in this group were those hired in Italy by C. H.
Graun: Giovanna Gasparini, Maria Camal ('Farinella'), Anna Loria Campolongo,
the castratos Giovanni Triulzi and Ferdinando Mazzanti, and the bass Gaetano
Pinetti.[54]

A third group is designated under the rubric 'An die letzten *Capell Bediente* so
anno 1742 dazugekommen' (Members of the *Kapelle* who arrived in 1742). Among
them are the flautists Quantz and his pupil Johann Joseph Lindner, both from
Dresden, as well as the flautist Friedrich Wilhelm Riedt, the cellist Ignaz Mara,
the oboist Joachim Wilhelm Döbbert, the scenery painter Fabri, two *souffleurs*
(prompters), two copyists, and a keyboard tuner. Singers who arrived in 1742
included the soprano Benedetta Molteni, a pupil of Hasse, and the castratos 'Porporino' (Anton Hubert), 'Paulino' (Paulo Bedeschi), and 'Stefanino' (Stefano Leonardi). Quantz had resisted joining Friedrich's *Hofkapelle* but accepted upon being
offered extraordinary privileges, including an annual salary of 2,000 *Thaler*, ex-

14 December 1739. Friedrich wrote to his sister exclusively in French. This letter, and several
others that are lost, are translated from Volz's German renditions.

[51] Johann David Erdmann Preuss, *Œuvres de Frédéric le Grand* (Berlin, 1846–56), 1: 67,
letter from Algarotti dated 15 September 1749. Bini became concertmaster at the court of
Württemberg-Stuttgart; see Marpurg, *Historisch-kritische Beyträge*, III, 'Erstes Stück' (1757), 65.

[52] D-Bga, I. HA Rep. 36 No. 2435 (1742/3), p. 19: 'An die ersten *Capell* bediente'. See Oleskiewicz, 'Like Father, Like Son', 260–61.

[53] 'Schale (Christian Friedr.)', in Ledebur, *Tonkünstler-Lexicon Berlin's*, 498–9; 'Seyffarth
(Joh. Gabriel)', ibid., 546.

[54] Ledebur, *Tonkünstler-Lexicon Berlin's*, 84, gives Farinella's name as Maria Camal or
Comati. After performing Graun's *Rodelinda*, she left Berlin, along with Mazzanti and Triulzi.

emption from performing at the opera, extra payments for providing compositions and flutes, and freedom from taking orders from anyone but the king. Since the Ruppin years, Quantz had exercised considerable influence in the court's musical matters and the choice of personnel. At Berlin he would earn more than any other musician at court, apart from the highest-paid opera singers.

Information in the 'Capelletats' about personnel and payments must be considered alongside the accounts of the king's *Schatoulle* (privy purse), from which many musicians received salaries or supplements.[55] Failure to consult the *Schatoulle* records and misunderstandings about Friedrich's personnel practices have led to the conclusion, for example, that Emanuel Bach was underpaid and unappreciated. The status and pay of musicians were based on seniority and assignment. It is true that in 1741 Schaffrath, receiving 400 *Thaler* annually, outranked Bach, who received 300 *Thaler* according to the 'Capelletats'. But, contrary to most accounts, Bach was not hired as 'first' harpsichordist, and no such title ever existed. Members of the *Hofkapelle* could advance to a higher salary or position when a death or departure created a vacancy or, more rarely, by negotiating a supplement. Christoph Nichelmann, hired in 1745 to compose vocal music as well as to play keyboard, received 500 *Thaler*. Upon Nichelmann's departure, Bach requested, and received, a supplement of 25 *Thaler* per month from the *Schatoulle* and 200 *Thaler* per year for teaching. This brought his annual income to 800 *Thaler*, one of the highest in the *Hofkapelle*, similar to that of Franz Benda. Only Quantz and both Grauns received more.[56]

The proportions of the royal *Hofkapelle* in 1745 closely reflect those recommended by Quantz in 1752. In addition to a keyboard, which is understood, he suggests the following:

> Zu zwölf Violinen geselle man: drey Bratschen, vier Violoncelle, zweene Contraviolone, drey Bassons, vier Hoboen, vier Flöten; und wenn es in einem Orchester ist, noch einen Flügel mehr, und eine Theorbe. Die Waldhörner sind, nach Beschaffenheit der Stücke, und Gutbefinden des Componisten, so wohl zu einer kleinen als großen Musik nötig.

> With twelve violins one takes three violas, four violoncellos, two 'Contraviolone' (contrabasses), three bassoons, four oboes, and four flutes, and when it is in an orchestra [that is, a theatre], one more keyboard and a theorbo. Horns are necessary in both small and large ensembles according to the nature of the composition and the views of the composer.[57]

[55] There is no complete study of the 'Schatoull-Rechnung', D-Bga, Rep. 47 Nos. 893–943 [1742–86]. In 1994, Herbert Heyde published an impressive study of its records on music and instruments in *Musikinstrumentenbau in Preußen*; other studies have followed. A list of payment records published in Christoph Henzel, 'Die Schatulle Friedrichs II. von Preußen und die Hofmusik', *Jahrbuch des Staatlichen Instituts für Musikforschung, Preußischer Kulturbesitz* (1999), 38–66, (2000), 175–209, is not complete and overlooks this previous literature.

[56] Oleskiewicz, 'Like Father, Like Son', 260–64.

[57] Johann Joachim Quantz, *Versuch einer Anweisung, die Flöte zu spielen* (Berlin, 1752), 'Hauptstück XVII', 'Abschnitt I', §16.

The royal *Hofkapelle* as constituted in 1745 (see Table 4.2) comprised eleven or twelve violinists; four viola players; four to five cellists (one gambist); two contrabassists; two keyboardists; one theorbist; one harpist; two flautists (not counting Quantz); four oboists; three bassoonists; and two horn players. The vocalists included four female singers, four castratos, and one tenor. With the expansion to four flautists in 1756, Quantz's ideal proportions for the theatre were fulfilled.

The expenditures for Friedrich's Rheinsberg *Kapelle* can be deduced from the *Hofstaatskasse* for 1740/41, which records the salaries of the members of the 'first' or Rheinsberg *Kapelle* (shown in Table 4.2, under 1740). These salaries total about 7,000 *Thaler*. Between 1741 and 1742 raises were given to the Grauns and to Franz Benda for their new roles as *Kapellmeister*, concertmaster, and 'Premier' violinist of the chamber ensemble. In 1744/5, the total expenditure recorded in the 'Capelletats' was just over 47,000 *Thaler*. The instrumentalists' salaries as a whole had more than doubled to 15,587 *Thaler*. Salaries for the *Hofoper* this year, including singers, dancers, court poet, copyists, and ancillary theatre personnel totalled nearly 32,000 *Thaler*.[58] Amounts spent on musicians and dancers in the 'Capelletats' would remain relatively stable, apart from the Seven Years' War, when many positions remained vacant. By 1751/2 the total expenditure had stabilized to about 56,605 *Thaler*, but this amount now included about 6,800 *Thaler* for actors of the French *Comédie*.

The *Hofkapelle*'s primary duties included performing for opera, ballet, and grand court concerts. Select musicians performed in the chamber and for intermezzos. As there was no *Hofkirche* (court church), sacred music was relegated to occasional special performances or commemorations.

## *The Hofoper, 1741–56*

In 1741 C. H. Graun's *Rodelinda* was performed in the theatre of the Berlin *Stadtschloß*. From 1742 the Italian *Hofoper* performed in a prestigious new opera house on the site of the present Berlin Staatsoper. The main opera season was Carnival, from December until February, which featured two opera productions, with two performances per week. Performances by the French *Comédie* and the Italian *Intermezzo* alternated with court masked balls (*Redouten*). Carnival typically saw an opera premiere by *Kapellmeister* Graun, whose works dominated the programme, but operas by the Dresden *Kapellmeister* Hasse were also staged, including *La clemenza di Tito* (1743), *Arminio* (1746/7), and *Didone abbandonata* (1752/3). Special occasions, including the birthday of the queen mother, weddings, and important court visits called for operas, intermezzos, serenatas, and pastorales (*Schäferspiele*). Some of these were composed by Christoph Nichelmann and Johann Friedrich Agricola; others were collaborations. The serenata *Il re pastore*, jointly composed by Quantz, Nichelmann, C. H. Graun, and Friedrich himself, introduced the singer Giovanna Astrua, the court's most highly paid *prima diva*.

---

[58] These figures contain neither the fluctuating salaries for the *Intermezzo*, nor the sometimes considerable 'Zulagen' (salary supplements) paid from the king's 'Schatoull-Rechnung'.

The performances, during August 1747, took place in Charlottenburg in honour of the queen mother and were repeated for Wilhelmine's visit from Bayreuth.[59]

Graun's *Merope*, staged for the queen's birthday in March 1756, was the final opera performed before the *Hofoper* closed for the war. The king's French draft preceded the libretto by Giampietro Tagliazucchi, to judge from Friedrich's letter of 18 December 1755: 'j'ai gâté la tragédie de Mérope en en faisant un opéra' (I have spoilt the tragedy of *Mérope* [by Voltaire] by making an opera out of it).[60] The king is also known to have drafted librettos for Graun's *Ifigenia in Aulide*, *Angelica e Medoro*, *Coriolano*, *Il giudizio di Paride*, *Semiramide*, *Montezuma*, and *I fratelli nemici*.[61]

The opera singers, selected and in some cases trained by Friedrich himself, were divided into primary and secondary roles. From 1741 the *prima donna* was Giovanna Gasparini (who remained active in the *Hofkapelle* until 1776). She was superseded in 1747 by Astrua, who remained until 1756. The leading castratos were Giuseppe Santarelli (1741–2), Stefano Leonardi ('Stefanino', 1742–3), Felice Salimbeni (1743–50), Giovanni Carestini (1750–54), Giovanni Amadori (1754–5), Domenico Luini (1755–7), and Giovanni Conciolini (1765–86). In April 1751, Astrua's pay was raised to 4,725 *Thaler* per year, in striking contrast to Gasparini, who never received more than 1,800 *Thaler*.[62] Of the lead castratos, Carestini — recruited from Dresden to replace Salimbeni — was the most highly paid, with an annual salary equal to Astrua's and exceeding that of his successor, who received at most only 4,440 *Thaler*.[63]

The Italian librettist Angelo Cori, who had revised librettos for the Opera of the Nobility and probably also for Handel, was engaged in London in May 1743, after the First Silesian War, in which England had sided against Friedrich.[64] As the king's cabinet minutes make clear, Cori was hired as a diplomatic favour to John, Baron

---

[59] Louis Schneider, *Geschichte der Oper und des Königlichen Opernhauses in Berlin* (Berlin, 1852), 119.

[60] See Preuss, *Œuvres de Frédéric le Grand*, XXVII: 284. Marpurg, 'Zweyte Fortsetzung der Nachricht von den Opern in Berlin', *Historisch-kritische Beyträge* (1758–9), IV, 'Fünftes Stück' (1759), 426, attributes *Merope*'s libretto to Graun's 'eigne[r] Feder' (own pen).

[61] Steffen Voss demonstrated in an unpublished paper, 'Voltaire — Wilhelmine — Villati: Zur Genese des Librettos zu Grauns drama per musica *Semiramide* (Berlin, 1754)', presented at *Opernkonzeptionen zwischen Berlin und Bayreuth: Das musikalische Theater der Markgräfin Wilhelmine*, musicological symposium hosted by the Universität Bayreuth (October 2009), that Friedrich's sister Wilhelmine drafted the text upon which Graun's *Semiramide* was based; this is contrary to Christoph Henzel, *Graun-Werkverzeichnis*, 2 vols. (Beeskow: Ortus, 2006), I: 395, who attributes the poetry to Tagliazucchi after Voltaire. Voss's finding is supported by a letter of March 1754, in which Friedrich credits his sister with the ideas for the opera (see Volz, *Friedrich der Große und Wilhelmine von Baireuth: Briefe*, II: 266).

[62] On Astrua's salary, see D-Bga, Brandenburg-Preußisches Hausarchiv, I. HA. Rep. 36 Nos. 2451–8.

[63] Salimbeni was paid for Prussian service through August 1750; see D-Bga, I. HA Rep. 36 No. 2449. Neither he nor Carestini appears in the *Königl. Polnischer und Churfürstl. Sächsischer Hof- und Staats-Calender*, but their contracts are documented in D-Dla, Loc. 907/5, 'Die italienischen Sänger und Sängerinnen . . .', vol. III, fols. 188ᵛ (1750), 150ʳ (1748) respectively.

[64] Lowell Lindgren's entry on Cori in *Grove Music Online*, <www.oxfordmusic.com> (accessed June 2009) documents his activity only up to 1741.

Carteret, later Earl Granville (1690–1763), a friend of George II and from 1742 to 1744 British secretary of state. Friedrich wrote: 'Ce n'est pas que je cherche d'avoir cet homme pour son savoir faire dans l'Opera, mais uniquement pour faire plaisir a Mylord Carteret ... et a quelques autres gens de distinction' (It's not that I seek to have this man because of his competence in opera, but solely to please Lord Carteret ... and some other people of distinction).[65] Cori, who served in a partly administrative capacity, remained a member of the *Hofkapelle* until his death in November 1775.[66]

The *Hofoper* employed only Italian singers. Most of those recruited in Italy by C. H. Graun in 1740 proved unacceptable and were released after the Carnival season. New singers were sought through agents in Italy, mature singers being lured to the Prussian capital through lucrative salaries. However, a few very young castratos were 'verkauft' (sold) by their families or teachers and brought to Berlin to be groomed to Friedrich's taste. An example will demonstrate how this young talent was sought and acquired.

Salimbeni's departure to Dresden in 1750 was a devastating blow, and the search for a replacement proved difficult. His successor, Giovanni Carestini, soon left for Russia. In 1754 Friedrich engaged Amadori as *primo uomo*. Friedrich's search for a young, malleable singer ended in May, a month before Amadori arrived in Berlin.[67] Wilhelmine informed Friedrich about a young castrato that the singer Stefanino had found:

> Stephanino m'a parlé d'un jeune home qui n'a que 15 ans qui a dit il la plus Belle voix quil ait entendu de sa vie. Ce n'est qu'un Ecollier. Il est a Folgno dans l'etat du Pape et apartient au Maitre de Chapell de cett endroit. J'ai crû peut etre il seroit propre pour recruter avec le tems votre Opera. La voix doit etre Infiniment plus Belle que celle de notre nouveau chanteur. Mais il lui faut encore 2 ou 3 ans pour le former[.]

> Stephanino spoke to me about a young man who is only fifteen years old, who has the most beautiful voice that he has ever heard. He's only a schoolboy. He's at Foligno in the Papal States and belongs to the *maestro di cappella* of that place. I thought that perhaps it would be proper in time to recruit [him] [for] your opera. His voice should be infinitely more beautiful than that of our new singer. But it will take two or three more years to train him[.][68]

Stefanino, a contralto, had served in Friedrich's *Hofoper* from November 1742 to 1 December 1743 before entering the Bayreuth *Kapelle* in 1744.[69] From 18 to 20

---

[65] D-Bga, Rep. 96 B No. 26 (1 January 1743), fol. 3ᵛ, No. 10.

[66] D-Bga, I. HA Rep. 36 No. 2480 (1775/6), where he is listed as having been paid in full for the first two quarters; but the entry for the next quarter reads 'Cessat, ist gestorben' (To cease: has died).

[67] D-Bga, I. HA Rep. 36 No. 2455 (1754/5). Amadori's salary (4,000 *Thaler*) commenced in June 1754, but he remained for only ten months, debuting in the title role of *Montezuma*.

[68] D-Bga, Brandenburg-Preußisches Hausarchiv, Rep. 46 W No. 17, vol. III, 5, fol. 13ʳ⁻ᵛ ([Bayreuth], 6 May 1754).

[69] Stefanino is listed as a member of the *Kapelle* in Bayreuth for the years 1744–60. See

June, Friedrich visited Bayreuth, where he saw *L'uomo*, with arias and libretto by Wilhelmine, and finalized the matter of the young castrato with Stefanino. Upon his return to Berlin, Friedrich wrote the following to his *Cammerdiener* Fredersdorf, who helped manage artistic personnel and other important affairs:

> ich habe in bareit Mit Steffanino abgeredet, er Sol mihr einen Jungen buben Kaufen in Rohm, der eine Schöne Stime hat. mache ihm dorten doch Credit und Schreib ihm darum. dann So ist ein Sänker in Neapoli, der heißet Menzoni; den Mus Man Skreibe, ob er sich Wil angagir vohr Künftig jar, denn der Monsieur Amador mihr nit gefal; und der andere Sol Sink, wie ein enkel. . . .

> I have arranged in Bayreuth with Stefanino to purchase for me in Rome a boy who has a beautiful voice; provide him with a loan and write to him about it. There is also a singer in Naples named Menzoni whom one must ask whether he wishes to be engaged for the coming year, as Mr Amadori doesn't please me and the other one is supposed to sing like an angel. . . .[70]

Menzoni declined the engagement, and Friedrich arranged for Stefanino to come from Bayreuth in the following season to substitute. However, the fifteen-year-old soprano from Rome – Giuseppe Tossoni – was hired and paid from 17 February 1755 with funds from the position vacated the previous January by the singer Anna Loria Campolongo. Tossoni's salary was set at 650 *Thaler*, of which 228 *Thaler* were set aside annually to compensate his former teacher Nicolini in Italy. Agricola, his instructor at Berlin, also received a share. Tossoni's training ended in 1760; from 1761 he earned 1,500 *Thaler* per year.[71]

### *Chamber music: The Potsdam Musici (1740–60)*

A small, select group of virtuosos performed in the king's evening concerts, which took place in his private apartments from the beginning of his reign. Friedrich played three to six flute concertos each evening, and two vocalists sang arias with string and keyboard accompaniment. Quantz oversaw the concerts, composing hundreds of sonatas and concertos for the king's private use, and occasionally performed himself. Franz Benda led the ensemble as 'Premier' violin, joined at least part of the time by Joseph Benda or Joseph Blume as second violin and, from 1744, Franz Caspari Benda on viola. Johann Georg Speer and Christian Ludwig Hesse alternated on *basso*. The keyboard players were Schaffrath (until 1745), Emanuel Bach (1741–67), Nichelmann (1745–55), and Carl Friedrich Fasch (1756–86). The singers Porporino, Paulino, and from 1757, Tossoni, were regularly called upon to perform before the king. Gottfried Silbermann's fortepianos replaced harpsichords

*Hochfürstlich-Brandenburg-Culmbachischer Address- und Schreib-Calender* (Bayreuth, 1738–68), 'Hofkapell- und Kammermusik'.

[70] D-Bga, Brandenburg-Preußisches Hausarchiv, Rep. 47 No. 225, letter to Fredersdorf (end of June 1754), reproduced in Johannes Richter, *Die Briefe Friedrichs des Grossen an seinen vormaligen Kammerdiener Fredersdorf* (Berlin-Grunewald: Klemm, 1926), 297.

[71] D-Bga, Brandenburg-Preußisches Hausarchiv, Rep. 36 No. 2467.

in these performances from 1746 in the Potsdam *Stadtschloß* and from 1747 in Schloß Sanssouci. In the 1750s the harpist Franz Brennessell attended, as did the bassoonist Marks, who played new parts added to some of Quantz's flute concertos.[72] Per diem payments and receipts recorded in the *Schatoulle* indicate that players attended on a rotating basis for roughly two to four weeks at a time, and that concertos were performed with one player to a part. Surviving sets of manuscript parts for flute concertos, copied for each of the palaces, likewise point to one player per part. Attendance at these concerts was rare and by invitation only, even for the court *Kapellmeister*. Foreign visitors, such as Charles Burney in 1772, were at most permitted to listen from an adjoining room.[73]

## Grand Court Concerts

The *Hofkapelle* performed not only at the opera but in frequent court concerts hosted by the king or the queen (at the Berlin *Stadtschloß* or Schloß Schönhausen), the queen mother (at Monbijou), and Princess Amalie. Members of the royal family and high nobility attended and sometimes performed with virtuosos of the *Hofkapelle*, and the public was also permitted to attend:

> Wenn bey der Königin und der verwittweten Prinzessin von Preußen große Concerte gegeben werden, welches öfters geschiehet, so ist es jedermann erlaubt, zuzuhören. Ein Fremder wird die gute Gelegenheit, die Königl. Sänger und Sängerinnen, und die vornehmsten Virtuosen der Königl. Kammer musik zu hören, nicht vorbeylassen.

> When the queen and the widowed princess of Prussia hold grand concerts, which happens often, everyone is permitted to attend. A visitor will not wish to forego the opportunity to hear the royal singers and the best virtuosos of the royal chamber music.[74]

Newspapers gave cursory reports of some of these concerts, but many private court concerts were not announced. The grand concerts normally began with a sinfonia and continued with instrumental works, cantatas, or arias. A court inventory of sinfonias lists works by members of the *Hofkapelle*, including Emanuel Bach and J. G. Graun, which were probably performed at these concerts.[75] Local music academies — some of which were hosted by members of the *Hofkapelle*, including Agricola, Riedt, and Janitsch — offered concerts in imitation of the court; here, too, amateurs and virtuosos performed together.[76]

[72] Most of Quantz's flute concertos are preserved today in D-B; see *QV*.
[73] Burney, *The Present State of Music*, II: 151–2. Burney's account avoids directly disclosing this fact, but contemporary reports confirm it; see Mary Oleskiewicz, 'Like Father, Like Son', 255, 271 n. 9.
[74] Friedrich Nicolai, *Beschreibung der königlichen Residenzstädte Berlin und Potsdam* (Berlin, 1786), 718. The princess was Luise Amalie, the widow of Prince August Wilhelm.
[75] D-B, Mus. ms. theor. Kat. 584.
[76] See Mary Oleskiewicz, 'Chamber Music and Piano Music / Kammermusik und Klaviermusik', in *The Archive of the Sing-Akademie zu Berlin: Catalogue / Das Archiv der Sing-Akademie*

## Music for the Intermezzo

In 1745, Friedrich had Knobelsdorff build a small theatre for the performance of comic intermezzos as part of the renovations of the Potsdam *Stadtschloß*; its decoration was completed by the court *Dekorateur* Bellavita in 1748.[77] The *Intermezzo* troupe, which Friedrich engaged in 1747, resided in Potsdam and at first comprised only two singers: buffo-bass and director Domenico Cricchi, and soprano Maria (Rosa) Ruvinetti Bon, wife of the theatre architect Girolamo Bon (see Table 4.3, pp. 127–8 below). The little troupe made its Potsdam debut on 15 March 1748 with Pergolesi's *La serva padrona*.[78] Two years later they sang to great acclaim in Agricola's comic intermezzo *Il filosofo convinto in amore*, which led to Agricola's appointment as court composer in May 1751.[79] Potsdam also saw performances of intermezzos by Hasse, including *Carlotta e Pantaleone* (1749) and *Don Tabarano* (1750). Each Carnival season the troupe was also ordered to Berlin to perform in the *Komödiensaal* of the *Stadtschloß*.[80]

Ballets embellished the intermezzos, with appearances by the famous solo dancer Barbarina Campanini before her dismissal in May 1748.[81] Music was supplied by select members of the *Hofkapelle*; like the dancers and other performers needed on these occasions, they received a per diem for their expenses from the king's *Schatoulle*.

In 1753, Friedrich engaged more singers for the intermezzos, which had up to now been executed with just two singers.[82] *Schatoulle* payments indicate that Carlo and Angelo Paganini and the buffo-bass Filippo Sidotti arrived in October 1753, followed by a 'Signor Croce' in January 1754. All three left Prussian service in April 1756, after which Friedrich hired eight new performers (Table 4.3); all were dismissed in 1757.

*zu Berlin: Katalog*, ed. Axel Fischer and Matthias Kornemann (Berlin: Walter de Gruyter, 2009), 108–10, 204–7.

[77] On the *Stadtschloß* theatre, see Herbert Frenzel, *Brandenburg-Preußische Schloßtheater* (Berlin: Gesellschaft für Theatergeschichte, 1959), 52–8.

[78] Ibid., 80.

[79] Marpurg, 'Lebensläuffe, Joh. Friedr. Agricola', *Historisch-kritische Beyträge*, I, 'Zweytes Stück' (1754), 148–52, at 151.

[80] Since the king financed the *Intermezzi* from his *Schatoulle*, these singers are not listed in the 'Capelletats'. The first payment to the Bons is recorded in D-Bga, Brandenburg-Preußisches Hausarchiv, Rep. 47 No. 901 (1748), fol. 6r. See Frenzel, *Brandenburg-Preußische Schloßtheater*, 76, for an overview of the *Intermezzo*.

[81] In performances on 19 and 25 April 1748. See Hans Droysen, 'Tageskalender Friedrichs des Großen vom 1. Juni 1740 bis 31. März 1763', *Forschungen zur brandenburgischen und preußischen Geschichte*, 29 (Munich: Duncker & Humblot, 1916), 95–157, at 118.

[82] As reported in the *Berlinische Nachrichten von Staats- und gelehrten Sachen* (2 April 1754).

## The Royal Ballet

The royal ballet performed for opera, Italian intermezzos, and French comedies.[83] Rehearsals were accompanied by a violinist from the *Hofkapelle*. During the Carnival season of 1744/5, Johann Gottlieb Freudenberg earned six ducats for rehearsals of *Alessandro e Poro*, half of which was paid for four weeks of rehearsals with the solo dancers Barbarina and Barthélemy Lani. Johann Gabriel Seyffarth composed and copied the court's ballet music. For Carnival performances in 1744/5 he received 25 and 30 *Thaler*, respectively, for copying eighteen part-books each for the ballets in C. H. Graun's operas *Alessandro e Poro* and *Lucio Papirio*.[84]

## Redouten: Janitsch and the Hautboisten

Janitsch, Friedrich's contrabassist since 1736, composed and oversaw music for the *Redouten* (masked balls) during Carnival as well as other court festivities in Berlin.[85] Twenty *Thaler* were paid out to *Hautboisten* for each ball; the twenty-four musicians who performed on these occasions comprised four regimental bands of six musicians each, each band receiving 5 *Thaler*. Five *Redouten* during January 1745 are documented by receipts signed alternately by two of the musicians, Rohde and Mulley, and in July of that year the 'Hautboisten vom 2ten Bataillon Guarde' (*Hautboisten* of the Second Bataillon Guarde), members of the king's *Leibgarde*, received 5 *Thaler*, 12 *Groschen* for an unspecified event.[86]

## Special Visits

During the 1740s and 1750s, the exchange of musicians between the courts of Berlin, Bayreuth, and Dresden continued as before. Such visits facilitated a lively cultural cross-fertilization through the exchange of musical manuscripts. Works by Quantz and the Grauns were especially favoured in Dresden, as evidenced today by copies of their music from the collection of the Dresden court. Several visitors stand out among the numerous guests received before the war; Hiller mentions one:

> Um seine alten Freunde zu besuchen, und zugleich die, bey Gelegenheit des Beylagers der vorigen Königen von Schweden, zu Berlin aufgeführten vier Opern zu hören, kam Pisendel im Jahre 1744 noch einmal nach Berlin. Da

---

[83] D-Bga, I. HA, Rep. 36 No. 2634.

[84] D-Bga, I. HA, Rep. 36 No. 2368, two signed receipts, dated 11 January 1745, not paginated.

[85] Marpurg, 'Lebensläuffe, Johann Gottlieb Janitsch', *Historisch-kritische Beyträge*, I, 'Zweytes Stück' (1754), 152–6, at 156.

[86] D-Bga, Brandenburg-Preußisches Hausarchiv, Rep. 36 No. 2638, fols. 19ʳ–22ʳ, four signed receipts dated 13, 18 (two), and 20 January 1745, not paginated. In 1743 the *Hautboisten* Rühle, Buch, and Krumel received payments for three *Redouten*; see Rep. 47 No. 896, No. 31 (January 1743). For the July payment, see D-Bga, Brandenburg-Preußisches Hausarchiv, Rep. 47 No. 898, No. 5.

der König von Preussen es erfuhr, ließ er ihn immer zu seiner Kammermusik einladen, unterheilt sich oft mit ihm überhaupt mit solcher Gnade, als die Verdienste dieses braven Tonkünstlers würdig waren.

In 1744, [the Dresden concertmaster] Pisendel made one more trip to Berlin [his last] in order to visit his old friends and to hear four operas being performed in Berlin on the occasion of the marriage of the king of Sweden. Upon learning of this, the king of Prussia continually had him invited to his chamber music and conversed often with him with as much grace as the worthy musician deserved.[87]

The most famous musical visit to Friedrich's court was that of Johann Sebastian Bach and his son Wilhelm Friedemann in May 1747, during which Bach improvised on a theme provided by the king. The visit led to the *Musikalisches Opfer* (Musical Offering), published by Bach with a dedication to the king; it comprises canons, two ricercars, and a trio sonata for flute and violin, all based on the royal theme. The work contains musical references to the king's repertoire, his Silbermann pianos, and his extraordinary two-keyed flutes built by Quantz. Its existence also underscores the respect for the erudition of German instrumentalists that Friedrich had expressed in his youthful correspondence.[88]

Hasse and the Dresden singer Angelo Maria Monticelli were Friedrich's guests in March 1753 as a result of successful performances of Hasse's *Didone abbandonata* at the Berlin *Hofoper*. Both men were called upon to sing privately before the king, who found that 'Hasse a chanté ... divinement' (Hasse sang divinely), by contrast to Monticelli, whom he judged to be a 'mauvais chanteur' (bad singer). The *Berlinische Nachrichten von Staats- und gelehrten Sachen* (7 April 1753) reported that the king presented Hasse with a superb diamond ring and Monticelli with a precious gold tabatière (snuffbox).[89]

The year 1750 marked an important visit by Friedrich's sister Wilhelmine from Bayreuth. Famously represented in Menzel's painting *Das Flötenkonzert* (1852), her stay occasioned numerous performances, including a private concert led by the king in his Potsdam palace *Sanssouci* in her presence. Wilhelmine was accompanied by her *Kapellmeister* Johann Pfeiffer and another chamber musician.[90]

---

[87] Hiller, 'Pisendel (Johann Georg)', *Lebensbeschreibungen*, 182–99, at 198. Hiller names the operas here as Graun's *Rodelinda*, *Artaserse*, and *Cato in Utica*, and Hasse's *La clemenza di Tito*.

[88] Regarding Quantz's flutes and Silbermann's pianos, see Mary Oleskiewicz, 'The Trio in Bach's *Musical Offering*: A Salute to Frederick's Tastes and Quantz's Flutes?', in *Bach Perspectives*, IV: *The Music of J. S. Bach: Analysis and Interpretation*, ed. David Schulenberg (Lincoln: University of Nebraska Press, 1999), 79–110.

[89] Letter to Wilhelmine dated 29 March 1753, in Preuss, *Œuvres de Frédéric le Grand*, XXVII: 225–6 and note b.

[90] D-Bga, Brandenburg-Preußisches Hausarchiv, Rep. 36, No. 828: '4. Zu des Quartier bey Ms. Buzano an Hofrath Ebauer ist ausgezahlet, kommt 1 Capellmeister und 1 Cammer Musicus vom Marggrafen zu logieren welche mit der Suite sind aufgekommen und hier aufm [sic] Schloße speisen und auch ihro Quartier haben' (4. Paid to *Hofrat* Ebauer for lodging at Buzano's, for 1 *Kapellmeister* and 1 *Cammermusicus* belonging to the retinue of the margrave, who will eat and lodge here in the palace).

## Teaching within the Kapelle

It is extraordinary that the king himself instructed the court's singers, particularly in ornamentation. A manuscript copy of the aria 'Digli ch'io son fedele' from Hasse's *Cleofide* containing Friedrich's autograph embellishments and cadenzas was prepared for the castrato Anton Hubert, known as 'Porporino' for his studies with Porpora. Porporino entered Prussian service in 1742 as a mezzo-soprano, but the aria reaches the note *b"* several times, indicating that his tessitura surpassed this range.[91]

Teaching was also an important part of the activity for many of the court musicians. Although much of it occurred privately, members of the *Hofkapelle* were paid by the court to instruct young or prospective new members. Instruction financed by the court meant that the teacher — one of the court's virtuosos — received some or all of the young musician's salary. In some cases apprentices received room and board from the instructor. For example, from June 1740 until May 1750, J. G. Graun received 360 *Thaler* per year on behalf of the Russian violinist Ivan Böhme; Böhme subsequently received the same amount as salary. Similarly, from April 1749 until November 1750, Graun was paid 300 *Thaler* per year for the violinist Balthasar Christian Bertram, after which Bertram drew a salary of 200 *Thaler* per year. Emanuel Bach received 200 *Thaler* annually from 1755 until 1763 for instructing the chamber harpist Brennessell, half of the latter's salary.[92] Bach undoubtedly taught him ornamentation, accompaniment, and figured-bass realization.[93] Agricola received payments for instructing the young castrato Tossoni.[94]

Franz Benda taught violin to Johann Leonhardt Hesse (from May 1753 until 1761/2), and, from February 1745 until May 1747, gave voice instruction to the young castrato Belling.[95] The castrato Paulino was taught and housed first by C. H. Graun (June 1743 – May 1749), and then by Franz Benda (June 1749 – May 1752).[96]

---

[91] Marpurg, 'Nachricht von dem gegenwärtigen Zustande der Oper und Musik des Königs', *Historisch-kritische Beyträge*, I, 'Erstes Stück' (1754), 78, calls Porporino a 'tiefer sopran' (low soprano); for the range of the aria, see Hasse, *Cleofide: Digli ch'io son fedele*, facs. with edn by Wolfgang Goldhan (Wiesbaden and Leipzig: Breitkopf & Härtel, 1991).

[92] Christoph Henzel, 'Neues zum Hofcembalisten Carl Philipp Emanuel Bach', *Bach-Jahrbuch*, 85 (1999), 171–7, lists the payments to Bach for Brennessell.

[93] *Carl Philipp Emanuel Bach: Solo Sonatas*, ed. Mary Oleskiewicz, *The Complete Works*, II/1 (Los Altos, Calif.: Packard Humanities Institute, 2008), pp. xvii–xviii; and Oleskiewicz, 'Like Father, Like Son', 263–4 and n. 51.

[94] Agricola received 140 *Thaler*, 16 *Groschen* (35 *Thaler*, 4 *Groschen* per month) for teaching Tossoni from February to May 1755, according to the 'Capelletats', D-Bga, I. HA Rep. 36 No. 2455. The 'Schatoull-Rechnung', D-Bga, Brandenburg-Preußisches Hausarchiv, Rep. 47 No. 909, No. 20, fol. 10ʳ, records additional payments of 5 *Thaler* per month, paid out in a lump sum of 75 *Thaler* in June 1756.

[95] The rubric 'Vor den Hesse an den ältern Benda' (To the elder Benda for Hesse) always precedes the salary of 400 *Thaler* listed in the 'Capelletats' for these years. D-Bga, I. HA Rep. 36 No. 2441 (1745/6) designates Belling as a singer. He was not a violinist, nor did he receive violin lessons from Benda, as Henzel states in 'Die Schatulle Friedrichs II' (1999), 43.

[96] First Graun, then Benda received Paulino's salary (400 *Thaler* per year) and from June 1747 also his supplement of 83 *Thaler*, 14 *Groschen*. However, a communication between Friedrich and Fredersdorf of February 1754 indicates that Benda had already been mentoring the

Quantz mentored Pisendel's nephew, the young flautist Lindner, whom he brought with him in 1742 from Dresden. From January 1742 until May 1748, Lindner received 300 *Thaler* every year as Quantz's 'Pfeifer Scholare', after which time he is listed as 'Flautenist' in the *Hofkapelle*. Quantz's instruction extended to the Bayreuth court; Margrave Friedrich, himself Quantz's former pupil, sent the flautist Georg Gotthelf Liebeskind to study with him in Berlin for several years.[97]

Members of the *Hofkapelle* also taught members of the nobility and musicians from other courts, as well as informally instructing one another. Benda, for example, counted J. G. Graun in Rheinsberg as his second teacher of the violin, and Quantz gave instruction in composition to Agricola and Nichelmann. Schaffrath enjoyed being in demand as a teacher from professionals and amateurs alike. The court's operatic *divo* Salimbeni, a master of the embellished adagio, owed his renowned skill in free ornamentation in part to the study of harmony with Schaffrath.[98]

Sydow, director of the *Hautboistenschule*, received a *Douceur* of 50 *Thaler* from Friedrich's *Schatoulle* for delivery of musicians to the king's regiments, and he occasionally trained musicians for the *Hofkapelle*. Beginning in October 1748 he received payments for a bassoonist, including 60 *Thaler* in 1753 for 'des jungen Marchs Instrumenta, wie auch Information' (young [Johann Christian] Marks's instruments and instruction). In 1748 the king purchased a wig and in 1754 a 'Basson' at 16 *Thaler* for 'der junge Marks in der Capelle' (young Marks in the *Kapelle*).[99] Both he and Carl Philipp Emanuel Bach received 'Diäten' (per diem payments) for a stay in Potsdam from 25 March until 30 August 1756, during which time the two may have accompanied the king's flute playing.[100]

## Friedrich and his Kapelle at War

Friedrich embarked upon the First Silesian War in December 1740. On 18 January 1742 he was welcomed in Dresden with a performance of Hasse's new opera *Lucio Papiro* and expressed his enthusiasm for it subsequently in letters to Algarotti.[101] On 18 December 1745, during the Second Silesian war (1744–5), Friedrich occupied Dresden, taking the Lubomirsky Palais as his quarters, where he held a concert. The next day he heard a *Te Deum* by Hasse in the Kreuzkirche and ordered a performance of Hasse's *Arminio*, in which Faustina sang and the composer (her

singer for years without remuneration; see Richter, *Die Briefe Friedrichs des Grossen an seinen vormaligen Kammerdiener Fredersdorf*, 363.

[97] Hiller, *Wöchentliche Nachrichten*, I, '24. Stück' (9 December 1766), 184.

[98] Hiller, 'Einige Nachrichten von dem Leben des berühmten Sängers Herrn Felice Salimbeni', *Wöchentliche Nachrichten*, I, '27. Stück' (30 December 1766), 205–9, at 208.

[99] D-Bga, Brandenburg-Preußisches Hausarchiv, Rep. 47 No. 901 (October 1748), entry no. 39 (3 *Thaler*); No. 906 (August 1753), entry no. 15; No. 901 (November 1748), entry no. 28 (2 *Thaler*, 12 *Groschen*); and Rep. 47 No. 907 (August 1754), entry no. 34.

[100] D-Bga, Brandenburg-Preußisches Hausarchiv, Rep. 47 No. 909 (1756), fols. 5ᵛ (No. 34), 8ᵛ (No. 32), 10ᵛ (No. 30), 12ᵛ (No. 34), 14ᵛ (No. 37), and 16ᵛ (No. 30).

[101] Sven Hansell, 'Johann Adolf Hasse', *Grove Music Online* (accessed 7 August 2009).

husband) Hasse directed.[102] Friedrich remained in the city until spring or summer 1746, ordering Hasse to play keyboard every night at his concerts and rewarding him with a diamond ring and 1,000 *Thaler*.[103] In July, Wilhelmine reported that Hasse, then in Bayreuth, 'est tres charmé de votre Flute mon tres cher Frere mais surtout de votre façon d'agir en saxe ou vous etes adoré et plus aimé que le Roy même' (is very charmed by your flute my very dear brother but especially by your actions in Saxony, where you are adored and more loved than the king [of Poland] himself).[104]

The Third Silesian War, unlike the first two, virtually halted formal musical life in Berlin. Better known as the Seven Years' War (1756–63), it saw the opera closed and left musicians and other court employees with little or no pay for long periods. The grand court concerts ceased, although private music making continued at court and at the campaign. During the winter, when fighting stopped, Friedrich resumed his nightly *soirées* with his chamber musicians.

On 9 September 1756 Dresden fell once again to Friedrich, and the king of Poland fled to Warsaw. On 22 November Friedrich heard the Saxon *Hofkapelle* perform a work by Hasse in the Catholic *Hofkirche* for the feast of St Cecilia. He attended services on other occasions as well, especially when Hasse directed; Fürstenau reports that the *Hofkapelle* performed frequent concerts in which Friedrich played flute and Hasse accompanied.[105] Friedrich attended services in the Frauenkirche, where he heard a motet, and he also heard the opera singers Pilaja and Albuzzi – finding neither good – and attended a few oratorios and several beautiful masses.[106] After Hasse's departure on 20 December, Franz Benda and Quantz were ordered to Dresden.

'Capelletats' survive for every year of the war except 1762/3.[107] These accounts show that during the fiscal year 1757/8 the musicians and other court employees received their normal salaries for only the first two quarters (Crucis, 1 June – 31 August, and Lucia, 1 September – 30 November). In the columns for the remaining two quarters (Reminiscere and Trinitas), however, one reads 'Bleibet annoch zu bezahlen' (Still remains to be paid). For these and subsequent periods, those who were not paid cash were issued 'Cassenscheine' – payment vouchers – to be bartered or redeemed after the war. This system was not limited to the *Hofkapelle* but extended across the entire civil service. Only those called to serve in the campaign were paid.[108]

[102] Schneider, *Geschichte der Oper*, 112.
[103] Preuss, *Œuvres de Frédéric le Grand*, III: 172; and Hansell, 'Johann Adolf Hasse'.
[104] D-Bga, Brandenburg-Preußisches Hausarchiv, Rep. 46 W No. 17, vol. II, 5, fols. 57ᵛ–58ʳ (dated 12 July 1746); Volz, *Friedrich der Große und Wilhelmine von Baireuth: Briefe*, II: 101.
[105] Moritz Fürstenau, *Zur Geschichte der Musik und des Theaters am Hofe der Kurfürsten von Sachsen und Könige von Polen*, 2 vols. (Dresden, 1861–2), II: 363.
[106] Volz, *Friedrich der Große und Wilhelmine von Baireuth: Briefe*, II: 337, letters to Wilhelmine dated Dresden, 6 and 10 December 1756.
[107] D-Bga, I. HA Rep. 36 Nos. 2460–67.
[108] D-Bga, I. HA Rep. 36 No. 401, 'Rechnung über Einnahme und Ausgabe bey der Königlich Preußischen Hoff Staats Casse von Trinitatis 1757 bis Trinitatis 1758', p. 48. The same held for officers actively serving the king.

Thus only a few musicians were paid for 1757/8. Franz Caspari Benda received his full salary 'weil er beständig in der Campagne sich aufhält' (because he resides constantly with the campaign). Caspari – unrelated to the other Bendas at court – appears from May 1744 with a salary of 150 *Thaler*.[109] In the 'Capelletats' he is listed invariably as a viola player, although he probably also played violin. To distinguish him from the elder Franz Benda (Benda senior) who played the violin, in the 'Capelletats' he is called Franz Benda 'der jüngere' (the younger) or Franz Caspari 'sonst Benda genannt' (otherwise called Benda). During this same year several others also served at the king's winter quarters in Breslau (Wrocław): Quantz (flute), Franz Benda senior (violin), C. F. Fasch (keyboard), Joseph Benda (violin), and Johann Georg Speer (cello). Each received his pro-rated salary 'vor eine Reise nach Breslau laut *Ordre* vom 24 Dec: 1757' (for a trip to Breslau, according to the order of 24 December 1757)' between December 1757 and March 1758.[110] These five, together with Franz Caspari, comprised the usual chamber ensemble that accompanied the king's private *soirées* in Potsdam. At Breslau the chamber ensemble was completed by the three singers who also ordinarily performed arias at these concerts: Porporino, Tossoni, and Paulino, all of whom received orders to come to Breslau. Thus in the early stages of the war Friedrich continued his nightly concerts in the usual fashion.

During the next fiscal year, 1758/9, only Franz Caspari remained with the king and received his full salary. Soon, however, a system of reduced salaries was introduced. From June 1759 until May 1762, musicians whose salaries totalled 400 *Thaler* or less received their full contractual amounts in cash. But those who earned more than 400 *Thaler* annually were paid only three-quarters of their salary, receiving the remainder as 'Cassenscheine'. Thus the concertmaster Johann Gottlieb Graun was paid 900 of his contractual 1,200 *Thaler*, and Franz Benda senior received 600 of his usual 800 *Thaler*.[111]

This system reduced Emanuel Bach's salary in the 'Capelletats' from 500 to 375 *Thaler* per year. As a result, he received less than a number of lower-salaried musicians, such as the flautist Lindner, who continued to be paid his usual 400 *Thaler*. Bach's actual annual salary, which included a teaching honorarium and a supplement of 25 *Thaler* each month from the king's *Schatoulle*, totalled 800 *Thaler*. But the summary account for the *Schatoulle* during these years leaves it unclear to what extent he and other musicians continued to receive such supplements. A rubric of January 1762 indicates that *Schatoulle* payments were issued as 'Cassenscheine'.

During 1760/61 the 'Capelletats' show that Quantz, Benda senior, and the singers Porporino, Paulino, and Tossoni were again called to winter headquarters

---

[109] D-Bga, I. HA Rep. 36 No. 2460. For each of four quarters Caspari received 37 *Thaler*, 12 *Groschen* (150 *Thaler* altogether). Ledebur, *Tonkünstler-Lexicon Berlin's*, 86, incorrectly gives his date of entry into the *Kapelle* as 1766. Franz Caspari is sometimes confused with Franz Benda (sen.), most recently in Tobias Schwinger, *Die Musikaliensammlung Thulemeier und die Berliner Musiküberlieferung in der zweiten Hälfte des 18. Jahrhunderts* (Beeskow: Ortus, 2006), 417.

[110] D-Bga, I. HA Rep. 36 No. 2460, p. 3. These musicians were not called back the next year. Apart from Franz Caspari, no musicians received any pay for the year 1758/9.

[111] D-Bga, I. HA Rep. 36 No. 2464–7.

in Leipzig after the battle of Torgau. For June to November they received three-quarters of their salary, the remainder in 'Cassenscheine'. But for December to March they were paid their full salaries because each received orders to come to Leipzig, and likewise in April and May when each was required to return to Leipzig.[112] From May 1762, Porporino was paid his full salary without 'Cassenscheine', which indicates that he was with the king. He also received a yearly supplement of 1,000 *Thaler* – a remarkable figure at a time when only 'Cassenscheine' were issued to the rest of the *Hofkapelle* and the majority of the *Hofstaat* (court personnel).

In 1761/2 Fasch and the rest of the ensemble were again called to winter quarters in Leipzig, but no special adjustment was made in the 'Capelletats' for those with reduced salaries. Although he was again receiving his full salary, Zelter reported that Fasch did not go because he could not afford the journey.[113]

Musicians not ordered to the campaign were free to travel. In 1759, the flautist Kottowsky went to London, and Emanuel Bach took refuge in Zerbst for several months, occupying himself with composition. Beginning in 1761, Franz Benda appeared at the courts of Weimar, Gotha, and Rudolstadt, receiving gifts totalling 2,000 *Thaler*.[114] Schaffrath, now in the service of Princess Amalie, remained in Berlin and gave private music lessons to the nobility, fleeing to Magdeburg with the court during the occupation of Berlin.

During the war, many musicians died or left the court's service. By 1761 the *Hofkapelle* had accumulated twelve vacant positions (see Table 4.2). Those who died in 1757 included the decorator Giuseppe Galli Bibiena, the bassoonist Alexander Lange, and the *prima donna* Astrua, who had been pensioned in January due to illness at 1,000 *Thaler* per year. The violinist Böhme passed away in 1758, the theorbist Baron and the *Kapellmeister* C. H. Graun in 1759. After the war, Agricola assumed Graun's duties but not his title. In 1760 the violinist Koch died, and then the *Hautboistenschule* director Pauly in 1762. Others who did not return included the singer Luini, the cellist Hock, and the viola player Gebhardt. The violinist Czarth, paid until May 1758, went to Meiningen before joining the *Hofkapelle* at Mannheim.[115]

In 1763 Friedrich returned to Berlin victorious. He revived the *Intermezzo*, engaged a *Comédie* troupe from the court at Bayreuth, and began to reorganize the *Hofoper*, which was in a shambles. He also resumed his famous nightly chamber *soirées*, albeit performing flute concertos with noticeably less stamina than before. Vacancies in the *Hofkapelle* were filled, and the reorganization and recopying of royal musical manuscripts damaged during the occupation of Berlin was begun. Agricola led the opera in Graun's stead, but without Graun's title or pay, until

[112] D-Bga, I. HA Rep. 36 No. 2466, p. 5. The rubrics for each musician read: 'weil er nach Leipzig zu kommen beordert worden, laut *Ordre* vom 9ten Dec: 1760' and 'weil er wieder retourniret gewesen'.

[113] Carl Friedrich Zelter, *Karl Friedrich Christian Fasch* (Berlin, 1801), 19.

[114] 'Franz Benda's Autobiography', *Forgotten Musicians*, ed. Paul Nettl (New York: Philosophical Library, 1951), 204–45, at 227–8.

[115] Ledebur, 'Czarth (Georg)', *Tonkünstler-Lexicon Berlin's*, 101; on Czarth at Mannheim, see Chapter 5, 'The Palatine Court in Mannheim', p. 139 below.

1775, when Johann Friedrich Reichardt replaced him as *Kapellmeister*; with the exception of a few works by Agricola, the repertory continued to feature works by Graun and Hasse. During the war, both Friedrich's sister Wilhelmine and his mother had died, but Queen Elisabeth Christine and other members of the royal family resumed sponsorship of grand court concerts. After the war, the king rarely travelled to Berlin, preferring the exclusion of Sanssouci. From 1768, intermezzos, an oratorio by Hasse, and the king's own private musical performances would also take place in an ostentatious new palace at Potsdam.

Berlin continued to prosper and grow as a musical centre, and public and private amateur music-making in 'academies' and *Salons* created an artistically fertile and financially rewarding environment for the court's virtuosos.[116] Music-making in Berlin was assured a future under Friedrich's nephew and successor Friedrich Wilhelm II, an avid cellist who, like his predecessor, had formed a large princely *Kapelle* of his own before ascending the throne. After Friedrich's death in 1786, he reorganized the *Hofoper*, created a national theatre, and merged the princely and royal *Hofkapellen* into one large orchestra; the era of Graun and Hasse was over.

## EXCURSUS: THE BERLIN *HOFKAPELLEN* OF THE MARGRAVES OF BRANDENBURG-SCHWEDT

Brandenburg-Schwedt was a cadet line of the House of Hohenzollern, some of whose members maintained significant *Hofkapellen* in Berlin during the reigns of Friedrich Wilhelm I and Friedrich II. The first princes of this line, four sons by the second marriage of the 'Great Elector' Friedrich Wilhelm I of Brandenburg (r. 1640–88), held the title of margrave of Brandenburg but no power. The eldest was Margrave Philipp Wilhelm (1669–1711), who was succeeded by his sons Friedrich Wilhelm (r. 1731–71) and Friedrich Heinrich (r. 1771–88); when the latter died without an heir, the Schwedt property reverted to the crown. The Great Elector's third-born son by his second marriage was Margrave Albrecht Friedrich (1672–1731). His son Karl Friedrich (1705–62), an officer in the Prussian army under Friedrich II, resided in Berlin and also maintained a *Hofkapelle*. Few court records before 1760 that concern musicians survive for any of these members of the Schwedt line. Nevertheless it is possible to establish complete rosters of musicians for certain years.

The Great Elector's fourth son in this line was Margrave Christian Ludwig (1677–1734), to whom J. S. Bach dedicated his six so-called Brandenburg Concertos in 1721. Christian Ludwig maintained a *Hofkapelle* in the Berlin *Stadtschloß*, where he continuously resided during the reign of his step-brother Friedrich Wilhelm I. His musicians undoubtedly performed for and with other members of the royal family, particularly as the royal court did not maintain its own *Kapelle*. As

[116] See Mary Oleskiewicz, 'Introduction to Part IV (Keyboard and Instrumental Music)', in *The Archive of the Sing-Akademie zu Berlin: Catalogue*.

noted above, several of these musicians entered the *Hofkapelle* of Crown Prince Friedrich upon Christian Ludwig's death in 1734.

Sources for Christian Ludwig's *Hofstaat* were destroyed in World War II, but records concerning his burial and the division of his estate in 1734 name six '*Cammer-Musici*': Emmerling, Kottowsky, Hagen, Kühlthau, Emis, and Ellinger (see Table 4.4).[117] Emmerling was employed by the margrave as a composer, keyboardist, and gamba player.[118] Whether Hagen could be the violinist Bernhard Joachim Hagen, in the *Hofkapelle* in Bayreuth from at least 1738, is not certain. It has not been previously noticed, however, that Emis must be the violinist Ehmes who entered Friedrich's *Hofkapelle* at this time along with Kottowsky, identified above as a bassoonist.[119] Ludwig's *Nachlass* (estate) contained a double-manual harpsichord by Michael Mietke with blue and silver lacquer, a large bass violin ('Bass Geige'), eleven music stands, and a large collection of instrumental and vocal music.[120]

Friedrich Wilhelm, eldest son of Philipp Wilhelm, inherited Schwedt in 1711, where he developed a residence that possessed several music rooms and an opera theatre. His younger brother Friedrich Heinrich resided in Berlin, where he maintained an instrumental ensemble of moderate proportions. In 1754 Marpurg published the roster of Friedrich Heinrich's *Hofkapelle* together with brief biographical information about its musicians. This *Hofkapelle* has been confused with that of the king's brother Prince Friedrich Heinrich. The error stems from confusion between the title 'Prince and Margrave Heinrich', with which Marpurg and other contemporary writers consistently describe Margrave Friedrich Heinrich of the Schwedt line, and that of the king's younger brother Heinrich, who was properly styled 'Prince Heinrich' alone.[121]

Marpurg's roster (see Table 4.4) shows that Heinrich's *Kapelle* has the general proportions of string and keyboard players that Quantz had recommended two years earlier: five violins, one viola, one cello, one contrabass, and one keyboard.[122] The *Hofkapelle* also included one flautist and one oboist. The keyboard player was J. S. Bach's pupil Johann Philipp Kirnberger (1721–1783), whose name stands

---

[117] D-Bga, Brandenburg-Preußisches Hausarchiv, Rep. 35 V 119, fol. 191ʳ.

[118] Walther, *Musicalisches Lexicon*, 'Emmerling', 206.

[119] Heinrich Besseler, 'Markgraf Christian Ludwig von Brandenburg', *Bach-Jahrbuch*, 43 (1956), 18–35, at 23, suggests that Kühltau is the bassoonist of that name who joined the Prussian *Hofkapelle* in 1752, but this is unlikely.

[120] D-Bga, Brandenburg-Preußisches Hausarchiv, Rep. 35 V 119.

[121] Marpurg qualifies references to Prince Heinrich as 'Prinz Heinrich, Bruder des Königes' (Prince Heinrich, brother of the king). The Margrave Friedrich Heinrich's customary title is confirmed by the title page of the 'Nachlass', drawn up at his death in 1788, 'Inventarium der verstorbenen Prinzen von Preußen, Markgrafen zu Brandenburg . . .' (Inventory of the deceased Prince of Prussia, Margrave of Brandenburg); see D-Bga, Brandenburg-Preußisches Hausarchiv, Rep. 36 No. 278. Ledebur, *Tonkünstler-Lexicon Berlin's*, 283–6, at 283, correctly reports that Kirnberger 'trat . . . mit K[öniglicher] Erlaubniss in die Kapelle des Markgrafen Heinrich dasselbst um 1754 ein' (entered . . . the *Kapelle* of Margrave Heinrich in 1754 with royal permission).

[122] Quantz, *Versuch*, 'Hauptstück XVII', 'Abschnitt I', §16.

at the top of the list, although neither he nor any other musician are designated *Kapellmeister*. Before joining Margrave Heinrich's *Hofkapelle* in April 1754, Kirnberger, who had also studied with the Dresden violinist Johann Georg Fickler, was engaged by Friedrich in March 1752 upon the death of Johann Georg Benda. Kirnberger received Benda's salary of 300 *Thaler* per year but remained in the *Hofkapelle* for only twelve months before entering the *Hofkapelle* of Margrave Heinrich. Kirnberger remained in the latter's *Kapelle* until 1758, when he became *Hofmusicus* to the king's sister Princess Amalie.[123] Contrary to modern biographical accounts, which have confused the two Heinrichs, Kirnberger never worked for the king's brother in Rheinsberg.[124] By 1769, Margrave Heinrich's *Hofkapelle* had grown to twenty-three players, including six violinists, two viola players, two cellists, two violone players, two oboists, three flautists, three bassoonists, two horn players, and one keyboardist.[125]

In 1754 Marpurg also reported on the *Hofkapelle* of Margrave Heinrich's cousin Karl Friedrich (see Table 4.4). His *Hofkapelle* had proportions similar to Heinrich's but featured more winds: five violins; one viola, cello, contrabass, keyboard, harp, and flute each; three oboes, two horns, and two bassoons. Presumably one oboist also doubled on flute. Strong connections existed between these musicians and those in the king's *Kapelle*. In particular, the harpist Theresa Petrini, one of the very few women instrumentalists of the time to hold a permanent appointment in a German *Hofkapelle*, was the daughter of the royal harpist Petrini. Taught by Agricola in voice and continuo playing, she accompanied her own singing and appeared frequently in Berlin. In 1753 she sang at a court concert hosted by Count Lehndorff, *Oberhofmeister* to the queen, and on 27 March 1755 she performed the second soprano part in C. H. Graun's *Tod Jesu*.[126] Raab, Hempel, Aschenbrenner, and Jacobi, a member of Janitsch's academy, were also former pupils of virtuosos in the king's *Hofkapelle*.

Both Margraves Heinrich and Karl hosted grand concerts in Berlin, but unlike those of the royal Prussian court, these were by invitation only. Their *Hofkapelle* are just two examples of many others in and around Berlin at this time, which, through the exchange of music, musicians, musical instruction, and collaborative performances, all contributed to Berlin's vibrant musical life.

[123] Eighteenth-century sources and prints give Kirnberger's title as *Hofmusicus*, not *Kapellmeister*. Amalie granted the title 'Kapellmeister von Haus aus' to Emanuel Bach, upon the latter's departure for Hamburg.
[124] See for example Howard Serwer's article on Kirnberger in *Grove Music Online* (accessed August 2009).
[125] Nicolai, *Beschreibung der königlichen Residenzstädte*, 217.
[126] Wieland Giebel, ed., *Die Tagebücher des Grafen Lehndorff* (Berlin: Berlin Story, 2007), 131; and Ledebur, 'Petrini (Therese)', *Tonkünstler-Lexicon Berlin's*, 415.

TABLE 4.1. Membership of the Royal Prussian Court Music in 1713 and 1715, and the Ruppin *Hofkapelle* of Crown Prince Friedrich in 1733

| Year | 1713 | 1715 | 1733 |
|---|---|---|---|
| Ruler | King Friedrich I (r. 1701–13) | King Friedrich Wilhelm I (r. 1713–40) | Crown Prince Friedrich (b. 1712) |
| Numeric Overview | 1 director of chamber music<br>24 instrumentalists<br>Regimental music (*Hautboisten*)<br>6 *Jagdmusikanten* (horns)<br>25 court and chamber trumpeters & 2 kettledrummers<br>4 vocalists (1 doubling as instrumentalist)<br>7 additional personnel | 1 *Kapellmeister* & 'Staabs-Hautboist'<br>Regimental music (12 *Hautboisten*, 6 per batallion in the king's *Leibgarde*)<br>1 court trumpeter<br>2 additional personnel | 5 instrumentalists (1 doubling as vocalist)<br>1 vocalist |
| *Kapellmeister* and 'Staabs-Hautboist, Hautboisten-Chor der Königl. Leibgarde' in Potsdam | | Heinrich Gottfried Pepusch (vn), also 'Cammer-Musicant' (500 *Thaler*)[a] | |
| Director of chamber music | Johann Trumpff, 'Senior des Cammer Concerts' (bn and tpt) (450 *Thaler*) | | |
| 'Sur-Intendant des Orgues' (Superintendent of the organs) | Christian Ernst Rieck, also *Cammermusicus* (org and kbd) (352 *Thaler*) | | |

| Year | 1713 | 1715 | 1733 |
|---|---|---|---|
| **Instrumentalists** | | | |
| *Cammermusici* | | | |
| Violin 1 | Justus Bernhard Gottfried Wiedemann (400 *Thaler*)<br>Joseph Spieß (300 *Thaler*)<br>Heinrich Gottfried Pepusch (300 *Thaler*)<br>Nicolas Mathes Jourdain (300 *Thaler*)<br>Ephraim Linicke (300 *Thaler*)<br>Martin Friedrich Marcus (Marcks) (200 *Thaler*) | | Johann Gottlieb Graun<br>Franz Benda (also tenor)<br>Georg Cazrth (also fl) [from December 1733] |
| Violin 2 | Friedrich Carl Rieck (jun.) (152 *Thaler*)<br>Johann Georg Linicke (200 *Thaler*)<br>Johann Philipp Schlesing (100 *Thaler*) | | Joseph Blume |
| Viola | *See* Soprano<br>*See Hofmusici* | | |
| Violoncello | Christian Bernhard Linicke (300 *Thaler*)<br>Gottlieb Hayne (also kbd) (300 *Thaler*)<br>Gottlieb Michael Kühnel (also vdg and lute) (200 *Thaler*) | | *See* Flute |

| Instrument | | | |
|---|---|---|---|
| Viola da gamba | See Violoncello | | |
| Contrabass | [possibly played by violoncellist] | | |
| Flute | See Oboes 1 and 2 | | [Crown Prince Friedrich (also va and hpd)] [Johann Joachim Quantz, visiting artist] See Violin 1 |
| Oboe 1 | Peter Glösch (also fl?) (400 Thaler) Friderich Schüler (also fl?) (150 Thaler) | | |
| Oboe 2 | Carl Ludwig Fleischer (also fl?) (150 Thaler) Ludwig Rose (also fl?) (150 Thaler) | | |
| Bassoon | Johann Michael Schüler (150 Thaler) Christoph Torbey ('Torley') (150 Thaler) See Director of chamber music | | |
| Horn | See Jagdmusik | | |
| Trumpet | See Director of chamber music and Cammer- und Hoftrompeter | See Cammer- und Hoftrompeter | |
| Lute | See Violoncello | | |
| Harpsichord/ Keyboard | See Violoncello | Gottlieb Hayne (?)[b] | Gottlieb Hayne |
| Organ | See 'Sur-Intendant des Orgues' See 'Sur-Intendant des Orgues' | | See Flute |

| Year | 1713 | 1715 | 1733 |
|---|---|---|---|
| *Hofmusic*[c] | | | |
| Violin 2 | Johann Christian Schultze (100 *Thaler*) | | |
| | Georg Friedrich Hager (100 *Thaler*) | | |
| | Salomon Lentz (100 *Thaler*) | | |
| | Peter Krause (100 *Thaler*) | | |
| Viola | Gottfried Dümler (100 *Thaler*) | | |
| Violoncello | Johann Ernst Güldenmeister (100 *Thaler*) | | |
| Hautboisten | *See Regimental music* | *See Regimental music* | |
| Regimental music | Exact number of musicians and names unknown | 12 *Hautboisten* (from two battalions, each band comprising 3 oboes, 2 bassoons, and 1 trumpet); names of musicians unknown | |
| Jagdmusik | 6 unnamed horn players, two of whom also played with the *Hofmusik* | | |
| Cammer- und Hoftrompeter | Johann Christoph Schobert[d] | Johann Friedrich Beyersdorff (200 *Thaler*) | |
| | Johann Friedrich Beyersdorff | | |
| | Johann Salomon Beyersdorff | | |
| | Martin Schobert | | |
| | Johann Gabelentz | | |

Christoph Brunner

Johann Jacob Wisian

Jacob Klingelhoffern

Christoph Daniel Weil

Simon Johann Tschack

Burchardt Reinhardt

Johann Christoph Arendt

Melchior Köhler

Johann Joachim Engelhardt

Johann George Moritz

Wilhelm Lehmann

Johann Heinrich Hermuth

Johann Christoph Schmidt

Johann Rudolff Naffziger

Maximilian Christian Bersch

Samuel Krause

Christian Friedrich Thies

Johann Ziegenhagen

Johann Jacob Moritz

Jacob Moritz

See Director of chamber music

Dannies

Gurck

*Hofpaucker*

| Year | 1713 | 1715 | 1733 |
|---|---|---|---|
| Vocalists | | | |
| *Cammermusici* | | | |
| Soprano | Johann Pustardt (also vn)[e] | | |
| Alto | Antonio Gualandi ('Campioli') (500 *Thaler*) | | |
| Tenor | Augustin Reinhard Stricker (300 *Thaler*) (also copyist, 30 *Thaler*)[f] | | [Carl Heinrich Graun, regular visiting artist] *See* Violin 1 |
| Bass | Christian Frohböse (Frobese) (100 *Thaler*) (also 'Reisekantor', travel *Kantor*) | | |
| Additional Personnel | | | |
| 'Dom Cantor' (*Kantor* at the cathedral) | Petraeo (100 *Thaler*) | Petraeo (50 *Thaler*) | |
| *Calcant* | Elisaeus Mergener (50 *Thaler*) Caspar Ziegeler (50 *Thaler*) Heinrich Erdman Fister (40 *Thaler*) | | |
| Copyist | Johann Kreyser *See* Tenor | | |
| *Hoforgelbauer* | Arp Schnitger, also tuned organs (150 *Thaler*) | | |
| Organ tuner | *See Hoforgelbauer* | Arp Schnitger (30 *Thaler*) | |
| *Hofinstrumentenmacher* | Michael Mietke (70 *Thaler*) | | |

*Sources*

1713: The information in this table is drawn from the *Adreß-Kalender der Königlich Preußischen Haupt- und Residentz-Städte Berlin und Daselbst befindlichen Koenigl. Hofes, Auch anderer hohen und niedern Collegien auf das Jahr 1713*; D-Bga, I. HA Rep 36 No. 339 'Königlich Preußische Hoff Staats Cassen Rechnung von Trinitatis 1712 bis Trinitatis 1713', p. 4 o f. ('Königl. Cammer Musicanten'), and pp. 67–72 ('Königl. Cammer und Hoff Trompeter'; and the similarly entitled document for the year 1711/12. Other details are taken from Sachs, *Musik und Oper*, esp.177–86. The salaries shown (in *Thaler*) are recorded in 1711/12 for a full year. In 1712/13, the year of the *Kapelle*'s dismissal, several musicians received less, perhaps because they departed before the end of the fiscal year: Justus Bernhard Gottfried Wiedemann (300), Joseph Spieß (100), Johann Georg Linicke (100), Gottlieb Hayne (300), Gottlieb Michael Kühnel (100), Peter Glösch (200), Carl Ludwig Fleischer (100), Ludwig Rose (150), Friderich Schüler (100), and Christoph Torbey (100). Pensioners are not included in this table, nor are 30 *Thaler* 'Kleidergeld' (clothing expenses) paid out to a number of the chamber musicians in 1713.

1715: Personnel information is taken from D-Bga, I. HA Rep 36 No. 69, 'Hoffstaats Etat von Trinitatis 1713 bis Trinitatis 1714', pp. 16–17, and No. 70 (1715/16), p. 27; see also Heyde, *Musikinstrumentenbau in Preußen*, 49.

1733: Information for the crown prince's *Hofkapelle* is based on the personal correspondence of Crown Prince Friedrich and his sister Wilhelmine and biographies published by Marpurg, *Historisch-kritische Beyträge*, I (1754–5); Johann Adam Hiller, *Wöchentliche Nachrichten und Lebensbeschreibungen*; and Ledebur, *Tonkünstler-Lexicon Berlin's*.

[a] Pepusch is always listed as violinist in the *Hofstaat* (courtly household) of Friedrich I; during the reign of Friedrich Wilhelm I, he received the title 'Staab-Hautboist' (leader of the *Hautboisten*), but his instrument is not specified. Some modern accounts describe him as an oboe player, but this cannot be confirmed by court documents. See, for example, Bruce Haynes, *The Eloquent Oboe: A History of the Hautboy, 1640–1760* (Oxford: Oxford University Press, 2001), 323, who suggests that the portrait of an unknown oboe player is Pepusch; Haynes does not mention Pepusch's court contract as violinist. Interesting in this regard is that the six *Hofmusici* in 1713 from the king's *Leibgarde* (life guards or personal bodyguard) were string players (see n. c below).

[b] Hayne, who gave musical instruction to the princes and princesses, was probably retained in the queen's *Hofstaat*, but records from this period do not survive.

[c] 'Hofmusicus' was a lower title given only to the six string players in the 'Leibgarde zu Fuß' who supplemented the *Hofkapelle*. They received 100 *Thaler* in addition to their regimental pay.

[d] In 1713, each of the twenty-five *Cammer- und Hoftrompeter*, as well as the two *Hofpaucker*, received a salary of 223 *Thaler*.

[e] In 1712/13 Pustardt received 52 *Thaler* 'Kostgeld' (expense money).

[f] In the *Adreß-Kalender* he is listed under vocalists, as a 'Tenorist'; in Ledebur, *Tonkünstler-Lexicon Berlin's*, 580, he is said to be a tenor and composer.

TABLE 4.2. Membership of the Royal Prussian Court Music Establishment in 1740, 1745, 1756, and 1760

| Year | 1740 | 1745 | 1756 | 1760 |
|---|---|---|---|---|
| Ruler | Crown Prince Friedrich (king from May 1740) | King Friedrich II (r. 1740–86) | | |
| Numeric Overview | 1 *Kapellmeister* <br> 1 concertmaster <br> 1 *Kapellmeister of the Potsdam Hautboistenschule* <br> 23–5 instrumentalists (2 doubling as vocalists) <br> 24 *Hautboisten* <br> 1 additional person | 1 *Kapellmeister* <br> 1 concertmaster <br> 1 director and composer of chamber music <br> 1 *Kapellmeister of the Potsdam Hautboistenschule* <br> 37 instrumentalists (\*denotes chamber duties) <br> 24 *Hautboisten* <br> 12 vocalists <br> 9 additional personnel | 1 *Kapellmeister* <br> 1 concertmaster <br> 1 director and composer of chamber music <br> 1 court composer <br> 1 *Kapellmeister of the Potsdam Hautboistenschule* <br> 38 instrumentalists (\*denotes chamber duties) <br> 24 *Hautboisten* <br> 9 vocalists <br> 12 additional personnel | [1 *Kapellmeister*] <br> 1 concertmaster <br> 1 director and composer of chamber music <br> 1 court composer <br> 1 *Kapellmeister of the Potsdam Hautboistenschule* <br> 33 instrumentalists (\*denotes chamber duties) <br> 24 *Hautboisten* <br> 6 vocalists <br> 11 additional personnel |
| *Kapellmeister* | Carl Heinrich Graun (also high tenor and vc) (800 *Thaler*; from May) | Carl Heinrich Graun (2,000 *Thaler*) | Carl Heinrich Graun | Vacant [Carl Heinrich Graun died 8 Augsut 1759] |
| Concertmaster | Johann Gottlieb Graun (800 *Thaler*; from May) | Johann Gottlieb Graun (1,200 *Thaler*) | Johann Gottlieb Graun | Johann Gottlieb Graun |
| Director of chamber music and *Kammercomponist* | | Johann Joachim Quantz (also fl and royal flute maker) (2,000 *Thaler*)\* | Johann Joachim Quantz (also fl and royal flute maker)\* | Johann Joachim Quantz (also fl and royal flute maker)\* |

| | | | |
|---|---|---|---|
| **Court composer** | Johann Friedrich Agricola | Johann Friedrich Agricola (400 *Thaler*) | | |
| **Kapellmeister, Potsdam Hautboistenschule** | Friedrich Wilhelm Pauly (also ob), 'Cammer-Musikant' | Friedrich Wilhelm Pauly (also ob), 'Cammer-Musikant' (400 *Thaler*) | Sydow, 'Cammer-Musikant' | Sydow, 'Cammer-Musikant' (400 *Thaler*)[a] |
| **Instrumentalists** | | | | |
| **'Premier' chamber violinist** | Franz Benda (sen.)* | Franz Benda (sen.)* | Franz Benda (sen.)* | Franz Benda (sen.) (also tenor) (500 *Thaler*) 'Premier' violin from May 1740 (800 *Thaler*) |
| **Violin** | Vacant | Georg Czarth | Georg Czarth (400 *Thaler*) | Georg Czarth (400 *Thaler*) |
| | Joseph Blume* | Joseph Blume* | Joseph Blume (300 *Thaler*)* | Joseph Blume (300 *Thaler*) |
| | Balthasar Christian Bertram | Balthasar Christian Bertram (200 *Thaler*) | Ehmes (400 *Thaler*) | Ehmes (400 *Thaler*) |
| | Johann Gabriel Seyffarth (400 *Thaler*) | Johann Gabriel Seyffarth | Johann Gabriel Seyffarth (300 *Thaler*) | Johann Caspar Grundke (300 *Thaler*) |
| | Johann August Koch | Johann August Koch (200 *Thaler*) | Georg Benda (250 *Thaler*) | [Georg Gustav?] Christiani [vn?][b] (300 *Thaler*) |
| | Joseph Benda* | Joseph Benda (400 *Thaler*) | Joseph Benda (250 *Thaler*)* | |
| | Johann Leonhardt Hesse | Johann Leonhardt Hesse (300 *Thaler*) | Johann Georg Benda ('Benda jun.') (300 *Thaler*) | |

| Year | 1740 | 1745 | 1756 | 1760 |
|---|---|---|---|---|
| Violin (cont.) | | Johann Gottlieb Freudenberg (sen.) (200 Thaler) | Johann Gottlieb Freudenberg (sen.) | Johann Gottlieb Freudenberg (sen.) |
| | | Ivan (Iwan) Böhme, 'Scholar' | Ivan (Iwan) Böhme (360 Thaler) | Vacant |
| Viola | Johann Georg Benda ('Benda jun.') (150 Thaler) | Franz Caspari Benda ('Franz Benda der jüngere') (150 Thaler)* | Franz Caspari Benda ('Franz Benda der jüngere')* | Franz Caspari Benda ('Franz Benda der jüngere')* |
| | Richter (Reich?)c | Georg Heinrich Gebhardt (150 Thaler) | Georg Heinrich Gebhardt | Vacant |
| | | Christian Carl Rolle (150 Thaler) | Hans Georg Steffani | Hans Georg Steffani |
| | | Johann Samuel Encke (140 Thaler) | Johann Samuel Encke | Johann Samuel Encke |
| Violoncello | Antonius Hock (400 Thaler) | Antonius Hock (400 Thaler) | Antonius Hock | Vacant |
| | See Kapellmeister | Ignaz Mara (600 Thaler) | Ignaz Mara | Ignaz Mara |
| | | Johann Georg Speer (300 Thaler)* | Johann Georg Speer* | Johann Georg Speer* |
| | | Christian Friedrich Schale (200 Thaler) | Christian Friedrich Schale | Christian Friedrich Schale |
| Viola da gamba | | Christian Ludwig Hesse (300 Thaler)* | Christian Ludwig Hesse* | Christian Ludwig Hesse* |
| Contrabass | Johann Gottlieb Janitsch (350 Thaler) | Johann Gottlieb Janitsch (350 Thaler) | Johann Gottlieb Janitsch | Johann Gottlieb Janitsch |

| Instrument | | | | |
|---|---|---|---|---|
| Flute | [Crown Prince Friedrich] | Johann Christoph Richter (160 *Thaler*) | Johann Christoph Richter | Johann Christoph Richter |
| | [Johann Joachim Quantz, visiting artist] | Friedrich Wilhelm Riedt (300 *Thaler*) | Friedrich Wilhelm Riedt | Friedrich Wilhelm Riedt |
| | | Johann Joseph Friedrich Lindner, 'Scholar' | Johann Joseph Friedrich Lindner (300 *Thaler*) | Johann Joseph Friedrich Lindner |
| | | *See* Director of chamber music *and Kammercomponist* | August Neuff (400 *Thaler*) | August Neuff |
| | | | Georg Wilhelm Kottowsky (120 *Thaler*) | Georg Wilhelm Kottowsky |
| Oboe | Carl August (120 *Thaler*) | Carl August (120 *Thaler*) | Carl August | Carl August |
| | Friedrich Wilhelm Pauly (120 *Thaler*) | Friedrich Wilhelm Pauly (120 *Thaler*) | Vacant (*see Kapellmeister*, Potsdam *Hautboistenschule*) | Vacant (*see Kapellmeister*, Potsdam *Hautboistenschule*) |
| | Binckowsky [ob?]d (120 *Thaler*) | Binckowsky (120 *Thaler*) | | |
| | Johann Caspar Grundke (300 *Thaler*) | Johann Caspar Grundke (300 *Thaler*) | Johann Caspar Grundke | Johann Caspar Grundke |
| | Joachim Wilhelm Döbbert (300 *Thaler*) | Joachim Wilhelm Döbbert (300 *Thaler*) | Joachim Wilhelm Döbbert | Joachim Wilhelm Döbbert |
| Bassoon | Christoph Julius Friedrich Dümler (120 *Thaler*) | Christoph Julius Friedrich Dümler | Christoph Julius Friedrich Dümler | Christoph Julius Friedrich Dümler |
| | Alexander Lange (120 *Thaler*) | Alexander Lange | Alexander Lange | Vacant |

| Year | 1740 | 1745 | 1756 | 1760 |
|---|---|---|---|---|
| Bassoon (cont.) | Kottowsky[e] (100 Thaler) | | Samuel Kühltau (120 Thaler); Johann Christian Marks* | Samuel Kühltau; Johann Christian Marks* |
| Horn | Johann Ignatius Horzitzky (156 Thaler); Görbich (156 Thaler) | Johann Ignatius Horzitzky; Görbich/Christian Mengis[f] (156 Thaler) | Johann Ignatius Horzitzky; Christian Mengis | Elias Encke (156 Thaler); Schober (156 Thaler) |
| Keyboard | Christoph Schaffrath (400 Thaler); Carl Philipp Emanuel Bach[g] | Christoph Nichelmann (500 Thaler)*; Carl Philipp Emanuel Bach (300 Thaler)* | Carl Friedrich Fasch (300 Thaler)*; Carl Philipp Emanuel Bach (600 Thaler)*[h] | Carl Friedrich Fasch*; Carl Philipp Emanuel Bach* |
| Theorbo | Ernst Gottlieb Baron (300 Thaler) | Ernst Gottlieb Baron | Ernst Gottlieb Baron | Ernst Gottlieb Baron (died 26 August 1760) |
| Harp | Petrini (400 Thaler) | Petrini (400 Thaler) | Franz Brennessell, 'Scholar' (400 Thaler) | Franz Brennessell, 'Scholar' |
| Instrument not specified | Richter[i] (120 Thaler) | Richter | | |
| Hautboisten | | 24 Hautboisten[j] | 24 Hautboisten | 24 Hautboisten |
| Vocalists | | | | |
| Soprano | | Giovanna Gasparini (1,700 Thaler); Benedetta Emilia (Amalie) Molteni (1,700 Thaler) | Giovanna Gasparini; Benedetta Emilia Molteni | Giovanna Gasparini (1,800 Thaler); Benedetta Emilia Molteni (600 Thaler) |

| Voice | | | |
|---|---|---|---|
| | Venturini (female) (1,000 *Thaler*; until 1 May 1745) | Giovanna Astrua (4,725 *Thaler*) | Vacant |
| | Maria Masi (1,500 *Thaler*)[k] | Agatha Collizzi (2,000 *Thaler*)[l] | |
| | Felice Salimbeni (4,440 *Thaler*) | Giuseppe Tossoni (422 *Thaler*)* | Giuseppe Tossoni (1,500 *Thaler*)* |
| | Paulo Bedeschi ('Paulino') (400 *Thaler*)* | Paulo Bedeschi ('Paulino') (2,000 *Thaler*)* | Paulo Bedeschi ('Paulino')* |
| | Antonio Cassati (240 *Thaler*) | Domenico Luini (4,000 *Thaler*) | Vacant |
| | Belling (male), 'Scholar' (96 *Thaler*) | | |
| Mezzo-soprano | Anton Hubert ('Porporino') (2,000 *Thaler*)* | Anton Hubert ('Porporino')*[m] | Anton Hubert ('Porporino') (1,500 *Thaler*)* |
| | Pasqualino Bruscolini (600 *Thaler*)[n] | | |
| Contralto/alto | Anna Loria Campolongo (600 *Thaler*)[o] | | |
| High tenor | *See Kapellmeister* | | |
| Tenor | Antonio Romani (1,200 *Thaler*) | Antonio Romani (2,000 *Thaler*) | Antonio Romani |
| | *See 'Premier' chamber violinist* | | |

| Year | 1740 | 1745 | 1756 | 1760 |
|---|---|---|---|---|
| **Additional Personnel** | | | | |
| Opera administrator | | Angelo Cori (1,200 *Thaler*) | Angelo Cori | Angelo Cori |
| Copyist | | Name not specified (Siebe?) (60 *Thaler*) | Siebe (60 *Thaler*) | Siebe |
| Calcant | | Name not specified | Ziegler (30 *Thaler*; also kbd tuner); Guillaume (30 *Thaler*) | Schmidt (30 *Thaler*) |
| *Hofinstrumentenmacher* and keyboard tuner in Berlin | | Christian Friedrich Hildebrand (100 *Thaler*; from December) | Christian Friedrich Hildebrand (also repaired instruments in Potsdam) | Christian Friedrich Hildebrand |
| *Hofinstrumentenmacher* and keyboard tuner | | Johann Friedrich Rost (jun.) (30 *Thaler*) | Johann Friedrich Rost (jun.) | Johann Friedrich Rost (jun.) |
| Keyboard tuner in Potsdam | | | Petzold | Petzold |
| Keyboard tuner | | | *See* Calcant | |
| Royal flute maker | | *See* Director of chamber music and *Kammercomponist* | *See* Director of chamber music and *Kammercomponist* | *See* Director of chamber music and *Kammercomponist* |
| *Souffleur* (prompter) | | Name not specified (40 *Thaler*) | Louvrieres (60 *Thaler*) | Doudiet (160 *Thaler*) |
| | | Name not specified (40 *Thaler*) | Siebe (80 *Thaler*) | Siebe |
| Court Poet | Johann Gualbert Bottarelli (?) | | Giampietro Tagliazucchi (400 *Thaler*) | Giampietro Tagliazucchi |

| Costume maker | Clezenne (400 *Thaler*) | Hermann (400 *Thaler*) | Hermann |
| Scenery painter/ *Dekorateur*; machinist | Giacomo Fabri (700 *Thaler*)P | Giuseppe Galli Bibiena (2,400 *Thaler*) | |
| *Avertisseur* (stage manager) | Jean Jean (400 *Thaler*) | Jean Jean | |

*Sources*

The information in this table is drawn from primary sources in D-Bga, I. HA Rep 36 Nos. 372 and 374, 'Rechnung über Einnahme und Ausgabe bey der Königlich Preußischen Hoff Staats Casse von Trinitatis 1740 bis Trinitatis 1741'; and No. 375 (1741/2); the 'Capelletats' in D-Bga. I. HA Rep. 36 Nos. 2441 (1744/5), 2443 (1745/6), 2455 (1754/5), 2456 (1755/6), 2464 (1759/60) and 2466 (1760/61); the king's 'Schatoull-Rechnung', D-Bga, Brandenburg-Preußisches Hausarchiv, Rep. 47 Nos. 895–911 (1742–61). Additional details are taken from Marpurg, *Historisch-kritische Beyträge*, I (1754–5); Ledebur, *Tonkünstler-Lexicon Berlin's*; Herbert Heyde, *Musikinstrumentenbau in Preußen* (Tutzing: Hans Schneider, 1994).

* Musicians known to have been called to serve in the king's private concerts are designated with an asterisk, but this information is based on incomplete records.

a  Ledebur, *Tonkünstler-Lexicon Berlin's*, 546, reports that 'Sidow' (Sydow) is probably the son of Samuel Peter Sydow, *Kapellmeister* to Elector Friedrich III. Samuel Peter Sydow was engaged as Elector Friedrich Wilhelm I of Brandenburg's director of music in 1679 and appears in court personnel lists until 1701. Bruce Haynes, *The Eloquent Oboe: A History of the Hautboy from 1640–1760* (Oxford: Oxford University Press, 2001), 426, confuses father with son in his discussion of the Potsdam *Hautboistenschule*.

b  Christiani's instrument is not specified; he served in the *Hofkapelle* until September 1743, when the remainder of his salary was assigned to a new violinist, Georg Benda. Christiani, who received 300 *Thaler* per year, the same amount as many other violinists, may be the violinist Georg Gustav Christiani listed in the *Hofkapelle* of Prince Ferdinand by 1755.

c  A Reich is mentioned as playing 'Bratsche' (viola) in Friedrich's Rheinsberg *Kapelle* (see Carl Wilhelm Hennert, *Beschreibung des Lustschloßes und Gartens . . . zu Reinsberg* [sic] (Berlin, 1778), 21; he might be identical to Richter (no instrument specified), who is listed among musicians of the first *Kapelle* in 1740.

d  Binckowsky, whose instrument is not specified, received 120 *Thaler*, the same amount as other oboists and bassoonists. He was replaced by the bassoonist Kühltau in 1752.

e  In 1740/41, Kottowsky is listed with a salary (perhaps a pension) of only 100 *Thaler* per year. In 1741/2, he is no longer listed in the 'Capelletats'.

f  Mengis took over the position beginning with Trinity quarter 1745 (1 March).

g  Emanuel Bach, though performing at court from 1740, does not appear in the 'Capelletats' until 1741. He must at first have been paid from the king's 'Schatoulle-Rechnung', which does not survive for 1740 or 1741.

h  In addition to the 600 *Thaler*, Bach received 200 of the 400 *Thaler* shown under Brennessell's name in 1745.

i  Richter's instrument is not specified; he received a salary of 120 *Thaler*, the same amount as other bassoonists and oboists and is paid through February 1750.

j  During these years twenty-four *Hautboisten* were drawn from four regimental bands of six musicians each to perform for court balls.

k  Masi remained at court only twelve months (April 1747 – March 1748). Her married name was Maria Giura, according to K. J. Kutsch and Leo Reimens with Hansjörg Rost, *Großes Sängerlexikon*, 4th expanded and updated edn, 7 vols. (Munich: K. G. Saur, 2003), IV: 2970.

l  Collizzi was paid from the 'Schatoull-Rechnung' from 1 October 1756 to at least May 1759 (for the period during the war the records of the 'Schatoulle-Rechnung' are incomplete). She was probably engaged as a replacement for Astrua, whose ill health forced her to leave Prussian service in January 1757.

m  The Italianized version of his name was Huberti.

n  Pasqualino received a payment from the 'Schatoull-Rechnung' in August 1743 (50 *Thaler*) and in November 1743 received what appears to be his salary for seven months; see D-Bga, Brandenburg-Preußisches Hausarchiv, Rep. 47 No. 896, and I. HA Rep. 36 No. 2437. He therefore did not arrive in Berlin at the end of December 1743, as stated by Henzel, 'Die Schatulle Friedrichs II.', 39.

o  Her name is spelt in various ways, including Anna Laura Campolungo and Lorio [*sic*] Campolongo; sources give her range as alto or contralto.

p  Marpurg, *Historisch-kritische Beyträge*, 1, 'Sechstes Stück' (1755), 503, reports that Fabri was a Venetian scenery painter and built operatic stage machinery.

TABLE 4.3. Membership of the *Intermezzo* Troupe in Potsdam in 1748, 1756, and 1760

| Year | 1748 | 1756 | 1760 |
|---|---|---|---|
| Numeric Overview | 1 director (also first 'Bassist'), 1 soprano, 1 additional person | 1 director (also first 'Bassist'), 4 sopranos, 3 tenors, 1 buffo-bass, 3 vocalists with unspecified ranges | 1 soprano, 1 tenor, 1 buffo-bass |
| Director | Domenico Cricchi (also first 'Bassist') (1,500 *Thaler*) | Domenico Cricchi (also first 'Bassist'; departed July)[a] | |
| Soprano | Maria (Rosa) Ruvinetti Bon (1500 *Thaler*)[b] | Ninetta Rosenau (550 *Thaler*) — Armellina Mattei (550 *Thaler*) — Oktavia Gehry (Gherri) (550 *Thaler*) — Maria Angela (Angiola) Paganini (1,258 *Thaler*; departed May) | Oktavia Gehry (Gherri) (?) |
| Tenor | | Carlo Paganini (250 *Thaler*, departed May) — Andrea Masno (893 *Thaler*, 18 *Groschen*)[c] | |
| Buffo-bass | | Francesco Paladini (550 *Thaler*) | Francesco Paladini (?) |
| Bass | *See* Director | Filippo Sidotti (400 *Thaler*) — *See* Director — [Giovanni?] Croce (350 *Thaler*; departed May)[d] | Filippo Sidotti (?) |

| Year | 1748 | 1756 | 1760 |
|---|---|---|---|
| Vocal range not specified | | Barbara Affabili (577 *Thaler*; 12 *Groschen*) | |
| | | Ferrari (550 *Thaler*)[e] | |
| | | [Christiano Koerbitz?] Tedeschini (550 *Thaler*) | |
| **Additional Personnel** | | | |
| Theatre architect | Girolamo Bon | | |

*Sources*

Information for this table comes from the king's 'Schatoull-Rechnung', from which the *Intermezzo* salaries were paid; Ledebur, *Tonkünstler-Lexicon Berlin's*; Claudio Sartori, *I libretti italiani a stampa dalle origini al 1800: Catalogo analitico con 16 indici*, 7 vols. (Cuneo: Bertola & Locatelli, 1990– ), VII (1994), *Indici II: Cantanti*; and K. J. Kutsch and Leo Reimens with Hansjörg Rost, *Großes Sängerlexikon*, 4th expanded and updated edn, 7 vols. (Munich: K. G. Saur, 2003), VII.

1756: Maria and Carlo Paganini, Croce, and Sidotti were dismissed in May. They received 'Reisegeld' (travel expenses) in May, recorded in D-Bga, Brandenburg-Preußisches Hausarchiv, Rep. 47 No. 909, fol. 8ᵛ, and were replaced in July and August by a new *Intermezzo* troupe that included Sidotti. 1760: The 'Schatoull-Rechnung' is not complete during the war. Four singers listed in 1756 received payments in 1764: Sidotti, Paladini, and Marianne Gehry; see 'Beläge zur Königl. Chatoulle Rechnungen', D-Bga, Brandenburg-Preußisches Hausarchiv, Rep. 36 Nos. 580–81. They were joined by two new singers, the director of the Potsdam *Intermezzo* and buffo-bass, Johann August Christoph Koch, and Armellina Koch.

[a] Droysen, 'Tageskalender Friedrichs des Grossen', 141, gives Cricchi's last performances as *Il impresario* (7 and 16 July 1756); however, no payments are recorded for him in the 'Schatoull-Rechnung' after 1754.

[b] This salary was shared with her husband, the theatre architect Girolamo Bon.

[c] Masno, paid for service from September 1756 until February 1757, is probably the singer listed by Sartori, *I libretti italiani*, 417, whose whereabouts are not reported between 1756 and 1758, when he went to Hamburg.

[d] Croce entered Prussian service in October 1753. Kutsch and Reimens, *Großes Sängerlexikon*, report that a Giovanni Croce (bass) was active in Hamburg, Leipzig, and Copenhagen from 1748 until 1753 but record no activity for him after this date.

[e] A baritone, Giuseppe Ignacio Ferrari, performed intermezzos in Naples from 1701 to 1715 (Kutsch and Reimens, *Großes Sängerlexikon*, 11: 1440), but a connection here cannot be determined.

TABLE 4.4. Membership of the Court Music Establishments of the Margraves of Brandenburg-Schwedt in Berlin in 1734 and 1754

| Year | 1734 | 1754 | 1754 |
|---|---|---|---|
| Ruler | Christian Ludwig (1677–1734) | Karl Friedrich (1705–1762) | Friedrich Heinrich (b. 1709; r. 1771–88) |
| Numeric overview | 6 instrumentalists (at least) | 17 instrumentalists (1 doubling as vocalist) | 11 instrumentalists<br>1 vocalist |
| **Instrumentalists** | | | |
| Violin | Ehmes (Ems or Emis)<br>Ellinger (vn?) | Friedrich Leopold Raab<br>August Kohne<br>Jacob Ludewig Ebel<br>Carl Wilhelm Ramnitz<br>Zachaus Wilhelm Albrecht | Jakob Le Fevre<br>Georg Bernhard Leopold Zeller<br>Christian Gottlob Fiebiger<br>Johann Hermann Vogt<br>Christian Friedrich Rackemann[a]<br>See Keyboard |
| Viola | | Christian Wilhelm Heinrich | Johann Joseph Dieterich |
| Violoncello | | Johann Christian Schwedler | Georg Bandow |
| Viola da gamba | Emmerling (also kbd) | | |
| Contrabass | | | |
| Flute | | Carl Ludewig Bewerich<br>Johann Friedrich Aschenbrenner (also kbd)<br>See Keyboard | Friedrich Krause<br>Friedrich Wilhelm |
| Oboe | | Johann Christian Jacobi<br>Joachim Friedrich Rodemann<br>Georg Erhard Fischer<br>Johann Friedrich Richter | Johann Friedrich Kannenberger |
| Bassoon | Kottowsky | | |

| Year | 1734 | 1754 | 1754 |
|---|---|---|---|
| Horn | | Antonius Hoetzel | |
| | | Johann Blassick | |
| Keyboard | *See* Viola da gamba | Christian Wilhelm Hempel (also fl) | Johann Philipp Kirnberger (also vn) |
| | | *See* Flute | |
| Harp | | Theresa Petrini (also soprano) | |
| Instrument not specified | Hagen | | |
| | Kühltau | | |
| Vocalists | | | |
| Soprano | | | |
| Bass | | *See* Harp | Carl Rudolph Vreden |

*Sources*

1734: D-Bga, Brandenburg-Preußisches Hausarchiv, Rep. 35 V 123.

1754: Personnel lists for Margraves Karl and Heinrich in Marpurg, *Historische-kritische Beyträge*, I (1754), 'Zweytes Stück', 156–60, and 'Erstes Stück', 85–7, respectively; additional details from Ledebur, *Tonkünstler-Lexicon Berlin's*; and Walther, *Musicalisches Lexicon*.

[a] Rackemann does not appear in Marpurg's personnel list of 1754; however, shortly thereafter he describes Rackemann as a member of the *Hofkapelle* of the Margrave Heinrich in his 'Entwurf einer ausführlichen Nachricht von der Musikübenden Gesellschaft zu Berlin', *Historische-kritische Beyträge*, I (1755), 'Fünftes Stück', 410; and in the 'Sechstes Stück', 505, Marpurg mentions that Rackemann recently joined the margrave's *Kapelle*.

# 5

# The Palatine Court in Mannheim

## *Bärbel Pelker*

THE RELOCATION OF THE PALATINE COURT by Elector Carl Philipp (1661–1742, r. from 1716) from Heidelberg to Mannheim, in 1720, marked the beginning of courtly musical life for the new residential town. It was, however, during the reign of his successor, the music-loving Elector Carl Theodor (1724–1799, r. from 1743), that between the years 1747 and 1778 a *Hofkapelle* of a unique character developed. To this day, it is identified internationally as the 'Mannheim School'. As this chapter will show, this *Hofkapelle* was not the result of an amalgamation of the Innsbruck and Düsseldorf *Hofkapellen*, as is commonly assumed, but, in fact, a new creation that began in 1747. Thanks to the elector's generous support, which, in addition to reasons of prestige, was clearly shaped by his own serious interest in music, the residential town of Mannheim advanced to become one of the leading musical centres of Europe during the second half of the eighteenth century.[1]

## THE *HOFKAPELLE* UNDER ELECTOR CARL PHILIPP (1720–42)

Before Carl Philipp succeeded his brother, the Düsseldorf-based Elector Johann Wilhelm of the Palatinate (1658–1716, r. from 1685), he maintained his own *Hofkapelle* – initially at his court in Breslau and then as Governor of Tirol in Innsbruck – which was amalgamated with his brother's Düsseldorf *Hofkapelle* following the latter's death in 1716. The negotiations were drawn out until the final takeover in

---

[1] Since 1990, the Mannheim *Hofkapelle* has been the focus of a research centre hosted by the Heidelberger Akademie der Wissenschaften; see <www.hof-music.de> (including a comprehensive list of publications). See also Bärbel Pelker, 'Die kurpfälzische Hofmusik in Mannheim und Schwetzingen (1720–78)', in *Süddeutsche Hofkapellen im 18. Jahrhundert*, Schriften zur Südwestdeutschen Hofmusik, 1 (Heidelberg: Universitätsverlag Winter, forthcoming). For an introduction to the topic in English, see Roland Würtz and Eugene K. Wolf, 'Mannheim School', *Grove Music Online*, <www.oxfordmusiconline.com> (accessed 10 September 2009); see also John Spitzer and Neal Zaslaw, *The Birth of the Orchestra: History of an Institution, 1650–1815* (Oxford: Oxford University Press, 2004), 256–62.

1718.[2] Initially, in 1716, Carl Philipp ordered a considerable reduction of the Düsseldorf court's household. The business of government was carried out by a locally appointed interim administration of privy councillors, which, among other things, decreed the dismissal of the court musicians.[3] In a letter from Innsbruck dated 11 September 1716, Carl Philipp asked the Dowager Electress Anna Maria Luisa de' Medici (1667–1743) for indulgence, since, owing to the fact that he already employed numerous musicians at his own court, he found himself unable to fulfil everyone's wishes to remain in service.[4] In May 1717, Carl Philipp left Innsbruck, initially relocating his court to Neuburg. In that same year, for reasons unknown, he reinstated the majority of the Düsseldorf musicians. This is confirmed by two extant, although undated, salary lists from Düsseldorf that were probably prepared at the end of 1717 or perhaps in early 1718.[5] The musicians from the Innsbruck and Düsseldorf *Hofkapellen* can be identified with the help of an overview dating from 1723, the earliest known list of Mannheim musicians (see Table 5.1, pp. 156–60 below).[6]

In November 1718, Carl Philipp moved his seat of government from Neuburg to Heidelberg, or, more precisely, to Schwetzingen – since Heidelberg Castle had been severely damaged in 1689 and 1693 during the War of the Palatine Succession (1688–97) and only partially repaired. The terrible state of the building, as well as disputes with the Protestant population of the town regarding the surrender of the Heiliggeistkirche to their Catholic counterparts, compelled the elector to choose Mannheim as his new seat of government. When, however, Carl Philipp ordered the relocation of his residence along with all government offices from Heidelberg to Mannheim on 12 April 1720, considerable inconvenience was experienced by the entire court, as the building of the massively-proportioned Mannheim palace had only just begun and, moreover, progress was slow. It was not until 22 November 1731 that the court moved into the new palace. The summer months had been spent in the small residential residence in Schwetzingen, while during the winter, the Palais Oppenheimer (later known as the Palais Hillesheim) on Mannheim's

[2] D-DÜha, Jülich-Berg II, No. 2225. On the Düsseldorf *Hofkapelle*, see particularly Alfred Strahl, *Die Hofmusik Jan Wellems 1679–1716: Eine historisch-genealogische Betrachtung mit Herkunfts- und Nachfahrentafeln*, Sonderheft (Düsseldorf: Düsseldorfer Verein für Familienkunde, 1988); regarding the Innsbruck *Hofkapelle*, see Walter Senn, *Musik und Theater am Hof zu Innsbruck: Geschichte der Hofkapelle vom 15. Jahrhundert bis zu deren Auflösung im Jahre 1748* (Innsbruck: Österreichische Verlagsanstalt, 1954).

[3] Letter from Düsseldorf, dated 19 July 1716, containing the so-called 'Entlassungsliste' (list of dismissals) of 1716, actually a final invoice itemizing services rendered from April to June 1716, which encloses a list of back payments for several musicians from March 1716, in D-Mhsa, Abt. III, Geheimes Hausarchiv, Korrespondenzakten 1155/1, fols. 129$^{r-v}$ and 131$^r$–132$^r$; facsimile available in Strahl, *Die Hofmusik Jan Wellems*, 135–7.

[4] Hermine Kühn-Steinhausen, 'Der Briefwechsel der Kurfürstin Anna Maria Luise von der Pfalz', *Düsseldorfer Jahrbuch*, 40 (1938), 15–256, at 171.

[5] D-DÜha, Jülich-Berg II, No. 2225; see also Gerhard Steffen, *Johann Hugo von Wilderer (1670 bis 1724), Kapellmeister am kurpfälzischen Hofe zu Düsseldorf und Mannheim*, Beiträge zur rheinischen Musikgeschichte, 40 (Cologne: Arno Volk, 1960), 93–4.

[6] D-Mbs, Cgm 1665, pp. 46–50.

market square had served as Elector Carl Philipp's interim quarters since 14 November 1720.[7]

Using only the sparse documentation which remains extant for this period, it is impossible to provide furnish a detailed reconstruction of the *Hofmusik*.[8] We can, however, be certain that lack of space would have prevented large-scale theatrical entertainments until 1742. In this respect, an evaluation of the few contemporary reports and extant librettos reveal that the *Hofmusik* was essentially restricted to concerts and sacred music. In particular, Carl Philipp's daughter, the music-loving Princess Elisabeth Auguste Sophie (1693–1728), frequently gave concerts in the afternoon.[9] Performances of short pastoral operas or serenatas containing congratulations and blessings on the occasion of birthdays and name days, or in homage to a distinguished guest, contributed further to the enrichment of the court's entertainment. Extant librettos also indicate performances, including oratorios, in Mannheim during Carl Philipp's reign (see Table 5.2, pp. 161–2 below).[10]

The premiere of the opera *Meride* by *Hofkapellmeister* Carlo Grua (actually Pietragrua) on 18 January 1742 was the first musically significant event to take place during the final year of reign of the ageing Elector Carl Philipp. This opera also marked the festive opening of the splendid new opera house built by Alessandro Galli da Bibiena (1686–1748) in the west wing of the Mannheim palace, which was inaugurated on the occasion of the double wedding of Carl Philipp's heir and greatnephew twice removed, Carl Theodor, and his granddaughter Elisabeth Augusta of Pfalz-Sulzbach (1721–1794), and that of her sister Maria Anna of Pfalz-Sulzbach (1722–1790) and Duke Clemens Franz of Bavaria (1722–1770). According to the extant libretto, Carl Philipp had obviously engaged guest artists for the two female lead roles in honour of the special occasion.[11] The role of the *prima donna* was performed by Rosa Pasquali from the Munich court opera, while the *seconda donna*, Rosa Gabrieli (d. 1783) from Bologna, eventually advanced to the position of first vocalist at the Mannheim *Hofoper*. The lead role was sung by the soprano castrato Mariano Lena (d. 1781), who became director of the *Hofmusik* in 1764. This festive opera *Meride*, the music for which is now lost, was repeated on 19 November 1742 for Princess Elisabeth Augusta's name day, despite freezing temperatures. After this

---

[7] Cf. Hermann Wiegand, '1716–42: Auf dem Weg zur Residenz unter Kurfürst Karl Philipp', in *Geschichte der Stadt Mannheim*, I, ed. Ulrich Nieß and Michael Caroli (Ubstadt-Weiher: Verlag Regionalkultur, 2007), 332–43, 346–71, at 340–42.

[8] Regarding *Hofmusik* during the reign of Carl Philipp, see also Friedrich Walter, *Geschichte des Theaters und der Musik am kurpfälzischen Hofe*, Forschungen zur Geschichte Mannheims und der Pfalz, I (Leipzig: Breitkopf & Härtel, 1898), 71–92.

[9] Karl Ludwig von Pöllnitz, *Des Freyherrn von Pöllnitz Neue Nachrichten welche seine Lebens-Geschichte und eine ausführliche Beschreibung von seinen ersten Reisen in sich enthalten, wie sie nach der neuesten Auflage aus dem Frantzösischen in das Hoch-Deutsche übersetzet worden*, part I (Frankfurt am Main, 1739), 570–71.

[10] Librettos held in D-MHrm and D-HEu; the music for these works is now lost. Cf. also the list provided in Walter, *Geschichte des Theaters und der Musik am kurpfälzischen Hofe*, 364.

[11] Librettos extant in US-Wc, ML 48 S 8167; D-W, Textb. 209 (in Italian); D-HEu, B 5054-1, *Palatina*, Sammelband III; and D-RT, Q 35, p. 315 (in German translation).

performance, Elector Carl Philipp became seriously ill.[12] He died at midnight on 31 December, at the age of eighty-one.

With the completion of the opera house, together with the court chapel and the courtly concert hall (the so-called 'Rittersaal'), Carl Philipp's young successor was provided from the outset with all the performance venues necessary for the comprehensive and ongoing cultivation of sacred and secular music in Mannheim.[13]

## THE *HOFKAPELLE* UNDER ELECTOR CARL THEODOR (1743–78)

Thanks to the generous support of Elector Carl Theodor, during his reign in Mannheim the *Hofmusik* developed into one of the leading musical ensembles in Europe. The elector himself, together with Friedrich II in Prussia, belonged among the ranks of the most musically well-educated rulers of the eighteenth century. Like Friedrich, Carl Theodor played the transverse flute, having initially taken lessons with Matthias Cannabich (*c.*1690–1773), and later with Johann Baptist Wendling (1723–1797), one of the best flute virtuosos of the time; in addition, the elector had played the violoncello since childhood. His participation as a soloist in musical academies (concerts at court) and in chamber music performances is referred to in contemporary reports.[14] Electress Elisabeth Augusta also possessed knowledge of music. From early childhood on, music and dance lessons were a normal part of the range of educational subjects that she enjoyed, chiefly at the summer residence of Schwetzingen, as was also the case for her two sisters, Maria Anna and Maria Franziska (1724–1794). Thus Elisabeth Augusta received harpsichord lessons from *Hofkapellmeister* Carlo Grua, as well as music lessons from the violoncellist Carlo Perroni (d. 1761) and the soprano castrato Mariano Lena.[15] Until 1769, the electress was also responsible for theatrical performances at court.[16]

---

[12] Andreas Felix von Oefele, 'Reisetagebuch', extant in D-MHsa, Kleine Erwerbungen 690.

[13] The opera house in the west wing of the palace was destroyed by the Austrian army in November 1795 and never rebuilt; an illustration of this venue is reproduced, among others, in Ferdinand Werner, *Die kurfürstliche Residenz zu Mannheim* (Worms: Wernersche Verlagsgesellschaft, 2006), 338–41. Despite having also suffered substantial damage during the Second World War, the baroque palace was reconstructed and restored, including the 'Rittersaal' in the *corp de logis* and the palace chapel (with different interior decoration) located in the west wing of the palace. For a 1758 city map of Mannheim, see Paul Corneilson, 'Reconstructing the Mannheim Court Theatre', *Early Music*, 25 (1997), 63–81, at 68.

[14] See, for example, the reports of the Dresden diplomats Christian Ludwig von Hagedorn and Andreas von Riaucour, in D-Dla, 10026 Geheimes Kabinett, Loc. 2621/1–6 (1745–8); Loc. 2622/1–5, 2623/1–5, 2624/1–6, 2625/1–4, 2626/ 1–4, 2627/1–3, 2628/1–5 (1748–78); Christian Friedrich Daniel Schubart, *Leben und Gesinnungen* (Stuttgart, 1791 and 1793; repr. Leipzig: VEB Deutscher Verlag für Musik, 1980), part I, p. 209.

[15] Supporting evidence is extant in D-KAg, 77/1658; D-Mhsa, Abt. III, Geheimes Hausarchiv, Korr. Akt 882 V b, fol. 112ᵛ; see also Walter, *Geschichte des Theaters und der Musik am kurpfälzischen Hofe*, 229; Stefan Mörz, *Die letzte Kurfürstin: Elisabeth Augusta von der Pfalz, die Gemahlin Karl Theodors* (Stuttgart: Kohlhammer, 1997), 18–22.

[16] Diplomatic reports of Count Riaucour (hereafter Riaucour file), letter from 13 January 1770 in D-Dla, 10026 Geheimes Kabinett, Loc. 2626/3, 1770.

## THE DEVELOPMENT OF THE *HOFKAPELLE*[17]

### *The Early Years (1743–46)*

During the early years of Elector Carl Theodor's reign, musical life at the court was only a shadow of its later self. This is remarkable considering the extraordinary love of music exhibited by the electoral couple. There were, for example, no performances at the opera house for almost six years, until Electress Elisabeth Augusta's birthday on 17 January 1748, when the opera *La clemenza di Tito* by Carlo Grua saw the recommencement of operatic productions.[18]

Nor did the court orchestra in these years have much in common with the legendary ensemble of the 1770s.[19] The young elector's musical knowledge and interest in music can be seen, however, in the first pioneering innovation he introduced, when as early as the summer of the first year of his reign, Carl Theodor named the 26-year-old violin virtuoso Johann Stamitz (1717–1757) as acting concertmaster.[20] It was not until Carl Offhuis' retirement, which dragged out until 1745, that Stamitz was listed officially in that capacity. According to the extant salary lists from 1744 and 1745, the court orchestra comprised between twenty-four and twenty-six musicians, divided into the following groups: two concertmasters, nine violinists, one to two violoncellists, one double bassist, four oboists, one bassoonist, four to five horn players, and two lutenists.[21] The configuration of the orchestra, which remained baroque in terms of its sound, cannot be described as numerically balanced, nor are all the instrumental sections fully represented: violoncello, double bass, and bassoon are only marginally filled, while violas and flutes are completely absent (at least officially), not to mention clarinets.

In 1746 the situation became even worse.[22] Including the two concertmasters, the membership of the orchestra had reached a historical low point in terms of

---

[17] Cf. Eugene K. Wolf, 'On the Composition of the Mannheim Orchestra, c.1740–78', *Baseler Jahrbuch für historische Musikpraxis*, 17 (1993), 113–38. The court calendars also list retired personnel, but the numbers provided in this chapter apply only to those musicians in active service, as calculated using information given in salary tables and personnel files for the years under consideration.

[18] Libretto in D-HEu, G 3077 Q, and D-MHrm, Mh 1737.

[19] The examination which follows in this chapter focuses on the significant development of the orchestra, with the vocal ensemble mirroring the demands of courtly musical life. The trumpeters and kettledrum players did not belong to the *Hofmusik* personnel, but rather to the staff of the court stables (the 'Obrist-Stallmeisterstab'; in modern German, *Oberstallmeisterstab* [Editors' note: the equivalent at the English court is led by the Master of the Horse]). In Mannheim, the latter comprised the equerries, page boys, dancing masters, Italian and French language teachers, fencing masters, carriage masters, horse trainers, grooms and stable boys, coachmen and fodder masters, as well as chamber and travel lackeys. These individuals will only be taken in consideration if they also played with the orchestra.

[20] D-Mhsa, Staatsverwaltung 910, 'Conferenz Protocolla' 1743, fol. 232.

[21] Salary lists from 1 January 1744 and 1745 are extant in D-KAg, 77/1648 (1744) and 77/1647 (1745).

[22] A list of court musicians dating from 1746 is extant in D-Mhsa, Abt. III, Geheimes Hausarchiv, Handschrift 206 II.

numbers, comprising only sixteen musicians. The nine violinists had been reduced to six, and instead of four horn players, there were now only two. From the earlier personnel of the Düsseldorf and Innsbruck *Hofkapellen* only two musicians (Georg Wenzel Ritschel and Matthias Cannabich) remained – thus, it becomes evident that the commonly-held belief that the famous Mannheim court orchestra resulted from the amalgamation of the Düsseldorf and Innsbruck *Hofkapellen* does not correspond with the facts. Regarding the composition of the up-to-date orchestra which developed in the years that followed, it is particularly noteworthy that lutes were absent for the first time. Moreover, the engagement of the highly gifted Christian Cannabich (1731–1798), a pupil of Stamitz who had entered the orchestra as a student in 1744 and now received a permanent position, marks a key turning point on the ensemble's path to becoming an orchestra of virtuosos.

The drastic reduction in the *Hofkapelle*'s personnel in 1746 may have been a result of the imminent relocation of the court to Düsseldorf. Initially, Carl Theodor found it difficult to settle in Mannheim, favouring instead his duchy of Jülich and Berg and the splendid court of Cologne, which was nearby. In September 1746, therefore, the elector ordered the departure for Düsseldorf, where life was filled with theatrical performances, masquerades, court balls, and the extremely popular *parforce* hunting.[23] However, an event that took place on 31 August 1747 was almost certainly a decisive influence on the subsequent resolution to return to Mannheim. According to reports of the Dresden diplomat Christian Ludwig von Hagedorn (1712–1780), the ceiling of the elector's private chamber (*Kabinett*) collapsed – at exactly the spot where the elector usually practised the cello.[24] After this experience, Carl Theodor surrendered to the strong insistence of Electress Elisabeth Augusta and, at the end of September 1747, ordered the move back to Mannheim.

## *The New Mannheim Hofkapelle (1747–78)*

In Mannheim, during the autumn of that same year, the printing of the new *Chur-Pfältzischer Hoff- und Staats-Calender* commenced with the calendar for 1748.[25]

[23] Reports of the Dresden diplomat Christian Ludwig von Hagedorn in D-Dla, 10026 Geheimes Kabinett, Loc. 2621/3–5 (1746–7).

[24] D-Dla, 10026 Geheimes Kabinett, Loc. 2621/5. Report of Hagedorn dated 1 September 1747.

[25] The *Chur-Pfältzischer Hoff- und Staats-Calender auff das Jahr . . .*, Mannheim, gedruckt in der Churfürstl. Hoff-Buchdruckerey (and its French version, *Almanach Electoral Palatin pour l'Année . . .*) covered the years 1750–77. Calendars pertaining to 1748–52 and 1754–78 (1753 is no longer extant) are housed in D-MHrm, D-Heu, and D-MHu, while the *Almanachs* for 1759, 1770, and 1771 are in D-Mbs. Copies are also held at the Forschungsstelle Südwestdeutsche Hofmusik (Heidelberg). An overview of the institutions that possess copies of these calendars is provided in Volker Bauer, *Repertorium territorialer Amtskalender und Amtsbücher im Alten Reich*, III: *Der Westen und Südwesten*, Studien zur europäischen Rechtsgeschichte, 147 (Frankfurt am Main: Vittorio Klostermann, 2002), 455–84; see also Heinz E. Veitenheimer, *Druckort Mannheim: Mannheimer Verleger und ihre Drucke von 1608 bis 1803* (Frankfurt am Main: Peter Lang, 1996).

Through the creation of this official publication Carl Theodor ensured the dissemination of detailed information on an annual basis regarding the electorate's court and state agencies, including the relevant ceremonial protocols, timing, and locations of court festivities, as well as the names of all members of the courtly household.

The institutionalization of the court signalled by this new court calendar also marked a new beginning for the *Hofmusik*. To begin with, the skeleton-like ensemble needed to be transformed into a fully functional orchestra. This task was entrusted primarily to concertmaster Johann Stamitz. He came up with a simple, quick, and effective solution that, while not necessarily concerned with quality, was certainly good value for money. Trumpeters and kettledrum players from the 'Obrist-Stallmeisterstab' were commanded to serve with the orchestra.[26] This strategic move resulted in the sudden increase of violinists from six to eleven, plus three additional cellos. Moreover, the violas and the woodwinds were now doubled, with the transverse flutes and oboes divided for the first time (see Table 5.1).[27] With the exception of the clarinets, which were still absent, all instrumental sections were now represented.

From this time on, this was to be the structure to which the orchestra would adhere. In this context, the appointment of oboist Alexander Lebrun (d. *c.*1770) is particularly noteworthy, as it revealed the strategy employed from the very beginning in order to expand the orchestra: the leading positions within the instrumental sections were given to musicians whose skills ranged from good to excellent. Initially, it was necessary to recruit virtuosos from outside Mannheim, for example, Jean Nicolas Heroux, Innocenz Danzi, Anton Fils, and the brothers Johann Baptist and Franz Wendling. But subsequently, at least since the middle of the 1760s – with the second generation of students – the best musicians from Mannheim's own orchestral school succeeded them, including the violinists Wilhelm Cramer, Carl and Anton Stamitz, and the oboists Friedrich Ramm and Ludwig August Lebrun.[28] At first, the latter had been accepted on probation, as was the case with the vocalists (for example, Franziska Danzi and Vincenzo Caselli). The violin section included string-playing trumpeters and kettledrummers, several ageing violinists from an earlier generation (Georg Wenzel Ritschel, Jacob Friedel, and Domenico Basconi), and young, newly appointed musicians who still needed to be trained in ensemble playing (for example, Johann Daniel Eyttner, Johannes Bittner, Nicolas Lerch, and Heinrich Ritter). That this was no dream ensemble for

[26] The certificate of apprenticeship for the trumpeter Franz Anton Brunner, dated 29 May 1749, contains all the signatures and sigla of the trumpeters and kettledrum players; see D-MHrm, MAV U/G 150. A list of the latter for the year 1746 is extant in D-Mhsa, Abt. III, Geheimes Hausarchiv, Handschrift 206 II. For a definition of the 'Obrist-Stallmeisterstab', see n. 19 above.

[27] *Chur-Pfältzischer Hoff- und Staats-Calender* (1748), 24–6. Note that since the court calendar was prepared the year prior to publication, it provides information current in 1747.

[28] Bärbel Pelker, 'Mannheimer Schule', in *Die Musik in Geschichte und Gegenwart: allgemeine Enzyklopädie der Musik*, 2nd rev. edn, 17 vols. (Kassel: Bärenreiter, 1994–2008; hereafter *MGG* 2), Sachteil, V: 1655–6.

an orchestral director – in particular a virtuoso of Johann Stamitz's stature – is obvious. Perhaps in recognition of his services, but certainly as an incentive not to lessen his zeal, Elector Carl Theodor appointed Stamitz the *Hofmusik*'s director of instrumental music on 27 February 1750.[29]

This had virtually no impact upon the state of the violin section between 1747 and 1753, with the sole exception occurring in 1750, when the violinist Carlo Giuseppe Toeschi (1731–1788) joined the orchestra, the second of Stamitz's students to do so. The reasons behind this stagnation are not known.

Two fundamental changes in the court's musical life occurred in 1753. On the one hand, a second opera stage had been erected at the summer residence of Schwetzingen, thus necessitating an increase in the number of singers employed, while also enriching the court's operatic repertoire with comic operas. On the other hand, for the first time (and from then on) the musical academies were integrated into the sequence of name-day celebrations for the electoral couple in November and during Carnival season. This resulted in an increased demand for newly composed works, in particular sinfonias and concertos, and necessitated the engagement of a second *Kapellmeister*, thereby relieving Stamitz, who had served in this office from 1751 to 1753 – to consider the move in a positive light. In the summer of 1753, the *Vicekapellmeister* position was given to the Viennese composer Ignaz Holzbauer (1711–1783), after he had distinguished himself with the successful premiere of his opera *Il figlio delle selve* in Schwetzingen for Princess Maria Franziska of Pfalz-Sulzbach's birthday on 15 June.[30] With the appointment of the 41-year-old Holzbauer, the elector had engaged a comprehensively educated artiste who could not only recite Horace from memory, but also was fluent in several languages, in addition to having studied the keyboard, violin, violoncello, and singing, as was customary. Holzbauer's early career at the Mannheim court can only be called brilliant. His newly composed operas dominated the repertoire performed during the 1750s, as did his large-scale oratorios for Good Friday.[31] Christian Friedrich Daniel Schubart thus considered Holzbauer, who according to his appointment decree was responsible for all matters pertaining to music, the person who had contributed 'das meiste zur Vollkommenheit dieses grossen Orchesters' (the most toward the perfection of this great orchestra).[32]

An examination of the court calendars indicates that, given the division of labour with Stamitz, Holzbauer's approach to expanding the ensemble up until 1758

[29] Appointment decree for Johann Stamitz as director of instrumental music, dated 27 February 1750, in D-Mhsa, Pers. Sel. Urk. Stamitz 1750 Feb. 27, Cart. 420.

[30] Riaucour file, in D-Dla, 10026 Geheimes Kabinett, Loc. 2623/2 (1753), Letter No. 7.

[31] On the life and works of Holzbauer see also Bärbel Pelker, 'Holzbauer, Ignaz (Jakob)', in *MGG* 2, Personenteil, IX: 265–75; Pelker, ed., *Ignaz Holzbauer: Günther von Schwarzburg*, 2 vols., Quellen zur Musikgeschichte in Baden-Württemberg: Kommentierte Faksimile-Ausgaben, 1 (Munich: Strube, 2000); Deanna D. Bush, 'The Orchestral Masses of Ignaz Holzbauer (1711–1783): Authenticity, Chronology, and Style with Thematic Catalogue and Selected Transcriptions' (PhD diss., University of Rochester, 1982).

[32] Christian Friedrich Daniel Schubart, *Ideen zu einer Ästhetik der Tonkunst* (Vienna: Degen, 1806; 2nd repr., ed. Fritz and Margrit Kaiser, Hildesheim and New York: Olms, 1990), 131. Holzbauer's appointment decree is extant in D-KAg, 77/1656.

did not focus initially on the violins but concentrated instead on the other sections of the orchestra.[33] This is evident, for example, in the increase in woodwind players in 1753, which now included three oboists, three bassoonists, and four flautists. The systematic expansion of the entire *Hofkapelle* also involved the appointment of four new singers, predominantly from Italy. As a result, the woodwind and vocal sections were now not only sufficient to carry out all the large-scale tasks associated with the court's musical life, but were filled once more to an excellent standard thanks to the engagement of highly-qualified musicians such as the flute virtuoso Johann Baptist Wendling and his wife, the soprano Dorothea Wendling (1736–1811). These virtuosos remained at the court and – in what can be considered an exceptionally fortunate circumstance – they also taught. Dorothea Wendling probably trained most of the Mannheim sopranos, as a result of which Felix Joseph Lipowsky referred to a 'Wendling-Schule'.[34]

By 1753, the strings ranked as the worst group in terms of overall quality. For them to become an orchestra of virtuosos, significant improvements were necessary, and these took place between 1754 and 1756. Stamitz's active contribution to the changes made during this phase of expansion must, however, be regarded as relatively minor, as he spent the period between August 1754 and autumn 1755 (that is over a year) in Paris. That Stamitz was permitted to be absent for such a lengthy interlude, indicates – at least according to the terms of the court's strict employment code – either that his presence was not required or that a substitute was in place. Officially, this meant that there were now only two individuals in charge of the violin section: *Kapellmeister* Holzbauer, who as the director of the orchestra was also responsible for new appointments, and concertmaster Alessandro Toeschi (before 1700–1758). Moreover, according to their salaries – which at the Mannheim court reflected a strictly hierarchical and achievement-oriented approach – Carlo Giuseppe Toeschi, Ignaz Fränzl (1736–1811), Jean Nicolas Heroux (1720–1769), and Franz Wendling (1733–1786) may well have assisted occasionally. Such teamwork would become an important part of the educational system employed by the 'Mannheim School' in the years to come.

The crucial turning point on the way to becoming a modern, efficient orchestra occurred in 1758, a year after Stamitz's death: Cannabich (violin 1) and Toeschi (violin 2), both students of Stamitz, now shared the position of concertmaster, while the violin section was comprised primarily of young musicians from the Mannheim orchestral school. The leading positions in each instrumental section were held by specialists on that instrument. In that same year, the court had also hired Georg Zarth (Čart or Czarth; 1708–1779/80), a further excellent violin virtuoso and violin teacher. Two clarinettists, Michael Quallenberg (c.1726–1786) and Johannes Hampel, were now officially included in the list of musicians for the first time.[35] Thus, the creation of the legendary court orchestra was now finally

[33] See the section 'Hof-Music' in the *Chur-Pfältzischer Hoff- und Staats-Calender* (1754–9).

[34] Felix Joseph Lipowsky, *Baierisches Musik-Lexikon* (Munich: Jacob Giel, 1811; repr. Hildesheim and New York: Olms, 1982), 386.

[35] A petition for gala uniforms made by the two court clarinettists, dated 6 October 1757 (D-KAg, 61/8744), implies that they were appointed that year and thus should have been

complete (see also Table 5.1, 1760). In the summer of 1763, Leopold Mozart became acquainted with this young orchestra in Schwetzingen and characterized it as follows:

> das Orchester ist ohne widerspruch das beste in Teutschland, und lauter junge Leute, und durch aus Leute von guter Lebensart, weder Säufer, weder Spieler, weder liederliche Lumpen; so, daß so wohl ihre Conduite als ihre production hochzuschätzen ist.

> the orchestra is, without doubt, the best in Germany, and [composed] entirely of people who are young and lead decent lives, are neither drunks, nor gamblers, nor slovenly rascals; hence, their conduct as well as their performance must be rated very highly.[36]

According to the court calendars, the Mannheim *Hofkapelle* continued to expand over the course of the following two decades. In 1762, the ensemble numbered more than seventy members, and in 1770, comprised more than eighty court musicians. The highest membership was reached in 1773 and 1774 with eighty-nine salaried musicians, after which the number levelled off at seventy-five. The ensemble thus was one of the largest *Hofkapellen* anywhere in Europe during the eighteenth century — making size an important characteristic of the Mannheim *Hofkapelle*.

A second major characteristic, which was frequently praised by contemporaries, was the orchestra's performance culture, often perceived as sensational.[37] As in any orchestra, this was an achievement for which the orchestra's director deserves credit above all. In Mannheim, Carl Theodor had put two top orchestral trainers in charge: Stamitz and, most importantly, Cannabich, who, according to Wolfgang Amadeus Mozart, was the best director 'den er je gesehen' (he had ever seen).[38] Indeed, from 1758, Cannabich in particular distinguished himself as an inspired orchestral leader. According to Schubart, a 'Nicken des Kopfes' (nod of the head) and a 'Zucken des Ellenbogens' (twitch of the elbow), were enough to ensure the

---

mentioned in the 1758 court calendar, although this was not the case. As a rule, clarinets found a permanent home in other *Hofkapellen* only during the last quarter of the eighteenth century, above all during the 1780s; however, they were still not employed in Stuttgart in 1789, and it was not until 1797 that they were used in Dresden on a regular basis. Cf. Ottmar Schreiber, *Orchester und Orchesterpraxis in Deutschland zwischen 1780 und 1850* (Berlin: Junker and Dünnhaupt, 1938; reprint Hildesheim and New York: Olms, 1978), 133–4.

[36] Letter from Schwetzingen dated 19 July 1763, in *Mozart: Briefe und Aufzeichnungen*, complete edn, ed. Internationale Stiftung Mozarteum Salzburg, collected by Wilhelm A. Bauer and Otto Erich Deutsch, commentary by Joseph Heinz Eibl (Kassel: Bärenreiter, 1962), I: 79, Letter No. 56.

[37] Cf. e.g. Friedrich Nicolai, *Beschreibung einer Reise durch Deutschland und die Schweiz im Jahre 1781*, VI (Berlin and Stettin, 1785), 702–3; Schubart, *Ideen zu einer Ästhetik der Tonkunst*, 130–31; Lorenz von Westenrieder, 'Von dem Zustand der Musik in Muenchen', *Jahrbuch der Menschengeschichte in Bayern*, 1/2 (1783), 366–80, at 377.

[38] Letter from Paris dated 9 July 1778, in *Mozart: Briefe und Aufzeichnungen*, II: 395, Letter No. 462.

precise performance of a composition.[39] Cannabich trained his 'Soldaten' (soldiers) in the perfect execution of works and the exquisite performance of frequent dynamic contrasts within a very short space of time, to the point that these were cultivated as a unique style.[40] In recognition of his services, Carl Theodor promoted Cannabich to director of instrumental music in 1773.[41]

In retrospect, also beneficial to this precise musical execution was the fact that entire families, if not dynasties of instrumentalists, singers, and composers, including the Cannabich, Cramer, Danzi, Fränzl, Grua, Lang, Lebrun, Ritschel, Ritter, Stamitz, Toeschi, Wendling, and Ziwny families remained with the *Hofkapelle* over several decades. Numerous friendships and family ties among the court musicians are documented, further strengthening the impression of close relationships.[42] This strong sense of community was yet another important reason for the extraordinary musical prowess of the court orchestra. Moreover, the above-mentioned strategy of recruiting virtuosos who were specialists on their instruments for leading positions, laid the foundation for this exemplary performance culture right from the start of 1747. After all, these top quality performers remained in Mannheim and passed on their knowledge to talented students, usually for more than a quarter of a century. Thus, Cannabich's strict orchestral discipline, the lengthy periods of service, the use of the same training methods in the so-called 'Mannheim School', as well as the musicians' specialization on only one instrument together with the associated emphasis on the quality of playing and technical virtuosity, are ultimately the secret of the exceptional performance culture of the Mannheim court orchestra.

The education of the younger musicians occurred during the expansion phase described above. Supervised first by Johann Stamitz from 1747, and then by Ignaz Holzbauer from 1753 until 1760, they included:[43] the violinists Christian Cannabich, Wilhelm Cramer (1746–1799), Ignaz Fränzl, Ferdinand Götz (1737–1763), Arnold Mayer,[44] Georg Ritschel (1744–1805), Johannes Ritschel (1739–1766), Jacob Ritter,[45] Sigismund Strauss (1740–1775), Carlo Giuseppe Toeschi, Johannes Toeschi (1735–1800), the double bassist Johann Wendelin Schäffer (d. 1769), the oboist Friedrich Ramm (1745–1813), and the bassoonist Sebastian Holtzbauer (1736–1800).

The training provided by the 'Mannheim School' also included composition lessons, which resulted in Mannheim boasting the highest number of composers and virtuosos within a court orchestra throughout the whole of Europe. Not only did

---

[39] Schubart, *Ideen zu einer Ästhetik der Tonkunst*, 137.

[40] The reference to soldiers is W. A. Mozart's; see letter cited in n. 38 above.

[41] *Chur-Pfältzischer Hoff- und Staats-Kalender* (1774), 49.

[42] Baptismal and wedding records are extant in Mannheim, Katholisches Kirchenbuchamt. These indicate that the Wendling, Toeschi, and Holzbauer families were close friends, as were the Richter and Ziwny families.

[43] A detailed examination is provided in Pelker, 'Mannheimer Schule', 1645–62.

[44] Mayer received an allowance towards his tuition fees ('Lehrgeld'); see D-KAg, 61/8744a.

[45] A son of the bassoonist Heinrich Adam Ritter, he was 'Accessist' (expectant) until 1760; see D-KAg, 77/1657.

the *Kapellmeister* and concertmasters in Mannheim compose, but also the regular court musicians. Between 1747 and 1760, this 'army of generals'[46] included Christian Cannabich, Wilhelm Cramer, Georg Zarth, Innocenz Danzi (*c.*1730–1798), Anton Fils (1733–1760), Ignaz Fränzl, Carlo Grua, Ignaz Holzbauer, Friedrich Ramm, Franz Xaver Richter (1709–1789), Georg and Johannes Ritschel, Johann Stamitz, the Toeschi family, and Johann Baptist Wendling.[47] This dual function – composer and performing musician – is a third important characteristic of the Mannheim *Hofkapelle* and explains, according to Ludwig Finscher, 'the dual significance of Carl Theodor's *Hofkapelle* – for the history of the orchestra and for the history of the symphony.'[48] Charles Burney had also associated this distinct feature of the court orchestra with the new style of the Mannheim concert symphony. He praised it above all for its 'variety, taste, spirit, and new effects produced by contrast and the use of *crescendo* and *diminuendo*', noting,

> At the court of Manheim [*sic*], about the year 1759, the band of the Elector Palatine was regarded as the most complete and best disciplined in Europe; and the symphonies that were produced by the maestro di capella, Holtzbaur, the elder Stamitz, Filtz, Cannabich, Toeski, and Fräntzel, became the favourite full-pieces of every concert, and supplanted concertos and opera overtures, being more spirited than the one, and more solid than the other. Though these symphonies seemed at first to be little more than an improvement of the opera overtures of Jomelli, yet, by the fire and genius of Stamitz, they were exalted into a new species of composition.[49]

This assessment continues to hold true today.[50]

[46] Charles Burney heard the Mannheim *Hofkapelle* in Schwetzingen in 1772 and described it as follows: 'I cannot quit this article, without doing justice to the orchestra of his electoral highness, so deservedly celebrated throughout Europe. . . . indeed there are more solo players, and good composers in this, than perhaps in any other orchestra in Europe; it is an army of generals, equally fit to plan a battle, as to fight it.' See Burney, *The Present State of Music in Germany, The Netherlands and United Provinces* (London, 1775; facs. repr., New York: Broude Brothers, 1969), 94–5.

[47] Additional secondary literature on the above-mentioned musicians is available at <www.hof-musik.de>, under 'Publikationen'.

[48] Ludwig Finscher, 'Mannheimer Orchester- und Kammermusik', in *Die Mannheimer Hofkapelle im Zeitalter Carl Theodors*, ed. Ludwig Finscher (Mannheim: Palatium Verlag and J&J Verlag, 1992), 141–76, at 144.

[49] Charles Burney, *A General History of Music from the Earliest Ages to the Present Period*, IV (London, 1789), 582.

[50] On the Mannheim symphony, see also Joachim Veit, 'Zur Entstehung des klassischen und romantischen Orchesters in Mannheim', in *Die Mannheimer Hofkapelle im Zeitalter Carl Theodors*, 177–95; Eugene K. Wolf, 'On the Origins of the Mannheim Symphonic Style', in *Studies in Musicology in Honor of Otto E. Albrecht*, ed. J. W. Hill (Kassel: Bärenreiter, 1980), 197–239; and Wolf, *The Symphonies of Johann Stamitz: A Study in the Formation of the Classic Style* (Utrecht: Bohn, Scheltema, & Holkema, 1981).

## THE ORGANIZATION OF THE *HOFMUSIK*[51]

### *Hierarchy*

To ensure that musical performances at the court ran smoothly, a set of strict regulations described the tasks and duties of *Hofkapelle* members, which, according to extant court documents, were clearly defined when musicians in leading positions were first appointed. The resulting well-defined areas of responsibility were based on a clear hierarchical order among the *Hofmusik* personnel. Until 1760, these comprised administrators (artistic director, court poet, and secretary), court music positions (two *Kapellmeister*, two concertmasters, two organists, male and female vocalists, and orchestral musicians), as well as copyists, *Calcanten*, and instrument makers.

### *Areas of Responsibility and Duties of the Court Musicians*

The tasks to be carried out were diverse and numerous, corresponding to the rich musical life at court, which kept the musicians busy primarily during the winter season from November until the end of Carnival. In addition to playing for large-scale musical events such as operas, plays with ballet, and concerts, the participation of the *Hofmusik* was required for performances of chamber and sacred music, as well as for *parforce* hunts, court balls, *Tafelmusiken*, and entertainment evenings (*Apartements*).[52]

The areas of responsibility for each office holder were considerable. According to the 1753 appointment decree of *Kapellmeister* Holzbauer, his duties comprised the composition, rehearsal, and direction of sacred music and, above all, of musico-dramatic works, as well as the specific task of providing the sole direction and organization of the orchestra.[53] The director of instrumental music did not just lead the first violin section during operas and the first symphony performed in court concerts, but was also responsible for all other instrument-related matters. These included the preparation of the orchestra's duty roster (which was not to overlap with vocal rehearsals), the purchase and repair of instruments, and the availability of supplies such as rosin and strings. The concertmaster led the second violin section during operas and in arias performed at court concerts; however, for solo concertos he directed from the first violin seat.[54]

As a rule, the allocation of musicians to executive positions was made with

---

[51] Cf. Roland Würtz, 'Die Organisation der Mannheimer Hofkapelle', in *Die Mannheimer Hofkapelle im Zeitalter Carl Theodors*, 37–48.

[52] In this context, *Apartement* refers to the French model of a court entertainment, accompanied by music and gambling.

[53] Appointment decree from 26 July 1753, D-KAg, 77/1656.

[54] Cf. also Georg Joseph Vogler, [ed.], 'Instrumentalmusik-Director', in *Deutsche Encyclopädie, oder Allgemeines Real-Wörterbuch aller Künste und Wissenschaften*, 23 vols. (Frankfurt am Main: Varrentrapp Sohn & Wenner, 1793), XVII: 657.

achievement-oriented criteria in mind.[55] While these appointments were certainly an acknowledgement of services rendered, the court typically failed to express its appreciation of past achievements. Rather, a promotion was understood as an unambiguous order to continue to fulfil one's duty to the best of one's abilities. In 1750 we read, for example, in Johann Stamitz's commission as director that

> die ihme anvertraute Directoren Stelle, seinem besten Verstandt und Wißenschafft nach, vertretten, forth im übrigen dasjenige in acht nehmen und Verrichten solle, was einem getrewen, aufrichtigen und fleißigen Instrumental-Music Directoren pflichten und amts halber, Zu Thuen obliget.

> the position of director to which he has been appointed, requires his best efforts in terms of intelligence and knowledge, and that from now on he is to ensure that he shall undertake what is officially required from a faithful, sincere, and diligent director of instrumental music.[56]

Office holders were not only required to perform music, as is evident from the appointment decree for Holzbauer, for instance, but were also ordered by the elector to contribute their own compositions to the *Hofmusik* repertoire. That strict regulations regarding position and oeuvre were in effect at the Mannheim court was illustrated by the extant works of court musicians. Only a *Hofkapellmeister* (Carlo Grua, Holzbauer, Johannes Ritschel, and Georg Joseph Vogler) was permitted to compose in all musical genres, but with a clear focus on vocal music (operas, passion settings for Good Friday, masses, cantatas, and motets). The directors of instrumental music (Johann Stamitz and Christian Cannabich) and the concertmasters (Carl Offhuis and Ignaz Fränzl, as well as Alessandro, Carlo Giuseppe, and Johannes Toeschi) were required to compose in all instrumental genres, with symphonies and ballet productions being of central importance. As a rule, the remaining members of the orchestra wrote music for their own instruments without being specifically asked to do so (solo concertos or chamber music works).[57]

[55] This can be seen in the distribution of the gratuities paid for additional services; see also the section on social structure in the present chapter.

[56] Appointment decree of Johann Stamitz, D-Mhsa, Pers. Sel. Urk. Stamitz 1750 Feb. 27, Cart. 420.

[57] Additional secondary literature on the musicians and their works, including editions of a selection of the latter, is available at <www.hof-musik.de>. For editions of vocal music, see, for example, *Ignaz Holzbauer: Günther von Schwarzburg, Oper in drei Akten*, ed. Hermann Kretzschmar, Denkmäler deutscher Tonkunst, 1st ser. 8–9 (Leipzig: Breitkopf & Härtel, 1902); *Gian Francesco de Majo: Ifigenia in Tauride*, ed. Paul Corneilson, Recent Researches in the Music of the Classical Era, 46 (Madison, Wisc.: A-R Editions, 1996); *Kirchenmusik der Mannheimer Schule*, ed. Eduard Schmitt, Denkmäler der Tonkunst in Bayern (hereafter DTB), new ser. 2–3 (Wiesbaden: Breitkopf & Härtel, 1980–82). Editions of sinfonias are included in *Mannheim Symphonists: A Collection of Twenty-four Orchestral Works*, ed. Hugo Riemann, 2 vols. (New York: Broude Brothers, 1956; repr. of DTB III/1, VII/2, and VIII/2); five sinfonias by Christian Cannabich are available in DTB, new ser. 11, ed. Stephan Hörner (Wiesbaden: Breitkopf & Härtel, 1996). See also *The Symphony 1720–1840*, ed. Barry S. Brook, Ser. C, III, IV, XI, XIV (New York and London: Garland, 1982–5); *Mannheimer Kammermusik des 18. Jahrhunderts*, ed. Hugo Riemann, DTB, old ser. 15–16; *Die Flötenkonzerte der Mannheimer Schule*, ed.

## THE STRUCTURE OF COURTLY MUSICAL LIFE[58]

### *Sacred Music*

Regarding the performance of sacred music at this Catholic court, the Mannheim *Hofcalender* (extant from 1748) provide evidence of a clear and stable structure regulated by the church year and other festive occasions.[59] Accordingly, on all Sundays and feast days, a 'Musicalische[s] hohe[s] Ambt' (a musical setting of the ordinary) followed the sermon; in the evening, both before and after the benediction, the 'Lauretanische Litaney [wurde] ebenfals musicalisch abgesungen' (a musical setting of the Litany of Loreto [in honour of the Virgin Mary] was also sung).[60] A local Mannheim phenomenon is illustrated, for example, in settings of the mass by Carlo Grua and Ignaz Holzbauer, which always omit the *Benedictus* – in its stead, the organ was played.[61] On high feast days, such as the birthdays and name days of the electoral couple, the high mass was celebrated in a particularly festive manner: according to descriptions in the court calendars, a sung *Te Deum* replaced the organ music usually played after the elevation. Moreover, on these important occasions, the *Gloria*, the *Te Deum*, and the last benediction were all accompanied by canon shots fired from the ramparts.

Interestingly, a hierarchy can be identified among certain feast days. Besides the above-mentioned festive worship services, Holy Week was the most important and extensive liturgical event at court. All members of the courtly household, dressed in mourning clothes, were required to take part, with the attendant ceremonial detailed in the court calendars on an annual basis. The Good Friday oratorio, undoubtedly one of the musical highlights, was performed around either eight

Walter Lebermann (Wiesbaden: Breitkopf & Härtel, 1964); and the Artaria editions, ed. Allan Badley, <www.artaria.com>. See also the series *Ballet Music from the Mannheim Court*, ed. Paul Corneilson and Eugene K. Wolf, Recent Researches in the Music of the Classical Era (Madison, Wisc.: A-R Editions, 1996–8).

[58] For a more detailed examination, see Bärbel Pelker, 'Zur Struktur des Musiklebens am Hof Carl Theodors in Mannheim', in *Mozart und Mannheim: Kongreßbericht Mannheim 1991*, ed. Ludwig Finscher, Bärbel Pelker, and Jochen Reutter, Quellen und Studien zur Geschichte der Mannheimer Hofkapelle, 2 (Frankfurt am Main: Peter Lang, 1994), 29–40.

[59] See Eduard Schmitt, 'Die Kurpfälzische Kirchenmusik im 18. Jahrhundert' (PhD diss., Universität Heidelberg, 1958); Jochen Reutter, 'Die Kirchenmusik am Mannheimer Hof', in *Die Mannheimer Hofkapelle im Zeitalter Carl Theodors*, 97–112; Johannes Theil, . . . *unter Abfeuerung der Kanonen: Gottesdienste, Kirchenfeste und Kirchenmusik in der Mannheimer Hofkapelle nach dem Kurpfälzischen Hof- und Staatskalender* (Norderstedt: Books on Demand, 2008).

[60] *Chur-Pfältzischer Hoff- und Staats-Calender* (1749), 'Anmerckungen', fol. A 2ʳ. The references to 'musicalisch abgesungen' and 'das Musicalische hohe Ambt' appear to indicate the performance of concerted church compositions – including repertoire that is no longer extant – that would have required the participation of vocalists and instrumentalists of the *Hofmusik*.

[61] Cf. the edition of a mass by Carlo Grua and the thematic catalogue of sacred music composed by Mannheim court musicians in the eighteenth century in Schmitt, ed., *Kirchenmusik der Mannheimer Schule*; Jochen Reutter, ed., *Ignaz Holzbauer: Missa in C* (Stuttgart: Carus, 1995).

or nine o'clock at night, in a large-scale setting (with vocal soloists, chorus, and orchestra). The extraordinary significance of this performance is illustrated by the text booklets printed specifically for these occasions, as well as the fact that the title and the composer were included in relevant archival documents.[62] That was generally not the case for regular performances of sacred music.[63]

Three feast days – Epiphany (6 January), Easter Sunday, and Christmas Day – were specially emphasized in Mannheim through a second musical worship service, Vespers, in addition to the high mass that featured a musical setting of the ordinary. On 31 December, the entire court household attended a celebratory worship service including a performance of a festive *Te Deum*. Afternoon church services that featured music (above all devotions and litanies) were abolished altogether during the second half of the 1750s, a move that had a significant and lasting impact on the sacred music repertoire. The only works now required were in the following genres: *Missa solemnis* (customarily with trumpets and kettledrums), *Missa brevis*, *Te Deum*, oratorio, compositions for Tenebrae, *Miserere*, and instrumental music (including pastoral symphonies). Worship services at court took place in the palace chapel; the Jesuit Church was referred to as the *Hofkirche* (court church) in the calendars, and, for the most part, it was reserved for use by the order.[64]

## Secular Music

It is much more difficult to describe the structure of the annual theatrical and concert performances at the Mannheim court, because the numerous visits of important guests and the extraordinary efforts made by the court with regard to representative displays of splendour on such occasions made it impossible to maintain a regular schedule of events. The court calendars provide a framework for the festive calendar of birthday and name-day celebrations of the princely family, as well as for the Carnival season. Between 1748 and 1762, there were eight official court celebrations. Besides the large-scale gala days in honour of the electoral couple, the court also commemorated, albeit on a lesser scale, the name days and birthdays of Prince Friedrich Michael of Zweibrücken (1724–1767) and his wife, Princess Maria Franziska, with a smaller gala, including the performance of either a ballet-pantomime or a French play. From 1763 onward, the number of feast days began to be reduced, until only the two name-day celebrations of the electoral

[62] Riaucour file 1748–78; Traitteur file, D-Mhsa, Abt. III, Geheimes Hausarchiv, Korr. Akt 882 V b; and the diaries of Freiherr von Beckers from 1770, 1775, 1776, and 1777, D-Mhsa, Kasten blau 1/57 und Kasten blau 433/7½.

[63] A list of oratorio performances is given, for example, in Karl Böhmer, 'Das Oratorium *Gioas, re di Giuda* in den Vertonungen von Johannes Ritschel (Mannheim 1763) und Pompeo Sales (Koblenz 1781)', in *Mannheim: Ein Paradies der Tonkünstler? Kongressbericht Mannheim 1999*, ed. Ludwig Finscher, Bärbel Pelker, and Rüdiger Thomsen-Fürst, Quellen und Studien zur Geschichte der Mannheimer Hofkapelle, 8 (Frankfurt am Main: Peter Lang, 2002), 227–51, at 250.

[64] The 'Reglement' mandated that the court attend the Jesuit church only twice a year: on Shrove Tuesday and on the anniversary of the church's consecration in October. Both churches, the chapel at the palace and the Jesuit church, were rebuilt after the Second World War.

couple, on 4 and 19 November, respectively, remained. The ceremonial protocol ordered a 'grosse Galla bey Hof' (a large-scale gala at court) on those days. In addition to the festive worship service mentioned above, a public *Tafel* was held as well, 'zu welcher die Churfürstl. Cammer-Herrn die Speisen tragen' (for which the electoral gentlemen-in-waiting served the food).[65] Up until 1756, a large-scale operatic performance took place on such days, at around five o'clock in the afternoon; from 1757, the first day of celebration concluded with a 'grand Apartement'. The opera became the central event of the following day. With this regulation, an additional fourth day of celebration was created, since the 'Gala-Akademie' (a large-scale concert at court that lasted up to four hours) and the 'Gala-Komödie' (a French play with ballet) gave a festive character to the two days that followed. However, reducing the courtly gala festivities to the two name days also meant a simultaneous increase in the celebrations, given that a second opera was now performed.

A second temporal constant in the court's musical life came with the Carnival season. The weekly Carnival entertainments at court, which usually began on 6 January, included (initially at least) a 'grand Apartement', two masked balls, and a play and an opera on Sunday – although an exception was made on major Carnival days, when the opera was moved to the Monday, framed by masked balls given on the two days each side. Until 1752, the opera for the electress's birthday (17 January) was also designated as the annual Carnival opera and then, from 1753 on, the festive opera performed for the elector's name day (4 November) was repeated as the opera for the Carnival which followed. Throughout the electoral reign in Mannheim, masked balls and operas appeared on an annual basis during Carnival season. In 1753, the musical academy was added to these for the first time and continued to be included, in contrast to the 'grand Apartement' which was dropped during the second half of the 1750s. The definitive Carnival schedule was printed every year in the *Mannheimer Zeitung* and small printed flyers were distributed to the court and the general public.[66] Judging from the courtly theatrical and concert events listed, operas, ballets, symphonies, and solo concertos were especially in demand from composers.[67]

The opening of the second court theatre in Schwetzingen in the summer of 1753 resulted in a major restructuring of the annual performance schedule of the court's musical life.[68] Until then, it had been customary to open the theatre season with

---

[65] *Chur-Pfältzischer Hoff- und Staats-Calender* (1749), unpaginated.

[66] Two printed flyers of the 'Reglement du Carneval' are reproduced in Pelker, 'Zur Struktur des Musiklebens', 36. The Carnival entertainments were described on a regular basis by Count Riaucour (Riaucour file, 1748–78); and were also reported on by Palatine ministers; these are extant from 1754; see D-Mhsa, Gesandtschaft Wien and Gesandtschaft Berlin.

[67] An exact reconstruction of the *Hofmusik* repertoire is impossible: all court music inventories and catalogues have been lost, and, owing to the high demand from outside of Mannheim, musicians composed not only for the Palatine court. Fortunately, information provided in extant librettos as well as references to performance allow us to verify the presentation of oratorios, operas, and ballets. That the electoral couple also required chamber music for their own private performances is a given (cf. Finscher, 'Mannheimer Orchester- und Kammermusik', 164–74).

[68] On the one hand, these remarks are based primarily on the extant librettos, the title

a new opera to mark the electress's birthday on 17 January. With the existence of a second opera house, the court now divided its musical life into two seasons: the winter season in Mannheim (November to early May) and the summer season in Schwetzingen (May to October).

The winter season focused entirely on representation and the display of courtly splendour in order to impress the public. This was achieved primarily through a new, large-scale festival opera,[69] which, until 1752, remained the only opera to be performed during the winter season. Visitors from out of town arrived in Mannheim as early as late October and usually stayed until the end of Carnival season, seeking to secure seats for the opera performances as early as was possible.[70] The festival opera was famous for its particularly elaborate productions: the extant librettos refer to at least eight different stage sets as well as large-scale ballet performances presented after each act, each with their own plots, separately printed text booklets, specially composed music, and additional stage decorations.[71] For these prestigious performances the number of participants exceeded one hundred.

The varied history of the Mannheim court opera began with the premiere of the first festival opera, *Meride*, by Carlo Grua, on 18 January 1742 (see above). During Carl Theodor's reign, the residence town developed into an operatic centre of European renown at which, beginning in the 1750s, primarily Italian operas based on librettos by Metastasio were cultivated — as was the case at virtually all large courts (such as Berlin, Dresden, Vienna, Madrid, Naples, Lisbon, and Copenhagen). In Mannheim, these included works by Johann Adolf Hasse (*Demofoonte*), Niccolò Jommelli (*Artaserse*, *L'Ifigenia* [*in Aulide*], and *Il Demetrio*), Baldassare Galuppi (*Antigona* and *L'Olimpiade*) as well as Ignaz Holzbauer (*La clemenza di Tito*, *Nitteti*, and *Ippolito ed Aricia*). At the same time, however, a renewal of opera

pages of which also indicate the occasion of performance for a festive opera; on the other hand, they draw from diplomatic reports, which provide the most reliable information regarding exact dates of performances of operas in Schwetzingen, including proof that they actually took place. In addition to the Riaucour file, the diplomatic reports of Palatine ministers for the period 1748–78 are significant in this respect (D-Mhsa, Gesandtschaft Berlin 136–56, Gesandtschaft Wien 649–706, Gesandtschaft London 235–49). Regarding the performance list, see Bärbel Pelker, 'Theateraufführungen und musikalische Akademien am Hof Carl Theodors in Mannheim: Eine Chronik der Jahre 1742–77', in *Die Mannheimer Hofkapelle im Zeitalter Carl Theodors*, 219–59.

[69] Nicole Edwina Ivy Baker, 'Italian Opera at the Court of Mannheim, 1758–70' (PhD diss., University of California, 1994); Paul E. Corneilson, 'Opera at Mannheim, 1770–78' (PhD diss., University of North Carolina, 1992); and Corneilson, 'Die Oper am Kurfürstlichen Hof zu Mannheim', in *Die Mannheimer Hofkapelle im Zeitalter Carl Theodors*, 113–29.

[70] The upper level of the opera house located in the west wing of the Mannheim palace was open to the public; see the description of an opera performance recorded in the diary of a quartermaster, lost after the Second World War but reproduced in Walter, *Geschichte des Theaters und der Musik am Kurpfälzischen Hofe*, 103–4. In 1795, the music from the Mannheim opera house that had been left behind when the court moved to Munich in 1778 was destroyed when the opera house burned down; see D-Mhsa, Abt. III, Geheimes Hausarchiv, Korr. Akt 882 V b, fols. 105^v–106^r.

[71] On ballet, see also Sibylle Dahms, 'Das Mannheimer Ballett im Zeichen der Ballettreform des 18. Jahrhunderts', in *Die Mannheimer Hofkapelle im Zeitalter Carl Theodors*, 131–40.

took place to which Holzbauer contributed in particular, in an attempt to implement the reform ideas of Francesco Algarotti, who demanded that all elements of opera focus solely on the drama. At the very latest by 1762, when the reform opera *Sofonisba* by Tommaso Trajetta was premiered, the court of Mannheim played an important role among operatic centres in Europe.[72]

In contrast to the splendid winter season, the summer sojourn at Schwetzingen was characterized by the diversity of performances and the intimate atmosphere enjoyed by the court.[73] During these months, there were no official grounds for chronologically fixed annual festivities; however, the court nonetheless sought to regulate the schedule of events during this time, at least in the first season of the palace theatre. The constantly changing flow of princely visitors and the special events presented in their honour was reason alone that this attempt failed. In the mind of the elector, the Arcadian surroundings of the summer residence in Schwetzingen, where the atmosphere was largely free from court ceremony, evidently required a different kind of operatic repertoire than that of the large-scale, prestigious court opera in Mannheim. Holzbauer's opera for the inauguration of the court theatre there, *Il figlio delle selve* (1753), which focuses on the transformation of a naive 'Sohn der Wildnis' (son of the wilderness) unaware of his royal origin into a noble, responsible prince, was definitely somewhat programmatic. An evaluation of the extant operatic repertoire clearly indicates that with this choice of topic Carl Theodor had already decided unequivocally upon the very premise of Schwetzingen: the motif of 'becoming human' through knowledge, an especially topical one during the Enlightenment – with the refinement and perfection of the human character also representative of masonic ideals.

The majority of operas that were performed thereafter in Schwetzingen reflect the different classes of society in various ways. Nowhere else in Europe was a summer residence's opera programme as diverse as that in Schwetzingen, with Italian opera buffa, French *opéra comique*, and German *Singspiel*. Indeed, as noted by Silke Leopold, 'Schwetzingen's repertoire focuses European operatic history as though viewed through a magnifying glass.'[74] The ongoing production of comic operas of Italian and French provenance at a summer residence, as occurred in Schwetzingen from 1753 until the court moved to Munich in 1778, was a unique occurrence in European music history.[75]

Finally, according to diplomatic reports, the *divertissements* of Schwetzingen

---

[72] See Baker, 'Italian Opera at the Court of Mannheim, 1758–70'; Silke Leopold, 'Von der Hofoper zur West Side Story: Mannheims Musiktheaterrepertoire', in *Mannheim und sein Nationaltheater: Menschen – Geschichte(n) – Perspektiven*, ed. Liselotte Homering and Karin v. Welck (Mannheim: Reiss-Museum, 1998), 86–105; Leopold, 'Europa unterm Brennglas: Oper in Schwetzingen zur Zeit Carl Theodors', in *Hofoper in Schwetzingen: Musik, Bühnenkunst, Architektur*, ed. Silke Leopold and Bärbel Pelker (Heidelberg: Universitätsverlag Winter, 2004), 55–70.

[73] For more detailed information on Schwetzingen's musical life and operatic performances, see *Hofoper in Schwetzingen*.

[74] Leopold, 'Europa unterm Brennglas', 57.

[75] For detailed information on librettos and music, see *Hofoper in Schwetzingen*, 87–154, 391–405.

court society also included plays and ballet performances, musical academies in the 'Mozartsaal' (as the venue is now called) in the southern *Zirkelgebäude*, as well as a passion for hunting (either *parforce* with hounds or shooting rounded-up game) which is rather difficult to understand by today's standards.[76]

## SOCIAL STRUCTURE[77]

### Incomes and Salaries of Court Musicians

Musical life at the electoral Palatine court profited from a provision made by the wife of Elector Johann Wilhelm, Anna Maria Ludovica (Luisa) de' Medici: the so-called 'mediceische Stiftung' allocated 52,000 *Gulden* a year to the 'Kapellen Musik'.[78] Schubart even named the impressive sum of 80,000 *Gulden* and concluded: 'Dieses Vermächtniß ist so fest gegründet, daß es kein Churfürst mehr umstoßen kann. Daher darf es niemand wundern, wenn die Musik in der Pfalz in kurzem zu einer so bewundernswürdigen Höhe aufstieg' (This legacy has been so firmly established, that no elector can ever overturn it. Therefore, it is not surprising that music in the Palatinate rose to such impressive heights so quickly).[79] An examination of the numerous petitions made by court musicians and the extant salary lists clearly shows that over the course of decades the *Hofmusik* personnel were able to draw upon a fixed and seemingly untouchable budget which could be increased by further funds from the general treasury, the privy purse, and the cabinet treasury.[80]

Each court musician received an annual salary according to their position and relative significance, which, thanks to the 'mediceische Stiftung', was paid regularly in cash every quarter.[81] Compared to other *Hofkapellen*, as for example, in Dres-

---

[76] [Editors' note: The *Zirkelgebäude* at Schwetzingen are two symmetrical curved outbuildings initially intended to serve as orangeries, but later used for performances and receptions.] Following the completion of the idyllically situated bath house in the palace grounds in 1773, chamber music performances were a regular part of Schwetzingen's diverse entertainment programme. The palace and its grounds have been preserved and include the historical performing venues: the concert hall (referred to as the 'Mozartsaal' since 2006), the bath house, and the small theatre, possibly the world's oldest *Rangtheater* (galleried theatre). For illustrations and an extensive discussion of the latter, see the volume *Hofoper in Schwetzingen*; Monika Scholl, 'Das Schwetzinger Schloßtheater: Der Idealtypus eines Sprech- und Musiktheaters des 18. Jahrhunderts', in *Theater um Mozart*, ed. Bärbel Pelker (Heidelberg: Universitätsverlag Winter, 2006), 83–99.

[77] Additional information is provided in Bärbel Pelker, 'Ein "Paradies der Tonkünstler"? Die Mannheimer Hofkapelle des Kurfürsten Carl Theodor', in *Mannheim: Ein Paradies der Tonkünstler?*, 9–33, at 22–33.

[78] D-Mhsa, Abt. III, Geheimes Hausarchiv, Korr. Akt 882 V b, fol. 71ᵛ.

[79] Schubart, *Ideen zu einer Ästhetik der Tonkunst*, 128–9.

[80] For the petitions, see D-KAg, Bestand 77 'Pfalz Generalia'. Salary lists from 1744, 1745, and 1759 are extant in D-KAg, 77/1648, 77/1647, and 77/6193 respectively; for 1746, in D-Mhsa, Abt. III, Geheimes Hausarchiv, Handschrift 206 II; and for both 1776 and 1778, in D-Mhsa, HR I, Fasz. 457/13.

[81] *Taschenbuch für die Schaubühne, auf das Jahr 1777* (Gotha, 1777), 248.

den, where some of the musicians had to wait for their wages for several years, the situation in Mannheim must have been like paradise.[82] Particularly favourable was the circumstance allowing additional family members to acquire positions within the orchestra or in the opera, ballet, and acting troupe, as can be seen, for example, with the Cannabich, Fränzl, Toeschi, Friedel, Wendling, and Danzi families. In such cases, their total income could reach a very substantial amount. The annual earnings of the Toeschi family in 1759 were 1,500 *Gulden*, while Johann Baptist Wendling and his wife Dorothea made even more, 2,000 *Gulden* – a handsome amount compared to *Kapellmeister* Holzbauer's yearly salary of 1,500 *Gulden*.[83]

Court musicians could increase their wages considerably by applying for gratuities, paid either as a lump sum or in instalments over a certain period of time. The importance of this additional source of remuneration is emphasized by the high number of extant petitions.[84] As is evident from minutes taken at meetings of the *Hofkammer* and the privy council, petitions were received and then either officially approved or 'abgeschlagen' (refused).[85] The granting of supplementary payments, which as a rule were paid in *Gulden* rather than in kind, depended on the *Hofkapelle* members' performance (in a general sense) or need. The odds of receiving a bonus were the highest when a member of the *Hofkapelle* had died, since that salary did not revert back to the state treasury, but was divided among the musicians.[86] In July 1760, for example, several court musicians, among them Ferdinand Götz, Anton Eytner (d. 1763), and Sebastian Holtzbauer, as well as the 'Accessisten' (expectants) Sigismund Strauss, Georg Ritschel, Arnold Mayer, and Jacob Ritter received financial supplements drawn from the salary of the late Anton Fils.[87] This policy was clearly modelled on the directives of the 'mediceische Stiftung', which stipulated that the money was to benefit the members of the *Hofkapelle*.

However, the surest way for individuals to receive a salary bonus was to go beyond the call of duty and provide extra services, such as the additional copying of music, the rastration of music paper and, in particular, teaching. Vocational training at the Mannheim court was truly exemplary. Apart from the children of musicians, who were usually first taught by a family member, the elector granted a premium ('Lehrgeld') towards the tuition fees of other talented children. For

---

[82] Cf. Richard Petzoldt, 'Zur sozialen Lage des Musikers im 18. Jahrhundert', in *Der Sozialstatus des Berufsmusikers vom 17. bis 19. Jahrhundert*, ed. Walter Salmen, Musikwissenschaftliche Arbeiten, 24 (Kassel: Bärenreiter, 1971), 64–82, at 68–9. [English trans. by Herbert Kaufman and Barbara Reisner in *The Social Status of the Professional Musician from the Middle Ages to the 19th Century* (New York: Pendragon Press, 1983).]

[83] Salary list dated 28 July 1759, D-KAg, 77/6193.

[84] D-KAg, Bestand 61 and Bestand 77.

[85] Numerous decisions are recorded in the minutes of the *Hofkammer* and privy council for the years 1742–78; see D-KAg, Bestand 61/874off.

[86] Numerous relevant personnel files ('Dienstbestellung- und Besoldungs-Acta') are extant in D-KAg, Bestand 77/1656 (*Hofkapellmeister*, from 1739), 1657 (violinists, from 1744), 1658 (concertmaster, from 1739), 1660 (violoncellists, from 1754), 1661 (*Waldhornisten*, clarinettists, bassoonists, and oboists, from 1743), 1665 (*Hofsängerinnen*, from 1742), and 1666 (*Hofsänger*, from 1746).

[87] Letter dated 23 July 1760, D-KAg, 77/1657.

those gifted enough to be considered for participation in the *Hofkapelle*, the court would pay all educational expenses, including lengthy study trips to Italy for the highly gifted, such as Christian Cannabich (from 1753 to 1756 or early 1757),[88] Johannes Ritschel (1758–61),[89] and Franz Wendling (1758–9).[90]

The most successful means of increasing their income was for court musicians to contribute their own compositions, and even *Hofkapelle* members who were obliged to compose for the court, enjoyed these bonuses.[91] It was certainly possible to earn a comparatively large amount of money through composition. The works of Mannheim court musicians (for example, Christian Cannabich, Fils, Holzbauer, Richter, Johann Stamitz, Carlo Giuseppe Toeschi, and Johann Baptist Wendling) became very popular, and from approximately 1755 onwards, publishers from abroad secured printing privileges for new repertoire.[92] However, the demand for handwritten compositions was much greater, obtained not only directly from the composers themselves but above all from the full-time court copyists specially hired for this purpose.[93] For the period until 1760, the following copyists are known by name: Jacob Cramer (from 1746), Johann Lochner (1753–74), Reinhard (first name unknown, 1754–9), and Wilhelm Sepp (from 1760). Ferdinand Fränzl was responsible for the rastration of manuscript paper.[94]

---

[88] Cannabich first studied with Niccolò Jommelli (1714–1774) in Rome and then probably with Giovanni Battista Sammartini (1700/1701–1775) in Milan; see Adolf Sandberger, 'Aus der Korrespondenz des pfalzbayerischen Kurfürsten Karl Theodor mit seinem römischen Ministerresidenten', in *Festschrift Hermann Kretzschmar zum siebzigsten Geburtstage* (Leipzig: C. F. Peters, 1918), 128–31. Sandberger examines the correspondence of the court with the foreign agent and resident representative Giovanni Antonio Coltrolini between 1750 and 1758; see also D-Mhsa, Kasten blau 76/2. On Cannabich, see also Mary Alyce Groman, 'The Mannheim Orchestra under the Leadership of Christian Cannabich' (PhD diss., University of California, Berkeley, 1979), 77.

[89] Ritschel received 300 *Gulden* travel money, 400 *Gulden* tuition money, and 100 *Gulden* of his previously drawn salary; see letter dated 4 October 1757 in D-KAg, 77/1657. Letters from the period 1758–61 by Franz and Johannes Ritschel to Giovanni Battista (Padre) Martini (1706–1784) are extant in I-Bc, H.86.150–58 and I.23.61; see also the 1761 correspondence of the court with Giovanni Antonio Coltrolini regarding Ritschel in D-Mhsa, Kasten blau 76/3.

[90] Per quarter Wendling was paid 300 *Gulden* travel money, 500 *Gulden* salary, and a teaching premium of 15 *Dukaten*; see letter dated 8 January 1760, D-KAg, 77/1657.

[91] Vogler received 300 *Gulden* for 'für abgelieferte Kompositionen' (for supplying compositions), a considerable cash injection in view of his annual salary of 450 *Gulden*; see letter dated 15 June 1773, D-KAg, 77/1656.

[92] Until 1760, Mannheim compositions appeared primarily in the publishing houses of La Chevardière, Huberty, and Le Clerc in Paris, as well as also from 1759 with Hummel in Amsterdam; cf. Cari Johansson, *French Music Publisher's Catalogues of the Second Half of the Eighteenth Century*, Publications of the Library of the Royal Swedish Academy of Music, 2 (Stockholm: Almquist & Wiksell, 1955); Johansson, *J. J. & B. Hummel, Music-Publishing and Thematic Catalogues*, 2 vols., Publications of the Library of the Royal Swedish Academy of Music, 3 (Stockholm: Almquist & Wiksell, 1972).

[93] Cf. the foundational philological examinations of primary sources carried out by Eugene K. Wolf, *Manuscripts from Mannheim, c.1730–78: A Study in the Methodology of Musical Source Research*, Quellen und Studien zur Geschichte der Mannheimer Hofkapelle, 9 (Frankfurt: Peter Lang, 2002).

[94] Evidence for 1753 and 1759 in D-KAg, 77/1657 and 77/6193.

Alongside these possibilities for gaining additional income, the court also offered further privileges and gifts from the court. During the summer months in Schwetzingen, board and lodging was paid for the resident musicians, while those who came from Mannheim were reimbursed for their travel expenses.[95] Furthermore, after each opera and theatrical performance, the singers, dancers, and chorus members were each given a bottle of wine, while the principal actors even received two bottles of burgundy as a special reward.[96]

## *Pension and Death Benefits Paid by the Court*[97]

The employment of a court musician usually ended only at his or her death. Neither a set retirement age nor a regulated pension plan was provided for. Only when musicians were no longer able to provide high-quality service due to old age (for example, vocalists and wind players) or illness, were they released from their duties. Long-term service did not necessarily result in a pension, but in order for one to be granted, approval on the highest level was required. Carl Theodor's generosity as an employer is once again evident in this context. He even allowed *Hofkapelle* members from abroad to receive their pension in their native country. As a rule, retired musicians received approximately fifty percent of their salary. When, for example, illness forced the alto castrato Stefano Pasi to resign from service in 1751, he continued to receive 500 *Gulden* in superannuation – half of his former salary – a sum that was sent to him in Italy.[98] In contrast, widows of musicians usually found themselves in much more difficult circumstances. Still, in this case as well the court sought to alleviate their dismal situations through the establishment of a type of fund for widows and orphans.[99]

In summary, the courtly system of benefits and pensions (whose solid foundation was provided by the 'mediceische Stiftung') functioned in a manner that was tightly organized, performance oriented, and as fair as possible. Consequently, each of the court musicians must have been able to lead an average middle-class life, if they lived within their means. Finally, the social commitment on the part of the electoral government deserves recognition. Because their needs were usually sufficiently met by the court, the majority of musicians were in the agreeable position of being able to focus on carrying out their duties, a fact that, in turn, had a positive impact on the quality of the musical performances.

---

[95] Lists of living quarters from 1758 and 1762 in D-KAg, 77/8506. The 1758 list is also reproduced in Bärbel Pelker, 'Sommer in der Campagne: Impressionen aus Schwetzingen', in *Hofoper in Schwetzingen*, 9–38, at 19.

[96] D-Mhsa, Abt. III, Geheimes Hausarchiv, Korr. Akt 882 V b, fol. 71ʳ.

[97] Numerous entries pertaining to subsidies and pensions can be found in D-KAg: for the period until 1760, see Bestand 61/8741–45; in Bestand 77, see specifically the salary list from 1759 (77/6193); numerous reports from 1770s onwards are found in 77/2647, 2654, 2657–61, 7598, 7599, 7601–5, 7607.

[98] Letter dated 1 June 1751, D-KAg, 77/1666.

[99] Names are provided, for example, in the salary list from 1759, D-KAg, 77/6193. It includes the pensioners Matthias Cannabich and Carl Offhuis, as well as the widows of the musicians Eyttner, Lederer, Johann Stamitz, Friedel, Lerch, and Basconi.

## CONTACT AND NETWORKS WITH OTHER COURTS

The Europe-wide exchange of information occurred then, as now, with the help of publications and through personal contacts. Among important publications in print, the *Hof- und Staatskalender* (1748–78) were of particular relevance for the courtly sphere and were available for purchase by any interested buyer. Since these provided the names of every member of the courtly household, arranged systematically by office or area of responsibility, they were an indispensable resource, especially where the preparation of visits by foreign virtuosos was concerned – an *entrée* at court, in particular at a *Musenhof* such as Mannheim, as a rule required careful planning. Only those individuals who maintained influential personal contacts or produced a recommendation by a high-ranking aristocrat could count on being invited by the court; others would be rejected. The court and state calendars also provided virtuosos with the names of relevant contacts: members of the reigning family and the *Hofmusik* personnel, as well as the names of ministers, diplomats, and agents.

The last mentioned group – the ministers, diplomats, and agents – were, in retrospect, of great importance with regard to the networks among princely houses. In 1760, for example, electoral Palatine ministers and servants visited Brussels, The Hague, Frankfurt, Cleves, Cologne, London, Milan, Munich, Naples, Paris, Regensburg, Rome, Saxony, Tuscany, Wetzlar, and Vienna. In turn, prior to 1760, Mannheim hosted foreign diplomats from the courts of Ansbach, Dresden, Paris, Rome, and Vienna.[100] These men sent regular reports – about two to three times a week – back to their own courts, containing the latest news and, if controversial in nature, in code. The range of mandatory topics discussed in these diplomatic missives included not only political issues, but also news on courtly life, such as the visits of princes or other famous personalities; of course, court gossip and scandals were also included. The reports generally finished with the latest information on cultural life: plays and musical performances were regularly listed, together with news on the latest appointees and their future plans. Drawing upon these numerous and precisely dated accounts, it is possible in the case of the Mannheim court to reconstruct not only the structure of musical life, but also an exact schedule of operatic productions.[101] Thanks to a well-functioning postal system, letters would arrive on the desk of the addressee between two to six days later. Consequently, princely courts were always well informed about recent events in Europe.[102]

[100] *Chur-Pfältzischer Hoff- und Staats-Calender* (1760), 43–6. During the 1760s, diplomats from Prussia, Denmark, and Hesse-Kassel arrived, followed by diplomats from Bavaria in 1772.
[101] Cf. the following articles by Pelker in *Hofoper in Schwetzingen*: 'Zur Struktur des Musiklebens', 29–40; 'Theateraufführungen und musikalische Akademien', 219–59; 'Chronologie zu Musik und Theater in Schwetzingen (1743–2003)', 389–432.
[102] The directory of the letter-post network, which was printed together with the stagecoach schedule at the end of the electoral Palatine *Hof- und Staatskalender*, illustrates Mannheim's far-reaching network of existing lines of communication; see 'Kaiserliche Briefpost zu Pferde', *Chur-Pfälzischer Hoff- und Staats-Kalender* (1777), 304–15.

Also beneficial in view of a European network were the numerous and in part fairly lengthy concert tours undertaken by court musicians since the 1750s (for example, Johann Stamitz, Richter, and Johann Baptist and Dorothea Wendling), primarily to Paris, London, and Italy. Once the heavy performance schedule of Carnival came to an end, and given that the small, almost intimate performance venues in Schwetzingen meant that the presence of the entire *Hofmusik* was not required in the summer months, the virtuosos were graciously permitted to travel by their employer. Carl Theodor would surely not have minded approving such leave, knowing full well that the fame earned by his virtuosos would shed a positive light back onto his own court.

The 'Golden Age' of the electoral Palatine *Hofmusik* ended in 1778, when Elector Carl Theodor succeeded the childless Bavarian Elector Maximilian III Joseph (1727–1777, r. from 1745). In compliance with inheritance laws, he was required to relocate his entire court to Munich. The majority of court musicians followed Carl Theodor to his new residence; those musicians who stayed on must be credited for beginning a new chapter of local musical history in the former residential town of Mannheim, one that from now on would, however, be written by its citizens.

TABLE 5.1. Membership of the Electoral Palatine Court Music Establishment in 1723, 1747, and 1760

The court of Mannheim relocated from Heidelberg only in 1720; the geographical references in the 1723 column denote musicians originally from either Carl Philipp's own earlier *Hofkapelle* in Innsbruck or that of his brother, Elector Johann Wilhelm (d. 1716), in Düsseldorf.

| Year | 1723 | 1747 | 1760 |
|---|---|---|---|
| Ruler | Elector Carl Philipp (r. 1716–42) | Elector Carl Theodor (r. 1743–99) | |
| Numeric Overview | 2 *Kapellmeister*<br>2 concertmasters<br>37 instrumentalists<br>12 vocalists<br>2 additional personnel | 1 *Kapellmeister*<br>2 concertmasters<br>30 instrumentalists<br>11 vocalists<br>2 additional personnel | 2 *Kapellmeister*<br>2 concertmasters<br>46 instrumentalists<br>16 vocalists<br>2 additional personnel |
| *Intendant* (artistic director) | Frantz Wolfgang Freiherr von Stechau | Matthäus Freiherr von Vieregg | Carl Christian Freiherr von Eberstein |
| *Kapellmeister* | *from Innsbruck*<br>Jacob Greber<br>*from Düsseldorf*<br>Johann Hugo Wilderer | Carlo Grua | Carlo Grua<br>Ignaz Holzbauer |
| Concertmaster | *from Innsbruck*<br>Gottfried Finger | Alessandro Toeschi<br>Johann Stamitz | Christian Cannabich<br>Carlo Giuseppe Toeschi |
| Vice-concertmaster | *from Düsseldorf*<br>Johann Sigismund Weiss | | |
| Instrumentalists | | | |
| Violin | *from Innsbruck*<br>Ignaz Grüber<br>Friedrich Muffat | Domenico Basconi<br>Jacob Friedel<br>Philipp Ernst Reyer<br>Christian Cannabich | Johann Paul Mayer<br>Jacob Cramer (also copyist)<br>Wilhelm Schwarz<br>Franz Anton Brunner |

| | | | |
|---|---|---|---|
| | *from Düsseldorf*<br>Carl Peter Thoma<br>Christian Hein<br>Johann Reinhard Bullman<br>Joseph Fischer<br>Franz Fischer<br>Philipp Heinrich Schneider<br>Matthias Niclas Stulick<br>Philipp Duruel (also *Tanzmeister*)<br><br>Carl Offhuis | Johann Philipp Bohrer (also tpt)<br>Wilhelm Schwarz (also tpt)<br>Franz Anton Brunner (also tpt)<br>Gerhard Heymann (also tpt)<br>Wilhelm Sepp (also tpt)<br>Johann Paul Mayer (also timp)<br>Jacob Cramer (also timp)<br>Johann Wilhelm Duruel (also *Tanzmeister*) | Johannes Toeschi<br>Ignaz Fränzl<br>Jean Nicolas Heroux<br>Johann Georg Danner<br>Franz Wendling<br>Johannes Ritschel<br>Wilhelm Cramer<br>Sigismund Strauss<br>Ferdinand Götz<br>Georg Zarth (Czarth)<br>Jacob Ritter<br>Georg Wilhelm Ritter<br>Georg Ritschel<br>Arnold Mayer<br>Felix Anton Sartorii<br>Conrad Brummer |
| Viola | *from Düsseldorf*<br>Anton Dönninger<br>Frantz Schubaur<br>Niclas Krieger | Ferdinand Fränzl (also tpt)<br>Joseph Götz (also tpt) | Ferdinand Fränzl<br>Johann Lochner (also copyist)<br>Wilhelm Sepp (also copyist)<br>Johann Philipp Bohrer |
| Violoncello | Carlo Perroni<br>Giuseppe Pellandini | Johann Daniel Fyttner<br>Johannes Bittner ('Bassettel')<br>Johannes Nepomuk Fürst (also tpt)<br>Wilhelm Friedel (also tpt) | Johannes Fürst<br>Wilhelm Friedel<br>Innocenz Danzi<br>Anton Eytner<br>Joseph Reßler |
| Contrabass | *from Innsbruck*<br>Jacob Halsegger<br>Georg Wenzel Ritschel<br>Philipp Ernst Reyer (possibly from Düsseldorf) | Georg Wenzel Ritschel<br>Georg Anton Hönisch (also tpt) | Johann Wendelin Schäffer |

| Year | 1723 | 1747 | 1760 |
|---|---|---|---|
| Flute | | Matthias Cannabich<br>Nicolas Lerch | Georg Ludwig Sartorii<br>Johann Baptist Wendling |
| Oboe | *from Innsbruck*<br>Johann Caspar Meyer<br>Johann Carl Daniels<br>Johann Niclas Findeis<br>Anselm Beyermüller<br><br>*from Düsseldorf*<br>Johann Frantz Knabi<br>Matthias Cannabich<br>Johannes Nolda<br><br>Nicolas Lerch<br>Franz Aloys Beck | Johannes Bleckmann<br>Alexander Lebrun | Johannes Bleckmann<br>Alexander Lebrun<br>Friedrich Ramm |
| Clarinet | | | Michael Quallenberg<br>Johannes Hampel |
| Bassoon | *from Innsbruck*<br>Johann Matthias Altensperger<br><br>*from Düsseldorf*<br>Swibertus Holtzbaur | Johann Heinrich Lederer<br>Heinrich Adam Ritter | Heinrich Adam Ritter<br>Anton Strasser<br>Sebastian Holtzbauer |
| Waldhorn | *from Innsbruck*<br>Daniel Otto<br>Georg Schwoboda<br><br>Christian Hindenlang | Johannes Matuska<br>Jacob Ziwny | Jacob Ziwny<br>Johannes Matuska<br>Wenzeslaus Ziwny<br>Joseph Ziwny |

| | | | |
|---|---|---|---|
| Trumpet | | *See* Violin, Viola, Violoncello, *and* Contrabass | |
| Lute/Theorbo | *from Düsseldorf*<br>Johann Jacob Weiss (lute)<br>Carlo Romanini (theorbo) | | |
| Organ | *from Innsbruck*<br>Christian Christoph Eggman | Franz Ritschel<br>Anton Marxfelder | Franz Ritschel<br>Anton Marxfelder |
| | *from Düsseldorf*<br>Paolo Grua | | |
| Timpani | | *See* Violin | |
| Vocalists | | | |
| Soprano | *from Innsbruck*<br>Eleonora Scio | Rosa Gabrieli | Rosa Gabrieli-Bleckmann<br>Dorothea Wendling<br>Franziska Schöpfer<br>Susanna Toeschi |
| Soprano castrato | *from Innsbruck*<br>Joseph Lasinsky | Mariano Lena<br>Enrico Pessarini | Mariano Lena<br>Lorenzo Tonarelli<br>Philippus Saparosi |
| | *from Düsseldorf*<br>Alessandro Mori | | |
| Alto | Eleonora Borosini | | |
| Alto castrato | Filippo Sicardi | Filippo Galletti<br>Stefano Pasi | Filippo Galletti<br>Jean Baptiste Coraucci |
| Tenor | *from Düsseldorf*<br>Lorenzo Santorini<br>Angelo Zuccarini<br>Matthias Zinzheim | Jacob Schöpfer<br>Pietro Sarselli | Pietro Sarselli<br>Jacob Schöpfer<br>Pietro Paolo Carnoli<br>Leopold Krieger |

| Year | 1723 | 1747 | 1760 |
|---|---|---|---|
| Bass | from Düsseldorf<br>Bertram Reuter<br>Johannes Krebsbach<br><br>Giovanni Battista Palmerini (possibly from Düsseldorf)<br><br>Johann Paul Meyer | Johannes Krebsbach<br>Natale Bettinardi (Bettinardo)<br>Franz Anton Lutz<br>Franz Xaver Richter | Franz Anton Lutz<br>Franz Xaver Richter<br>Joseph Giardini |
| **Additional Personnel** | | | |
| Court poet | | | Mattia Verazi |
| Secretary | | | Johann Spengel |
| Copyists | | | See Violin and Viola |
| Calcant | Hans Georg Harris | Jacob Rauch<br>Franz Arnold Harris | Name not specified |
| Lautenmacher (lute maker) | Jacob Rauch | | |
| Tanzmeister | See Violin | See Violin | |

Sources

1723: Based on information in D-Mbs, Cgm 1665, pp. 46–50.

1747: Based on the listing in Chur-Pfältzischer Hoff- und Staats-Calender (1748), 24–6; not including pensioners. The year 1747, rather than 1745, was chosen here, as 1747 marks the beginning of the most important phase in the development and history of the Mannheim Hofmusik.

1760: See Chur-Pfältzischer Hoff- und Staats-Calender (1761), 27–30; without pensioners.

TABLE 5.2. Documented Performances of Vocal Works at the Court of Mannheim, 1720–42

| | |
|---|---|
| *c.*1720–30 | *La giustizia, la pace, la poesia protette,* 'Componimento drammatico', for Elector Carl Philipp's birthday |
| 1721 | *Il ritratto della Serenissima Principessa Elisabetta Augusta*, a cantata for four voices in one act by Johann Jacob Greber (*c.*1673–1731), for Princess Elisabeth Auguste Sophie's birthday |
| 3 November 1721 | Cantata in one act, text by Lorenzo Santorini (*c.*1672–1764), performed to celebrate the close of the autumn hunting season and for Elector Carl Philipp's birthday |
| 19 November 1721 | *Il concilio de' pianeti,* 'Componimento per musica' in one act by Lorenzo Santorini, for Princess Elisabeth Auguste Sophie's name day |
| Lent 1722 | *Il trionfo di placido,* oratorio in two parts by Johann Hugo von Wilderer (*c.*1671–1724) |
| 1722 | *Coronide,* 'Pastorale eroica' in three acts, for the visit of the Elector of Cologne, Joseph Clemens of Bavaria (1671–1723) |
| | Cantata in one act by Johann Hugo von Wilderer, also in honour of the Elector of Cologne |
| | Cantata in one act by Johann Hugo von Wilderer, in honour of the visit of the Coadjutor Archbishop of Cologne and Prince-Bishop of Münster, Clemens August I of Bavaria (1700–1761) |
| | *Amor sul monte, ovvero Diana amante di Endimione,* pastorale in three acts |
| | *I felici inganni d'amor' in Etolia,* 'Favola boschereccia' in three acts |
| 4 November 1723 | Cantata in one act by Johann Jacob Greber, for Elector Carl Philipp's name day |
| 17 March 1724 | *Ester,* 'Dramma sacro per musica' in two parts by Johann Hugo von Wilderer, for Princess Elisabeth Auguste Sophie's birthday |
| 1724 | *Il giudicio di Paride,* 'Festa teatrale per musica' in one act with prologue by Johann Hugo von Wilderer, and containing ballets by Carl Offhuis and choreography by Paul de Fleuris |
| Carnival 1726 | *Li quattro arlichini,* 'Commedia' in three acts with three musical intermedi after Molière, a performance by the gentlemen of the court |
| Carnival 1731 | *Divertimento teatrale per musica* in one act, after Molière |
| 11 April 1732 | *Cristo pendente dalla croce,* oratorio in two parts |
| 15 April 1740 | *La conversione di S. Ignazio,* oratorio in two parts by Carlo Grua (*c.*1695/1700–1773), text by Lorenzo Santorini |
| Lent 1741 | *Bersabea, ovvero Il pentimento di David,* 'Azione tragico-sacra' by Carlo Grua |
| 1741 | *Jaele,* oratorio in two parts by Carlo Grua, text by Lorenzo Santorini |

| 18 January 1742 | *Meride*, 'Dramma per musica' in three acts by Carlo Grua, text by Giovanni Claudio Pasquini (1695–1763) |
| 23 March 1742 | *Il figliuol' prodigo*, 'Azione sacra per musica' in two parts by Carlo Grua, text by Giovanni Claudio Pasquini |
| 19 November 1742 | *Meride*, repeat performance |

# DUCHIES

# 6

# The Court of Württemberg-Stuttgart

## Samantha Owens

T HE YEARS 1715 TO 1760 represent a rather unsettled period in the musical life of the south-west German court of Württemberg, based primarily at palaces in Stuttgart and Ludwigsburg. Nevertheless, the surviving archival documentation, held by the Hauptstaatsarchiv Stuttgart and covering the reigns of three successive dukes – the Lutheran absolutist Eberhard Ludwig (r. 1693–1733), his cousin, the Catholic convert Carl Alexander (r. 1733–37), and the latter's son, the undeniably extravagant, opera-loving Carl Eugen (r. 1744–93) – illuminates many of the central themes of Western musical history. These include the emergence of the orchestra, the rise in the importance of chamber music, and the increasing numbers of Italian musicians employed in German *Hofkapellen* during the eighteenth century.

Described by Peter H. Wilson as 'one of the weaker middle ranking territories within the Empire', the rulers of the duchy of Württemberg nevertheless made significant efforts to keep abreast of the latest cultural trends.[1] The final decades of the seventeenth century therefore witnessed an increasing awareness on the part of the court of the fashionable French style, resulting in the employment of French musicians, festive performances of large-scale *Singballette* (modelled loosely on the *ballet de cour*), the adoption of new baroque woodwind instruments, and the institution of a Lullian string band – all of which helped to prepare the way for the eventual appearance of the orchestra at the court.[2] As befitted a German prince of his rank, Eberhard Ludwig (1676–1733) had received an education that stressed the importance of French style and manners, and he continued to provide support for French culture at his court despite France's periodic acts of aggression.[3] In 1700,

---

[1] Peter H. Wilson, 'Women and Imperial Politics: the Württemberg Consorts, 1674–1757', in *Queenship in Europe, 1660–1815: The Role of the Consort*, ed. Clarissa Campbell Orr (Cambridge: Cambridge University Press, 2004), 221–51, at 223.

[2] For further details, see Samantha Owens, 'The Württemberg *Hofkapelle*, c.1680–1721' (PhD diss., Victoria University of Wellington, 1995).

[3] On the concerns of the Württemberg estates regarding this educational policy (which included French dancing lessons for the prince and his two sisters), see D-Sha, A21, Büschel 609, decree of 30 June 1686; James Allen Vann, *The Making of a State: Württemberg, 1593–1793* (Ithaca, N.Y.: Cornell University Press, 1984), 152–3.

embarking somewhat belatedly on his *Kavaliersreise*, Eberhard Ludwig made sure not to miss the sights of France's royal splendour: a contemporary account of his travels noted that he had seen incognito 'einen guten Theil Franckreichs besonders Pariß und den Königl. Hof zu Versailles' (a good deal of France, especially Paris and the royal court at Versailles).[4] By the turn of the eighteenth century, no doubt influenced by Europe-wide cultural trends, the Württemberg court's musical taste began to turn increasingly towards Italy, a move highlighted in an ambitious series of operatic productions directed by Johann Sigismund Cousser (or Kusser, 1660–1727) between 1698 and 1702.[5] But such extravagant expenditure came to an abrupt end with the resumption of military activity following the outbreak of the War of the Spanish Succession (1701–14), a conflict that was to have a considerable impact on the nature of music at the court.

## THE EMERGENCE OF THE ORCHESTRA

Little documentation remains regarding the court musical establishment during the first decade of the eighteenth century. As shown by the numeric overview in Table 6.1 (pp. 183–95 below), by 1715 the membership of the Württemberg *Hofkapelle* is known to have stood at three *Kapellmeister*, twenty-two instrumentalists, eleven vocalists, and two *Kapellknaben*. There was also a complement of seven trumpeters and one kettledrummer, although, strictly speaking, the latter group was not part of the *Hofkapelle*.[6] A troika of music directors perhaps seems unwarranted given the reasonably small size of the musical establishment, but this may be explained, at least in part, by an unseemly dispute that had arisen between the two incumbent *Kapellmeister*, Theodor Schwartzkopff (1659–1732) and his former pupil Johann Georg Christian Störl (1675–1719). In January 1706, Störl attempted to have Schwartzkopff and his family ousted from the *Kapellhaus*, claiming that his own residence was unsuitable for rehearsals of 'Opern' (operas, destined for the fast-approaching Carnival season), while composition was virtually impossible due to the cacophony created when the *Kapellknaben* hosted by his family practised their various instruments.[7] It is obvious that neither the (admittedly rather small) Stuttgart castle nor the *Lusthaus* located in the nearby ducal pleasure gardens were available to the musicians for day-to-day rehearsals.

At the time this exchange took place, Eberhard Ludwig was in Munich, wit-

---

[4] [Andreas Matthäus Wolffgang], *Abbildung und kurtze Lebens-Beschreibung aller biß dahin Regierenden Durchleuchtigsten Herzogen zu Würtemberg*... (Stuttgart, 1704), 246.

[5] See Samantha Owens, Introduction to *Johann Sigismund Kusser: Adonis* (Middleton, Wisc.: A-R Editions, 2009), pp. xi–xxvii.

[6] See D-Sha, A21, Büschel 607, Johann Christoph Pez, 'Lista. Der ganzen Würtemberg: Hochfürstl: Musicorum', 14 January 1714; Anon., 'Lista. Der ganzen Würtenb: Hfrtl: Hof Music', c.December 1714–July 1715; 'Etat der Hof Musik', 11 March 1715, transcribed in Josef Sittard, *Zur Geschichte der Musik und des Theaters am württembergischen Hofe*, 2 vols. (Stuttgart: Kohlhammer, 1890–91), I: 90–95.

[7] Letter of Johann Georg Christian Störl to Duke Eberhard Ludwig, 20 January 1706, transcribed in Sittard, *Zur Geschichte der Musik*, I: 324–5.

nessing at first hand the disintegrating fortunes of the ruling Wittelsbach family. Elector Maximilian II Emanuel (1662–1726) and his brother Joseph Clemens (1671–1723), the elector-archbishop of Cologne, had sided with the French in the War of the Spanish Succession and suffered defeat at the Battle of Blenheim in 1704. Forced to seek asylum in France, by 1706 they had been declared imperial outlaws.[8] It seems probable that while in Munich during the winter of 1705–6, Eberhard Ludwig (or perhaps one of his aides) became aware of the Bavarian court musician Johann Christoph Pez (1664–1716), to whom, among other duties, fell the responsibility of instructing the Wittelsbach children in music.[9] By May 1706 the entire Bavarian *Hofkapelle* had been released by imperial decree, and on 12 November Pez was engaged as Württemberg 'Rath und Oberkapellmeister', a higher rank than held by either Schwartzkopff or Störl.[10] Having been sent by Max Emanuel to study violin and composition in Rome during the 1690s, Pez's new (and extremely generous) salary package of 2,000 *Gulden* not only reflected the suitability of his training and experience to date, but also included wages for both his daughter, the singer Maria Anna Franziska Pez (b. 1689), and his personal copyist, Antonÿ Meister.[11]

Pez's term as Württemberg *Oberkapellmeister* lasted until his death in 1716 and resulted in a considerable expansion of the *Hofkapelle*, particularly in terms of the types of instruments regularly employed. As shown in Table 6.1, all of the instrumentalists were capable of playing more than one instrument, with a full range of woodwinds (recorder, flute, oboe, clarinet, bass recorder, and bassoon), plucked and bowed strings (violin, viola, viola d'amore, viola da gamba, French *basse de violon*, violoncello, lute, and theorbo), keyboards, horns, trumpets, and kettledrums.[12] This growth occurred despite the considerable toll of the ongoing War of the Spanish Succession, which affected Stuttgart residents most directly in 1707, when a major invasion caused the ducal family to flee temporarily to Switzerland. The financial burden of military expenditure coupled with the expense of building a new

[8] Samuel John Klingensmith, *The Utility of Splendor: Ceremony, Social Life, and Architecture at the Court of Bavaria, 1600–1800*, ed. Christian F. Otto and Mark Ashton (Chicago: University of Chicago Press, 1993), 41.

[9] Klaus Merten, *Schloß Ludwigsburg / Ludwigsburg Palace* (Munich and Stuttgart: Deutscher Kunstverlag, 1992), 2; Ulrich Iser, '"Wie du ein französisches lied vor meiner gesungen": Zur musikalischen Erziehung der Wittelsbacher Prinzen', in *Die Bühnen des Rokoko: Theater, Musik und Literatur im Rheinland des 18. Jahrhunderts*, ed. Frank Günter Zehnder (Cologne: DuMont, 2000), 87–112, at 97.

[10] Iser, '"Wie du ein französisches lied"', 98; Robert Münster, 'Die Musik am Hofe Max Emanuels', in *Kurfürst Max Emanuel, Bayern und Europa um 1700*, 2 vols., ed. Hubert Glaser (Munich: Hirmer, 1976), 1: 295–316, at 297; Bertha Antonia Wallner, ed., *Ausgewählte Werke des Alt-Münchener Tonsetzers Johann Christoph Pez*, Denkmäler der Tonkunst in Bayern, 35 (Augsburg: Filser, 1928), p. xxxviii.

[11] Wallner, *Ausgewählte Werke*, p. xxxviii; as *Kapellmeister* in 1699, Schwartzkopff had earned only 300 *Gulden* plus payments in kind; see D-Sha, A21, Büschel 607, 'Verzaichnüß', c.1699.

[12] For further details, see Owens, 'The Württemberg *Hofkapelle*'; Samantha Owens, 'Upgrading from Consort to Orchestra at the Württemberg Court', in *From Renaissance to Baroque: Change in Instruments and Instrumental Music in the Seventeenth Century*, ed. Peter Holman and Jonathan Wainwright (Aldershot: Ashgate, 2005), 227–40.

palace at Ludwigsburg (the foundation stone for which was laid in 1704) soon put a serious strain on the court's resources. In 1709 a major retrenchment took place that saw a number of musicians released and Pez's salary reduced by 500 *Gulden*.[13] Even following the Peace of Utrecht in 1713, the excesses of a prolonged period of military conflict were still to be paid for. It seems that a proposal was made to further economize spending on the *Hofkapelle* at this time, since in a report of January 1714 Pez felt moved to comment,

> vier stundt taffel *Music*, zweÿ biß drithalbstundt *Cammer Music*, widerumb Taffel *Music*, und biß weilen noch einen Ball darzu, das khönnen 8: *Musici* ohne abwexlung nicht außthauren, welches doch Unsere *Musici* mit gröstem fleiß, und *punctualit*ät thuen; Mann khan zwar *Music* machen mit 2: und 3: Persohnen, das khan auch ein Burger haben, aber einen Durchleüchtigsten *regir*enden Hertzogen von Würtemberg seine Hochfürstl: Cappell- und Hof *Music* zu *fourniren* (verstehe ich nach *decor*, und Ehr Seines Hochfürstl: Hauses) da gehören mehrers alß 8: *Musici* darzu.

> four hours of *Tafelmusik*, two to three and a half hours of chamber music, *Tafelmusik* once again, and from time to time a ball as well, that [is a workload] eight musicians could not manage without alternation, which is what our musicians do with the utmost diligence and punctuality; one can, to be sure, make music with two or three people, which is also [the number of musicians] a burgher can afford, but a Most Serene Ruling Duke of Württemberg providing for His Most Princely *Kapelle* and *Hofmusik* (as I understand the setting and glory of his most princely house) must have more than eight musicians belonging to his musical establishment.[14]

Yet at the same time, despite the financial restraints suffered since his initial appointment, Pez was clearly proud of the instrumentalists under his command. Possibly referring to Lullian-style string discipline he noted,

> alle in 3: 4: biß 5:erleÿ *sort*en der *instrument*en *versirt* sein, streichen auch mit sauberen französischen Zug so net und *unit:*te zusamen, das ich ein[e] *Music* in gantzem Röm: Reich mir getraue herauszufordern, seÿe[n] möchte noch 5: mahl so starkh sein, die es der Unserigen bevor thuen solte.

> all are experienced on three, four, to five different types of instruments, [and] also bow [on string instruments] with clean French characteristics so nicely and unitedly together, that I dare to challenge any musical establishment in the [Holy] Roman Empire, even if they are five times the size of us, to be better than us.[15]

Extant documents indicate that the duties performed by Pez's *Hofkapelle* centred on the provision of music for the church, *Tafel*, and ducal chambers. But while

---

[13] Sittard, *Zur Geschichte der Musik*, I: 86.
[14] D-Sha, Pez, 'Lista'. I would like to thank Barbara M. Reul and Brian Clark for their assistance with translations.
[15] Ibid.

expressing great confidence in his instrumentalists, Pez clearly had genuine concerns regarding the vocalists employed by the court, writing in 1714,

> *Vocalisten* haben wür so wenig, das wür just, ein *quatuor* mit seiner *Ripien* in der Hof*cappella* khönnen besetzen, solte aber ein oder der ander krankh werden, so khan dises auch nicht geschehen, das mann also nur mit 2: oder 3: etwas machen khan, welches ja für eine so vornembe Hochfürstl: *Cappella* nicht anständig ist, und [ich] offt gezwungen bin, auß denen *Instrumenti*sten alles hervor zu suchen, was nur singen khan, wann ich andst alle Stimmen besetzen will.

> We have so few vocalists, that we can only just fill a quartet with its ripieno in the *Hofkapelle*; should one or the other become ill, this cannot take place either, [and while] it is possible to perform something with only two or three [vocalists], this is not really appropriate for such a distinguished Most Princely *Kapelle*, and I am often forced to seek out those instrumentalists who can sing when I want to fill all vocal parts.[16]

Rather than relating exclusively to the number of singers employed, this problem may have been further exacerbated by the occasional absences of Catholic musicians employed by the court. This had certainly been the case in 1688, when the *Kapellmeister* Johann Friedrich Magg (fl. 1655–*c*.1690) complained that three French members of the *Hofkapelle* had failed to attend a single church-music performance the entire year.[17] As a Catholic himself, Pez perhaps chose not to mention this particular difficulty in his report. It seems likely that Giovanni Maria Ricci could be counted among the culprits, since in 1717 Schwartzkopff described him as follows:

> ein Italianer, singt einen schönen *Bass*, besonders beÿ den *Cammer Musi-*qüen, weilen er aber nicht wohl Teütsch singen kan, auch Catholischer *Re-ligion* ist, und dahero öffters über Feld in seine Kirch geht, alß kann er nicht beständig, und jedesmahlen in der Cappell gebraucht werden.

> an Italian, [who] sings a beautiful bass, especially as part of chamber music [performances]; however, because he cannot sing in German very well, and is also of the Catholic religion, he frequently goes across the field to his church, therefore he cannot be used constantly and every time in the chapel.[18]

Eberhard Ludwig was a particularly enlightened ruler in this regard. Pez's employment contract specifically guaranteed freedom from religious persecution: 'daß ich und die Meinige, wegen der von Unß *profiti*renden Römisch-Catholischen *Religion*, von niemanden angefochten, oder *tourbirt* werde, sondern selbige in einen benachbarten Dorff *exercire*' (that neither myself nor my wife will be attacked or

---

[16] Ibid.
[17] D-Sha, A21, Büschel 631, letter of Magg to the prince regent, Duke Friedrich Carl of Württemberg-Winnenthal, *c*. 10 February 1688.
[18] D-Sha, A21, Büschel 609, Theodor Schwartzkopff, 'Die Hoff und Capell Music', 27 May 1717.

troubled because of our profession of the Roman Catholic religion; therefore, the same shall be practised by us in a neighbouring village).[19] Yet there was at least one significant repercussion to Pez's Catholicism: the waiving of the customary requirement that he provide lodgings for a number of the court *Kapellknaben*, although he did remain their overall supervisor. Accordingly, during Pez's tenure at the court the importance of the *Kapellknaben*'s role declined markedly, to the point where in 1715 only two were employed. Friedrich Ludwig Mayer (Maier) possessed a weak bass singing voice and played oboe, viola, and the *basse de violon*, while Georg Heinrich Schmidbauer (a tenor who was able to stand in for his father as *Kantor* when required) performed on the viola, gamba, and keyboards. Both were paid 75 *Gulden* per annum, a little under one-third of an ordinary musician's wage.[20]

In contrast to many other Lutheran parts of the German-speaking lands, the Württemberg court reached a partial solution to the resultant shortage of treble voices by employing a succession of young, unmarried women as vocalists. Known as *Lehr-Discantistinnen* (and occasionally referred to as *Kapellknaben* despite that term's masculine gender), these musicians received a salary rate roughly equivalent to that of a *Kapellknabe*, and were given intensive musical training with the expectation that they would eventually become permanent members of the Württemberg music establishment.[21] A further sign of the court's relatively progressive attitude towards the employment of females was the engagement of the trumpeter Elisabetha Schmid. According to a report supplied by Schwartzkopff in 1717, she could play 'etliche Stück' (quite a number of pieces) on the instrument alongside her father and brother, but in general understood little about music.[22]

It is likely that women vocalists also figured in the troupe of French *Comödianten* engaged by Eberhard Ludwig between 1713 and 1716, in a nod towards the court's large-scale theatrical entertainments during former times. Significantly though, the duke never returned to large-scale opera, perhaps having learnt his lesson from the vast sums expended during Cousser's stay in Stuttgart early in his reign. According to his own testimony, Pez was required to compose for this group and to rehearse them for hours on end, although further details of the performances themselves are lacking.[23] As the century progressed, the annual celebration of the duke's hunting order – established in 1702 and named after St Hubert, the patron saint of the hunt – was to become one of the most important festivities in the life of the court. Serenatas and other entertainments were staged on these occasions at the ever-expanding palace in Ludwigsburg. While no music or librettos remain, a document detailing accommodation for this event in 1715 gives an idea of

[19] D-Sha, A21, Büschel 612, Anon., 'Staat und Ordnung' for Pez, 25 April 1711.

[20] On Mayer and Schmidbauer, see D-Sha, Pez, 'Lista'; D-Sha, Schwartzkopff, 'Die Hoff und Capell Music'; D-Sha, A21, Büschel 607, J. G. C. Störl, 'Lista. Der Jenigen *personen*, so der mahlen beÿ Hochfstl: Hoff-*Capell* sich befinden', 19 May 1717.

[21] See Samantha Owens, 'Professional Women Musicians in Early Eighteenth-Century Germany', *Music & Letters*, 82 (2001), 32–50.

[22] D-Sha, Schwartzkopff, 'Die Hoff und Capell Music'.

[23] Letter of Pez to Duke Eberhard Ludwig, 21 October 1715, transcribed in Sittard, *Zur Geschichte der Musik*, 1: 87–9.

the forces involved. *Oberkapellmeister* Pez was lodged in the *corps de logis*; 'die völlige Music' (all of the musicians) were packed into one large room; and the *Comödianten* had been divided into those married and single, with the former (together with their wives) housed in the orangery, and the latter in a nearby inn.[24] Given the traditional association of the horn with the hunt, the music on these occasions presumably featured the two horn players appointed by Pez in 1713, for whom he is known to have scored parts in his 'concerti graßi' [*sic*].[25]

Increasingly, in contrast to the elaborate *Singballette* and operas which had earlier been staged to celebrate ducal birthdays, by the second decade of the eighteenth century smaller-scale musical presentations were becoming the norm. The court had clearly readjusted its attitudes regarding the extent to which 'Cammer-Musique' was able to reflect a ruler's wealth and sophistication. This shift coincided with a perceptible increase in instrumental specialization within the *Hofkapelle* – apparently influenced by the employment of foreign musicians. In 1715 the latter group comprised the violinist Francesco Venturini and the French *basse de violon* player François La Rose. Both specialized primarily on their first instrument, but are also known to have played at least one other instrument as well (the violoncello and violin, respectively). The practice of instrumental specialization was also on the rise at other larger German courts in the early decades of the century, with Dresden acting as a vanguard in this respect. An important step in this process at the Württemberg court appears to have been the formalization of service 'auf dem Land', at the ruling family's country estates, which was specifically mentioned as part of the duties of *Hofmusici* for the first time in 1711.[26] By 1715, this was causing financial ructions in Stuttgart, with the ducal ecclesiastical authorities, from whose coffers the musicians were largely paid, registering their unwillingness to provide remuneration for this exclusively secular duty. In an effort to rein in expenditure, a rotational system was proposed in which a keyboardist and a copyist were on call at all times, with three groups each consisting of a violinist, an oboist, and a string bass player alternating every four weeks.[27]

At this early stage, rather than being officially appointed at a separate, higher rank, the Württemberg court musicians involved in this extra service were simply referred to jointly as 'Hof- und Camer-Musicanten' (court and chamber musicians). That there was some differentiation between members of the *Hofkapelle*

[24] Friedrich Kübler, *Die Familiengalerie des Württembergischen Fürstenhauses im Kgl. Residenzschloß zu Ludwigsburg* (Ludwigsburg: Eichhorn, 1905), 76; D-Sha, A21, Büschel 150, 'Ludwigsburger Zimmer-Außtheiler auf St: Hubert d. 3.tn Novbr: 1715'.

[25] Johann Wilhelm Lumpe and Johann Christoph Biener, appointed 26 June 1713 and 11 July 1713 respectively; see Walther Pfeilsticker, *Neues Württembergisches Dienerbuch*, I (Stuttgart: Cotta, 1957) §§886, 902; D-Sha, Pez, 'Lista'.

[26] D-Sha, A21, Büschel 611, Anon., 'Concept Staats vor die Sambtl: Hoff Musicos', 25 April 1711.

[27] D-Sha, A21, Büschel 632, Anon., 20 July 1715, 'Was denen Musici, so auff das Land gehen, statt der Natural Verpflegung, zur besold. zuschlagen ware'. In essence this was a travelling ensemble along the lines of the Saxon court's Polish *Kapelle*, organized by August II around this same time, albeit on a much smaller scale; see Chapter 3, 'The Saxon Court of the Kingdom of Poland', p. 55 ff. above.

can be seen in their annual salary rate. The latter is the sole criterion for their (ana-chronistic) separation into 'Cammer-Music' and 'Hof-Music' in the 1715 column of Table 6.1.[28] It is clear, however, from a selection of documents dating from May 1717 (following Pez's death in September 1716), that both Schwartzkopff and Störl considered chamber music a major function of the court's musical establishment, alongside church music and table music. Their reports confirm Pez's view of the *Hofkapelle* as a pool of multi-talented musicians, each capable of performing on an assortment of instruments, from which a variety of ensembles could be created depending upon the occasion.[29] But in the case of church and table music, the pre-ferred instrumentation did appear relatively fixed in the minds of the two *Kapell-meister*. By 1717, then, the concept of the orchestra as an institution with relatively set personnel and instrumentation was beginning to crystallize at the court.

## THE RISE OF *CAMMER-MUSIQUE*

The increasing importance of chamber music at the Württemberg court was further signalled approximately one month after Pez's death, when a young Italian virtuoso violinist and composer, Giuseppe Antonio Brescianello (*c.*1690–1758), was engaged under the newly created title 'director of chamber music'. He had come from Ven-ice to Munich in April 1715 in the entourage of the electress of Bavaria, Theresa Ku-nigunde (1676–1730), and possibly heard of the Württemberg *Oberkapellmeister*'s death (and the vacancy this created) from Pez's former colleagues at the Bavarian court.[30] Somewhat unusually, Brescianello's initial Württemberg appointment ap-pears to have existed outside the jurisdiction of the *Hofkapelle*. Not only is he absent from Störl's 1717 report, but Schwartzkopff's concurrent account of the mu-sical establishment mentions him only in passing, as 'Concertmeister Brescianello' in an entry on another musician, a situation that may possibly reflect his exclusion from church music performances.[31] Elsewhere, Schwartzkopff describes Brescia-nello as 'Cammer und Tafel-Music Concert Meister', but it is clear from surviving documents that the young Italian had grander plans, actively seeking promotion to the vacant post of *Oberkapellmeister*.[32] He was, however, destined to face some stiff competition from the celebrated opera composer Reinhard Keiser (1674–1739), who appeared in Stuttgart during the summer of 1719 with equally high hopes of

---

[28] Of the musicians referred to in the 20 July 1715 document, two were receiving 400 *Gul-den*, a further four 300 *Gulden*, while the remaining five men received the so-called 'ordinary' salary of 247 *Gulden* per annum.

[29] D-Sha, Schwartzkopff, 'Die Hoff und Capell Music'; D-Sha, Störl, 'Lista'.

[30] Samantha Owens, '". . . nicht so leicht in einer Protestantischen Hoff Cappell einen Ca-tholischen Cappell Meister . . .": Notes on the Early Career of Giuseppe Antonio Brescianello (*c.*1690–1758)', *Musik in Baden-Württemberg Jahrbuch*, 15 (2007), 199–214.

[31] D-Sha, Schwartzkopff, 'Die Hoff und Capell Music'.

[32] D-Sha, A21, Büschel 612, letter of Schwartzkopff to Duke Eberhard Ludwig, 1 March 1718.

gaining the position. This is documented through a collection of letters uncovered by Josef Sittard towards the end of the nineteenth century.[33]

Keiser began his campaign with a successful performance of a piece of church music and a small theatrical work. In August 1719, he wrote to the court chamberlain, Friedrich Wilhelm von Grävenitz – the brother of the duke's mistress, Christiane Wilhelmine von Grävenitz (1686–1744) – requesting support for a serenata he hoped to perform on the duke's name day (St Ludwig's day, 25 August). While the composer claimed this event would be his farewell audience, it was, in fact, to be several years before he departed the court permanently.[34] One consequence of Brescianello and Keiser's struggle over the vacant post of *Oberkapellmeister* was the increased factionalization that occurred within the *Hofkapelle*. The two sides appeared to be split largely along national lines, with Keiser notably referring to 'meine Feinde, die hiesigen Italiener' (my enemies, the local Italians), while the tenor Johann Christoph Höflein contributed a letter of support 'im nahmen braver Teutschen in der fürstlichen Capell' (in the name of the virtuous Germans of the princely *Kapelle*).[35] Having presented the duke with the score of an Italian-language opera pastorale, *Piramo e Tisbe*, in 1718, Brescianello was presumably well aware by the early 1720s that Eberhard Ludwig's artistic priorities were focused on less expensive options, possibly one reason why Keiser, a renowned composer of German opera, ultimately failed in his bid to gain the position. Brescianello was appointed *Oberkapellmeister* in February 1721, making him the first Italian to be placed in charge of the Württemberg *Hofkapelle*.[36] Keiser's frustration was released in a very public manner, when he insulted Brescianello in front of the ducal family and assembled courtiers during a *Bauernhochzeit* (a popular type of festivity imitating a 'peasant wedding'), an incident that led to his arrest and detention for several days.[37]

Brescianello's strategy for the revitalisation of the *Hofkapelle* saw a string of musicians appointed in the succeeding decade at the new rank of *Cammermusicus*.[38] The first of these long-term appointments had actually been made in 1719, when Maria Dorothea St Pierre was engaged 'beÿ dero Cammer Musique, als eine Lautenistin' (with Your Chamber Music, as a lutenist). Her salary stood at 500 *Gulden*, plus free accommodation and the right to eat at 'die Tafel bei Hoff' (the so-called 'free table' at court) at a time when the average Württemberg *Hofmusicus* received only 247 *Gulden* per annum.[39] Four chamber musicians were engaged in the year

---

[33] Josef Sittard, 'Reinhard Keiser in Württemberg', *Monatshefte für Musikgeschichte*, 18 (1886), 3–12.

[34] Letter of Keiser to Friedrich Wilhelm von Grävenitz, 16 August 1719, transcribed ibid., 4.

[35] Ibid., 10 and 6.

[36] D-Sha, A21, Büschel 612, decree of Duke Eberhard Ludwig, 1 February 1721.

[37] See D-Sha, A21, Büschel 630, documents dated 21, 22, and 28 February 1721, and 18 March 1721.

[38] See Samantha Owens, 'On the Concept of the *Kleine Cammer-Musique* in Early Eighteenth-Century German Court Music', in *Johann Friedrich Fasch als Instrumentalkomponist*, ed. Konstanze Musketa, Schriften zur mitteldeutschen Musikgeschichte, 14 (Beeskow: Ortus, 2007), 95–107.

[39] D-Sha, A21, Büschel 616, appointment decree of Duke Eberhard Ludwig, 18 September

of Brescianello's promotion: Eleonore Eisentraut (vocalist), her husband Augustus Eisentraut (violoncellist), Franz Joseph Greÿl (violinist), and Franciscus Holzbaur (bassoonist). The year 1724 saw the employment of two further violinists (Sebastian Bodinus and Haumale Des Essarts) and two male vocalists (Le Long and Barre, first names unknown). Three more *Cammermusici* – the singer Giovanna Toeschi, her husband Alessandro Toeschi (before 1700–1758), a violinist, and the gambist Johann Daniel Hardt (1696–1763) – were engaged in 1725. A bassoonist, Louis D'Etri (D'Etry or Detrÿ), and an oboist, 'Sonnetti' (probably 'Gulielmo' Schiavonetti), followed in 1727, while two years later Wenceslaus Spurni, a string bass player, and the celebrated woodwind specialist Johann Michael Böhm (b. c.1685), joined the *Kapelle*.[40]

The superior talents of these musicians were frequently showcased at special evening gatherings (*Assembléen*), hosted by individual members of the ducal family in their own private rooms. From the mid-1720s onwards, key events in the life of the court, including ducal birthdays and name days, were consistently celebrated in this manner. An example is the name day of Duchess Johanna Elisabetha in 1732, which occurred not long after her reinstatement following the imprisonment of the duke's long-term mistress the previous year.[41] As described by an official chronicler, 'Abends ware in Ihro. Fstl: Dhl: der Herzogin Zimer große *Assemblée*, worbeÿ auch ein angenehmer Camer *Music*' (In the evening Her Most Princely Serene Highness, the duchess hosted a large gathering in her rooms, which also featured a pleasant chamber music [performance]).[42]

In 1730, a visitor to the court, Baron Karl Ludwig von Pöllnitz (1692–1775), had described the hectic schedule of entertainment on offer:

> Se[ine] Durchl. lassen Französische Comödie halten, wo jederman frey zu-gelassen wird, und haben wir über das fast beständig *Ball*, Verkleidung, und Musicalisches *Concert*. Alle Tage ist grosse Gesellschaft bey der *Maitresse* des Herzogs, und spielet man in ihrem Zimmer *Piquet*, *Quadrille* und *Pha-*

1719; see also Owens, 'Professional Women Musicians', 46–7. Filippo Antonio Scandalibene had been employed at the rank of chamber musician (instrument or voice not specified) in November 1715, but was released one year later; see Pfeilsticker, *Dienerbuch*, §908.

[40] For details of the documentation for these appointments, see Owens, 'On the Concept of the *Kleine Cammer-Musique*', Table 3: 'Appointments at the level of *Cammermusicus* at the Württemberg court, 1715–29'. Regarding 'Gulielmo' Schiavonetti, see D-Sha, A21, Büschel 609, Alessandro Toeschi (?), 'les qualités, et habilités, de ses Musiciens Instrumentistes', c.January 1729. For further information on the Schiavonetti (Schiavonetto) family, the violoncellist Giovanni Baptista Schiavonetti (d. 1730), his wife, soprano Elisabetta Pilotti-Schiavonetti (d. 1742), and their oboe-playing son, see Norbert Dubowy, 'Italienische Instrumentalisten in deutschen Hofkapellen', in *The Eighteenth-Century Diaspora of Italian Music and Musicians*, ed. Reinhard Strohm (Turnhout: Brepols, 2001), 61–120, at 78; Winton Dean, 'Elisabetta Pilotti-Schiavonetti', *Grove Music Online*, <www.oxfordmusic.com> (accessed 20 December 2008). Cf. also Chapter 11, 'The Court of Würzburg', p. 309 below.

[41] Hans Jürgen Rieckenberg, 'Grävenitz, Christiane Wilhelmine Friedricke Gräfin', in *Neue Deutsche Biographie*, VI (Berlin: Duncker & Humblot, 1964), 720–22.

[42] D-Sha, A21, Büschel 149, name-day celebrations of Duchess Johanna Elisabetha, November 1732.

*raon*, so daß man hier alle Lustbarkeiten, welche an grossen Höfen sonst im Schwange gehen, zu geniessen hat.

His Serene Highness has French plays performed, to which everyone is admitted free, and apart from these there are almost continual balls, masquerades, and musical concerts. Every day there is a large gathering [hosted] by the mistress of the duke, and in her rooms one plays piquet, quadrille, and pharaon, so that here one can enjoy all the pleasures which are in vogue at large courts.[43]

It was undoubtedly Eberhard Ludwig's first-hand experience of other larger courts, particularly that of Louis XIV at Versailles, that inspired him to convert one of his hunting lodges, some fifteen miles north of Stuttgart, into his new ducal residence. This was a decision that brought him among the ranks of an increasing number of German princes who chose to abandon their traditional ruling seats around this time in favour of building magnificent baroque palaces.[44] The burgeoning service requirements of the new residence required the construction of an adjacent town, Ludwigsburg, with prospective inhabitants encouraged by the offer of free building materials, exemption from taxes for twenty years, and complete religious freedom.[45] The duke's liberal approach to the latter can be witnessed to this day in the town's market square, where two baroque churches still face each other: Protestant and Catholic. This situation was mirrored at the court itself, with a Lutheran preacher for the majority of the nobility, a Calvinist minister for the duke's daughter-in-law, Hereditary Princess Henriette Marie, and a Catholic priest for his cousin Prince Carl Alexander, a son of Friedrich Carl of Württemberg-Winnenthal (1652–1698), the former prince regent.[46] Whereas in the aftermath of the 1688 invasion *Kapellmeister* Magg had been shunned as a Catholic proselyte and French collaborator, Eberhard Ludwig surely realized that the creation of a cultured baroque court required the employment of Catholic artists and artisans from across Europe. The positive impact of this attitude on the *Hofkapelle* can also be seen in the increased number of foreign musicians appointed in these years, above all Italian and French (see Table 6.1).

By the early 1720s performances were increasingly taking place in the splendour of the duke's new palace at Ludwigsburg, and in 1725 the musicians were ordered to reside there on a permanent basis.[47] In addition to the introduction of new, more spacious performance venues, music at the court was further enriched

---

[43] Karl Ludwig von Pöllnitz, *Des Freyherrn von Pöllnitz Brieffe: welche das merckwürdigste von seinen Reisen und die Eigenschaften derjenigen Personen woraus die vernehmsten Höfe von Europa bestehen, in sich enthalten: aus der letzten vermehrten französischen Auflage ins deutsche übersetzet*, 1 (Frankfurt am Main, 1738), 380–81.

[44] See Charles Burney, *The Present State of Music in Germany, The Netherlands and United Provinces*, 2nd edn (London, 1775; facs. repr. New York: Broude Brothers, 1969), 1: 99–100.

[45] See contemporary documents reproduced in Oscar Paret, *250 Jahre Ludwigsburg, 1704–1954* (Ludwigsburg: Stadt Ludwigsburg, 1955), 20–21, 23–6.

[46] Pöllnitz, *Des Freyherrn von Pöllnitz Brieffe*, 1: 372–3.

[47] See D-Sha, A21, Büschel 632, decree of Duke Eberhard Ludwig, 28 July 1725.

through the presence of Eberhard Ludwig's son, Hereditary Prince Friedrich Ludwig (1698–1731). Having spent much of his youth abroad, at first at school in Lausanne and Turin (safe from invading French forces), and subsequently on a lengthy *Kavaliersreise*, the prince had returned home permanently in 1716. He brought with him not only a new bride, Princess Henriette Marie of Brandenburg-Schwedt (1702–1782), but also a substantial music collection featuring the latest works from the printing presses of Amsterdam and Paris. By the early 1730s, Friedrich Ludwig's collection encompassed a rich selection of manuscript and printed music from the best German and foreign composers, the full extent of which is documented in a series of inventories completed following the prince's death.[48] The surviving remnants of this sizeable collection are now held at the Universitätsbibliothek Rostock, carried north by Friedrich Ludwig's daughter, Princess Louisa Frederica (1722–1791), upon her marriage in 1746 to the future duke of Mecklenburg-Schwerin, Friedrich II (1717–1785).[49] These sources also reveal the results of decades of composing and bartering by successive Württemberg *Kapellmeister*, providing evidence of the many links between *Hofkapelle* members and their counterparts elsewhere in Europe.[50] A keen dilettante, the prince took both composition and practical music lessons with various ducal musicians and also participated in chamber music sessions with them, playing the flute. While his contribution may not have been significant financially, owing to the tight control exercised by his father over his household expenditure, there can be no doubt that Friedrich Ludwig lent unparalleled general support to the *Hofkapelle*.[51]

As can be seen from Table 6.1, the *Hofkapelle* grew in size between 1715 and 1730, particularly in the quantity of instrumentalists employed.[52] Both the appointment of Brescianello and the increased number of musicians whose training

---

[48] D-Sha, G218, Büschel 14, 'Protocollum ... den 19. Maÿ 1732'; 'Inventarium ... Anno 1732'; 'Inventarium ... Septembri et Octobri p. 1737'; 'Inventarium ... Anno 1737'.

[49] See Ekkehard Krüger, *Die Musikaliensammlungen des Erbprinzen Friedrich Ludwig von Württemberg-Stuttgart und der Herzogin Luise Friederike von Mecklenburg-Schwerin in der Universitätsbibliothek Rostock* (Beeskow: Ortus, 2006), vol. 1.

[50] There are, for example, pieces by Pez, Brescianello, and Toeschi in the former Saxon court music collection in D-Dl; works by Brescianello are also listed in the facsimile edition of the *Concert-Stube des Zerbster Schlosses, Inventarverzeichnis aufgestellt im März 1743*, published as Studien zur Aufführungspraxis und Interpretation der Musik des 18. Jahrhunderts: Dokumentationen/Reprints, 4, ed. Eitelfriedrich Thom (Michaelstein/Blankenburg: [no publisher], 1983). See also Samantha Owens, '"zum Fürstl: Hoff Staat gehörige Musicalien": The Ownership and Dissemination of German Court Music, 1665–c.1750', in *Musik an der Zerbster Residenz*, ed. Konstanze Musketa and Barbara M. Reul, Fasch-Studien, 10 (Beeskow: Ortus, 2008), 103–15.

[51] See Ortrun Landmann, '"Pour l'usage de Son Altesse Serenissime Monseigneur le Prince Hereditaire de Wirtemberg": Stuttgarter Musikhandschriften des 18. Jahrhunderts in der Universitätsbibliothek Rostock', *Musik in Baden-Württemberg Jahrbuch*, 4 (1997), 149–73; Samantha Owens, '"Und mancher grosser Fürst kan ein Apollo seyn": Erbprinz Friedrich Ludwig von Württemberg (1698–1731)', *Musik in Baden-Württemberg Jahrbuch*, 10 (2003), 177–90. On Friedrich Ludwig's expenditure, see Wilson, 'Women and Imperial Politics', 236.

[52] See D-Sha, A21, Büschel 609, letter of Brescianello to Duke Eberhard Ludwig, '... sur les Musiciens Instrumentale d'Arché', 21 January 1729; Anon., 'Concept Anbringen ... der Instrumental Music', 29 January 1729; D-Sha, Toeschi (?), '... les qualités, et habilités'; A6, Büschel

had taken place beyond the Württemberg court undoubtedly led to an expansion
of repertoire and awareness of the latest foreign performance practices. Despite
this, however, by June 1729 the focus on employing select virtuosos, often at great
expense, had resulted in a perceived decline in the standards of the larger instrumental group, with Brescianello calling for the urgent appointment of at least five
'good' string players, including two violinists, one viola player, one violoncellist,
and a double bass player.[53] In a report focusing on the *Hofkapelle*'s string players
(including chamber and ordinary musicians alike), Brescianello wrote,

[le corp de nos Musiciens Instrumental d'Arché,] qui semble peut-être d'ail-
leur bien grand, et nombreux reduit à 8, ou 9 personnes serviables [e]taut
au plus, dont s'il n'en manque quelqune (comme il arrive bien souvent) il
est absoulument impossible que je puisse produir avec honneur un des mes
Concerts, malgres tous les efforts, que je puisse faire pour le soûttenir; et
êtants memme tous ensemble il ne sauroit jammais reussir comme il faut. Il
est vrai qu' aux Musique de Table il y a presque toujours l'aide de quelque
Hautboist dont l'on ne sauroit se passer, mais, outre qu' Entre ces gens
(comme ils changent souvent) il y en a d'ordinaire contre un bon deux, ou
trois de mauvaix, qui non obstant servent bien pour remplir dans une Sinphonie, mais gattent, plus qu'ils soûtiennent un Concert ou il faut avoir des
Gens fermes, et accoutumés à cela, l'on ne sauroit pas non plus compter sur
Eux, non que quelque fois, ou ils y viennent trop tard, ou il n'en vien point
du tout: C'est allors aussi que je suis bien embarassé, et obbligé à faire aider
par tout ce qu'il y a present, jusque par des Garcons apprentifs, car les seuls
Musiciens de la Cour nes suffisent pas non plus à produire une tollerable Sinphonie de Table, qui doit être un peu forte.

though [the body of string instrumentalists] might seem quite good and
numerous, [they] reduce to eight or nine serviceable people at most; if any
of them are missing (as happens quite often), it is absolutely impossible for
me to be able to mount one of my concertos honourably in spite of all the
efforts I am able to make to support them; and even having them all together,
it would never be possible to succeed in the way that they should. It is true
that at a *Tafelmusik*, I am often helped by some *Hautboist*, which we cannot
do without, but ordinarily for every good one amongst them (as they often
change) there are two or three bad, who might be good enough to complete
a symphony, but they spoil more than they improve in a concerto, where
reliable people are needed, and accustomed to this, one cannot count on
them; sometimes they arrive late, or they do not come at all. That is why I am
very embarrassed and obliged to accept help from anyone who happens to
be about, even apprentice boys, for the court musicians alone are no longer

79, Anon., 'Specification', 24 January 1731; Anon., *Hofkapelle* register, 1731, transcribed in Sittard, *Zur Geschichte der Musik*, I: 123–4.

53  D-Sha, Brescianello, '. . . sur les Musiciens Instrumentale d'Arché'.

capable of producing an acceptable *Sinphonie de Table*, which ought to be quite impressive.[54]

A second contemporary report, almost certainly supplied by concertmaster Alessandro Toeschi, agreed with Brescianello's view: 'foibles à la verité, tant en quantité, qu'en leus qualités, et si en cas, deux ou trois venoient à manquer, soit par Maladie, Morts, ou autrement, on ne pourroit faire aucun Concert' (in truth [they are] weak both in quantity and quality; and in the event that two or three happened to be missing, whether from illness, death, or for some other reason, it would not be possible to mount any concert at all).[55]

Given the difficulty of this situation, it appears that despite the official distinction made between ordinary and chamber musicians in both title and salary, all – regardless of rank – were expected to participate in everyday *Hofkapelle* performances, due to the small size of the musical establishment. The appointment decrees of a number of musicians referred explicitly to this condition, such as that of Wenceslaus Spurni, appointed 'zu einem Bassisten beÿ Dero zu Cammer alß größeren Hof-Music' (as a [string] bass player with Your chamber [music] as well as the larger *Hofmusik*).[56] As pointed out by Brescianello in his 1729 report, musicians from outside the *Hofkapelle* regularly took part in court performances throughout the first half of the century, including members of various local *Hautboistenbanden* (some on a more permanent basis than others), the resident trumpeters and kettledrummers, other court employees, students, and local *Stadtmusicanten* (civic musicians). With the rise in specialization from the 1720s and 1730s, it seems that the 'old guard' (consisting primarily of *Hofmusici* and *Hautboisten*) was increasingly left behind, eventually being useful only as fairly rudimentary ripieno players.[57] In 1730, a direct attempt was made to improve discipline, and with it performance standards, through the appointment of an aristocratic 'Ober-Music-Director', Christian Adolf von Ziegesar. Unfortunately, this move was not a success, severely undermining Brescianello's authority and causing widespread dissension within the musical establishment.[58]

## THE TRIUMPH OF ITALIAN OPERA

By the end of 1733, the duke, his son Friedrich Ludwig, and his grandson Prince Eberhard Friedrich had all died (tragically, the latter lived for only a matter of months, in 1718–19). The ducal seat passed to Carl Alexander (1684–1737), Eberhard Ludwig's Catholic cousin from the family's Winnenthal line. Recalled to

[54] D-Sha, Brescianello, '... sur les Musiciens Instrumentale d'Arché'.

[55] D-Sha, Toeschi (?), '... les qualités, et habilités'.

[56] D-Sha, A21, Büschel 617, decree of Duke Eberhard Ludwig, 8 June 1729.

[57] See, for example, the career of Caspar Heinrich Hetsch, outlined in Samantha Owens, 'Regimental and Courtly Oboe Bands in Early Eighteenth-Century Württemberg', *ABA Journal of Band Research*, 34/2 (1999), 1–18, at 12.

[58] See Samantha Owens, 'Censorship of the *Goût Moderne* in 1730s Ludwigsburg and the Music of Giuseppe Antonio Brescianello', *Eighteenth-Century Music*, 2 (2005), 299–310.

Stuttgart from his post as imperial governor of Belgrade, the new duke was known more for his military exploits than for his interest in cultural matters, a state of affairs that took an unexpected turn in 1736 with the engagement of a contingent of Italian vocalists (predominantly female).[59] These musicians, together with the opera composer Riccardo Broschi (brother of the celebrated castrato Farinelli) who was appointed *maestro di capella* alongside Brescianello, formed the basis of an Italian opera company.[60] Yet this venture was destined to be short-lived, due to the duke's unexpected death in March 1737. Carl Rudolph of Württemberg-Neustadt (r. 1737–38), the first of the two administrator dukes who followed, re-leased all the court's musicians; some months later he re-established the *Hofkapelle*, but it was substantially reduced both in size and in the levels of individual salaries. For *Oberkapellmeister* Brescianello in particular, the duke's sudden demise was catastrophic, since it resulted in his replacement by the gamba player Hardt – a chain of events that serves to highlight the often erratic nature of court employment.

Luckily for Brescianello, this period of retrenchment (and personal humiliation), during which the administrator dukes sought to bring the duchy back on a secure footing following Carl Alexander's financially reckless reign, came to an end when the latter's eldest son obtained his majority in 1744. Having spent the years immediately prior to his accession at the Prussian court of Friedrich II, the new duke, Carl Eugen (1728–1793), returned to Stuttgart from Berlin with a handful of musicians including the lutenist Johann Friedrich Daube, the violinist and keyboardist Jacob Senger (Sänger), the copyist Johann Friedrich Baltz, and the violinist Joseph Lang.[61] While he is known to have taken keyboard lessons with C. P. E. Bach whilst in Berlin, Carl Eugen's musical interests appear to have been wide-ranging. This is indicated in a letter from Georg Wilhelm Weißmann in 1748 regarding a 'Bock-Music' consisting of bagpipers and fiddle players that had served the hereditary prince in both Berlin and in Stuttgart earlier in his reign. With its origins in Eastern European traditional music, this group was only one of a number of diverse ensembles that contributed their unique musical flavour to the wider sound world of the early-eighteenth-century court beyond the confines of the *Hofkapelle*. The latter also included the trumpeters and kettledrum players, horn players assigned to the hunt, and the court and regimental oboe bands.[62]

[59] Angelica Cantelli, her father 'Anshelm' Cantelli, Margaretha Furiosi, Ginevra Poli, Staggi (first name unknown, employed together with her husband, the oboist Carlo Staggi), 'Tedeschina', Carlina Valvassori, and Giovanni Philippo Galetti; see D-Sha, A21, Büschel 609, Brescianello, '*Specification* Sämtliche beÿ der Fürstl: Camer- und Hoff-*Music*', 13 November 1736; D-Sha A7, Büschel 44, Anon., 'Besoldungs Reglement vor die Neü-Beschriebene u. anzunehmende *Virtuosinnen*', 31 August 1736.

[60] D-Sha, A7, Büschel 50, decree of Duke Carl Alexander, 10 November 1736: '*Compositore di Musica Riccardo Broschi* in dero dienste gdgst. beruffen u. zum *Maestro di Capella* wegen seiner besitzenden guthen Geschicklichkeit u. *virtù* bestelt u. angenommen haben' (*Compositore di musica* Riccardo Broschi, who, due to the good skill and virtue which he possesses, has been graciously taken into your service as *maestro di capella*).

[61] Stephan Morens, 'Herzog Carl Eugen von Württemberg und die Stuttgarter Oper um 1750', *Musik in Baden-Württemberg Jahrbuch*, 11 (2004), 83–98, at 94.

[62] See Owens, 'Regimental & Courtly Oboe Bands'; Samantha Owens, '"Gedancken für

Although the figures for the year 1745 in Table 6.1 depict the state of the Würt-temberg musical establishment very early in Carl Eugen's reign, it is evident that the young ruler was already starting to make his mark.[63] Presumably influenced both by his experience of his father's foray into the world of Italian opera in the 1730s, as well as his own familiarity with theatrical music at the Prussian court, two lists from published court calendars for the years 1744 and 1746 signal the direction of the future changes Carl Eugen was to introduce. He began by reinstating Brescianello to the position of *Oberkapellmeister* and restoring the *Hofkapelle* to more or less its size and constitution at the time of his father's death in 1737 (with the exception of the troupe of Italian opera singers, although that development was to come).

The duke then commenced appointing virtuosos, including three musicians fresh from the service of the exiled king of Poland based in Lorraine, Stanisław Leszczyński (1677–1766): the Italian oboist Ignazio Ceceri, the horn player Franz Spurni, and his wife, lutenist Maria Dorothea (née St Pierre).[64] This marked the return of the Spurnis to the Württemberg court, which they had left during the late 1730s (together with their young daughter Dorothea, later Wendling) after many years of what they considered inadequate remuneration.[65] Among the most notable of these early engagements was the soprano Francesca Cuzzoni (1696–1778), more than a little past her prime, hired in December 1745. She was to be the first in a seemingly never-ending string of Italian opera singers employed by Carl Eugen, in what was to emerge as one of his all-consuming passions. Further fostered through an impressive theatrical building programme, the 1750s and 1760s saw a series of large-scale Italian-language operas produced under the direction of Niccolò Jommelli (appointed *Oberkapellmeister* in 1753) and the celebrated ballet master Jean Georges Noverre, entertainments that have largely been examined in detail elsewhere.[66]

During Carl Eugen's notoriously extravagant reign – even his wife, Elisabeth

ein gantzes Leben": *Polnischer Bock* Music at the Württemberg Court, *c.*1730', *The Consort: European Journal of Early Music*, 54 (1998), 43–56.

[63] Anon., *V. Continuatio . . . oder Beschreibung was dermahlen vor Standes-Persohnen . . . so die Hoch-Fürstl. resp. Herr und Dienerschafft ausmachen . . . des Jahrs 1744* (Eßlingen, [1744]), 30–31; Anon., register of the *Hofkapelle*, 1 February 1745, transcribed in Sittard, *Zur Geschichte der Musik*, II: 29–31; D-Sha, A21, Büschel 614, Anon., 'Besoldungen beÿ Hochfürstl: Cammer Music', *c.*1744–5; and Anon., *VII. Continuatio . . . oder Beschreibung, was dermahlen vor Standes-und andere Persohnen . . . bey Hoch-Fürstlich-Württembergischen Hof . . . bey dem Anfang des Jahrs 1746* (Heilbronn, [1746]), 39–40.

[64] On Ceceri, see Owens, 'An Italian Oboist in Germany – Double Reed Making *c.*1750', *Early Music*, 28 (2000), 65–70.

[65] See documents relating to the Spurnis in D-Sha, A21, Büschel 617.

[66] See, for example, Audrey Lyn Tolkoff, 'The Stuttgart Operas of Niccolò Jommelli' (PhD diss., Yale University, 1974); Ute Christine Berger, *Die Feste des Herzogs Carl Eugen von Württemberg* (Tübingen: Silberburg-Verlag, 1997); Friedrich Lippmann, 'La "Didone abbandonata" di Niccolò Jommelli (Stoccarda, 1763)', *Rivista italiana di musicologia*, 38 (2003), 257–81; Stefan Morens, 'Herzog Carl Eugen von Württemberg und die Stuttgarter Oper um 1750', *Musik in Baden-Württemberg Jahrbuch*, 11 (2004), 83–98.

Friderique Sophie of Brandenburg-Bayreuth (1732–1780), was so disgusted by his profligate behaviour that she left him in 1754 – the musical establishment expanded considerably. Music was frequently employed to enhance the pomp and ceremony surrounding virtually every aspect of the duke's everyday life. Accordingly, a comparison of the *Hofkapelle* in the years 1715 and 1760 reveals a marked increase in the number of vocalists and instrumentalists; indeed, the figures more or less doubled during that time (excluding the largely ceremonial trumpet and kettledrum ensemble, which remained a fairly static entity). In stark contrast to the first few decades of the century, when Württemberg court musicians were expected as matter of course to perform on a variety of instruments, by the 1750s a highly stratified division of musical personnel had become the norm, from the *Oberkapellmeister* down to the lowliest *Calcant*. Printed court calendars provide unambiguous evidence of this increasingly strict hierarchy, with the main body ranging from specialist 'Cammer Virtuosen' down to ordinary 'Hof-Musici'.[67]

That the personnel required for such sumptuous musical display included a significant proportion of highly paid foreigners – largely, although not exclusively, Italian – is undoubtedly one of the most striking aspects of the 1760 column in Table 6.1. In 1715 only a small handful of the musicians had come from non-German speaking backgrounds.[68] However, the costly splendour of 1760 belied a less than savoury backdrop, having been paid for 'in blood': the capital raised in part through an agreement with France to provide an army of 6,000 infantrymen, the large majority of whom were peasants pressed into military service against their will.[69] Leopold Mozart, perhaps somewhat unfairly, laid the blame for the extraordinary number of Italians squarely at the feet of Jommelli, writing in 1763,

> Ich sehe die ganze Sache als ein Werk des Jomelli an, der sich alle Mühe giebt, die Deutschen an diesem Hofe auszurotten. Es ist ihm auch schon fast gelungen und wird ihm immer mehr gelingen. . . . Ueberdiess hat er bey seiner Musik unumschränkte Macht, und das ist es, was die Musik gut macht. Wie sehr aber Jommelli für seine Nation eingenohmen ist können sie daraus schlüssen, weil er und andere seiner Landsleute, deren sein Haus immer voll ist, um ihm aufzuwarten, sich vernehmen liessen, daß es zu verwundern und kaum glaublich seye, daß ein kind teutscher Geburt so ein Musik: genie und so viel geist und feuer haben könne, ridete amici!

> I regard the whole business as the work of Jommelli, who is doing his best to eradicate the Germans at this court. He has almost succeeded too, and will succeed completely . . . Moreover, he has unlimited control over his *Musik* [ensemble] and that explains the music's excellence. Indeed you can judge how partial Jommelli is to his country from the fact that he and some of his

---

[67] See, for example, the list of Württemberg court musicians signed by 'Music Director und Ober Capell Meister' Niccolò Jommelli, c.1750, in D-Sha, A21, Büschel 607.

[68] Georg Ernst Bürckh, *Jetzt-florirendes Würtemberg, oder Herzogl. Würtembergisches Adress-Hand-Buch* . . . (Stuttgart, 1760), 58, 64–6, 69.

[69] Daniel Heartz, *Music in European Capitals: The Galant Style, 1720–80* (New York: W. W. Norton, 2003), 448–9.

compatriots, who are ever swarming at his house to pay him their respects, were heard to say that it was amazing and hardly believable that a child of German birth [W. A. Mozart] could have such unusual genius and so much understanding and passion, *ridete amici*![70]

Yet despite this condemnation, the early decades of Carl Eugen's rule were still remembered by some as the halcyon days of music in Württemberg. Certainly, the poet Christian Friedrich Daniel Schubart (1739–1791) saw the situation in a rather more positive light, while having more reason than most to think ill of the duke's regime. Writing during his ten-year incarceration in the fortress of Hohenasperg (after reportedly insulting one of duke's mistresses), he nevertheless considered Carl Eugen's reign to have been

> die eigentliche blühende Epoche der Wirtembergischen Musik ... Er [Carl Eugen] verschrieb viele Sänger und Sängerinnen aus Italien, besetzte sein Orchester mit den trefflichsten Meistern, und nahm den grossen Jomelli mit einem Jahrgehalt von 10[,]000 fl [*Gulden*] als Obercapellmeister in seine Dienste — Von dieser Zeit an wurde der musikalische Geschmack in diesem Lande ganz *welsch* ... Unter Jomelli ward die Wirtembergsiche Hofmusik eine der ersten der Welt.

> the most flourishing epoch in the music of Württemberg ... He [Carl Eugen] recruited many male and female singers from Italy, filled his orchestra with the most excellent masters, and took the great Jommelli into his service as *Oberkapellmeister* with a yearly salary of 10,000 *Gulden*. From this time on-wards musical taste in the region was totally Italian ... [and] under Jommelli the Württemberg *Hofmusik* became one of the foremost in the world.[71]

There can be no doubt, however, that this proud musical tradition was depend-ent not only on Carl Eugen, Jommelli, and their 'most excellent masters' both vocal and instrumental. Schubart, in fact, described all the dukes of Württemberg as great supporters and lovers of music. Indeed, in many senses its success owed as much to the foundations laid by earlier rulers, and, perhaps even more importantly, to the successive ranks of *Kapellmeister*, *Cammermusici*, and *Hofmusici* employed at the court during the first six decades of the eighteenth century.[72]

[70] Letter of Leopold Mozart to Lorenz Hagenauer, 11 July 1763, in *Mozart: Briefe und Aufzeichnungen: Gesamtausgabe*, ed. Wilhelm Adolf Bauer and Otto Erich Deutsch, 1 (Kassel: Bärenreiter, 1962), 76. Translation adapted from Emily Anderson, *The Letters of Mozart and His Family*, 3rd edn, rev. and ed. by Stanley Sadie and Fiona Smart (London: W. W. Norton, 1985), 23.

[71] Christian Friedrich Daniel Schubart, *Ideen zu einer Ästhetik der Tonkunst* (Vienna: Degen, 1806), 2nd repr., ed. Fritz and Margrit Kaiser (Hildesheim and New York: Olms, 1990), 149–50.

[72] Ibid., 147.

TABLE 6.1. Membership of the Württemberg-Stuttgart Court Music Establishment in 1715, 1730, 1745, and 1760

| Year | 1715 | 1730 | 1745 | 1760 |
|---|---|---|---|---|
| Ruler | Duke Eberhard Ludwig (r. 1693–1733) | | Duke Carl Eugen (r. 1744–93) | |
| Numeric Overview | 3 Kapellmeister / 1 concertmaster / 21 instrumentalists (1 doubling as vocalist) / 7 trumpeters & 1 kettledrummer / 11 vocalists (3 doubling as instrumentalists) / 2 Kapellknaben[a] / 2 additional personnel | 2 Kapellmeister / 2 concertmasters / 26 instrumentalists / 9 trumpeters & 1 kettledrummer / 9 members of Hautboistenbande / 12 vocalists[b] / 4 Kapellknaben / 2 additional personnel | 2 Kapellmeister / 2 concertmasters / 25 instrumentalists (1 doubling as vocalist) / 6 trumpeters & 1 kettledrummers / Hautboistenbande (c.9 members?) / 9 vocalists (including 2 Kapellknaben) / 2 additional personnel | 2 Kapellmeister / 49 instrumentalists / 8 trumpeters & 2 kettledrummers / 16 vocalists / 2 additional personnel |
| 'Ober-Music-Director'[c] | | Christian Adolf von Ziegesar | | |
| Oberkapellmeister | Johann Christoph Pez | Giuseppe Antonio Brescianello | Giuseppe Antonio Brescianello | Niccolò Jommelli, 'Music-Director und Ober-Capell-Meister' |
| Kapellmeister | Theodor Schwarzkopff / Johann Georg Christian Störl (also organist at the Stuttgart Stiftskirche, civic church) | Theodor Schwarzkopff | Johann Daniel Hardt | Johann Daniel Hardt |

| Year | 1715 | 1730 | 1745 | 1760 |
|---|---|---|---|---|
| Concertmaster | Giuseppe Antonio Brescianello (vn) | Haumale Des Essarts (vn?) | Stephan Freudenberg (vn) | |
| | | Alessandro Toeschi (vn) | Johann Michael Böhm (fl, rec, and ob) | |
| **Instrumentalists** | | | | |
| *Cammermusici* | | | | |
| Violin | Francesco Venturini (also vc) | Franz Xavier Blam (*Cammerdiener* visiting from the Bavarian court) | *See* Concertmaster | Pietro Martinez |
| | Franz Anton Maximilian Pez (also va, va d'am, and cl) | Stephan Freudenberg | | Andreas Curz |
| | Stephan Freudenberg (also rec, ob, and fl) | Francesco Venturini (also vc) | | Pietro Pieri |
| | *See* Concertmaster, Oboe, *and Basse de violon* | Eisenhuth, 'Hoff und Cammermusicus' | | Angelo Giura |
| | | *See* Concertmaster | | Angelo Vio |
| | | | | Antonio Lolli |
| | | | | Martial Greiner |
| | | | | Florian Johann Deller (Döller) |
| | | | | Philipp David Stierlen |
| | | | | Johann Georg Glanz |
| | | | | Angelo Emiliani |

| Instrument | | | | |
|---|---|---|---|---|
| | | | See Concertmaster | Pietro Poli / Joseph Stenz |
| Viola | See Violin | | | |
| Violoncello | | Wenceslaus Spurni / Augustus Eisentraut / See Violin | | Johann Heinrich Botthof / Ignaz Voschitka / Eberhard Malterre / Planti |
| *Basse de violon* | François La Rose (also vn) | | | |
| Viola da gamba | See Violin | Johann Daniel Hardt / See Violin | | |
| Contrabass | | | | Angelo Conti / Gasparo Giannini |
| Flute | See Violin *and* Harpsichord | Johann Michael Böhm (also rec and ob; also secretary with the chamber music) | See Concertmaster | |
| Recorder | See Violin, Oboe, *and* Harpsichord | See Flute | See Concertmaster | |
| Oboe | Johann Eberhard Hildebrand (also rec and vn) | 'Gulielmo' Schiavonetti | Ignazio Ceceri | Joseph Plà |
| | See Violin *and* Harpsichord | See Flute | See Concertmaster | Juan Baptiste Plà |
| Clarinet | See Violin | | | |

| Year | 1715 | 1730 | 1745 | 1760 |
|---|---|---|---|---|
| Bassoon | | Louis D'Etri (D'Etry or Detrÿ) | | |
| Horn | | Franz Spurni | Franz Spurni | Franz Spurni |
| Lute/Theorbo | Johann Gumprecht (lute/theorbo; also 'Tutelar Rath'd) | Maria Dorothea Spurni (née St Pierre) (lute) | Maria Dorothea Spurni (née St Pierre) (lute) | |
| | | | Johann Friedrich Daube (lute/theorbo) | |
| Harpsichord | Johann Nicola Nicolai (also rec, fl, and ob) | | Jacob Senger | |
| *Hofmusici* Violin | Georg Albrecht Kreß (also va d'am, va, and rec) | Johann Eberhard Dunz (also va and copyist) | Johann Eberhard Dunz | Johann Eberhard Dunz |
| | Georg Christoph Hildebrand (also va) | Friedrich Ludwig Mayer | Johann Michael Himmelreich | Luigi Schiatti |
| | Georg Christoph Bleßner (also ob, rec, cl, va, and bass singer) | Georg Christoph Bleßner | [Johann Balthasar?] Enßlinᵉ (also bass singer) | Caspar Heinrich Hetsch |
| | Johann Georg Zahn (also va, rec, and kbd) | Albrecht Andreas Fischer | Albrecht Andreas Fischer (also tpt) | |
| | Georg Philipp Schwahn (also va and 'musical' *Paucker* – that is, musically literate) | Georg Philipp Schwahn (also va) | Johann Ernst Lang | |

| | | | | |
|---|---|---|---|---|
| | Jean Mamere (dismissed by July 1715) | Sigmund Castenbauer (also va and 'Instrument Verwalter', steward of the instruments) | Francesco Venturini (possibly retired) | |
| | See Concertmaster, (Instr.) *Cammermusici*, Oboe, *Waldhorn*, *Hautboisten*, Hoftrompeter, Alto (*Hofmusici*), Tenor (*Hofmusici*), and Copyist | See Concertmaster *and* Copyist | See Concertmaster *and* Copyist | See (Instr.) *Cammermusici* |
| Viola | See (Instr.) *Cammermusici*, *Violin*, *Waldhorn*, *Hautboisten*, Alto (*Hofmusici*), *Kapellknaben, and* Copyist | See Violin | | Johann Michael Himmelreich[f] |
| Viola d'amore | See (Instr.) *Cammermusici and Violin* | | | Johann Ferdinand Herdtlen (Herdlein); Albrecht Andreas Fischer |
| Violoncello | Johann Christoph Grott (also court painter); See (Instr.) *Cammermusici* | Carl Gustav Radauer; Johann Christoph Grott (also court painter); See (Instr.) *Cammermusici* | Carl Gustav Radauer; Franz Christian Jahn (jun.) | Carl Gustav Radauer; See (Instr.) *Cammermusici* |

| Year | 1715 | 1730 | 1745 | 1760 |
|---|---|---|---|---|
| *Basse de violon* | *See* (Instr.) *Cammermusici,* Oboe, *and Kapellknaben* | | | |
| Viola da gamba | *See Hoftrompeter and Kapellknaben* | *See* (Instr.) *Cammermusici* | | |
| String bass (generic) | *See Hautboisten* | | | |
| Contrabass | Erhardt Eberlen[g] | | Johann Christoph (or Christian) Jahn (sen.) (also 'Instrumenten-Verwalter') | Johann Christoph (or Christian) Jahn (sen.) |
|  | *See Hoforganist* | | | Franz Christian Jahn (jun.)<br>*See* (Instr.) *Cammermusici* |
| Flute | *See* (Instr.) *Cammermusici* | *See* (Instr.) *Cammermusici* | *See* Concertmaster | [Georg Friedrich?] Enßlin<br>Johann Friedrich Daube[h] |
| Recorder | *See* (Instr.) *Cammermusici,* Oboe, Violin, *and Hautboisten* | *See* (Instr.) *Cammermusici* | *See* Concertmaster | |
| Oboe | Johann Michael Glockhardt (also vn, rec, and *basse de violon*)<br>*See* (Instr.) *Cammermusici,* Violin, *and Kapellknaben* | Johann Eberhard Hildebrand<br>Adam Friedrich Commerell<br>Caspar Heinrich Hetsch | Adam Friedrich Commerell<br>Caspar Heinrich Hetsch<br>*See* Concertmaster *and* (Instr.) *Cammermusici* | Adam Friedrich Commerell<br>Christoph Hetsch |

| Instrument | | | | |
|---|---|---|---|---|
| Clarinet | *See* (Instr.) *Cammermusici,* Violin, *and* Copyist | *See* (Instr.) *Cammermusici* | | *See* (Instr.) *Cammermusici* |
| Bassoon | *See Waldhorn and Hautboisten* | *See* (Instr.) *Cammermusici* | Johann Christoph Biener (Bühner) | Johann Conrad Zobel |
| *Waldhorn* | Johann Wilhelm Lumpe (also vn)<br>Johann Christoph Biener (Bühner) (also va and bn) | Johann Christoph Biener (Bühner) | Johann Midlar (Millars)<br>Johann Conrad Zobel<br>Andreas Schacke (Zschacke)<br>*See* (Instr.) *Cammermusici and* Hautboisten | *See* (Instr.) *Cammermusici* |
| Lute/Theorbo | *See* (Instr.) *Cammermusici* | *See* (Instr.) *Cammermusici* | *See* (Instr.) *Cammermusici* | |
| Harpsichord/ Keyboard | *See* (Instr.) *Cammermusici,* Violin, *and* Kapellknaben | *See* (Instr.) *Cammermusici* | *See* (Instr.) *Cammermusici* | |
| *Hoforganist* | Isaac Seidel (also cb for opera accompaniment) | Isaac Seidel | Johann Stierlen | Johann Stierlen |
| *Hautboisten* | Georg Friedrich Bamberg<br>Sigmund Castenbauer (vn, va, bn, and string bass) | Georg Friedrich Bamberg | Georg Friedrich Bamberg<br>[Georg Friedrich?] Enßlin | Georg Friedrich Bamberg<br>Jacob Senger |

# SAMANTHA OWENS

| Year | 1715 | 1730 | 1745 | 1760 |
|---|---|---|---|---|
| *Hautboisten (cont.)* | Carl Gustav Radauer (large and small string bass, va, bn, and bass rec) | | Johann Ferdinand Herdtlen (Herdlein) (also hn) | |
| | | | Friedrich Martin Keßler (also 'Hof-Musicus')i | |
| *Hoftrompeter*i | Georg Melchior Fenchel (played with *Hofkapelle*; also vn and vdg) | Johann Friedrich Otto (official member of *Hofkapelle*) | Johann Friedrich Otto | Johann Friedrich Otto |
| | Johann Friedrich Otto (from July 1715 played with *Hofkapelle*; also vn) | Georg Andreas Steinmarck (official member of *Hofkapelle*) | Johann Leonhard Dürr | Johann Gottfried Greber |
| | Johann Casimir Gundel | Johann Casimir Gundel | Johann Christoph Hellwig | Johann Andreas Barth |
| | Johann Jacob Grimminger | Johann Christoph Hellwig | Georg Andreas Steinmarck | Johann Christoph Hellwig |
| | Johann Heinrich Schachtenbeck | Johann Leonhard Dürr | Johann Gottfried Greber | Andreas Martini |
| | Philipp Heinrich Riecker | Domini (Dominique) Acostak | Andreas Martini | Andreas Bloß |
| | Daniel Rousselin (probably retired) | Johann Heinemann (sen.) | *See Violin* | Georg Andreas Steinmarck |
| | | 'Trompeterin R[H?]einemænnin' (female trumpeter)l | | Johann Heinemann (jun.) |

| | | | | |
|---|---|---|---|---|
| *Hofpaucker* | Jeremias Christian Reusinger<br>*See* Violin | | Johann Michael Beumelburg<br>Jeremias Christian Reusinger<br>Eberhard Wilhelm[k] | Ernst Wilhelm Schwartz<br>Heinrich Gottlieb Eckhard (Eccardt), 'Jagd-Paucker' (kettledrummer for the hunt) |
| *Hautboistenbande* | | The 'Bande Hautbois von der Garde Fusiliers' (9 musicians)[m] | Georg Friderich Enßlin and the *Hautboisten* 'von der Fürstl. Garde zu Fuß' (from the ducal infantry guard)[n] | |
| Vocalists<br>*Cammermusici*<br>Soprano | Maria Anna Franziska Pez<br>Eleonore Eisentraut | | Maria Johanna Frankenberg<br>Francesca Cuzzoni | Maria Masi-Giura<br>Monaca Bonani<br>Aloysia Louise Josepha Pircker<br>Ferdinando Mazzanti<br>Francesco Guerrieri<br>Francesco Bozzi<br>Joseph Paganelli<br>Arcangelo Cortoni |
| Alto | | | | |
| Tenor | | | Johann Christoph Höflein (also chamber secretary) | Johann Ignatius (Cajetano) Neusinger[o] |

| Year | 1715 | 1730 | 1745 | 1760 |
|---|---|---|---|---|
| Tenor (*cont.*) | | | | Johann Ignatius (Cajetano) Neusinger |
| Bass | Giovanni Maria Ricci | Giovanni Maria Ricci | | |
| Range not specified | | Le Long<br>Barret (soprano?) | | |
| *Hofmusici* | | | | |
| Soprano | Maria Dorothea Kornbeck<br><br>Johanna Dorothea Sybilla Schmidbauer<br><br>Susanna Margaretha Scharnizki, 'Lehr-Discantistin' (trainee vocalist) | Johanna Dorothea Sybilla Rueff (née Schmidbauer)<br><br>Christina Louisa Mayer (née Schmidbauer)<br><br>Maria Dorothea Schulz, 'Lehr-Discantistin'<br><br>Madelaine Le Febure, 'Lehr-Discantistin' | Johanna Dorothea Sybilla Rueff (née Schmidbauer) | Maria Johanna Franckenberg[er]<br><br>Johanna Dorothea Sybilla Rueff (née Schmidbauer) |
| Alto | Matthias Gabrielis (also vn)<br><br>Johann Christian Arnold (also copyist and va)<br>Johann Frohmäyer (probably retired) | Matthias Gabrielis<br><br>Johann Christian Arnold | Matthias Gabrielis | Matthias Gabrielis<br><br>Johannes Wangner |
| Tenor | *See Hofkantor*<br>*See Kapellknaben* | | | *See Hofkantor* |

| | | | | |
|---|---|---|---|---|
| **Bass** | Johann Franz Wagner (also imperial notary)<br>*See* Violin *and* Kapellknaben | | [Friedrich Ludwig?] Mayer (also copyist)<br>*See* Violin | [Johann Balthasar?] Enßlin<br>Glantz (*cf.* Glanz among *Cammermusici above*) |
| **Hofkantor** | Johann Georg Schmidbauer (tenor; also vn) | Johann Joseph Reuss (Reis) (at Ludwigsburg)<br>Vetter (at Stuttgart) | Johann Christoph Seemann | Johann Georg Stözel (in the Lutheran court chapel) |
| **Kapellknaben** | Friedrich Ludwig Mayer (ob, va, *basse de violon*, and bass singer)<br>Georg Heinrich Schmidbauer (va, vdg, kbd, and tenor) | Johann Caspar (both vocal and instrumental music)<br>[Christoph or Johann Leonhard?] Hetsch<br>Johann Achilles Strauss<br>Philipp David Stierlen | Megger (vocal range not specified)<br>Johannes Wangner (castrato) | [Martin Mohr ('Capell-Knab' in the Catholic court chapel) P] |
| **Additional Personnel** | | | | |
| *Copyist* | Anthonÿ Meister (also vn, va, and cl)<br>*See* Alto (*Hofmusici*) | Carl Coraro Belleroche (also vn)<br>*See* Violin | Carl Coraro Belleroche (also vn)<br>*See* Bass (*Hofmusici*) | Johann Friedrich Baltz |
| *Calcant* | Johann Philipp Jungheimb (also 'Instrument Verwalter', steward of the instruments) | Schwartzkopff | Name not specified | Conrad Remp |

[notes to table overleaf]

*Sources*

1715: Based on information in D-Sha, Pez, 'Lista'; D-Sha, 'Lista. Der ganzen Würtenb: Hfrtl: Hof Music'; and the 'Etat der Hof Musik'.

1730: Based on information in D-Sha, Brescianello, '... sur les Musiciens Instrumentale d'Arché'; D-Sha, 'Concept Anbringen . . . der Instrumental Music'; D-Sha, Toeschi (?), '... les qualités, et habilités'; D-Sha, 'Specification'; and *Hofkapelle* register, 1731.

1745: Based on information in *v. Continuatio . . . des Jahrs 1744*, 30–31; *Hofkapelle* register, 1745; D-Sha, 'Besoldungen beÿ Hochfürstl: Cammer Music'; and *VII. Continuatio . . . des Jahrs 1746*, 39–40.

1760: Based on information provided in Bürckh, *Jetzt-florirendes Würtemberg . . . Adress-Hand-Buch*, 58, 64–6, 69.

a  In 1715 and 1730, the *Kapellknaben* performed as both instrumentalists and vocalists on a regular basis and are thus listed separately here.

b  Although select instrumentalists and vocalists undoubtedly continued to perform as vocalists and instrumentalists (that is, vice versa), as the eighteenth century progressed extant court records relating to the musicians increasingly do not mention this, presumably a sign of specialization within the *Hofkapelle*.

c  For further details regarding this position (newly created in 1730), see Owens, 'Censorship of the *Goût Moderne*'.

d  A member of the chief supervisory body for the care of orphans in Württemberg, see Karl Pfaff, *Geschichte Wirtenbergs*, II (Reutlingen, 1820), 201.

e  The exact identity of the two musicians with the surname Enßlin is difficult to establish; both appear in the anonymous *Hofkapelle* register, 1745, p. 30: one as 'Musicus und Bassist Enslin', the other as 'Hautboist Enßlin'.

f  Himmelreich, Herdtlen, and Fischer are listed under the rubric 'Violette'.

g  While the terminology used for this instrument around 1715 differed, for example 'violone' (Pez, 1714), 'Grossen Violon' (Schwartzkopff and Störl, 1717), and 'Contra Bass' (Störl, 1717), it is clear from extant documents that all these terms referred to the same 16' pitch instrument; see Owens, 'The Württemberg *Hofkapelle*', 179 ff. In 1729, Brescianello identified the lack of 'une bonne Grosse Basse'; see D-Sha, Brescianello, '... sur les Musiciens Instrumentale d'Arché'.

h  On Daube's descent from 'Cammer-Theorbist' to ordinary flute player, see Susan P. Snook-Luther, *The Musical Dilettante: A Treatise on Composition by J. F. Daube* (Cambridge: Cambridge University Press, 1992), 2–4.

i  Former *Hautboist* with the ducal guard (see D-Sha, A21, Büschel 615, appointment decree, 1 November 1745), who thus would have played a variety of instruments to a professional standard; he is not associated with any particular instrument in archival records, hence his inclusion here among the *Hautboisten*.

j  Strictly speaking, the *Hoftrompeter* and *Hofpaucker* were not part of the *Hofkapelle*; however, there always appears to have been two trumpeters (often designated 'musical' trumpeters) who performed on a regular basis with the *Hofkapelle*. In 1731, Otto and Steinmarck were described as members of the latter (see D-Sha, 'Specification').

k  Both Acosta and Eberhard Wilhelm were described in court accounts as 'moors' and were probably of African descent; for a discussion of two further 'Mohren' employed at the Württemberg court during the seventeenth century – the kettledrum player Eberhard Christoph and the trumpeter Christian Real – see Monika Firla and Hermann Forkl, 'Afrikaner und Africana am württembergischen Herzogshof im 17. Jahrhundert', *Tribus: Jahrbuch des Linden-Museums Stuttgart*, 44 (1995), 149–93.

<sup>l</sup> Presumably the daughter of Johann Heinemann (sen.). The D-Sha 'Specification' dated 1731 lists 'Trompeterin R[?H]einemæennin' immediately after Johann Heinemann (sen.), although it is clear that the feminine indicators – the 'in' at the end of 'Trompeterin' and 'R[?H]einmæennin', together with the 'e' joined after 'a' to make 'æ' – are later additions. The accompanying comment that this trumpeter was to be released from service because 'Er sich gar nicht hören läst' (he [*recte* she] is never heard), may be a further reason as to why the court official charged with writing this report was somewhat confused regarding the trumpeter's identity. Strikingly, the salary of 150 *Gulden* allocated to this musician (the only trumpeter listed as receiving this amount) is exactly the same as that paid to a young female trumpet player employed at the Württemberg court between 1717 and 1722, Elisabetha Schmid; for further details, see Owens, 'Professional Women Musicians', 45–6.

<sup>m</sup> D-Sha, A21, Büschel 23, 'Fourier Zettel' for visit of Hereditary Prince Friedrich Ludwig to the Liebenzell spa, *c.*1730/31.

<sup>n</sup> D-Sha, A21, Büschel 618, 12 April 1745, 'Rent Cammer' protocol.

<sup>o</sup> Listed among the *Hofmusici* in the *VII. Continuatio . . . des Jahrs 1746*; however, his substantial salary (450 *Gulden* – see the *Hofkapelle* register, 1745, p. 30) and his later description as a *Cammermusicus* indicates this may have been a mistake.

<sup>p</sup> The nature of this position is not clear, given that Mohr is not listed with the musicians.

# 7

# The Court of Saxony-Gotha-Altenburg

## *Bert Siegmund*

F OR OVER THREE HUNDRED YEARS, Gotha was the residential town of the dukes of Saxony-Gotha and Saxony-Gotha-Altenburg as well as Saxony-Coburg and Gotha. Saxony-Gotha was founded in 1639, with Duke Ernst I (1601–1675), later known as 'der Fromme' (the Pious), elevating Gotha to the rank of residential town on 9 April 1640. Throughout his reign, this prince focused on promoting the overall welfare of Saxony-Gotha and its subjects, eliminating the devastation wrought by the Thirty Years' War, and establishing a functional state. He thought of his court primarily as a ruler's household and led a virtuous existence that served his subjects as a model for their own lives, thus making Saxony-Gotha a prime example of the so-called 'hausväterlicher Hof'.[1] Significantly, Duke Ernst gave the name Friedenstein ('Stone of Peace') to the residential palace he had erected between 1643 and 1655, which replaced its predecessor, Castle Grimmenstein ('Stone of Wrath'):

> Denn der erste Grundstein, der zum Fürstlichen Schlosse Friedenstein geleget wurde, war zugleich der Grundstein von der Friedensteinischen Schloß-Kirche, und ward Anno 1643 den 26. Octobr. Mittags um 12 Uhr an der Ecke gegen Morgen, wo die Kirche noch stehet, 52 Schuhe tief in die Erden geleget, auch der Anfang sothaner Arbeit Nachmittage 3 Uhr vom Herzog selbst, indem er auf einer Leiter hinab stiegen, in Augenschein genommen. Wiewohlen sich nun diesem Kirch- und Schloß-bau nicht geringe Hindernisse in den Weg legten, . . . dennoch . . . im September 1646 die Kirche eingeweyhet . . .

> The first foundation stone that was laid for the princely palace of Friedenstein was at the same time the foundation stone of the Friedenstein palace chapel, and was laid 52 *Schuhe*[2] deep into the earth at noon on 26 October 1643, at the east corner, where the chapel stands to this day. At around 3

---

[1] Volker Bauer, *Die höfische Gesellschaft in Deutschland von der Mitte des 17. bis zum Ausgang des 18. Jahrhunderts: Versuch einer Typologie* (Tübingen: Max Niemer, 1993), 66 ff., at 69. See also Chapter 1, 'An Introduction to German *Hofkapellen*', p. 2 n. 3 above.

[2] As a measurement of length, the *Schuh* (shoe) is synonymous with the *Fuß* (foot); a Saxon foot was *c.*28.3 cm long, therefore 52 *Schuhe* equates roughly to 14.72 m.

o'clock that afternoon, the duke himself inspected the initial work, climb-ing down a ladder in order to do so. Although major obstacles hindered the building of the chapel and the palace, . . . nevertheless, . . . the chapel was consecrated in September 1646 . . .³

## THE DEVELOPMENT OF THE GOTHA *HOFKAPELLE* UNTIL 1715

The consecration of the court chapel on 17 and 18 September 1646 was one of the first large-scale musical events of Duke Ernst I's reign (1640–75) and included the involvement of musicians from other courts, town musicians from Gotha, and local school choirs. It also marked the birth of the *Hofkapelle*: first documented in 1651, it comprised two trumpeters (Hans Georg Wagner and Hans Rauchmaul), a *Hofkantor* and a *Hoforganist* (Johann Krauße), male sopranos (*Discantisten*), a church choir (*Kantorei*), and four adjunct musicians ('Adjuvanten').⁴ This ensem-ble would continue to exist until the twentieth century.

It is likely that Wolfgang Carl Briegel (1626–1712) served as *Kantor* from the very outset, since he was identified as *Hofkantor* in 1652.⁵ By 1658 he was referred to as 'Der Music Directore', in 1660 as 'Der Fürstlich sächsischen Hofcapell zu Gotha Directore' (director of the princely Saxon *Hofkapelle* at Gotha), and then as 'Capellmeister' in 1664.⁶ In 1671, Briegel was called to Darmstadt.⁷ Georg Ludwig Agricola (1643–1676) succeeded him as director of the *Hofkapelle*, but several deaths in the ducal family hampered the further development of musical life at court, and by the time Ernst 'the Pious' died in 1675, the *Hofkapelle* – which in any case was not equipped to handle more challenging tasks and thus needed to be augmented by external musicians on special occasions – was in need of reform.

As a result of the distribution of the duke's inheritance following his death, in 1680 Saxony-Gotha was divided into seven lines, Saxony-Gotha-Altenburg among

³ Johann Georg Brückner, *Sammlung verschiedener Nachrichten zu einer Beschreibung des Kirchen- und Schulenstaats im Herzogthum Gotha*, Part 1 (Gotha, 1753), '1. Stück', p. 92.

⁴ D-GOtsa, Immediate Kammer-Sachen 11/11/4. The name of the *Hofkantor* as well as the number of treble voices and members of the *Kantorei* are not provided.

⁵ *1652 Erster Theil: Darinnen begriffen x. Paduanen, x. Galliarden, x. Balleten und x. Cou-ranten; Mit 3. oder 4 Stimmen, Componirt Von Wolffgang Carl Briegeln, Fürstl. Sächsischen bestalten Hoff-Cantore* . . . (Erfurt: Birckner, 1652), cited in Armin Fett, 'Musikgeschichte der Stadt Gotha von den Anfängen bis zum Tode Gottfried Heinrich Stölzels' (Diss., Universität Freiburg im Breisgau, 1951), 418 n. 250 (referring to p. 111).

⁶ See Fett, 'Musikgeschichte der Stadt Gotha', 112; *Haupt- und Trost-Spruch, welcher der weiland wol-edlen und viel-ehren-tureichen Jungfer Annen Christinen Wildin, so wol im Leben als auch im Sterben, sehr lieb und angenehm gewesen . . . von Wolffgang Carl Briegeln, Fürstl. Sächs. Capellmeister auff Friedenstein* ([without location], 1664), copy in D-B, 5 an: 4"@Ee 636.

⁷ Oswald Bill, 'Briegel, Wolfgang Carl', in *Die Musik in Geschichte und Gegenwart: allge-meine Enzyklopädie der Musik*, 2nd rev. edn (Kassel: Bärenreiter, 1994–2008; hereafter *MGG* 2), Personenteil, III: 894–900.

them.[8] Ernst's son and successor, Friedrich I (1646–1689, r. from 1675), followed the advice of *Hofkapellmeister* Wolfgang Michael Mylius (1636–1713, appointed in 1676) and drastically reshaped the *Kapelle*. Of utmost importance for the repertoire and constitution of the musical ensemble was the court theatre, which was set up in the former ballroom of the west tower of the Friedenstein palace in accordance with a decree issued by Friedrich I in 1681.

According to contemporary records, performances had already taken place at the court of Gotha as early as 1646 and continued until 1675. However, Ernst 'the Pious' was opposed to theatrical productions and balls in principle. According to Elisabeth Dobritzsch, 'the expenses would only burden his subjects', and 'he firmly believed that simply banning the *Possenspiele* (farces) and comedies that were so beloved by his court and his subjects would achieve nothing. Therefore, he focused on lending such pieces a meaningful content.'[9]

In marked contrast to this approach, the palace theatre built by his son from 1681 boasted an impressively outfitted auditorium and the most advanced stage technology of the day, including sophisticated machinery to facilitate stage changes (even when the curtains were open), flying machines, trap doors, and wave machines, to name but a few.[10] Completed in 1687, this theatre was in fact so advanced in its design that the same stage machinery remained in use until 1755, when minor improvements were made to the mechanics. And even today, it is still extensively preserved.[11] Following the premiere of a *Kurtzes Schäffer-Spiel* at the theatre in April 1682,[12] the first baroque opera to be performed at the court, *Die geraubete Proserpina*, was presented on 22 April 1683 to mark the duchess's birthday.[13] These two productions were followed by further operas, *Singspiele*, and ballets, which were to have a positive impact on the constitution of the *Hofkapelle*, now permanently comprising between six to eight vocalists, a *Hoforganist*, and four to five additional instrumentalists, as well as a *Kapellmeister*.[14] Substantial developments in 1686 shaped the future of the ensemble even further, specifically the establishment of an *Hautboistenbande* and the appointment of Christian Friedrich Witt (*c.*1660–1717) as chamber organist.[15]

---

[8] When the Saxon duchies were reorganized in 1826, the new principality of Saxony-Coburg and Gotha was created; it continued to exist until 1918.

[9] Elisabeth Dobritzsch, *Barocke Zauberbühne: Das Ekhof-Theater im Schloß Friedenstein Gotha*, Gothaisches Museums-Jahrbuch, 8 (2005) (Weimar: Hain Verlag, 2004), 13.

[10] Ibid., 57; on the stage machinery, see p. 22 ff.

[11] The main seating area was repainted only in 1761, in the rococo style.

[12] *Kurtzes Schäffer-Spiel, in dem glücklich erlebten Geburts-Tage der Frauen Christinen ... auf dem Friedensteinischen Theatro vorgestellet* (Gotha, [without date]), libretto in D-GOl, Sign. Poes. et Lit. 2164, No. 23. Regarding the year, see Erdmann Werner Böhme, *Die frühdeutsche Oper in Thüringen* (Stadtroda: Richter, 1931), 92.

[13] Dobritzsch, *Barocke Zauberbühne*, 59–60.

[14] See the respective entries in D-GOtsa, Kammerrechnungen 1685/6 and 1699/1700.

[15] D-GOtsa, E xi/65: A diary entry written by Duke Friedrich I, dated 14 November 1686, reads: 'Mittags die Capelle Wieder zum Ersten Mahl aufwartten lassen. Und die neue[n] Hauboix' (The *Kapelle* served [that is, performed] again for the first time at midday. So did the new 'Hauboix' [*Hautboisten*]). The latter were identified as *Hofhautboistenbande* for the first time in 1697, making them one of the first oboe bands in existence in the German-speaking

During the reign of Friedrich II (1676–1732), who was still a minor at the time of his father's death and succeeded him only in 1691, the gradual expansion of the *Hofkapelle* continued. It is important to realize, however, that we are not dealing here with the emergence of a large orchestra, at least as the concept is understood in a modern sense. During these decades a *modus operandi* had already begun to develop in Gotha that can be observed throughout the period under review: the permanently employed musicians formed the core personnel of the *Hofkapelle*, which could then be either augmented or modified depending on the type of music that was performed. During the early years of Friedrich II's rule, this included musical-theatrical genres such as opera and *Singspiel*, as well as sacred music, specifically passion settings and sacred concertos. On special occasions, Latin church music (including masses and *Magnificat* settings), sacred cantata cycles (labelled, especially during Mylius' tenure, as 'musicalische Concerten'), and diverse chamber music works were performed.[16] Accordingly, the *Hofkapelle* comprised only seventeen individuals in 1692, namely the *Kapellmeister*, a court organist and a chamber organist, four vocalists, four instrumentalists, three *Kapellknaben*, a *Schloßkirchner* (the sexton in charge of the palace chapel), and two *Calcanten* who operated the organ bellows.[17] The ensemble was augmented from the ranks of the chamber valets, the court *Hautboisten* and, on special occasions (such as the performance of operas), by members of *Hofkapellen* from outside Gotha as well.[18]

The reign of Duke Friedrich II also saw Pietism begin to prevail in Gotha, represented in particular by Gottfried Vockerodt (1665–1727), the principal of the Gotha *Gymnasium illustre* (grammar school). In this context, the year 1697 is of special significance for the development of the *Hofkapelle*. Numerous polemical papers — authored not only by Vockerodt but also Johann Christoph Lorber (1645–1702) in Weimar and Johann Beer (1655–1700) in Weißenfels — sharply attacked music as well as theatre, and brought opera performances to a standstill. Only serenatas and serenata-like 'Singe-Gespräche' continued to be performed. Armin Fett's claim that the latter were also discontinued as of 1704 and only resumed after Gottfried Heinrich Stölzel's appointment in 1719 cannot be supported in light of recently uncovered primary source evidence.[19] The Historische Bibliothek in Rudolstadt holds numerous, hitherto-unknown librettos from the period 1709 to 1716 that document performances of such works; the majority were

---

lands; the number of *Hautboisten* is not indicated, see Fett, 'Musikgeschichte der Stadt Gotha', 136. On Witt, see Peter Wollny, 'Witt, Witte, Christian Friedrich', in *MGG* 2, Personenteil, XVII: 1046–8.

[16] For example, sonatas and suites with various chamber music scorings, as well as solo keyboard music, see Wollny, 'Witt', 1047.

[17] D-GOtsa, Kammerrechnungen 1691/92, cited in Fett, 'Musikgeschichte der Stadt Gotha', 339.

[18] See, for example, Fett, 'Musikgeschichte der Stadt Gotha', 116, 134, 135, 137.

[19] Ibid., 178.

set to music by Christian Friedrich Witt at the express command of members of the ducal family.[20]

After Mylius' death in 1713, Witt succeeded him, having served as director of the *Kapelle* alongside him since 1694. He assumed control of a *Hofkapelle* that comprised nineteen members, including the *Kapellmeister*, as well as four vocalists and seven instrumentalists (specifically four string players and three woodwind players).[21] While the size of the ensemble stayed virtually the same, the internal distribution of forces had changed, with the number of bassoonists, *Kapellknaben*, and *Calcanten* being reduced by one each. Furthermore, the two organist positions had been cut altogether, probably because Witt was an excellent organist himself and because the violinist Johann Gottfried Golde (1679–1759) was officially listed as court and chamber organist from 1720.[22] The five vacant positions, as well as the additional ones, were all filled with instrumentalists – two violinists, a violoncellist, and two oboists – with priority given to musicians who were accomplished on more than one instrument (see Table 7.1, pp. 217–21 below). These were joined by a *Hofkantor* and an *Orgelmacher* (organ builder). It is particularly striking that two oboists were also appointed to the *Hofkapelle*, despite the fact that there was a *Hofhautboistenbande*. Unfortunately, the extant primary sources fail to provide detailed information on this ensemble, as is also the case with the court trumpeters and kettledrum players.[23] Only a very few of these individuals can be identified, making it impossible to determine the total number of musicians employed at the court at this time.[24]

Nevertheless, it is safe to assume that the constitution of the *Hofkapelle* virtually stayed the same during Witt's brief tenure. On the one hand, the Gotha historian Johann Georg August Galletti (1750–1828) confirmed that 'Die herzogliche Kapelle bestand um das Jahr 1715 aus dem Kapellmeister Witten, 4 Sängern und 7 Instrumentalisten, von welchen der größte Theil auch zu andern Diensten gebraucht werden konnte' (Around 1715, the princely *Kapelle* consisted of the *Kapellmeister* Witt, four vocalists, and seven instrumentalists, the majority of whom were also

---

[20] D-RUhb, Sammelband 212 'Carmina'; it contains, among other items, the serenatas *Die grünende Beständigkeit der lieblichen Zufriedenheit* (Gotha, 1711), *Entsetzlichste Tieffen! abscheulichste Höhen!* (Gotha, 1712), and *Der wohl-beygelegte Streit* (Gotha, 1713).

[21] D-GOtsa, Kammerrechnungen 1712/13, cited in Fett, 'Musikgeschichte der Stadt Gotha', 340.

[22] D-GOtsa, Kammerrechnungen 1719/20, cited in Fett, 'Musikgeschichte der Stadt Gotha', 341.

[23] D-GOtsa, Kammerrechnungen 1641/42 ff., cited in Fett, 'Musikgeschichte der Stadt Gotha', 183.

[24] See, for example, the application letter of the trumpeter Gottfried Kohl, dated 20 November 1695, D-GOtsa, Geheimes Archiv, UU XXIX/5. On the basis of information contained in a further document dating from 1695, which names eight trumpeters (Adam, Prinz, Heinrich, Abraham, Opel, Volckmar, Hermann, and Madelung) as well as one kettledrum player (Stettfeld), Fett conjectures that a similar number of trumpeters and kettledrum players were employed at the court of Gotha in succeeding years; see D-GOtsa, Immediate Kammersachen IX/1/44, cited in Fett, 'Musikgeschichte der Stadt Gotha', 185.

able to carry out other tasks).[25] On the other hand, the 1717/18 court account lists most of members of the *Hofkapelle* by name, including all the instrumentalists. Previously unknown names appear only among the vocalists and the *Kapellknaben*.[26] Therefore, it is highly likely that the configuration from 1713 was still the same in 1715. A lack of clarity exists regarding the exact musical expertise of Johann Laurentius Stengel: identified as 'Musicus' in the 1713 'Kammerrechnungen' (where he was listed after the vocalists, but before the instrumentalists), he was first explicitly labelled 'Falcetist' in 1729. Moreover, Stengel's salary of 65 *Gulden* amounted to only one third of a regular vocalist's wage, a circumstance which implies that he was employed as a junior vocalist. In later years both Stengel and the falsettist Johann Andreas Westphal also distinguished themselves as poets and librettists.[27]

These changes in the constitution of the *Hofkapelle* are strong indicators of its artistic priorities at that time. As mentioned above, operatic productions in Gotha had come to a halt in the early years of the eighteenth century. The performance of church music continued to be a major focus, but with the number of instrumentalists now holding permanent, full-time positions, more and more instrumental music – including concertante works that went beyond chamber music – must have been performed by the *Hofkapelle*. This argument is supported by information provided in various diaries kept by the dukes of Gotha, which convey the wide range of occasions upon which the musicians were required to perform, on an almost daily basis.[28] Moreover, a comparative examination of Mylius' output with that of his successor, Witt, yields much insight.

While only one work by Mylius is extant – his theory treatise, *Rudimenta musices, das ist Eine kurtze und grundrichtige Anweisung zur Singe-Kunst* (Gotha, 1685; 2nd edn, Mühlhausen, 1686) – the composer did compile an overview of his sacred works, listed in a document entitled 'Musicalische Opera, welche mit der Hülffe Gottes erhoffes nach und nach getrucket werden sollen' (Musical works, which, with the help of God, are to be printed in stages).[29] In contrast, apart from his famous *Psalmodia sacra* (Gotha, 1715), Witt's oeuvre comprises a much greater

---

[25] Johann Georg August Galletti, *Geschichte und Beschreibung des Herzogthums Gotha*, Part I (Gotha, 1779), 331.

[26] Johann Andreas Westphal, listed as 'Registrator und Falcetist' in 1713, is missing from the court records in 1718. Instead, a bass singer named Metzger appears in the 'Kammerrechnung' for that year; according to Fett, 'Musikgeschichte der Stadt Gotha', 275, Metzger was active in Gotha from 1714 until 1718. The places of two *Kapellknaben*, Straubel and Gebhardt, listed in the 1713 'Kammerrechnung', were taken in 1718 by Erdmann, König, and Güldner (no first names are provided), as well as a further, unidentified junior musician.

[27] Stengel, for example, is named as librettist of Stölzel's serenata *Die beschützte Irene* (Altenburg, 1722; libretto in D-RUkb, Sign. SB 212), as well as other (untitled) cantatas and serenatas from 1722 and 1723 listed in Gottfried Christian Freiesleben's *Kleine Nachlese zu des berühmten Herrn Prof. Gottsched's nötigem Vorrathe zur Geschichte der deutschen dramatischen Dichtkunst* (Leipzig, 1760), 64–78. Westphal's dates are unknown, but he is referred to as a poet in D-GOtsa, Immediate Kammersachen IX/I/36, cited in Fett, 'Musikgeschichte der Stadt Gotha', 286.

[28] D-GOtsa; see, for example, Sign. E XI/5, E XI/7, E XI/15, E XI/17, E XI/20, and E XI/65.

[29] Cited in Fett, 'Musikgeschichte der Stadt Gotha', 212–13; while the original document is lost, Fett believes that this undated primary source dates from Mylius' tenure in Gotha.

number of sacred and secular vocal works (the latter extant only as librettos), as well as instrumental concertos, orchestral suites, sonatas, and keyboard music, including organ works.[30]

Yet, even when a (presumably) significant loss of source material is taken into account, the general tendency is nevertheless clear: from a small *Hofkapelle* centred on vocalists in order to provide regular church music (which needed to be augmented for the musical-theatrical performances that took place up until the end of the seventeenth century), the court musical establishment had grown considerably by 1715 and was now primarily oriented towards instrumentalists. This new *Kapelle* was much more versatile, and it not only carried out the traditional task of providing sacred music but also successfully tackled the challenges inherent in the fashionable instrumental genres of the early eighteenth century. Significantly, no fewer than ninety-seven instruments had been acquired by the court up until 1713, including thirteen trumpets and four trombones.[31] However, the extent to which this collection of instruments – whose contents can be deduced using extant records of purchase – was in fact available and in actual use remains uncertain.

## THE DEVELOPMENT OF THE GOTHA *HOFKAPELLE* FROM 1715 UNTIL 1730

Witt's untimely death in 1717 interrupted the *Kapelle*'s development. Friedrich II did endeavour to replace him with a suitable candidate – attempts were made, for example, to secure both Georg Philipp Telemann and the *Kapellmeister* in Hanover, Francesco Venturini (1675–1745).[32] However, the duke's efforts were unsuccessful for a lengthy period; as a result, the *Hofkapelle* remained without a director for two years. Finally, on 24 November 1719, Gottfried Heinrich Stölzel (1690–1749) became the new court *Kapellmeister*, a position that he held until his death.[33]

The two-year vacancy of the *Kapellmeister*'s position left its mark on the *Hofkapelle*; Stölzel initially set about addressing deficiencies, before gradually

[30] Cf. the section listing Witt's compositions in Wollny, 'Witt'.

[31] See Christian Ahrens, *'Zu Gotha ist eine gute Kapelle . . .': Aus dem Innenleben einer thüringischen Hofkapelle des 18. Jahrhunderts* (Stuttgart: Franz Steiner, 2009), 45–6: forty-eight string instruments, six plucked instruments, thirty-nine wind instruments, and four unspecified instruments, plus seventeen keyboard instruments.

[32] See Georg Philipp Telemann's autobiography in Johann Mattheson, *Grundlage einer Ehren-Pforte* (Hamburg, 1740, repr. ed. Max Schneider, Berlin: Liepmannssohn, 1910), 354–69, at 363–4: 'Als ich ohngefehr, 1716. durch Gotha reisete, und der geschickte Capellmeister, Christian Friedrich Witt, gestorben war, sollte mir dessen Platz wieder werden. Ich dachte daran, wie warm ich in Franckfurt bey 1600 fl. saß, und reisete weiter' (When, in about 1716, I passed through Gotha, where the skilful *Kapellmeister* Christian Friedrich Witt had [recently] died, his position was to be offered to me. But then I thought about my comfortable salary of 1,600 *Gulden* in Frankfurt, and moved on); incidentally, Telemann made an error regarding Witt's date of death: the latter died on 3 April 1717. On Venturini, see Fett, 'Musikgeschichte der Stadt Gotha', 143.

[33] D-GOtsa, Kammerrechnungen 1719/20, fol. 182r.

expanding the ensemble and its repertoire. His primary focus initially was on church music, and within a month of assuming office he had composed a cycle of six Christmas cantatas, followed by large-scale passions in 1720, 1723, and 1725, as well as mass settings and his first complete cantata cycles.[34] Moreover, in 1723, opera performances once again began to take place in Gotha. The first was the musical drama, *Der Musenberg*, presented on the occasion of Duke Friedrich's birthday on 28 July, and by autumn a second work had already been performed, the pastoral opera, *Die beglückte Tugend*, marking the birthday of Duchess Magdalena Auguste on 23 October.[35]

Not surprisingly, this soon had an impact on the *Hofkapelle* – not only with regard to its constitution, but also on the selection of instruments at its disposal. As early as Stölzel's first years in office, there are numerous entries in the 'Friedensteinische Kammer-Rechnungen über das baare Geld', the court account books detailing cash transactions, specifically in the section headed 'Ausgabe-Geldt Fürstl: Hoff-Capell' (cash expenditures for the princely *Hofkapelle*), made in relation to the purchase of instruments, including:

> vor 2 neuerhandelte Waldhörner, welche z. F. Hof-Capell geliefert (for two newly acquired hunting horns which were delivered to the princely *Hofkapelle*);[36]

> Vor *Musicali*en und ein paar *per force* Hörner, welche von Wien aus durch den Hn. Rath Gottern anhero zur Fürstl. Capelle geliefert worden (for music and several *parforce* horns, which were delivered from Vienna for the princely *Hofkapelle* by Councillor [Ludwig Andreas] Gotter [1661–1735]);[37]

> vor 3. zur Fürstl. Hof-Capelle erhandelt- und gelieferter neür Hautbois (for three new oboes which were purchased and delivered to the princely *Hofkapelle*).[38]

This change in the status of musical life at the court of Gotha can also be seen in the elaborate staging of musical-theatrical performances, which alongside opera

---

[34] These included the cantata cycles *Gott-geheiligtes Singen und Spielen des Friedensteinischen Zions* (1720/21, text: Johann Oswald Knauer), libretto in D-Gs, Sign. Poet. Germ. III, 746; *Neue Geistliche Gedichte* (probably in 1722/3, text: Erdmann Neumeister), libretto, for example, in D-Gs, MA 88-57:608; *Das Saiten-Spiel des Hertzens am Tage des Herrn* (1724/5, text: Benjamin Schmolck), for the court of Anhalt-Zerbst, libretto in D-ZEo, Sign. A 549; and *Musicalische Kirchen-Andachten* (1725/6, text: Erdmann Neumeister and Lorenz Reinhardt), libretto in D-GOl, Sign. Cant. spir. 884/10); as well as *Texte zur Kirchen-Music* (1728/9, text: G. H. Stölzel), libretto in D-GOl, Sign. Cant. spir. 891 a–891 zz.

[35] On *Der Musenberg*, see Johann Christoph Gottsched, *Nöthiger Vorrath zur Geschichte der deutschen dramatischen Dichtkunst, oder Verzeichniß aller deutschen Trauer- Lust und Singspiele, die im Druck erschienen von 1450 bis zur Hälfte des jetzigen Jahrhunderts gesammlet und ans Licht gestellet von Johann Christoph Gottscheden*, 2 vols. (Leipzig, 1757–65), I: 299; on *Die beglückte Tugend*, see Freiesleben, *Kleine Nachlese*, 70.

[36] D-GOtsa, Kammerrechnungen 1719/20.

[37] D-GOtsa, Kammerrechnungen 1720/21, entry from 26 June 1721.

[38] D-GOtsa, Kammerrechnungen 1724/25, fol. 252ᵛ, entry from 15 August 1725.

also included serenatas and *Tafelmusiken*, the majority of which were also presented dramatically: most probably not on a stage – and thus without theatrical
scenery – but with costumes. From 1723, there was even a specially designated
tailor, the 'Comoedien Schneider', responsible for the latter.[39]

These details also clearly demonstrate a growing need for both admiration and
prestige on the part of the princely house of Gotha, a trend which must also be
viewed as a gradual turning away from the ideal of the 'hausväterlicher Hof' that
had once dominated the rule of Ernst 'the Pious'. The path taken by the dukes of
Gotha in order to finance their need for prestige illustrates this perfectly. After
Friedrich I had, for example, almost ruined state finances by building the *Lustschloß* Erffa-Friedrichswerth and maintaining an army of over 10,000 men, his
successors, Friedrich II and Friedrich III, set about successfully tapping into new
sources of cash through a flourishing trade in soldiers, supplying them to France,
Prussia, and rulers elsewhere. As a result, 3,000 men from Gotha fought in the War
of the Spanish Succession (1701–14), and in 1733 as many as 5,000 soldiers took
part in the War of the Polish Succession (1733–8), as part of the forces of Emperor
Charles VI.[40]

Nevertheless, in cultural terms this period can be regarded as one of brilliance in
the history of Gotha. As Jenny von der Osten notes,

> At the beginning of the eighteenth century, among all Saxon residences
> Schloß Friedenstein already ranked second behind the electoral court of
> Dresden with regard to external splendour. The year 1729 – when Princess
> Luise Dorothée of Saxony-Coburg-Meiningen [1710–1767] returned to her
> ancestral home by marrying Hereditary Prince Friedrich, the future Duke
> Friedrich III of Saxony-Gotha – outwardly marks the beginning of a golden
> age, defined by an enlightened as well as sophisticated approach to culture.[41]

In 1676, Wolfgang Michael Mylius had made concrete suggestions regarding the
constitution of the *Hofkapelle*; now, more than half a century later, the numbers
he had envisioned were reached for the first time.[42] Although no relevant archival
records (in particular the 'Kammerrechnungen') remain extant for the year 1730, in
1732 the permanently employed members of the *Hofkapelle* included five vocalists,
five violinists, one violoncellist, three oboists, two bassoonists and the continuo
group – a total of eighteen musicians in all, plus the *Kapellmeister* and the so-
called 'Zusatzkräfte' (additional personnel) comprising the *Hofkantor*, *Hofkirchner*, *Hoforgelmacher*, and the *Calcant* (see Table 7.1). Otherwise, the singer Sidonia
Dorothea Cramer, daughter of bassoonist Johann Andreas Cramer (d. 1748) and
the first female vocalist documented at the court of Gotha, participated exclusively

---

[39] Dobritzsch, *Barocke Zauberbühne*, 45.

[40] Anon., 'Fremdentruppen', *Meyers Konversationslexikon*, 4th edn, 19 vols. (Leipzig and
Vienna, 1885–92), VI: 665–6.

[41] Jenny von der Osten, *Luise Dorothee, Herzogin von Sachsen-Gotha, 1732–67* (Leipzig:
Breitkopf & Härtel, 1893), 13.

[42] See Mylius' 'Memorial' from 1 April 1676, D-GOtsa, Geheimes Archiv, UU XXXVII/1,
reproduced in full in Fett, 'Musikgeschichte der Stadt Gotha', 362–7.

in musico-dramatic performances between 1729 and 1738, for which she was paid separately.[43]

The constitution and moderate size of the Gotha *Hofkapelle* around this time were typical for its day; indeed, when one disregards the trumpeters and kettledrum players, it came close to the requirements outlined by Johann Sebastian Bach for a 'well-appointed church music' in Leipzig in 1730.[44] However, this did not quite mirror the reality of the situation. Like his predecessors, Stölzel had at his disposal not only the actual members of the *Hofkapelle*, but also other court servants who were proficient on instruments, as well as court trumpeters, kettledrum players, and the entire *Hautboistenbande*. Stölzel's famous Concerto grosso 'a quattro chori' in D major, for example – featuring two choirs that each comprise three trumpets and kettledrums, a woodwind choir (transverse flute, three oboes, and bassoon), a string choir (four violins, viola, violoncello, and violone), plus two harpsichords – was undoubtedly conceived with the court trumpeters in mind.[45] Beyond their daily duties with regard to the provision of fanfares, their participation was apparently not limited to important special occasions. In 1732, the trumpeters requested a pay raise due to the fact that 'bekanndtermaßen iedesmahl bey der Tafel Music mit der Capelle aufwarten müssen und unter die Capelle in ordentlicher Weise mit gerechnet werden' (as everyone knows, [we] have to serve together with the *Kapelle* for each *Tafelmusik* and are considered an integral part of the *Kapelle*).[46]

Stölzel himself did not seem to be fully convinced of their skills, however, as indicated in his assessment of a newly-recruited trumpeter:

> daß er nicht allein die Trompete ziemlich fertig bläst, sondern auch bey ferner weiter Übung, immer je mehr und mehr stärcker zu werden verspricht. Dahero selbigen wohl zu gönnen, wenn Serenissimus in Absicht, daß sehr wenige beym Trompeter-Corps bey der Music mit ihrem Instrument zu gebrauchen sind, ihm die anjetzo verledigte Trompeter-Stelle angedeyhen zu lassen geruhen.

> not only is he already a fairly accomplished trumpeter, but his skills should improve steadily as he continues to practise. If Your Serene Highness offered him the trumpeter position that is currently vacant, he would certainly be very deserving of it, as there are very few members of the *Trompeter-Corps* who are actually accomplished enough to participate in musical performances.[47]

[43] Fett, 'Musikgeschichte der Stadt Gotha', 263.

[44] Johann Sebastian Bach, *Kurtzer, iedoch höchstnöthiger Entwurff einer wohlbestallten Kirchen Music: Nebst einigem unvorgreiflichen Bedencken von dem Verfall derselben, Leipzig, 23. August 1730*, ed. Werner Neumann, Faksimile-Reihe Bachscher Werke und Schriftstücke, 1 (Leipzig: Deutscher Verlag für Musik, 1955).

[45] An edition of this work is included in *Instrumentalkonzerte deutscher Meister*, ed. Arnold Schering, Denkmäler deutscher Tonkunst, 29/30 (Leipzig: Breitkopf & Härtel, 1907), rev. edn by Hans Joachim Moser (Wiesbaden: Breitkopf & Härtel, 1958).

[46] Fett, 'Musikgeschichte der Stadt Gotha', 187.

[47] Ibid., 186.

## THE DEVELOPMENT OF THE GOTHA *HOFKAPELLE*
## FROM 1730 UNTIL 1745

Duke Friedrich II died in 1732. The claim made in secondary literature that the *Hofkapelle* suffered a serious rupture as the consequence of a drastic reduction following the accession of Friedrich III (1699–1772), is not supported in extant primary sources.[48] But one ensemble was indeed negatively affected, namely the *Hautboistenbande*, which was apparently terminated in 1733 for unknown reasons. It could not have been due to a lack of demand, since Friedrich III re-established the band soon after, on 28 July 1734. The 'Specification der neün [neuen] Hoff Banta Hauboisten' (Specification of the new court *Hautboistenbande*) listed as its members Johann Nicolaus Neuenhahn, Matthes Hartrock, Johann Christoph Hoffmann, Bartholomäus Poß, Johann Daniel Walther, and Johann Friedrich Nohrs.[49]

By and large, a modest, yet systematic expansion of the *Hofkapelle* can be discerned after 1733, starting with the permanent appointment of two *Waldhornisten* in 1734, and followed by a violinist, Johann Andreas Schieck (d. 1787), and a bassoonist, David Abraham Böhmer (1707–1786).[50] Moreover, the *Kapellknabe* and vocalist Gottfried Diestel was 'genöthigt, die Laute zu erlernen' (ordered to learn [how to play] the lute) in 1743, and, in the years that followed, was listed as 'Accompagnist'.[51] The court also ensured that the instruments at the *Hofkapelle*'s disposal met the ongoing needs of its musicians.[52]

In fact, the number of instruments owned by the court illustrates particularly convincingly that the information on the *Hofkapelle* members contained in extant archival records reflects only partially the actual musical possibilities on offer. For example, transverse flutes were in use before Stölzel's appointment and are also present in his works; however, both the surviving registers of the *Hofkapelle* members and the *Hof- und Adreßkalender* fail to list a single flautist until 1775.[53] References to viola players are similarly absent, despite the fact that parts for viola are always included in scores. And, not least, it is difficult to imagine that following the death of lutenist Georg Friedrich Meusel (or Meisel, 1688–1728), no lutenist would have been available until Gottfried Diestel was appointed in 1743.[54]

---

[48] Cf. Armin Fett, 'Gotha', in *Die Musik in Geschichte und Gegenwart: allgemeine Enzyklopädie der Musik*, 1st edn, 17 vols. (Kassel: Bärenreiter, 1949–87; hereafter *MGG*), V: 553–61, at 557.

[49] D-GOtsa, Geheimes Archiv, UU XXXVII/5.

[50] The *Waldhornisten* were Johann Caspar Hötzel (dates unknown) and Anton Ferdinand Weisse (d. 1768); see D-GOtsa, Kammerrechnungen 1734/35, 218. On Schieck and Böhmer, see D-GOtsa, Geheimes Archiv, UU XXXVII/60a.

[51] See Fett, 'Musikgeschichte der Stadt Gotha', 263; *Hoch-Fürstlicher Sachsen-Gothaisch- und Altenburgischer Hof- und Adress-Calender* (Gotha, 1744 ff.).

[52] Cf. Ahrens, 'Zu Gotha ist eine gute Kapelle', 167 ff.

[53] On the flute at the court prior to Stölzel, see ibid., 50; the relevant court *Calender* are: *Hoch-Fürstlicher Sachsen-Gothaisch- und Altenburgischer Hof- und Adress-Calender* (Gotha, 1744–64); *Herzoglich Sachsen-Gothaisch und Altenburgischer Hof- und Adreß-Calender* (Gotha, 1765–67); *Herzoglich-Sachsen-Gotha- und Altenburgischer Hof- und Adreß-Calender* (Gotha, 1768–1825).

[54] Meusel was listed as a member of the Gotha *Hofkapelle* from 1718, cf. Fett, 'Musikgeschichte der Stadt Gotha', 275.

The years up until 1745 were particularly productive for Stölzel as a composer — although much of his instrumental music has now been lost. No fewer than six cycles of church cantatas, including two double cycles, date from the period after 1730 alone.[55] His extant output comprises masses, passions, and serenatas, as well as no fewer than seven operas composed between 1729 and 1744.[56] It is evident from this oeuvre that in contrast to works intended for regularly scheduled musical performances (such as Sunday cantatas, *Tafelmusiken*, and the like), which were scored for a modest ensemble, at times sacred and secular festivities warranted tremendous musical effort.

This leads to the conclusion that permanent members of the Gotha *Hofkapelle* were, on the one hand, joined in great numbers on special occasions not only by *Hofhautboisten*, *Hoftrompeter*, and kettledrum players, but also by other court servants. On the other hand, the regular musicians were able to cope successfully with the varying demands of daily musical life by themselves. In view of the diverse challenges presented in the compositions written for the *Hofkapelle*, as well as the surviving evidence regarding the extant instruments at their disposal, it is safe to assume that musicians in Gotha were required to be proficient on at least two or three instruments as a general rule rather than the exception, as was also the case at other courts.

Although reports on musicians who played multiple instruments are sporadic at best in the extant archival records, they do emphasize the great importance that was attached to this requirement within the context of the application and appointment process for musicians. And, not surprisingly, this held not only for the *Hofkapelle* members, but also for the court *Hautboisten*. For example, when, on 12 June 1738, the former dragoon Simon Oßwaldt requested a place in the *Hautboistenbande*, Stölzel replied to the duke:

> Hochfürstl. gnädigsten Befehl unterthänigst zu befolgen haben auch den dritten Hautboisten Nahmens Geyer gehört, und finde ihn auf der Violine fast so stark als Harttrocken, auf der Hautbois mögte er ihm gleich seyn, auch bläset Oswald ein beßer Waldhorn als Geyer.

Following the prince's most gracious order to hear [an audition by] the third

---

[55] *Benjamin Schmolckens Nahmen-Buch Christi und der Christen* (double cycle, 1731/2, text: Benjamin Schmolck), libretto in D-GOl, Sign. Cant. spir. 176; two single cycles for 1732/3 and 1733/4, referred to in Georg Benda, 'Specification dererjenigen Musicalien, so an Serenissimum überlaßen worden' (undated), extant in D-GOtsa, appointment lists and salary tables for 1750, fols. 108f[r], 108f[v], 108g[r], notarized copy from 25 March 1778 in D-GOl, Sign. Cod. Chart. A 1332 (3); *Erbauliche Kirchen-Andachten* (double cycle, 1735/6, text: Johannes Caspar Manhardt), libretto in D-GOl, Sign. Cant. spir. 5; and two single cycles, *Musicalische Lob- und Danck-Opfer* (1737/8) and *Erbauliche Kirchen-Andachten* (1743/4), both set to Stölzel's own texts, in D-GOl, Sign. Cant. spir. 878 and 876a.

[56] Stölzel's most festive scoring for mass settings comprised SATB, three trumpets, kettledrum, two horns, two oboes, strings, and basso continuo. The seven operas were: *Die triumphierende Liebe* [*Acis und Galathea*] (1729), *Adonis* [*Venus und Adonis*] (1730), *Thersander und Demonassa, oder Die glückliche Liebe* (1733), *Narcissus* (1734 and 1735), *Endymion* (1740), *Die gekrönte Weisheit* (1742), and *Die mit Leben und Vergnügen belohnte Tugend* (1744).

*Hautboist*, Geyer, I found him to be almost as strong as Harttrocken on the violin, about the same on the oboe, but Oswald is a better *Waldhorn* player than Geyer.[57]

Moreover, a further application for an *Hautboist* position made by Georg Christoph Stubenrauch in 1747 indicates that,

> [zur] beßeren habilitierung, die Violine bey Dero Cämmerierer und Concertmaster, die Flaute traverse und Hautbois aber bey dem hiesigen Cammermusico Hempel vollkommen zu erlernen beflissen gewesen.

> in order to be better qualified, [he] was eager to learn [how to play] to perfection the violin from the chamberlain and concertmaster [Johann Wilhelm Hien], and the transverse flute and the oboe from the local *Cammermusicus* [Johann Friedrich] Hempel.[58]

Even if the ability of some of its musicians to play more than one instrument allowed the Gotha *Hofkapelle* to be a flexible ensemble able to cope successfully with many demands, it is important to note that a certain risk also lay in the fairly modest number of members. The absence of a single musician could have far-reaching consequences for the performance of an entire series of works. In Stubenrauch's application we also read that the duke

> gnädigst bekannt seyn wird, daß die neuesten Kirchen-Jahrgänge auf die Flaute traverse gesetzt sind und dieses Instrument bey jetziger Unpässlichkeit des Cammer-Musici Hempels und biß zu dessen Wieder Geneßung zum Abbruch der Harmonie bey denen jetzigen Kirchen Musiqven gäntzlich erlieget.

> will be graciously aware, that most recent cantata cycles have included a transverse flute part; however, due to the present indisposition of the *Cammermusicus* Hempel, the current performances of church music will suffer greatly due to the removal of this instrument from the harmony, until [Hempel] has fully recovered [from his illness].[59]

Last but not least, such reports draw attention to the fact that the *Hofkapellmeister* was in charge of the *Hautboisten*, at least in musical matters, even though they were officially still under the authority of the military; indeed, they were viewed as regular members of the *Kapelle*, who participated, for example, in performances of sacred music. During the 1740s (the exact date is unknown), two additional musicians joined the *Bande* bringing the total to eight members, at least three of whom are known to have played other instruments.[60]

Armin Fett has claimed that 'the expansion of the *Hofkapelle* was brought to an

---

[57] D-GOtsa, Geheimes Archiv, UU xxxvii/5, dated 1 July 1738.
[58] D-GOtsa, Geheimes Archiv, UU xxxvii/47.
[59] Ibid.
[60] Johann Sebastian Hartwig played the bassoon and Johann Matthäus Harderoth the horn; see D-GOtsa, Geheimes Archiv, UU xxxviii/5, cited in Fett, 'Musikgeschichte der Stadt

end around 1743', specifically referring to the number of musicians, as well as to the instruments available to them.[61] In fact, during the period in which Stölzel's last large-scale operas and cantata cycles were performed, four musicians joined the ensemble (see Table 7.1) and new instruments continued to be purchased. Therefore, despite the fact that Fett's wording gives the impression that the long-term and goal-oriented expansion of the *Kapelle* had been completed and come to a halt, such a conclusion is inaccurate.

In terms of its personnel, the overall development of the *Hofkapelle* during the preceding decades is characterized by an ongoing sense of stability, despite at times politically unfavourable conditions. With the exception of the brief termination of the *Hautboistenbande* in 1733–4 (the cause of which remains unclear), no further disruptions or dramatic phases of expansion can be observed. As a rule, musicians who were appointed members of the Gotha *Hofkapelle* could assume that these were posts for life. Even during turbulent times, the constitution of the ensemble fluctuated remarkably little. The violinist Johann Nicolaus Specht, for example, was employed from 1733 until 1795, a total of sixty-two years. Furthermore, there appear to be no records – at least among those that remain extant – to indicate the dismissal of a musician when the instrument he played was no longer needed. In any case, such drastic steps would have been unnecessary, owing to the fact that the musicians generally played more than one instrument. When demands changed in the long term, a musician's focus simply shifted to his secondary instrument, or (as was the case with the vocalist-turned-lutenist Diestel), he would be asked to take lessons on another instrument. This practice can be traced back many years: Christian Ahrens, for example, has located a record from 1711 that indicates that two *Hautboisten* were instructed on the horn.[62] In this way, the *Kapellmeister* was able to respond to the musical-stylistic developments of the time in a sufficiently flexible manner, despite the modest number of newly-appointed musicians.

## THE DEVELOPMENT OF THE GOTHA *HOFKAPELLE* FROM 1745 UNTIL 1760

Parallel to this development, the number of instruments owned by the court continued to increase at a comparable rate after 1745. As Ahrens has shown, the expansion focused not only on supplementing and replacing instruments that already belonged to the *Kapelle* – particularly horns (in 1734, 1738, and 1744) – but also on acquiring entirely new instruments.[63] In 1741, serpents were even introduced

Gotha', 269. Simon Oßwaldt played both the bassoon and the horn; see statements made by Stölzel, pp. 208–9 above, and by Benda, p. 212 below.

[61] Fett, 'Gotha', 557.

[62] On 9 March 1711, 25 *Thaler* were paid to 'Zweÿen Hautbois [als] Zubuße [Zuschuss] zu erlernung der Waldhörner' (two *Hautboisten* as a subsidy so they could learn how to play the *Waldhorn*); see D-GOtsa, Geheimes Archiv, E. XII, 12 h, No. 6, Schatullrechnungen 1711, fol. 20ʳ, cited in Ahrens, 'Zu Gotha ist eine gute Kapelle', 167.

[63] Ahrens, 'Zu Gotha ist eine gute Kapelle', 175–6.

into the *Hofkapelle*, followed shortly thereafter (in 1742 and 1749) by clarinets for the *Hautboistenbande*.[64] Oddly enough, however, Stölzel's oeuvre does not include clarinets, while parts for serpents exist only in the performance material that survives for four sacred cantatas he wrote for Sondershausen.[65] The context in which these instruments were used in Gotha therefore remains unclear. It is, however, important to point out that the clarinets and other instruments at the court's disposal by the late 1740s constituted the complete, 'classic' *Harmoniemusik* ensemble: two oboes, two clarinets, two horns, and two bassoons, all available for the court *Hautboistenbande*. Unfortunately, no music has survived, making it impossible to draw conclusions regarding its repertoire.

Thus, by the end of the 1740s, *Hofkapellmeister* Stölzel had laid important foundations for that particular decade and for the future development of his *Hofkapelle*. In fact, although Stölzel has largely remained in the shadow of his better-known contemporaries — above all Bach, Handel, and Telemann — this information offers us a new facet to our understanding of the composer: while maintaining a successful network of musical colleagues and remaining ever open to new ideas, Stölzel was able to carefully plan ahead, step by step, to ensure that 'his' orchestra would come to rank among the best at the time.

In 1750, Georg Anton (Jiří Antonín) Benda (1722–1795) succeeded Stölzel as Gotha's *Hofkapellmeister*. Shortly thereafter, in 1751, the employment contract of the *Hautboistenbande* was changed to a civilian one — so that its members were no longer under the jurisdiction of the military. While it is tempting to credit Benda with this change, viewing it as one of his first acts in office, this was not, in fact, the case. The impetus was instead provided by the 'Kriegs-Commissions-Director' (director of the War Commission) and tax official, Johann August von Beneckendorff, who requested — with the 'utmost devotion' — in a letter of 8 September 1751, 'Die Bezahlung der Hof Hautboisten-Bande aus F. Herzogl. Cassa betr.' (that the court *Hautboistenbande* should be paid from the ducal coffers), rather than from the 'Kriegs-Cassa'. Friedrich III's reply from 13 September 1751 reads: 'daß ... die Bande der Hof-Hautboisten künfftig lediglich und allein zu Hof- und nicht zu Militair-Diensten ... gebrauchet werden dürffen' (that ... from now on the band of court *Hautboisten* shall be permitted to be used solely in the service of the court and not for the military). With regard to payments, the duke decreed that 'ihr tractament zeithero aus der Kriegs-Cassa erhalten, ... solche nunmehr aus Unserer Fürstl. Rentcamer allhier salariret und hiernach das nöthige verfüget werden mögte' ([although] in the past their wages had been supplied from the war coffers, ... from now on their salaries will be paid by our princely treasury, which, accordingly, will hereafter supply all that is necessary).[66] This is in marked opposition to other courts, where *Hautboisten* generally held military posts and thus also served

---

[64]  Ibid., 196, 209.

[65]  Held in D-SHm: *Gott ist die Liebe, und wer in der Liebe bleibet*, Mus. A 15:224; *Selig seid ihr Armen, denn das Reich Gottes ist euer*, Mus. A 15:223; *Weil wir in der Hütten sind, sehnen wir uns*, Mus. A 15:242; *Wohltun ist wie ein gesegneter Garten*, Mus. A 15:241. All of the cantatas belong to the 1736/7 cycle.

[66]  See the relevant documents in D-GOtsa, Geheimes Archiv, UU XXXVIII/7.

as military musicians when required. The designation 'Hofhautboistenbande' remained in use until well after 1751, with the suffix 'Bande' being dropped only in
1781, and the same number of *Hautboisten* — eight — employed in Gotha well into
the nineteenth century.

Soon after Benda began his tenure, a number of additions were made to the
*Hofkapelle*. Particularly noteworthy is the inclusion of the two permanently appointed Italian vocalists, Giovanni Andrea Galletti 'di Toscano' and Maria Elisabetha Galletti.[67] Moreover, a group of Bohemian musicians was active in Gotha,
which included Benda himself, his sister Anna Franziska, the two horn players
Johann Caspar Hötzel and Anton Ferdinand Weisse, as well as the violinist Dismas Hattasch (1724–1777).[68] The latter had wed Benda's sister in 1751 and was accepted into the *Hofkapelle* shortly thereafter, remaining a member until his death.
Apparently an excellent string player, Hattasch also composed: several 'Parthien'
for wind instruments by him as well as additional works ascribed to 'Hattasch'
or 'Johann Hattasch' are extant in the well-known collection of Count Christian
Philipp von Clam-Gallas at Schloß Friedland in Bohemia (now Zámek Frýdlant,
Czech Republic).[69] Unfortunately, it is impossible to confirm whether these compositions were written for Gotha's *Hofhautboistenbande*.

Benda also continued to place a high value on achieving the greatest possible
versatility when selecting musicians to be appointed. In a report on the *Hautboist*
Henckel, Benda notes:

> dergestallt, daß ersterer [Oßwaldt] in Ansehung des Tones auf dem Fagott
> vorzuziehen, letzterer Henckel aber in Betracht, daß er nächst dem Fagott
> auch andere Instrumente als den großen Violon und Violoncello spielet . . .
> auch gut zugebrauchen [*sic*] wäre.

> the first [applicant, Oßwaldt] is preferable because of his tone on the bas-
> soon, but the latter, Henckel, should be given consideration as he can play
> other instruments in addition to the bassoon, such as the double bass and the
> violoncello . . . and therefore would also be very useful.[70]

When examining Benda's output during his early tenure in Gotha, it becomes
apparent that, for the most part, he continued to compose in the same musical
genres that had served Stölzel: above all, sacred music and instrumental works.[71]

---

[67] *Hoch-Fürstlicher Sachsen-Gothaisch- und Altenburgischer Hof- und Adress-Calender*
(1751).

[68] *Hoch-Fürstlicher Sachsen-Gothaisch- und Altenburgischer Hof- und Adress-Calender*
(1752).

[69] Rudolf Quoika, 'Hattasch (Hatass, Hataß, Hataš), Dismas', in *MGG*, V: 1815–18. The
family's genealogy remains unclear; see also Undine Wagner, 'Hataš, Hatasch, Hattasch,
Hatass', in *MGG* 2, Personenteil, VIII: 850–51.

[70] D-GOtsa, Geheimes Archiv, UU XXXVIII/9, Georg Benda, 'Pro Memoria', 19 May 1756;
there were four applicants for the vacant position.

[71] Among his sacred works were the following cantata cycles: *Das Nahmen-Buch Christi
und der Christen* (1750/51, text: Benjamin Schmolck) music lost, but libretto extant in D-GOl,
Cant. spir. 879; *Poetische Andachten* (1753/4, text: Johann Jacob Rambach), the majority of the

Moreover, numerous other compositions by Stölzel were repeated, including his double cantata cycle from 1728/9 in 1752/3, 1763/4, and 1765/6[72], as well as other cantata cycles, Lenten cantatas, and passion settings up until 1768.[73] It should also be noted that Benda 'worked' with Stölzel's performance materials, occasionally inserting new chorales into cantatas, leaving out entire cantata movements, and even creating entirely new cantatas by taking individual movements from two existing cantatas as his starting point. In so far as the extant librettos can be taken to provide meaningful evidence, they appear to indicate that Benda did not alter the musical substance of the movements from which he drew. Frequently, in fact, the respective title pages expressly indicate that the poetry and music was provided by Stölzel, 'weyl. F. S. Capellmeister' (former princely Saxon *Kapellmeister*).[74]

These findings provide evidence that the ongoing stability which had shaped the development of the *Hofkapelle* in previous decades remained ongoing. Only in 1765 did another noteworthy growth in personnel occur, although this time not within the *Hofkapelle* itself. Following the departure from the court of the 'Wanderkomödiant' Franz Anton Berger (a travelling actor who was a guest in Gotha from July 1764 to March 1765), Benda's only opera, *Il Xindo riconosciuto*, was performed, on 11 August 1765. Soon after, the court engaged a small Italian ensemble of singers and actors. The latter included Leopoldo Burgioni and Nicolina Rosa (from 1765) as well as Paulo Sibylla, and a married couple by the name of Bianchi (from 1767).[75] In the main, this ensemble performed Italian intermezzos; its members were dismissed soon after the death of Duchess Louise Dorotheé of Saxony-Coburg-Meiningen (1710–1767).

The spirited and highly educated wife of Duke Friedrich III, Louise Dorothée had been at the centre of cultural life during the preceding decades. A correspondent of many of the leading personalities of the day, eminent men honoured her with their visits (including Voltaire in 1757), and even her services as an international diplomat were appreciated and sought after.[76] It is therefore no exaggeration to describe the court of Gotha in these decades as a centre of the Enlightenment. As pointed out by Dobritzsch, 'During the 1730s . . . , the ideas of French Enlightenment philosophers gained a foothold at the court of Gotha, thus weakening

music is lost, but the libretto is in D-GOl, Cant. spir. 872; and *Cantaten über die Sonn- und Festtäglichen Evangelia* (1760/61, text: Balthasar Münter), libretto in D-GOl, Cant. spir. 883a–d.

[72] Librettos extant as *Texte zur Kirchen-Music in Hoch-Fürstl. Schloß-Capelle zum Friedenstein nach der Epistel und dem Evangelium des* [respective liturgical Sunday] *abgefasset von Gottfried Heinrich Stöltzeln, F. S. Capellmeistern* (Gotha, 1728[–9]), copies in D-GOl, Cant. spir. 891a–891zz. Librettos for the repeat performances are extant in D-GOl, Cant. spir. 877 (for 1752/3), Cant. spir. 877b (for 1763/4), and Cant. spir. 877a (for 1765/6).

[73] It was customary in Gotha to celebrate an additional afternoon service on Quinquagesima (*Esto mihi*), the six Sundays during Lent (*Invocavit, Reminiscere, Oculi, Laetare, Judica,* and *Palmarum*) as well as Annunciation or *Mariae Verkündigung* (25 March). This resulted in a number of so-called 'Paßions-Andachten' (passion devotions), which were performed in addition to the regularly scheduled cycles of church cantatas by Stölzel.

[74] See, for example, the libretto for the 1763/4 cycle, in D-GOl, Cant. spir. 877b.

[75] Dobritzsch, *Barocke Zauberbühne*, 176.

[76] Von der Osten, *Luise Dorothee*, 283.

interest in opera, which in any case had become outmoded by this time. At the duchess's suggestion, French plays appeared on the stage more and more frequently ... performed by members of the court.' Dobritzsch has established that these included Regnard's *Démocrit* in 1733, the year of Friedrich III's accession to power, as well as Voltaire's tragedies *Mahomet* (1751), *Zayre* (1755), *Le Mort de César* (1757), and *Alzire, ou Les Américains* (1760). In addition, comedies by Molière, Destouches, and de Graffigny were given.[77]

There can be no doubt that increasingly in the years after 1733, a shift occurred in Gotha with regard to the performance of dramatic works: away from opera towards spoken theatre. The personal preferences of the ruling couple were definitely an important contributing factor, but, in any case, early German opera was already in general decline, so that this development must be viewed as a trend typical of its time. However, such an apparent change in taste should not draw attention away from the following remarkable detail. As reported by Christoph Gottsched in around 1738, 'Die Opern vermindern sich merklich' (Operas have decreased considerably), before going on to observe, 'wie sehr die deutschen Opern abnehmen, oder dünne werden' (how markedly German-language operas have declined or become watered down).[78] Then, commenting specifically on the opera *Atalante* (Danzig, 1741), Gottsched wrote: 'NB. Hiermit hören die deutschen Opern gar auf...' (N.B.: This marks the end of performances of operas in German).[79] In direct contrast to this last statement, however, Stölzel's opera *Die mit Leben und Vergnügen belohnte Tugend* was performed in Gotha for Duchess Louise Dorothée's birthday some three years later, on 9 August 1744.[80] It seems clear, therefore, that early German-language operas were performed much longer in Gotha than elsewhere, making the court, in a manner of speaking, one of the last refuges of Central German baroque opera.

Alongside performances of operas and theatrical works, which were presented by courtiers and servants alike (including the *Hofkapelle* and its singers), there are records of frequent guest performances by 'Wanderkomödianten' (travelling players). For example, as noted by Dobritzsch, 'In August 1745, the court of Gotha engaged the ensemble of the famous theatre reformer, Friederike Caroline Neuber, who was travelling through Saxony on her way to Frankfurt where a new emperor was to be crowned.'[81] In April 1750, and again in August 1753, the actor and theatrical impresario Franciscus Schuch (*c*.1716–1764) visited Gotha with his troupe, whose extensive repertoire ranged from works by Voltaire, Corneille, Racine, and Molière to Gottsched and Grimm.[82]

To date, no evidence has come to light that provides information as to why Benda did not compose or perform operas after taking over the *Hofkapelle* in 1750, thus breaking the pattern set by his predecessor, Stölzel. Possible reasons include

---

[77] Dobritzsch, *Barocke Zauberbühne*, 171.
[78] Gottsched, *Nöthiger Vorrath*, I: 311–12.
[79] Ibid., 314.
[80] Libretto (Gotha, [1744]), in D-HAu, Sign. Pon. FK (Wd 615).
[81] Dobritzsch, *Barocke Zauberbühne*, 174.
[82] Ibid., 174–5.

historical events unrelated to music, such as the Seven Years' War (1756–63). There can also be no doubt that the death of Duchess Louise Dorothée in 1767 had a significant impact on all aspects of cultural life at court, as did the accession of Duke Ernst II of Saxony-Gotha-Altenburg (1745–1804), following the death of his father in 1772.

This situation changed fundamentally when – after a massive fire in the palace at Weimar in 1774 – the court of Gotha engaged the famous theatre troupe of Abel Seyler (1730–1800), initially for three months, and then until July 1775, after which Ernst II appointed them permanently.[83] The troupe comprised eleven actresses and twelve actors, as well as the music director Schweitzer, a ballet master, and a female solo dancer.[84] The permanent establishment of the Gotha *Hoftheater* marks not only the beginning of Benda's composition of *Singspiele* and melodramas (some of which, including *Ariadne auf Naxos* and *Medea*, were successful across Europe), but also led to a further expansion of the *Hofkapelle*, which evolved into a standard classical orchestra under Benda's successor Anton Schweitzer (1735–1787).

As the above examination has shown, the history of the *Hofkapelle* of Gotha was shaped by the fact that only two rulers led the duchy of Saxony-Gotha-Altenburg between 1715 and 1760: Friedrich II and his son Friedrich III. The number of *Kapellmeister* was also remarkably low, with Stölzel holding the post for thirty years, and his successor, Benda, for twenty-eight years; indeed, with the exception of the two years after Witt's death in 1717, the *Hofkapelle* was never without an exceptionally gifted director. For this reason, 'ongoing stability' is the phrase best employed as the leading characteristic of the ensemble's development.

Naturally, the important intellectual shifts that occurred during the eighteenth century – subsumed now by expressions such as 'the end of the baroque era' and 'Enlightenment' – did not pass Gotha by. Their impact on the *Hofkapelle* was, however, surprisingly limited: step by step, the number of musicians increased slightly over these decades, and changes in repertoire led to modifications in both scoring and the instruments available. Furthermore, throughout this period, the *Hofkapelle* experienced no major upheavals, let alone any episodes of complete disruption. Even politically precarious situations such as the Seven Years' War had virtually no effect on the ensemble itself; rather, their primary impact was on the repertoire that was performed.

At the same time, musical life at Schloß Friedenstein was by no means peripheral to the life of court, and, in common with the court's cultivation of art, literature, and science, must not be regarded as having been provincial. Quite to the contrary, both during the 'hausväterlicher Hof' led by Ernst I of Saxony-Gotha, as well as later under Ernst II, whose court clearly began to approach a 'Musenhof',

---

[83] On 17 July 1775, with the establishment of a permanent theatre in Gotha, the first geographically fixed theatrical ensemble in Germany came into being; cf. Helga Raschke, 'Conrad Ekhof: Ein Schauspieler des 18. Jahrhunderts', in *Die Residenzstadt Gotha in der Goethe-Zeit*, ed. Hans Erkenbrecher and Helmut Roob (Bucha bei Jena: Quartus-Verlag, 1998), 85–94, at 94.

[84] Ibid., 93. Among them was Hans Conrad Dietrich Ekhof (1720–1778), the so-called 'Vater der deutschen Schauspielkunst' (the father of dramatic arts in Germany); see Joseph Kürschner, 'Ekhof', in *Allgemeine Deutsche Biographie*, V (Leipzig, 1877), 788.

highly educated dukes bestowed upon music generous amounts of attention and support.[85]

As recommended by Volker Bauer, 'It seems advisable, therefore, to scrutinize the widespread view that German princes imitated the court and lifestyle of Louis XIV and thus can be considered, more or less, as ridiculous miniature versions of the Sun King.'[86] At the court of Gotha, music was an important part of daily life, supported by dukes who themselves engaged in artistic activities. To this end, they maintained a highly successful *Hofkapelle* that, despite its modest size, was very versatile, thanks to the ability of many of its members to play more than one instrument and due to the participation of court trumpeters and kettledrum players, and the *Hofhautboistenbande*, as well as other musically-proficient court employees. A nineteenth-century assessment of Duke Ernst II illustrates this perfectly:

> Allerdings war ihm alle rauschende Musik zuwider, aber die sanften und lieblichen Töne der Harmonie liebte er wie irgend Einer. In seiner Jugend blies er sogar die Flöte vortrefflich . . . und an seinem Hofe unterhielt er eine ausgezeichnete Kapelle.

> Although any loud [literally, roaring] music was not to his liking, he did enjoy the soft and lovely tones of the *Harmonie* [that is, wind ensemble] like none other. As a youth he even excelled in playing the transverse flute . . . and at his court he maintained an excellent *Kapelle*.[87]

Today, the Thüringen Philharmonie Gotha can rightly call itself 'a young orchestra with a 350-year old tradition' — a tradition that, not least, has bequeathed to the musical world an abundant legacy of musical works of extraordinary quality.[88]

---

[85] On the terms 'hausväterlicher Hof' and 'Musenhof', see Bauer, *Die höfische Gesellschaft*, 69, 75.

[86] Ibid., 39.

[87] August Beck, *Ernst der Zweite, Herzog zu Sachsen-Gotha und Altenburg als Pfleger und Beschützer der Wissenschaft und Kunst* (Gotha, 1854), 321–2.

[88] 'Das Orchester', *Thüringen Philharmonie Gotha* [website], ed. Gesellschaft der Freunde und Förderer der Thüringen Philharmonie Gotha, <www.thphil.de/orchester.html> (accessed 3 October 2009).

TABLE 7.1. Membership of the Gotha Court Music Establishment in 1713, 1732, 1745, and 1756

| Year | 1713 | 1732 | 1745 | 1756 |
|---|---|---|---|---|
| Ruler | Duke Friedrich II (r. 1691–1732) | | Duke Friedrich III (r. 1733–72) | |
| Numeric Overview | 1 *Kapellmeister* / 9 instrumentalists / c.7 trumpeters & 1 kettledrummer / *Hofhautboistenbande* (exact number unknown) / 7 vocalists / 3 additional personnel | 1 *Kapellmeister* / 1 concertmaster / 11 instrumentalists / c.7 trumpeters & 1 kettledrummer / *Hofhautboistenbande* (exact number unknown) / 7 vocalists / 3 additional personnel | 1 *Kapellmeister* / 1 concertmaster / 16 instrumentalists / 7 trumpeters & 1 kettledrummer / 8 members of the *Hofhautboistenbande* / 4 vocalists / 3 additional personnel | 1 *Kapellmeister* / 16 instrumentalists / 7 trumpeters & 1 kettledrummer / 8 members of the *Hofhautboistenbande* / 8 vocalists / 4 additional personnel |
| *Kapellmeister* | Christian Friedrich Witt (also org) | Gottfried Heinrich Stölzel | Gottfried Heinrich Stölzel | Georg Anton Benda |
| Concertmaster | | Johann Wilhelm Hien, 'Premier-Violinist' | Johann Wilhelm Hien | Vacant |
| Instrumentalists Violin | Henning (first name unknown) / Johann Christoph Wenig [jun. or sen.?] (also bn) / Johann Gottfried Golde (also org) / *See Hautboisten* | Johann Georg Straubel / Nicolaus Bauer / Johann August Engert / Johann Nicolaus Specht | Johann Georg Straubel / Nicolaus Bauer / Johann August Engert / Johann Nicolaus Specht | Johann Georg Straubel / Nicolaus Bauer / Johann August Engert / Johann Nicolaus Specht |

| Year | 1713 | 1732 | 1745 | 1756 |
|---|---|---|---|---|
| Violin (*cont.*) | | | Johann Andreas Schieck | Johann Andreas Schieck<br>Dismas Hattasch<br>*See Hautboisten* |
| Violoncello | Johann Sebastian Lange | Johann Sebastian Lange | Johann Sebastian Lange | *See Hofhautboistenbande* |
| Contrabass | | | *See Hofhautboistenbande* | *See Hofhautboistenbande* |
| Flute | | | *See Oboe* | *See Hautboisten* |
| Oboe | | | Johann Friedrich Hempel, 'Cammermusico' (also fl) | |
| Bassoon | Johann Andreas Cramer<br>*See Violin* | Johann Andreas Cramer<br>Christian Heinrich Stölzel | Johann Andreas Cramer<br>Christian Heinrich Stölzel<br>David Abraham Böhmer<br>*See Hofhautboistenbande* | Christian Heinrich Stölzel<br>David Abraham Böhmer<br>*See Hofhautboistenbande* |
| Waldhorn | | | Johann Caspar Hötzel<br>Anton Ferdinand Weisse<br>*See Hofhautboistenbande* | Johann Caspar Hötzel<br>Anton Ferdinand Weisse<br>*See Hofhautboistenbande* |
| Lute | | [Georg Friedrich Meusel, d. 1728] | Gottfried Diestel, 'Accompagnist' | Gottfried Diestel, 'Accompagnist' |
| *Hoforganist* in Gotha | [*See Kapellmeister and Violin*] | Johann Gottfried Golde (also chamber organist) | Johann Gottfried Golde | Johann Gottfried Golde<br>Johann Gottfried Golde (jun.) |

| | | | | |
|---|---|---|---|---|
| *Hoforganist* in Altenburg | | | | Johann Christian Kluge |
| Substitute | | | Johann Christian Hofmann | |
| *Hautboisten* | Johann Siegmund Wenig<br>Johann Conrad Dölle (also vn) | Johann Matthäus Cramer<br>Johann Conrad Dölle | Samuel Böhmer | Samuel Böhmer<br>Georg Christoph Stubenrauch (also vn and fl) |
| *Kapellknaben*[a] | Johann Georg Straubel<br>Johann Gottfried Gebhardt | Friedrich Schüler ('Schieler') | | |
| *Hoftrompeter* | Names and exact number unknown | Names and exact number unknown | Nicolaus Schreck, 'Concert-Trompeter'<br>Johann Christoph Eccardt<br>Valentin Schulz<br>Johann Caspar Seyring<br>Johann Wilhelm Starckloff<br>Jeremias Brand<br>Heinrich August Schneider | Nicolaus Schreck, 'Concert-Trompeter'<br>Johann Christoph Eccardt<br>Johann Wilhelm Starckloff<br>Jeremias Brand<br>Johann Gottfried Schneider<br>Christian Wilhelm Hien<br>Tobias Krafft |
| *Hofpaucker* | Name unknown | | Johann Heinrich Schneider | Johann Heinrich Schneider |

| Year | 1713 | 1732 | 1745 | 1756 |
|---|---|---|---|---|
| *Hofhautboistenbande* | Names and exact number unknown | Names and exact number unknown | Johann Nicolaus Neuenhahn, 'Premier-Hautboist'; Johann Georg Beck; Johann Matthäus Harderoth (also hn); Bartholomäus Poß; Johann Daniel Walther; Simon Oßwaldt (also hn, bn, vc, and cb); Johann Sebastian Hartwig; Johann Georg Ihme | Johann Nicolaus Neuenhahn, 'Premier-Hautboist'; Johann Georg Beck; Bartholomäus Poß; Johann Daniel Walther; Simon Oßwaldt (also hn, bn, vc, and cb); Johann Sebastian Hartwig (also bn); Johann Georg Ihme; Johann Georg Bremser |
| Vocalists | | | | |
| Soprano (falsetto) | Johann Andreas Westphal; Johann Laurentius Stengel, 'Musicus' | Johann Laurentius Stengel | Johann Thielemann Cramer, 'Discantist' | Johann Thielemann Cramer, 'Sopranist' |
| Soprano | | | | Anna Franziska Hattasch (née Benda) |
| Alto | Johann Nicolaus Michaelis | Johann August Hebert | Johann August Hebert | Johann August Hebert |
| Tenor | Valentin Burckhardt; Nicolaus Schlechtweg | Valentin Burckhardt | Johann Christian Ziegeldecker | Johann Christian Ziegeldecker |

| | | | | |
|---|---|---|---|---|
| Bass | Johann Ernst Göldel / Metzger (first name unknown) | Joseph Ambrosius Huber | Johann Gottfried Weidler | Georg Nicolaus Otto |
| Range not specified | | Sidonia Dorothea Cramer | | Giovanni Andrea Galletti 'di Toscano' / Maria Elisabetha Galletti |
| *Hofkantor* | Georg Zacharias Busius | Georg Zacharias Busius | | Carl Göpel |
| Additional Personnel | | | | |
| *Hofkirchner* (caretaker) | Johann Michael Retzmann | Johann Michael Retzmann | | Heinrich Andreas Fladung / Johann Gottfried Schütz |
| *Calcant* in Gotha | Johann Georg Fabarius | | Christian Thieme | |
| *Calcant* in Altenburg | | Christian Thieme | | |
| *Orgelmacher* in Gotha | Christoph Thielemann | Christoph Thielemann | Christoph Thielemann | Johann Christian Hofmann |
| *Orgelmacher* in Altenburg | | | Heinrich Gottfried Trost | Heinrich Gottfried Trost |

*Sources*

Based on information found in the extant 'Hofkammerrechnungen' for 1712/13 and 1732/33 (as cited in Fett, 'Musikgeschichte der Stadt Gotha', 340, 342) and the *Hoch-Fürstlicher Sachsen-Gothaisch- und Altenburgischer Hof- und Adress-Calender* (Gotha, 1744–64) for the years 1745 and 1756.

[a] In the absence of primary source material, it is difficult to determine the exact duties of *Kapellknaben* at Gotha. Ahrens, '*Zu Gotha ist eine gute Kapelle*', 33–5, believes that they carried out support tasks such as the copying of music; some were presumably also hoping for an official appointment with the *Kapelle* (see, for example, Fett, 'Musikgeschichte der Stadt Gotha', 262, who notes that Johann Thielemann Cramer began as a *Kapellknabe* in 1733, before being appointed as a vocalist with the *Kapelle*). Only those who showed real musical talent continued to receive lessons and appear primarily to have played instruments, rather than having sung, at least on a regular basis. It is also likely that the basic musical training received by the *Kapellknaben* was sufficient for them to gain general employment later on 'bei Schuldiensten' (at a school; see Johann Brückner (1757), cited in Ahrens, p. 34); in other words, they could become *Kantoren*.

# 8

# The Courts of Saxony-Weißenfels, Saxony-Merseburg, and Saxony-Zeitz

## *Wolfgang Ruf*

OVER 350 YEARS AGO on 1 May 1657, in accordance with a directive in the will of Elector Johann Georg I (1585–1656), the three duchies of Saxony-Weißenfels, Saxony-Merseburg, and Saxony-Zeitz were established for the collateral lines of the Albertine-Saxony dynasty in order to provide for the sons born after the actual successor (see the genealogical overview in Table 8.1, p. 250 below): the so-called secundogeniture principalities.[1] At that time, Dukes August of Saxony-Weißenfels (1614–1680), Christian of Saxony-Merseburg (1615–1691), and Moritz of Saxony-Zeitz (1619–1681) each received small portions of the electorate of Saxony to govern autonomously for their own economic benefit. Their first-born brother, Elector Johann Georg II of Saxony (1613–1680), who resided in Dresden, inherited not only the largest part of the territory, but also retained supremacy over the whole of Saxony (including those areas left to his brothers) in legal and military matters, as well as foreign policy. Thus the secundogeniture dukes received only a restricted sovereignty; that is, they held the genuine rights of rulers, and governed territories, without actually possessing them. Their estates continued to suffer from the consequences of the devastating Thirty Years' War: the populations of towns and villages were decimated, administrative structures either had not been re-established or were completely rebuilt, and the region's economic base — founded mainly on agriculture and trade — was meagre. These adverse conditions forced the dukes to concentrate their rule on the formation of an effective administration and the welfare of their subjects. However, despite economic constraints, these dukes carried out extensions to their splendid royal palaces that were widely visible as impressive symbols of their rank and magnificence, both to their own people and to high-ranking foreign guests. This approach brought the need to establish a courtly apparatus befitting their rank, including the cultivation of music. Such measures of prestige were necessary, since despite their

---

[1] For an explanation of the historical context, see the articles in the exhibition catalogue *Barocke Fürstenresidenzen an Saale, Unstrut und Elster*, ed. Museumverbund 'Die fünf Ungleichen' and the Museum Schloß Moritzburg Zeitz (Petersberg: Michael Imhof, 2007).

restricted power in real terms, the Saxon dukes held the same status as the elector of Saxony in the imperial hierarchy. Indeed, thanks to the age and the former glory of their lineage they were counted by their contemporaries as being among 'denen vornembsten teutschen Fürsten ... als mitregierende Herren der Churfürstl. Sächsischen Lande' (the most distinguished German princes ... as co-reigning rulers of the electoral Saxon lands).[2]

Each of these three so-called 'kleine', albeit ambitious, central German courts drew upon a number of tenured musicians who participated in performances in the church, at the *Tafel*, in the chamber, and for official ceremonies, as well as occasionally in theatrical productions also. They were united under the generic terms (*Hof-*) *Kapelle* or *Hofmusik*, which in the broadest sense referred to all performing musicians who received a salary from the court, provided that it was a musical community that was at least structured hierarchically, had been institutionalized permanently over a substantial period of time, and, above all, was committed to artistic quality with contractually regulated rights and duties. In addition to those employed primarily as musicians, the court relied on adjunct musicians who were called upon only when the occasion demanded; these individuals were either court employees or musicians from the local town. The *Kapelle* as a whole comprised a collection of musically accomplished individuals organized into several groups, many of whom were not only active as musicians, but who frequently carried out other functions as well, including those of 'Reise- oder Jagdbegleiter' (travel or hunting companion), 'Hof-' or 'Reisefourier' (a quartermaster in charge of provisions at court, particularly during travel), 'Cammerschreiber' (court secretary), court poet, diplomatic envoy, 'Pagenhofmeister' or 'Pageninformator' (teacher of the court pages), 'Cammerdiener' (chamber valet), and chamber lackey.

The highest-ranking member, the *Kapellmeister*, was responsible for the selection of the musicians; the duke issued the decree for their engagement. The authority of the *Kapellmeister* to issue directives — which the other musicians had to obey — was confined solely to artistic decisions. He was also in charge of the composition and direction of the ensemble, the selection of repertoire, and the acquisition of music. That the *Kapellmeister* also contributed his own compositions alongside the works of other composers is self-evident; many of these presumably remained in his possession, or in the case of larger scores became the property of his employer. Vocalists and instrumentalists were usually specialists in a certain voice type or instrument, but it was also not uncommon for the latter to be competent on two or more instruments (for example, on the violin and oboe). A number of musicians were also employed as both instrumentalists and singers. The permanent appointment of musicians was made without any set end date, with the duke's approval required for voluntary resignations from the court's service and for permission to

---

[2] Zacharias Zwantzig, *Theatrum Praecedentiae* (Frankfurt, 1709), cited by Peter-Michael Hahn, 'Dynastische Legitimation und höfische Pracht: Strategie und Verhalten der Herzöge von Sachsen-Weißenfels', in *Johann Beer: Schriftsteller, Komponist und Hofbeamter, 1655–1700*, ed. Ferdinand van Ingen and Hans-Gert Roloff, Jahrbuch für Internationale Germanistik, Series A: Congress Reports, 70 (Bern: Peter Lang, 2003), 41.

travel (including holidays). Only the office of *Kapellmeister* seems to have included a mutually agreed period of notice of six months.[3]

In principle, the death of a ruler meant the end of one's employment contract, even if this was not specifically noted in the appointment letter. However, a change in regime did not, as a rule, affect the employer–employee relationship; rather, it remained intact via a renewal of the employee's 'Vokation' (that is, appointment to a particular office). While superannuation was not an automatic entitlement, it was common to grant pensions to long-serving musicians and to continue listing their names along with all their professional titles in the salary registers until their death.

Members of such *Kapellen* were divided into groups ranked according to their musical function: (1) the chamber musicians, the highest-ranking group, which included the vocalists and select instrumentalists; (2) the remaining court musicians (instrumentalists); (3) the court trumpeters (who were also called 'Musikalische Trompeter') and the kettledrummers associated with them; (4) the group of *Hautboisten* and violinists; (5) the *Kapellknaben* (usually numbering between two and four). With regards to the singers, the high vocal parts were performed by female sopranos, male falsettists, and *Kapellknaben*.[4] The designation 'Cammermusicus' was used for vocalists and instrumentalists alike; the epithet 'Cammer' referred to the venue: the ducal chambers, in which solo performances by (permanently appointed) vocalists, string players, wind players (oboists, 'Cammer' or 'Concert' trumpeters, and *Waldhornisten*), lutenists, or harpists took place. The internal move from court to chamber trumpeter (that is from the third to the first group) was viewed as an honour, since it entailed a promotion in both rank and salary. *Hoftrompeter* were only responsible for providing relatively simple ceremonial music (including fanfares), whereas *Cammertrompeter* performed elaborate, soloistic music in the princely chambers. Differentiated from among the trumpeters as a sixth group were the 'Heer' and 'Feld' (army and field) musicians. These were either still in military service or were allowed to continue carrying that honorary title after having served in that capacity, despite the fact they were now employed as a chamber or court trumpeter. In Weißenfels we also encounter combined job designations such as 'Cammer-, Hof- und Feldtrompeter', 'Cammer- und Hoftrompeter', and 'Hof- und Feldtrompeter', as well as the single titles 'Hoftrompeter' and 'Feldtrompeter'.[5] Military musicians were a special case in this respect, given that when undertaking civil service at court they were supervised by the ducal *Kapellmeister*; however, when participating in military actions as members of the electoral Saxon army, they were subordinate to the commander of the regiment.

The 'Bande der Violons und Hautbois' (the fourth group), which had been

[3] Cf. the appointment of Johann Philipp Krieger, cited by Arno Werner, *Städtische und fürstliche Musikpflege in Weißenfels bis zum Ende des 18. Jahrhunderts* (Leipzig: Breitkopf & Härtel, 1911), 152.

[4] Torsten Fuchs, *Studien zur Musikpflege in der Stadt Weißenfels und am Hofe der Herzöge von Sachsen-Weißenfels*, Quaderni di Musica/Realtà, 36 (Lucca: LIM Editrice, 1997), 74–7.

[5] The different types of trumpeters are outlined in Johann Ernst Altenburg, *Versuch einer Anleitung zur heroisch-musikalischen Trompeter- und Paukerkunst* (Halle, 1795), 26–30.

established according to the fashion of the time in Weißenfels in 1695, held an intermediate position. It consisted of musicians who played the oboe, bassoon, recorder, or violin and who served at the *Tafel* or outdoors, entertaining with suites, single dances, or marches. They were normally subordinate to the *Hofmarschall* (court chamberlain), but when ordered to do so they also reinforced the *Kapelle* at official musical performances; naturally, on such occasions they were required to follow the *Kapellmeister*'s instructions.[6] Their professional status is uncertain, but they were at least not bound to a trade guild and presumably counted among those 'Schriftlose' who left behind virtually no music, performing predominantly dance tunes or other simple music from memory.[7] Primarily (but not exclusively) responsible for providing light-hearted instrumental music, this does not, however, exclude the possibility that these *Hautboisten* may also have played ripieno parts in operatic performances or performed chorales on wind instruments during devotions.

The *Kapellen* of the three Saxon ducal courts, the electoral seat in Dresden, the neighbouring Saxon-Thuringian residences (Weimar, Gotha, and Eisenberg, among others), and those of the Anhalt courts (Köthen and Zerbst) were loosely interconnected, a situation that resulted in guest performances, temporary substitutions, or the recruitment of individual musicians by one of the other courts. Furthermore, close ties existed with the opera company in Leipzig, which had been founded in 1693.[8] Among the most remarkable pieces of evidence regarding connections in personnel beyond territorial boundaries are Johann Sebastian Bach's documented visits to, and works written for, Weißenfels; these occurred in 1712 or 1713, when Bach was active in Weimar, and in 1725 when he was in Leipzig.[9] In addition, we must consider Bach's appointment as 'Hochfürstlich Sachsen-Weißenfelsischer Kapellmeister' (Most Princely *Kapellmeister* of Saxony-

---

[6] Werner Braun, 'Entwurf für eine Typologie der "Hautboisten"', in *Der Sozialstatus des Berufsmusikers vom 17. bis 19. Jahrhundert*, ed. Walter Salmen (Kassel: Bärenreiter, 1971), 47 ff. [English trans. by Herbert Kaufman and Barbara Reisner, *The Social Status of the Professional Musician from the Middle Ages to the 19th Century* (New York: Pendragon Press, 1983)].

[7] Werner Braun, 'Die sächsischen Sekundogeniturfürstentümer und die geschichtliche Regionalität ihrer Musik', in *Musik der Macht – Macht der Musik: Die Musik an den sächsisch-albertinischen Herzogshöfen Weißenfels, Zeitz und Merseburg*, ed. Juliane Riepe, Schriften zur mitteldeutschen Musikgeschichte, 8 (Schneverdingen: Karl Dieter Wagner, 2003), 38.

[8] See also Michael Maul, *Barockoper in Leipzig (1693–1720)* (Freiburg im Breisgau: Rombach, 2009), 2 vols.

[9] Eva-Maria Ranft, 'Zur Weißenfelser Hofkapelle im Hinblick auf die Bach-Forschung', in *Weißenfels als Ort literarischer und künstlerischer Kultur im Barockzeitalter*, ed. Roswitha Jacobsen, Chloe: Beihefte zum Daphnis, 18 (Amsterdam and Atlanta: Rodopi, 1994), 97–107, at 103 ff. It is well known that Bach composed the cantatas *Was mir behagt, ist nur die muntre Jagd*, BWV 208 (probably in 1713), and *Entfliehet, verschwindet, entweichet, ihr Sorgen*, BWV 249a (1725), for the celebration of Duke Christian's birthday in those years. Reimer views Bach's 'Hunt' Cantata as a perfect example of court music intended for a *divertissement* and shaped by its function; see Erich Reimer, *Die Hofmusik in Deutschland 1500–1800: Wandlungen einer Institution*, Taschenbücher zur Musikwissenschaft, 112 (Wilhelmshaven: Noetzel, 1991), 151–68. However, one question arises: can these special occasions at the small court of Weißenfels be considered typical for institutional parameters at absolutistic courts?

Weißenfels) 'von Haus aus' (by proxy) in 1729, as well as the activities of the Dresden court *Kapellmeister* Heinrich Schütz in that same capacity for the court of Zeitz (from 1663 onwards).

## THE WEISSENFELS *HOFKAPELLE*

Among the three secundogeniture principalities, Saxony-Weißenfels ranked first. Its founder, Duke August, as the second-born brother, was next in line for the electorship. Thanks to this *spes successionis* he was able to lay claim to certain advantages of rank when compared to the other immediate descendants of Elector Johann Georg I. Indeed, August considered himself equal to the Dresden elector, of whom he was a serious competitor, thanks also to the rather peculiar dual role he played as both the administrator of the important archbishopric of Magdeburg and as duke of Saxony-Weißenfels. Having been elected as archbishop of Magdeburg at the age of twelve, August was represented by the cathedral chapter until he reached his majority in 1635. However, owing to the Thirty Years' War, he was only able to take up the archbishop of Magdeburg's residence in Halle on the Saale in 1642. On the occasion of the Peace of Westphalia (1648), the secularized archbishopric was not granted to him, but to Elector Friedrich Wilhelm of Brandenburg (1620–1688), with the concession that August would continue to rule Magdeburg (now a duchy) until his death, although, admittedly, under restricted conditions. August's capacity for decision making on matters concerning the territory of Magdeburg was limited by the control of the Magdeburg cathedral chapter and by the Brandenburg troops stationed in the region. Furthermore, the members of the local Estates (which comprised representatives from both the landed nobility and the civic authorities) enjoyed voting rights regarding the raising of taxes and use of tax revenue. From 1657 onwards, August was able to reign much more freely when exercising his sovereign rights in the areas that bordered his duchy of Saxony-Weißenfels. However, his rule was still subject to the supremacy of his elder brother, Elector Johann Georg II of Saxony, as mentioned earlier. This state of affairs also had an economic impact on both territories (that is, the archbishopric of Magdeburg and the duchy of Saxony-Weißenfels), as August provided only modest financial support for the population over the course of several decades. Nevertheless, he was responsible for the emergence of a vibrant court life in Halle, in which music and opera played particularly significant roles.

After August's death in 1680, his son, Johann Adolph I, moved the ducal residence to Weißenfels. Only a few kilometres from Halle, and located outside of the electoral Brandenburg territory, the capital of Saxony-Weißenfels was already home to a substantial palace that offered further possibilities for expansion. While Halle had now permanently lost the coveted status of *Residenzstadt* (that is, the seat of power) owing to the change in rulership, the palace of Neu-Augustusburg together with the town of Weißenfels, located at the bottom of the palace hill, began to flourish and became the most important cultural hub in the western part of the entire Saxon territory. Johann Adolph (r. 1680–97) and his sons, who in turn each succeeded him as duke – Johann Georg (r. 1697/8–1712), Christian (r. 1712–36), and Johann Adolph II (r. 1736–46), respectively – continued the politics of August (Johann Adolph I's father). They demonstrated their high rank and station both inwardly and externally, and manifested their equality in rank with the elector both in terms of dynastic ties and a certain mental detachment (in the sense of their continual consideration of, and emphasis on, their independence). This led to ongoing tensions between the electoral house in Dresden and the secundogeniture rulers in Weißenfels. However, the ever-increasing extravagance of their courtly life took a heavy toll on the princes' financial situations. Finally, from the time of Christian's reign, a commission appointed by the emperor to investigate debts took control of the principality's administration and announced massive reductions in expenditure.[10]

As had been the case earlier in Halle, and continued to be so in Dresden, in Weißenfels music and theatre were the most important vehicles for princely self-aggrandizement, spiritual edification, and secular entertainment. The secular or sacred occasions that involved musical or theatrical performances at the Neu-Augustusburg palace were manifold: birthday and name-day celebrations of the princely couple, births, baptisms, weddings of the princes and princesses, funerals of members of the ruling family or of high-ranking officials, visits of high-ranking guests, and anniversaries. In addition, major feast days of the church, Reformation Day, New Year's Day, commemorative services, or services of thanksgiving for important events in the electorate or in the Holy Roman Empire were celebrated. Consequently, the repertoire encompassed diverse musical and theatrical genres: sacred cantatas, passions, and mass settings as well as operas, *Singspiele*, serenatas, comedies, tragedies, *Schäferspiele* (pastorales), masquerades, *Possenspiele* (farces), and dances.

The main performance venue for sacred music was the court chapel. Consecrated in 1682, it was lavishly furnished and, as the ruling family's burial place, served as a symbol of the dynasty's unity. Music for the *Tafel* and the chamber was performed in the so-called *Tafelgemach* (an area used for both dining and entertaining) or in the spacious *Festsaal*, while across from the chapel a relatively small *Komödiensaal* had been set up in 1685 as a venue for theatrical performances. The performers were permanent court employees or visiting professionals, including vocalists, instrumentalists, dancing masters, and actors. Several *Kapellknaben* also participated; they were sometimes labelled 'Choralisten', at other times 'Altaristen' (altar boys), without any clear differentiation between the two terms. Musical performances could also involve travelling musicians who happened to be in town, choral singers from the civic church (*Stadtkantorei*) and local school choirs, as well as from the choir at the *Gymnasium illustre*, an institution established by

---

[10] Hahn, 'Dynastische Legitimation', 51. The lavish courtly life of the Weißenfels residence was examined by Rashid-S. Pegah, using travel reports dating from 1719, in 'Bei Hofe und in der Stadt: Von zwei markgräflichen Reisen im Herbst 1719', a paper presented at the international scholarly conference *Komponisten im Spannungsfeld von höfischer und städtischer Musikkultur*, Magdeburg, 18–19 March 2010. I should like to thank the author for very kindly sending me his manuscript.

Duke August to provide higher schooling for the children of aristocrats and civil servants.[11] The dukes of Weißenfels also took musicians with them while on their travels, primarily trumpeters, but also chamber musicians or the *Hautboistenbande*. These included, for instance, visits to the nearby Neuenburg castle (near Freyburg on the Unstrut) which served as a hunting lodge, their secondary residences in Querfurt and Sangerhausen, or to adjacent Saxon or Thuringian towns and residences. Occasionally, they also ventured to locations outside central Germany, such as Karlsbad (Karlovy Vary) in Bohemia.

The diary of the musician and poet Johann Beer (1655–1700) paints a lively picture of the demanding workload of musicians at the Weißenfels court, which frequently involved non-musical duties, and of their dependency on the good will of the current ruler.[12] In his novels and writings on music, Beer depicted the varied and exhausting activities required of a court musician as being much more advantageous than a civic musician's service with all its petty constraints.[13] We have him to thank for the information that following the death of Duke August in 1680 and the ensuing dissolution of the *Kapelle* in Halle, only a few of the approximately twenty singers and instrumentalists became part of the Weißenfels *Kapelle* that was established through a decree of 23 December 1680.[14] Among them were Johann Philipp Krieger (1649–1725), who had been promoted to *Kapellmeister*, and Beer himself. Beer was active initially as an alto vocalist and in 1685 advanced to the position of concertmaster, making him the second most important musician in the *Hofkapelle* at that time.[15] From 1697 onwards, he carried out the even higher ranking office of ducal *Bibliothecarius* (librarian), a vocation that corresponded more closely to his exuberant poetic talent. Beer's far-reaching reputation as a composer is evidenced by commissions he received for celebrations held at courts located outside of the Weißenfels territory, including Eisenberg (1683), Weimar (1697), and Jena (1697), as well as distinguished offers of employment from Coburg (1684) and Copenhagen (1691). It is puzzling, however, that Beer apparently did not write operas for Weißenfels. Beer was a perceptive observer of the hustle and bustle of courtly life and eventually could no longer condone the ongoing excessive extravagance of the Weißenfels court, as shown in his heartfelt prayer on the occasion of an opera performance in 1700: 'Gott erleuchte doch alle großen Herren, dass sie anstatt solcher

---

[11] Otto Klein, *Gymnasium illustre Augusteum zu Weißenfels: Zur Geschichte einer akademischen Gelehrtenschule im Herzogtum Sachsen-Weißenfels*, I (2nd edn) and II (1st edn) (Weissenfels: Arps Verlag, 2003, 2007).

[12] Johann Beer, *Sein Leben von ihm selbst erzählt*, ed. Adolf Schmiedecke (Göttingen: Vandenhoeck & Ruprecht, 1965).

[13] Richard Alewyn, *Johann Beer: Studien zum Roman des 17. Jahrhunderts*, Palestra, 181 (Leipzig: Mayer & Müller, 1932), 192 ff.

[14] Krieger's appointment is cited by Werner, *Städtische und fürstliche Musikpflege in Weissenfels*, 151 ff.

[15] A 'Vicecapellmeister', Gottfried Grünewald (1673–1739), is documented only for the period 1709–11. It is likely that the position was created specifically to provide Grünewald (the son-in-law of Johann Philipp Krieger) with a title in order to assist with his applications for positions elsewhere. In 1713, Grünewald became *Vicekapellmeister* at the Darmstadt court.

einreissender Eitelkeiten Allmosen geben! Amen!' (May God enlighten all great lords, so that instead of such very expensive vanities, they give alms! Amen!)[16]

It is impossible to provide exact details of the Weißenfels *Hofkapelle*'s membership for the entire period of its existence, as very few personnel registers pertaining to later years remain extant and these – for 1726 and 1732–43 – only cover those employed primarily as musicians. Adjunct musicians, as well as those called in from the town of Weißenfels, are only partially documented. Nevertheless, there can be no doubting the close correlation between the aristocratic-courtly and civic-urban cultivation of music essential for a small court such as Weißenfels. The following overview (as seen in Table 8.2, pp. 251–5 below) begins with 1681, the first full year following the foundation of the *Kapelle*. Further fixed points are the final years of the reigns of the first two dukes, 1697 and 1712, while the dates 1726 and 1742 represent the two years during the terms of the last two dukes for which personnel registers have survived. This data enables the tracking of changes within nearly identical periods over the course of sixty years. The fact that some names appear twice indicates that a musician either served in two different musical functions or was employed for a longer period; missing entries denote either a vacant position or an unverifiable appointment. The small number of entries for the year 1742 can be explained by the radical reduction of the *Kapelle* that occurred when the last duke took office in 1736, with only the trumpeters (who were considered indispensable) and several *Hautboisten* being retained.

Drawing upon research carried out to date – in particular the work of Arno Werner, Eva-Maria Ranft, and Torsten Fuchs[17] – it is possible to organize the musicians into groups based on their positions and to identify the majority of the employees. However, it should be noted that the value of this overview is somewhat limited, given that it is not always possible to determine whether a person was active primarily as a *Kapelle* musician at any set date or whether he held another position and only participated in musical performances when ordered to do so. Table 8.2 indicates that the trumpeters were not only the largest and most stable group, but clearly also the best documented; they were, after all, held in high regard, being of the utmost importance to princely representation. In Weißenfels (as at other Saxon courts, for example, in Zeitz), this group as a rule numbered eight court trumpeters and one kettledrum player. If sufficiently proficient and appointed at the appropriate rank, they could also be used for chamber music or in 'Feldmusik' (music on the battle field). In later years the highest-ranking trumpeters were Johann Caspar Altenburg (1689–1761) and Christian August Nicolai (d. 1760), who both carried the title 'Hochfürstlich. Sächsisch Wohlbestallter Musikalischer Cammer-, Hof- und Feldtrompeter' (Princely Saxon well-appointed musical chamber, court, and field trumpeter). From 1729 onwards, Nicolai was also

[16] Beer, *Sein Leben*, 90.

[17] See Werner, *Städtische und fürstliche Musikpflege in Weißenfels*; Adolf Schmiedecke, 'Zur Geschichte der Weißenfelser Hofkapelle', *Die Musikforschung*, 14 (1961), 416–23; Eva-Maria Ranft, 'Zum Personalbestand der Weißenfelser Hofkapelle', *Beiträge zur Bach-Forschung*, 6 (1987), 5–36; Ranft, 'Zur Weißenfelser Hofkapelle im Hinblick auf die Bach-Forschung', 97–107; Fuchs, *Studien zur Musikpflege in der Stadt Weißenfels*, 153–72.

listed as 'Geheimer Cammerdiener' (valet of the Privy Chamber).[18] Nicolai and Altenburg can be used to illustrate the close family ties that often existed among trumpeters. Two of Altenburg's sons were likewise court trumpeters in Weißenfels, and his youngest son, Johann Ernst (born in Weißenfels in 1736), has provided us with the best documentation of the state of the art of trumpet playing in the later eighteenth century (including its decline). The latter ranks Nicolai among the nine most celebrated German trumpeters,[19] and with good reason: Nicolai won fame when performing in Leipzig in 1731 for the Saxon elector and king of Poland, Friedrich August I (1670–1733), together with his fellow trumpeter Johann Caspar Altenburg. Shortly thereafter, Nicolai received an offer to enter the Dresden *Hofkapelle*, but the duke of Weißenfels refused to release him.[20] His brothers, Johann Friedrich Nicolai and Christian Joseph Nicolai, were also trumpeters at the Weißenfels court, and his wife was a daughter of the trumpeter Johann Caspar Wilcke. A further two of Wilcke's four daughters married the trumpeters Georg Christian Meißner and Andreas Krebs, while the fourth, Anna Magdalena Wilcke (1701–1760), became the second wife of Johann Sebastian Bach shortly after being appointed princely singer in Köthen in 1721.

This survey of the *Hofkapelle* and its sub-groups does not, however, include all persons who contributed their talents to musical performances on an everyday basis as well as on special occasions at the Weißenfels residence. In addition to permanently engaged and visiting artists, groups of folk musicians and wandering minstrels performed for the court, above all at larger festivities and carnival entertainments. Among them were the 'Altenburger Spielleute', the 'Zeitzer Pfeifer', a 'Leipziger Musik', a 'Lustige Musik', a 'Schweizer Musik', and a 'Bocksmusik' consisting of 'Sackpfeifer' (bagpipers), plus 'Bergsänger' from the Ore Mountains (the *Erzgebirge*). They appeared at the court neither by chance nor of their own free will, but rather were specifically requested to perform. While we cannot be certain which instruments and repertoire they played, these individuals clearly added a further layer to the highly stratified music at court, ranking below the *Hautboisten* (who did not belong to a guild and largely performed from memory), and expanding the already broad spectrum of performance in Weißenfels by playing popular, folk, and picturesque music, much to the delight of locals.[21]

Musical life at the court of Weißenfels was shaped first and foremost by opera and sacred music. Music performed during worship services followed the Lutheran model of Dresden: the foundation was four-part singing, primarily psalms with texts by Cornelius Becker set to music by Heinrich Schütz. An adaptation of Becker's Psalter for soprano and figured bass formed part of the *Hoch-Fürstliche Sachsen-Weißenfelsische Vollständige Gesangs- und Kirchen-Buch*, which the local Superintendent Johann David Schieferdecker (1672–1721) published in 1714 in

[18] Ranft, 'Zur Weißenfelser Hofkapelle', 99.
[19] Altenburg, *Versuch einer Anleitung*, 58.
[20] Ibid.
[21] Werner, *Städtische und fürstliche Musikpflege in Weißenfels*, 100–101; Fuchs, *Studien zur Musikpflege in der Stadt Weißenfels*, 74–5; Braun, 'Die sächsischen Sekundogeniturfürstentümer', 40 ff.

Weißenfels on the occasion of the consecration of the court chapel in Sangerhausen.[22] With regard to concerted music, specifically sacred cantatas, the 'concerto aria cantata' was a genre performed regularly. Previously unknown in Protestant circles, it combined a biblical text set as a sacred concerto for multiple parts with strophic *Lied* poetry set as a solo aria. Conceived in Italy, this new genre had found its way to central Germany via the Dresden court. Featuring German instead of the customary Latin text, in around 1665 it was also adopted by the *Hof- und Konsistorialrat* (court and consistorial councillor) and poet David Elias Heidenreich (1638–1688) and *Kapellmeister* David Pohle for use during worship services at the court of Halle.[23]

Between 1704 and 1706, the theologian Erdmann Neumeister (1671–1756) served as court deacon at the Weißenfels court. Originally from the nearby village of Üchteritz, Neumeister had previously taught poetics at the University of Leipzig, and in 1704 published his first collection of *Geistliche Cantaten statt einer Kirchenmusic*.[24] Following his time at the Weißenfels court, Neumeister served as preacher at the court of Count Balthasar Erdmann von Promnitz at Sorau (now Żary) in Upper Silesia, who also employed Georg Philipp Telemann around this time. In 1715, he became head pastor at the St Jacobi Church in Hamburg. Neumeister's poetry provided the foundation for another important type of sacred Protestant cantata, the 'madrigalian cantata', which was employed not only by Telemann, but also by Johann Sebastian Bach, Philipp Heinrich Erlebach (1657–1714), and Gottfried Heinrich Stölzel (1690–1749). Comprising an alternation of recitatives and arias, this form of cantata can be traced back to the Italian chamber cantata and opera.[25] The Weißenfels *Kapellmeister* Johann Philipp Krieger set seventy-nine of Neumeister's texts as solo cantatas, although no music has survived, as is the case with the majority of his other sacred works, which originally numbered more than 2,250 in total. These were listed by Krieger in an inventory of sacred vocal works performed by him in Weißenfels, a document that thus provides evidence of the vibrant and diverse musical life of the court chapel.[26] A further composer of sacred vocal works was David Heinrich Garthoff (*c.*1670–1741), from whose

[22] Braun, 'Die sächsischen Sekundogeniturfürstentümer', 35.

[23] Wolfram Steude, 'Anmerkungen zu David Elias Heidenreich, Erdmann Neumeister und den beiden Haupttypen der evangelischen Kirchenkantate', in *Weißenfels als Ort literarischer und künstlerischer Kultur*, 45–54.

[24] On Neumeister see *Erdmann Neumeister (1671–1756): Wegbereiter der evangelischen Kirchenkantate*, ed. Henrike Rucker, Weißenfelser Kulturtraditionen, 2 (Rudolstadt: Hain-Verlag, 2000).

[25] Steude, 'Anmerkungen zu David Elias Heidenreich', 54–61.

[26] Klaus-Jürgen Gundlach, 'Johann Philipp Krieger: Das geistliche Vokalwerk', in *Weissenfels als Ort literarischer und künstlerischer Kultur*, 63–73; and Gundlach, ed., *Das Weißenfelser Aufführungsverzeichnis Johann Philipp Kriegers und seines Sohnes Johann Gotthilf Krieger (1684–1732)* (Sinzig: Studio-Verlag, 2001). Werner Braun considers Krieger's inventory to be unique among extant courtly music collections; see 'Die sächsischen Sekundogeniturfürstentümer', 36 ff.

output forty-four cantatas remain extant.[27] Garthoff's musical versatility saved his professional career. Appointed initially as an oboe player at the court in 1698, he later switched to the post of organist after suffering the loss of his lower lip while bird shooting. (Incidentally, Johann Beer was accidentally killed on that same occasion when a captain's shot went wide). In 1713, Garthoff became *Director musices* at the local *Gymnasium illustre* and remained in charge of the school's choir and orchestra until his death in 1741.

Of comparable importance to sacred music at the Weißenfels court was the court opera, which under the auspices of the first three dukes of Weißenfels became a splendid home for early German opera. As a non-permanent establishment financed exclusively by the dukes, attendance was reserved for the ducal family, noble guests, and high-ranking court employees. Between 1682 and 1736, an average of two to three performances were given per year, usually on the occasion of birthdays celebrated by the ducal couple or for the visits of foreign aristocrats.[28] At times, members of the aristocratic court circle and the ducal family appeared on the stage themselves. It is difficult to pinpoint the exact genre of the works that were performed, for not only did their labels vary (for example, opera, *Singspiel*, *Schäferei*, *Pastorelle*, masquerade, *Tafelmusik*, and serenata), but the musical scores have all been lost.[29] Only two printed collections have survived, both featuring music by Johann Philipp Krieger: *Auserlesene in denen dreyen Sing-Spielen Flora, Cecrops und Procris enthaltene Arien*, published in Nuremberg in 1690, with a second part to this publication, the *Ander Theil*, appearing in Nuremberg two years later, in 1692.[30] The extant text booklets confirm that in contrast to operatic establishments at other German courts, texts were always sung in German in Weißenfels. This was necessary in order to comply with a condition of the *Fruchtbringende Gesellschaft* in which each member should 'die Hochdeutsche Sprache in jhrem rechten wesen und stand, ohne einmischung frembder außländischer wort, auffs möglichste und thunlichste erhalte' (preserve to the best of one's ability the true nature and standing of the High German language without the interference of

---

[27] On Garthoff's life and works, see Fuchs, *Studien zur Musikpflege in der Stadt Weißenfels*, 103–14.

[28] Klaus-Peter Koch, 'Das Jahr 1704 und die Weißenfelser Hofoper: Zu den Umständen der Aufführung von Reinhard Keisers Oper *Almira* anlässlich des Besuches des pfälzischen Kurfürsten am Weißenfelser Hof', in *Weißenfels als Ort literarischer und künstlerischer Kultur*, 75–95.

[29] Regarding the diversity of early opera performance in Weißenfels, the body of source material, and the connections to the Hamburg and Leipzig opera houses, see Fuchs, *Studien zur Musikpflege in der Stadt Weißenfels*, 89–100; Eleonore Sent, ed., *Die Oper am Weißenfelser Hof*, Weißenfelser Kulturtraditionen, 1 (Rudolstadt: Hain-Verlag, 1996). Additional information and an overview of works performed between 1681 and 1708, during the reigns of Johann Adolph I and Johann Georg respectively, can be found in Bernhard Jahn, *Die Sinne und die Oper: Sinnlichkeit und das Problem ihrer Versprachlichung im Musiktheater des nord- und mitteldeutschen Raumes (1680–1740)*, Theatron: Studien zur Geschichte und Theorie der dramatischen Künste, 45 (Tübingen: Max Niemeyer, 2005), 328–78.

[30] D-Mbs, 4 Mus. pr. 403; PL-Kj, Mus. ant. prac. K 328; information taken from inventory included in Jahn, *Die Sinne und die Oper*, 405.

strange foreign words).[31] Duke August, the founder of the duchy, was a member of this important literary academy and as such bore the name 'der Wohlgeratene' (literally 'He who turned out well'); from 1667 until his death in 1680 he was also the Society's last head. August's descendants adhered to this linguistic ruling, which was not a product of parochial or patriotic thinking, but rather reflected German cultural identity and self-confidence within a wider European context. The opera librettists were courtiers or men of letters who lived in the surrounding area, such as Paul Thiemich (or Thymich, 1656–1694), a teacher at the Leipzig *Thomasschule*; Johannes Riemer (1648–1714), who taught at the *Gymnasium illustre* in Weißenfels; the poet August Bohse (alias Talander, 1661–1740); and Heinrich Anselm von Ziegler und Klipphausen (1663–1696). Erdmann Neumeister and Friedrich Christian Feustking (1678–1739) may also have been involved.[32] Christian Friedrich Hunold (1680–1721, pseudonym: Menantes), another poet of some importance in the field of music, incorporated into his writings experiences that had shaped his youth during the reign of Duke Johann Georg. Indeed, the majority of his first novel, *Die verliebte und galante Welt* (Hamburg, 1700) was conceived in Weißenfels.[33] It was also Hunold who published Neumeister's poetic writings as *Die allerneueste Art, zur reinen und galanten Poesie zu gelangen* in Hamburg in 1707.[34] Hunold's texts for cantatas, operas, and oratorios were set to music by Reinhard Keiser, Johann Friedrich Fasch, Georg Philipp Telemann, and Johann Sebastian Bach.

The most prominent among the composers of opera in Weißenfels was court *Kapellmeister* Johann Philipp Krieger. Nineteen theatrical works written between 1684 and 1707 can be attributed to him.[35] His student, the chamber musician and court composer Johann Augustin Kobelius (1674–1731), also contributed twenty-one works between 1705 and 1729. Further operas for Weißenfels were composed by the Dresden *Kapellmeister* and director of the Leipzig Opera, Nikolaus Adam Strungk (1640–1700), as well as by three important composers born in the duchy of Weißenfels who, after having receiving their musical education at the Leipzig *Thomasschule*, all made important contributions to German musical life elsewhere: Reinhard Keiser, Johann Christian Schieferdecker (1679–1732), and Johann David Heinichen (1683–1729).[36] The son of an organist from the small town of Teuchern, Keiser acquired renown as a composer of operas in Braunschweig before becoming director of the Opera at the Gänsemarkt in Hamburg, where he supervised

[31] *Der Fruchtbringenden Gesellschaft Vorhaben, Nahmen, Gemählde und Wörter* [1629], facsimile of the 'Gesellschaftsbuch' of Prince Ludwig I of Anhalt-Köthen, I, ed. Klaus Conermann (Weinheim: VCH Verlagsgesellschaft, 1985), Preface, sig. A iij[v].

[32] Koch, 'Das Jahr 1704 und die Weißenfelser Hofoper', 81–2.

[33] Hanns H. F. Schmidt, 'Menantes in Weißenfels', in *Menantes: Ein Dichterleben zwischen Barock und Aufklärung*, ed. Cornelia Hobohm, Palmbaum Texte, 21 (Bucha bei Jena: Quartus-Verlag, 2006), 96–107.

[34] Bernhard Jahn, 'Hunold, Christian Friedrich', in *Die Musik in Geschichte und Gegenwart: allgemeine Enzyklopädie der Musik*, 2nd rev. edn (Kassel: Bärenreiter, 1994–2008; hereafter *MGG 2*), Personenteil, IX: 531.

[35] Inventory in Torsten Fuchs, 'Krieger, Johann Philipp', in *MGG 2*, Personenteil, X: 720.

[36] Koch, 'Das Jahr 1704 und die Weißenfelser Hofoper', 81.

and mentored the young Georg Friedrich Händel. Schieferdecker was the son of Christian Schieferdecker, *Kantor* of Teuchern and later organist at the court of Weißenfels. Involved with the Gänsemarkt Opera during the early 1700s, he became organist at Lübeck's Marienkirche in 1707, succeeding his father-in-law Dieterich Buxtehude. Heinichen hailed from the small township of Krössuln near Weißenfels, where his father was a pastor. Following a period of study in Venice and Rome, Heinichen was appointed to the venerable post of *Kapellmeister* at the Dresden court in 1716.

The Weißenfels residence both attracted and fostered the development of musical talent, including the children of the court falsettist Daniel Döbricht and his wife, the former vocalist Katharina Elisabeth Grosse. Their son, Ernst Samuel Döbricht (*c.*1680–1751), succeeded his father-in-law Nikolaus Strungk as director of the Leipzig Opera, while two of his sisters, together with Strungk's three daughters, were highly successful members of the Leipzig Opera ensemble.[37] Johanna Elisabeth Döbricht (1692–1786 [1774?]), the youngest daughter, first received acclaim when singing in Christoph Graupner's opera *Telemach* at the opening of the Darmstadt opera house in 1711 and from that time rated among the finest German vocalists. In 1713, she became the wife of the famous viola da gamba player Ernst Christian Hesse (1676–1762).[38] The most important singer in Weißenfels was Pauline Kellner (d. 1736), who had previously enjoyed great successes in Braunschweig, Stuttgart, and Hamburg. The duke had engaged her specifically for celebrations held in Weißenfels on the occasion of his sister Magdalena Sybille's wedding with Johann Wilhelm of Saxony-Eisenach in June 1708. In 1710 Kellner was hired permanently as 'Cantatricin für Kirche, Tafel und Theater' ([female] singer for the church, table, and theatre), receiving an exceptionally high salary and special privileges such as the ongoing use of a ducal carriage for both official engagements and private excursions.[39]

When the last duke of Saxony-Weißenfels, Johann Adolph II, took power in 1736, the golden days of opera in Weißenfels were finally over; according to the evidence of surviving librettos, the last musico-dramatic performance appears to have taken place during that same year.[40] The halt in operatic productions presumably owed less to a disinterest on the regent's part, but rather more to the court's rampant debts and the duke's ongoing military service as a general of the electoral infantry.[41]

[37] On this topic, see Maul, *Barockoper in Leipzig*, Textband, 254–308.

[38] Elisabeth Noack and Dorothea Schröder, 'Döbricht, Johanna Elisabeth', in *Grove Music Online*, <www.oxfordmusiconline.com> (accessed 6 August 2009).

[39] Werner, *Städtische und fürstliche Musikpflege in Weißenfels*, 77–8; Fuchs, *Studien zur Musikpflege in der Stadt Weißenfels*, 98.

[40] For an overview of extant librettos, see Fuchs, *Studien zur Musikpflege in der Stadt Weißenfels*, 173–81.

[41] Ibid., 24–5.

## THE MERSEBURG *HOFKAPELLE*

The duchies of Saxony-Merseburg and Saxony-Zeitz ranked below Weißenfels, both in terms of dynastic relations as well as political power, even though their founders — as former administrators of two bishoprics — were also bound to an honourable tradition. The basis of their rule differed from that of the duke of Weißenfels, inasmuch as there was no prospect of their ever inheriting the estate of the Dresden elector. Therefore, these dukes had no incentive to go into deficit through lavish expenditure on external representation, in order to compensate for a lack of power. The display of splendour in Merseburg and Zeitz was therefore much inferior to Dresden and also differed noticeably from Weißenfels, where the strong desire for prestige had exceeded the court's limited economic resources from the time of the duchy's foundation. The efforts of the Dresden and Weißenfels residences to draw level with one another can really only be seen in the sphere of palace architecture.

The first dukes, Christian I of Saxony-Merseburg and Moritz of Saxony-Zeitz, had a great deal in common. Like their older brothers, both had experienced the early glory days of the Dresden court during their youth. In 1642, Christian and Moritz went together on a three-year *Kavaliersreise* that took them through northern Germany, Denmark, and Holland, and led them to the important musical centres of Copenhagen and Gottorf. In 1650, the two brothers married two sisters, Christiana and Sophie Hedwig of Schleswig-Holstein-Sonderburg-Glücksburg, in a splendid double wedding with accompanying celebrations that lasted for four weeks. The Dresden festivities on this occasion included the performance of a *Singballett* entitled *Paris und Helena*; set to a text by David Schirmer, the music (by an unknown composer) is now lost.[42]

Indicative of Christian's penchant for music is his appointment as inspector of the Dresden *Hofkapelle* following the wedding. That same year he established his own small court in Dresden which included several musicians. Wolfram Steude provided the first detailed study of musical life at the Merseburg court, upon which the following section is based. He considers that the official appointments of David Pohle and his brother Samuel by the electoral prince and then duke, Christian, on 1 October 1650 mark the beginning of the *Hofkapelle*.[43] David Pohle (1624–1695), son of a *Stadtpfeifer* from the *Erzgebirge*, was an 'Instrumentalist' and also a competent composer. He belonged to the circle of students surrounding

---

[42] Uta Deppe, *Die Festkultur am Dresdner Hofe Johann Georgs II. von Sachsen, 1660–1719* (Kiel: Ludwig, 2006), 413 n. 392.

[43] Wolfram Steude, 'Bausteine zu einer Geschichte der Sachsen-Merseburgischen Hofmusik (1653–1738)', *Musik der Macht — Macht der Musik*, 76–7. Christoph Henzel supplemented Steude's study in his article 'Zur Merseburger Hofmusik unter Herzog Moritz Wilhelm', in *Mitteldeutschland im musikalischen Glanz seiner Residenzen: Sachsen, Böhmen und Schlesien als Musiklandschaften im 16. und 17. Jahrhundert*, ed. Peter Wollny, Ständige Konferenz Mitteldeutsche Barockmusik: Jahrbuch, 2004 (Beeskow: Ortus, 2005), 95–103.

Schütz and in 1650 served briefly at the court of Landgrave Wilhelm V of Hesse-Kassel.[44]

When in 1653 Duke Christian relocated to Merseburg, the brothers Pohle, together with the vocalist Heinrich Groh (d. 1690), who had also formerly been employed at Dresden, moved to the new court. The origins of a further six musicians named in a list of the 150 employees of the Merseburg court in 1653 are uncertain.[45] It is known that the *Kapelle* initially consisted of a vocalist (a falsettist) and four instrumentalists (probably two string players and two musicians who were proficient on both strings and woodwinds), as well as three trumpeters and a kettledrum player. Moreover, there were at least two *Kapellknaben* (referred to in the previously mentioned salary lists), who were apparently used as sopranos in Weißenfels. It remains unclear whether the position of court organist existed from the start or whether the organist who served at the cathedral adjacent to the palace was paid by the court or by the consistory. But it is possible that the organist and theologian Johann Friedrich Alberti held such a position from 1666, when the new cathedral organ was consecrated.[46] In any case, the small band of musicians would have met the basic requirements of a princely court with regards to music for the church and *Tafel*, as well as for fanfares and processions.

The first director of the Merseburg *Kapelle* was David Pohle; in 1660 he relocated to Halle, where he initially served as 'Fürstlich Magdeburgischer Concertmeister' (princely Magdeburg concertmaster) and where, from 1661, he served as 'Capellmeister' until relinquishing the post (probably not entirely voluntarily) to Johann Philipp Krieger in 1680. In addition, from the 1670s Pohle had already been working 'von Haus aus' for both Weißenfels and Zeitz between 1678 and 1682. The court in Halle, which offered many more opportunities for the composition of sacred polyphonic vocal music and *Singspiele*, was clearly much more attractive to the ambitious Pohle than the rather modest court of Merseburg. Nevertheless, he returned to Merseburg in 1682 to resume the position of *Kapellmeister*, probably until his retirement in 1691.[47] In the intervening period (most likely from 1660 to 1682), Heinrich Groh, who distinguished himself as both vocalist and composer, appears to have directed the Merseburg ensemble. Walther describes Groh as the 'Fürstl. Sächs. Merseburgischen Capell-Director' (princely Saxon-Merseburg 'Capell-Director') and refers to his *Tafel-Ergötzung*, a collection of twelve suites published in 1676.[48]

The further development of the *Kapelle* can only be surmised from a few

[44] More detail on David Pohle is provided in Walter Serauky, *Musikgeschichte der Stadt Halle*, 2 vols. in 3 (Halle: Waisenhaus-Verlag, 1935–43; repr. Hildesheim and New York: Georg Olms, 1971, Beiträge zur Musikforschung, I, 6/7, 8/9), II/1: 218–46; Michael Malkiewicz, 'Pohle, David', in *MGG* 2, Personenteil, XIII: 714–16.

[45] Steude, 'Bausteine zu einer Geschichte', 79.

[46] Ibid., 81, 83.

[47] Ibid., 84. Malkiewicz, 'Pohle, David', claims that Pohle served as *Kapellmeister* until his death in 1695; however, this appears to be inaccurate in light of Johann Theile's appointment in 1691.

[48] Johann Gottfried Walther, *Musicalisches Lexicon* (Leipzig, 1732), 292.

surviving reports that describe special occasions celebrated at the court. These included a 'grosse Taffel' (large-scale *Tafelmusik*) and a 'solenne Music' (solemn music) performed for the birthdays of the duchess and the duke in 1674, in which Princes Philipp and Heinrich both took active roles as instrumentalists. Moreover, in 1676, on the occasion of a visit made to the court by several princes – relatives from Schleswig-Holstein – the guests 'durch Musicalische Concerts und Ball . . . mit hiesiger jungen Herrschaft sich divertirten' (had been entertained with musical concerts and a ball . . . together with the local young princes).[49]

The initial flowering of the *Hofkapelle* of Merseburg both reached its high point and subsequently experienced a sudden decline during the reign of Christian II (1691–94), when the distinguished Johann Theile (1646–1724) took over the position of *Kapellmeister* from David Pohle, serving in that capacity until the duke's death. Theile, an experienced composer of both sacred and all forms of secular music, was famous for his mastery of counterpoint.[50] After receiving his first musical instruction in Magdeburg with Johann Scheffeler, he undertook further study with Heinrich Schütz some time between 1666 and 1672, as well as training as a jurist in Leipzig. Theile also spent time in Stettin and Lübeck, prior to serving as court *Kapellmeister* of Gottorf from 1673 to 1675.[51] He then went to Hamburg, where in early 1678 his sacred *Singspiel* entitled *Der erschaffene, gefallene und auffgerichtete Mensch* was performed, and possibly also the secular opera *Orontes* (which may have been composed by Nikolaus Adam Strungk). From 1685 onwards, Theile was once again charged with the composition and direction of sacred music as part of his duties as *Kapellmeister* at the court of Braunschweig-Wolfenbüttel. His move to Merseburg, probably in 1691, was presumably tied to plans for making the court's musical life as vibrant as that of Gottorf and Wolfenbüttel. Theile was assisted by his capable concertmaster, the violinist Christian Heinrich Aschenbrenner (1654–1732), a former student of the famous Johann Heinrich Schmelzer (1623–1680) in Vienna. Following a period of employment in Zeitz from 1677, Aschenbrenner had entered the Merseburg *Kapelle* in 1683.[52]

However, the death of Duke Christian II in 1694 put a temporary end to the activities of the *Kapelle*: all the musicians were dismissed. Theile, who was granted a small pension, remained active nevertheless, making contacts with the courts of Berlin and Vienna. Continuing to use the title 'Hochf. Sächsisch-Mersburgischer Capellmeister' (Most princely Saxon-Merseburg *Kapellmeister*), he dedicated his *Andächtige Kirchen-Music* (c.1701–5) to King Friedrich I in Prussia, whom he supposedly instructed on the oboe.[53] Theile also supplied the Viennese imperial court

---

[49] References in Steude, 'Bausteine zu einer Geschichte', 82.

[50] Johann Adlung, *Anleitung zu der musikalischen Gelahrtheit* (Erfurt, 1758), 184 n. m, refers to Theile as the 'Vater der Contrapunctisten, wie ihn einige nennen' (father of all contrapuntalists, as some call him).

[51] Regarding Theile, see Ulf Grapenthin, 'Theile, Johann', in *MGG* 2, Personenteil, XVI: 728–32.

[52] Karl-Ernst Bergunder, 'Aschenbrenner, Christian Heinrich', in *Grove Music Online*, <www.oxfordmusiconline.com> (accessed 6 August 2009).

[53] Grapenthin, 'Theile, Johann'.

with several sonatas and a mass setting.[54] In addition, for a brief period in 1709 until 1710, as *Musices Magister*, he taught students at the up-and-coming Prussian university in Halle.[55]

At the time of Duke Christian II's death, his six-year-old son and heir, Moritz Wilhelm (1664–1718), was too young to rule or maintain his own court. Until he reached the age of his majority in 1708, he was placed under the guardianship of the Saxon elector. It is possible that around this time or perhaps shortly before, the *Hofkapelle* may have become active once again. At the beginning of this second phase of the Merseburg *Kapelle*'s history, only three musicians can be identified by name. Jacob Christian Härtel (dates unknown) had previously served as *Kapellmeister* in Oettingen and may have possibly already directed the Merseburg ensemble for an indefinite period (at least between 1720 and 1727).[56] Christian Heinrich Aschenbrenner, who like Theile had been dismissed in 1695, returned in 1713 as *Hofkapellmeister* and served in that capacity until his retirement in 1719. The third musician was the court and cathedral organist Georg Friedrich Kauffmann (1679–1735), who appears to have been Aschenbrenner's successor.[57] Before long, the *Kapelle* comprised between twenty-five and thirty individuals, with whom it was possible to perform large-scale chamber and church music and carry out the necessary representative functions (for example, when special occasions were celebrated at the court) at full strength. Of two salary registers transcribed by Wolfram Steude, dated 1720 and 1727 respectively, that from 1720 lists at least twenty-three persons under the heading 'Capelle'.[58] Thirteen musicians are specified by name, including the 'Musicus' Härtel, organist Kauffmann (spelled incorrectly, as 'Haußmann'), violinist (Johann Christoph) Förster (a former student of both Kauffmann and Heinichen), and the 'Stadt Pfeiffer Fleischhack'. Moreover, a 'Capell Knabe', a *Calcant* (bellows blower), and eight 'Hautboisten Jungen' (apprentice *Hautboisten*) are listed, with names also provided for eight 'Trompeter und Paucker'.[59] Under the heading 'Außerordentliche Besoldungen und Pensionen' (Extraordinary Salaries and Pensions) only the retirees 'Capellmeister Aschenbrenner' and 'Capellmeister Theil[e]' are mentioned.

The list from 1720 also sheds light on the constitution of the ensemble. It included four vocalists (bass, tenor, alto, and probably also the 'Cantor Luther' as falsettist), two 'Violisten', an 'Hautboist', one bassoonist, and one lutenist. The *Stadtpfeifer* was involved as well, most likely with his journeymen and apprentices; he received a modest stipend from the court in addition to his regular salary paid

[54] Johann Mattheson, *Grundlage einer Ehren-Pforte* (Hamburg, 1740, repr., ed. Max Schneider, Berlin: Liepmannssohn, 1910), 370.

[55] Werner Braun, 'Theile-Studien', in *Festschrift Arno Forchert*, ed. Gerhard Allroggen and Detlef Altenburg (Kassel: Bärenreiter, 1986), 77–8.

[56] Steude, 'Bausteine zu einer Geschichte', 92.

[57] Ibid., 89.

[58] Ibid., 88–91.

[59] Regarding Förster, see Pippa Drummond, 'Förster, Christoph', in *Grove Music Online*, <www.oxfordmusiconline.com> (accessed 6 August 2009); Undine Wagner, 'Förster, (Johann) Christoph (Friedrich)', in *MGG* 2, Personenteil, VI: 1495–9.

by the town. From 1708 until 1715 Johann Joachim Quantz trained with *Stadtmusicus* Fleischhack, apparently a less than inspiring experience. Quantz commented in 1755 that the Merseburg *Hofkapelle* was rather modest in size at the time of his apprenticeship and required augmenting by civic musicians 'sowol in der Kirche, als bey der Tafel' (in the church as well as at the *Tafel*).[60] In 1727, the constitution of the *Kapelle* was virtually the same as it had been in 1720, except for a modest decrease in the number of *Hautboisten* and trumpeters, from eight down to six. More importantly, in 1726 or 1727, 'Capell-Director Graun' superseded Kauffmann; the latter stayed on as organist at a lower salary.[61] Like Pohle and Theile, the violinist Johann Gottlieb Graun (1702/3–1771) was yet another Merseburg musician of extraordinary artistic significance. A student of Pisendel in Dresden and briefly also of Tartini in Padua, Graun had apparently already made a name for himself as a virtuoso when assuming his post in Merseburg; otherwise, Johann Sebastian Bach would never have sent his son Wilhelm Friedemann to study the violin with Graun for over a year, in 1726–7.[62] According to Christoph Henzel, the undated print of Graun's *Sei sonate per il violino, e cembalo* can be attributed to his Merseburg period, and the music was probably written in 1726.[63] Graun soon began to look around for more attractive posts. This led him first to Arolsen, residence of the prince of Waldeck, where Graun became 'concert director' in 1731. He was appointed to the *Kapelle* of the Prussian crown prince in Ruppin in 1732 and then, from 1736, in Rheinsberg; upon Friedrich's accession to the throne in 1740, Graun took over the highly remunerated (with 1,200 *Thaler*) position of royal concert master.[64]

Working alongside Graun in Merseburg was the above-mentioned Christoph Förster (1693–1745), a second violinist in the court *Kapelle*, who had become acquainted with the Italian concerto and vocal style when studying with Heinichen in Weißenfels, as well as in Dresden and in Prague. Förster adapted this style in his *Sei Duetti*, op. 1 (1737), published by Telemann in Paris, and possibly also in the twelve *Concerten von verschiedenen Instrumenten* that were dedicated to the Merseburg duchess, Henriette Charlotte, but whose composer cannot be clearly identified.[65] Italian instrumental and vocal music had now gained acceptance at this court, and Johann Gottfried Walther reported in his detailed article on Förster that in Merseburg at that time 'bey Taffel- und Cammer-Musicken keine andere als in dieser Sprache abgefaßte Cantaten, gedultet werden' (when it came to music at the *Tafel* and in the chamber, only cantatas conceived in that particular language

[60] Quantz's autobiography in Friedrich Wilhelm Marpurg, *Historisch-kritische Beyträge zur Aufnahme der Musik* (Berlin, 1754–78), I, 'Drittes Stück' (1755), 197–250, at 201; see also Steude, 'Bausteine zu einer Geschichte', 85, 89.

[61] Henzel, 'Zur Merseburger Hofmusik', 96.

[62] Christoph Henzel, 'Graun, Johann Gottlieb', in *MGG* 2, Personenteil, VII: 1511.

[63] Ibid.

[64] See also Chapter 4, 'The Court of Brandenburg-Prussia', pp. 79–130 above.

[65] Walther, *Musicalisches Lexicon*, 251. Regarding Förster's output, see Henzel, 'Zur Merseburger Hofmusik', 99–102; Wagner, 'Förster, Christoph'.

[Italian] were admissible).[66] Förster remained a member of the Merseburg *Kapelle* until its demise in 1738, his last position being that of concertmaster, although the exact date of his promotion is not known.

The duke's great enthusiasm for music is reflected in an inventory made in the year following his death in 1731, entitled 'An Musicalischen Sachen und Instrumenten' (Regarding Musical Items and Instruments).[67] Recorded in this document are the contents of four large boxes containing music as well as numerous outmoded and relatively new string instruments: fifty-one 'Violons von unterschiedener Größe' (*Violons* of different sizes – presumably violins and violas), thirteen 'Viole de Gambe und Viole de Cello, Theils gut theils untüchtig' (violas da gamba and violoncellos, some good, some unfit for playing) , fifty-eight 'allerhand Violinen, theils unbrauchbar' (all sorts of violins, some of them unusable), three 'Brazschen' (violas), and one 'Violon de Cello'. Moreover, we find a 'Chalcedon' (calichon or mandora), a 'Spinett', an 'alt[es] Clavier' (old keyboard instrument), and numerous woodwind instruments, including two 'Fleutes douces' (recorders), five 'Fleuten-Bäße' (bass recorders), seven 'Bassons', six 'Hautbois', one 'Schallmey' (shawm), and six 'Pommer' (larger sizes of shawm). Finally, six trumpets, twelve trombones, and five pairs of kettledrums are listed. Details regarding the repertoire and the whereabouts of these instruments are not known. We can, however, safely assume that this mixed collection of both old and new instruments had been acquired by the court gradually, and that it comprised instruments played by the court musicians, as well as some that had already been discarded by them. Thus the instruments did not form part of a private collection maintained by the duke.

The final years of the Merseburg *Hofkapelle* remain obscure. But Duke Heinrich, who died childless at the age of seventy in 1738 (and who had succeeded his nephew Moritz Wilhelm, who had left no heirs), did seem willing to continue with musical activities to the same extent as before. Not only did Duke Heinrich bring the capable organist and composer Johann Theodor Roemhildt (1684–1756) with him from his former residence at Spremberg in Lower Lusatia, the most remote area of the widely scattered duchy, but he also increased the membership of the *Kapelle* to roughly thirty musicians.[68] This number included *Hautboisten* as well as additional trumpeters and kettledrum players; thus the ensemble reached the average size of court *Kapellen* at Central German residences. A comparison of the salary ordinance from 1727 and the salary overview from 1738 – the year in which the *Kapelle* was dissolved – indicates a minimal increase in the number of vocalists, strings, and *Kapellknaben*, and also shows that two clarinettists had been added to the six resident *Hautboisten*. Also documented is a small honorarium for 'Cantor Graun', that is none other than August Friedrich Graun (1698–1765), *Kantor* at the cathedral and older brother of the former *Kapellmeister* Johann Gottlieb Graun. Finally, the customary eight trumpeters and two kettledrum players are listed by

[66] Walther, *Musicalisches Lexicon*, 251.
[67] Steude, 'Bausteine zu einer Geschichte', 93–5.
[68] On Roemhildt, see Eduard Mutschelknauss, 'Roemhildt, Johann Theodor', in *MGG* 2, Personenteil, XIV: 259–60.

name, as well as an unusually large group of fifteen 'Berg Musicanten', probably once again singing miners and their accompanying instrumentalists from the *Erzgebirge*.[69]

The dynastic end of the Merseburg secundogeniture brought about by Moritz Wilhelm's death also meant the annulment of all employment contracts. After their dismissal, the majority of *Kapelle* members and *Hautboisten* requested further support (probably in the form of pension payments) from the electoral government in Dresden, which was apparently granted to them temporarily, in some cases until 1739.[70] The two directors of the *Kapelle* were more fortunate: Roemhildt remained titular *Kapellmeister* and cathedral organist in Merseburg until his death in 1756, while concertmaster Förster established successful contacts with the princely court of Schwarzburg-Sondershausen and later on also with the court of Schwarzburg-Rudolstadt, where he served as *Vicekapellmeister* until his death in 1745. What happened to the other musicians is not known.[71]

## THE ZEITZ *HOFKAPELLE*

The duchy of Saxony-Zeitz was the shortest-lived of the three 'Sekundogenituren': it existed for only two generations, following which it reverted back to the electorate of Saxony in 1718. The first duke, Moritz, maintained close contacts with the elector in Dresden; however, during the reign of his son and successor Moritz Wilhelm, this relationship turned into an ongoing dispute when Elector Johann Georg III (1647–1691) attempted to curtail the sovereign rights of his cousin in Zeitz. In 1657, Moritz, who also administered the bishopric of Naumburg-Zeitz, erected the palace of Moritzburg on the Elster where the old bishop's castle had once stood. Magnificent to this day, it is, however, noticeably more modest than the Neu-Augustusburg residence in Weißenfels. Six years later, in 1663, he moved his court from Naumburg to the residential palace in Zeitz, which was only partly ready for occupancy, its construction being not yet fully complete. Naumburg remained Moritz's secondary residence, which he visited regularly together with a large entourage, so that a courtly life was also maintained there – albeit it in a rather limited fashion – above all during the annual Peter and Paul Fair. That same year, in 1663, the duke, a rather frugal individual who was not particularly enthusiastic about music, established a *Hofkapelle*, most likely with the intention of keeping the costs low and ensuring only that basic musical requirements were met with, for example, at worship services, the ducal *Tafel*, and a limited number of court festivities.

The development of the Zeitz *Kapelle* has yet to be examined in detail; for the time being, we must rely on preliminary studies produced by Arno Werner

[69] Steude, 'Bausteine zu einer Geschichte', 97–9.
[70] Ibid., 99–101.
[71] See Chapter 10, 'The Court of Sondershausen', pp. 287–303 below.

and Adolf Schmiedecke.[72] Extant documents indicate that the 'Churfürstl. Sächß. Capellmeister' (electoral Saxon *Kapellmeister*) Heinrich Schütz was the force behind the foundation of the Zeitz *Hofkapelle*. Schütz – well-known to the duke of Zeitz, who had spent his youth in Dresden – had been released from most of his duties pertaining to the Dresden *Kapelle* in 1656 and was thus able to advise the duke as 'Kapellmeister von Haus aus' (*Kapellmeister* by proxy) on all questions relating to the constitution of the *Kapelle* and musical activities within the life of the court. Specifically, he arranged for the purchase of new instruments, supervised the renovation of the organ in the palace chapel, gave advice on how the choir loft should be built in order to ensure good acoustics, made suggestions regarding the systematic arrangement of the music library, concerned himself with the vocal training of the *Kapellknaben*, and provided the court with his own compositions.[73] Most importantly, he contributed to a draft *Kapellordnung* (a set of rules for the *Kapelle*) and recommended suitable musicians (see below).

However, choosing two of his own protegées – Johann Jacob Löwe (1629–1703, known as the 'Lion [Löwe] of Eisenach') and Clemens Thieme (1631–1668) – as *Kapellmeister* and concertmaster respectively turned out to be a mistake. They quickly began to quarrel, for reasons unknown. Löwe, born in Vienna where he also received his initial musical training, was the son of a diplomat (originally from Eisenach) in the service of the Saxon elector. After studying in Dresden for three years, Löwe was recommended by Schütz in 1655 for the post of *Kapellmeister* at the court of Duke August the Younger (1579–1666) in Wolfenbüttel. There he composed numerous sacred concertos and Italian-influenced suites. In 1663, Löwe accepted employment in Zeitz, having once again been recommended by Schütz.[74] According to the latter, Löwe was 'ein auffrichtiger Ehrlicher mensch' (a sincere and honest person) with a refreshing sense of humour, who preferred, however, 'gerne alles nach seinem Embsigen sinn haben' (for everything to proceed in his own industrious manner).[75] The self-assured Thieme had, like Löwe, received solid training in vocal and instrumental music in Dresden, first of all with the theorbo player Philipp Stolle (1614–1675) and with Schütz, and then later with Christoph Bernhard (1627 or 1628–1691), who instructed him in composition. Moreover, in 1642, Stolle, Schütz, and Matthias Weckmann (1618 or 1619–1674) had gone to the court of Copenhagen, taking the eleven-year-old *Kapellknabe* Thieme along with

---

[72] Arno Werner, *Städtische und fürstliche Musikpflege in Zeitz bis zum Anfang des 19. Jahrhunderts* (Bückeburg and Leipzig: Siegel, 1922); Adolf Schmiedecke, 'Aufführungen von Opern, Operetten, Serenaden und Kantaten am Zeitzer Hof', *Die Musikforschung*, 25 (1972), 168–74; Michael Märker, 'Zeitz', in *MGG* 2, Sachteil, IX: 2275–8; Wolfgang Ruf, 'Musik am Zeitzer Hof', in *Musik der Macht – Macht der Musik*, 102–16.

[73] Memoranda from Schütz to Duke Moritz, dated 14 July and 29 September 1663, D-Dl, Loc. 8592; memorandum to the Superintendent of Zeitz (without date, 1667?), D-WERa, Rep. A 29d 1, No. 19, fols. 22ʳ–23ʳ.

[74] Arndt Schnoor and Horst Walter, 'Löwe von Eisenach, Johann Jakob', in *MGG* 2, Personenteil, XI: 526–8.

[75] Letter to Duchess Sophie Elisabeth of Braunschweig-Lüneburg, 24 July 1655, D-Wa, 1 Alt 25 No. 294, fols. 9ʳ–11ᵛ; reproduced in Heinrich Schütz, *Gesammelte Briefe und Schriften*, ed. Erich H. Müller (Regensburg: Gustav Bosse, 1931), 253–6.

them. Following his return to Dresden (which cannot be dated exactly), Thieme
served as instrumentalist in the Saxon *Hofkapelle* from 1651 until 1663. When
Thieme's attempt to find employment in Hamburg failed, he accepted the position in Zeitz in 1663, yet another position Schütz had procured for him, although
Thieme may have considered it unsatisfactory as he ranked second to Löwe. When
the court failed to produce official appointment letters outlining the responsibilities of all musicians in a timely fashion, an inevitable conflict ensued between
the opinionated Thieme and the hard-working *Kapellmeister*, and even Thieme's
promotion to concertmaster and the expansion of his duties were insufficient to
resolve the problem.[76]

With regard to the music performed at the court, the 'Fürstl. S. Capellordnung'
(Princely S[axon] *Kapelle* regulations), issued in 1664, failed to provide information on the organization of music for the *Tafel* and chamber, or indeed any other
secular music at the court in Zeitz. It did, however, regulate the order of worship
services throughout the church year, from festive weddings to simple 'Betstunden'
(devotions), as well as outlining the distribution of duties among the leading court
musicians in an appendix.[77] It also determined the extent to which, in addition to
the pastor, the members of the *Kapelle*, the *Kapellknaben*, the town *Kantorei*, and
the congregation were involved and at which points during the service specific
vocal genres were to be performed and in which language. These included, for
example, 'ein lat. oder Teutzsch Concert oder Motetto' (a Latin or German [sa-
cred] concerto or motet), a 'Teutzsch Lied' (German song), a 'lateinischer Psalm
musicaliter' (Latin psalm set to music), a 'Missa teutzsch' (German mass setting),
a 'Magnificat teutzsch oder lateinisch' (*Magnificat* in German or Latin), or a 'Li-
tanei Teutzsch, figuraliter oder choral' (German litany, figural or choral [that is, in
either a concerted or unison choral setting]). During the Vespers services held on
the first day of Christmas and on Easter Sunday, 'figuraliter' (concerted) settings of
Schütz's *Historien* were to be sung, while for devotions and services with sermons
held during the week, 'Ein Psalm D. Cornelii Beckers nach den Melodien des
Capellmeisters Schütz' (a psalm by D[irector] Cornelius Becker employing melo-
dies of *Kapellmeister* Schütz) was scheduled. Despite the modest forces available,
Schütz's contributions in all musical styles, ranging from the sacred concerto to the
simple sacred songs (of the type often gathered together in a *Cantional*), were performed regularly in the court chapel and provided a musically diverse programme
that included the participation of the congregation.

The order of worship for Christmas Day (opposite) provides an example of the
exacting nature of these regulations conceived in 1664:[78]

---

[76] Hans-Joachim Buch (and editors), 'Thieme, Clemens', in *MGG* 2, Personenteil, XVI:
756–7.
[77] The text of the Zeitz *Kapellordnung* is found in Werner, *Städtische und fürstliche Musikpflege in Zeitz*, 67–71. Werner suspects that the numbering system is inaccurate.
[78] Ibid., 67.

Am heiligen Christtage wird der Gottes-
dienst in der Kirchen folgend. Ordnung nach
verrichtet.

1. Introitus. Motetto de tempore.
2. Kyrie. Christe. Kyrie.
3. Intonirt d. Priester vor dem Altar das
   Gloria.
4. Missa.
5. Allein Gott in der Höh.

6. Collecte u. die Epistel.
7. Gelobet seyst du Jesu Christ.

8. Evangelium.
9. Concert von d. Capelle.

10. Intonirt d. Priester das Credo.
11. Glaube.
12. Predigt u. vor derselben: Ein Kindlein
    so löblich. Und ist zu notiren, daß von
    hiervon biß uf Purif. Mariae vor allen
    Sonntags-Predigten itzermeldetes Lied
    zu singen.

13. Ein groß Concert.
14. Collecte u. d. Seegen.
15. Zum Beschluß: Ach mein hertzliebes
    Jesulein.

In der Vesper gehet der Gottesdienst halbweg
zwey Uhr an. Und

1. intonirt d. Priester vor dem Altar: Deus in
   adjutorium, worauf d. Chor antwortet.

2. Die Geburt Unsers Herrn und Heilands
   Jesu Christi; figuraliter.

3. Predigt, u. für dem Vater Unser: Ein Kindelein so löbelich.

4. Magnificat, wo zwischen die gewöhnlich
   Teutzschen Lied[er], als: 1. Lobt Gott,
   ihr Christen allzu gleich. 2. Wir Christenleut. 3. In dulci jubilo.

5. Collecte.
6. Benedicamus Deo.

On the first feast-day of Christmas the following order of service is to be followed in
the church:

1. Introit. Motet assigned for that day.
2. *Kyrie. Christe. Kyrie.*
3. The priest intones the *Gloria* in front of
   the altar.
4. Mass.
5. 'Allein Gott in der Höh' [All glory be to
   God on high].
6. Collect and Epistle.
7. 'Gelobet seyst du Jesus Christ' [Praise to
   thee, O Jesus Christ].
8. Gospel.
9. [Sacred] concerto performed by the
   *Kapelle.*
10. The priest intones the *Credo* [in Latin].
11. The Creed [in German].
12. Sermon and prior to that: 'Ein Kindlein
    so löblich' [A child so praiseworthy]. It
    must be noted that from now until [the
    feast day of] the Purification of Mary
    this chorale shall be sung prior to all
    Sunday sermons.
13. A large-scale concerto.
14. Collect and the Benediction.
15. In closing: 'Ach mein herzliebes Jesulein'
    [O my darling little Jesus].

Vesper services begin at half past one o'clock
in the afternoon. And

1. The priest intones in front of the altar:
   *Deus in adjutorium* to which the choir
   replies
2. 'Die Geburt Unsers Herrn and Heilands
   Jesu Christi' [The birth of our Lord and
   Saviour Jesus Christ]; [in a] figural [set-
   ting].
3. Sermon, and prior to the Lord's Prayer:
   'Ein Kindelein so löbelich' [A child so
   praiseworthy].
4. *Magnificat*, which is sung between the
   customary German hymns: 1. 'Lobt Gott,
   ihr Christen allzu gleich' [Praise God,
   you Christians, all together]. 2. 'Wir
   Christenleut' [We Christian people].
   3. 'In dulci jubilo'.
5. Collect.
6. *Benedicamus Deo* [Benediction].

Despite the fact that the *Kapellordnung* detailed the duties of the senior court
musicians, the discord between Löwe and Thieme continued as before. It eventually divided the court's musicians and led *Kapellmeister* Löwe to quit his position

in 1665, after which concertmaster Thieme led the *Kapelle* until his death three years later. In 1664 or 1665 the small court ensemble at Zeitz included the former *Kantor* of Naumburg, Gottfried Kühnel (d. 1684) as alto, the bass Christoph Dörffel, and the viola da gamba player August Kühnel (1645–c.1699), the son of a *Cammermusicus* from Mecklenburg (and, incidentally, not related to the above-mentioned vocalist). They were assisted by Johannes Bohl, previously a 'Churfürstlicher Brandenburgischer Cammer Musicus' (chamber musician in the service of the elector of Brandenburg) and Ludwig Sulze, formerly an instrumentalist with the Dresden *Hofkapelle*, together with four *Kapellknaben* and an organist.[79] These places of origin indicate that even a small court such as Zeitz held a certain attraction for young musicians. In 1668, Gottfried Kühnel was promoted to 'Fürstliche[r] Capelldirektor', a position equivalent to that of *Kapellmeister*, which he occupied until the *Kapelle* folded in 1682, following the death of the duke. From 1678 onwards, he was assisted by David Pohle, as *Kapellmeister* 'von Haus aus'. After his tenure in Zeitz, Kühnel became organist at Leipzig's Thomaskirche, while the talented August Kühnel went first to England to perfect his viola da gamba playing prior to working in the cities of Darmstadt, Weimar, and Kassel, in each case for only a few years.[80] The dismissal of more than a dozen musicians was, as suggested in a corresponding overview dating from 1682, a welcome means of reducing court expenses.[81] Even a 'Musikalischer Trompeter' named Schober was laid off, despite the fact that court trumpeters were not usually considered members of the *Kapelle* and generally enjoyed the security of a permanent position, safe in the knowledge that they belonged among the indispensable (external) symbols of princely power.

After Duke Moritz Wilhelm had reached his majority and began his reign in 1685, it took considerable time before a regulated musical life existed once more at the court.[82] The ducal *Hofordnung* from 1688, for example, mentions only trumpeters. One of these was Johann Caspar Wilcke, who later appeared in Weißenfels (in 1716). Not until 1691 does the court 'Diarium' mention 'die Musicanten nebst der Capell' (the musicians who served alongside the *Kapelle* [members]). This comment indicates that a *Kapelle* had begun to re-emerge and that a number of musicians who did not belong to the ensemble were also active at the court – most likely *Hautboisten*, who are also sporadically documented in Zeitz.

Following the marriage of the prince with Maria Amalia, a daughter of Friedrich Wilhelm I, elector of Brandenburg, in 1689, life at the court of Zeitz appears to have flourished once more with renewed splendour. A decade later, the demand for representation rose considerably with the elevation of the duchess to the rank of 'Her Royal Highness', following her brother's accession to the throne of Prussia. For the time being, however, the court of Zeitz was rather hesitant about re-engaging past *Kapelle* members or recruiting new musicians. The former

---

[79] Werner, *Städtische und fürstliche Musikpflege in Zeitz*, 64.

[80] Haniko Itoh, 'Kühnel, August', in *MGG* 2, Personenteil, x: 833–4.

[81] Werner, *Städtische und fürstliche Musikpflege in Zeitz*, 78.

[82] This and the following paragraph are based on Werner, *Städtische und fürstliche Musikpflege in Zeitz*, 78 ff.

members included the bass vocalist Johann Franciscus Beyer, who was allowed to carry the title 'Capell-Director', as well as the violinist Christian Aschenbrenner, who in 1695 was entrusted with the position of *Kapellmeister*. Although he moved to Merseburg in 1703, he remained at the court's disposal 'von Haus aus'. Duke Moritz Wilhelm undoubtedly valued Aschenbrenner, since he granted him an old-age pension even after Aschenbrenner had resigned from his Merseburg position and the duke himself was forced to move from Zeitz to his secondary residence in Weida, having converted to Catholicism.

Music at the court of Zeitz experienced one last golden age from the turn of the eighteenth century, when operas began to be performed. In 1701, a hall for operatic performances was fitted out at the Moritzburg, and in Naumburg a theatre was built by the duke for this purpose and leased to a local businessman. Since the *Hofkapelle* lacked both the necessary forces for a performance and an accomplished opera composer, the court engaged visiting artists for special occasions. And although Theile — now retired and living in Merseburg — acted as an adviser, it is possible that he may have felt too old to contribute more fully. Prior to the establishment of a theatrical venue within the Moritzburg, the first opera performed in Zeitz was probably *Camilla, Königin der Volsker*, performed on 3 and 9 February 1699; its composer and librettist are unknown. Adolf Schmiedecke suspects that this work had previously been performed in Weißenfels in 1694 and was thus already known to the musicians there.[83] Moreover, at times the duke engaged 'Hofcompositeure' (court composers) from elsewhere in central Germany to write specifically for Zeitz and Naumburg; generally these individuals were either his own subjects or had come to his attention during his visits to the Leipzig Fair. Known performances in Zeitz included *Cupido und Psyche* by Johann Magnus Knüpfer (1705; libretto by Johann Ulrich König) and *Lucius Verus* (1711) by Johann Friedrich Fasch.[84] Fasch, who hailed from Thuringia, had spent a year as falsettist in the Weißenfels *Kapelle* led by Johann Philipp Krieger, before moving to Leipzig in 1701. After graduating from the *Thomasschule* in 1708, he founded the town's second collegium musicum and was said to have been recommended to Zeitz by Johann David Heinichen.[85] Heinichen himself had composed the operas *Olimpia vendicata* (1709) and *Paris und Helena* (1710) for the Peter and Paul Fair in Naumburg, followed by Fasch's *Clomire* (1711) and *Die getreue Dido* (1712), and Gottfried Heinrich Stölzel's *Valeria* (1712) and *Orion* (1713).[86] Only very few librettos or selected arias survive from these operas. Renate Brockpähler and Schmiedecke have been able to determine some titles, but the identities of librettists and

[83] Schmiedecke, 'Aufführungen von Opern', 169.

[84] Michael Maul, 'Knüpfer, Sebastian', in *MGG 2*, Personenteil, x: 356. Knüpfer was a son of the Leipzig *Thomaskantor* Sebastian Knüpfer and had been organist at St Wenzel's Church in Naumburg since 1691.

[85] Stephan Blaut, 'Fasch, Johann Friedrich', in *MGG 2*, Personenteil, vi: 759–75; see also Chapter 9, 'The Court of Anhalt-Zerbst', pp. 259–86 below.

[86] See Wolfgang Horn, 'Heinichen, Johann David', in *MGG 2*, Personenteil, viii: 1185–6; Bert Siegmund, 'Stölzel, Gottfried Heinrich', in *MGG 2*, Personenteil, xv: 1553.

the theatrical forms employed by composers are uncertain.[87] The last opera performance is believed to have taken place on the occasion of the duchess's birthday in November 1713: *Berenice*, set to music by an unknown composer.[88]

Henceforth, the court settled — as they had done in earlier times — for dramatic cantatas, serenatas, or selected arias for those special occasions that necessitated musical performances, led by the tenor and organist Ernst Nikolaus Thaur (d. 1726), also a poet and composer who excelled as the creator of panegyric musical works. As the last *Kapelldirector*, Thaur organized the musical performances presented as part of the festivities held in September and October 1717 for the wedding of Princess Dorothea Wilhelmina with the Prince Wilhelm, the future landgrave of Hesse-Kassel. These included string players, oboists, horn players, trumpeters, *Bockpfeifer*, and *Bergmusikanten*.[89] The brief history of the Zeitz *Hofkapelle* came to an end in 1717 when the ducal family was compelled to move to Weida. The fate of the musicians, all of whom lost their jobs, is unknown.

The residences of the Saxon 'Sekundogenituren' whose brief flowering lasted for only a few generations, coinciding for the most part with the European High Baroque period, were among the so-called 'kleine' German courts. While of little consequence in terms of political power play, their rulers nevertheless pursued highly ambitious cultural goals. As is obvious from this chapter, musical performances at court were outranked only by the construction of impressive palaces. Otherwise court music was an explicit sign of absolutistic self-aggrandizement for the dukes, with culture serving as a perfect means through which they could assert themselves. Music was also an imperative, indeed an indispensable requirement for these small courts, and thus formed an integral part of sacred and secular daily life, as well as on frequent special occasions. The formalization of court music in the shape of a *Kapelle* had great symbolic significance, despite the fact that the strict observance of formalities and ceremonial procedures was usually rather limited when compared to larger, more established courts: musical performances were viewed as regular occurrences rather than as ritual (formal) representative events, and thus can be seen as having set a trend for the future. The workload of the musicians was a heavy one, given that they frequently also held other, non-musical jobs. Owing to their small forces and limited financial means, the *Kapellen* of the courts examined in this chapter had to rely heavily on nearby residences in the form of reciprocal assistance, as well as the exchange of musicians and musical works, with the frequent close family ties among princely families being particularly conducive to such arrangements. Moreover, they depended on the support of those towns that were either home to, or situated near, a princely residence. While civic communities enjoyed some independence in terms of legal and financial matters, they were, of course, required to provide assistance at the courts of local rulers in order

---

[87] Renate Brockpähler, *Handbuch zur Geschichte der Barockoper in Deutschland* (Emsdetten/ Westfalen: Lechte, 1964), 288–9; Schmiedecke, 'Aufführungen von Opern'.

[88] Schmiedecke, 'Aufführungen von Opern', 172.

[89] Ibid., 174; Horn, 'Heinichen, Johann David'. For more detail regarding Heinichen's activities in Naumburg and Leipzig, see Maul, *Barockoper in Leipzig*, Textband, 353–472.

to ensure the splendour and magnificence of musical performances. The fact that the number of court employees was relatively small resulted in a certain personal intimacy between the duke and his musicians, which, naturally, would never have broken the social barrier of rank. A welcome change to musical life at court came with travelling vocalists and instrumentalists who performed either voluntarily or upon the prince's invitation; they often hailed from within the duchy and presented genres from the realm of folk music. The crossing of boundaries between aesthetic and socially defined styles must be viewed as another basic element of the musical life at small courts. A tremendously dense musical-cultural network of communication and interaction existed not only between the relatively few large residences, but also included countless smaller courts similar in kind to the Saxon 'Sekundogenituren', as well as numerous towns, and even villages.[90] It is largely thanks to this circumstance that during the baroque period music from Central Germany attained an outstanding reputation that reached far beyond its borders.

[90] Johann David Heinichen, a pastor's son from the village of Krössuln near Weißenfels, reported that prior to his training with Kuhnau in Leipzig, he himself had 'allbereit an kleinen Orten starcke Kirchen-Musiquen componiret, und selbst dirigirt hatte' (had already composed well-appointed pieces of church music and conducted them himself in small communities); see Heinichen, *Der Generalbaß in der Komposition* (Dresden, 1728), 840 note f.

TABLE 8.1. Genealogical Overview of Saxon Rulers

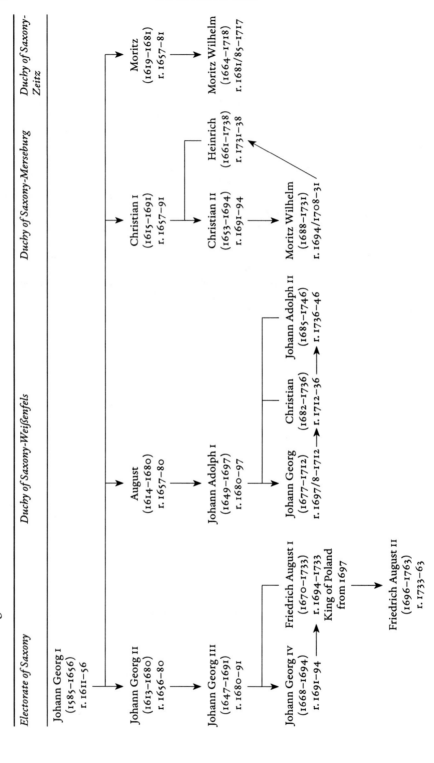

TABLE 8.2. Membership of the Weißenfels Court Music Establishment in 1681, 1697, 1712, 1726, and 1742

| Year | 1681 | 1697 | 1712 | 1726 | 1742 |
|---|---|---|---|---|---|
| Ruler | Duke Johann Adolph I (r. 1680–97) | | Duke Johann Georg (r. 1697/98–1712) Duke Christian (r. 1712–36) | Duke Christian | Duke Johann Adolph II (r. 1736–46) |
| Numeric Overview | 1 *Kapellmeister* 2 instrumentalists 2 trumpeters 5 vocalists 1 additional person | 1 *Kapellmeister* 1 concertmaster 13 instrumentalists 6 trumpeters & 1 kettledrummer 8 vocalists | 1 *Kapellmeister* 1 concertmaster 19 instrumentalists 8 trumpeters & 1 kettledrummer 6 vocalists | 1 *Kapellmeister* 15 instrumentalists 11 trumpeters & 1 kettledrummer 9 vocalists | 7 instrumentalists 10 trumpeters & 1 kettledrummer 1 vocalist |
| *Kapellmeister*/ 'Capelldirector' | Johann Philipp Krieger | Johann Philipp Krieger | Johann Philipp Krieger | Johann Gotthilf Krieger | |
| Concertmaster | | Johann Beer | Johann Georg Linike (Linicke) | | |
| Instrumentalists | | | | | |
| *Cammermusici* | Conrad Höffler (vdg) | Johann Augustin Kobelius Johann August Leizmann Gottlob Edelmann (lute) | Johann Simon Unger Anton Balthasar König Otto Gerhardt Verdion Johann Anton Dürr (lute) | Johann Simon Unger (ob) Johann Adam Falckenhagen (lute) Johann Anton Dürr (lute) | Johann Georg Koppe (harp) |

| Year | 1681 | 1697 | 1712 | 1726 | 1742 |
|---|---|---|---|---|---|
| **[Hofmusici]** | | | | | |
| Violin | Johann Hoffmann | Johann Hoffmann | Johann Hoffmann | Johann Adam Andreae | Leonhard Pardoffsky |
| | | Johann Wolfgang Barth | Johann Wolfgang Barth | | Johann Adolf Unger |
| | | | Johann Balthasar König | | |
| | | | Justus Werner | | |
| Viola | | | See Hautboisten | | |
| Violoncello/Viola da gamba | See Cammermusici | | | Georg Caspar Mangold (sen.) (vc) | |
| Oboe | | | | See Cammermusici | |
| Waldhorn | | | | Georg Christoph Veith | Johann Franz Trappe |
| | | | | Jacob Junige | |
| Lute | | See Cammermusici | See Cammermusici | See Cammermusici | See Cammermusici |
| Harp | | | | | |
| Hoforganist | | Christian Edelmann | David Heinrich Garthoff | David Heinrich Garthoff | Georg Caspar Mangold (jun.) |
| Hautboisten | | Arnold Schumann | Georg Wilhelm Köhler | Georg Wilhelm Köhler (jun.) | Georg Wilhelm Köhler (jun.) |
| | | Martin Böttcher | Christoph Heinrich Köhler (also va) | Christoph Heinrich Köhler | Christoph Heinrich Köhler |

| | | | | | |
|---|---|---|---|---|---|
| | Christian Buder<br>Johann Valentin Hopf<br>Johann Kühne<br>Hans Schautzer<br>Johann Friedrich Seyffart | Johann Christian Geißler<br>Johann Jacob Prager<br>Adam Friedrich Belldorf<br>Johann Christoph Frisch<br>Johann Valentin Hopf<br>Johann Hilsefunk<br>Johann Rosenbaum | Johann Christian Geißler<br>Johann Jacob Prager<br>Adam Friedrich Belldorf<br>Johann Christoph Frisch<br>Leonhard Pardoffsky | | |
| *Cammertrompeter* | | | Christian Melchior Nicolai<br>Johann Christian Biedermann<br>Johann Ernst Scheller | Christian Melchior Nicolai<br>Johann Caspar Altenburg<br>Christian August Nicolai<br>Johann Caspar Wilcke (sen.) | Andreas Krebs<br>Johann Caspar Altenburg |
| *Hoftrompeter* | Wolfgang Gottfried Förster<br>Johann Jacob Starzmann | Ernst Friedrich Renisch<br>Johann Elias Uhrlaub<br>Johann Christoph Heininger | Ernst Friedrich Renisch<br>Johann Elias Uhrlaub<br>Johann Christoph Heininger | Ernst Friedrich Renisch<br>Johann Elias Uhrlaub<br>Johann Nicolaus Bettstedt | Christoph Arnoldt<br>Johann Christian Günther<br>Johann Nicolaus Bettstedt |

| Year | 1681 | 1697 | 1712 | 1726 | 1742 |
|---|---|---|---|---|---|
| *Hoftrompeter (cont.)* |  | Hans Carl Klinkert; Johann Caspar Stubenrauch; Christian Wilhelm Thiess | Johann Caspar Altenburg; Georg Christian Meißner | Johann Christoph Altenburg; Georg Christian Meißner; Johann Friedrich Nicolai; Georg Friedrich Rehbock | Johann Christoph Altenburg; Johann Rudolph Altenburg; Christian Joseph Nicolai; Johann Friedrich Löffler; Christian Ernst Kettner |
| *Hofpaucker* |  | Jacob Mändel | Ernst Friedrich Reinisch | Johann Heinrich Thalacker | Johann Heinrich Thalacker |
| Vocalists |  |  |  |  |  |
| Soprano |  | Philippine Döbricht | Pauline Kellner | Pauline Kellner; Clara Elisabeth Grohe; Johanna Aemilia Falckenhagen |  |
| Treble | Daniel Döbricht; Johann Flemming | Adam Immanuel Weldig; Samuel Weldig | Adam Immanuel Weldig; Gottfried Wendebaum | Gottfried Wendebaum |  |
| Alto | Johann Beer | Gottlob Edelmann |  | Johann Gottfried Geißler |  |

| | | | | | |
|---|---|---|---|---|---|
| Tenor | Samuel Grosse | Andreas Schele | Johann Wolfgang Barth | Johann Ebert / Johann Franciscus Lehmann | |
| Bass | Donath Rössler | Nathan Lüders | Gottfried Grünewald | Andreas Elias Ehrhardt | |
| Hofkantor | | Jacob Mändel / Israel Gräffner | Jacob Mändel | Johann Christoph Schieferdecker | Johann Christoph Schieferdecker |
| Additional Personnel | | | | | |
| Tanzmeister | Johann David Wagner | | | | |

*Sources*

Based on information provided in Werner, *Städtische und fürstliche Musikpflege in Weißenfels*; Schmiedecke, 'Zur Geschichte der Weißenfelser Hofkapelle'; Ranft, 'Zum Personalbestand der Weißenfelser Hofkapelle'; Ranft, 'Zur Weißenfelser Hofkapelle'; Fuchs, *Studien zur Musikpflege in der Stadt Weißenfels*, 153–72.

# PRINCIPALITIES
## AND
# PRINCE-BISHOPRICS

# 9
# The Court of Anhalt-Zerbst
## *Barbara M. Reul*

ANHALT-ZERBST, a principality situated about 90 km north-west of Leipzig, is best known as the childhood home of Catherine the Great of Russia (1729–1796) and the workplace of its long-time *Hofkapellmeister* Johann Friedrich Fasch (1688–1758). This chapter presents a systematic re-evaluation of the expansion of the Anhalt-Zerbst *Kapelle* between 1715 and 1760.[1] It will draw heavily from extant account books ('Kammerrechnungen'), intact for the period 1662 to 1790, and numerous other hitherto unknown primary sources held at Dessau and Zerbst/Anhalt.[2] First to acknowledge publicly the importance of *Hofmusik* was Prince Carl Wilhelm (b. 1652, r. 1676–1718) in 1699. His son, Johann August (b. 1677, r. 1718–42), possessed an even greater interest in the arts and during his reign provided the long-term financial support for a well-appointed *Hofkapelle* and an entrepreneurial *Kapellmeister* to flourish. Catherine's father, Prince Christian August (1690–1747), and his cousin Johann Ludwig (1688–1746) followed in Johann August's footsteps in this respect, especially after Catherine (formerly Princess Sophie Auguste Friedericke of Anhalt-Zerbst) married the future tsar of Russia in 1745. A clear shift in priorities occurred after their deaths, when Catherine the Great's mother, Dowager Princess Johanna Elisabeth (1712–1760) began to rule in 1747 on behalf of her younger child, Friedrich August (b. 1734, r. 1752–93). But it was the Seven Years' War (1756–63) that marked the beginning of the end in terms of a musical *Blütezeit* at the court. In 1758, Friedrich August and

---

[1] Earlier studies include Hermann Wäschke, 'Die Zerbster Hofkapelle unter Fasch', *Zerbster Jahrbuch*, 2 (1906), 47–63; Nigel Springthorpe, 'Passion Compositions and Composers of Passion Music Associated with the Court of Anhalt-Zerbst' (PhD diss., University of Surrey, 1997), chap. 2; Konstanze Musketa, 'Musik am Zerbster Hof', in *Mitteldeutschland im musikalischen Glanz seiner Residenzen: Sachsen, Böhmen und Schlesien als Musiklandschaften im 16. und 17. Jahrhundert*, ed. Peter Wollny, Jahrbuch der Ständigen Konferenz Mitteldeutsche Barockmusik, 2004 (Beeskow: Ortus, 2005), 107–26.

[2] D-DEla (referred to in German sources as LHASA, DE), Kammer Zerbst, Kammerrechnungen 1654/55, 1662/63–1789/90. I should like to thank Dr Andreas Erb, director of the Landeshauptarchiv Sachsen-Anhalt, and his staff, as well as the Internationale Fasch-Gesellschaft (International Fasch Society) for their ongoing support of my research activities. Brian Clark and Samantha Owens commented extensively on an earlier version of this chapter, for which I am grateful.

his mother went into exile, *Kapellmeister* Fasch died after thirty-six years of service, and Zerbst was besieged by thousands of Prussian soldiers. By the end of 1760, the *Kapelle* had turned into a skeleton ensemble, and even the continued efforts of acting *Kapellmeister* Johann Georg Röllig (1710–1790) could not prevent a steady decline in musical performances and repertoire.

## THE *KAPELLE* BEFORE 1715 UNDER CARL WILHELM

Musical performances at the court of Anhalt-Zerbst during the second half of the seventeenth century seemed to have involved only brass instruments, specifically trumpets.[3] The situation changed when on 24 June 1699 the 'Stadt Musico' (civic musician) Johann Christoph Grahmann was promoted to court musician and commissioned to put together a small musical ensemble.[4] Specifically, at least one vocalist and five musicians playing their own instruments were to present music in the following configurations: a string band plus a 'Baß *Violons*' [*sic*], an oboe ('*Hautbois*') band, including a dulcian; a consort of recorders ('*Fleutes Douces*'), and a group of two or three violas da gamba. No mention is made of a keyboard instrument or lute, but these six players would have been able to provide all the types of music that were commonly performed at courts at this time. It can also be inferred from the above list that the musicians were expected to perform on more than one instrument or both play and sing – an important prerequisite for anyone who wished to secure a *Kapelle* position at the court of Anhalt-Zerbst during the eighteenth century. Repertoire performed at the 'Taffel', during *Assembléen*, and for visiting foreign nobility and other aristocrats, was to include 'die neuesten arthen' (the newest types) of music (perhaps in the highly popular French style?), and was not to be performed elsewhere. A stable income, even if musical performances should cease for several months during times of general mourning at the court, was to be Grahmann's reward.[5]

In addition to the court's own musical ensemble, a steady stream of musicians from outside Anhalt-Zerbst performed at the court from 1701 onward, an important trend that continued for half a century.[6] An official collection of musical instruments may also have been begun in 1701, when a trumpeter named Scheckel was reimbursed for an oboe and a violin.[7] The celebrations held for the wedding of Hereditary Prince Johann August and Princess Friedericke of Saxony-Gotha-

---

[3] See D-DEla, Kammerrechnungen 1673/74–1677/78.

[4] D-DEla, Kammer Zerbst, No. 2872, Part 2, fols. 684ʳ–687ʳ, and Barbara M. Reul, 'Musical Life at the Court of Anhalt-Zerbst: An Examination of Unknown Primary Sources at the Landeshauptarchiv Sachsen-Anhalt, Abteilung Dessau', in *Musik an der Zerbster Residenz*, ed. Konstanze Musketa and Barbara M. Reul, Fasch-Studien, 10 (Beeskow: Ortus, 2008), 197–222, at 199–204.

[5] D-DEla, Kammer Zerbst, No. 2872, Part 2, fols. 686ᵛ, 687ʳ.

[6] Various entries in D-DEla, Kammerrechnungen 1701/02–1708/09, document visits by musicians from Freiberg (Saxony), Weimar, Merseburg, Zeitz, Weißenfels, Magdeburg, and Gotha.

[7] D-DEla, Kammerrechnungen 1701/02, fol. 59ʳ, No. 884; fol. 60ᵛ, No. 912.

Altenburg (1675–1709) that same year featured a *Singspiel* entitled *Des Frühlings Liebessieg* and involved musicians from Gotha and possibly Leipzig also.[8] In 1707, the kettledrummer Johann Anton Richter first appears on the court's payroll, and a year later, a new organist, Johann Ulich, replaced Burckhard Meyer at the Bartholomäikirche where the court worshipped.[9] One of Ulich's duties was the provision of sacred vocal music on the occasion of birthdays celebrated by the princely family, a task that in future years would be carried out primarily by the *Kapellmeister*. The first musician to be labelled 'Cammer *Musico*' was Johann Gottfriedt Rauhfus (Rauchfus or Rauffuß), who may have been recommended by Christiane Eberhardine, the Saxon electress and Queen of Poland (1671–1727).[10] With regard to the further purchase of new instruments, in 1714/15 the *Hoftrompeter* Schmied was reimbursed for buying six trumpets and two *Waldhörner*, and there was also a 'Basson' in need of repair; the latter belonged to an unspecified 'Collegio Musico' (possibly a reference to a member of Grahmann's ensemble).[11]

EXPANDING THE KAPELLE

The first official *Kapellmeister*, Johann Baptist Kuch from Hamburg, was appointed on 29 September 1715.[12] That fiscal year, Rauhfus received 800 *Thaler* for a 'von ihm erhandelten kleinen Bande *Hautboisten*' (a small band of *Hautboisten* negotiated by him).[13] Since he had previously been paid a 'Lehrgeld' of 100 *Thaler* for teaching a single private student in 1714/15, these funds were certainly intended for the recruitment, room and board, and tuition of talented young players. This supposition is backed up by a letter from 11 June 1715, in which Electress Christiane Eberhardine of Saxony recommended Rauhfus and six boys to her brother at the court of Bayreuth.[14] A 'Stimmwerck *Instr*[ument]' (consort set of [unspecified] instruments) for 'denen kleinen *Hautboisten*' (the young *Hautboisten*) was purchased two years later.[15] It is more than likely that one, some, or all of Rauhfus's students

[8] See Erdmann Werner Böhme, *Die frühdeutsche Oper in Thüringen* (Stadtroda: Richter, 1931), 110; D-DEla, Kammerrechnungen 1701/02, fol. 63ʳ, No. 965, 29 July 1702; fol. 62ᵛ, No. 949.

[9] D-DEla, Kammerrechnungen 1707/08, fol. 29ᵛ, No. 102. See also Cordula Timm-Hartmann, 'Johann Ulich in Zerbst', in *Musik an der Zerbster Residenz*, 91–102; Michael Maul, 'Zwei Clavierbücher aus der Herzogin Anna Amalia Bibliothek Weimar als Quellen zur Zerbster Musikpflege um 1680', ibid., 41–68.

[10] D-DEla, Kammerrechnungen 1711/12, fol. 28ᵛ, No. 113.

[11] D-DEla, Kammerrechnungen 1714/15, fol. 63ᵛ, Nos. 931, 936.

[12] D-DEla, Kammerrechnungen 1715/16, fol. 30ʳ, No. 98; 1714/15. See also Hermann Wäschke, 'Rölligs Kantate für St. Jakobs-Tag', *Zerbster Jahrbuch* (1908), 6–19, at 8; Bernhard Engelke, 'Johann Friedrich Fasch: Versuch einer Bibliographie', *Sammelbände der Internationalen Musikgesellschaft*, 10/2 (1908/9), 263–83, at 276.

[13] D-DEla, Kammerrechnungen 1715/16, p. 74, No. 1315; their names are not provided.

[14] D-DEla, Kammerrechnungen 1714/15, vol. II, p. 57, No. 880. See also Chapter 14, 'The Court of Brandenburg-Culmbach-Bayreuth', p. 397 below.

[15] D-DEla, Kammerrechnungen 1717/18, p. 127, No. 1304.

stayed on permanently as *Hautboisten* attached to the elite princely Grenadier (or 'Schloß') Guard (see Table 9.1, pp. 283–4 below).

Three new musicians were appointed in 1716, the most substantial annual budget increase since the *Kapelle*'s inception in 1699. Specifically, the singer 'Monsieur Boll' (Samuel Gottlieb Poll), the trumpeter Kühne (replacing Schmied, who had died, from Easter 1716), and the 'Cammer Musico' Sattler are first listed in the court's account books.[16] (Curiously, a draft of Sattler's official appointment decree was prepared only on 22 March 1721; it indicates that he was required not only to play the violin, but also to instruct the court pages in fencing.[17]) Meanwhile, in 1716/17, Kuch arranged for a new harpsichord ('Clavicembel') from Bremen.[18] This may have been for the personal use of Prince Johann August, a student of Burckhard Meyer on the 'Clavicordium' between 1688 and 1704.[19] A 'contra violone' was purchased in 1717/18, but it is unclear which *Kapelle* members would have played it.[20] On 24 June 1717, Johann Caspar Wilcke (1691–1766) took up a post as trumpeter at Zerbst, which he held until his death.[21] He may have been involved in the celebration of the 200th anniversary of the Augsburg Confession from 31 October to 2 November 1717. References to several (untitled) pieces of music are included in the order of worship decreed by Carl Wilhelm – his last 'Verordnung', as he died on 3 November 1717.[22]

Johann August, Carl Wilhelm's son and successor, was the most important and consistent supporter of the Anhalt-Zerbst *Hofkapelle* during the eighteenth century, especially in the first decade of his reign. In 1719/20, for instance, employees of the court who worked in the *Schloßkirche* (palace chapel), which included all clergy, musicians, the *Kantor*, and other personnel (such as the *Hofkirchner* or caretaker, and the *Calcant*) began to be acknowledged as a separate class of servants in the Zerbst 'Kammerrechnungen'.[23] They were heavily involved in the consecration of the new *Schloßkirche* on 18 October 1719, performing music most likely

---

[16] D-DEla, Kammerrechnungen 1716/17, p. 54, Nos. 105, 106, 112, 'halbjährlich' (for half the year). On the topic of recruitment and retention, see Barbara M. Reul, 'Court Musicians at Anhalt-Zerbst: New Sources for Eighteenth-Century Employment Practices', in *Proceedings of the 2008 Annual Conference of the Society for Eighteenth-Century Music*, ed. Sterling Murray (Ann Arbor, Mich.: Steglein), forthcoming.

[17] D-DEla, Kammer Zerbst, Facharchiv Zerbst, Fach 12 No. 7/2, fols. 227ʳ–228ᵛ.

[18] D-DEla, Kammerrechnungen 1716/17, p. 138, No. 1285.

[19] D-DEla, Kammerrechnungen 1686/87, p. 59, No. 666.

[20] See D-DEla, Kammerrechnungen 1717/18, p. 125, No. 1305.

[21] Wilcke must not be confused with either his father, Johann Caspar Wilcke sen. (then a trumpeter in Zeitz), or the musician of the same name (1707–1758), a tenor employed at the court of Sondershausen; see Chapter 10, pp. 294, 296 below. Wilcke sen. and his daughter Anna Magdalena, a vocalist at the court of Anhalt-Köthen and future wife of Johann Sebastian Bach, performed at Zerbst in 1720/21, not in winter 1716 as claimed by Wäschke, 'Die Zerbster Hofkapelle', 48; see D-DEla, Kammerrechnungen 1720/21, p. 141, Nos. 1169–70.

[22] See D-DEla, Konsistorium Zerbst IV, No. 10, fols. 3ʳ–16ᵛ, at fols. 5ᵛ–9ʳ.

[23] D-DEla, Kammerrechnungen 1719/20, p. 64: 'Besoldungen auff die zur Hochfürstl. Schloß Kirche gehörige Geistl. und auf die *Capelle*'.

composed by *Kapellmeister* Kuch.[24] His annual salary rose by over fifty per cent to 300 *Thaler* between 1718 and 1721 in light of his increased workload, a sum that also covered the expense of acquiring music for the court.[25] Several new musicians were recruited as well, including (Johann) Christian Brasch, and Johann Vent (also the local 'Stadtpfeifer' and a viola player).[26] Employment contracts for Vent and Brasch are extant and illustrate their employer's vision for a well-appointed and versatile *Kapelle*.[27] Brasch was not only proficient on the violin, the oboe, the viola da gamba, the transverse flute, and the recorder, but he was also required to perform at least three times a week in a specially adapted 'Concert Zimmer' — its exact location in the palace is now unknown. That Brasch, like Kuch and Grahmann before him, was also expected to procure new music for the court may indicate that this was a standard clause in the contracts of court musicians. Brasch was also paid for teaching the oboe and violin to the '*Hautboisten* Bande', but not for long: he departed in 1724, with the *Waldhornist* Köth supposedly taking his place.[28] Vent, who had officially replaced Grahmann as 'Hof-Musikus' (that is leader of the court ensemble first established in 1699) on 29 September 1719, received the same salary as his predecessor: 60 *Thaler*. While he was not paid during general times of mourning, at least his accommodation (shared by his family, journeymen, and apprentices) at the top of the Bartholomäiturm (St Bartholomew's Tower) was free.

Curiously absent from the payrolls of the courtly household after 1719/20 are the court trumpeters and kettledrummers. Nigel Springthorpe has suggested that this could have been due to a shift of emphasis from primarily ceremonial music to court entertainment.[29] However, Wilcke carried the title 'Zerbstischer Hoff u. Feld-Trompeter, auch Camer u. Hoff Musicus' (Zerbst court and field trumpeter, also chamber and court musician), and three other individuals are referred to as

---

[24] D-DEla, Konsistorium Zerbst IXa, vol. 378. See also D-DEla, Kammerrechnungen 1718/19, p. 79, No. 1468: sixteen music stands were painted at this time, which may indicate the number of musicians who performed on this occasion, if performing one voice or instrument per part.

[25] D-DEla, Kammerrechnungen 1719/20, p. 64, Nos. 162, 163; 1720/21, p. 78, No. 175. References to the purchase of sacred cantata cycles appear in 1721/22, p. 155, Nos. 1306 (Telemann), 1308a (the 'Liebich-Erlebachsche' cycle, a collection of cantatas by the *Kapellmeister* of Schleiz, Gottfried Sigismund Liebich and Philipp Heinrich Erlebach).

[26] Günther Schmidt-Jescher, 'Als es in Zerbst noch Stadtpfeifer gab . . .', *Zerbster Heimatkalender* (1960), 62. Wäschke, 'Die Zerbster Hofkapelle', 61, mistakes Johann Andreas Friedrich Vent (d. 1757, at the age of thirty-four) with his father Johann Vent; see the Anhalt-Zerbst 'Sterberegister der Schloßkirche' (hereafter 'Sterberegister'), housed in D-ZEsb, vol. 1746–69, pp. 201–2.

[27] D-DEla, Facharchiv Zerbst, Fach 12 No. 7/2, fols. 103ʳ–105ʳ, 111ʳ–113ʳ; Reul, 'Court Musicians at Anhalt-Zerbst', forthcoming.

[28] D-DEla, Kammerrechnungen 1723/24, p. 76, No. 227ᵇ: Brasch must have been the unidentified 'abgegangene Cammer-Musico', as he does not appear on the 1724/5 payroll. Wäschke, 'Die Zerbster Hofkapelle', 51, claims that Köth joined the *Hofkapelle* in March (Easter?) 1724, but he is not listed on any payroll and may, therefore, never have been a member of the *Hofkapelle*. Köth did, however, perform on the occasion of Prince Johann August's funeral; see D-DEla, Kammerrechnungen 1742/43, p. 252, No. 34.2070.

[29] Springthorpe, 'Passion Compositions', 114–15.

field trumpeters in the *Schloßkirche*'s death registers.[30] Resident trumpeters also received an annual general New Year's bonus and from time to time individual 'Verehrungen' (cash gifts for services rendered) as well.[31]

Their participation in performances at the chapel is evident from entries in a series of volumes labelled 'Verzeichnis' (inventory), which chronicles all worship-related activities at the *Schloßkirche* from 1719 to 1747 and from 1749 to 1773.[32] Specifically, trumpeters and kettledrum players performed settings of the *Te Deum* and congregational chorales on major feast days such as Christmas, Easter, Pentecost, New Year's Day, and 'Cantate' Sunday, the fourth Sunday after Easter.[33] But it was the *Kapelle* that, on a regular basis, premiered or repeated cantata cycles that had been newly composed by local composers or acquired externally. Repertoire included collections by Fasch, Röllig, Telemann, Stölzel, and Erlebach, as well as two cycles comprising cantatas by more than one composer.[34] The *Kapelle* performed concerted music in a minimum of three worship services per week: one on Saturday evenings (Vespers) and two on Sundays (morning and afternoon). Each featured a cantata; during certain church years, so-called double cycles, consisting of two cantatas composed as a set, were performed on Sunday mornings and afternoons respectively. Lutheran *Missae breves* (settings of the *Kyrie* and *Gloria*) were presented in morning services on all feast days as well as on major and minor holidays.[35] The *Kapelle* also performed cantatas on 'Aposteltage' (the feast days of Jesus' twelve apostles). Moreover, the Passion Gospel was divided into self-contained cantatas that were presented at different services throughout Holy Week, with each of the four Gospel texts allocated annually in turn between 1720 and 1743. This was followed in subsequent years by a 'Passion aus den Vier Evangelisten', a so-called gospel-harmony setting that merged all four canonical accounts of the life of Jesus.[36]

The performance of solemn cantatas and secular pieces to be performed by the *Kapelle* on the birthdays of the reigning prince and his family was customary at the court even in the absence of the person being honoured.[37] The composition and

[30] D-ZEsb, 'Sterberegister', vols. 1719–45, 1746–69, entries on Scheckel, Clausius, and J. H. Thieß.

[31] Rüdiger Pfeiffer, *Johann Friedrich Fasch (1688–1758)* (Wilhelmshaven: Noetzel, 1994), 39.

[32] D-DEla, Konsistorium Zerbst IXa, Nos. 351–77.

[33] Wäschke, 'Rölligs Kantate für St. Jakobs-Tag', 18.

[34] See Barbara M. Reul, 'Musical-Liturgical Activities at the Anhalt-Zerbst Court Chapel from 1722 to 1758: The Konsistorium-Zerbst Rep. 15A IXa Primary Source at the Landesarchiv Oranienbaum', in *Johann Friedrich Fasch und sein Wirken für Zerbst*, ed. Internationale Fasch-Gesellschaft, Fasch-Studien, 6 (Dessau: Anhaltische Verlagsgesellschaft, 1997), 59–70.

[35] Settings of the *Credo* were customarily performed on major feast days such as Christmas Day and Easter Sunday instead of a cantata, and Fasch also composed at least one setting of a Lutheran mass in German ('Deutsche Messe').

[36] Nigel Springthorpe, 'The Zerbst Passion Tradition', in *Johann Friedrich Fasch und sein Werken für Zerbst*, 101–13, Tables 1 and 2 at 103–4.

[37] See Barbara M. Reul, 'Performances of Sacred Birthday Cantatas by J. F. Fasch (1688–1758) at the Court of Anhalt-Zerbst', *Lumen*, 22 (2003), 27–46; Stephan Blaut, 'Geburtstags-serenaten für den Anhalt-Zerbster Hof in der ersten Hälfte des 18. Jahrhunderts', in *Musik an der Zerbster Residenz*, 236–68.

direction of such works was normally the responsibility of the *Kapellmeister*, but in the spring of 1722, when Kuch suddenly left Zerbst, the *Kapellmeister* in nearby Köthen, Johann Sebastian Bach, stepped in and supplied a secular work for Prince Johann August's birthday on 8 August. It is possible that the interim *Kapellmeister* Johann Friedrich Wagner directed the work's premiere.[38]

On 29 September 1722, the court of Anhalt-Zerbst appointed Johann Friedrich Fasch as its new *Kapellmeister*.[39] A graduate of Leipzig's *Thomasschule*, he founded a second collegium musicum in the town (modelled after that of his idol Telemann) and later read law and theology at the University of Leipzig.[40] He had also taken composition lessons with Darmstadt's *Kapellmeister* Christoph Graupner and concertmaster Gottfried Grünewald in 1714, and subsequently worked in the celebrated orchestra of Count Wenzel Morzin in Prague.[41] Fasch's starting salary in Zerbst was 350 *Thaler* (50 more than had been paid to Kuch), even though his responsibilities and duties were (presumably) identical. Moreover, Fasch wrote both the text and the music for the sacred cantata *Die Gerechten müssen sich freuen* to celebrate Princess Hedwig Friederike's birthday in autumn 1722.[42] In the next year, he turned down the offer to become Johann Kuhnau's successor as *Thomaskantor* in Leipzig, having just begun his tenure in Zerbst, and being unwilling to teach Latin.[43]

In exchange for Fasch's loyalty, the prince allowed him to travel in 1725, as evident from account books of his former employer in Prague, Count Morzin, as well

[38] On Kuch's departure, see Wäschke, 'Die Zerbster Hofkapelle', 48; D-DEla, Kammerrechnungen 1721/22, p. 68, Nos. 188, 189, 190; p. 155, No. 1309. Regarding the 1722 birthday cantata, see Michael Maul, 'Neues zu Georg Balthasar Schott, seinem Collegium Musicum und Bachs Zerbster Geburtstagskantate', *Bach-Jahrbuch*, 93 (2007), 61–103, at 91–4. On Wagner, see D-DEla, Kammerrechnungen 1720/21, p. 68, No. 180; Reul, 'Musical Life at the Court of Anhalt-Zerbst', 197–8.

[39] D-DEla, Kammerrechnungen 1722/23, p. 73, No. 193. The most comprehensive article is Stephan Blaut's entry on 'Fasch, Johann Friedrich', in *Die Musik in Geschichte und Gegenwart: allgemeine Enzyklopädie der Musik*, 2nd rev. edn (Kassel: Bärenreiter, 1994–2008), Personenteil, VI: 760–75.

[40] Werner Gottschalk, 'Johann Friedrich Fasch (1688–1758): Ein Beitrag zur Genealogie des Komponisten und Zerbster Hofkapellmeisters', *Ekkehard Familien- und regionalgeschichtliche Forschungen*, 12/2 (2005), 33–41; Andreas Glöckner, 'Johann Sebastian Bach und die Universität Leipzig: Neue Quellen (Teil 1)', *Bach-Jahrbuch*, 94 (2008), 159–202, at 170–4.

[41] Fasch copied two ripieno violin parts for Graupner's cantata *Gott will mich auch probieren* for *Reminiscere* Sunday, which is extant in D-DS, Mus. ms. 422/06. See Chapter 12, 'The Court of Hesse-Darmstadt', p. 340 below. Regarding Fasch's time in Prague, see Undine Wagner, 'Johann Friedrich Fasch und sein Wirken für Prag', in *Das Wirken des Anhalt-Zerbster Hofkapellmeisters Johann Friedrich Fasch (1688–1758) für auswärtige Hofkapellen*, ed. Internationale Fasch-Gesellschaft, Fasch-Studien, 8 (Dessau: Anhalt-Edition, 2001), 126–45.

[42] Barbara M. Reul, 'Johann Friedrich Faschs in Darmstadt überlieferte Geburtstagskantaten für Fürstin Hedwig Friederike von Anhalt-Zerbst', in *Das Wirken des Anhalt-Zerbster Hofkapellmeisters*, 191–210.

[43] Ulrich Siegele, 'Bachs Stellung in der Leipzig Kulturpolitik seiner Zeit', *Bach-Jahrbuch*, 69 (1983), 7–50; (1984), 7–43, at (1984) 7–13.

as those of the court of Köthen.[44] The court of Anhalt-Zerbst also paid for Fasch to spend six months in Dresden from October 1726 until around Easter 1727.[45] There, he polished his own advanced compositional skills with the assistance of his old friends from Leipzig, *Kapellmeister* Johann David Heinichen (1683–1729) and concertmaster Johann Georg Pisendel (1687–1755). There is no documentation regarding who directed the Zerbst *Kapelle* during this period. When Fasch, a widower, returned home, he was a changed man: deeply touched by the teachings of Count Nicolaus Ludwig von Zinzendorf (1700–1760), he had become a follower of Pietism and chosen a second bride who shared his religious views, Johanna Helena Simers. However, the news that Fasch had turned his back on Lutheran Orthodox beliefs was not welcomed by the clergy in Zerbst. They made his working environment uncomfortable to the point where the *Kapellmeister* sought positions elsewhere (including in Copenhagen), albeit unsuccessfully.[46]

Fasch's connection with Dresden, specifically with Pisendel, continued to thrive during this time: Fasch regularly supplied the Saxon court with instrumental compositions until 1755.[47] Money never seems to have exchanged hands, implying that Fasch was probably 'paid' with musical scores, a scenario supported by the contents of the Zerbst *Hofkapelle*'s vast music library (the so-called 'Concert-Stube'), to be discussed in more detail below.[48] Furthermore, the court reimbursed Fasch for shipping and handling costs, which document his commitment to the organiza-

---

[44] Wagner, 'Das Wirken Johann Friedrich Faschs für Prag', 127; Friedrich Smend, *Bach in Köthen* (Berlin: Christlicher Zeitschriftenverlag, 1951), 153 n. 30.

[45] See Wäschke, 'Die Zerbster Hofkapelle', 51; Elena Sawtschenko, 'Briefe von Johann Friedrich Fasch im Archiv der Frankeschen Stiftungen Halle', in *Das Wirken des Anhalt-Zerbster Hofkapellmeisters*, 85–110, at 110. For a more detailed discussion, see Reul, 'Court Musicians at Anhalt-Zerbst', forthcoming.

[46] Fasch corresponded with Zinzendorf in the 1730s; nine letters by Fasch, but none by Zinzendorf, are extant. See Thilo Daniel, 'Fasch und Zinzendorf: Bemerkungen zur Geschichte eines Briefwechsels', in *Das Wirken des Anhalt-Zerbster Hofkapellmeisters*, 74–84; Martin Petzoldt, 'Fasch als Briefkorrespondent Zinzendorfs: ein Beitrag zur theologischen Lokalisierung Faschs', in *Johann Friedrich Fasch (1688–1758): Wissenschaftliche Konferenz in Zerbst am 5. Dezember 1983 aus Anlaß des 225. Todestages*, ed. Günther Fleischhauer, Walther Siegmund-Schultze, and Eitelfriedrich Thom, Studien zur Aufführungspraxis und Interpretation, 24 (Michaelstein/Blankenburg: Rat des Bezirkes Magdeburg, 1984); Pfeiffer, *Johann Friedrich Fasch*, 54–73. For a discussion of Fasch's sacred extant cantatas viewed through a Pietist lens, specifically his cantata cycle *Das in Bitte, Gebeth, Fürbitte und Dancksagung bestehende Opffer* (premiered at the *Schloßkirche* in 1735/6), see Elena Sawtschenko, *Die Kantaten von Johann Friedrich Fasch im Lichte der pietistischen Frömmigkeit: Pietismus und Musik* (Paderborn: Schöningh, 2009).

[47] Manfred Fechner, 'Vom Dresdner Umgang mit Faschs Kompositionen', in *Das Wirken des Anhalt-Zerbster Hofkapellmeisters*, 9–28; Fechner, 'Die Dresdner Hofkapelle als Fasch-Orchester', *Musik an der Zerbster Residenz*, 141–8. See also Barbara M. Reul, 'Catherine the Great and the Role of Celebratory Music at the Court of Anhalt-Zerbst', *Eighteenth-Century Music*, 3/2 (2006), 269–309, at 273–6. The digitalization of the numerous works still extant has been part of an extensive three-year Deutsche Forschungsgemeinschaft project currently underway at the Sächsische Landesbibliothek – Staats- und Universitätsbibliothek, Dresden; see <www.slub-dresden.de>.

[48] Ortrun Landmann, 'Zur Spezifik der Fasch-Handschriften in der Sächsischen Landesbibliothek', in *Johann Friedrich Fasch (1688–1758)*, 94.

tion of a 'Music-Wechsel' (music exchange), primarily in Central Germany as well as with Prague.[49] But it is difficult, if not impossible, to determine how many of these works the entrepreneurial *Kapellmeister* had supplied to which colleagues in the hopes of receiving scores in return.

With regard to instruments purchased and new appointments made prior to 1730, in 1724 Fasch was reimbursed by the court for a violone, and he probably facilitated the purchase of two *Waldhörner* and two *Waldhautbois* (oboes da caccia) from Leipzig as well as two chalumeaux from Dresden.[50] The following year, the *Hautboist* Johann Christoph Richter (Ritter) was hired.[51] An alto soloist named Karl (Johann?) Ludwig Weißflock joined at Easter 1727, and the chamber musician Johann Georg Fröde (Frödel) appears on the court's payroll from 29 September 1727 onwards; the court purchased an oboe and a violin specifically for him.[52] Moreover, Richter and Fröde are the most likely performers for those works by Fasch that featured recorders and transverse flutes – three of the latter had been purchased in 1721.[53]

## THE *KAPELLE* FLOURISHES UNDER PRINCE JOHANN AUGUST

Fasch's *Kapelle* had more than doubled by 1730 and continued to grow (see Table 9.1). The *Cammermusicus* Benjamin Gottlob Gutbier (also 'Cammer Calculator' or accountant) joined in 1730; his musical expertise is not specified in the payroll, but Fasch identified him as a former servant of Count Zinzendorf in 1732.[54] Gutbier died on 19 June 1733 and may have been replaced by the Austrian Carl Höckh (1707–1773), an expert violinist who joined the *Kapelle* either in late 1733 or in early 1734.[55] Also proficient on the *Waldhorn* and the oboe, he had been recommended by Franz Benda (1709–1786), one of many guest artists performing

---

[49] See, for example, D-DEla, Kammerrechnungen 1725/26, p. 298, No. 34/1695; 1754/55, p. 298, No. 27.2831; and Fasch's request published in Johann Mattheson, ed., *Der musicalische Patriot* (Hamburg, 1728), 340–42. Fasch's works may also have been performed in Halle, Karlovy Vary, and Teplice (Bohemia) (see Sawtschenko, 'Briefe von Johann Friedrich Fasch', 104–5), Vienna (see Petzoldt, 'Fasch als Briefkorrespondent Zinzendorfs', 39), and Copenhagen (see Gottfried Gille, 'Neue Fasch-Kantate in Kopenhagen entdeckt', *Faschiana*, 13 (June 2009), 2).

[50] D-DEla, Kammerrechnungen 1723/24, p. 168, Nos. 1335, 1336; Wäschke, 'Die Zerbster Hofkapelle', 52.

[51] D-DEla, Kammerrechnungen 1725/26, p. 89, No. 236.

[52] D-DEla, Kammerrechnungen 1726/27, p. 97, No. 246; 1727/28, p. 97, No. 229 ('Frödl', listed as an *Hautboist* only from 1744/45; see p. 104, No. 169); p. 243, Nos. 35.2109 and 52.2110.

[53] Wäschke, 'Die Zerbster Hofkapelle', 48; Nigel Springthorpe, 'Recorders in the Repertoire of the Court of Anhalt-Zerbst', *The Recorder*, 29/3 (2009), 90–98.

[54] D-DEla, Kammerrechnungen 1730/31, p. 93, No. 213. Wäschke, 'Die Zerbster Hofkapelle', 53, notes that Gutbier had been referred to Zerbst from Gotha. See also Pfeiffer, *Johann Friedrich Fasch*, 68.

[55] D-ZEsb, 'Sterberegister', vol. 1719–45, p. 168. See also Undine Wagner, 'Carl Höckh: ein Musiker der Zerbster Hofkapelle', in *Musik an der Zerbster Residenz*, 293–312; D-DEla, Kammerrechnungen 1733/34, p. 99, Nos. 234, 235; Brian Clark, 'Keeping it in the Family', in *Carl Friedrich Christian Fasch (1736–1800) und das Berliner Musikleben seiner Zeit*, ed.

at Zerbst in the 1730s.[56] A bassoonist, Johann Christian Klotsch (Klotzsch), re-placed the (deceased?) violinist Sattler in 1734/5, which may have inspired Fasch to focus more on the bassoon and subsequently on the French double-reed trio in his compositions.[57] In 1736/7 Johann Peter Möhring, a violinist, succeeded the late *Hofkirchner* Goldammer (presumably also a string player), and in 1737/8 Johann Simon Unger replaced Klotsch (who had moved to Darmstadt).[58] That same year, the multi-talented gambist/violoncellist, organist, copyist, and composer Johann Georg Röllig first appeared on the court's *Kapelle* payroll. He may have replaced Johann Friedrich Wagner (d. 13 July 1737), listed as 'Hofforganist' in the death reg-istration records.[59] Röllig, a composition pupil of Jan Dismas Zelenka in Dresden, studied theology for several years in Leipzig, where he also supposedly met J. S. Bach, who performed Röllig's St Matthew Passion and kept sixty-five of his canta-tas in the music library of the *Thomasschule*.[60] In his autobiographical sketch from 1777, Röllig claimed that Prince Johann August had appointed him as 'Hoforga-nist und Kammermusikus', but entries in the Zerbst account books indicate that he was paid only for his services as music copyist that year; the designation 'organist' did not appear until 1738/9.[61]

Concerning the lower-ranking musicians of the *Kapelle*, four *Choralknaben* (choral scholars) positions are documented over the course of several decades, but names are never specified in the Zerbst account books. Fortunately, the Zerbst native Ernst Christian Paul Rockenfuß indicated in a letter addressed to Prince Johann August from 1738 that he had sung (as a *Choralknabe*) with the *Kapelle* for the past six years.[62] A *Kapellknabe* named Johann Friedrich Harnisch was instructed (probably on the keyboard) by the organist Ulich, while the soprano Poll taught Harnisch singing from 1724 to 1730.[63] But Harnisch was never listed

---

Internationale Fasch-Gesellschaft, Fasch-Studien, 7 (Dessau: Anhaltische Verlagsgesellschaft, 1999), 25–48.

[56] D-DEla, Kammerrechnungen 1732/33, p. 233, No. 44.1868.

[57] D-DEla, Kammerrechnungen 1734/35, p. 98, No. 231. For a preliminary overview of Fasch's extant compositions, see Rüdiger Pfeiffer, *Verzeichnis der Werke von Johann Friedrich Fasch (FWV)*, Kleine Ausgabe, Dokumente und Materialien zur Musikgeschichte des Bezirkes Magdeburg, 1 (Magdeburg: Rat des Bezirkes Magdeburg, 1988). A new online *Fasch-Verzeichnis* is in preparation; for updates, see <www.fasch.net>.

[58] Wäschke, 'Die Zerbster Hofkapelle', 56, confused *Hofkantor* Gattermann with *Hofkirch-ner* Goldammer; see D-DEla, Kammerrechnungen 1736/37, p. 99, No. 223. See also Kammer-rechnungen 1737/38, p. 109, No. 229: Klotsch was still paid by the Zerbst court for the full year, until June 1736; it is unclear who took his place in 1736/37.

[59] D-ZEsb, 'Sterberegister', vol. 1719–45, p. 212. Cf. D-DEla, Kammerrechnungen 1737/38, p. 109, Nos. 223, 224. The payment for Röllig covered the period from 24 June to 23 December 1737.

[60] Wäschke, 'Die Hofkapelle unter Fasch', 55–6. For an updated biography, see Nigel Springthorpe, 'Who Was Röllig? Röllig and the Sing-Akademie Collection', in *Musik an der Zerbster Residenz*, 117–40, at 117–24.

[61] Wäschke, 'Die Hofkapelle unter Fasch', 55; cf. D-DEla, Kammerrechnungen 1737/38, p. 228, No. 11.1838; 1738/39, p. 109, Nos. 203–6.

[62] Reul, 'Court Musicians at Anhalt-Zerbst', forthcoming.

[63] Wäschke, 'Die Zerbster Hofkapelle', 51. Ulich, however, received not just 3 *Thaler* but

as a member of the *Kapelle*, in contrast to the two sons of Christian Carl Kettner (1687–1760). They appear as *Kapellknaben* on payrolls from Michaelis (29 September) 1737 to Michaelis 1745, at which time (Martin Wilhelm) 'Zipprich' was accepted; he stayed until mid 1749.[64] The average training period for junior musicians at the court seems to have been six years, depending on prior skills and progress. To what extent Fasch's private composition student Johann Gabriel Seyffarth (1711–1797) was involved in performances at the court during the 1730s, is unclear, but he may have facilitated the performance of eleven cantatas from a 1735/6 cycle by Fasch in Kaufbeuren in 1744/5.[65]

In 1737/8, Prince Johann August granted his *Kapellmeister* a raise of 50 *Thaler* (increasing Fasch's annual salary to 400 *Thaler*), and a one-off additional payment or 'Nachschuß' of 442 *Thaler* for services rendered since 29 September 1722.[66] This must have delighted Fasch, who, for unknown reasons, continued to carry a heavy debt from his Leipzig days, which in 1733 amounted to 1,000 *Thaler* – close to three times his annual salary.[67] Perhaps the cash injection was also meant to motivate Fasch to put his plans to leave Zerbst to rest, or at least on hold. In addition, Fasch must have appreciated the extra income generated by composing princely birthday music for the court of Köthen between 1730 and 1755.[68]

Let us now turn to the repertoire of the *Kapelle* prior to 1745. Both the music and instruments at Fasch's disposal are detailed in one of the most remarkable music inventories still extant from the first half of the eighteenth century. The Zerbst 'Concert-Stube', prepared in 1743, lists almost five hundred compositions.[69] These include masses, ouverture suites, solo and ensemble concertos, sonatas, and sinfonias; cantata cycles are referred to by title only. Of the nearly ninety different

more than 30 *Thaler* per quarter; see D-DEla, Kammerrechnungen 1724/25, p. 177, Nos. 1387–90.

[64] See the respective entries in D-DEla, Kammerrechnungen 1737/38–1745/46, and Reul, 'Court Musicians at Anhalt-Zerbst', forthcoming.

[65] Wagner, 'Carl Höckh', 304, and Siegmund, 'Zu Johann Friedrich Faschs Kantatenjahrgang', 227–30. The performance materials remain there to this day.

[66] Wäschke, 'Die Zerbster Hofkapelle', 55; see also D-DEla, Kammerrechnungen 1737/38, p. 109, Nos. 215, 216.

[67] See also Konstanze Musketa, 'Johann Friedrich Faschs letzte Lebensjahre, dargestellt an Dokumenten aus dem St. Bartholomäi-Stift zu Zerbst', in *Johann Friedrich Fasch und sein Wirken für Zerbst*, 312–22; *Was dieser Geldmangel uns vor tägl. Kummer machet: Briefe, Johann Friedrich Fasch betreffend, aus dem St. Bartholomäi-Stift zu Zerbst (1752 bis 1757)*, ed. Konstanze Musketa with Dietrich-Karl Bischoff, Schriftenreihe zur Mitteldeutschen Musikgeschichte, I/3 (Oschersleben: Ziethen, 1997), 7–15. See also Barbara M. Reul, '"Forgive us our debts": Viewing the Life and Career of Johann Friedrich Fasch (1688–1758) through the Lens of Finance', *Eighteenth-Century Music*, 8/2 (2011), forthcoming.

[68] Maik Richter, 'Die Köthener Hofmusik zur Zeit des Fürsten August Ludwig', in *Musik an der Zerbster Residenz*, 167–82, at 177–8.

[69] See D-DEla, Kammer Zerbst, No. 4520b, fol. 42r; the facsimile edition of the *Concert-Stube des Zerbster Schlosses, Inventarverzeichnis aufgestellt im März 1743*, ed. Eitelfriedrich Thom, Studien zur Aufführungspraxis und Interpretation der Musik des 18. Jahrhunderts: Dokumentationen/Reprints, 4 (Michaelstein/Blankenburg: [no publisher], 1983). For a transcription of the inventory's contents, see Bernhard Engelke, *Johann Friedrich Fasch: Sein Leben und seine Tätigkeit als Vokalkomponist* (Halle: Kämmerer, 1908), app. 2.

composers mentioned, Fasch is the best represented, followed by Vivaldi and Telemann.[70] Only a fraction of this music has survived as part of the so-called 'Zerbster Musikstube', a collection of scores now held in Dessau. Among them are 'Aposteltage' cantatas and Lutheran *Missae breves* by Fasch as well as sacred works by Heinichen, Zelenka, Röllig, and Stölzel.[71]

Despite its size, the 'Concert-Stube' is not a true representation of the number of musical compositions to which the *Kapelle* had access in 1743. Sacred cantatas and secular serenatas written on the occasion of princely birthdays are only referred to generically, and works for Holy Week are omitted altogether – as is Telemann's 'Sicilian' cantata cycle from 1719/20, which was presented five times during Fasch's 36-year tenure.[72] Works by Graupner are curiously absent as well, and only one cantata by J. S. Bach was performed at the Zerbst court chapel (*Ich hatte viel Bekümmernis*, BWV 21, in 1726/7), even though the *Thomaskantor* was familiar with Fasch's instrumental works.[73] In addition, Fasch and other accomplished composers in the *Hofkapelle* – such as Höckh and Röllig – could have accumulated scores that they were willing to share.

During the 1730s, the court also purchased many new instruments, including strings, brass and woodwind instruments, and had ageing keyboards refurbished.[74] The 'Concert-Stube' specified thirty instruments in 1743: a pair of kettledrums, a 'clavicimbal', a violone, two violoncellos, eight violins, three violas, four flutes, two bass recorders, two bassoons, two oboes, two oboes da caccia ('Wald-*Hautbois*'), and three *Waldhörner*.[75] This respectable number of instruments for a court the size of Anhalt-Zerbst emphasizes that many, if not all of the full-time instrumentalists and possibly also the two *Kapellknaben* must have been proficient in a second (or third) unrelated musical area.

[70] To date only a few, usually composer- or style-specific investigations of music listed in the 'Concert-Stube' have been undertaken, as the information provided in the inventory (genre, scoring, composer's surname) is often too general to identify a specific work. See the various relevant chapters in *Johann Friedrich Fasch und der Italienische Stil*, ed. Internationale Fasch-Gesellschaft, Fasch-Studien, 9 (Dessau: Anhalt-Edition, 2003); Ute Poetzsch, 'Telemann-Werke in der Zerbster *Concert-Stube*', in *Das Wirken des Anhalt-Zerbster Hofkapellmeisters*, 71–82.

[71] D-DEla, Zerbster Musikstube. A brief description by Brian Clark is available online; see <http://sites.google.com/site/thefaschproject/>. See also Springthorpe, 'The Passion Compositions', 134–7 and Tables 2.7 and 2.8.

[72] See Springthorpe, 'The Passion Compositions', 132–3; Brit Reipsch, 'Anmerkungen zum sogenannten "Sizilianischen Jahrgang" von Georg Philipp Telemann', in *Telemann in Frankfurt*, ed. Peter Cahn (Mainz: Schott, 2000), 74–92.

[73] Regarding Graupner, see Reul, 'Catherine the Great', 277, for a list of scenarios that could explain such an imbalance. On Bach and Fasch, see Stephan Blaut, 'Die 1898 von Hugo Riemann in der Leipziger Thomasschul-Bibliothek gefundenen Fasch-Ouverturen-Suiten: Verlorene Quellen, verlorene Werke?', in *Johann Friedrich Fasch als Instrumentalkomponist*, ed. Konstanze Musketa, Schriften zur mitteldeutschen Musikgeschichte, 14 (Beeskow: Ortus, 2007), 17–26; Peter Wollny, 'Aufführungen Bachscher Kirchenkantaten am Zerbster Hof', in *Bach und seine mitteldeutschen Zeitgenossen*, ed. Rainer Kaiser (Eisenach: K.-D. Wagner, 2001), 199–217, at 204–7.

[74] Wäschke, 'Die Zerbster Hofkapelle', 53–4, 56–7. In 1738, Fasch also purchased a Cremonese violin in Eisenach, but it is unclear whether he did so on the court's behalf or for himself.

[75] Reul, 'Music at the Court of Anhalt-Zerbst', Table 2, 216–17.

In addition to enjoying the musical talents and technical skills of his own musicians, Prince Johann August seemed keen on hearing guest artists from the immediate region and further afield on a regular basis. These were usually identified by instrument or vocal range and home town only, rather than by name, in the Zerbst account books. Franz Benda, Christian Ferdinand Abel (father of the Köthen gambist Carl Friedrich Abel), and Johann Christian Hertel, *Kapellmeister* of Mecklenburg-Strelitz, are among the notable exceptions.[76] Fasch's well-developed networking skills must have also helped attract travelling musicians and he perhaps offered to exchange compositions with or write new music for them, or both.

On 7 November 1742, Prince Johann August died. A double cantata was performed by the *Hofkapelle* at the court chapel on 13 December, but neither its text nor music is extant.[77]

### SHIFTING PRIORITIES UNDER JOHANN LUDWIG II, CHRISTIAN AUGUST, JOHANNA ELISABETH, AND FRIEDRICH AUGUST

The year 1745 marked the single historically most significant event in the history of the principality – the marriage of Catherine (formerly Princess Sophie Auguste Friedericke of Anhalt-Zerbst) and Grand Duke Peter of Russia (1728–1762). In Zerbst, Catherine's nuptials were celebrated in style, with the *Hofkapelle* taking centre stage.[78] Fasch composed a serenata in thirty-two movements to mark the occasion, *Weichet! Ihr verdickten Schatten*, using a text by Johann Jacob Ulisch (c.1708–1767), deputy sexton at the Bartholomäikirche, rather than by the Magdeburg native Christian Gotthilf Jacobi (c.1696–1750), who provided the court with poetry for princely birthday music on an annual basis between 1730 and 1751.[79] The serenata's premiere must have involved all musicians specified on the payroll that year (including the newly installed 'clavicymbalist' and chamber musician Christoph Heinicke; see Table 9.1) as well as additional paid and unpaid musicians who augmented the *Hofkapelle* on that occasion. Among them were the violinist (Johann Heinrich) 'Heil', several 'Capell-Adjuvanten' (adjunct musicians), and

---

[76] Wäschke, 'Die Zerbster Hofkapelle', 47–63; Springthorpe, 'The Passion Compositions', Table 2.4.

[77] D-DEla, Konsistorium Zerbst IXa, vol. 364. All musicians received special bonuses, ranging from 30 *Thaler* (Fasch) to 8 *Thaler* (*Hofkirchner* Möhring); see D-DEla, Kammerrechnungen 1742/43, p. 251, Nos. 2047–56.

[78] Reul, 'Catherine the Great', 278–301.

[79] Only the printed text of the wedding serenata survives in D-ZEo, A.3e. Extant texts for musical settings from Zerbst do not usually specify the poet or composer, but regular payments to Jacobi are documented in D-DEla, Kammerrechnungen. On Ulisch's activities as a poet in the early 1750s, see Barbara M. Reul, 'Unbekannte Dokumente zu J. F. Fasch und dem Musikleben am Zerbster Hof', in *Johann Friedrich Fasch als Instrumentalkomponist*, 153–86, at 174–82. Of the numerous serenatas that Fasch composed before 1745, the music is extant only in his *Freuden-Bezeugung der Vier Tages-Zeiten* to commemorate Prince Johann August's birthday in August 1723. Opera performances were not customary at Zerbst, but in 1738 Fasch did revive his opera *Berenice*, first performed as *Lucius Verus* (Zeitz, 1711).

probably a number of musically proficient senior students from the Bartholomäischule and the local university college, the *Gymnasium illustre*; Johann Wilhelm
Hertel (1727–1789), who attended the latter and also studied with Höckh in the
1740s, comes to mind.[80] The 'Hofthürmer und Musico' Johann Andreas Friedrich
Vent and his ensemble may have participated as well.

In 1745/6, the court purchased new instruments: six new trumpets and a viola
from Leipzig and a transverse flute from Berlin were added to the six violins and
the bassoon that had been bought the year before.[81] Perhaps the players of these
woodwind instruments had also inspired Fasch to feature the French double-reed
trio prominently in his orchestral suites. Johann Adolph Scheibe (1708–1776)
commented in 1745, 'Unter den Deutschen haben sich wohl Telemann und Fasch
in dieser Art von Ouverturen am meisten gewiesen (among the Germans, Telemann and Fasch have excelled the most in this type of ouverture [suite]).[82]

Of the princes who reigned between 1745 and 1759, Johann Ludwig II (1688–
1746) appreciated music the most. As is evident from his extant music collection at
Jever — an enclave of Anhalt-Zerbst that he had previously governed — the prince
owned a variety of musical scores of works by Italian and German composers, including vocal, keyboard, and flute music.[83] Fasch is known to have held him in high
esteem and may have presented Johann Ludwig with copies of Zerbst cantatas and
sent to him printed text booklets for cantata cycles written during his first year as
*Kapellmeister*.[84]

Prince Johann Ludwig's support of the *Kapelle* was, however, short-lived, as
he died on 5 November 1746, followed shortly thereafter by his siblings Christian
August on 16 March 1747 and Sophia Christiana on 3 May 1747. The musicians
were naturally involved in the funeral commemorations; the service held at the
court chapel after Johann Ludwig's death apparently featured organ music and

---

[80] D-DEla, Kammerrechnungen 1745/46, p. 297, No. 28.2779. See also Clark, 'Keeping it
in the Family', 27; Reul, 'Catherine the Great', 297–8; Wagner, 'Carl Höckh', 298–301. Musical
performances were customary at the Bartholomäischule from the 1720s until the 1740s, marking important events such as birthdays of the school's pastor and vice-principal.

[81] See the respective entries in D-DEla, Kammerrechnungen 1745/46, p. 298; 1744/45,
p. 297.

[82] Johann Adolph Scheibe, *Critischer Musikus* (Leipzig, 1745), '73. Stück', p. 673.

[83] Dirk Hermann, 'Johann Ludwig (II.): Oberlanddrost zu Jever und Regent von Anhalt-
Zerbst', *Zerbster Heimatkalender*, 2005, <www.schloss-zerbst.de>, 'Publikationen' (accessed
11 August 2009); Sybille Heinen, 'Katalog der ehemaligen Bibliothek der Fürsten von Anhalt-
Zerbst im Schloß zu Jever', in *Bibliophile Kostbarkeiten: Die Bibliothek der Fürsten von Anhalt-
Zerbst im Schloß zu Jever*, ed. Antje Sander and Egbert Koolman, Ferne Fürsten: Das Jeverland
in Anhalt-Zerbster Zeit, 1 (Oldenburg: Isensee, 2003), catalogue entries pertaining to music,
shelfmarks MGJ 34, 35, 36, 37, 1605–7, 1610–12. See also Günther Hoppe, '"Marches", "heu-
rige Venetianische Opern" und andere Spuren einer militärischen und einer frühen Italien-
Begeisterung bei Zerbster und Köthener Prinzen', *Cöthener Bach-Hefte*, 10 (2002), 181–98.

[84] See Michael Maul, 'Johann Friedrich Fasch und das Freiberger Kantorat', in *Johann
Friedrich Fasch als Instrumentalkomponist*, 237–50; Heinen, 'Katalog der ehemaligen Bibliothek der Fürsten von Anhalt-Zerbst', 565–6; the catalogue in Sander and Koolman, *Bibliophile
Kostbarkeiten*, shelfmarks MGJ 59, 70, 71 (cantatas; only the wrappers are extant), MGJ 379,
381 (cantata cycles by Erlebach and Fasch respectively).

chorales only (perhaps an oversight by the scribe?), in contrast to the special music performed at the equivalent ceremonies for both Christian August and Sophia Christiana.[85] The court remunerated *Kapelle* members for contributing to un-specified 'Trauer und Begräbnis' (mourning and funeral) activities organized for Christian August in the spring of 1747 — possibly a flat fee acknowledging their involvement in all funeral-related music during 1746 and 1747, which also included performances at the princely *Gymnasium illustre*.[86] The latter featured the chamber musician Johann Michael Sciurus ('bassist [bass vocalist] Scuerus'), a valued member of the Köthen *Kapelle* since May 1725.[87]

When Princess Sophia Christiana died, two services were also held at Zerbst's Trinitatiskirche.[88] Its geographic location — on the other side of the river Nuthe, the town's natural dividing line — required the musicians, clergy, and palace congregation to travel across one of the town's bridges for a performance of a 'Trauer-Gesang' (actually a sacred solo cantata) and a lengthy double cantata.[89] Furthermore, the period of mourning observed by the court following Christian August's and Sophia Christiana's deaths impacted upon the music customarily performed in honour of Archduchess Catherine of Russia. Her birthday was acknowledged by the *Kapelle* annually between 1746 and 1773, with the exception of 1747, the year of her father's death.[90]

Several changes occurred in the *Kapelle* personnel in the late 1740s. First, a male soprano ('discantist') from Magdeburg named Borthmüller assisted between 1 January and 9 April 1748. He replaced the elderly soprano and court secretary Kettner, who took over the solo alto parts of the late Weißflock. In June 1748, the soprano Johann Michael Teicher from Dresden (who also served as music copyist) joined the *Kapelle*; he may have been recommended by Johann Georg Röllig's brother, Christian August Röllig, 'Hof-Cantor' at Dresden.[91] Six months later, the *Kapelle*

[85] D-DEla, Konsistorium Zerbst IXa, vol. 364, services held on 16 December 1746 for Johann Ludwig, 17 May for Christian August, and 18 June for Sophia Christiana.

[86] D-DEla, Kammerrechnungen 1746/47, p. 317. As early as 21 July 1724, the death of Prince Johann August's mother Sophia had been commemorated at the *Gymnasium illustre*; see D-ZEo, A.12.a., fols. 248ʳ–249ᵛ. Otherwise, see D-ZEo, A.11.c., fols. 88ʳ–90ᵛ (for the death of Johann Ludwig, 3 February), 107ʳ–109ᵛ (for that of Christian August, 21 June).

[87] See D-DEla, Kammer Köthen, Kammerrechnungen 1724/25, p. 25/fol. 48ᵛ, No. 283; 1735/36, p. 118, No. 624; cf. D-DEla, Kammer Zerbst, Kammerrechnungen 1746/47, p. 334, No. 47.3363. Sciurus may also have performed in Christian August's funeral service held at the court chapel; see D-DEla, Konsistorium Zerbst IXa, vol. 364, 17 May 1747; D-ZEo, A.11.c., fol. 107ʳ (the text of the double cantata). Sciurus returned to perform in Zerbst as a vocalist in the 1750s; see D-DEla, Kammerrechnungen 1752/53, p. 256, No. 19.2377; 1753/54, p. 283, No. 42.2554.

[88] D-ZEo, A.11.c., fols. 119ʳ–120ʳ, 120ᵛ–121ᵛ.

[89] D-DEla, Konsistorium Zerbst IXa, vol. 364, 18 May 1747. The Trinitatiskirche was most likely also the location to which Fasch referred in 1752 when noting that one of his cantata cycles was performed 'in der Stadtkirchen' (in the town church); see Engelke, *Johann Friedrich Fasch*, 39.

[90] Reul, 'Catherine the Great', 301–3.

[91] Reul, 'Court Musicians at Anhalt-Zerbst', forthcoming; Springthorpe, 'Who was Röllig?', 134–40.

benefited albeit briefly, from the death of *Waldhornist* Köth (even though he had never been an official member): a new position was created for the musician who replaced him, the lutenist Malachovsky, an individual of questionable character.[92] J. W. Hertel performed at the palace in early 1750 and may have personally escorted the *Kapellmeister*'s musically gifted son, Carl Fasch (1736–1800), to Strelitz, where he taught him for the remainder of the year.[93] In the meantime, the Anhalt-Zerbst court – and perhaps the *Kapelle* which possibly provided incidental music – enjoyed the theatrical productions presented by the famous actress Friederike Caroline Neuber (1697–1760) and her troupe in the palace's large dining room (the 'Kirch-Saal').[94]

Johann August's widow, Princess Hedwig Friederike, passed away on 14 August 1752. The composition of the double cantata presented in her memory at the court chapel on 22 September would have formed part of Fasch's responsibilities, and therefore he was not remunerated separately.[95] Nor had he received additional compensation for transforming a single cantata cycle into a shorter double cantata cycle to be premiered during the 1751/2 church year, a direct result of the court's newly adopted policy regarding the court chapel, which also required the clergy to keep their sermons short.[96] On the other hand, funds for new music were provided between 1752 and 1756, and the court paid for new instruments while also ensuring that others, including string, brass, woodwind, and keyboard instruments, were maintained.[97]

The most exciting event to be celebrated at the court in the early 1750s was undoubtedly the wedding of Prince Friedrich August and Princess Carolina Wilhelmina of Hesse-Kassel, festivities for which were held in Zerbst on 17 and 18 November 1753.[98] The court brought in additional trumpeters from Coswig and Wittenberg, and five unspecified musicians from Magdeburg augmented the *Ka*-

---

[92] D-DEla, Kammerrechnungen 1749/50, p. 108, Nos. 190, 191; Wäschke, 'Die Zerbster Hofkapelle', 61.

[93] D-DEla, Kammerrechnungen 1749/50, p. 271, No. 31.2387; see also Wagner, 'Carl Höckh', 298–301. Carl Fasch's first teacher had been concertmaster Höckh, who was also his godfather; see D-ZEsb, 'Schloß Kirchenbuch', p. 40, 22 November 1736; this source lists all children baptized at the Zerbst court chapel between 1736 and 1742.

[94] Wäschke, 'Die Zerbster Hofkapelle', 62, and Engelke, 'Johann Friedrich Fasch: Versuch einer Biographie', 280.

[95] D-DEla, Konsistorium Zerbst IXa, vol. 366, 22 September 1752. Neither the text nor the music remains extant.

[96] See Fasch's letter to Johann Friedrich Armand von Uffenbach, 1 March 1752, reproduced in Engelke, *Johann Friedrich Fasch*, 38–42; Reul, 'Unbekannte Dokumente', 174–82; Brian Clark, 'When Brevis isn't Short Enough: Fasch's Re-workings of Mass Settings for the Zerbst *Schloßkirche*', in *Johann Friedrich Fasch und sein Wirken für Zerbst*, 136–41.

[97] D-DEla, Kammerrechnungen, 1752/53, p. 287, No. 32.2756; 1753/54, p. 310, No. 26.2864; 1754/55, p. 267, No. 25.2459; 1755/56, p. 270, No. 23.2541. See also Wäschke, 'Die Zerbster Hofkapelle', 61–2.

[98] Musketa, 'Musik am Anhalt-Zerbster Hof', 121–2; Musketa, 'Johann Friedrich Fasch und die Zerbster Feierlichkeiten zur Hochzeit des Fürsten Friedrich August von Anhalt-Zerbst 1753', in *Johann Friedrich Fasch als Instrumentalkomponist*, 187–206.

*pelle* members who received new livery for the occasion.[99] Musical premieres included *Sacro Dio*, an Italian 'Drama per musica' by Fasch; *Brich aus und laß Dein Jauchzen schallen*, a sacred work in two parts composed by Telemann; and *Die Glücksäligkeit eines Landes*, a serenata by Röllig.[100] Otherwise, the *Kapelle* played while the bridal party and their guests dined, performed concerts in the private chambers of both the groom and his mother, and provided music for a 'Fackeltanz' (torch dance) and several minuets. Moreover, Vent's ensemble and that of civic musician Reinsdorff (Reinßdorf) played for nightly balls, as they did regularly throughout the 1740s and 1750s.[101]

One of the busiest musicians at the court, not only at times of celebration, was Johann Georg Röllig. According to his autobiographical sketch prepared in 1777, he became *Vicekapellmeister* in 1742.[102] However, there are no corroborating entries regarding this promotion in the Zerbst court records or printed materials, nor does Röllig mention this honour in extant correspondence. His workload does, nevertheless, indicate increased responsibilities, but without proper remuneration. In March 1755, Röllig complained to his employer about having to step in constantly for elderly or sick colleagues, play instruments he was not proficient on, and sing, probably solos assigned to J. J. Ulisch.[103] Röllig had also composed two entire cantata cycles, one for the church year 1754/5, and one to be premiered in 1755/6 – all in addition to his daily duties at the chapel and without payment![104] It was Röllig's health that ultimately paid the price: in 1755, he was still recovering from 'jährliche Krankheiten' (annual illnesses), the treatments for which had eaten up most of his wages, and between 1756 and 1759, when he instructed Princess Carolina Wilhelmina on the keyboard for two and a half years, he fell ill for an entire winter.[105]

By the spring of 1756, the court had addressed the shortage of musicians by actively looking for a new bass singer – Johann Caspar Creuzburg was paid to serve in that capacity for seven weeks – but it took two more years until a permanent appointment was made. Georg Peter Weimar (Weymar) joined the *Kapelle* as bass soloist and substitute *Kantor* in late June 1758.[106] Meanwhile, Fasch's son Carl had

---

[99] Musketa, 'Johann Friedrich Fasch und die Zerbster Feierlichkeiten', 194 and 201–2; Wäschke, 'Die Zerbster Hofkapelle', 62; Reul, 'Unbekannte Dokumente', 183–5.

[100] D-ZEo, A.II.c, fols. 130ʳ–133ʳ (text); Musketa, 'Johann Friedrich Fasch und die Zerbster Feierlichkeiten', 197–9, 201. The music to *Sacro Dio* is not extant, but the label 'Drama per musica' implies a sacred opera, which would have been unusual at the time.

[101] Musketa, 'Johann Friedrich Fasch und die Zerbster Feierlichkeiten', 203.

[102] Wäschke, 'Die Zerbster Hofkapelle', 55–6.

[103] Reul, 'Court Musicians at Anhalt-Zerbst', forthcoming. Ulisch substituted for the ailing Gottfried Förster between 1754 and 1756.

[104] Reul, 'Musical Life at the Court of Anhalt-Zerbst', 204–10.

[105] Brian Clark, 'Eine kleine Nachtmusik', in *Musik an der Zerbster Residenz*, 281–92, at 291. See also Barbara M. Reul, 'Das vakante Organistenamt an der St. Bartholomäi-Kirche zu Zerbst und die "liederliche Lebensart" von Johann Heinrich Heil (1706–1764)', *Mitteilungen des Vereins für Anhaltische Landeskunde*, 19 (2010), 129–43. Johann Friedrich Kolbe had assisted at the court chapel when Röllig had been ill.

[106] See Reul, 'Court Musicians at Anhalt-Zerbst', forthcoming; Helga Brück, 'Weimar, Georg Peter', in *Biographisch-bibliographisches Kirchenlexikon*, 33 vols. (Nordhausen: Bautz,

returned to Zerbst from Strelitz and, in 1753, assisted the *Kapelle* on the occasion of Friedrich August's wedding festivities, albeit without pay. That he joined them on other occasions as well, such as on princely birthdays and high feast days, is very likely. In early 1756 at the latest, Carl Fasch left Zerbst for Berlin to serve as second harpsichordist in King Friedrich II's *Hofkapelle*.[107]

This brings us to the overview of the Zerbst *Kapelle* that Marpurg published in his *Historisch-kritische Beyträge* of 1757 (see also Table 9.1).[108] Names, instruments, and voice types, plus brief biographical information for nineteen musicians (from a total of twenty positions) are listed – in comparison to the eleven musicians who appear on the 1756/7 payroll, which clearly identifies Teicher, rather than Kettner, as the resident soprano.[109] However, the greatest revelation is the constitution of the string section. Four of the six violinists were, in fact, court trumpeters, one was the resident kettledrummer, and another the *Hofkirchner*.[110] Had these individuals formed the string section in 1753 or even 1745, when wedding festivities were held at the court?[111] One also wonders who had provided Marpurg with this information, and whether Fasch had access to all nineteen musicians on a regular basis or only on special occasions.

The exact number of participants in the premiere of the serenata *Beglückter Tag* in 1757, the only extant work in this genre composed by Fasch in honour of Catherine, is unclear. Since the reigning Russian Tsarina Elisabeth, Catherine's mother-in-law, is praised by the poet, J. J. Ulisch, he had either written it prior to the onset of the Seven Years' War in 1756, or, more likely, it was meant as an incentive for Catherine to protect the principality of Anhalt-Zerbst during her brother's reign.[112] In early 1758, when Friedrich August refused to deliver a French spy to the Prussian king, within six weeks a total of 1,500 foot soldiers descended upon

---

1990–2010), XXII: 1508–10, accessible online at <http://www.bautz.de/bbkl/w/weimar_g_p. shtml>. Weimar was apparently also a skilled performer on brass and string instruments.

[107] See articles in *Carl Friedrich Christian Fasch (1736–1800) und das Berliner Musikleben seiner Zeit*: Clark, 'Keeping it in the Family', 25–48; Christoph Henzel, 'Carl Friedrich Christian Fasch als Hofmusiker', 72–80. In 1791, Carl Fasch founded the famous choral society 'Singakademie zu Berlin'.

[108] Friedrich Wilhelm Marpurg, *Historisch-kritische Beyträge zur Aufnahme der Musik*, 5 vols. (Berlin, 1754–78; repr. Hildesheim and New York: Olms, 1970), III, 'Zweytes Stück' (1757), 130–31, 'IV. Die Hochfürstliche Anhalt Zerbstische Capelle'.

[109] D-DEla, Kammerrechnungen 1756/57, p. 109.

[110] See, for example, D-DEla, Kammerrechnungen 1753/54, p. 282, No. 3.2545 (Nicolai and Rühlmann); 1754/55, p. 298, No. 24.2836 (Vollund). See also D-DEla, Konsistorium Zerbst 1b, No. 5, fol. 3ʳ: Rühlmann was also a 'Hoffourier', a designation given to the 'älteste und vornehmste' (oldest and most noble) of the trumpeters at a court. See Johann Heinrich Zedler, *Grosses vollständiges Universal-Lexicon aller Wissenschaften und Künste* (Halle and Leipzig, 1731–54), 64 vols., 'Trompeter', XLV: 1120; 'Fourier', IX: 1587.

[111] D-DEla, Kammerrechnungen 1752/53, p. 287, No. 30.2752. Six new violins were purchased from the instrument dealer Anton.

[112] Elena Sawtschenko, 'Zwei bisher unbekannte Werke von Johann Friedrich Fasch in dem aus Kiew zurückgegebenen Archiv der Singakademie zu Berlin', in *Johann Friedrich Fasch und der Italienische Stil*, 225–42, at 230–42.

Zerbst.[113] Frightened, Friedrich August and his mother (who, incidentally, never took up residence in Coswig as was customary for dowager princesses) escaped on 8 April 1758 – his wife, Princess Carolina Wilhelmina, was informed by a court official that she was to fend for herself until further notice.[114]

In the summer of 1758 Fasch welcomed both C. P. E. Bach and Carl Fasch to Zerbst; the exact dates cannot be determined. They had fled a war-torn Berlin for the (presumably) much safer Zerbst. During his stay Bach composed six keyboard sonatas, which reflect new stylistic features that he would later develop more fully in his Hamburg works.[115] Bach and Carl Fasch may have performed with the *Kapelle* on occasion; Fasch senior and Bach also appear to have taught G. P. Weimar.[116] In addition, a report of the highest-ranking clergyman of Anhalt-Zerbst indicates that a 'berühmter Tonkünstler aus Berlin' (a famous composer from Berlin) was present when several applicants auditioned for the vacant organist's position at Bartholomäikirche in September of 1758.[117]

The visitors from Berlin returned home just days before 16,000 Prussian soldiers descended on 4 December 1758 upon the roughly 6,400 people who lived in Zerbst – an unequivocal message from Friedrich II for Catherine the Great and her brother living in exile.[118] The very next day, *Kapellmeister* Fasch died at the age of 70. In early October, he had prepared an up-to-date inventory of the music and musical instruments belonging to the court. It reveals that the number of instruments and especially the number of musical scores had increased substantially over the years, particularly in the genres of orchestral suites, trio and solo sonatas, as well as German and Latin masses. Works in the sinfonia genre had shown the greatest increase, from eight to 140 scores, further details of which are not provided. Not only does this emphasize that works displaying the abilities of the entire ensemble (rather than individual virtuosity) were now preferable to Fasch, but also his knowledge of the latest trends and developments.[119]

Preparations for Fasch's quiet funeral were overshadowed by the astounding demands made by a Prussian general on 7 December 1758: 100,000 *Thaler*, 800 recruits, and 811 horses.[120] Nonetheless, the privy council executing the wishes of the exiled Friedrich August adopted a 'business as usual' policy in 1759, with the *Kapelle*'s regular performance schedule being maintained, and concertmaster Höckh and court organist Röllig sharing duties. The latter was in charge of music

[113] Friedrich Wilhelm Sintenis, *Die Chronik von Zerbst 1758–1830*, ed. Hannelore Seidler (Zerbst: Verlagsbuchhandlung Friedrich Gast Zerbst and Anhaltische Verlagsgesellschaft Dessau, 1995), 14.

[114] Clark, 'Eine kleine Nachtmusik', 281–92.

[115] David Schulenberg, 'C. P. E. Bach in Zerbst: The Six Sontatas of Fall 1758; With Contributions on the Early Biography and Compositions of Carl Fasch', in *Johann Friedrich Fasch als Instrumentalkomponist*, 131–52.

[116] Brück, 'Weimar, Georg Peter', 1508–10.

[117] D-DEla, Konsistorium Zerbst, No. 275, fol. 20ʳ; Reul, 'Das vakante Organistenamt', 136–7.

[118] Sintenis, *Chronik der Stadt Zerbst*, 15.

[119] Reul, 'Musical Life at the Court of Anhalt-Zerbst', 210–19.

[120] Sintenis, *Die Chronik von Zerbst*, 15.

for special occasions, with the exception of the spring of 1759, when J. W. Hertel, now *Kapellmeister* of the Mecklenburg-Schwerin court, was commissioned to compose a birthday serenata, *Das Glück der Völker*, in honour of Princess Carolina Wilhelmina. Was this perhaps an audition piece for the vacant *Kapellmeister* position?[121] If so, the princess's death on 22 May 1759 prevented an appointment.[122]

Finally, a brief examination of the court's overall spending habits over the course of four decades demonstrates an emphasis on external, lasting splendour. Interestingly, the wages of the *Kapelle* members increased only by 35.5, compared to 94.25 per cent for court servants in general, while costs for maintaining various palaces (Zerbst, Dornburg, and Friederikenberg) had risen by 80.6 per cent, almost 20 per cent more than the amount the court spent on the poor (62.5 per cent).[123]

### DECLARING MUSICAL DEFEAT — THE *KAPELLE* IN 1760

Musical life at the court took a turn for the worse in 1760 (see Table 9.1). The oboist Ritter and the alto Kettner died, and four musicians were designated for release, ranging from Weimar, the most recent appointee, to the oboist Fröde, who had joined the *Kapelle* in 1727/8.[124] Would these dismissals have eased the financial burden placed on the town by the continued presence of Prussian soldiers and the prince's outrageous demands from exile?[125] No, on the contrary, the government official von Köseritz worried about dismissing Weimar, who had substituted for the elderly *Hofkantor* Gattermann.[126] Nevertheless, all four discharged musicians were still involved in a memorial service for the late Princess Johanna Elisabeth on 22 December 1760, albeit at a reduced fee; to what extent the trumpeters, kettledrummer, and *Hofkirchner* listed in Marpurg's 1757 overview assisted on this occasion or in general, remains unclear.[127] Otherwise, Röllig was paid handsomely by the court for composing birthday music for the princely family (and a much smaller *Kapelle*) between 1759 and 1764, and for writing a work to commemorate Catherine's accession to the Russian throne in 1762.[128]

Performances at the *Schloßkirche* on Saturdays, Sundays, and feast days featuring the *Hofkapelle* ceased on the first Sunday of Advent in 1765. Until 1773,

[121] Clark, 'Eine kleine Nachtmusik', 281–92.

[122] D-DEla, Konsistorium Zerbst IXa, vol. 369, memorial service held on 10 August 1759.

[123] Bettina Schmidt, 'Musikpflege am Zerbster Hof um die Mitte des 18. Jahrhunderts', in *Johann Friedrich Fasch und sein Wirken für Zerbst*, 323–30.

[124] D-ZEsb, 'Sterberegister', vol. 1746–69, pp. 266 (Ritter), 271 (Kettner); D-DEla, Kammer Zerbst, No. 2975, fol. 1ʳ. The latter provides an overview of all twenty-two court employees who were dismissed, including the bassoonist Unbescheid and the soprano Teicher.

[125] See D-DEla, Kammerrechnungen 1760/61, p. 97: Prince Friedrich August had nearly 75,000 *Thaler* transferred to Paris that year. See also Sintenis, *Die Chronik von Zerbst*, 13–91.

[126] D-DEla, Kammer Zerbst, No. 2975, fol. 7ʳ.

[127] D-DEla, Kammerrechnungen 1760/61, p. 243, Nos. 1774–88. They received half of their usual honorarium.

[128] Reul, 'Catherine the Great', 303–4; Reul, 'Court Musicians at Anhalt-Zerbst', forthcoming. Neither the music nor the text of the work is extant.

when entries in the court chapel chronicles come to an end, concerted music was presented only on special occasions, such as princely birthdays, including those of Catherine, her children, and her grandchildren.[129] Röllig was finally promoted to *Kapellmeister* in 1777, almost four years after Höckh's death.[130] Meanwhile, Prince Friedrich August, supposedly 'geistig-wirr' (mentally confused), hired out over 1,000 soldiers from Anhalt-Zerbst to fight for Britain in the American War of Independence in exchange for 30,000 *Thaler*.[131] Röllig passed away before the death of Friedrich August in 1793, an event accompanied by general rejoicing in Anhalt-Zerbst; remarkably, after 1758 the prince had never again set foot on Zerbst soil. Had Catherine's brother continued to live at the palace, the slow and painful death of a once vibrant *Hofkapelle* would perhaps have been prevented.

[129] Reul, 'Catherine the Great', 307–9.
[130] Reul, 'Musical Life at the Court of Anhalt-Zerbst', 221–2.
[131] Clark, 'Eine kleine Nachtmusik', 282; Specht, *Geschichte der Stadt Zerbst*, 81; Reul, 'Catherine the Great', 303.

TABLE 9.1. Membership of the Anhalt-Zerbst Court Music Establishment in 1715, 1730, 1745, and 1760

| Years | 1715 | 1730 | 1745 | 1760 |
|---|---|---|---|---|
| Rulers | Prince Carl Wilhelm (r. 1674–1718) | Prince Johann August (r. 1718–42) | | Prince Friedrich August (r. 1752–93) |
| Numeric Overview | 1 *Kapellmeister* / 3 instrumentalists / 3 trumpeters & 1 kettledrummer / 'Kleine Hautboistenbande' / 2 vocalists | 1 *Kapellmeister* / 7 instrumentalists / 5 trumpeters (at least) / 7 *Grenadiere* (at least) / 9 vocalists (1 doubling as instrumentalist) / 2 additional personnel | 1 *Kapellmeister* / 9 instrumentalists / 6 trumpeters (at least) / 4 *Grenadiere* (at least) / 9 vocalists (1 doubling as instrumentalist) / 3 additional personnel (1 doubling as instrumentalist) | [1 acting *Kapellmeister*] / 1 concertmaster / 6 instrumentalists / 1 *Grenadier* (at least) / [1757: at least 6 trumpeters & 1 kettledrummer] / 9 vocalists (2 doubling as instrumentalists) / 2 additional personnel |
| *Kapellmeister* | Johann Baptist Kuch, 'Capell Director' | Johann Friedrich Fasch | Johann Friedrich Fasch | [Johann Georg Röllig, org, vdg, and vc; also copyist; acting *Kapellmeister*[a]] |
| Concertmaster | | | | Carl Höckh (vn; also hn and ob) |
| Instrumentalists | | | | |
| *Cammermusici* | | | | |
| Violin | | Johann George Sattler, *Cammermusicus* (also fencing instructor) | Carl Höckh, *Cammermusicus* from 1746 (vn; also hn and ob) | [1757: *See Hoftrompeter, Hofpaucker, and Hofkirchner*][b] |

| | | | |
|---|---|---|---|
| | See Oboe and Hofmusici | See Oboe, Hofmusici, and Hofkirchner | See Harpsichord, Hofmusici, Concertmaster, and Oboe |
| Viola | See Hofmusici | See Hofmusici | See Hofmusici |
| Viola da gamba/Violoncello | See Soprano | See Soprano | See Alto |
| | | See Hoforganist and Hofkirchner | See Hoforganist and Hofkirchner |
| Contraviolone | | | [1757: vacant] |
| Flute/Recorder | See Oboe | See Oboe | See Oboe |
| Oboe | Johann Georg Fröde (Frödel) (also vn; fl and rec?) | Johann Georg Fröde (also vn; fl and rec?) | Johann Georg Fröde (also vn; fl and rec?) |
| | Johann Christoph Richter (also fl and rec?) | Johann Christoph Ritter (also fl and rec?) | Johann Christoph Ritter (also fl and rec?; d. 19 August 1760) |
| | [See Bassoon] | See Violin | See Concertmaster |
| Bassoon | [Johann Christian Klotsch, 1734/35–36/37, also ob] | Johann Simon Unger | Johann Bernhard Unbescheid |
| Waldhorn | See Violin | See Violin | See Concertmaster |
| Lute | | [Malachovsky, December 1749–September 1752] | |

| Years | 1715 | 1730 | 1745 | 1760 |
|---|---|---|---|---|
| Harpsichord | | | Christoph Heinicke, 'Clavicembalist', *Cammermusicus* (also organist at the Bartholomäikirche) | Johann Heinrich Heil, 'Clavicembalist' (also vn; organist at the Bartholomäikirche) |
| *Hoforganist* | Johann Ulich, *Cammermusicus* (also organist at the Bartholomäikirche) | Johann Ulich, *Cammermusicus* (also organist at the Bartholomäikirche); Johann Friedrich Wagner, *Cammermusicus* (also copyist)[d] | Johann Georg Röllig, *Cammermusicus* (also vdg, vc, and copyist) | Johann Georg Röllig *Cammermusicus* (also vdg, vc, and copyist) |
| Instrument(s) not specified | Johann Gottfried Rauhfus (Rauchfus or Rauchfuß), *Cammermusicus* and *Hofmusicus* (ob?) | Benjamin Gottlob Gurbier (vn?; also 'Cammer-Calculator', accountant) | | *See Bass* |
| *Hofmusici* | Johann Christoph Grahmann (instruments not specified) | Johann Vent (va; also vn?; other brass instruments as *Stadtpfeifer*) | Johann Andreas Friedrich Vent (va; vn?) | George Gottlieb Giel (vn?; va?) |
| *Kapellknaben* | | [Johann Friedrich Harnisch, *c*.1724–30] | Karl Christian Wilhelm Kettner (until September 1745); Johann Christian August Kettner (until September 1745) | |

| | | | | |
|---|---|---|---|---|
| *Hoftrompeter*[e] | Christian Scheckel<br>David Clausius<br>Johann Christoph Schmied | Johann Caspar Wilcke<br>David Clausius<br>Johann Wolfgang Jacobi ['musicalischer *Hofftrompeter*'; also at Dornburg]<br>Johann Friedrich Sauerland<br>Johann Balthasar Schneider<br>Johann Gottlieb Viepeck | Martin Wilhelm Zipprich (September 1745–49)<br>Johann Caspar Wilcke<br>Friedrich Wilhelm Thieß<br>Johann Andreas Gregorius Fliedner<br>Ernst Wilhelm Schlag<br>Johann August Preller<br>Johann Gottlieb Viepeck<br>Johann Heinrich Thieß | [1757: Johann Caspar Wilcke[f] (vn)]<br>[1757: Friedrich Wilhelm Thieß (vn)]<br>[1757: Johann Andreas Gregorius Fliedner (vn)]<br>[1757: Christian August Nicolai (vn)]<br>[1757: Gottfried Rühlmann (vn)]<br>Johann Gottlieb Viepeck<br>[1757: Johann Christian Wolland (Vollund)]] |
| *Hofpaucker* | Johann Anton Richter | | | |
| 'Kleine Hautboistenbande' | 'six boys' (names unknown) | | | |
| *Grenadiere* ('Schloßguarde')[g] | Carl Wilhelm Haucke (ob; vn?)<br>Johann George Kuhblanck (ob; vn?)<br>Johann Friedrich Schalge (ob; vn?) | | Johann Friedrich Dalchör (Dalchau) (ob; vn?)<br>Johann Adolph Schröder (ob; vn?)<br>George Rudolph Kötteritz (ob; vn?) | Johann Christian Friedrich Ulrich (ob; vn?) |

| Years | 1715 | 1730 | 1745 | 1760 |
|---|---|---|---|---|
| *Grenadiere (cont.)* | | Johann Peter Friedrich Schulze (ob; vn?) | Johann [Christian?] Friedrich Ulrich (ob; vn?) | |
| | | Johann Sigismund Srzelyl (ob; vn?) | | |
| | | Johann Adolph Heuer (Heyer or Hoyer) (ob; vn?) | | |
| | | 'Hautboist Siegelius' | | |
| **Vocalists** | | | | |
| Soprano | | Christian Carl Kettner (also vdg) | Christian Carl Kettner (also vdg; court secretary since 1738) | Johann Michael Teicher (also copyist) |
| Alto | | Karl (Johann?) Ludwig Weißflock, *Cammermusicus*[h] | Karl (Johann?) Ludwig Weißflock, *Cammermusicus* | Christian Carl Kettner, *Cammermusicus* (also vdg and court secretary; d. 22 November 1760) |
| Tenor | | Samuel Gottlieb Poll, *Cammermusicus* and *Hofmusicus* | Samuel Gottlieb Poll, 'Tenorist' and *Cammermusicus* | Samuel Gottlieb Poll, *Cammermusicus* and *Hofmusicus* (also 'Inspector') |
| Bass | | Christian Friedrich Horn, *Cammermusicus*[i] | Gottfried Förster, *Cammermusicus* | Georg Peter Weimar (Weymar) (also *Hofkantor* and unspecified brass and string instruments) |

| | | | | |
|---|---|---|---|---|
| Range not specified | [one member of Grahmann's 1699 ensemble] | | | |
| Hofkantor | [Daniel Roxer, Kantor at the Bartholomäikirche] | Michael Gattermann | Michael Gattermann | Michael Gattermann <br> See Bass |
| Choralknaben | 'the four choral scholars'j | 'the four choral scholars' | 'the four choral scholars' | 'the four choral scholars' |
| **Additional Personnel** | | | | |
| Hofkirchner (caretaker) | Johann Christian Goldammer | | Johann Peter Möhring (also vn and vdg)k | Johann Peter Möhring (also vdg) [1757: vn] |
| Copyist | See Hoforganist^l | | Johann Wilhelm Gottfried Biesenbruch (also organist at the Trinitatiskirche) | See Soprano |
| | | | See Hoforganist | See Hoforganist |
| Calcant | Johann Müller | | Johann Müller (also librarian) | [Johann Christian?] Schöne |

*Sources*

Based on information provided in D-DEla, Kammer Zerbst, Kammerrechnungen 1715/16, pp. 30, 53; 1729/30, p. 97, and 1730/31, p. 93; 1744/45, p. 104, and 1745/46, p. 104; and 1759/60, p. 112, and 1760/61, p. 109, as well as the marriage and death registers ('Trau Register', 'Sterberegister') of the Anhalt-Zerbst *Schloßkirche*, housed in D-ZEsb. First names of musicians have been gleaned from various other sources, primarily Wäschke, 'Die Zerbster Hofkapelle', 47–63.

a According to Röllig's autobiographical sketch from 1777; see Wäschke, 'Die Zerbster Hofkapelle', 56.

b The constitution of the Anhalt-Zerbst *Hofkapelle* as published in Friedrich Wilhelm Marpurg, *Historisch-kritische Beyträge zur Aufnahme der Musik*, III, '2. Stück' (Berlin, 1757), 130–31, is included in this column to emphasize that the actual forces available to the *Kapellmeister* may have been much greater than is apparent from related entries in the 1759/60 and 1760/61 Kammerrechnungen.

c It is unclear from the entries in the respective Kammerrechnungen whether Johann Christoph Richter was, in fact, Johann Christoph Ritter.

d 'Sterberegister', vol. 1719–45, p. 212: 'Hoch-fürstl. Cammer *Musicus*[,] Hofforganist und *Notist*'. Given that musicians appointed at the court typically played more than one instrument, Wagner may have been proficient on string or brass instruments or both.

e Another trumpeter listed in the Kammerrechnungen was Georg Jägersdörffer (1668/69, p. 73); the 'Cammer-Pauker' von Kosewitz (1751/52, p. 264) may have been the 'Heer-Pauker' referred to in 1753/54, p. 281, No. 27:2524.

f Spelt 'Wüllicke' in Marpurg, *Historisch-kritische Beyträge*, III: 131.

g See the respective entries in the 'Trau Register', vol. 1719–44, which indicates that Haucke and Kuhblanck were married in 1728, Schalge in 1729, Ulrich in 1742, and Kötteritz in 1744. Also identified as 'Hautboisten' are Gottfried Lebrecht Köckeritz and Christian Könnicke (Könnecke) who both married in 1739 and could still have been active with the *Grenadier Garde* in 1745. In the respective entries in the 'Sterberegister', vols 1719–45 and 1746–69, family circumstances, rather than biographical details, are given for Schulze, Srzelyl, Dalchöi, Heuer, and Schröder. A reference to an 'Hautboist' named Siegelius (no first name is provided) appears in D-DEla, Kammer Zerbst, No. 8457, fols 15–16, a document prepared in Zerbst on 15 (25?) January 1739 by A. [Anton Günther?] Möhring, possibly the 'Bauschreiber' and father-in-law of copyist Biesenbruch, see Wäschke, 'Die Zerbster Hofkapelle', 58. The 'Trau Register', specifically vol. 1745–60, also refers to a drummer or 'Tambour', Johann Adolph Schütze, who got married in 1756, but it is unclear whether he would still have been active in 1760.

h Wäschke, 'Die Zerbster Hofkapelle', 54 (as Karl Ludwig); 'Sterberegister', vol. 1746–69, p. 39 (as Johann Ludwig).

i Label specified in the 'Sterberegister', vol. 1719–45, p. 269 (Horn, d. 1740), vol. 1746–69 (Förster, d. 1755).

j 'Denen vier Choralknaben [bezahlt]' (paid to the four choral scholars), see the respective payroll entries in the 1729–31, 1744–6, and 1759–61 Kammerrechnungen.

k Möhring – and vocalist C. C. Kettner – participated in performances at the court, playing their own violas da gamba at 'Concerten' and 'Tafelmusiquen' (concerts and as table music), see the autograph letter by J. F. Fasch from 29 April 1756 in D-DEla, Kammer Zerbst, No. 8457, fol. 55.

l See Maul, 'Neues zu Georg Balthasar Schott', 94: Johann Friedrich Wagner already identified himself as 'Notist' (copyist) in 1722. Cf. Wäschke, 'Die Zerbster Hofkapelle', 49, who lists him (incorrectly) as 'Johann Gottfried Wagner'.

# 10
# The Court of Sondershausen
### Michael Maul

WHILE THE SONDERSHAUSEN *HOFKAPELLE* undoubtedly counts among the smaller court orchestras of central Germany, it was nevertheless an ensemble that could call upon a long tradition – one that continues to the present day. Yet tracing the *Kapelle*'s early history up until the second half of the eighteenth century is at times problematic. Not only does the information provided by the extant primary sources vary widely in terms of its quality and comprehensiveness, but documentation is extremely sparse for the first half of the eighteenth century. Virtually no archival material exists to document the appointments and activities of individual musicians, shed light on the musical life of the residence, or indeed provide a general understanding of cultural representation at the court.

Only the 'Rentereirechnungen' (treasury accounts) have survived intact, although unfortunately without the corresponding volumes of receipts.[1] While these accounts provide continuous insight into the life of the court, it is impossible to draw conclusions regarding expenditure from the count's (and later the prince's) privy purse. In contrast to the rather sketchy archival documentation, the extant musical scores associated with the *Hofkapelle* are virtually unparalleled in terms of their variety within a central German context. The remnants of the court's music library – today stored partly in the Schloßmuseum Sondershausen and partly at the Thüringisches Staatsarchiv Rudolstadt – comprises representative portions of the performance material used by the *Hofkapelle* from around 1700. In addition, we are fortunate that the court organist from 1775 onwards, Ernst Ludwig Gerber (1746–1819), carefully collected biographical information on the most important members of the orchestra for inclusion in his well-known *Historisch-biographisches Lexikon der Tonkünstler* (1790–92 and 1812–14).[2] Thus, despite some severe lacunae, the primary source situation for the Sondershausen *Hofkapelle* is, on the

---

[1] D-RUl, Rentereirechnungen; further relevant documents can also be found under the following categories: Regierung Sondershausen, Geheimes Consilium Sondershausen, Hofmarschallamt Sondershausen, and Kanzlei Sondershausen.

[2] Ernst Ludwig Gerber, *Historisch-biographisches Lexicon der Tonkünstler, welches Nachrichten von dem Leben und Werken musikalischer Schriftsteller . . . enthält*, 2 vols. (Leipzig, 1790–92); Gerber, *Neues historisch-biographisches Lexikon der Tonkünstler: welches Nachrichten*

whole, unusually wide-ranging and has already been the focus of several scholarly studies.[3]

EARLY HISTORY UNTIL 1715

During the thirteenth century, the dominion of Sondershausen came into the possession of the counts of Schwarzburg, with many future Schwarzburg regents choosing the town of Sondershausen as their residence. The existence of a small *Hofkapelle*, admittedly comprising initially only a small group of court musicians – lutenists, 'Musicanten', and *Cammermusici* – can be traced back to the sixteenth century.[4] During the course of the seventeenth century, the shape of the ensemble became clearer. In 1619, reference was made to five court employees who received an annual allowance for the purchase of strings; from this time onwards, specially appointed court organists are also mentioned in the documents.[5] The claim made by some scholars that a *Hofkapelle* was first mentioned in a document dating from 1637 is based on a reference to an unnamed 'Fürstl[icher] Capellmeister' (princely *Kapellmeister*) – except that the counts of Sondershausen were only made princes in 1697 – together with five further musicians and a *Kapellknabe*.[6] However, this turns out to be a mistaken conclusion, since the file in question contains documents from throughout the seventeenth century; furthermore, this specific undated folio must have been prepared around 1730, given the musicians it names: Bona, Rothe, Öfftiger, Wolff, and Ziegenbein (see Table 10.1, pp. 300–303 below).[7]

Consequently, according to information currently available, the appointment decree issued in 1659 for the future 'Hoff Musicus' Holtzner (who was concurrently deputy principal of the *Stadtschule*)[8] must be viewed as possibly the earliest indication of the existence of a *Hofkapelle* of some kind. According to this document, Holtzner was ordered '[zu] dirigieren' (to direct) the 'Chorum musicum' in performances of both *Tafel* and sacred music (the latter in the town church and the court chapel) and 'abzurichten' (to provide) vocal training for the 'Adjuvanten'

*von dem Leben und den Werken musikalischer Schriftsteller, berühmter Komponisten, Sänger . . . enthält*, 4 vols. (Leipzig, 1812–14).

[3] See Friedrich Wilhelm Beinroth, *Musikgeschichte der Stadt Sondershausen* (Innsbruck: Universitätsverlag Wagner, 1943); Fritz Hennenberg, *Das Kantatenschaffen von Gottfried Heinrich Stölzel*, Beiträge zur musikwissenschaftlichen Forschung in der DDR, 8 (Leipzig: Deutscher Verlag für Musik, 1976); Karla Neschke, *Johann Balthasar Christian Freislich (1687– 1764): Leben, Schaffen und Werküberlieferung*, Schriftenreihe zur mitteldeutschen Musikgeschichte, 3 (Oschersleben: Ziethen, 2000); Neschke, 'Das Leben und Schaffen von Johann Balthasar Christian Freislich (1687-1764) in seiner Amtszeit als Kapellmeister am Sondershäuser Hof (1717–31)', *Sondershäuser Beiträge*, 6 (2001), 15–55.

[4] Beinroth, *Musikgeschichte der Stadt Sondershausen*, 93–4.

[5] Ibid., 97.

[6] See ibid., 98; Neschke, *Johann Balthasar Christian Freislich*, 40.

[7] D-RUl, Kanzlei Sondershausen, No. 1794, fol. 54r, salaries of *Hofdiener* at Sondershausen in 1637 and 1639–1707.

[8] This document is included in Beinroth, *Musikgeschichte der Stadt Sondershausen*, 100–101.

(adjutants) and 'Schulknaben' (school boys). His appointment was only possible because the town *Kantor* and the town organist had been forced by the counts to accept a reduction in their wages, so that Holtzner's appointment as 'Director der Music bey Hofe' (music director at court) actually appears to be an indication of the specialization and emancipation of music at the court.

The situation at the beginning of eighteenth century had barely changed at all. At the head of the court's musical establishment was a *Kapellmeister*, the Frankenhausen-born Elias Christoph Stock (1655–1715), who had taken over the position in 1692 following the death of his predecessor Jeremias Koch (1637–1693); the latter had served as *Hofkantor* until his appointment as *Kapellmeister* in 1682.[9] He was assisted by a *Hofkantor*, a court organist (concurrently employed as a clerk), an alto and a tenor vocalist, as well as an indeterminate number of musicians – perhaps between one and four individuals – who also carried out other roles, for the most part clerical duties. The latter were usually referred to as *Cammerdiener* (chamber valets) or *Cammerschreiber* (chamber clerks) in the account books, as the members of the *Hofkapelle* were not yet listed in a separate category. In addition, there were almost a dozen trumpeters, although very few of these would have participated in concerted music at court. The core of their duties centred on service as messengers and *Fourier* (quartermasters). With regard to vocalists, the most proficient singers at the local *Gymnasium* (grammar school) – one or two students – were apparently 'abgerichtet' (trained) as *Kapellknaben* for the sacred music in the court chapel.[10]

Let us now turn from the account books to the extant musical sources. The latter can be divided into two groups, which provide information on the nature of the performance practices at the court and in the immediate vicinity. The oldest surviving musical documents are the autograph score, together with various performance materials, for a German-language setting of the St Matthew Passion composed in 1697 by Johann Christoph Rothe (1653–1700), described as a 'Fürstl. Schwartzburg. Cammer-Diener, wie auch Hoff- und Cammer-Musicus' (princely Schwarzburg chamber valet, as well as court and chamber musician).[11] This work, one of the earliest extant concerted settings of the Passion, continued to be performed well into the eighteenth century.[12] The oldest layer of performing parts reveals musical forces of at least nine vocalists (who performed eleven parts), four viola da gamba parts, and a basso continuo group.[13] The second set of musical

[9] See ibid., 102 ff.

[10] See ibid., 14 ff.; D-RUl, 'Jahres-Rechnung über Einnahme und Ausgabe-Geld Bey Fürstl: Schwartzburg: RenthCammer zu Sondershausen von Michael. 1729. usqu: 1730' (hereafter 'Jahres-Rechnung 1729/30').

[11] The titles used here are cited as they appear in the record of his death (on 21 June 1700) in D-SHst, 'Sterbebuch 1691–1741', 49. The date of J. C. Rothe's death provided in Gerber's *Historisch-biographisches Lexicon der Tonkünstler* (and subsequently repeated by many scholars) is inaccurate.

[12] Music extant in D-SHm, Mus. A 13:1.

[13] Several literary sources also point to the participation of a significant number of musicians. In a description of festivities held for the official opening of a new *Fasanenhaus* (pheasant-house) on 30 August 1694, we read that 'acht Sänger und zwanzig Instrumentalisten

sources comprises predominantly secular vocal compositions dating from around 1710, the majority of which appear to have been copied by *Kapellmeister* Stock.[14] Contemporary repertoire dominates here, above all chamber cantatas by Georg Philipp Telemann, music from Leipzig's opera house and collegia musica, as well as works by Reinhard Keiser (1674–1739) and numerous anonymous composers.[15]

## 'EIN ORCHESTER VON 30 WACKERN VIRTUOSEN': THE HEYDAY OF THE *HOFKAPELLE* DURING THE REIGN OF PRINCE GÜNTHER I (1720–40)

*Kapellmeister* Stock died on 4 December 1715.[16] His successor was Johann Balthasar Christian Freislich (1687–1764), born in Salzungen (Thuringia), who had apparently already been employed at the Sondershausen court for a number of years (possibly from 1714).[17] In contrast to Stock, Freislich was also active as a composer. Numerous scores from his tenure (which lasted until 1731) remain extant in Sondershausen, while others found their way to Danzig, where Freislich held the position of *Kapellmeister* at St Mary's Church from 1732 until his death in 1764, and are now held in the Biblioteka Gdańska Polskiej Akademii Nauk.[18] His documented extant output for Sondershausen centred on:

1. sacred cantatas – of which sixty-seven are extant in Sondershausen, with texts by Salomo Franck, Erdmann Neumeister, Johann Jacob Rambach, and Gottfried Ephraim Scheibel;[19]
2. Passion music – with a setting of St Matthew's Gospel from 1720, as well as one of the text by Barthold Heinrich Brockes (1680–1747), probably dating from before 1726, still extant;[20] and
3. birthday cantatas for members of the princely family – three survive in musical form and thirteen as text only.[21]

In addition, works by other composers were also performed during Freislich's tenure, including at least one sacred cantata cycle by Telemann (his *Geistliches Singen und Spielen*, Eisenach, 1710–11), regular or pasticcio settings of the Passion

---

ein in Musik gesetztes lateinisches Gedicht' (eight vocalists and twenty instrumentalists [had performed] a Latin poem set to music) at the accompanying feast, as cited in Neschke, *Johann Balthasar Christian Freislich*, 58–9.

[14] Further detailed information can be found in Michael Maul, *Barockoper in Leipzig (1693–1720)*, 2 vols. (Freiburg im Breisgau: Rombach, 2009), Textband, 113–51.

[15] See the overviews of these sources ibid., 124, 132–3, 149–51.

[16] See the church records held in D-SHst; the dates provided in older secondary sources (such as Gerber, *Neues historisch-biographisches Lexikon der Tonkünstler*, IV: 286; Beinroth, *Musikgeschichte der Stadt Sondershausen*, 105) are inaccurate.

[17] Neschke, *Johann Balthasar Christian Freislich*.

[18] See the thematic catalogue ibid., 113 ff.

[19] See ibid., esp. 134 ff.; Maul, *Barockoper in Leipzig*, Textband, 534.

[20] Neschke, *Johann Balthasar Christian Freislich*, 302.

[21] Detailed information can be found in the thematic catalogue included ibid., 113 ff.

by Reinhard Keiser (including one to Brockes's text), Rothe's setting for Sondershausen of 1697 (see above) in a version adapted by Freislich, and possibly Stölzel's *Brockes-Passion*.[22] Operas and musical-theatrical performances were also given, albeit on a small scale.[23] Unfortunately, it is impossible to comment on the cultivation of purely instrumental music during the first half of the eighteenth century, as no relevant musical sources have survived from that period.

What can be gathered from the surviving documents is a transformation of the *Hofkapelle* and its musical repertoire following the accession of Prince Günther I (Count Günther XLIII, 1678–1740), who succeeded his father, Christian Wilhelm I (1645–1721, r. from 1666, prince from 1697) in 1720, while the latter was still alive. These changes were, however, reflected less in the size of the ensemble – since, as before, only a small number of musicians were engaged – but rather more in their evident specialization: the account books now listed the musicians in their own separate category, under the heading 'die Bedienten bey der Fürstl: Capelle betreffend' (concerning the members of the princely *Kapelle*). Moreover, the salaries paid to those in leadership roles were considerably higher, and almost all the musicians were now labelled as such, although many of them also continued to occupy other posts at court (see Table 10.1).[24]

The reason behind this drastic change in artistic policy appears to have been that Prince Günther held a different, rather more modern view of the signficance of a *Hofkapelle* and, indeed, of the general importance of courtly cultural representation. A highly educated individual (who had studied Oriental languages), the prince had travelled extensively throughout Europe, including a visit in 1702 to France and then on to England, where Oxford University supposedly conferred upon him the honorary degree of Doctor of Laws.[25] The journey to England also seems to have had a concrete impact on the repertoire of the *Hofkapelle*. Gerber noted in 1812 in his *Lexikon* that while in London the hereditary prince had 'ums Jahr 1720 [*recte* 1702]' (in around 1702) acquired twenty volumes containing Italian operas and cantatas and brought them back to Sondershausen. These included numerous compositions by Giovanni Bononcini, Francesco Bartolomeo Conti,

---

[22] See ibid., 48 ff.

[23] The best example is Freislich's *Die verliebte Nonne* (date of premiere unknown), an 'operina' of which fragments are extant; see ibid., 357–8. In this context, see also Erdmann Werner Böhme, *Die frühdeutsche Oper in Thüringen* (Stadtroda: Richter, 1931), 178–89; Renate Brockpähler, *Handbuch zur Geschichte der Barockoper in Deutschland* (Emsdetten/Westfalen: Lechte, 1964), 344–8; Herbert A. Frenzel, *Thüringische Schloßtheater: Beiträge zur Typologie des Spielortes vom 16. bis zum 19. Jahrhundert*, Schriften der Gesellschaft für Theatergeschichte, 63 (Berlin: Selbstverlag der Gesellschaft für Theatergeschichte, 1965); Neschke, *Johann Balthasar Christian Freislich*, 94 ff.

[24] D-RUl, 'Rechnung Der Hochfürstl: Schwartzburg: Rentherey zu Sondershausen über Beschehene Einnahme und Ausgabe Geldt, Von Michaelis 1714. bis dahin 1715'.

[25] See Günter Lutze, *Aus Sondershausens Vergangenheit: Ein Beitrag zur Kultur- und Sittengeschichte früherer Jahrhunderte*, II (Sondershausen: Eupel, 1909), 109. Additional biographical information is provided in Christian August Junghans, *Geschichte der Schwarzburgischen Regenten* (Leipzig, 1821), 328–9.

Alessandro Scarlatti, and Francesco Mancini.[26] To this day, the influence of Italian operatic repertoire remains clearly recognizable in the collection, even if it is impossible to explain in individual cases how the surviving Italian music is connected to the hereditary prince's trip.[27] In any case, according to Heinrich Frankenberger, one of Prince Günther I's first tasks as the new ruler was 'die vorgefundene, minder bedeutende Hofkapelle [zu vervollständigen] und auf eine hohe künstlerische Stufe [zu bringen]' (to round out the already existing, mediocre *Hofkapelle* and raise it to a higher artistic level).[28] Retrospectively, Gerber referred to the prince as a 'Beschützer der Künste' (protector of the arts), a view which is also confirmed by a number of further sources.[29] Among these is the revenue and expenditure of the princely treasury. A comparison shows that in around 1715 annual expenditure ranged from 32,000 to 40,000 *Gulden* with a surplus of 800 *Gulden*; by 1730, this outlay had increased to *c*.100,000 *Gulden*, resulting in an annual loss of 6,000 *Gulden*.[30] Prince Günther was clearly also a lover of the writings of the Hamburg poet Barthold Heinrich Brockes, elevating him to the rank of imperial *Pfalzgraf* (count palatine) and poet laureate in 1730 (a situation that coincidentally explains the numerous settings of Brockes's passion oratorios performed in Sondershausen during his reign).

The court of Sondershausen then decided to send *Kapellmeister* Freislich to Dresden for one year in order to take lessons on the pantaleon (a type of dulcimer) with the instrument's inventor, the famous Pantaleon Hebenstreit (1668–1750).[31] Freislich's departure in 1731 resulted in a curious situation at the court: the small *Hofkapelle* was now without a *Kapellmeister*, since no replacement for Freislich had been hired. Was this an economy measure? Apparently not. Rather, it should be viewed as a deliberate decision on Prince Günther's part. For, having earlier wasted a chance to gain Gottfried Heinrich Stölzel for his court, the prince now promoted

---

[26] See the article 'Alveri' in Gerber, *Neues historisch-biographisches Lexikon der Tonkünstler*, I: 81–2.

[27] See Helen Geyer, 'Italienische Spuren im Repertoire der Hofmusik', in *Residenzstadt Sondershausen: Beiträge zur Musikgeschichte*, ed. Karla Neschke and Helmut Köhler (Sondershausen: Starke-Druck, 2004), 23–32; Geyer, '"Nach dem neuesten Geschmacke": Überlegungen zum italienischen Hofmusikrepertoire des frühen 18. Jahrhunderts am Beispiel des Hofes zu Sondershausen', in *Mitteldeutschland im musikalischen Glanz seiner Residenzen: Sachsen, Böhmen und Schlesien als Musiklandschaften im 16. und 17. Jahrhundert*, ed. Peter Wollny, Ständige Konferenz Mitteldeutsche Barockmusik Jahrbuch, 2004 (Beeskow: Ortus, 2005), 65–79.

[28] Heinrich Frankenberger, 'Die Musikzustände zu Sondershausen unter Fürst Günther I. in den Jahren 1720–40', in *Heinrich Frankenbergers Abhandlungen über musikwissenschaftliche Fragen*, ed. Hermann Gresky (Sondershausen: Eupel, 1925), 23; cf. Manfred Fechner, 'Gottfried Heinrich Stölzels Wirken für den Hof Schwarzburg-Sondershausen', in *Jahrbuch der Ständigen Konferenz Mitteldeutsche Barockmusik, 2002*, ed. Peter Wollny (Schneverdingen: Karl Dieter Wagner, 2004), 203–28.

[29] See the article 'Rothe (August Friedrich)' in Gerber, *Historisch-biographisches Lexicon der Tonkünstler*, II: 333.

[30] D-RUl, 'Rechnung Der Hochfürstl: Schwartzburg: Rentherey zu Sondershausen über Beschehene Einnahme und Ausgabe Geldt, Von Michaelis 1714. bis dahin 1715'; 'Jahres-Rechnung 1729/30'.

[31] Gerber, *Historisch-biographisches Lexicon der Tonkünstler*, I: 441.

him, so to speak, to the post of external *Kapellmeister*, despite the fact that Stölzel had been *Hofkapellmeister* in Gotha since 1719. Regarding this situation, Gerber wrote (referring to Stölzel's original application for the post, apparently made in 1719):

> Im Jahre 1719 [*recte* Januar 1718[32]] trat er [Stölzel] in die Dienste des Gräflichen Hofes zu Gera. . . . Er bot darauf dem hiesigen [d. h. Sondershäuser] Hofe seine Dienste an. Zum Unglück hatte sich Freislich der hernachmals als Kapellmeister in Danzig starb, vorher schon durch verschiedene gefällige Kompositionen und durch sein Betragen, die Gunst der vornehmsten des Hofs zu erlangen gewußt. Stölzel fand als ein Unbekannter wenig Unterstützung. Freislichs Gönner brachten es bey dem Fürsten dahin, daß selbiger zum Kapellmeister ernannt wurde. Sobald Stölzel keine Hofnung mehr vor sich sah, gieng er noch im selbigen Jahre nach Gotha, und wurde daselbst sogleich zum Kapellmeister ernannt. Kaum aber hatte ihn unser Fürst [Günther I.] aus seinen Kompositionen näher kennen gelernt, als er es sehr bereuete, ihn nicht in Dienste genommen zu haben, und er hielt sich in Ermangelung seiner in der Folge dadurch schadlos, daß er ihn außer zwey vollständigen Doppeljahrgängen, Paßionen und Tedeums für die Kirche, die mehresten solennen Gelegenheitsmusiken verfertigen lies.

> In the year 1719 [*recte* January 1718] he [Stölzel] entered the service of the Count of Gera. . . . He then offered his services to the local [Sondershausen] court. Unfortunately, Freislich (who later died as *Kapellmeister* in Danzig) had already impressed the highest-ranking individuals at court with various pleasing compositions and by his conduct. Being unknown at the court, Stölzel found little support. Freislich's patrons eventually persuaded the prince to appoint him as *Kapellmeister*. As soon as he had lost all hope, Stölzel left for Gotha that same year and was immediately appointed *Kapellmeister*. However, when our prince [Günther I] had familiarized himself with [Stölzel's] compositions, he regretted not having offered him permanent employment and compensated by commissioning from him two complete double cycles of sacred cantatas, Passions, and *Te Deum* settings for the church as well as several solemn works for special occasions.[33]

Entries in the account books during the 1730s confirm that from 1732/3 onwards, Stölzel actually composed the annual birthday music for the princely couple on a regular basis and was remunerated appropriately for his services. He was also well paid for sending numerous musical works – including several cantata cycles – to Sondershausen, composing a double cycle specifically for the court in 1735/6.[34] To date, works by Stölzel surviving in Sondershausen comprise more than 330

---

[32] Maul, *Barockoper in Leipzig*, Textband, 583.

[33] Gerber, *Historisch-biographisches Lexicon der Tonkünstler*, II: 589.

[34] See the Rentereirechnungen in D-RUl, specifically the cantata cycles listed between 1732/3 and 1738/9. Stölzel apparently received 36 Gulden, 12 Groschen per cycle; further details are provided in Hennenberg, *Das Kantatenschaffen von Gottfried Heinrich Stölzel*, 24–5.

cantatas, two Passions, a German *Te Deum*, and at least nine secular occasional works written for festive occasions.[35]

Gerber – almost certainly relying on information provided by his father, Heinrich Nikolaus Gerber (1702–1775), who had succeeded Freislich as court organist in 1731 – also acknowledged that the Sondershausen *Hofkapelle* reached its peak during the 1730s. On the one hand, this is evident from the admiration he expressed in the biographical articles on the main members of the *Kapelle*: Rödiger, Wilcke, and the two Rothes.[36] But, on the other hand, the information Gerber supplied on the early years of his father as Sondershausen *Hoforganist* in particular provides a brief glimpse into the musical practices of the court:

> Hier [d. h. in Sondershausen] hatte sich unterdessen [d. h. um 1730] alles zu seinem Vortheil verändert. Am Hofe des damals regierenden Fürst Günthers, hörete man ein Orchester von 30 wackern Virtuosen und Sängern, für welches ein Stölzel, Förster und Freißlich arbeiteten, unter welchem sich die ersten und größten Virtuosen Deutschlands hören ließen, und wobey ein [Johann Philipp] Kirnberger [1738–40] und [Johann Adolph] Scheibe [1736] eine Zeitlang lebten, um ihre Kenntnisse zu erweitern.... Nach einem anderthalbjährigen Aufenthalte auf dem Lande, erhielt er [d. h. Gerbers Vater] den Ruf zu seinem Fürsten als Hoforganist in Sondershausen, zu welchem Amte er an den drey Weynachtsfeyertagen des 1731sten Jahres zur Zufriedenheit des Fürsten und des Hofs, die Probe ablegte. Er fand endlich hier, was er so lange gesucht hatte: hinlängliche musikalische Beschäftigung. Er hatte nemlich, außer den Wochen- und Sonntagskirchen, noch wöchentlich in zwey Hofassembleen den Flügel zu spielen. Ueberdies übergab ihm der Fürst ein vortrefliches junges Genie, Namens Oeftger, den er auf dem Klavier und in der Komposition unterrichten mußte. Der Tod vernichtete aber die Erwartungen, die man sich von desselben Talenten gemacht hatte, während der Reise, welche ihn der Fürst, um der Kunst willen, thun ließ.

> Meanwhile [in around 1730], here [in Sondershausen] everything had changed for the better. During the reign of Prince Günther, an orchestra of thirty valiant virtuosos and singers could be heard at the court, for which Stölzel, Förster, and Freislich toiled, [and] under whom some of the leading and most respected virtuosos of Germany performed, and among whom [Johann Philipp] Kirnberger and [Johann Adolph] Scheibe lived for a time in order to expand their knowledge [from 1738 to 1740 and in 1736 respectively]. ... After a period of approximately one-and-a-half years in the countryside, he [Gerber's father] was called by his prince for the position of court

[35] See Fechner, 'Gottfried Heinrich Stölzels Wirken für den Hof Schwarzburg-Sondershausen', 207; Hennenberg, *Das Kantatenschaffen von Gottfried Heinrich Stölzel*, 23; Maul, *Barockoper in Leipzig*, Textband, 143; Bert Siegmund, 'Zu Chronologie und Textgrundlagen der Kantatenjahrgänge von Gottfried Heinrich Stölzel', in *Alte Musik und Aufführungspraxis: Festschrift für Dieter Gutknecht zum 65. Geburtstag* (Vienna: LIT-Verlag, 2007), 81–92.

[36] See the respective articles on Rödiger, Wilcke, and the two Rothe brothers in Gerber, *Historisch-biographisches Lexicon der Tonkünstler*.

organist in Sondershausen, to which office he was appointed having given the necessary trial performances on the three feast days of Christmas in 1731, to the satisfaction of the prince and the court. He had finally found what he had been seeking for so long: satisfying employment as a musician. In addition to playing services on weekdays and Sunday, he had to perform every week on the *Flügel* [keyboard] for two court *Assembléen*. Moreover, the prince entrusted him with the care of an outstanding young genius named Oeftger, to whom he [Gerber] had to teach keyboard and composition. However, during a trip on which the prince had sent him for art's sake, death shattered those expectations which had been held for his [Oeftger's] talents.[37]

The information provided by Gerber on visiting musicians in Sondershausen can be augmented by entries in the treasury accounts of honoraria paid in 1736 to a musician named Kreß (most likely Ludwig Albrecht, b. 1718), as well as to Johann Ernst Süß (employed at Kassel from 1722) and Johann Scherer.[38] It is now also possible to solve the inconsistency between the number of performing musicians given by Gerber ('thirty valiant virtuosos and singers') and the barely more than fifteen full-time musicians employed at court during the 1730s (see Table 10.1). The latter were joined in part by their students, in part by lackeys, clerks, and secretaries at court (who are frequently not identified as musicians in the account books). The core of the *Kapelle* comprised a dozen individuals and it is questionable whether the regular performances (at the *Tafel*, in church, and in the chamber) involved for the most part only them. It is conspicuous at the very least that two of the leading members of the ensemble are generally labelled as 'Musici' in the account books, even though, according to Gerber, they were excellent singers, as well as being masters (and therefore also section leaders) of a particular instrument. Johann Christoph Rödiger (1704–1765), an alto soloist capable of a 'rührenden und edlen Vortrage des Adagios' (touching and noble performance of the Adagio) was also an accomplished violinist, who could improvise 'nach Locatelli's Manier' (in the manner of Locatelli). His colleague Johann Ernst Rothe (1688–1774) excelled as a bass singer and also played ripieno parts on the violin.[39] Whether or not it is a coincidence that in Stölzel's double cantata cycle for 1735/6 written for Sondershausen, 'die Begleitung der Arien außer dem Basse, größtentheils blos in 2 Violinen [bestand]' (the accompaniment of arias, apart from the bass [that is, basso continuo], comprised for the most part only two violins), deserves further consideration.[40]

---

[37] Gerber, *Historisch-biographisches Lexicon der Tonkünstler*, I: 493.

[38] A son of Johann Jacob Kreß (1685–1728), Ludwig Albrecht was in search of employment during the late 1730s; see Ekkehard Krüger, *Die Musikaliensammlung des Erbprinzen Friedrich Ludwig von Württemberg-Stuttgart und der Herzogin Luise Friederike von Mecklenburg-Schwerin in der Universitätsbibliothek Rostock*, 2 vols. (Beeskow: Ortus, 2006), I: 260–61. On Süß and Scherer, see Beinroth, *Musikgeschichte der Stadt Sondershausen*, 110; see also Max Seiffert's notes on Johann Philipp Kirnberger's *Stammbuch* (roughly equivalent to a commonplace book), under the heading 'Notizen', *Vierteljahrsschrift für Musikwissenschaft*, 5/2 (1889), 365–71.

[39] Cf. Gerber, *Historisch-biographisches Lexicon der Tonkünstler*, II: 304 ff., 331–2.

[40] See ibid., 590.

When conceiving the vocal parts, Stölzel must surely have taken into account the abilities of the Sondershausen vocalists, at least with regard to the parts performed by tenor Johann Caspar Wilcke (1707–1758).[41]

It is possible that Prince Günther may have only considered reappointing a *Kapellmeister* in around 1739. Christoph Förster, who had lost his job as concertmaster in Merseburg in 1738, appears to have been keen on securing this post while visiting Sondershausen in 1739–40. During that time, he composed serenatas for the Sondershausen princely couple (for which music is still extant), and the official funeral music performed by the *Hofkapelle* for Prince Günther in 1740.[42] That these activities failed to result in Förster's permanent appointment clearly relates to the changed circumstances at the court following the death of this artistically-minded ruler.

## 'NICHTS WENIGER, ALS VERSCHWENDERISCH': THE REIGN OF PRINCE HEINRICH (1740–58)

Beinroth portrayed the era of Heinrich I as one that continued to be productive for the *Hofkapelle*, most likely in an attempt to stress the orchestra's seemingly uninterrupted tradition from the early baroque period to the nineteenth century.[43] In reality, when Prince Heinrich I of Schwarzburg (1689–1758) took over as regent in 1740 following the death of his half-brother (with whom he had supposedly lived in continuous 'Disharmonie' due to the right of primogeniture introduced by Prince Christian Wilhelm), the musical life of the Schwarzburg residence took a clear step backwards.[44] The chronicler of the official history of the Schwarzburg rulers, Christian August Junghans, evaluated Heinrich retrospectively as a prince who had loved 'äußern Glanz und Pracht' (conspicuous glamour and splendour), had known 'keinen Stolz' (no pride), was 'äußerst leutselig' (extraordinarily affa-

---

[41] This Weimar-born musician was recommended to Sondershausen by Stölzel and, prior to his appointment there in 1732, had performed in Moscow (from 1722 onwards), in Gotha (1731/2), and possibly also earlier at the Hamburg Gänsemarkt Opera (around 1722); according to Gerber, *Historisch-biographisches Lexicon der Tonkünstler*, II: 807–11: 'Seine Stimme war ein hoher Tenor, so daß er das zweygestrichene c noch klar und deutlich, ohne den geringsten Zwang, angeben konnte. Deswegen hielt sich auch seine Stimme in dem von dem Kapellmeister Stoelzel für den hiesigen Hof gesetzten Kirchenjahrgange, durchaus in der eingestrichenen Octave auf. Sein Ton war äußerst zart und fein, dabey aber der schönste Silberton, den ich je gehöret habe. In der Biegsamkeit und Fertigkeit seiner Kehle suchte er seines Gleichen, und in der Deklamation war er Meister' (His voice was that of a high tenor, with which he could produce the C above middle C [$c''$] without any straining. This is also why his part remained in the octave above middle C in the cantata cycle set by *Kapellmeister* Stölzel for the local court. His [Wilcke's] sound was extremely tender and delicate, yet he was able to produce the most beautiful silvery tone that I have ever heard. The flexibility and skill of his throat had no equal, and he was a master with regard to declamation).

[42] See D-SHm, Mus. A 6:1–3; Mus. A 6:4 (serenatas); Mus. A 6:5 (funeral music).

[43] Beinroth, *Musikgeschichte der Stadt Sondershausen*, 110.

[44] Regarding the princes' relationship, see Junghans, *Geschichte der Schwarzburgischen Regenten*, 331.

ble), but was also 'nichts weniger, als verschwenderisch' (nothing less than extravagant) and loved 'muntere Scherze' (lively jokes). He also reportedly exercised the 'schöne Tugend der Wohltätigkeit' (the beautiful virtue of charity) and insisted on 'strengste Etiquette' (strict etiquette) at his court.[45]

However, these remarks conceal the fact that during the reign of Prince Heinrich (who, incidentally, was seldom present in Sondershausen), the *Hofkapelle* and indeed cultural life in general were subject to a rigid policy of retrenchment and forced to accept painful budget cuts.[46] The latter is already evident in figures from 1745: the recorded annual expenses taken from the *Rentkammer* for the *Hofkapelle* reached approximately 450 *Gulden* – whereas during Prince Günther's reign these had averaged at around 800 *Gulden* – from the court's total expenditure of 100,000 *Gulden*. Moreover, by this time the court's revenues amounted to around 140,000 *Gulden*.[47] The supply of music on the part of the Gotha *Kapellmeister* was also apparently no longer of interest; at least there are no documented payments to Stölzel following the accession of Heinrich I. Nor is it possible to determine the characteristic features of the music performed during the latter's reign from the surviving court repertoire. The court continued to lack a resident *Kapellmeister*, and the approximately twelve full-time musicians formerly recorded under the heading 'Fürstliche Capelle' (princely *Kapelle*) in the account books had now shrunk to four names: Rothe, Rödiger, Wilcke, and Gerber (see Table 10.1). It seems that the prince had released (or failed to reappoint) only a small number of those now missing from the listing of musicians. His policy of retrenchment required rather that a significantly higher number of musicians than before carry out additional duties. In any case, many of those previously employed exclusively as members of the *Hofkapelle* were now listed in the accounts as 'Kanzlisten' (clerks) in the princely chamber or among the lackeys (see Table 10.1).

That this was a real structural reform, and did not occur solely on paper, is supported by remarks made by Ernst Ludwig Gerber in his articles pertaining to Sondershausen court musicians. Reporting on the life of the court violoncellist Johann Wolfgang Wolff (1704–1740), Gerber emphasized that Wolff had been appointed to the Sondershausen *Kapelle* by Prince Günther in 1734; however, when the latter, 'der die Künste sehr schätzte, im Jahr 1740 mit Tode abgieng, und die Kapelle bey dem Regierungsantritte des Nachfolgers desselben, ein ähnliches Schicksal mit demjenigen hatte, welches vor wenigen Jahren die schöne Casseler Kapelle betraf; so wandte er sich nach Strelitz' (who was a connoisseur of the arts, died in 1740 and his successor came to power, the *Kapelle*'s fate began to resemble that of the fine *Kapelle* of Kassel only a few years ago; for that reason he [Wolff] moved to Strelitz).[48] By drawing upon the example of Hesse-Kassel, Gerber clearly likened the situation in Sondershausen to the complete dissolution of a *Kapelle*, since at the beginning of his reign Landgrave Wilhelm IX (r. 1785–1807) promptly

---

[45] Ibid., 331–2.

[46] Cf. Beinroth, *Musikgeschichte der Stadt Sondershausen*, 110.

[47] D-RUl, 'Jahres-Rechnung über Einnahme und Ausgabe-Geld Bey der Fürstl: Schwartzburg: RenthCammer zu Sondershausen von Michael. 1744. usqu: 1745'.

[48] Gerber, *Historisch-biographisches Lexicon der Tonkünstler*, II: 828–9.

closed the two theatres supported by the court, released the ballet troupe and the *Hofkapelle*, and paid off the musicians.[49] Gerber also offers a laconic commentary on the amalgamation of positions in Sondershausen. Referring to the change in the position of his father, who served as the sole court organist from 1731, he notes:

> Das Jahr 1749, wo er endlich alles Sträubens ohngeachtet, genöthiget wurde, ein Hofamt [d. h. das eines Kellerschreibers] anzunehmen, welches mit weit- läuftigen Rechnungen verbunden war, setzte allen seinen musikalischen Be- schäftigungen ein Ziel. Kaum, daß er außer der Kirche zu Hause dann und wann dem Klavier ein halb Stündgen widmen konnte.

> In the year 1749, despite great protest on his part, he had been forced to take on a court position [that of a clerk of the cellar] which involved the prepa- ration of copious numbers of invoices, taking a heavy toll on his musical activities. Except for playing at church, he was only very occasionally able to devote half an hour on the keyboard at home.[50]

### 'KLUGE SPARSAMKEIT': THE RULE OF PRINCE CHRISTIAN GÜNTHER III (1758–94)

The situation only changed with the end of Prince Heinrich's reign following his death in Frankfurt am Main in 1758. Having never married, Heinrich was suc- ceeded by his nephew Christian Günther, who ruled for almost four decades, and, according to Christian August Junghans, was well liked thanks to his 'kluge Sparsamkeit' (shrewd frugality).[51] However, this policy applied only in part to the *Hofkapelle*: treasury invoices from 1760 indicate that once again around 750 *Gul- den* were spent on the ensemble (from a total expenditure of 120,000 and revenue of 190,000 *Gulden*).[52] Moreover, close to a dozen musicians were once again em- ployed explicitly as members of the *Kapelle* (see Table 10.1). References regarding the *Kapelle*'s repertoire are also available for the period around 1760. Ernst Ludwig Gerber (b. 1746) commented in 1812 that he recalled 'noch mit Vergnügen, als Knabe [d. h. um 1760] manche schöne Arie [gesungen zu haben]' (with delight that as a boy [in around 1760] he had sung many a fine aria) from a cantata cycle by Christoph Förster (d. 1745) – the concertmaster at Merseburg, later *Viceka- pellmeister* in Rudolstadt – 'in der hiesigen [d. h. Sondershäuser] Stadtkirche' (in the local [Sondershausen] town church).[53] Around 1759, Johann Christian Con- tius (1714–1776), the former harpist of Count Heinrich von Brühl's *Kapelle* and

[49] Hartmut Broszinski, 'Kassel', in *Die Musik in Geschichte und Gegenwart: allgemeine Enzy- klopädie der Musik*, 2nd rev. edn (Kassel: Bärenreiter, 1994–2008; hereafter *MGG* 2), Sachteil, V: 5.

[50] Gerber, *Historisch-biographisches Lexicon der Tonkünstler*, I: 495.

[51] Junghans, *Geschichte der Schwarzburgischen Regenten*, 335.

[52] D-RUl, 'Rechnung über Einnahme und Ausgabe-Geld Bey Fürstl: Schwartzburg: Cam- mer zu Sondershausen Von Mich: 1759. bis dahin 1760'.

[53] Gerber, *Neues historisch-biographisches Lexikon der Tonkünstler*, II: 158; it is possible that

also an ambitious composer, was once again active for a short time in Sondershausen, admittedly in a private capacity. He received 27 *Gulden* from the *Rentkammer* in 1760/61 for 'Kirchenstücke' (sacred works) he had prepared, some of which are extant in Sondershausen.[54] According to Gerber, Contius composed 'in dieser Zeit einige Kirchenstücke für den dasigen Hof, wobey er zwar tieff aus Hassens Quellen trank, aber nichtsdestoweniger guten Geschmack und Beurtheilung und nicht gemeine Kenntnisse vom Contrapunkt, zeigte' (several sacred works for the local court during this time, whereby he drank deep from [Johann Adolf] Hasse's fountains, but nevertheless showed good taste and judgment and no mean contrapuntal skill).[55] In addition, the renowned violin virtuoso Leopold August Abel (1718–1794), brother of the famous Carl Friedrich Abel (1723–1787), was active as concertmaster in Sondershausen from 1758 onward, receiving 42 *Gulden* for six sinfonias (now lost) that he had composed during his tenure.[56] In 1767, he moved to the court of Margrave Friedrich Wilhelm of Brandenburg-Schwedt.

In short, musical life at the residence – which remained without a *Kapellmeister* – appears to have recovered during the reign of Christian Günther. Eventually, a change, indeed a modernization, occurred during the reign of Prince Günther Friedrich Carl I (1794–1835). From 1806 on the *Kapelle* performed in public as the 'Loh-Orchester', named after the location where their concerts first took place: in a small grove inside the park of the princely palace. And under this name the Sondershausen orchestra continues to perform to this day.[57]

this unidentified cantata cycle may have been acquired much earlier, perhaps during Förster's stay in Sondershausen.

[54] D-RUl, 'Rechnung über Einnahme und Ausgabe-Geld Bey Fürstl: Schwartzburg: Cammer zu Sondershausen Von Mich: 1760. bis dahin 1761', unpaginated. The original performance material for fourteen cantatas, plus scores, remains extant in D-SHm, Mus. A 4:1–14 and MS M 17:122a.

[55] Gerber, *Historisch-biographisches Lexicon der Tonkünstler*, 1: 298.

[56] See ibid., 3–4; Beinroth, *Musikgeschichte der Stadt Sondershausen*, 111; Walter Knape, 'Abel, Leopold August', in *MGG* 2, Personenteil, 1: 31–2.

[57] Beinroth, *Musikgeschichte der Stadt Sondershausen*, 111–40.

Table 10.1. Membership of the Sondershausen Court Music Establishment in 1715, 1730, 1745, and 1760

| Year | 1715 | 1730 | 1745 | 1760 |
|---|---|---|---|---|
| Ruler | Prince Christian Wilhelm (r. 1666–1720) | Prince Günther I (r. 1720–40) | Prince Heinrich I (r. 1740–58) | Prince Christian Günther III (r. 1758–94) |
| Numeric Overview | 1 *Kapellmeister* / 7 instrumentalists / 7 trumpeters & 1 kettledrummer / 3 vocalists (1 doubling as instrumentalist) / 1 unspecified musician | 1 *Kapellmeister* / 6 instrumentalists / 5 trumpeters (1 doubling as kettledrummer) / 3 vocalists (2 doubling as instrumentalists) / 5 unspecified musicians | 1 instrumentalist / 8 trumpeters & 1 kettledrummer / 4 vocalists (2 doubling as instrumentalists) / 1 unspecified musician | 1 concertmaster / 7 instrumentalists / 8 trumpeters & 1 kettledrummer / 4 vocalists (2 doubling as instrumentalists) / 2 unspecified musicians |
| *Kapellmeister* | Elias Christoph Stock | Johann Balthasar Christian Freislich (also *Hoforganist*) | | |
| Concertmaster | | | | Leopold August Abel |
| Instrumentalists[a] | | | | |
| Violin | | *See Alto and* Bass | *See Alto and* Bass | August Benjamin Rothe / *See Alto and* Bass |
| Violoncello | | Johann Wolfgang Wolff, 'Hoff- und Cammer-Musicus' | | Johann Benjamin Vonende |
| *Waldhorn*[b] | | | | Reinert / Bachmann / Ernst Ludwig Freyde / Johann Christoph Friedemann Spenß |

| | | | | |
|---|---|---|---|---|
| *Hoforganist* | Johann Christian Blettermann (also clerk) | [*See Kapellmeister*] | Heinrich Nikolaus Gerber[c] | ? [possibly no longer listed as such in the accounts] |
| *Hautboisten* | Johann Caspar Abel<br>Christoph Cramer<br>Sebastian Remper<br>Martin Hendrich<br>Johann Wilhelm Kraut<br>Johann Georg Öffiger (d. 1764)[d] | Christoph Cramer<br>Martin Hendrich<br>Johann Wilhelm Kraut<br>Johann Georg Öffiger | ? [possibly no longer listed as such in the accounts] | |
| *Hoftrompeter* | Johann Jacob Briegleb<br>Johann Georg Heyland<br>Johann Melchior Köhler<br>Heinrich Michael Mäder<br>Johann George Meißner<br>Paul Samuel Reichenbach<br>Johann Andreas Ziegenbein | Johann Melchior Köhler<br>Johann George Meißner<br>Köhler<br>Heinrich Michael Mäder | Johann Nicolaus Bräutigam<br>Johann Philipp Eißfeld<br>Hoffmann<br>Johann Melchior Köhler<br>Johann George Meißner<br>Heinrich Michael Mäder<br>Paul Samuel Reichenbach | Böttcher<br>Johann Philipp Eißfeld<br>Johann Bernhard Jaritz, 'Cammertrompeter'<br>Johann Wilhelm John<br>Albrecht Günther<br>Heinrich Köhler<br>Heinrich Michael Mäder |
| *Hofpaucker* | Johann David Döring, 'Musicalischer Hoff-Paucker' – that is, musically literate<br>*See Hoftrompeter* | Johann Andreas Ziegenbein | Wahl<br>Christian Wilhelm Lutze | Schlothauer<br>Christian Wilhelm Lutze |

| Year | 1715 | 1730 | 1745 | 1760 |
|---|---|---|---|---|
| Vocalists[a] | | | | |
| Soprano | | | | |
| Alto | Johann Georg Öffiger / Johann Christian Werner | Johann Christoph Rödiger (also vn), 'Cammer- und Hof-Musicus'[e] | Johann Christoph Rödiger (also vn) | Johann Christoph Rödiger (also vn) |
| Tenor | | | Johann Caspar Wilcke[f] | Albert Rudolph Rothe, 'Registrator und Capell Tenorist' (registrar and tenor in the chapel) |
| Bass | | Johann Ernst Rothe (also vn), 'Cancellist und Hoff-Musicus'[g] | Johann Ernst Rothe (also vn) | Johann Ernst Rothe (also vn) |
| Hofkantor | | | | |
| Kapellknaben[h] | Gustav Geußenhainer | Johann Sebastian Knaubel Ziegenbein | Johann Sebastian Knaubel | Johann Sebastian Knaubel Weidner |
| Duties not specified[a] | Johann Samuel Staude, 'Cammerdiener und Hofmusicus' | Heinrich Johann Bona, 'Secretarius'; Johann Matthias Tölcke, 'Cammerdiener' (chamber valet), also 'Hoff- u. Cammer-Musicus alhier'; [August Friedrich?] Rothe, listed as a lackey; Wilhelm Gottfried Sympher, 'Musicus' | August Friedrich Rothe, 'Canzellist und Cammer-Musicus' | August Friedrich Rothe |

*Sources*

Based on information contained in the extant 'Rentereirechnungen' (D-RUl) and church records held in D-SHst; this does not include unidentified personnel who may have been members of the *Kapelle*, but are not listed as such in the accounts.

a  Listed in the account books from 1730 under the rubric 'Hofkapelle'; but partly also under general court personnel. Occasionally, only last names are provided.

b  Entered in the account books under the rubric 'Jägerei' (the hunt); between 1722–23, a musician named Jelincke held the position of *Waldhornist* at the court.

c  From 1749 also 'Kellerschreiber' (clerk of the cellar).

d  Given that the *Hautboist* Johann Georg Öfftiger died in 1764, it seems likely that that the singer of the same name listed in 1715 was a different person, probably a relative.

e  Later 'Cammer-Verwalter' (chamber steward), also 'Hoff- und Cammer- Musicus'.

f  Mentioned as 'Cammer-Registrator' (chamber registrar) in 1752 and 1758; also as a 'Cammer- und Hoff-Musicus'.

g  Clerk and court musician; also listed in 1751 as 'Geheimer Regierungs-Canzellist' (clerk of the privy cabinet).

h  Two boy sopranos from the local *Gymnasium* were selected and specially trained to perform with the *Hofkapelle*.

# 11

# The Court of Würzburg

*Dieter Kirsch*

A PRINCIPAL DIFFERENCE between ecclesiastical governments and secular ones is the lack of dynastic succession. The consequences arising from this circumstance are illustrated, *pars pro toto*, by the Würzburg *Hofmusik*, an institution that continued to exist into the nineteenth century. The continual succession of rulers from different backgrounds prevented the ongoing pursuit of any specific long-term goals over the course of several reigns. This tendency was strengthened by the cathedral chapter, which, as the governing body, tended to let itself be guided by experiences gathered under the immediate predecessor when selecting a new ruler. Consequently, the prince-bishops who succeeded one another might hold entirely different, even contradictory interests, and this could affect the musical institutions of the court.

## THE SOURCES

During the bombing of Würzburg on 16 March 1945, great quantities of valuable primary sources were irretrievably lost, including the entire surviving musical repertory of the *Hofkapelle*, of which not even an inventory has been preserved. Important files from the State Archives, such as salary registers of the court servants, also went up in flames. Subsequently, given the decimation of the holdings, research in this area was hardly considered an encouraging prospect. On closer inspection, however, it became apparent that the pre-war researchers who were able to draw from the complete collection did not come close to uncovering all the sources: on the one hand, they appear to have overlooked a fair amount, while on the other, a meticulous examination of the sources undoubtedly required a great deal of time.

The untouched sources that do survive include, among others, the registration books for residents in the parishes of the Würzburg Diocese, as well as the civic property records ('Güterlagerbücher'), which provide information on house and land possession. In addition, extensive court files have recently emerged, such as those from the comprehensive collection of employee-related decrees issued by Prince-Bishop Adam Friedrich in 1758, and an exhaustive inventory of the court's musical instruments drawn up following the abdication of the last prince-bishop in 1802. The majority of these continue to be kept in the State Archives in Würzburg, while the State Archives in Bamberg hold material relevant to the periods during which these two dioceses were governed jointly. Furthermore, for the period under Bavarian rule during the nineteenth century, we can also draw upon isolated documents found in the collection of the Bavarian State Archives in Munich.

Until recently, Oskar Kaul's 1924 monograph *Geschichte der Würzburger Hofmusik im 18. Jahrhundert* was considered the fundamental scholarly work on the Würzburg court music establishment, and it continues to retain importance. Although Kaul's study was based on many documents that no longer exist, it has the disadvantage that he recorded very few source references. An attempt to remedy this deficiency was made by the present author in his *Lexikon Würzburger Hofmusiker*, which features an extensive chapter listing all available sources, including those that were cited by Kaul but are now lost.[1]

## FROM THE EARLIEST RECORDS
### TO THE EARLY EIGHTEENTH CENTURY

The earliest references to musicians at the prince-bishop's court in Würzburg can be found in the town's *Ratsakte* (council records) and *Steuerrechnungsbücher* (tax account books). From 1412 onwards, the wind players of the court were given an 'Opfergeld' (literally, offering money), presumably for their performance ushering in the New Year. As well, there is mention initially of the 'pfeiffern und büsewmer' (shawm and sackbut players, 1436), and later of 'Trumettern' (trumpeters, 1510 and 1609).[2]

From the sixteenth century onwards, the court's 'Standbücher' (an overview of employees according to rank) provide evidence of officially appointed organists; indeed, it is possible to trace an almost unbroken line of these from 1535, begin-

---

[1] Dieter Kirsch, *Lexikon Würzburger Hofmusiker vom 16. bis zum 19. Jahrhundert*, Quellen und Studien zur Musikgeschichte Würzburgs und Mainfrankens, 1 (Würzburg: Echter, 2002). The most important secondary literature includes Oskar Kaul, *Geschichte der Würzburger Hofmusik im 18. Jahrhundert* (Würzburg: Becker, 1924); Kaul, *Musica Herbipolensis: Aus Würzburgs musikalischer Vergangenheit*, ed. Frohmut Dangel-Hofmann (Marktbreit: Greß, 1980); Wilhelm Eckert, 'Fortunato Chelleri, sein Leben und Wirken besonders an den ehemaligen Höfen zu Würzburg und Kassel' (Diss., Universität Heidelberg, 1922); Andreas Scherf, *Johann Philipp Franz von Schönborn, Bischof von Würzburg (1719–24), der Erbauer der Residenz*, Schriftenreihe zur bayerischen Landesgeschichte, 4 (Munich: Verlag Kommission für bayerische Landesgeschichte, 1930); Fritz Zobeley, *Rudolf Franz Erwein Graf von Schönborn und seine Musikpflege*, ed. Gesellschaft für Fränkische Geschichte, Neujahrsblätter, 21 (Würzburg: Ferdinand Schöningh, 1949); Adam Gottron, *Mainzer Musikgeschichte von 1500 bis 1800*, Beiträge zur Geschichte der Stadt Mainz, 18 (Mainz: Stadtbibliothek Mainz, 1959); Burkhard von Roda, *Adam Friedrich von Seinsheim: Auftraggeber zwischen Rokoko und Klassizismus*, Veröffentlichungen der Gesellschaft für fränkische Geschichte, Ser. 8, 6 (Neustadt an der Aisch: Degener, 1880).

[2] D-WÜsa, Ratsakte 1436, No. 493, fol. 73$^r$; Steuerrechnungsbuch 1510, No. 9230, and 1609, No. 5537.

ning with the engagement of Johann Gerlach. An ensemble referred to by the term
'Cantorey' can first be verified through court accounts from the reign of Prince-
Bishop Julius Echter von Mespelbrunn (r. 1573–1617).[3] The *Kapellmeister* Gallus
Flaischberger (d. 1627) had under his command an organist, a player of the cornetto, a sackbut player, and five singers. With the exception of the organist, all carried out other duties at the court in addition to their musical responsibilities. Aside
from the three established positions of *Hoftrompeter*, organist, and *Kapellmeister*,
occasional references to courtly 'Musicanten' are found in court documents dating from the seventeenth century. Reinforcements were engaged on a short-term
basis as required from the ranks of civic musicians, choristers from Würzburg's
churches, school pupils, and students. When Emperor Ferdinand II visited the
town in September 1619 after his coronation in Frankfurt, '16 Knaben und Stu-
denten mit schönen Kleidern geziert mit allerley musicalischen Instrumenten'
(sixteen boys and students with a variety of musical instruments, wearing beautiful
clothes) performed at the *Ehrenpforte* (a triumphal arch).[4] Furthermore, during
the first quarter of the seventeenth century, the Jesuit academy entitled 'Academia
Juventute PP. Societatis Jesu' employed several court musicians to instruct their
students.[5] 'Fagot' players added a new tone colour when they joined the courtly
ensemble sometime prior to 1650, as shown by the civic *Steuerrechnungsbücher*.[6]
Even though the names of the latter performers, as well as those of individual court
vocalists and generic *Hofmusici*, appear in church registers and tax records, a significant Würzburg *Hofmusik* cannot be said to have existed during the seventeenth
century. At most, the number of the court trumpeters and kettledrum players
steadily increased: under Johann Gottfried von Guttenberg (r. 1684–98), six wind
players and a kettledrummer dined at the so-called *Rittertisch* (knights' table).[7]

As alluded to above, one particular feature regarding the history of the Würzburg *Hofmusik* in the eighteenth century requires mention here: during much
of this period, three Catholic prince-bishops governed not only the bishopric of
Würzburg, but also the neighbouring bishopric of Bamberg. As a result, under the
rule of Friedrich Carl von Schönborn (r. 1729–46) there were three possible contractual relationships for the court musicians: employment either in Würzburg, or
in Bamberg, or joint service in both places. Those engaged on the latter terms –
trumpeters and musical lackeys in particular – belonged to both courts and were
deployed in one place or the other, as required. This special relationship was dissolved in 1746 following the death of Schönborn, with the servants reassigned to

---

[3] D-WÜst, Standbuch 796, fol. 56[r-v].

[4] D-WÜsa, Ratsprotokoll 1619, p. 173.

[5] Cited in Carl Braun, 'Geschichte und Heranbildung des Klerus in der Diöcese Würzburg
seit ihrer Gründung bis zur Gegenwart', in *Festschrift zur dritten Säkularfeier des bischöflichen
Klerikalseminars ad Pastorem bonum*, I (Würzburg: Stürmer, 1889), 399.

[6] See, for example, the entry for the 'Fagot' player Georg Meggelein, who owned property
in the Bastheim quarter, in D-WÜst, Steuerrechnungsbuch 5680, or those for his colleague
Daniel Kempe in the Dietrich quarter, Steuerrechnungsbuch 5662 ff.

[7] D-WÜst, Historischer Verein, MS f. 680, 'Wie viel Tafel und Tisch bey Guttenbergisch,
Greiffenclau- und Schönbornischen Regierung gewesen'.

either one of the two courts. It is for this reason that Würzburg had at its disposal eight trumpeters and two kettledrum players in 1745, but no more than four trumpeters and a single kettledrum player in 1746. Under Adam Friedrich von Seinsheim (r. 1755–79), the two bishoprics were administered separately. And even if the key personnel of both *Kapellen* were deployed between the two in a reciprocal fashion, they remained clearly attached to one court or the other. This separation was also retained under Franz Ludwig von Erthal (r. 1779–95), but his lack of interest in music made such mutual service superfluous.

COURT MUSIC UNDER
JOHANN PHILIPP II VON GREIFFENCLAU (R. 1699–1719)
AND JOHANN PHILIPP FRANZ VON SCHÖNBORN (R. 1719–24)

The appointment of court organist Johann Andreas Degen (1657–1700) as *Kapellmeister* on 1 February 1700, early in the reign of Johann Philipp II (1652–1719), immediately signalled that more attention would be given to music at the Würzburg court. A detailed document (now lost, but reproduced by Kaul) lists the duties for which the *Kapellmeister* was responsible as organist, musical director, composer, custodian of music, and music teacher. But because of Degen's untimely death in June 1700 few of these responsibilities had been put into action; instead, it was the task of his successor, the clergyman Johann Martin Fegelein, who directed the *Hofmusik* until 1722, to uphold the regulations. The clause that 'er sich ständig bemühen, und auch eiffrigst angelegen seyn lassen solle, etwas neues bey die Handt zu bringen' (he should endeavour continually, and also assiduously concern himself with having something new at hand) illustrates that having up-to-date music for his court was clearly of some importance to the prince-bishop.[8] However, superb performances could hardly be expected from his *Hofkapelle* in the years around 1715, given that it was only sufficiently staffed to carry out its duties in the chapel (see Table 11.1, pp. 324–30 below). Remarkably, with the exception of the court trumpeters, the *Kapellmeister*, and the organist, all musicians also held other court positions, as is evident from personnel lists and court 'Standbücher'. Moreover, no singers' names are recorded, which implies that external reinforcements were necessary. The *Hofkapelle* of this time does not appear to have been a major burden on the household budget: from 1683 the annual costs for employing the court musicians ('Uncosten, welche auf die Hoff Musicos Jährlich verwendet werden') were reported as 1,152 *Gulden*, plus payments in kind.[9]

Life at the court became more lavish when Johann Philipp Franz von Schönborn (1673–1724) was elevated to the bishopric in 1719. Sophisticated, thoroughly educated, and a practising musician whose taste had been formed by Italian music

[8] Cited in Kaul, *Geschichte der Würzburger Hofmusik*, 14.

[9] D-WÜst, Domkapitelprotokolle 1683, p. 275. The *Naturalien* (payments in kind) comprised 4 *Malter* of grain and 4 *Malter* 'Küchenspeise' (a generic dish prepared by the court kitchen for employees), as well as 3 *Fuder* and 6 *Eimer* of wine.

while studying abroad as a young man, he adopted the principle, hitherto customary only at major courts, that through the deliberate promotion and fostering of
the arts his reign would be seen to have far-reaching influence.[10] The building of
a prestigious residence and the founding of a genuine court musical establishment
are the most conspicuous expressions of this endeavour.[11]

The ambitions of the prince-bishop's musical plans are apparent in his engagement of musicians from Italy, presumably with the intention of maintaining an
ensemble that could compete successfully with the best *Hofkapellen* on the Con-
tinent. The order of their appointments can be verified by extant decrees: the Italians Giovanni Francesco Benedetti (bass singer and *Cammermusicus*) and Carlo
Ricciarelli (alto) joined in 1721.[12] The following year, the bass singer Girolamo Bassano, the soprano Anna Maria Elisabetha Belotti (Pilotti; d. 1742), the vocalist and
copyist Carlo Antonio Capellani, *Kapellmeister* Fortunato Chelleri (1687–1757),
the oboists Giovanni Benedetto Platti (1697–1763) and Schiavonetto (jun.), the
alto Raphaele Signorini, and the cellist Giovanni Baptista Schiavonetto (d. 1730)
were hired. In 1723, the bass singer Filippo Ricchini arrived, followed by the tenor
and *Cammermusicus* Francesco Ambrosini in 1724. Two years earlier, according to the appointment decree, the French flautist and bassoonist Louis D'Etry
(D'Etri) was engaged. Other recruits who joined in 1720 included the bassoonist
Gottfried Carbach (d. 1728) and the viola da gamba player Johann Daniel Hardt
(1696–1763). In 1722, the violinist Johann Gottfried Vogler, the lutenist August
Wilhelm Heinrich Gleitsmann (1698–1756), and the oboist and copyist Johann
Hummel (1684–1764) were appointed; a year later, the court welcomed the violin-
ist and 'Studiosus' Johann Aull (b. 1700) and the vocalist Maria Theresia Platti.
The number of *Hoftrompeter* also increased, having been recruited in pairs: Johann
Zacharias Glatte and Johann Sigmundi arrived in 1720, while two years later, Jakob
Jaros und Anton Lippmann came to Würzburg from Vienna.[13]

Apart from the retention of musicians who had been employed by his predecessors, Johann Philipp Franz engaged exclusively 'Ausländer' (foreigners, to use
eighteenth-century terminology), as opposed to 'Inländer' (locals), a term which
applied only to those who lived within the diocese. This course of action emphasizes
the ruler's demand for quality, as do the varying levels of salary offered in contracts.
Thus, 1,000 *Reichsthaler* was paid to *Kapellmeister* Chelleri and to the vocalist
Signorini, as well as to the entire Schiavonetto (Schiavonetti) family (that is, the
vocalist Belotti (Pilotti), her husband, and son), who had been appointed *in toto*.[14]

[10] Particularly formative was a three-year period of study, together with his brother Friedrich Carl, at the Collegium Germanicum in Rome between 1690 and 1693; later travels took
him to political centres such as The Hague, Vienna, London, and Paris; see Scherf, *Johann
Philipp Franz von Schönborn*, 3 ff.

[11] The palace, designed by Balthasar Neumann, is today a UNESCO World Heritage Site.

[12] On appointments made during Johann Philipp Franz's tenure, see specifically D-WÜst,
Historischer Verein, MS f. 675/11, 'ältere Hof Music Decreta besonders sub Celmo Joanne
Philippo Francisco'.

[13] For additional information on all Würzburg court musicians, including those later in
service, see Kirsch, *Lexikon Würzburger Hofmusiker.*

[14] D-WÜst, Historischer Verein, MS f. 675/11, decrees dated 2 July 1722. [Editors' note: Cf.

In many letters to his relatives, the prince-bishop proudly included reports regarding 'his' Italians, who in 1722 and 1724 had accompanied him on trips to the spa town of Schlangenbad near Wiesbaden, an extravagance that surely excited the attention and admiration he so desired.[15] It is likely that they would have played Italian music during such visits, since *Kapellmeister* Chelleri and the virtuoso Platti were in charge of selecting compositions to entertain their employer on special occasions.[16] The prince-bishop's personal interest in ensuring the best working conditions for his musicians is also evident in several other decisions. As early as 1719 — the first year of his reign — he had transferred his own private collection of valuable musical instruments to the court and appointed Norbert Gedler as the first 'Hofgeigenmacher' (court luthier) to maintain the increased number of instruments.[17] In addition, Johann Philipp Franz ensured the ongoing professional education of his *Kapelle* members. In 1723, he sent the violinist Vogler to Italy and ordered *Kapellmeister* Chelleri, together with the famous architect Balthasar Neumann, to travel to Mannheim, 'dasigen Hoff und vornehmen Baw [zu sehen und] die so sehr gerühmte churfürstliche music zu höhren' (to see the court and the noble building [that is, the residential palace] there, and hear the much praised electoral music [*Hofmusik*]).[18]

Johann Philipp Franz von Schönborn, who had 'newen musique zimblich ursach zufrieden zu seyn' (every reason to be satisfied with [his] new *Hofmusik*), appears to have appointed his musicians more for chamber music — that is for secular purposes — rather than as a *Hofkapelle* for sacred music.[19] The few performance-related references that can be found (mostly in diaries of court quartermasters) mention pastorales, concertos, and serenatas that were presented to special guests during or after meals.[20] Only once is an oratorio referred to, even though musical performances at the cathedral were, naturally, part of the *Hofmusik*'s duties, especially when the prince-bishop celebrated high mass himself.[21] To that end, he

---

Chapter 6, 'The Court of Württemberg-Stuttgart', p. 174 n. 40 above, for a reference regarding further information on the violoncellist Giovanni Baptista Schiavonetti (d. 1730), his wife, soprano Elisabetta Pilotti-Schiavonetti (d. 1742), and their oboe-playing son.]

[15] See Zobeley, *Rudolf Franz Erwein Graf von Schönborn*, 43 ff.

[16] More than seventy works by Platti that were composed within the surroundings of the Würzburg court, above all the works for violoncello, are extant in the library of Count Rudolf Franz Erwein von Schönborn (1677–1754). See Fritz Zobeley and Frohmut Dangel-Hofmann, eds., *Die Musikalien der Grafen von Schönborn-Wiesentheid*, 3 vols. (Tutzing: Hans Schneider, 1967–92).

[17] On Gedler, see Dieter Kirsch, 'Füssener Lauten- und Geigenmacher in Würzburg', *Musik in Bayern*, 51 (1955), 27–40, at 14 ff.

[18] D-WÜst, Bausachen 355, vol. I/1, p. 14, 3 January 1723. See also Chapter 5, 'The Palatine Court in Mannheim', pp. 131–62 above.

[19] Letter of Johann Philipp Franz to his brother Rudolf Franz Erwein, 9 June 1722, cited in Zobeley, *Rudolf Franz Erwein Graf von Schönborn*, 45.

[20] D-WÜst, Historischer Verein, MSS f. 205, q. 176 a–d.

[21] For the reference to an oratorio, see the letter of *Hofrat* Fichtl to Rudolf Franz Erwein, March 1724, cited in Zobeley, *Rudolf Franz Erwein Graf von Schönborn*, 47.

had a separate podium built in the cathedral in order that both the music and its performers might be better presented.[22]

The sudden death of Johann Philipp Franz during a hunt, on 18 August 1724, brought the short-lived splendour of his *Hofmusik* to an abrupt end. Schönborn's lavish court had always been a thorn in the side of the cathedral chapter, which was responsible for governance during the interim period. Now it had the opportunity to implement changes, and so promptly took drastic measures. On 18 September 1724, the cathedral chapter decided to inform all court musicians

> daß man nunmehro nichtß mehr Versprechen könte, darumben sie sich selbsten zu berathen hätten, ob Es ihnen Vorträglicher seye, bey dem nächst künfftigen neuen Regenten hinwiederum zu Suppliciren, oder ihre fortun anderweitig zu suchen.

> that they [the chapter members] were no longer in the position to promise anything; therefore, they [the musicians] were to discuss among themselves whether they would rather, on the one hand, make a petition to the future new ruler, or, on the other, seek their fortune elsewhere.[23]

The news of the *Hofmusik*'s dissolution spread quickly. Under the heading 'Obitus celsissimi Principis Herbipolensis' (the death of His Most Serene Highness, the Prince-Bishop of Würzburg), the provost of the Unterzell monastery noted in his minute-book,

> Es erfolgte bei sothanem interregno eine gewaltige Änderung bey Hoff unter den Bedienten: Alle Hofmusicanten wurden cassiret, die Schantzarbeit und Bau an der Fortification und Residenz eingestellet, die Schatzung auf ein Simplum reduciret, die vile[n] Mundköch dimittiret, alle Jagten eingestellet ...

> A tremendous change in the court's workforce occurred during the interim period: all court musicians were released; the work on digging of trenches and the construction of the fortification and palace came to a halt; the levies were reduced to the bare minimum; several of the personal chefs were dismissed, [and] all hunts ceased ...[24]

## THE REIGNS OF CHRISTOPH FRANZ VON HUTTEN (R. 1724–29) AND FRIEDRICH CARL VON SCHÖNBORN (R. 1729–46)

The restrictions imposed by the cathedral chapter were continued with a similar determination by the newly elected prince-bishop, Christoph Franz von Hutten (1673–1729). As a consequence of the rigorous cost-cutting measures, Platti and

---

[22] D-WÜst, Domkapitelprotokolle 1724, pp. 227–8.

[23] Ibid., p. 272.

[24] Cited in Maria Fischer-Flach and Wolfgang Fischer, *Protokollbuch des Frauenklosters Unterzell bei Würzburg* (Würzburg: Echter, 1987), 199.

Bassano were the only Italian musicians who remained in Würzburg, having been
re-employed at lower salaries.[25] All other Italians had probably left the *Hofkapelle*
by 1724. Hardt and D'Etry sought their fortunes at the court in Stuttgart in 1724
and 1727 respectively. In 1725, the oboist Hummel returned to Ansbach, and the
violinist Vogler went to Darmstadt; *Kapellmeister* Chelleri had already left for
Kassel in 1724. Those musicians who stayed behind on reduced salaries would have
been more than sufficient to provide the mandatory sacred music. This would have
suited the ruler perfectly, as he cared little for music. Thus, the once promising and
ambitious project of establishing an Italian-dominated *Hofmusik* in Würzburg that
was capable of competing successfully with *Hofkapellen* at other major courts had
been reduced to next to nothing.

When the brother of Johann Philipp Franz, Friedrich Carl von Schönborn
(1674–1746), first ascended to the bishopric of Bamberg in 1729, and, shortly
thereafter, that of Würzburg as well, conditions for the cultivation of courtly art
and culture took a turn for the better. The new ruler had a particular liking for
Italian music, a fondness he had shared with his older brother and which they had
developed during their three-year stay at the Collegium Germanicum in Rome
(1690–93). Moreover, during his lengthy term as imperial vice-chancellor in Vienna from 1704 to 1734, Friedrich Carl was able to observe closely the magnificent
display of ceremonial and musical splendour of the Viennese court. Given such
models, he considered an accomplished *Hofkapelle* to be an indispensable part
of his household (see Table 11.1, 1730). However, to be able to pay for the costly
ongoing work on the residential palace, Friedrich Carl was forced to find a more
economical solution in order to maintain his *Hofmusik*.[26]

A decree issued on 15 January 1732 requested clarification on four important
points that concerned the *Hofmusik*:

1mo In welchen Personen diese bestehe, was jeder tractire und zur besoldung habe
2do welche aus dero fürstl. Würzburg. privat oder dermahlig gemeinschafft-
lichen Hoff Musique tüchtig zu würcklichen und was für Diensten,
oder welche nicht tüchtig seyen
3tio Was sonderlich an denen Stimmen abgehe und
4to wie solche ohne große Kostbahrkeit beygebracht und zum Teil pro
futuro wohl könnten dahier gelehret werden

1. Which persons it comprises, what each one plays, and what salaries they
have
2. Which persons from the princely Würzburg private or formerly joint

25 See D-WÜst, Historischer Verein, MS f. 675. Platti's salary was lowered from 600 to 400
*Gulden*, Bassano's from 720 to 580 *Gulden*.
26 According to Richard Sedlmaier and Rudolf Pfister, *Die fürstbischöfliche Residenz zu
Würzburg* (Munich: Georg Müller, 1923), 66, at the beginning of Friedrich Carl's reign the
construction costs amounted to approximately 296,000 *Gulden*; by the time the building was
finished, the amount had increased to 1,564,000 *Gulden*.

*Hofmusik* are capable of actual service and of what kind, and which persons are not capable of this

3. Which [instrumental or vocal] parts are particularly lacking, and
4. How these can be provided without spending a fortune and could possibly in part be taught here in the future.[27]

The details of matters relating to this review were, as with all music-related issues, handled by the prince-bishop's confidante, the 'Cammer-Herr' (chamberlain) Joseph Anton Komareck, who had come with him from Vienna. The list of court musicians prepared by Komareck in 1732 comprised twenty-five persons, including a court organ builder, a *Hofgeigenmacher*, and a *Calcant*.[28] Remarkably, *Kapellmeister* Wolfgang Händler (1694–1738) did not draw the highest salary, but rather the 'Virtuos Platti', who was paid twice as much, at 400 *Gulden*. Furthermore, Platti received additional income due to his duties as 'Cammer Tenorist' and second violinist. In accordance with the decree made by 'Celsissimus' (the prince-bishop) that all available forces were to be instructed in music, Platti was also remunerated for singing lessons given not only to boy trebles, but also to young girls.[29]

Friedrich Carl must have pursued his goal of involving as many of his court servants as possible for musical purposes right from the start of his reign. Upon his arrival in Würzburg in 1729 there had already been '7 Laquayen welche alle Musicanten außer Einem so ein Sattler gewesen' (seven lackeys who were all musicians except for one who was a saddler) included in his entourage, as noted by the court quartermaster Anton Glaser.[30] For a modest bonus payment ranging from 10 to 50 *Gulden* depending on their abilities, these individuals were obliged to serve with the *Hofmusik* as well as carrying out their own duties.[31] Some of the court musicians were similarly versatile, as is evident from entries in court minutes and 'Standbücher'. Thus, the lutenist Gleitsmann worked as secretary and translator, the musician Fegelein served simultaneously as court chaplain, and the violinist Wolff was also employed as the court's dancing master. Other musicians carried out clerical duties, such as the tenor Johann Baptist Roth, for example, while his colleague Georg Sebald, a violinist, served as a 'Schanzschreiber' (scribe serving the fortification works), and the bass singer Johann Georg Ley worked as *répétiteur* of the court's page boys.[32]

That the prince-bishop's plans for the expansion of the *Hofmusik* were followed through with is illustrated by a draft prepared by Komareck in 1740. He states that 'Zur Errichtung einer Compendiosesten Hoff-Capell oder Kirchen-Musique

[27] D-WÜst, Historischer Verein, MS f. 675/11.
[28] Reproduced in Kirsch, *Lexikon Würzburger Hofmusiker*, 11–12.
[29] D-WÜst, Historischer Verein, MS f. 675/1, decree dated 15 January 1732.
[30] D-WÜst, Historischer Verein, MS f. 30a, fol. 32ᵛ, 'Unterschiedliche Begebenheiten'.
[31] See Kirsch, *Lexikon Würzburger Hofmusiker*; cf. the entries on the lackeys Georg Kummerer, Paul Niemand, Adam Rupert, Johann Tilscher, Caspar Tritt, and Bernhard Ulrich, to name but a few examples.
[32] From 1750 on, Ley is listed as such in the court calendars; the majority of the latter are extant in D-WÜd.

werden erfordert' (For the establishment of a well-appointed *Hofkapelle* or church music [the following] are required):

| | |
|---|---|
| 1 Organista | 1 organist |
| 1 Tiorbista | 1 theorbist |
| 2 Violoncelli | 2 violoncellos |
| 2 Fagotti | 2 bassoons |
| 1 Violon | 1 *Violon* [string bass] |
| 3 Soprani | 3 sopranos |
| 3 Altisten | 3 altos |
| 3 Tenoristen | 3 tenors |
| 3 Baßisten | 3 bass singers |
| 4 zum Violino 1^mo | 4 for the 1st violin |
| 3 zum Violino 2^do | 3 for the 2nd violin |
| 2 zur Brazzia | 2 for the viola |
| 2 zur Oboe 1^mo | 2 for the 1st oboe |
| 2 zur Oboe 2^do | 2 for the 2nd oboe |
| 1 zum Cornu 1^mo | 1 for the 1st horn |
| 1 zum Cornu 2^do | 1 for the 2nd horn |
| 2 Posaunisten | 2 trombones |
| _____ | _____ |
| 36 Persohnen | 36 persons[33] |

Friedrich Carl's policy of austerity also made an impact on the court trumpeters. Despite being protected by an imperial privilege, at the time of their appointment they also now committed themselves 'nach erfordernus zur Kirchen- und Hof-Music williglich gebrauchen zu lassen' (to participate willingly in church and court music when required) on the other instruments on which they were proficient.[34] In spite of his ongoing commitment to cutting costs, the prince-bishop demonstrated generosity when it came to the professional development of his musicians. He willingly financed study trips, sending the boy soprano Busch to Vienna, and the violinist Georg Wenzel Bisetsky and the tenor Johann Georg Laudensack to Italy (see Table 11.1, 1745).[35] That music director Komareck was able to realize his plans for expansion can be seen in the personnel list of the Würzburg *Hofkapelle* published by Lorenz Christoph Mizler in his *Musikalische Bibliothek* (1746).[36] It provides the names of thirty-six individuals, among them many servants normally employed in other capacities at court, as well as a fair number of military musicians, all of whom were committed to playing with the *Hofmusik*, plus 'acht Trompeter und zwey Pauker, zusammen sechs und vierzig Personen' (eight trumpeters and two kettledrum players, [making] altogether forty-six persons).

---

[33] D-WÜst, Historischer Verein, MS f. 675/1, draft dated 20 January 1740.

[34] For the exact wording of the decree for *Hoftrompeter* Meergraf, see Kirsch, *Lexikon Würzburger Hofmusiker*, 138.

[35] See the relevant entries ibid.

[36] Lorenz Christoph Mizler, *Musikalische Bibliothek*, III/2 (Leipzig, 1746), 364 ff.

Insight into the repertoire of this 'compendiosesten *Hoff-Capell*' is provided by a 'Catalogus Deren Hoff Musicalien, So Unter glorreicher Regierung Sr Hoch-fürstl: Gnaden Friderici Caroli ... ab Anno 1730 biß Annum 1746 beygeschafft ... worden' (Catalogue of the court music which had been acquired during the glorious reign of his Most Princely Grace Friedrich Carl [von Schönborn] ... from 1730 until 1746).[37] Although it records only one-third of the compositions purchased jointly for Bamberg and Würzburg, it is possible nevertheless to detect a certain bias. Two-thirds are sacred works, including oratorios, mass settings, offertories, settings of Vespers, and motets, while the remaining third comprises secular works, above all serenatas and cantatas. A similar ratio is noticeable regarding the nationalities of the composers represented: twenty-eight are Italian, while fourteen are of German or Austrian origin. In addition to major local figures such as Georg Waß-muth, Wolfgang Händler, and Fortunato Chelleri, these composers were primarily musicians who had been active at the Viennese imperial court, including Fux, Conti, Caldara, Porpora, and Reutter – a sign of just how much the musical taste of the prince-bishop of Bamberg and Würzburg had been shaped by his thirty-year tenure as imperial vice-chancellor.

## COURT MUSIC UNDER
## ANSELM FRANZ VON INGELHEIM (R. 1746–49)
## AND CARL PHILIPP VON GREIFFENCLAU (R. 1749–54)

With the death of Friedrich Carl von Schönborn and the election of his successor, Anselm Franz von Ingelheim (1683–1749), came a problem that would also affect the *Hofmusik*. Since both Franconian dioceses were now once again each to be governed by their own ruler, the furniture and personnel of the combined households had to be divided. The music, musical instruments, and musicians were distributed according to a formula according to which two thirds went to Würzburg and one third to Bamberg. The financial consequences of the 'Schönbornischen Bau-wurmbs' (the Schönborns' obsession with building) also prompted the new ruler to carry out a 'Bestallungs-Moderation' (a regulation of appointments), which would affect above all the better-paid musicians.[38]

Anselm Franz's brief, three-year tenure left behind little of any lasting significance. One exception, however, was the *Hoff-, Stands- und Staats-Calender*, an annually revised, printed handbook listing all court offices and their associated personnel, which he introduced in 1747. From the time of its inception until 1802,

---

[37] See Dieter Kirsch, 'Das Bamberger Drittel: Zum Repertoire der Würzburger und Bamberger Hofmusik unter Fürstbischof Friedrich Carl von Schönborn (1729–46)', in *Im Dienst der Quellen zur Musik: Festschrift für Gertraut Haberkamp zum 65. Geburtstag* (Tutzing: Hans Schneider, 2002), 39–56.

[38] Zobeley, *Rudolf Franz Erwein Graf von Schönborn*, 43. [Editors' note: 'Schönbornischen Bauwurmbs' was a phrase used by members of the Schönborn family; it translates literally as 'the Schörnborns' building worm' – more idiomatically, 'the Schönborns' building bug']. Regarding the 'Bestallungs-Moderation', see D-WÜst, Hofkammerprotokoll 1746, fol. 767ʳ.

this publication included the *Hofmusik* in its various configurations. Its listing appears after the 'Hoff-Ku[e]chen-Ambt' (court kitchen office), an order which reflects the musicians' relatively insignificant rank under Anselm Franz von Ingelheim.

Carl Philipp von Greiffenclau (1690–1754) likewise achieved little of positive consequence for the *Hofmusik*. At least, he managed to bring the construction work on the residential palace to a close in 1753, but only by reducing expenditure in other areas. In that same year, after deeming the annual outlay for the *Hofmusik* too high at 11,000 *Gulden*, the prince-bishop instructed *Kapellmeister* Waßmuth to cut costs. To that end, a series of strict measures was devised which prescribed:

1) daß der oder diejenige Virtuosen, welcher oder welche jenige Dienste in der Music nicht mehr leisten, zu denen solche angenommen worden, oder wer sonsten von der Music ausser Stand zu dienen kommet, auf den halben Sold, von nun an, und also künfftig hin ebenmäßig gesezet, soforth der solcher gestalten eingehende halbe Sold der Person angewiesen werden solle, welche zu der wiederbestellung dieser Diensten anzunehmen ist.

2) daß derjenige Virtuos oder Musicus, welcher Von einer prob oder Music ohne genügliche Ursach, und ohne deren Vorgängige anzeig bey dem Capellenmeister ausbleibet, um den Betrag der ganzen bestallung für 1 Monath Von dem Capellenmeistern gestrafet, und mit gleicher Straf

3) auch jene angesehen und beleget werden, welche dem Capellenmeistern in seinen amts handlungen ungebührlich widerstehen, oder sonsten nachlässig in der Übung der Music sich erfinden lassen.

4) die solcher gestalten fallenden Strafgelder nach abgezogenen ⅓ alß welcher dem Capellenmeistern zu verbleiben hat, unter die Vor anderen mehr fleissige Jeden Jahrs Vertheilet werden sollen.

5) daß die unter denen banden deren Regimentern stehende mehr tüchtige Musici (so Viel deren zur Hof-Music noch nöthig seyn wollen) zu solcher beygezogen und darmit weiter befähiget, dagegen auch deren jedem monathlich 1 fl rh [*Rheinischer Gulden*] zulaag gereichet, und so dann diese zu seiner zeit nach Ihrem Wohlverhalten zu Hofbedienten angenohmen, dagegen

6) die anderweit sich erledigende derley sonders gebrödete Musicanten-Stellen nicht wiederum besetzet, wann jedoch

7) deren Ein oder der andere ferner aufzustellen wäre, von dem Capellenmeister nach genohmener Prob der pflichtmäsige Vorschlag jedes mahlen erstattet werden solle, und solchergestalten

8) wie Seine Hochfürstl. Gnaden dem Capellenmeister die Obsorg und Direction der Music überlassen, Er auch für deren gute bestellung hafften solle;

Als wird sothane S.er Hochfürstl. Gnaden höchste anordnung Ihm Capellenmeistern zu seiner nachachtung in gnaden hiermit ohnverhalten. Decretum Würtzburg den 4. Martij 1753.

1) That one or all of those virtuosos who can no longer carry out the musical duties for which they were first appointed, as well as those who are no longer able to serve as musicians, shall receive only half their salary from now on, and it shall remain at that level; the other half shall be assigned immediately to the person who has to be hired to carry out those duties.

2) that the virtuoso or *Musicus* who fails to report for a rehearsal or a musical performance without sufficient reason, and without informing the *Kapellmeister* in advance, will be penalized by the *Kapellmeister* the amount of one month's salary [including payments in kind]; and that same penalty

3) shall be applied to those who oppose the *Kapellmeister*'s official decisions in an improper manner, or who are found to be neglectful in their musical practice.

4) that such penalties which are ordered shall be distributed annually among those who are more diligent, following the subtraction of one third [of the full amount] which is to remain with the *Kapellmeister*.

5) that the more capable *Musici* who are members of the regimental bands (in as much as they are still required for the *Hofmusik*) shall continue to participate [in the latter]; and for this each of them shall receive a monthly bonus of 1 *Rheinischer Gulden*, and if their conduct is good, shall be engaged as court servants in due course.

6) that other vacant positions of musicians that are currently funded by other sources shall not be filled again, except when

7) one or the other should be considered for appointment, [then,] in each case, after having undertaken an audition, the *Kapellmeister* shall be required to present the recommendation [to the court], and inasmuch as

8) His Most Princely Grace entrusts the *Kapellmeister* with the care and direction of the *Hofmusik*, this also includes the responsibility for making suitable appointments.

The above highest decree of His Most Princely Grace is herewith graciously presented to the *Kapellmeister* for compliance. Decree Würzburg, 4 May 1753.[39]

Despite these financial restrictions, Carl Philipp appears to have nevertheless indulged his penchant for music featuring brass instruments. The trumpeters and *Waldhornisten* were ordered to perform daily during mealtimes, as noted by the court quartermaster Spielberger in his diary on 1 April 1750.[40] These instrumentalists were also the only group of musicians that increased in number during Carl Philipp's tenure. The horn parts, played initially by three lackeys, were eventually performed by four properly appointed court musicians. Moreover, the court calendars reveal that the number of trumpeters rose from four to seven.[41]

---

39 D-WÜst, Historischer Verein, MS f. 679, 'Conferenz Protocoll de 26ten Februarij 1753'.
40 D-WÜst, Historischer Verein, MS q. 176c, fol. 25ʳ.
41 See D-WÜd, court calendar from 1751, p. 51. The *Hoftrompeter* Schädel, Meergraf, Göp-

## THE *HOFMUSIK* UNDER
## ADAM FRIEDRICH VON SEINSHEIM (R. 1755–79)

When Adam Friedrich von Seinsheim (1708–1779) was elected prince-bishop of Würzburg in 1755 and bishop of Bamberg two years later, both dioceses were once again governed by one ruler whose veins ran with Schönborn blood (from the maternal side). And even though Adam Friedrich, unlike his two Schönborn predecessors, lacked practical musical knowledge, the art of music was a pleasure he could not do without. He was particularly partial to opera and relied on his brother Count Joseph Franz (1707–1787), who resided in Munich, to keep him informed regarding recent trends. The prince-bishop's remark, 'In meinem Sinn seynd die Opern die schönste[n] Spectacles' (in my opinion, operas are the most beautiful spectacles) reflects his genuine interest in this art form.[42] No wonder, then, that he fulfilled his own dream of having a theatre built in Würzburg's residential palace: at first in the 'Fürstensaal', and from 1770, in the palace's 'Nordoval' (today the *Nordoval-Galeriesaal*, or North Oval Gallery Hall). Moreover, in order to avoid having to do without his 'angenehmste Unterhaltung' (most pleasing entertainment) while in Bamberg, he had a garden theatre installed at his 'Marquardsburg', Schloß Seehof.[43]

Like Friedrich Carl, the new prince-bishop placed great emphasis on the comprehensive education of his musicians, with Italy remaining the measure of all things in this respect. Musicians sent there included the violinist Lorenz Joseph Schmitt (1737–1796), and the vocalists Anna Catharina Bayer (1738–1793) and Anna Catharina Laudensack (d. 1756, in Italy). Adam Friedrich also had the violinist Aloys Fracassini (c.1733–1798) and the vocalists Aloys Costa and Domenico Steffani (1738–1782) recruited from Italy. Steffani, a tenor, who had previously served as vocal teacher at the Ospedale della Pietà in Venice, was destined to lead theatrical performances to new heights. According to a short biography of the singer, 'Man gab nichts als italienische Stücke und Stephani, der ein Liebling Adam Friedrichs war, dirigierte diese Musiken mit unermüdlichstem Fleiße, und verdient wirklich die Stütze dieses Theaters genennet zu werden' (Nothing but Italian pieces were presented, and Stephani [*sic*], who was a favourite of Adam Friedrich, directed these musical performances with tireless effort, and truly deserves to be called the pillar of this theatre).[44] Indeed, it is possible to talk of a 'Würzburg School' with Steffani at the helm, which produced such renowned figures as the siblings Sabina (1752–1829) and Felicitas Ritz (1756–?, later Hayne), and Sabina Renk (1755–1817, later Hitzelberger). A further Italian engaged by the court was the dancing master

fert, Baßing, Ringelmann, Andreas, and Paulus Ritz (Rietz) are listed in the category 'Hof-Fourier-Amt' (office of the court quartermaster).

[42] Cited in Roda, *Adam Friedrich von Seinsheim*, 86.

[43] See also Emil Marschalk von Ostheim, *Die Bamberger Hof-Musik unter den drei letzten Fürstbischöfen* (Bamberg: Hübscher, 1885), 4 ff.

[44] In *Artistisch-Literarische Blätter von und für Franken*, ed. Bartholomäus von Siebold (Würzburg: C. P. Bonitas, 1808), 18.

Antonio Voltelino, who was required 'mit und nebst seiner Frau zu gleichmäßiger Producirung seiner Künste auf dem fürstlichen Hoftheater sich gebrauchen zu lassen' (to display his art regularly at the princely court theatre [both] by himself and with his wife).[45] Thus, everything was arranged so that the prince-bishop and his court, as well as his own subjects, could be entertained with musical and theatrical performances – for the cosmopolitan and philanthrophic Adam Friedrich had expressly made his two theatres open to the public.

The Würzburg *Hofmusik* was now in an excellent state, thanks to both the training offered on-site and the targeted recruitment of new personnel. New instrumental colours had also been added to the ensemble in the form of the transverse flute and the clarinet.[46] That the position of *Kapellmeister* remained vacant after Waßmuth's death in 1766 appears not to have been considered a deficiency. His duties were carried out by concertmaster Lorenz Schmitt in Würzburg and by Aloys Fracassini in Bamberg. For important occasions and the particularly favoured operatic performances, the leading members of both *Hofkapellen* were brought together, with productions premiered at the Würzburg palace repeated in the gardens of Schloß Seehof.[47] During the reign of Friedrich Carl von Schönborn the court had begun to move away from paying its musicians in accordance with an assessment of their level of performance. A trend can be discerned towards standardizing salaries for members of individual instrumental sections, but also among the vocalists.[48] This, however, did not prevent Adam Friedrich from making exceptions for musicians in whom he took a special interest. For example, he decreed that the salaries of the horn virtuoso Punto (Johann Wenzel Stich, 1746–1803) and the trumpeter Joseph Anton Bauer would be 708 and 520 *Gulden* respectively – amounts that were much higher than the average wage.[49] Moreover, the prince-bishop initially paid the clarinettists Martin Heßler and Stephan Blum from his privy purse, and also gave 600 *Gulden* to the heirs of *Kapellmeister* Waßmuth in order to acquire for Würzburg the disputed rights to the latter's compositions.[50]

In total, Waßmuth had composed 282 works for the Würzburg court, as revealed in negotiations with his heirs. Among them were probably numerous sacred works, but also compositions for specific occasions, as is evident from extant librettos commemorating the ordination of a new prince-bishop or wedding celebrations of his relatives. These also included other secular works such as burlesques and serenatas with primarily Italian texts which were translated into German by the

---

[45]  D-WÜst, Historischer Verein, MS f. 675/11, decree dated 1 March 1770.

[46]  D-WÜd, court calendar from 1764, pp. 62 and 67.

[47]  Unfortunately, virtually no repertoire from the prince-bishop's theatre remains extant, the sole exceptions being *La cantata e disfida di Don Trastullo* by Jommelli, presented on 16 February 1768 for the prince-bishop's birthday, and *Il barone di Torre Forte* by Joseph Willibald Michl, as well as *La finta giardinera* by Anfossi in August 1774. See Kirsch, *Lexikon Würzburger Hofmusiker*, 70–71.

[48]  See especially D-WÜst, Historischer Verein, MSS f. 675/1, 11; Standbuch 805.

[49]  D-WÜst, Historischer Verein, MSS f. 675/1, 11, decrees dated 22 May 1774 and 1 February 1764.

[50]  D-WÜst, Historischer Verein, MS f. 675/11, decree dated 22 January 1763; Hofkammer-protokoll 1767, pp. 585–6.

court lutenist Gleitsmann.[51] The music-loving prince-bishop's favourite was and continued to be opera, which had found a small, but exquisite centre of cultivation at the Würzburg residence.

## CONCLUSION

Although the history of the Würzburg *Hofmusik* came to an end only in the mid-nineteenth century, it is possible to assess its changing fortunes and dependence on the musical tastes of the respective prince-bishops.[52] After an era of great support for the musical life of Würzburg by Johann Philipp Franz von Schönborn (r. 1719–24), Friedrich Carl von Schönborn (r. 1729–46), and Adam Friedrich von Seinsheim (r. 1755–79), the *Hofmusik* immediately suffered. The length of an individual prince-bishop's tenure ultimately determined the extent to which the *Hofkapelle*'s performance standards increased or decreased. Furthermore, there can be no doubt that Adam Friedrich von Seinsheim deserves special credit for making it possible for musical theatre to flourish during the twenty-four years he governed, and for first opening his two theatres in Würzburg and Bamberg to the public.

Despite the various contingencies faced by the court musicians due to changing employers, a number of consistent features can be identified throughout this period. The court trumpeters, who belonged to a guild protected by an imperial privilege, were always administered separately from the *Hofkapelle*, at least until 1802. The trumpeters reported to the quartermaster's office, which was also in charge of the musical lackeys, whereas the court musicians' immediate superior was the *Hofkapellmeister* or music director. When, from the 1730s, trumpeters and lackeys were ordered to serve with the *Hofkapelle*, they were required to obey the *Kapellmeister* in this capacity only; in all other matters, they were subordinate to the quartermaster.

The salaries of all court servants, including the court musicians, were administered by the *Hofkammer*. Only in exceptional cases did 'Celsissimus' open his privy purse to engage musicians whom he especially favoured.[53] Over the course of the eighteenth century, a trend towards the standardization of musicians' salaries is also evident; however, the distinction between highly paid virtuosos and lower-

---

[51]  See Oskar Kaul, 'Die musikdramatischen Werke des Würzburgischen Hofkapellmeisters Georg Franz Waßmuth', *Zeitschrift für Musikwissenschaft*, 7 (1924/5), 390–408, 478–500; Reinhard Wiesend, 'Würzburger Libretti', *Musik in Bayern*, 15 (1977), 5–30. The latter mentions ten musical settings by Waßmuth, including the oratorios *La colpa originale*, *Giuditta*, and *Testamento di Nostro Signor Gesu Cristo sul Calvario*, as well as the burlesque *Il vecchio Alfeo, medico di campagna*.

[52]  On the history of the *Hofkapelle* in the late eighteenth and nineteenth centuries, see Dieter Kirsch, 'Die Würzburger Hofkapelle', in '... *meine angenehmste Unterhaltung': Musikinstrumente und Musikalien aus fränkischen Sammlungen; Zur Sonderausstellung des Mainfränkischen Museums Würzburg, 14. Mai–24. August 2003* (Würzburg: Mainfränkisches Museum, 2003), 9–16, at 13–16.

[53]  Among these exceptions were the above-mentioned horn player Punto and the clarinettists Heßler and Blum as well as the harpist Christian Peter Paul Grund (1722–1784).

paid court musicians remained in effect until the early nineteenth century when prince-bishops ceased to be in power.[54] Otherwise, a uniform basic salary became the rule in around 1730, especially among trumpeters. Musicians could also receive special bonuses from the court according to their level of performance and length of service – which could also include *Naturalien* (payments in kind) such as bread, wine, grain, wood, and candles. Würzburg court musicians during the eighteenth century continued to receive their salaries until the time of their death, after which their families often became impoverished, as is evident from numerous extant petitions made by widows and orphans. Occasionally, alms would be presented to them as payments in kind or cash, but a 'Sterbquartal' (that is, wages for the three months following the death) was approved only in exceptional cases.[55]

By an act of grace, orphaned children of court musicians were accepted into the 'Juliusspitälische Studentenmusäum'. This charitable foundation, initiated by Prince-Bishop Julius Echter von Mespelbrunn in 1576, provided needy and talented orphans with accommodation and an education. As early as 1579, the pupils were encouraged to sing so as to enrich musical performances at the institution's chapel, the *Spitalkirche*. Prince-Bishop Friedrich Carl von Schönborn considered the approximately thirty beneficiaries as additional forces for his *Hofmusik* and in 1733 entrusted *Kapellmeister* Wolfgang Händler with their musical education at the Juliusspital. Adam Friedrich von Seinsheim pursued this path with similar intensity: from 1766, the court violinist Ignaz Franz Xaver Kürzinger (1724–1797) was responsible for their training, and until its dissolution in August 1803 the 'Studentenmusäum' remained an effective augmentation of the *Hofmusik*, especially in the vocal sphere.[56]

The Würzburg *Hofkapelle* was also expanded under Friedrich Carl (r. 1729–46) through the means of jointly appointed musicians from Bamberg, who were obliged to serve at both courts. Adam Friedrich (r. 1755–79) ordered his best Bamberg musicians to Würzburg and *vice versa*, above all when operas were presented at the garden theatre of Schloß Seehof.[57] Musical ties were maintained with the courts of Mainz and Ansbach, but performances of foreign musicians at Würzburg

[54] Among the privileges of the virtuosos and other favoured court servants was that they appeared 'außer Livrée' (out of livery); that is, they were not required to wear clothing that would publicly identify them as court employees. See also D-WÜst, Historischer Verein, MS f. 675/1, 'Extractus Hof Protocolli', dated 20 January 1740, which lists the names of seventeen musicians holding this particular privilege.

[55] See D-WÜst, Hofkammerprotokoll 1730, fol. 640ʳ (widow of the bassoonist Carbach); Hofkammerprotokoll 1733, fol. 165ᵛ (widow of the court trumpeter Aßler, who received four *Malter* of grain in lieu of cash).

[56] See Remigius Stölzle, *Erziehungs- und Unterrichtsanstalten im Juliusspital zu Würzburg von 1580–1803* (Munich: C. H. Beck, 1914); Bernhard Janz, 'Von Vogler bis Fröhlich: Das Würzburger Julius-Spital als Zentrum der Musikausbildung in der zweiten Hälfte des 18. Jahrhunderts', in *Musikpflege und Musikwissenschaft in Würzburg um 1800*, ed. Ulrich Konrad (Tutzing: Hans Schneider, 1998), 17–28.

[57] Musicians from Bamberg included the violinist Aloys Fracassini, the singer Maria Barbara Bauerschmidt, and the oboist Johann Georg Janzer, while the vocalists Anna Catharina Fracassini, Aloys Costa, and Ignaz Doll, as well as the *Kapellmeister* and violinist Lorenz Schmitt all hailed from Würzburg.

were rare.[58] The few related diary entries made by *Hoffourier* Spielberger between 1747 and 1755 do not usually refer to names or musical programmes.[59]

For the three music-loving prince-bishops, Johann Philipp Franz, Friedrich Carl, and Adam Friedrich, the education and professional development of promising talents cost the court many thousands of *Gulden*.[60] In addition to training *in situ*, the preferred locations were the court of Mannheim and especially Italy – specifically Padua and Rome.[61] The individuals sponsored in this way were required to take an oath promising their return to service in Würzburg after the completion of their training, a sensible measure in view of the high costs.[62]

There were, of course, also musicians who travelled in the opposite direction, from Italy to Würzburg.[63] The most influential among these was Giovanni Benedetto Platti, who was the only Italian to remain in Würzburg until his death. He served six prince-bishops as oboist, violone player, vocalist, singing and oboe teacher, and also composed from 1722 until his death in 1763.[64] After that, Prince-

[58] The elector of Mainz, Franz Lothar von Schönborn (1655–1729), an uncle of the two prince-bishops of Würzburg, sent two horn players there to take composition lessons from Chelleri in 1723; one was his future *Kapellmeister* Johann Ondrascheck. See Gottron, *Mainzer Musikgeschichte von 1500 bis 1800*, 94. Good neighbourly relations with Ansbach had already been cultivated under Johann Philipp Franz. Reciprocal visits frequently included musicians among the entourage; in 1754, for example, seven Würzburg court trumpeters had been sent 'zu dem hochfürstl. Einzug' (in the princely entourage) to Ansbach. See D-WÜst, Historischer Verein, MS q. 176d, fol. 163ᵛ, entry of the *Hoffourier* (quartermaster) from 27 November 1754.

[59] On 25 December 1747, an entry in the diaries of the *Hoffourier* refers to the appearance of a female vocalist who accompanied herself on the dulcimer; on 18 February 1748, a daughter of the *Hofkammerrat* Gick played on the fortepiano; on 17 June 1748, musicians from Gerolzhofen performed a *Tafelmusik* at midday and a serenata in the evening; and on 14 August 1750, an unspecified number of *Waldhornisten* from Kempten were remunerated with '2 ganze Caroliner' [Editors' note: the *Carolin* was a variety of gold coin]. On 18 February 1751, a visiting *Waldhornist* was heard and considered 'so extra gut und stark' (especially good and strong), while on 21 September 1751, a virtuoso on the violoncello performed who apparently 'solle dieser nach dem Abaco der beste in Europa seyn' (was supposed to be the best in Europe after [Joseph-Marie-Clément Dall']Abaco). A Marquis von Werner, 'der beste Virtuosus auf der Violin und Viol d'amour' (the best virtuoso on the violin and viola d'amore) entertained the court on both instruments sometime in October 1751; on 5 October, the Mainz flute virtuoso Wolff and the Ansbach oboist Hummel had also performed. Finally, on 17 January 1754, the daughter of the barber Stapf, whose singing lessons were paid for by the court, had 'sich heute das Erstemahl in Ihrer Lehr hören lassen, und sich gefällig gemacht' (performed for the first time since she began her training and delighted the audience).

[60] D-WÜst, Historischer Verein, MS f. 675/1. The undated list indicates that Anna Catharina Bayer's stay in Italy from 1756 to 1758 cost 3,232 *Gulden*, 25 ⅗ *Kreutzer* – more than ten times what she would later earn as a court singer in Würzburg.

[61] Favoured vocal teachers were Giovanni Carestini (*c.*1704–*c.*1760) and Giovanni Battista Ferrandini (*c.*1710–1791), both of whom had close ties with Munich.

[62] D-WÜst, Hofkammerprotokoll 1756, fol. 233, 'Ayd-formul für beede Sängerinnen'. Among the musicians sent to Italy for further training were also the violinists Johann Georg Vogler, Georg Wenzel Bisetsky, and Lorenz Schmitt, the tenor Johann Georg Laudensack and his daughter, the vocalist Anna Catharina Laudensack.

[63] The lutenist Gleitsmann was, in all likelihood, also recruited for the Würzburg court in Venice. In addition to him, the court newly engaged eight Italians in 1722.

[64] The vast secondary literature on Platti includes the following items: Fausto Torrefranca,

Bishop Adam Friedrich recruited only three Italians: the vocalists Costa and Steffani, as well as the dancing master Voltelino. Viennese influences can also be discerned during Friedrich Carl von Schönborn's term of office, but otherwise younger musicians were usually recruited from within the diocese. In many cases, these youths came from musical or teaching families. Moreover, military musicians stationed in Würzburg took the opportunity to advance from casual staff to permanent members of the *Hofkapelle*.

Much of the repertoire of the Würzburg *Hofkapelle* has been lost, but the few extant sources indicate that the balance of sacred and secular music and the range of functions of the latter – whether chamber, theatrical, or *Tafel* music – depended upon the taste of the reigning prince-bishop. Chamber music was performed even when the ruler in question was less fond of music (and, as a result, the performers entertained themselves, rather than the prince-bishop). This is evident from a diary entry made by *Hoffourier* Spielberger on 19 August 1748, during the tenure of Anselm Franz von Ingelheim:

> Unter der Tafell war Music von denen Virtuosis aus Würzburg, H. Waßmuth, Enderle, Gleitsmann, Geiger und 2 Singerinnen nebst unter livrée laquayen. Die Music dauerte, biß Ihro hochf: Gnaden sich redirirten, nach welchen erst wiederum frisch angefangen worden. Sie dauerte bis 7 Uhr.[65]

> At the *Tafel* there was music [performed] by the virtuosos from Würzburg, [including the] *Herren* Waßmuth, Enderle, Gleitsmann, Geiger, and two female vocalists, as well as liveried lackeys. The music continued until His Grace, the prince-bishop, retired, after which they began anew, until 7 o'clock.

In the end, however, when examining the development of the Würzburg *Hofmusik* during the eighteenth century, it is the efforts of three music-loving individuals that must be emphasized: those of the two brothers von Schönborn and their distant relative Adam Friedrich von Seinsheim. They appear to have formed a kind of dynastic line, which, despite many bitter setbacks and lack of continuity, offered the Würzburg *Hofkapelle* the opportunity for artistic development.

*Giovanni Platti e la sonata moderna*, Istituzioni e monumenti dell'arte musicale italiana, 2 (Milan: Ricordi, 1963); Frohmut Dangel-Hofmann, '"Der guthe Houboist von Würtzburg, der platti . . .": Sein kompositorisches Schaffen im Spiegel der Schönbornschen Musikaliensammlung', *Musik in Bayern*, 47 (1993), 11–31; Alberto Jesuè's thematic catalogue, *Le opere di Giovanni Benedetto Platti (1697–1793)* (Padua: I Solisti Veneti, 1999).

[65]  D-WÜst, Historischer Verein, MS q. 176b, fols. 323ᵛ f.

TABLE 11.1. Membership of the Würzburg Court Music Establishment in 1715, 1730, 1745, and 1760

| Year | 1715 | 1730 | 1745 | 1760 |
|---|---|---|---|---|
| Ruler | Prince-Bishop Johann Philipp II von Greiffenclau (r. 1699–1719) | Prince-Bishop Friedrich Carl von Schönborn (r. 1729–46) | | Prince-Bishop Adam Friedrich von Seinsheim (r. 1755–79) |
| Numeric Overview | 1 *Kapellmeister* / 8 instrumentalists / 6 trumpeters & 1 kettledrummer | 1 *Kapellmeister* / 25 instrumentalists (3 doubling as vocalists) / 10 trumpeters & 2 kettledrummers / 7 vocalists / 2 additional personnel | 1 'Director der Hofmusik' / 26 instrumentalists (1 doubling as vocalist) / 8 trumpeters & 2 kettledrummers / 7 vocalists / 4 additional personnel | 1 *Kapellmeister* / 23 instrumentalists (1 doubling as vocalist) / 6 trumpeters & 2 kettledrummers / 9 vocalists / 4 additional personnel |
| 'Director der Hofmusik' | | | Joseph Anton Komareck (also 'Cammer-Herr', chamberlain) | |
| *Kapellmeister* | Johann Martin Fegelein | Wolfgang Händler | *See Hoforganist* | Georg Waßmuth |
| 'Hofkompositor' (court composer) | | | | |
| Instrumentalists[a] | | | | |
| Violin [no Violas specified] | Johann Boveri (also clerk) / Johann Jakob Degen (also bass singer and clerk) / Johann Salver (also copperplate engraver) | Johann Martin Fegelein (also chaplain) / Johann Georg Fegelein (also clerk) / Johann Georg Wolff (also *Tanzmeister*) | Johann Georg Retzer / Georg Wenzel Bisetsky / Johann Boveri | Johann Georg Retzer / Johann Jakob Degen (also clerk) / Johann Georg Wolff (vn; also *Tanzmeister*) |

| Instrument | | | |
|---|---|---|---|
|  | Johann Boveri (also clerk)<br>Johann Jakob Degen (also bass singer and clerk)<br>Johann Ludwig Geiger (also 'Protokollist', secretary)<br>Georg Sebald (also scribe)<br>Johann Georg Retzer<br>Georg Franz Waßmuth (vn; also organist)<br>Johann Franz Tilscher (also lackey; carried out unspecified musical service) | Johann Georg Fegelein (also registrar; carried out unspecified musical service)<br>Georg Sebald (also scribe)<br>Johann Georg Wolff (also *Tanzmeister*)<br>Johann Jakob Degen (also clerk)<br>Johann Ludwig Geiger (also secretary)<br>*See* Oboe | Lorenz Joseph Schmitt<br>Wilhelm Küffner<br>Joseph Ignaz Fackler (also 'Tenorist')<br>Johann Ludwig Geiger (also secretary) |
| Violoncello |  |  | Johann Georg Fegelein (also clerk) |
| Violone |  |  | Jacob Leo<br>Johann Wenzel Butzfeld (also 'Paraquen-Inspector', inspector of the barracks) |
| Flute | *See* Oboe |  |  |

| Year | 1715 | 1730 | 1745 | 1760 |
|---|---|---|---|---|
| Oboe | | Giovanni Benedetto Platti (also 'Cammer-Tenorist' and teacher of vn and singing) | Giovanni Benedetto Platti (also 'Cammer-Tenorist' and vn) | Giovanni Benedetto ('Johann') Platti |
| | | Johann Jakob Brack | Johann Jakob Brack | Johann Peter Cron |
| | | Caspar Tritt (also lackey and fl; carried out unspecified musical service) | Joseph Schweller | Johann Melchior Reinhard, 'Aushilfe' (temporary assistant) |
| | | | | Johann Anton Triebel, 'Aushilfe' |
| | | | | Martin Heßler[b] |
| Clarinet | | | | |
| Bassoon | | Anton Pfister (also civic 'Türmer', tower musician) | Anton Pfister (also civic 'Türmer') | Anton Baumgartner, 'Aushilfe'[b] |
| Waldhorn | | Johann Georg Boxleidner (also soprano) | Franz Barsisky | Joseph Boxleidner |
| | | Franz Barsisky (also lackey; carried out unspecified musical service) | Franz Lothar Dell (also lackey) | Franz Lothar Dell |
| | | Johann Christoph Brix (also lackey) | Anton Erdmann (also lackey) | Georg Diedel |
| | | Franz Lothar Dell (also lackey) | Kaspar Sandra (also lackey) | Friedrich Domnich |

| | | | | |
|---|---|---|---|---|
| Harp | | Anton Erdmann (also lackey)<br>Wenzeslaus Neumann (also lackey)<br>Jakob Stiger (also lackey)<br>Bernhard Ulrich (also lackey; carried out unspecified musical service) | Jakob Stiger (also lackey) | Christian Peter Paul Grund[c] |
| Lute | | August Wilhelm Heinrich Gleitsmann (also secretary and translator) | August Wilhelm Heinrich Gleitsmann (also secretary and translator) | |
| *Hoforganist* | Johann Baptist Schnapp | *See* Violin | Georg Franz Waßmuth (also 'Hofkompositor') | Albert Kette |
| Instrument(s) not specified ('Musici') | Johann Karl Braun (also 'Kanzlist', clerk)<br>Joseph Dennhöffer (also scribe)<br>Ignaz Dillinger (also 'Rezeptoratsdiener', servant of the revenue office)<br>Johann Georg Hausknecht (also scribe) | Johann Franz Herold (also chamber lackey)<br>Paul Niemand (also lackey) | Nikolaus Peter<br>Michael Joseph Fichtel (also lackey)<br>Johann Georg Keltz (also lackey and 'Musicus')<br>Ludwig Plago (also lackey) | Johann Georg Keltz, 'Musicus' |

| Year | 1715 | 1730 | 1745 | 1760 |
|---|---|---|---|---|
| Instrument(s) not specified (cont.) | | | Johann Georg Stadler (also lackey)<br>Johann Franz Tilscher (also lackey)<br>Caspar Tritt (also lackey) | |
| Hoftrompeter | Anton Aßler<br>Anton Cottmann<br>Franz Georg Eckstein<br>Johann Jakob Jüngling<br>Laurenzius Raaz<br>Johann Peter Schedel | Anton Aßler<br>Andreas Brochert<br>Wilhelm Eberlein<br>Joseph Natterer<br>Joseph Nußbaum<br>Johann Kaspar Rüdel<br>Johann Michael Schedel<br>Joseph Anton Schedel<br>Sebastian Schunder<br>Bernhard Steurer | Johann Michael Baßing<br>Georg Geiger<br>Wolfgang Göpfert<br>Matthias Meergraf<br>Joseph Natterer<br>Joseph Nußbaum<br>Joseph Anton Schedel<br>Bernhard Steurer | Wolfgang Göpfert<br>Bernard Ringelmann<br>Franz Andreas Ritz<br>Paulus Ritz (Rietz)<br>Franz Peter Ritz<br>Georg Geiger |
| Hofpaucker | Daniel Bedacht | Johann Philipp Gottlob<br>Franz Sebastian Schlegel | Anton Göser<br>Franz Sebastian Schlegel | Johann Michael Schlegel<br>Franz Sebastian Schlegel |
| Vocalists<br>Soprano | | Karl Liere, 'Discantist' (treble)<br>Johann Georg Appelius, 'Discantist'<br>Maria Theresia Platti | Maria Theresia Platti | Catharina Pfister<br>Margaretha Boxleidner<br>Anna Catharina Fracassini (née Bayer) |

| | | | |
|---|---|---|---|
| **Alto** | | *See Waldhorn*<br>Joseph Busch | Barbara Bongard<br>Maria Johanna Wolf | Magdalena Andre (née Kolb)<br>Francisca Beschel |
| **Tenor** | | Johann Baptist Roth (also clerk)<br>*See Oboe* | Karl Liere<br>Johann Georg Laudensack (also clerk)<br>*See Oboe* | Johann Georg Laudensack (also clerk)<br>Johann Georg Boxleidner<br>*See Violin* |
| **Bass** | *See Violin* | Wilhelm Düring<br>Johann Georg Ley (also *répétiteur*)<br>*See Violin* | Wilhelm Düring<br>Johann Georg Ley (also *répétiteur*) | Johann Martin Fischer<br>Johann Georg Ley (also *répétiteur*) |
| **Additional Personnel** | | | | |
| Copyists | | [1722–24: Carlo Antonio Capellani]<br>[1722: Johann Hummel] | Joseph Wehl | Joseph Wehl |
| *Calcant* | | | | |
| Instrument makers | | Benedikt Hornmeyer<br>Johann Georg Fischer, violin maker | Benedikt Hornmeyer<br>Johann Georg Fischer, violin maker<br>Johann Philipp Seuffert, organ builder | Benedikt Hornmeyer<br>Zacharias Fischer, violin maker<br>Johann Philipp Seuffert, organ builder |
| *Tanzmeister* | | *See Violin* | *See Violin* | *See Violin* |

*Sources*

1715: Compiled from church records held in D–WÜd and court records (particularly *Hofkammer* minutes) extant in D–WÜst.
1730, 1745: Compiled from decrees and court records in D–WÜst, Historischer Verein, MS f. 675/1, 11.

1760: The order of names is given as in the Würzburg *Hof- und Staatskalender* from 1761. Since these calendars always appeared in January, they provided information relating to the previous year. The *Hoftrompeter* and musical lackeys appear under the rubric 'Hof-Fourir-Amt:' (pp. 55–6), the court musicians under 'Hochfürstl. Hof- und Cammer-Musici' (p. 58).

[a] A clear distinction between court and chamber musicians (*Hofmusici* and *Cammermusici*) was only made during the reign of Prince-Bishop Johann Philipp Franz von Schönborn from 1719 to 1724; those from Italy, for example, were differentiated from others in decrees as 'musici da camera'. Otherwise, the general label 'Hof- und Cammermusic' (court and chamber music) appears to have become so established over the course of time that it was retained as a term in common use, for instance, in the *Hofkalender*. From 1740, the court distinguished only between musicians who wore livery and those who did not.

[b] D-WÜst, Historischer Verein, MS f. 675/II.

[c] D-WÜst, Historischer Verein, MS f. 675/I, II.

# LANDGRAVIATES
# AND
# MARGRAVIATES

# 12

# The Court of Hesse-Darmstadt

## *Ursula Kramer*

T HE PERIOD BETWEEN 1715 AND 1760 – the focus of the present volume – virtually coincides with that of the employment of Christoph Graupner (1683–1760) at the court of Hesse, from his initial engagement as a musician in Darmstadt in 1709, followed by his promotion to first *Hofkapellmeister* just two years later. His fifty-one years of service covered the reigns of two landgraves: Ernst Ludwig (1667–1739) for the first thirty years, and his son Ludwig VIII (1691–1768) for the remaining twenty-one until Graupner's death. Considering its size and compared to other *Hofkapellen*, in the period immediately following Graupner's arrival in particular, the Darmstadt court had at its disposal an extraordinarily high number of vocalists and instrumentalists.[1] However, the spirit of optimism which had initially accompanied Graupner's appointment began to disappear by the end of the second decade of the eighteenth century: opera performances came to a halt and from this time on opportunities for composition at the court were restricted to chamber music as well as to cantatas for the Sunday church service. Financial difficulties at the court became a long-term issue for the musicians who repeatedly called for their unpaid wages.

Over the course of the more than fifty years during which Graupner was active as a composer in the same location, he produced a total oeuvre of over 1,400 vocal works (including 10 operas) and 300 verified instrumental works (plus a further 90 anonymous and uncertain instrumental compositions). It is also remarkable that the majority of his output appears have survived substantially intact at only one library, the Hessische Universitäts- und Landesbibliothek in Darmstadt.[2] In

---

[1] See the fundamental research carried out by Joanna Cobb Biermann, 'Die Darmstädter Hofkapelle unter Christoph Graupner', in *Christoph Graupner: Hofkapellmeister in Darmstadt 1709–60*, ed. Oswald Bill, Beiträge zur mittelrheinischen Musikgeschichte, 28 (Mainz: Schott, 1987), 27–72; Cobb Biermann, 'Exkurs: Die Darmstädter Hofkapelle', in *Die Sinfonien des Darmstädter Kapellmeisters Johann Samuel Endler, 1694–1762*, Beiträge zur mittelrheinischen Musikgeschichte, 33 (Mainz: Schott, 1996), 11–49; Oswald Bill, 'Dokumente zum Leben und Wirken Christoph Graupners in Darmstadt', in *Christoph Graupner: Hofkapellmeister*, 73–212. Selective yet detailed accounts of the Darmstadt *Hofkapelle* forces had already been provided in earlier literature; see Elisabeth Noack, *Musikgeschichte Darmstadts vom Mittelalter bis zur Goethezeit* (Mainz: Schott, 1967).

[2] Following Graupner's death, his family and the landgrave entered in a dispute regarding

marked contrast, considerable losses of archival material during the Second World War, at the Stadtarchiv Darmstadt as well as at the Hessisches Staatsarchiv Darmstadt, make it impossible to trace the *Kapelle*'s changes in size and personnel with absolute certainty.


## PRELUDE

The musico-historical significance which Darmstadt earned as a result of the presence of Christoph Graupner during the first half of the eighteenth century had its roots in 1666. In that year, the widowed Landgrave Ludwig VI (1630–1678) married for the second time. His bride, Elisabeth Dorothea of Saxony-Gotha-Altenburg (1640–1709), was a spirited and artistically talented woman, who soon after her arrival in Darmstadt began to look after matters concerning the *Hofkapelle*, which was not in a particularly good state at the time. In 1671, the landgravine arranged for Wolfgang Carl Briegel (1626–1712), her long-time music teacher in Gotha, to join her in Darmstadt and even commissioned him to compose large-scale stage works (for example, *Triumphierendes Siegesspiel der wahren Liebe*, 1673), thus marking the beginning of theatrical performances at the Hessian residence.[3] When the landgrave died in 1678, he left behind Elisabeth Dorothea and their eight young children. Since the oldest of their sons, the future ruler Ernst Ludwig, was only eleven years old, his mother reigned on his behalf until 1688. Her artistic ambitions focused on the rebuilding of the theatre, issuing disciplinary regulations for the musicians, and ensuring that her children received an excellent musical education.

Hereditary Prince Ernst Ludwig, Graupner's future employer, received lessons in composition and keyboard from Briegel as well as learning to play the lute from another *Hofkapelle* member. In 1685, Ernst Ludwig and his brother Georg were sent to France on a *Kavaliersreise*; in November they reached Paris, where they remained until May 1686.[4] Not only the two princes but also two violinists who had accompanied them were able to gain local knowledge regarding the latest musical

his estate, since the landgrave considered the music his own property as a matter of course. The confrontation continued for over fifty years and ended with the purchase of the music by Grand Duke Ludwig I in 1819; see the preface of Oswald Bill and Christoph Großpietsch, eds., *Christoph Graupner: Thematisches Verzeichnis der musikalischen Werke; Graupner-Werke-Verzeichnis, GWV, Instrumentalwerke* (Stuttgart: Carus, 2005), pp. xxviii ff. In contrast, the majority of the music composed by other *Hofkapelle* members has been lost, with one exception being the work of Johann Samuel Endler; see Cobb Biermann, *Die Sinfonien des Darmstädter Kapellmeisters Johann Samuel Endler.*

   [3] The handwritten libretto is extant in D-DSsa (in German sources usually abbreviated HStAD), D 8 15/2.

   [4] D-DSsa houses several files containing travel reports prepared by the accompanying 'Hofmeister' addressed to Landgravine Elisabeth Dorothea; see D-DSsa, D 4 344/1–5. This correspondence, which has yet to be systematically and comprehensively assessed (particularly in light of the cultural and musical impressions gained by the princes), lists the various locations visited, although Paris was undoubtedly the actual destination of the tour.

developments. With the subsequent engagement in Darmstadt of four French musicians together with the Parisian-trained viola da gamba player August Kühnel (1645–1700?), the *Hofkapelle* fully embraced the French style.[5] This new orientation was exemplified by the performance of Lully's *Acis et Galatée* on the occasion of Ernst Ludwig's marriage with Dorothea Charlotte of Ansbach in December 1687; the prince had attended the work's premiere in Paris. In 1688, Ernst took over from his mother's regency, but owing to political circumstances (including a French invasion) he was forced that same year to move his residence to Gießen in Upper Hesse, returning to Darmstadt only a decade later. As a result of this development, the *Hofkapelle* was considerably reduced in size.

The landgrave's appointment of Ernst Christian Hesse (1676–1762) in 1694 went far beyond merely securing a young viola da gamba player for his *Hofkapelle*. Through Ernst Ludwig's personal support, Hesse was able to perfect his skills when the landgrave sent him on a three-year musical study trip to Paris in 1698; in later years, he would tour Europe extensively as a viola da gamba virtuoso, travelling to metropolitan centres such as Hamburg and London (1705/6), Dresden and Berlin (1709/10), and Vienna (1710). Promoted to *Kapelldirector* in 1707, while on his travels Hesse also acted as a kind of artistic advisor to his employer, regularly reporting in his letters about individual musicians he had encountered during his guest performances and whom he could recommend for an appointment in Darmstadt.[6] Writing from Vienna on 7 November 1710, for example, Hesse informed Ernst Ludwig of the trumpeter 'Scottschofsky, Hongrois de nation, encore Garcon . . . jouant en meme tems du Violon, et qui en un mot l'emporte de fort loin sur les autres Trompetes à Darmstadt' (Skotschoffsky, a Hungarian by birth, still a young-ster . . . playing the violin at the same time, and who in a nutshell far outshines all the other trumpeters in Darmstadt); soon after, Skotschoffsky did indeed relocate to Darmstadt.[7]

Ernst Ludwig also travelled a great deal himself — not at first, but increasingly following the death of his young wife in November 1705.[8] One of his most regular destinations was Hamburg; in the spring of 1708, he spent several weeks there,

---

[5] Noack, *Musikgeschichte Darmstadts*, 157–8.

[6] Hesse also travelled, for instance, to Mantua (where Ernst Ludwig's brother, Philipp, was governor) and Venice. In addition to his duties with the *Hofkapelle*, Hesse served as 'Accessist' (aspirant) at the *Hofkanzlei* (court chancellery). After 1714, Hesse served as a war commissioner and from 1726 as a war councillor, all the while undertaking lengthy concert tours as a virtuoso.

[7] Letter from Ernst Christian Hesse to the landgrave, D-DSsa, Personalakte Hesse, D 4 358/1.

[8] See the contemporary chronicle prepared by the archivist Johann August Buchner (hereafter Buchnersche Chronik) in D-DSsa, Best. C 1 C No. 32, pp. 1154–5. Regarding the period prior to 1705, see Hermann Kaiser, *Barocktheater in Darmstadt* (Darmstadt: Eduard Roether, 1951), 85. Between February 1708 and March 1709, all travel was painstakingly documented in D-DSsa, D 4 345/2; the destinations and places visited included Kassel, Hanover, Braunschweig, Wolfenbüttel, Schwerin, Hamburg, Celle, Homburg, Darmstadt, Nuremberg, Düsseldorf, Salzburg, Linz, Breslau, Leipzig, Arolsen, and Frankfurt am Main. In the absence of a substantive biography of Ernst Ludwig, it remains unclear whether this restlessness may have been a reaction to his personal life.

including visits to the opera at the Gänsemarkt.[9] At this time, Christoph Graupner not only was working there as a harpsichordist but, from 1707, had also premiered some of his own works.[10] Within the context of this visit, the landgrave offered Graupner a post with the Darmstadt *Hofkapelle*; since Briegel was still *Hofkapellmeister*, Ernst Ludwig initially appointed Graupner as 'Vice-Capellmeister' in January 1709. In 1711, he was promoted to *Kapellmeister* and from then on was in charge of 'die music sowohl in alß außer der Kirchen' (all the music both within as well as outside of the church).[11] One of his extant employment contracts details Graupner's duties: he was to direct ('dirigiren'), but in particular 'zum accompagniren auf dem Clavir, so offt es nöthig, gebrauchen laßen, wie nicht weniger componiren' (to make himself available for accompanying on the keyboard whenever necessary, and to compose no less).[12]

That this document refers first and foremost to the church as a fixed point of reference, may be somewhat surprising, given the context in which Ernst Ludwig had first become aware of Graupner (that is, the Gänsemarkt opera house). But it does provide a clear picture of the situation at the Hessian court at the time: Sunday worship services constituted a constant, and at the same time, fixed framework within which music was to be heard in the form of cantatas. Other occasions featuring music, especially large-scale secular ones, were not regulated. Regarding operatic performances – which the ambitious landgrave had undoubtedly envisioned for Darmstadt when appointing Graupner – little firm evidence remains that documents their frequency.[13] But Graupner's own compositional contribu-

---

[9] In 1709, Ernst Ludwig purchased from the widow of the former co-founder and later manager and director of the Hamburg Opera, Gerhard Schott, their imposing house at the Gänsemarkt for 22,000 *Reichsthaler*. Cf. Joachim R. M. Wendt, 'Neues zur Geschichte der Hamburger Gänsemarktoper', in *Beiträge zur Musikgeschichte Hamburgs vom Mittelalter bis in die Neuzeit*, ed. Hans Joachim Marx, Hamburger Jahrbuch für Musikwissenschaft, 18 (Frankfurt: Peter Lang, 2001), 178–81; Wendt, *Materialien zur Geschichte der frühen Hamburger Oper* (Aurich: Books on Demand, 2002), 36–41.

[10] *Dido, Königin von Carthago* and *L'amore ammalato / Die krancke Liebe, oder Antiochus und Stratonica* were independent compositions by Graupner that had been performed on stage in Hamburg as early as 1707. To what extent Graupner was also involved in the composition of *Der angenehme Betrug, oder Der Carneval von Venedig*, premiered in 1707, is unclear. It is possible that during his stay in Hamburg in 1708 the landgrave was present at the premiere of Graupner's next opera, *Il fido amico, oder Der getreue Freund Hercules und Theseus* (month of performance cannot be verified). The extant libretto for the fourth work by Graupner, *Bellerophon, oder Das in die preußische Krone verwandelte Wagen-Gestirn*, provides the date of its premiere, 28 November 1708. Cf. Hans Joachim Marx and Dorothea Schröder, eds., *Die Hamburger Gänsemarkt-Oper: Katalog der Textbücher* (Laaber: Laaber-Verlag, 1995).

[11] The three extant primary sources that provide details of Graupner's employment in Darmstadt are transcribed verbatim in Bill, 'Dokumente zum Leben', 107–11.

[12] For a copy of the contract from 1710, see ibid., 108–10.

[13] Documentation for the period during which opera performances took place at the Darmstadt court, between 1709 until 1719, is sparse. Later references, according to which performances were presented outside of the court's calendar of festivities (Pasqué, for example, mentioned two to three performances a week in 1711, while Kleefeld referred to sixty-one performances in 1712) could not be verified, but are cited in Andrew D. McCredie, 'Christoph

tion alone clearly demonstrates that this was significantly fewer than the number of his productions in Hamburg.[14]

## GRAUPNER'S ARRIVAL IN DARMSTADT IN 1709

Graupner's engagement in Darmstadt was at the core of Landgrave Ernst Ludwig's ambitious plans for fostering courtly musical life, which he made a priority from 1709 onwards. Originally, he had intended to build a new opera house, but this was successfully vetoed by the *Rentkammer* (court treasury); instead, the old opera house (a former riding hall) was renovated by the Hanover architect Louis Remy de la Fosse (*c*.1659–1726). The landgrave's campaign also included, above all, a significant increase in the membership of the *Hofkapelle*. By the early eighteenth century, the *Kapelle* had clearly not only recovered from the earlier reduction brought about by the war, but in the year of Graupner's arrival experienced an extraordinary revival. Seventeen highly qualified musicians were appointed within the space of twelve months, including a number of Graupner's former colleagues from his time in Hamburg and Leipzig.[15] In autumn 1709, two female singers from Hamburg joined the Darmstadt *Hofkapelle*, Anna Maria Schober (bap. 1672–1728) and Margaretha Susanna Kayser; an unidentified opera by Graupner was premiered.[16]

In the following year, Gottfried Grünewald (1673–1739) – formerly *Vicekapellmeister* in Weißenfels and earlier active for several years as a vocalist at the Hamburg Opera (during Graupner's time there) – first appeared as a guest bass vocalist in Graupner's *Berenice und Lucilla*. With the latter's promotion to the directorship of the *Hofkapelle*, Grünewald, who was also in demand as a virtuoso on both the harpsichord and the pantaleon, accepted the permanent postition of *Vicekapellmeister* at the Darmstadt court in 1711. In February that same year, the remodelled opera house was reopened with a glittering performance of Graupner's *Telemach*, an event which was assisted by the participation of an array of external musicians. Vocalists from the Leipzig Opera included the future wife of Ernst Christian Hesse, Johanna Elisabeth Döbricht (1690 or 1692–1774), and Konstantin Knöchel (1679–1725), both of whom were engaged permanently in Darmstadt immediately afterwards. Only Johann Georg Pisendel (1687–1755) as director of instrumental music eventually preferred Dresden over a permanent appointment at the Hessian residence, whereas his one-time colleague from Hoffmann's collegium musicum in Leipzig, Johann Michael Böhm (b. *c*.1685), stayed on until 1729.[17]

Graupners Opern: Hintergründe, Textvorlagen und Musik', in *Christoph Graupner: Hofkapellmeister*, 269–302, at 296.

[14] McCredie, 'Christoph Graupners Opern'; see particularly the comparison on pp. 270–71 and 297. During his stay in Hamburg, Graupner composed two operas each for the years 1707–9, in contrast to Darmstadt, where only five, or possibly six, were composed by Graupner between 1710 and 1719.

[15] Cobb Biermann, 'Die Darmstädter Hofkapelle', 47.

[16] Kaiser, *Barocktheater in Darmstadt*, 170.

[17] In addition, two singers from Frankfurt participated in this special occasion, which

In the mean time, Ernst Ludwig had sent Böhm to Hamburg in order to study operatic performance practice; back in Darmstadt he took up the position of concertmaster in 1718. Following Pisendel's rejection, Johann Jacob Kreß (1685–1728) from Oettingen was appointed as chamber musician in 1712. Two horn players are first mentioned in primary sources, together with an additional bassoonist, in 1714, the year in which the number of full-time *Kapelle* members reached its (documented) zenith at forty-six individuals, a figure that can be verified for only one other year, 1718.[18]

Landgrave Ernst Ludwig bestowed titles associated with other official court positions upon large numbers of his musicians, although the extent to which they were in fact employed by the privy council, government, or *Rentkammer* is unclear and may also have depended on the individual. (The rationale behind this practice was, at least in part, to provide musicians with the opportunity to increase their salaries by taking on additional duties). Some of these were listed as salaried members of the *Hofkapelle* – such as the future *Vicekapellmeister* Johann Samuel Endler (1694–1762), who also carried the designation of chamber secretary – while others were recorded under their secondary area of employment.[19] As a result, we cannot be entirely sure who participated in *Hofkapelle* performances, and the number of potentially available musicians may have been higher in certain years.[20] Moreover, there were younger musicians (for example, sons of *Kapelle* members) who played for free over extended periods of time. Extant private correspondence of the landgrave, specifically letters of thanks, also indicate that musicians from other *Kapellen* served occasionally at the Darmstadt court, although the exact numbers are not recorded.[21]

Officially, there were three different types of employment available to *Hofkapelle* members: first, as chamber musicians; second, as 'Anwärter' (aspirants for chamber musician positions); and third, as 'Anwärter auf Anwärterstellen' (candidates for the aspirant posts), a group that included, in particular, the children of *Kapelle* members.[22] The few orchestra lists that remain extant – including a 'Besoldungs-buch' (salary register) and excerpts from court account books that have since been lost – also differentiate between 'Hof Musicus' and 'fürstl. CammerMusicus'.[23] In any case, the court seems to have dispensed with such a subdivision in later years, given that while these designations are listed side by side in a *Rentschreiberei* invoice

motivated Graupner to make a special trip to the neighbouring town to supervise the learning of their parts.

[18] Cf. the diagram given by Cobb Biermann, 'Die Darmstädter Hofkapelle', 32, which traces the changing size and forces of the Darmstadt *Hofkapelle* throughout Graupner's tenure.

[19] Albrecht Eckhardt, 'Beamte und Diener der Zentral- und Hofverwaltung Hessen-Darmstadts 1704–28', *Hessische Familienkunde*, 9/1 (1968), 30–44.

[20] Cf. the information provided in Cobb Biermann, 'Die Darmstädter Hofkapelle', 27–72. The numbers she lists must be viewed as the minimum number of players.

[21] As described by Noack, *Musikgeschichte Darmstadts*, according to primary sources held at D-DSsa.

[22] Cobb Biermann, 'Die Darmstädter Hofkapelle', 41–2.

[23] The 'Besoldungsbuch' information is reproduced in Noack, *Musikgeschichte Darmstadts*, 188–9; regarding the court accounts, see D-DSa, Kasten 'Müller'.

from 1730, only *Cammermusici* are referred to in 1740.[24] This may also explain why in 1758, in response to disputes regarding rank that had arisen within the *Kapelle*, Graupner and Endler concluded that 'wir wißen hier nichts von sogenannten Hoff-Musicis; allen membris der hießigen Fürstlichen Hoff-Capelle vom ersten bis auf den letzten ist von jeher das praedicatum eines Cammer Musici beygeleget worden' (here, we know nothing of so-called *Hofmusici*; every single member of the local princely *Hofkapelle* has been bestowed with the title of *Cammermusicus*).[25] Evidently, the period during which the court had differentiated between these two designations, lay back so many decades that neither musician could recall it.

As shown earlier with the example of Böhm, who was appointed at Darmstadt in 1711 and was proficient not only on the oboe but also on the flute and recorder, from the early eighteenth century on there were already musicians in the Darmstadt *Hofkapelle* who played more than one instrument. That such (documented) cases increased considerably around the middle of the eighteenth century may not necessarily indicate an increase in this phenomenon, but simply be connected with the existence of a more extensive and highly detailed selection of primary sources. As part of the efforts of young musicians to obtain paid positions, countless petitions were written, which naturally emphasized the diverse qualifications of the applicants.[26] On the one hand, these display a certain tendency towards combinations of related instruments such as oboe/bassoon or violin/viola; on the other hand, they also provide evidence of the court's support for woodwind players such as Johann Christian Klotsch (Klotzsch), who after a 'zugestoßene[n] Fatalité an den Zähnen' – a major dental mishap – could no longer play the bassoon but 'in Ansehung seiner langwierigen guten Diensten nicht zu verstoßen' (in acknowledgment of his lengthy and excellent service was not to be dismissed); indeed the court was more than willing to employ him as a viola player.[27]

Graupner's appointment as *Hofkapellmeister* in January 1711 came with a salary of 500 *Gulden* (Frankfurt currency) as well as additional, extraordinarily high payments in kind, totalling 38 *Malter* of grain and cereal, 8 *Klafter* of wood, and three *Ohm* of high-quality wine, 'alles Darmstätter Maases' (all in Darmstadt measures).[28] Graupner was also allowed to dine at the *Hoftafel*, a privilege which cost the court a further 130 *Gulden* annually and, according to an extant list dated 1709, was bestowed upon only three musicians.[29] The contractual conditions for Johanna Elisabeth Döbricht from Leipzig were identical, in contrast to Konstantin Knöchel, who – like the other newly engaged *Kapelle* members Böhm and Kreß – received only 400 *Gulden* and lower payments in kind. Regular *Kapelle* musicians were paid significantly less: the bassoonist Johann Corseneck (formerly an

[24] D-DSa, Kasten 'Müller'. This did not apply to the *Hoftrompeter* and *Hofpaucker*, who continued to be listed in their own separate category.

[25] D-DSsa, D 8 16/1, reproduced in Bill, 'Dokumente zum Leben', 176–7.

[26] Cobb Biermann, 'Die Darmstädter Hofkapelle', 37.

[27] Ibid.

[28] Cf. the employment contract given in Bill, 'Dokumente zum Leben', 110–11. In Hesse, a *Malter* was 128 litres, a *Klafter* was 90–150 cubic feet, and an *Ohm* was 150 litres.

[29] D-DSsa, D 8 15/6.

*Hautboist* and trumpeter in the dragoon regiment) had been appointed in 1711 with an initial salary of 100 *Gulden*; in 1716, this was increased to 130 *Gulden*, 21 *Albus*, plus 2 *Gulden* for having taught a student shortly after his arrival. The latter appears to have been Johann Nikolaus Orth, who was eventually appointed officially as a horn player in the *Hofkapelle* in 1714. Thus, the instruction of younger musicians was probably a normal part of the Darmstadt musicians' duties.[30]

The systematic strengthening and expansion of the *Hofkapelle* up until the middle of the 1720s is also reflected in the acquisition of numerous instruments. In 1711, the organ builder Christian Vater (1679–1756) from Hanover was paid more than 2,700 *Gulden* (which amounts to more than five times the annual salary of the *Hofkapellmeister*) for an organ for the court chapel, a 'große[s] Opern Instrument' (large opera harpsichord), a 'schwartze[s] Instrument, welches in . . . Durchl. Cammer stehet' (a black harpsichord, which stands in the chamber of [His] Highness), a 'Clavicordij sambt dem Fueß . . . vor . . . Durchl[.] der Princessin' (a clavichord including a pedal for [Her] Highness the princess), and 'ein Instrument vor Hochfürstl. . . . Herrschafft' (a harpsichord for the most princely . . . family), as well as 'ein . . . Instrument . . . vor den Capellmeister' (a harpsichord . . . for the *Kapellmeister*).[31] In 1713, 'Waldhörner, Fagotten und Hautbois . . . in Dero [des Landgrafen] Gemach unterthänigst gelieffert' (hunting horns, bassoons and oboes . . . were most humbly delivered to [the landgrave's] chamber).[32]

It was during this phase of the Darmstadt *Hofkapelle*'s expansion that Johann Friedrich Fasch (1688–1758) visited for three and a half months, having been known to Graupner since his early days in Leipzig, when the latter was his prefect at the *Thomasschule*. In 1713, Fasch had embarked on a journey with the intention of perfecting his skills in the area of composition under Graupner and Grünewald. He received free instruction and accommodation; that he was also directly involved in weekly musical duties is demonstrated by the extant music for the cantata *Gott will mich auch probieren* from February 1714, in which individual orchestral parts are clearly copied in Fasch's own hand.[33]

Beyond the generic phrase 'within as well as outside of the church' that appears in the appointment contracts for Graupner and the vocalist Johanna Elisabeth Döbricht, few concrete details are known regarding occasions involving music at the Darmstadt court. It can be confirmed, however, that from 1709 on, Graupner and his deputy Grünewald regularly alternated the task of composing Sunday cantatas. Extant text booklets printed in Darmstadt for the years 1712 and 1713 provide evidence that two cantatas were performed every Sunday and feast day, one of which was a repeat of the corresponding cantata from the previous year's cycle in the afternoon. Moreover, according to the foreword for the 1713 cycle (which began on the first Sunday of Advent in 1712):

[30] Noack, *Musikgeschichte Darmstadts*, 174.
[31] D-DSa, Kasten 'Müller'; Kammerrechnungen 1711.
[32] D-DSa, Kammerrechnungen 1713.
[33] I should like to thank Oswald Bill for providing me with this information. See also Chapter 9, 'The Court of Anhalt-Zerbst', p. 265 above.

Sie haben sich's dabey gefallen lassen, in den Nachmittags-Andachten, jedes-
mahl ein Stuck aus dem letzteren Jahr-Gang auffzuführen, und wird solches
dem geneigten Leser zu seiner Nachricht hierbey mit angefüget, damit er,
wie zuvor, auch itzo noch seine Andacht durch deren Mitlesung stärcken
könne . . .

They [the congregation] enjoyed the fact that a composition from last year's
[cantata] cycle was always peformed during afternoon devotions, and [there-
fore these texts] have been added for the information of the gracious reader,
so that he, as before, can once more strengthen his devotions by reading
along . . .[34]

To what extent this practice was adhered to, and for how long, remains unclear.
In any case, one of the very few extant contemporary testimonies that contain
statements regarding musical performance at the Darmstadt court indicates that
'Sontags Nachmittags [wie] auch wohl in der Woche, Cammer Musiquen' (on
Sunday afternoons as well as during the week, chamber music) was performed.[35]
'Eine ordentliche Mittwochs-Probe' (a regular Wednesday rehearsal) had been
held for this purpose, at least initially, but it must have been abolished at some
point; the only related evidence dates from 1758 and demands its reintroduction.[36]
A special room in the palace was evidently used for small-scale musical perfor-
mances: in his handwritten diary, which primarily documents his correspondence,
Ernst Ludwig continually referred to a 'chambre de musique' (music room) and
occasionally the entry 'musique' is also recorded.[37]

The chronicle of the *Archivrat* Buchner also highlighted operatic performances
as being the residence's main musical attraction. However, despite the numerous
productions referred to in secondary literature, especially following the re-opening
of the theatre in 1711, concrete references regarding their frequency are no longer
available.[38] It is also surprising that, after *Telemach*, the next new opera by Graupner was not premiered until 1715; most recently, the later attribution of that year's
*La costanza vince l'inganno* as a work by the Darmstadt *Kapellmeister* has been
called into question (in any case, the overture and ballet music were composed by
Ernst Ludwig himself).[39] In 1719, this opera was repeated when the elector of Trier

---

[34] From the preface to Georg Christian Lehms's text booklet, *Das singende Lob Gottes*
(Darmstadt, 1712), extant in D-DS, W 3720.

[35] D-DSsa, Buchnersche Chronik, pp. 1155–6.

[36] See the letter of concertmaster Enderle, D-DSsa, D 8 15/6, cited in Cobb Biermann, 'Die
Darmstädter Hofkapelle', 44.

[37] D-DS, MS 1586, Ernst Ludwig, 'Diarium' (which comprises entries for letters both written and received during the period 1718–25, as well as occasional additional information).

[38] See D-DSsa, D 4 350/1, 'Cabinetts Cassa', which provides an overview of performances
between June 1713 and March 1715. Accordingly, 154 'Comödien' were staged, in contrast to
only two operas (the latter given in February and March 1715). It is possible that Pasqué and
Kleefeld respectively arrived at comparatively high numbers of performances in 1711 and 1712
because they also included stage plays; see McCredie, 'Christoph Graupners Opern', 296.

[39] *La costanza vince l'inganno* was originally transmitted as an anonymous work. Friedrich
Noack attributed the opera to Graupner; see his article 'Die Opern von Christoph Graupner in Darmstadt', in *Bericht über den 1. Musikwissenschaftlichen Kongreß der Deutschen*

visited the court. Also taking part on this occasion were vocalists and instrumentalists from outside of Darmstadt – letters of appreciation from the landgrave refer
to a female vocalist engaged in Kassel, as well as as an oboist from Braunschweig-
Wolfenbüttel and a violinist in the employ of a prince of Anhalt.[40] Furthermore,
a *ballet-divertissement* (1717) and a pastorale entitled *Adone* (1719) have also been
verified as works by Graupner.

The *ballet-divertissment* formed part of extensive wedding festivities, held over
the course of a week from the end of April until the beginning of May 1717, to
celebrate the marriage of Hereditary Prince Ludwig, the future Landgrave Ludwig
VIII, and Charlotte Christine of Hanau-Lichtenberg. An extant account of this
major event refers explicitly to the inclusion of music, not only during the morning church service ('eine schöne Musik gehalten', a beautiful [piece of] music was
performed), but also at the afternoon *Tafel*, where 'eine schöne Musik abgesungen'
(a beautiful [piece of] music was sung).[41] The latter work must have also been
a cantata, since 600 copies of its text had been printed and were to be distributed
among the guests for them to read along with during the performance.[42]

In addition to the operas by Graupner already mentioned, music remains extant for only two further theatrical works: a three-act opera, *La fedeltà coronata*,
as well as the 'Divertimento' *Apollo in Tempe*; however, performances of these in
Darmstadt cannot be verified.[43] Indeed, when measured against the ambitious beginnings of opera at the court, the number of operatic works known to have been
composed definitively for Darmstadt is surprisingly modest, given that leading
members of the Hamburg Opera ensemble were engaged. From 1712, a troupe of
French actors also resided at court, although the possible involvement of several
*Hofkapelle* members in their performances can only be inferred indirectly. The
French were led by their own *Kapellmeister*, Valoy, who died in 1715. The future
*Hofkantor* Johann Ludwig Hildebrandt had served as an associate member of the
*Hofkapelle* from 1712, according to his own report 'mit unermüdlichem Fleiß . . .
und zwar in der Kirche als auch im Orchester und bei Komödien' (with untiring
diligence . . . specifically in the church as well as in the orchestra and for comedies).[44]
Moreover, a highly paid dancing master continued to belong to the personnel of

*Musikgesellschaft in Leipzig vom 4. bis 8. Juni 1925* (Leipzig: Breitkopf & Härtel, 1926), 252–9.
However, Raymond Joly has indicated to the author that new circumstantial evidence now puts
Noack's attribution into question.

[40] Cf. Noack, *Musikgeschichte Darmstadts*, 184.
[41] A printed description of the festivities is given in D-DSsa, Best. C1 C No. 31.
[42] See the 'Kammerrechnung' from 1717, which refers to costs for the printer, Adolf Müller,
in D-DSa, Kasten 14, No. 227.
[43] D-DS, Mus. ms. 245 (*La fedeltà coronata*); Mus. ms. 1174 (*Apollo in Tempe*). These manuscript copies identify Ernst Christian Hesse as the composer, but these attributions appear
to have been made at a later date and are probably incorrect. I should like to thank Rashid-S.
Pegah for bringing this to my attention; see also his article '"Pasqués Phantastereien über
Opern" oder Das Gastspiel des Impresario Antonio Maria Peruzzi und seiner Operisten-
Truppe in Frankfurt am Main 1731/32 – und die Folgen', *Studi vivaldiani*, 10 (2010), forthcoming.
[44] D-DSsa, D 8 16/1, quoted after Noack, *Musikgeschichte Darmstadts*, 196.

the *Hofkapelle* until the mid-eighteenth century, despite the fact that Graupner's arrival in 1709 clearly signalled a move in the court's musical orientation away from the French and towards the Italian style (see Table 12.1, pp. 356–63 below).

The recognition that the court had occasionally relied upon Italian vocalists from comparatively early on – their names are not specified – comes thanks to the special manner in which performance materials for cantatas were prepared at Darmstadt.[45] The alto part of the cantata for 26 December 1709, for example, is the first to feature a version of the text in quasi-block letters supplementing the German spelling of the original. In a further cantata a few weeks later, German words in roman script were combined with phonetic annotations. This only makes sense when considered from the perspective of an Italian attempting to pronounce German properly. For example, 'Jesulein' was written out as 'Jesulain' to prevent a possible Italian misproununciation as 'Jesule-in'. It therefore appears likely that an Italian vocalist, whether male or female, participated in a cantata performance in Darmstadt for the first time around the turn of the year 1709/10. While this phenomenon occurred only sporadically at first – presumably indicating a comparatively brief stay by the artist in question at the Hessian residence – later on, it can be seen repeatedly for longer periods of time.[46]

The apparent presence of Italian singers early on also seems plausible because some of the arias of the opera *Berenice und Lucilla* were sung in Italian. A salary list from 1718 refers to the Italian alto castrato Campioli (Antonio Gualandi) as a permanent member of the Darmstadt *Hofkapelle*, receiving a salary of 400 *Gulden* plus 156 *Thaler* for meals.[47] It remains unclear whether he had already sung for the first time in Darmstadt in 1712 and then returned occasionally to the landgravial court in the years which followed. The phonetic transcriptions that appear regularly in alto parts once again from 1716 on indicate, however, that he was most likely engaged permanently from that year.[48] In 1719, Campioli left Darmstadt to travel north.[49] That same year, the singer Giovanna Toeschi (d. 1726), the wife of the violin virtuoso Alessandro Toeschi (c.1700–1758), came to Darmstadt – the use of her name in the score of a cantata from 1722 leaves no doubt regarding

[45] For an examination of the surviving cantata material, see Guido Erdmann, '"Eghiptens jamar": Über den beschwerlichen Einsatz italienischer Sänger in Graupners Kirchenmusik', *Mitteilungen der Christoph-Graupner-Gesellschaft*, 2 (2005), 3–29.

[46] This was the case throughout 1716, as well as from October 1717 until December 1719, occasionally also in 1720, and from the second half of 1721 until September 1722.

[47] This list is reproduced in Noack, *Musikgeschichte Darmstadts*, 188–9, at 189. Amongst the holdings of the (unfoliated) 'Cabinet Cassa' in D-DSsa, D 4 350/1, there is a hitherto unknown source which indicates that in 1717 the 'Casterat Campiole' [*sic*] was already paid an annual salary of 400 *Gulden*.

[48] Little is known regarding the life of Campioli. Moreover, there is conflicting information as to the vocalist's engagement prior to Darmstadt; cf. Erdmann, '"Eghiptens jamar"', nn. 42, 43.

[49] Campioli supposedly sang in Hamburg in 1719 and then went straight to Braunschweig-Wolfenbüttel; cf. Winton Dean, 'Antonio Gualandi', in *Grove Music Online*, <www.oxfordmusiconline.com> (accessed 25 October 2009). In contrast, Erdmann, '"Eghiptens jamar"', 22, states that he went from Darmstadt straight to Braunschweig-Wolfenbüttel.

Toeschi's participation as an alto soloist. The significant increase in phonetic transcriptions in the alto parts of cantatas from 1719 onwards should therefore be seen in the light of the Toeschis' arrival at the Hessian residence.[50] Names of other Italian singers are not known, although the salary list from 1718 contains an entry for 'der kleine Castrat' (the little [that is, young] castrato).[51] Most likely, this refers to a student of Campioli's. With the permanent cessation of opera performances in 1722, the principal reason for employing native Italian speakers finally disappeared. The previously Italian-dominated alto parts in the cantatas were now taken over by the newly appointed falsettist Johann Samuel Endler.

Just at the time when the Darmstadt *Hofkapelle* was in its phase of expansion came the appointment in 1712 of Georg Philipp Telemann at the Frankfurt Barfüßerkirche. He was also known to Graupner from his time in Leipzig, although contemporary reports documenting renewed contact between the two musicians are remarkably sparse.[52] At the very least, in early April 1716, when two large-scale performances of Telemann's setting of the *Brockes-Passion* were given at the Barfüßerkirche, the entire Darmstadt *Hofkapelle* including vocalists and orchestral musicians took part. Telemann clearly had fewer instrumentalists at his disposal in Frankfurt than the court of Darmstadt.[53] Several weeks later, the birth of Emperor Charles VI's only son, Leopold Johann (who unfortunately was to die in infancy), was celebrated with a festive cantata together with a serenata. The Darmstadt musicians once again participated, with a concert review describing 'die unvergleichliche Execution des Darmstädtischen Orchesters' (the incomparable execution of the Darmstadt orchestra).[54]

In the years and decades that followed, even after Telemann's departure from Frankfurt, members of the Darmstadt *Hofkapelle* continued to participate in performances there. It is evident from the correspondence of the Frankfurt patrician and music enthusiast Johann Friedrich Armand von Uffenbach (1687–1769) that Graupner continued to visit Frankfurt; he also supplied his own compositions to the collegium musicum of the local 'Zum Frauenstein' Society.[55] In turn, an extraordinarily high number of works by Telemann appear amongst the holdings of the Hessische Universitäts- und Landesbibliothek in Darmstadt. That these works, a number of which were copied by Graupner himself, were performed in the palace, at least in part, is a possibility.

[50] Cf. Erdmann, '"Eghiptens jamar"', 24.

[51] Reproduced in Noack, *Musikgeschichte Darmstadts*, 189.

[52] See ibid., 190 ff., where a very positive picture is painted of this musical relationship, one that Oswald Bill has interpreted more critically; see Bill, 'Telemann und Graupner', in *Telemann und seine Freunde: Kontakte – Einflüsse – Auswirkungen*; *Bericht über die Internationale Wissenschaftliche Konferenz anläßlich der 8. Telemann-Festtage der DDR, Magdeburg, March 1984*, 2 vols. (Magdeburg: Zentrum für Telemann-Pflege und -Forschung, 1986), II: 27–35.

[53] Noack, *Musikgeschichte Darmstadts*, 191, presumes that even Graupner, Grünewald, and Hesse actively participated.

[54] Cited ibid., 192.

[55] Letters from Graupner to Uffenbach in Bill, 'Dokumente zum Leben', 186–93.

## THE DEVELOPMENT OF THE DARMSTADT *HOFKAPELLE*
## FROM 1715 UNTIL 1730

In May 1715, the chancellery of the palace, which contained the living quarters of the landgrave and his family, burnt to the ground. Neighbouring buildings within the palace complex also caught fire and suffered heavy damage. Extensive repairs and new construction work had to be carried out, which consumed huge sums of money and dragged on beyond the death in 1726 of the architect Remy de la Fosse, until 1729. Even then, the palace continued to be a construction site in parts, with windows covered with wooden boards.[56] As late as the mid-1730s, the landgrave continued to reside in a house on the market square; the extent to which these construction problems also had an impact upon normal courtly life, including the role played by music, is not documented.

The strong growth of the *Hofkapelle* (see Table 12.1, 1715), in particular since Graupner's arrival in Darmstadt and the associated costs that followed (such as the renovation of the theatre and the ensuing lavish productions, as well as the acquisition of expensive musical instruments), had awakened scepticism amongst certain officials from comparatively early on.[57] Symptomatic in this regard was the refusal of the court treasury to grant approval for the building of a new theatre. A crisis point was reached just a few years later, when in the wake of the Peace of Rastatt in 1714 subsidy payments from Braunschweig ceased. Two years after that, state bankruptcy threatened, with the balance sheets from 1717 indicating a total debt of more than 2,000,000 *Gulden* for the court treasury and the war chest.[58] A direct consequence of this was that the musicians' salaries were no longer paid out, resulting in a never-ending series of complaints. As early as 1715, Ernst Ludwig had already complained to his minister, Privy Councillor Kameytsky that 'die Leuthe liegen mir . . . auf dem halß undt ist des anlauffens kein Ende . . .' (the people are pestering me and there is no end to these demands).[59]

This marked the beginning of a decades-long feud between members of the *Hofkapelle* and their employer, caused by a courtly lifestyle that went far beyond what was realistically feasible. The ones suffering were the musicians, who could do little to improve the situation. Some were able to supplement their income through concert tours; others were forced to ask for their dismissal in order to accept positions elsewhere.[60] Frequently, these requests were simply rejected by the court, and any subsequent announcements regarding leaving the residence,

[56] *Darmstadt in der Zeit des Barock und Rokoko*, II: *Louis Remy de la Fosse*, exhibition catalogue, ed. Magistrat der Stadt Darmstadt (Darmstadt: [no publisher], 1980), 99–111.

[57] An itemization of the costs for the opening production of *Telemach* in the opera house is extant in D-DSsa, D 8 17/2.

[58] Cf. Cobb Biermann, 'Die Darmstädter Hofkapelle', 48.

[59] D-DSsa, D 4 359/1.

[60] Cf. Cobb Biermann, 'Die Darmstädter Hofkapelle', 58–9; 'Specificatio, was die fürst[l]. Bedienten biß den letzten Xbris 1720 an Besoldung noch zu fordern haben', D-DSsa, E 14 A 3/1.

without permission if necessary, were met with threats and intimidation.[61] Over the years, unpaid wages had accumulated considerable arrears, which repeatedly left *Kapelle* members in desperate hardship. Little wonder then that several left the court in secret: the violinist and singer Fischer had already disappeared in 1717, leaving behind only his debts.[62] Campioli also appears to have departed in this manner, whereas the violinist Peter Ludwig Rosetter was granted a lengthy holiday from which he simply failed to return. The married couple Margaretha Susanna and Johann Kayser (a soprano and an oboist respectively) left the residence in 1718 to take up employment elsewhere. Kreß was owed an entire year's worth of salary (in his case 400 *Gulden*) in 1719, following seven years of service with the *Kapelle*. A register of debts dating from 1721, the 'Specificatio, was die fürst[l]. Bedienten biß den letzten Xbris 1720 an Besoldung noch zu fordern haben' (Specification of what the princely employees are still owed up until the end of December 1720), lists the sums actually owed to claimants alongside the amounts the court intended to pay out. In many cases, the outstanding payments amounted to far more than an annual salary, with a total debt of close to 59,000 *Gulden*, of which less than 38,000 *Gulden* were to be paid out.[63] As a result, the Darmstadt *Hofkapelle* had recorded a considerable drop in membership by the end of the second decade of the century. Furthermore, four of the seven musicians who were no longer available had been vocalists – hardly surprising then that the last elaborate opera had been staged in 1719.

Against a background of this kind, even the *Hofkapellmeister* sought to secure a position elsewhere, hardly surprising given the marked deterioration of the *Hofkapelle* both financially and in terms of personnel compared to the situation at the time of his appointment. Like others before him, in early 1723 Graupner used a fabricated request for holiday leave in order to disguise his application for the Leipzig *Thomaskantorat*. After successfully passing the trial composition round, the Leipzig town council first of all attempted to make Graupner's Darmstadt employer aware of the step he had undertaken in secret, before asking the landgrave to release him from the Hessian residence in favour of the Leipzig post.[64] But Ernst Ludwig did not approve the request for dismissal, and Graupner's Darmstadt employment contract was instead revised, resulting in an increased annual salary of 900 *Gulden* – payment of which was guaranteed before all other musicians. This clause led to considerable disagreement within the *Kapelle*. A further direct consequence of Graupner's actions was the appointment of two new musicians from his old Leipzig circle. In 1723, Endler was engaged as an alto vocalist, but, as per Graupner's wishes, was also to be utilized as a violinist, while two years later Johann Gottfried Vogler (b. 1691), another violinist, relocated to the Hessian residence. A further new admission into the Darmstadt *Hofkapelle* came from Stuttgart, with the tenor Johann Christoph Höflein entering into the landgrave's service in

[61] Cf. the respective reports written by Johann Michael Böhm in D-DSsa, D 4 356/24.

[62] Cobb Biermann, 'Die Darmstädter Hofkapelle', 50.

[63] Ibid., 51.

[64] Cf. the details on Graupner's application for Leipzig in Bill, 'Dokumente zum Leben', 122 ff.

early 1724.[65] Moreover, internal changes also occurred within the *Kapelle*: after the flautist and oboist Böhm had risen in the *Hofkapelle*'s hierarchy to become concertmaster in 1718 (a position which involved directing part of the court's chamber music performances), not long afterwards the violinist Kreß was also promoted to the rank of concertmaster, in 1723.

That the orchestra continued to face financial difficulties is further documented by letters written by Höflein as part of his parallel duties as chamber secretary. According to these, he presented his employers with suggestions for remedying the problems that had arisen and, in 1731, even turned to Friedrich Armand von Uffenbach, who reportedly knew of certain possibilities for consolidation.[66] Böhm had already departed from Darmstadt in a most spectacular fashion two years earlier: after submitting six unsuccessful written requests for permission to resign and with several years' worth of salary in arrears, he left the court under false pretences, travelled towards Ludwigsburg, and on that account was under the threat of arrest. He was accused of having taken music and instruments that belonged to the *Kapelle* without authorization; however, Böhm justified himself by stating that these were his own, private manuscripts.[67]

### THE DEVELOPMENT OF THE DARMSTADT *HOFKAPELLE*
### FROM 1730 UNTIL 1745

According to a decree from the landgrave, in addition to his regular duties Graupner was also required to look after the 'Taffel-piècen und Concerts' (pieces for table music and concerts) from 1730 onward, most likely due to the departure of concertmaster Böhm in 1729.[68] As indicated in a contemporary travel account by Baron Karl Ludwig von Pöllnitz, however, chamber music did not play a particularly important role at the Darmstadt court, given that Ernst Ludwig resided in a house on the market square. The landgrave only came 'auf die Sonn- und fest-Täge . . . nach Hoff, und speiset mit [s]einem Herrn Sohn an einer Taffel von 16. Personen zu mittag, Abends aber den Dames, welche niemahlen als auf Sonn- und Fest-Täge nach Hoff kommen' (to the court on Sundays and feast days . . . , and dined at midday together with his son at a table of sixteen people; in the evening, however, [he dined] with the ladies, who only ever came to court on Sundays and feast days).[69] Chamber music, therefore, must only have been required in this context.

---

[65] Contacts to the landgravial family had already existed years earlier and may have played a role in his appointment. Regarding Höflein, see Rashid-S. Pegah, 'J. C. Höflein und Christoph Graupners "Kleine Nacht-Musiquen"', *Mitteilungen der Christoph-Graupner-Gesellschaft*, 5 (2010), 49–58.

[66] Ibid. Nothing is known, however, regarding a reply from Uffenbach.

[67] Noack, *Musikgeschichte Darmstadts*, 213, drawing from sources in D-DSsa.

[68] The full decree is cited in Bill, 'Dokumente zum Leben', 182. In accordance with this, Grauper's allowance of writing materials was increased by fifty per cent.

[69] Karl Ludwig von Pöllnitz, *Nachrichten des Baron Carl Ludwig von Pöllnitz: Enthaltend was derselbe auf seinen Reisen besonderes anmercket, nicht weniger die Eigenschafften*

The dire financial situation continued throughout the 1730s and occasionally prompted very bizarre courses of action. In 1733/4, for example, the landgrave approved the minting of debased coinage, with the seigniorage being used to pay oustanding fees. Not surprisingly, the recovery brought about by this measure was only short-term. Nevertheless, the constitution of the *Kapelle* between 1728 and 1735 probably did not decline quite as seriously as the rather stringent listing of personnel suggested by Joanna Cobb Biermann, with a minimum of twenty-seven and twenty-four full-time musicians respectively. During difficult financial times the instrumentalists are particularly likely to have held an additional position at court in order to at least make ends meet, while continuing to be available as performers for musical events.

There was, however, a further series of new appointments to the *Hofkapelle* during the 1730s, including the vocalists Georg Balthasar Hertzberger and Maria Elisabeth Schetky-Eberhardt (both 1714–1769), as well as the violinist David Steger and the violoncellist Christoph Ehrenfried Riedel.[70] In 1731, Martin Schöne, formerly in the service of Count Friedrich Karl von Erbach (1680–1731), had been appointed as second violinist and performer on several other instruments. The count von Erbach and Ernst Ludwig had long been friends, dedicating their own compositions to one another, and Friedrich Karl is known to have borrowed Darmstadt musicians to augment his own *Kapelle* in 1726. When, following the deaths of the count and his wife in 1731 and 1738 respectively, a number of the Erbach servants were dismissed, one further musician, Jakob Friedrich Stolz, received a position as oboist with the Darmstadt *Hofkapelle* in 1738.[71]

By the end of the 1730s, the definitive number of musicians documented at the court had risen once more to forty. Of special significance was the appointment in 1735 of Klotsch from Zerbst, who was not only a virtuoso on the bassoon, but also excelled on the chalumeau. Graupner's compositions for bassoon (specifically the solo concertos) as well as his sonatas for mixed ensemble (which call for the bassoon and also the chalumeau), were presumably written in direct response to Klotsch's arrival in Darmstadt. That the composition of the orchestra was considered from a strategic angle and that Klotsch's skills would be used to the best possible advantage, is evident from the fact that he was very quickly given a student. From 1737, Jacob Führer took lessons from Klotsch, for which the latter received a financial bonus.[72] That the instruction apparently focused not only on the bassoon, but also on the chalumeau was indicated indirectly by a statement made by another *Kapelle* member, who referred to the performance of a work for three chalumeaux in 1738. The latter only mentions one player definitively by name: the newly appointed oboist Stolz. The use of the label 'Nacht-Musique' for this

*dererjenigen Personen, woraus die vornehmste Höfe in Europa bestehen*, part 2 (Frankfurt am Main, 1735), cited in Christoph Großpietsch, *Graupners Ouverturen und Tafelmusiken: Studien zur Darmstädter Hofmusik und thematischer Katalog* (Mainz: Schott, 1994), 73.

[70] Dates for Hertzberger and Schetky-Eberhardt as provided in Noack, *Musikgeschichte Darmstadts*, 215, 240, 270.

[71] Pegah, 'J. C. Höflein', 56.

[72] Noack, *Musikgeschichte Darmstadts*, 215.

composition also hints at its performance context, possibly a night time serenata presented outdoors.[73]

The fiftieth anniversary of Ernst Ludwig's reign was celebrated at great expense in February 1738. Included among the festivities were illuminations and fireworks as well as new musical compositions, with Graupner contributing a sacred cantata as well as a secular one, both of which featured elaborate orchestral scoring and a five-part vocal ensemble to mark the special occasion.[74]

A major turn of events, and one which had a significant impact on Graupner and the *Hofkapelle* in particular, occurred the following year, with the death of Landgrave Ernst Ludwig on 12 September 1739. Graupner composed two cantatas for the funeral proceedings, and according to an extant description detailing the order of ceremony, at least one of these was performed at the civic church, the destination of the funeral procession from the palace. Moreover, an overview survives that lists those court employees who were provided with mourning clothes and included among them are twenty-six musicians. Five of the latter can only be connected with the *Hofkapelle* thanks to their inclusion in this document, as they were not paid for their musical services and are therefore not included in any other list.[75]

In December 1739, Graupner also lost his *Vicekapellmeister* and friend Grüne-wald, with whom he had shared the task of composing of Sunday cantatas for many decades. The extent to which this brought about a deterioration in Graupner's own situation is apparent from a comment in his autobiographical essay for Johann Mattheson's *Grundlage einer Ehren-Pforte*:

> wobey mir die gantze Arbeit allein zugewachsen, nachdem der gute Grüne-wald vor einem halben Jahre verstorben ist . . . Ich bin also mit Geschäfften dermaassen überhäuffet, daß ich fast gar nichts anders verrichten kan, und nur immer sorgen muß, mit meiner Composition fertig zu werden, indem ein Sonn- und Fest-Tag dem andern die Hand bietet, auch noch öffters andre Vorfälle dazwischen kommen.

> whereby, following the death of good old Grünewald half a year ago, the entire work load fell to me, . . . I am now so overextended with work, that I can hardly get anything else done and always have to worry about finishing my compositions from one Sunday and feast day to the next, and frequently for the other events that occur in between as well.[76]

With the death of Ernst Ludwig and the accession of his son Ludwig VIII, the

---

[73] Letter from Johann Christian Höflein to Landgrave Ernst Ludwig, dated 11 June 1738, cited by Pegah, 'J. C. Höflein', 55.

[74] *Der Herr erhöre Dich* for two trumpets, four kettledrums, two horns, two chalumeaux, bassoon, two violins, viola, and basso continuo, as well as the even more opulent cantata, *Schallt tönende Pauken, klingt helle Trompeten,* for pairs of oboes, oboes d'amore, trumpets, kettledrums, horns, chalumeaux, bassoons, and violins, one viola, and basso continuo.

[75] D-DSsa, D 4 342/2: 'Acta die nach dem unterm 12ten Sept. 1739 erfolgten Absterben des Herrn Landgraven Ernst Ludwig gemachten TrauerAnstalten betr.'

[76] Johann Mattheson, *Grundlage einer Ehren-Pforte* (Hamburg, 1740; repr., ed. Max Schneider, Kassel: Bärenreiter, 1969), 412–13.

landgraviate's shattered financial situation came to light, with a total deficit of 2,000,000 *Gulden*. The new landgrave, although very much interested in music, nevertheless opted to cut back on expenditure associated with the *Hofkapelle*. A salary regulation that took effect in January 1740 in part mandated significant losses for individual *Kapelle* members. Thus the wage of the oboist Stolz, who had only just been appointed in mid-1738 with a salary of 400 *Gulden*, was now reduced by half.[77] According to this 'Regulierten Besoldungs-Ordnung', Graupner supposedly continued to receive the 900 *Gulden* guaranteed in 1723, Endler – referred to here for the first time as concertmaster – was paid the second-highest wage at 500 *Gulden*, followed by 400 *Gulden* each for Ludwig Christian Hesse (a gamba virtuoso like his father), concertmaster Lenzy (Lenzi), the cellist Riedel, Klotsch, and the two vocalists Schetky and Hertzberger. Other wages were lowered to 130 *Gulden*, while the services of *Kapelldiener* Dachmann warranted a mere 24 *Gulden*. Several musicians, including the younger Hesse, left the residence soon after, and by 1741, the documented number of *Hofkapelle* members had dropped down to seven. Those who remained frequently carried high debts, because their salaries had not been paid. Even Graupner was owed more than one year's salary in 1745, and virtually all the *Kapelle* members had valid claims still to be met. A report by a treasury clerk at the time sheds light on the court's practice: musicians were paid from taxes owed to the court, and if those were not received, then the salaries had to be deferred.[78]

Despite the ailing financial situation, Ludwig VIII led an extravagant lifestyle, reintroducing the *parforce* hunt and specifically employing a painter to record hunting scenes (which occasionally included individual *Hoftrompeter* wearing red uniforms). Ludwig's preferred residence was the hunting lodge in Kranichstein, and he only came to the Darmstadt palace for Sunday church services. Finally, in the 1740s (the exact date is unknown), the *Hofkapelle* was divided, with Endler being assigned to direct the musicians in Kranichstein; sometime prior to 1744 he was promoted to *Vicekapellmeister*. As a composer, Endler contributed a small handful of secular cantatas but, above all, a considerable number of overtures and sinfonias have been preserved.[79] It is likely that the latter were intended for Kranichstein.

Alongside the two *Kapellmeister* Graupner and Grünewald, a number of other *Kapelle* musicians had already made their mark as composers during the early decades of the eighteenth century. These included Johann Jacob Kreß, Ernst Christian Hesse, Johann Gottfried Vogler, (Johann Daniel?) Hauck, and a certain Kühfuß. In later decades, Friedrich Beringer (d. 1760) and Johann Georg Christoph Schetky (1737–1770) also composed, and works for the keyboard as well as sinfonias, con-

---

[77] The complete list is reproduced in Noack, *Musikgeschichte Darmstadts*, 218.
[78] Cobb Biermann, 'Die Darmstädter Hofkapelle', 55–6.
[79] For details, see Cobb Biermann, *Die Sinfonien des Darmstädter Kapellmeisters Johann Samuel Endler*.

certos for violin and harpsichord, chamber music works, and a number of cantatas by the concertmaster Wilhelm Gottfried Enderle (1722–1790) are also extant.[80]

## THE DEVELOPMENT OF THE DARMSTADT *HOFKAPELLE* FROM 1745 UNTIL 1760

The decline in personnel that occurred during 1740/41 continued during the years which followed (see Table 12.1), with the lowest level reached in 1746/47, when the number of musicians recorded was twenty-seven. From that point, the figure climbed steadily until 1760, with the court employing almost as many full-time *Kapelle* members in the late 1750s as it had only twice before: in 1714 and 1719.[81] This was, however, in no way synonymous with an general easing of the financial situation, as witnessed by the further letters of complaint written by individual musicians during these years, as well as a catalogue of debts from 1752. These documents indicate that the aging members of the *Kapelle* and their widows were particularly hard-hit by the massive deficit.[82] An extant salary list dating from 1749 sheds light on the salary levels of the time. They continued to remain at the reduced amounts set in 1741, with the oboist Stolz, Kühfuß, and Dubois all listed as receiving 200 *Gulden*, Graupner and Endler being paid 900 and 500 *Gulden*, respectively, the newly appointed violinist Deuter, 400 *Gulden*, and Christian Klotsch, 450 *Gulden*. Three of the vocalists (Maria Elisabeth Schetky, Hertzberger, and Lachmund) were also identified on this list as 'Secret.' (secretary) — since, as mentioned earlier, such secondary appointments would have served to improve their wages (which were set at 450, 490, and 300 *Gulden*, respectively).[83]

During the 1740s, however, the court once again began to appoint new musicians, including the violinist Maximilian August Heinrich Deuter (d. 1760) in 1742, the dancing master Friedrich J. Etienne (1747), and the cellist Johann Friedrich Gernand. Moreover, between 1741 and 1745, the son of Johann Ludwig Brauer is documented as having served as a bassoonist (like his father). During the latter half of the 1740s, a whole string of new names appear among the *Hoftrompeter*, most likely a direct result of the new ruler's increased interest in hunting. Despite existing debts, the violin virtuoso Enderle was appointed in 1753 at the extremely high salary of 750 *Gulden*, fifty percent above what the court paid his superior Endler, by way of comparison. That same year two musicians from the Bayreuth *Hofkapelle* relocated to Darmstadt: the oboist Christoph Metsch and the

---

[80] In contrast to Endler's oeuvre, little is known about the compositional activities of the other *Kapelle* members and their works for Darmstadt.

[81] Cobb Biermann, 'Die Darmstädter Hofkapelle', overview on p. 32.

[82] Regarding the catalogue of debts, cf. ibid., 56. Noack, *Musikgeschichte Darmstadts*, 214, 223, 224, refers to a series of complaints made by individual musicians regarding unpaid fees (as, for example, by Johanna Elisabeth Hesse, Klotsch, and Johann Philipp Mahler). The case of Georg Balthasar Hertzberger is described in Cobb Biermann, 'Die Darmstädter Hofkapelle', 56.

[83] The salary list (see D-DSsa, D 8 15/7) is reproduced in Bill, 'Dokumente zum Leben', 71.

bassoonist Beringer were each paid an annual salary of 300 *Gulden* and, from 1755, received an additional 50 *Gulden*.[84]

While some of these newly-appointed musicians are only documented for relatively brief periods, the membership of the small vocal ensemble, which was required particularly for the performance of cantatas on Sundays, remained remarkably constant. Beginning with the appointment of soprano Maria Elisabeth Schetky-Eberhardt in 1735, followed by the bass Georg Balthasar Hertzberger (in Darmstadt from 1737), the alto Johann Justus Hamberger, and the tenor Johann Friedrich Lachmund (both hired in 1739), all remained members of the *Kapelle* beyond 1760. Only after the death of soprano Maria Ludmilla Schetky-Vogel (1694–1751) did the court make a new appointment: her twelve-year-old granddaughter Charlotte Luise Schetky (1739–1765), engaged at 100 *Gulden*. In view of the usual fluctuation in membership, particularly with regard to vocalists, this stability is especially remarkable and must surely be connected to the fact that at this time vocalists in Darmstadt were no longer required for operatic roles.

In the decades around the middle of the eighteenth century, levels of virtuosity declined markedly among the orchestral musicians; in fact, a number of *Kapelle* members were required to perform on multiple instruments.[85] Also, having given employment to several musicians from Leipzig early on in Graupner's tenure, the preference in later years was for hiring instrumentalists locally, from the surrounding region, including in a few cases (as with cellist Johann Georg Christoph Schetky) the children of *Hofkapelle* members. Requests to participate without payment in the *Hofkapelle* or receive training from its members were continually received. These were then annotated by Graupner with appropriate assessments and recommendations; although, at times, the latter were ignored by the landgrave.[86] Just as before, individual *Kapelle* members, including Klotsch, provided instrumental tuition. *Kapellmeister* Endler also took on pedagogical duties: Johann Georg Christoph Schetky studied composition with him, and he was mentioned as a tutor to the two princesses.[87]

The steady growth in the number of musicians in Darmstadt, which resumed from the mid-1740s, must be viewed within the context of the fact that the court now comprised two households: the palace in town and the hunting lodge at Kranichstein. That a fairly impressive orchestra was also assembled at the latter residence is evident from a document dated 1757. Not only does this refer to a num-

---

[84] Noack, *Musikgeschichte Darmstadts*, 234.

[85] For example, Martin Schöne, Johann Gottlieb Schöne, and Johann Christian Klotsch; see Cobb Biermann, 'Die Darmstädter Hofkapelle', 36–7.

[86] Cf. Bill, 'Dokumente zum Leben', 163–70.

[87] It is unclear exactly which girls were instructed by Endler: Cobb Biermann, *Die Sinfonien des Darmstädter Kapellmeisters Johann Samuel Endler*, 45, names Caroline Luise (1723–1783) and Luise Auguste Magdalene (1725–1742), the two daughters of Ludwig VIII (at that time hereditary prince). According to Christoph Großpietsch (in his introduction to Bill and Großpietsch, eds., *Christoph Graupner: Thematisches Verzeichnis*, 15) these were not the two granddaughters of Ernst Ludwig, but rather his own children from his morganatic marriage with Louise Sophie von Spiegel: Louisa Charlotte (1727–1753) and Friederike Sophie von Epstein (1730–1770).

ber of instruments which the Imperial-Royal Regiment had sent to augment the existing collection, but it also gives the names of musicians who were to play them. These comprised five violins, one viola, one violoncello, two horns, two clarinets, two clarino trumpets, a pair of kettledrums, four oboes, and two bassoons, as well as two 'Engl. Wald Hautbois'. Shortly before this, the court had already arranged to purchase one lute, two cellos, one viola, one musette, and 'Zwey Pohlnische Böcke' (two Polish bagpipes).[88]

In 1754, Graupner became blind, bringing an end to his active directorship of the *Hofkapelle*. This change was thus also accompanied by a fundamental loss of authority, which by 1758 had led the musicians to quarrel openly about rank. Not only Graupner and Endler, but also the directly affected concertmaster Enderle responded by preparing written statements, which contain important and detailed information.[89] In this context, Enderle requested the reintroduction of regular rehearsals for the musicians, 'damit Niemand Ursach haben möge den Einwand zu machen, die Musicalien seyen nicht richtig geschrieben oder im Tempo über-macht' (so that no one could have cause to object that the music was not copied correctly or that the tempo was overwhelming [that is, unplayable]). He presented a proposal in which the musicians were each to be assigned a specific instrumental designation, in other words, a single allocation as opposed to performing on a vari-ety of different instruments. This is significant because, technically speaking, when considered from the perspective of the definitively available Darmstadt *Kapelle* personnel, it can be interpreted as an optimum. The 'Arrangement' (which does not include court trumpeters or vocalists) details a total of twenty-two musicians, each allocated to single instrument as follows: two oboes, two flutes, three first and four second violins, two violas, four bassoons, one violoncello, one violone, two horns, and one kettledrummer. While balance is achieved in the upper parts between the strings and the woodwinds doubling them, the clear dominance of the bassoons in the lower register is particularly striking.[90] The subheading of Endler's overview also describes the scope of the *Kapelle*'s duties: 'wie solches bey Aufführung [von] Kirch- Kammer und Taffel Musiquen bey der Instrumental Music zu observieren' (how such performances of church, chamber, and *Tafel* music are to be observed by the instrumentalists).[91]

A few weeks later, the landgrave announced a definitive ruling. In order to prevent renewed conflict among the musicians, a *Kapellmeister*, a concertmaster, or a representative nominated by them was to assume control and address the question of orchestral discipline.[92] At the same time, in context of visits made by guests from outside Darmstadt, the duties of the *Hofkapelle* with regard to the

---

[88]  Quoted in Noack, *Musikgeschichte Darmstadts*, 238.

[89]  The distinction between court and chamber musician has already been addressed above; when Graupner and Endler negated the existence of the title *Hofmusicus* in relation to the Darmstadt *Hofkapelle*, their memories must have been faulty.

[90]  D-DSsa, D 8 16/1. The 'Arrangement' is also reproduced in Cobb Biermann, 'Die Darm-städter Hofkapelle', 69–70.

[91]  Cobb Biermann, 'Die Darmstädter Hofkapelle', 69–70.

[92]  Reproduced in Noack, *Musikgeschichte Darmsstadts*, 244.

differentiation between 'Concert' and 'Taffel Musique' were specified more precisely. Beyond the sphere of the church, music was heard not only as a background
accompaniment to meals, but during concert performances it was also the centre of
the audience's attention. Thus in the spring of 1760, for example, the Swedish diplomat Count Ulrich zu Lynar heard the 'Comtesse von Epstein' (one of Ernst Ludwig's two daughters from his second marriage) perform Italian arias in a concert.[93]
    To date, Lynar's travel report is also the only known contemporary reference to
a particular attraction of the Darmstadt court, one which afforded foreign guests
a special musical treat:

> Daneben [neben dem Schloss] ist ein kleiner Garten und an demselben ein
> Lusthaus, darin die Herrschaft des Sommers speist und in dessen Mitte, wo
> die Tafel hinzustehen kommt, ein kleines rundes Loch ist, welches in ein
> Soutterain führt, daraus die Musik sehr schön klingen soll; zu dem Ende
> ist auch in allen vier Ecken eine Öffnung, daraus der Schall herauskommen
> kann.

> Next [to the palace] is a small garden and in it a *Lusthaus* where the land-
> gravial family dines during the summer, and in the middle of which, where
> the table is set up, there is a small round hole that leads to a basement, out of
> which music is meant to sound very beautifully. To that end, in each of the
> four corners there is also an opening from which the sound can come.[94]

This pavilion had been built sometime during the first decade of the eighteenth
century and may have been used during Ernst Ludwig's reign as a special entertainment for visitors. It was demolished in the nineteenth century, but a surviving
architectural plan indicates that there was an underground passageway from the
main building of the palace most likely intended for the musicians.[95]
    Twenty-one years after Graupner's death a biographical article was published
in the Hesse-Darmstadt *Staats- und Adreß-Kalender* for the year 1781, in which
tribute was paid to the importance of the *Hofkapellmeister*:

> er [brachte] in kurzer Zeit die hiesige Kirchen- und Theater-Musick sowohl
> durch seine Compositionen, als auch durch Herbeyziehung mehrerer Virtu-
> osen in ein solches Aufnehmen, daß sie damals für eine der vorzüglichsten in
> Teutschland gehalten wurden.

> within a short period of time, he had made such a positive impact on sacred
> and theatrical music hereabouts, not only with his compositions but also by

---

[93] Cf. Friedrich Noack, 'Eine Reise durch das Großherzogtum Hessen im Frühling 1760',
*Mitteilungen des Oberhessischen Geschichtsvereins*, new ser. 16 (1908), 3–22, at 15.
[94] Travel account written by Count zu Lynar, published in excerpts, ibid., as cited in
Großpietsch, *Graupners Ouverturen und Tafelmusiken*, 74.
[95] Lithograph reproduced in Ludwig Weyland, 'Geschichte des Großherzoglichen Resi-
denzschlosses zu Darmstadt', *Archiv für hessische Geschichte und Alterthumskunde*, 11/3 (1867),
447–520. The existence of this music pavilion is further documented in several paintings and
engravings dating from prior to the 1830s.

enlisting several virtuosos, that at the time it was held to be among the most excellent in all of Germany.[96]

The reputation of the Darmstadt *Hofkapelle* and its director did indeed reach far beyond the confines of the residence, and not only Mattheson referred to the 'berühmten' (famous) *Kapellmeister* Christoph Graupner, but Telemann also praised the quality of the Darmstadt musicians.[97]

In conclusion, Graupner's arrival in Darmstadt had provided an important impetus for musical life at court, but within a few years economic realities had put a significant curb on this rapid growth. Yet despite the adverse financial situation, over the course of the decades that followed, Graupner, together with his deputies, sought to maintain a suitable level of musical activity. Even though relatively few sources remain which describe these in greater detail, the astounding wealth of compositions by Graupner still extant themselves bear witness to the vibrancy of the musical culture in Darmstadt.

[96] *Hoch-Fürstlich Hessen-Darmstädtischer Staats- und Adreß-Kalender auf das Jahr 1781* (Darmstadt, 1781), reproduced in Oswald Bill, 'Christoph Graupners Biographie aus dem Jahre 1781', *Mitteilungen der Christoph-Graupner-Gesellschaft*, 1 (2004), 3–19, at 4.
[97] Mattheson, *Grundlage einer Ehren-Pforte*, 410.

Table 12.1. Membership of the Hesse-Darmstadt Court Music Establishment in 1715, 1730, 1745, and 1760

| Year | 1715 | 1730 | 1745 | 1760 |
|---|---|---|---|---|
| Ruler | Landgrave Ernst Ludwig (r. 1688–1739) | | Landgrave Ludwig VIII (r. 1739–68) | |
| Numeric Overview | 2 *Kapellmeister*<br>2 concertmasters<br>11 instrumentalists<br>7 trumpeters & 2 kettledrummers<br>8 vocalists<br>10 unspecified musicians<br>2 additional personnel | 2 *Kapellmeister*<br>8 instrumentalists<br>4 trumpeters & 1 kettledrummer<br>7 vocalists (1 doubling as instrumentalist)<br>4 unspecified musicians<br>2 additional personnel | 2 *Kapellmeister*<br>13 instrumentalists (1 doubling as vocalist)<br>4 trumpeters & 1 kettledrummer<br>6 vocalists (1 doubling as instrumentalist)<br>4 unspecified musicians<br>2–3 additional personnel | 1 *Kapellmeister*<br>1 concertmaster<br>21 instrumentalists (2 doubling as vocalist)<br>6 trumpeters & 2 kettledrummers<br>5 vocalists (plus 2 instrumentalists also employed as *Hofkantor* & 'Pädagog-Kantor')<br>2 unspecified musicians<br>3–4 additional personnel |
| *Kapellmeister* | Christoph Graupner | Christoph Graupner | Christoph Graupner | Christoph Graupner (d. May 1760)<br>Johann Samuel Endler |
| *Vicekapellmeister* | Gottfried Grünewald (also bass singer, hpd, org, and pantaleon) | Gottfried Grünewald (also bass singer, hpd, org, and pantaleon) | Johann Samuel Endler | |
| *Kapelldirector* | *See* Viola da gamba | | | |
| Concertmaster | Johann Jacob Kreß (vn)<br><br>Johann Michael Böhm (ob, fl, and rec) | | | Willhelm Gottfried Enderle (vn and hpd) |

Instrumentalists

| | | | | |
|---|---|---|---|---|
| **Violin** | Fischer (also voice, range unspecified) | Johann Gottfried Vogler (also org) | Maximilian August Heinrich Deuter (vn 1; also org) | Maximilian August Heinrich Deuter (vn 1; also org) |
| | Peter Ludwig Rosetter | *See* Alto | Ernst Gottlieb Schetky (vn 1; also tenor and secretary) | Ernst Gottlieb Schetky (vn 1; also tenor and secretary) |
| | Jean-Baptiste Tayault (also *Tanzmeister*) | Petrus Franziskus Demoll (also *Tanzmeister*) | Martin Schöne (vn 2; also wind player) | Martin Schöne (vn 2; also wind player) |
| | *See* Concertmaster | *See* Concertmaster | David Steger (also harp, chamber lackey, and possibly clarino tpt) | David Steger (also harp, chamber lackey, and possibly clarino tpt) |
| | | | | Ernst Christian Schüler (Schüller) (also clarino tpt and possibly fl) |
| | | | | Johann Gottfried Wilhelm Schwartz (vn 2, lute, hpd, and pantaleon) |
| | | | | Franz Christian Wicht (also org) |
| | | | | *See* Concertmaster, Oboe, *Hoftrompeter, and Hofpaucker* |
| **Viola** | *See Waldborn* | *See Waldborn* | *See Waldborn and* Tenor | Johann Heinrich Noell (also *Hofkantor*) |
| | | *See* Bassoon | *See* Bassoon | *See* Flute, Bassoon, *Waldborn, and* Tenor |

| Year | 1715 | 1730 | 1745 | 1760 |
|---|---|---|---|---|
| Viola da gamba | Ernst Christian Hesse (also *Kapelldirector*) | Ernst Christian Hesse (also 'Kriegsrat', war councillor) | Ernst Christian Hesse (also 'Kriegsrat', war councillor) | |
| Violoncello | | | Christoph Ehrenfried Riedel | Johann Georg Christoph Schetky |
| Contrabass | Johann Kaspar Braun *See Hoftrompeter* | | | *See Hoftrompeter* |
| Flute/Recorder | *See Concertmaster* | | | Johann Christoph Kühfuß *See Violin* Johann Gottlieb Schöne (also wind player and va) |
| Oboe | Johann Kayser *See Concertmaster and Bassoon* | *See Bassoon* | Jakob Friedrich Stolz | Christoph Metsch (also vn) Jakob Friedrich Stolz |
| Clarinet | | | | *See Bassoon* Johann Peter Schüler (also hn and musette) |
| Chalumeau | | | *See Bassoon* | *See Bassoon* |
| Bassoon | Johann Ludwig Brauer Johann Corseneck (also ob, tpt, and possibly hn) | Johann Ludwig Brauer Johann Corseneck (also ob, tpt, and possibly hn) | Johann Jakob Brauer Johann Ludwig Brauer | Friedrich Beringer Johann Christian Klotsch (also chalumeau and va) |

| | | | | |
|---|---|---|---|---|
| *Waldborn* | Johann Philipp Mahler (also va); Johann Nikolaus Orth | See Kapelldiener; Johann Philipp Mahler (also va); Gottfried Schwartz | Johann Christian Klotsch (also chalumeau and va); Johann Philipp Mahler (also va); Gottfried Schwartz | Johann Karl Andreas Maromerh (also ob); Friedrich Heyl (also chamber lackey); Johann Philipp Mahler (also va); Gottfried Schwartz |
| Clarino/Trumpet | | | | See Clarinet |
| Lute | | | | |
| Harp/Pantaleon | See Bassoon | See Bassoon | See Violin | See Violin |
| Harpsichord | See Bassoon | See Bassoon | See Violin | See Violin |
| *Hoforganist* | See Vicekapellmeister; See Vicekapellmeister; Johann Philipp Jung (also 'Geheimer Registrator', privy registrar); See Vicekapellmeister | See Vicekapellmeister; See Vicekapellmeister; Johann Philipp Jung (also 'Geheimer Registrator', privy registrar); See Violin; See Vicekapellmeister | See Violin; Johann Philipp Jung (also 'Geheimer Registrator', privy registrar); See Violin | See Violin; See Violin and Concertmaster; Jakob Friedrich Greiß (also 'Stallverwalter', stable manager); See Violin and Miscellaneous |
| *Hoftrompeter* | Johann Valentin Burckhardt; Georg Heinrich Ebel; Johann Wilhelm Christoph Ehrmann; Hieronymus Ritter | Albert Brausch; Johann Valentin Burckhardt; Johann Gröger; Hieronymus Ritter | Johann Berlick von Schasczyn; Johann Christoph Melchior Eisenschmitt; Johann Georg Keyl; Hieronymus Ritter | Johann Berlick von Schasczyn; Johann Christoph Albrecht (also cb); Johann Heinrich Gröger (also vn and cb); Friedrich Ferdinand Kahl |

| Year | 1715 | 1730 | 1745 | 1760 |
|---|---|---|---|---|
| Hoftrompeter (cont.) | Johann Christoph Kahl; Johann Gröger; Johann Georg Skorschoffsky (also cb) | | | J[ohann?] Paul Rudloff; Georg Ludwig Wiegand |
| Hofpaucker | See Bassoon; Johann Schüler; Georg Andreas Fick (also copyist) | See Bassoon; Johann Schüler | See Violin; Johann Schüler | See Violin; Johann Schüler; 'J. L. Würtz' (also vn) |
| **Vocalists** | | | | |
| Soprano | Johanna Elisabeth Hesse-Döbricht; Margaretha Susanna Kayser-Vogel; Anna Maria Schober; Maria Ludmilla Schetky-Vogel | Johanna Elisabeth Hesse-Döbricht; Maria Ludmilla Schetky-Vogel | Maria Elisabeth Schetky-Eberhardt; Maria Ludmilla Schetky-Vogel | Charlotte Luise Schetky; Maria Elisabeth Schetky-Eberhardt |
| Alto | | Johann Samuel Endler (also vn and chamber secretary) | Johann Justus Hamberger | Johann Justus Hamberger |
| Tenor | Gottfried Avianus Knöchel | Johann Christoph Billing; Johann Christoph Höflein | Johann Friedrich Lachmund (also va and secretary); See Violin | Johann Friedrich Lachmund (also va and secretary); See Violin |

| | | | | |
|---|---|---|---|---|
| Bass | See Vicekapellmeister | See Vicekapellmeister | Georg Balthasar Hertzberger (also secretary) | Georg Balthasar Hertzberger (also secretary) |
| Range not specified | Gottlieb Igel (also 'Geheimer Kanzlist') 'Gottlieb[in]' (female) | Gottlieb Igel (also 'Geheimer Kanzlist') | | Rivinus Dufosé (also chamber lackey) |
| | See Violin | | | Johann Heinrich Schön (also 'Stadtturmer') |
| *Hofkantor*[a] | Konstantin Knöchel | Johann Ludwig Hildebrandt | Johann Ludwig Hildebrandt | *See* Viola |
| Duties not specified[b] | Johann Kaspar Geibel (also 'Stadtturmer', civic tower musician) | Johann Adam Henning | Johann Heinrich Klepper | |
| | Franz Anton Kühfuß | Franz Anton Kühfuß | Johann Arnold Schemes (also *Kammerfourier*) | |
| | Johann Adam Ostheim (also secretary and copyist) | Johann Adam Ostheim (also secretary and copyist) | Eberhard Anton Helffmann (also secretary and copyist) | |
| | Johann Heinrich Gillmer (also clerk) | Eberhard Anton Helffmann (also secretary and copyist) | Johann Zahorsky | |
| | Johann Christoph Gorr (also 'Stadtturmer' and clerk) | | | |
| | Christoph Held | | | |
| | Jakob Kayser (also *Cammerdiener*) | | | |

| Year | 1715 | 1730 | 1745 | 1760 |
|---|---|---|---|---|
| Duties not specified (*cont.*) | Georg Philipp Sahlfeld (also secretary)<br>Johann Tobias Sahlfeld (also secretary)<br>Ferdinand Werner (also 'Geheimer Kanzlist', privy clerk) | | | Georg Gottfried Assmus<br>?<br>Johann Christian Dubuc |
| **Additional Personnel** | | | | |
| Copyist | *See Hofpaucker and* Instrument(s)/Voice not specified | *See* Instrument(s)/Voice not specified | *See* Instrument(s)/Voice not specified | *See* Instrument(s)/Voice not specified |
| *Hoforgelmacher* | Johann Anton Mayer | | | |
| *Glockenist* (bell-ringer) | Johann Nikolaus Assmus | Johann Nikolaus Assmus | Johann Christian Köhler | Johann Christian Köhler |
| *Tanzmeister*[c] | *See* Violin | *See* Violin | ? | |
| *Kapelldiener* (servant) | Jacob Führer (also bn) | Jacob Führer (also bn) | Johann Gerhard Schweitzer (unpaid volunteer) | |
| Miscellaneous | | | | Albrecht Ludwig Abele ('Pädagog-Kantor'; also org) |

*Sources*

This table follows the diagram provided by Cobb Biermann, 'Die Darmstädter Hofkapelle', 32. Only those musicians who could be verified as full-time members of the *Hofkapelle* during the years in question are listed here; individuals who were primarily employed elsewhere but may have also been at the *Hofkapelle*'s disposal are not included.

[a] In Darmstadt, as at many other courts, the *Hofkantor* was designated an 'Außerordentliches Mitglied' (extraordinary member) of the *Hofkapelle*.

b See Cobb Biermann, 'Die Darmstädter Hofkapelle', 41.

c See ibid., 61–6. Tayault served from 1709 to 1719 and Demoll from 1718 to 1740. Moreover, the two *Tanzmeister* 'Friedrich J. Etienne' and 'F. Dubois' were employed at court between 1747 and 1749 and from 1749 until 1759 respectively. See also Wilhelm Gottfried Enderle, 'Arrangement wie solches bey Aufführung Kirch-Cammer und Taffel Musiquen bey der Instrumental Musik zu observieren – aus dem Jahr 1758', reproduced in Bill, 'Dokumente zum Leben', 69–70. It is, therefore, highly likely that the court employed a *Tanzmeister* in 1745 and 1760, even if there are no primary sources extant to support this theory.

# 13

# The Court of Baden-Durlach in Karlsruhe

*Rüdiger Thomsen-Fürst*

I N 1535, THE MARGRAVIATE OF BADEN was divided into two territories: Baden-Durlach and Baden-Baden, which were Protestant and Catholic respectively. Initially, the Protestant branch of the house of Baden resided in Pforzheim, but in 1565 they transferred their seat to Durlach. In 1715, in the wake of the extensive devastation of Durlach during the War of the Palatine Succession (1688–97), including the destruction of its residential palace, the Karlsburg or 'Carolsburg', a new town was founded and a new palace built on the Rhine plain near Durlach, in what is today Karlsruhe. Similar action had been taken in the Catholic margraviate of Baden-Baden several years earlier, after its residence (also named Baden-Baden) had been burnt down by French troops in 1689: from 1700 onwards a new palace together with a 'planned' town were constructed in Rastatt, with buildings erected according to compulsory architectural guidelines. The relocation of the Baden-Durlach court to Karslruhe was completed by 1718.[1] And when, in 1771, following the death of the last margrave of Baden-Baden, the two territories were reunited under the conditions of the deed of inheritance, Karlsruhe remained the official residence until the end of World War I. For a short period of time, between 1803 and 1806, Baden became an electorate and then existed as a grand duchy until 1918; furthermore, as a member of the Confederation of the Rhine (1806–13), it had also gained large territories.

The *Hofkapelle* of Baden-Durlach, as with that of Baden, belongs to those institutions which can boast of a comparatively long and uninterrupted history: it continued as a court orchestra until 1918, and its place is occupied today by the Badische Staatskapelle Karlsruhe. After the Thirty Years' War, the employment of court musicians in Baden-Durlach can be traced back to at least the year 1662.[2]

---

[1] The court servants were required to relocate to Karlsruhe by the autumn of 1717; see Christina Wagner, 'Von der Stadtgründung zur großherzoglich badischen Haupt- und Residenzstadt', in *Karlsruhe: Die Stadtgeschichte*, ed. Stadt Karlsruhe (Karlsruhe: Badenia, 1998), 65–189, at 78.

[2] A summary overview of salaries for that year indicates that 428 *Gulden*, 30 *Kreutzer* (including both cash payments and payments in kind) were paid out for the 'Music der Hoff-Capellen', see D-KAg, 47/639, 'Naturalienabrechnung', reproduced in *340 Jahre Badische Staatskapelle Karlsruhe und 30 Jahre Gesellschaft der Freunde des Badischen Staatstheaters*

The reign of Margrave Friedrich VI (1659–77) saw performances held in the Dur-lach residence, above all ballets held during festivities celebrated by the margravial family.[3] The earliest documented example is a 'Tanz Spiel', *Glück und Tugend*, performed in 1666, the composer of which is unknown.[4] The period in office of his son Friedrich VII Magnus (1647–1709, r. from 1677) was rather less fortunate. The first true operatic performance on the 'Hoch-Fürstlichen Schau-Platz Carolsburg' (Most Princely Stage [in the] Karlsburg) took place in 1684, with *Der sich selbst besiegende Scipio* (composer unknown).[5] However, only a few years later, in August 1689, the residential palace was burnt down by French troops in the War of the Palatine Succession. For some years to come, a regular court musical life was im-possible; it was not until 1699 that the Karlsburg was provisionally reopened, while the onset of the War of the Spanish Succession further prevented a rapid improve-ment of conditions. Margrave Friedrich Magnus died in 1709 and was succeeded by his son Carl Wilhelm, whose accession inaugurated a long period of peace.

## 1715: THE FOUNDING OF KARLSRUHE AND THE EXPANSION OF THE *HOFKAPELLE*

The reign of Margrave Carl Wilhelm (1679–1738), who had married Princess Magdalena Wilhelmina of Württemberg (1677–1742) in 1697, is marked above all by the founding of the town of 'Carols-Ruhe' (literally 'Carl's Rest'). The margrave was especially passionate about musical theatre and ensured that during the 1720s Karlsruhe became an important performance venue for early German opera.

When assembling his *Hofkapelle* early in his reign, Carl Wilhelm was able to draw upon a number of musicians who had already served under his father. Among them was *Vicekapellmeister* Enoch Blinzig (1661–1737), who in 1708 attempted to secure a recommendation to the Prussian court, citing as his reason the lamentable condition of the margraviate.[6] It was, however, a journey to Italy that provided Carl Wilhelm with critical impetus for his court musical establishment when in 1712 he attended the carnival in Venice.[7] This stay appears to have also been intended to assist with the reorganization of his own ensemble, since the margrave brought back with him to Karlsruhe both Italian music and musicians (as will be discussed

---

*e. V.*, ed. Badisches Staatstheater Karlsruhe (Karlsruhe: Badisches Staatstheater Karlsruhe, 2002), 2–3.

[3] Ludwig Schiedermair, 'Die Oper an den badischen Höfen des 17. und 18. Jahrhunderts', *Sammelbände der Internationalen Musikgesellschaft*, 14 (1912/13), 191–207, 369–449, 510–50, at 204–5.

[4] Ibid., 204.

[5] Ibid., 205–6.

[6] In early July 1708, Blinzig submitted a written request for such a recommendation to Duke Moritz Wilhelm of Saxony-Zeitz; reproduced ibid., 207.

[7] Hans Leopold Zollner, '. . . *der sich in Carolsruh ein Eden hat erbaut*': *Ein Lebensbild des Markgrafen Karl Wilhelm von Baden-Durlach* (Karlsruhe: Badische Neueste Nachrichten Ba-dendruck, 1990), 25.

below).[8] Only a small handful of music inventories detailing the collection of the Karlsruhe *Hofkapelle* remain extant, making Armin Brinzing's recent discovery of an inventory of the Durlach palace, including music, all the more significant.[9] This inventory indicates that a substantial collection of works by Jean-Baptiste Lully — which until its destruction during World War II had been part of the music collection of the Badische Landesbibliothek — did not originally come from Rastatt, as had been assumed by Klaus Häfner, but rather had belonged to the Durlach *Hofkapelle*.[10] Featured among the inventory is music brought back from Margrave Carl Wilhelm's trip to Venice in 1712, including compositions by Antonio Vivaldi.[11] Giuseppe Boniventi (*c*.1670–after 1727) was most likely appointed *Hofkapellmeister* on 10 January 1712, presumably when the margrave was still in Venice.[12] Additional Venetian musicians, above all vocalists, including Maria Maddalena Frigieri, Giovanna Stradiotti, and Natale Bettinardo (Bettinardi), also came to Durlach at this time.

But the city of the lagoons also seems to have provided Carl Wilhelm's inspiration for the establishment of one particular institution in his new town, causing him to be portrayed in a poor light, especially since the nineteenth century. At issue here is his large ensemble of 'Hofsingerinnen' (female court singers), which had already upset the duchess of Orléans, 'Liselotte of the Palatinate' (1655–1722), the sister-in-law of King Louis XIV of France, who referred to it as a 'serail ridicule' (ridiculous seraglio):

> Ich habe schon von dem ridicullen serail gehört, so der margraff von Durlach helt. Wie ich jetzt von unßern Teütschen, es seÿe fürsten, oder ander herrn, höre, so seindt sie alle so närisch, alß wen sie auß dem dollhauß kämmen; ich schamme mich recht davor.

> I have already heard about the ridiculous seraglio maintained by the margrave of Durlach. According to what I've heard lately of our Germans —

---

[8] An inventory extant in D-KAg refers to specific works that the margrave brought back with him from Venice; cf. Martina Rebmann and Armin Brinzing, 'Musikalien, beschrieben von Martina Rebmann und Armin Brinzing', in *Vierzig Jahre Badische Bibliotheksgesellschaft e. V. Jubiläumsschrift und Begleitheft zur Ausstellung, 1966–2006: Kostbare Geschenke der Badischen Bibliotheksgesellschaft*, ed. Wolfgang Klose (Karlsruhe: Badische Bibliotheksgesellschaft 2006), 71–93. I am grateful to Armin Brinzing for providing me with this and other pieces of information.

[9] Ibid., 71.

[10] Klaus Häfner, 'Repertoire und Musikalien der Rastatter Hofkapelle im frühen 18. Jahrhundert: Zusammensetzung und Schicksal', in *J. C. F. Fischer in seiner Zeit: Tagungsbericht Rastatt 1988*, ed. Ludwig Finscher, Quellen und Studien zur Geschichte der Mannheimer Hofkapelle, 3 (Frankfurt am Main: Peter Lang, 1994), 21–43, at 34–6, which includes a complete list of works.

[11] Armin Brinzing, *Thematischer Katalog der Musikhandschriften (Signaturengruppe Mus. Hs.), mit einem vollständigen Verzeichnis der Werke Johann Melchior Molters (MWV)*, Die Handschriften der Badischen Landesbibliothek in Karlsruhe, 14 (Wiesbaden: Harrassowitz, 2010).

[12] See Norbert Dubowy, 'Boniventi', in *Die Musik in Geschichte und Gegenwart: allgemeine Enzyklopädie der Musik*, 2nd rev. edn (Kassel: Bärenreiter, 1994–2008; hereafter *MGG 2*), Personenteil, III: 342–3.

whether they are princes or aristocrats – they are all as crazy as if they had come out of the mad house; I am really quite ashamed by this. (15 December 1718)

Von deß margraffs von Durlaches dolles leben habe ich gehört; er ist gar zu narisch. Ich forcht, dießer herr sey gar zum nahren geworden, den närischer hatt mans nie erlebt undt habe nie von dergleichen gehört, alß einen mahler zu Paris, so Santerre hieß; der hatte keine mahlerjungen noch knechte, so ihm dinten, lautter junge medger, so ihn auß- undt ahnzogen; er war aber nicht geheüraht.

I have heard about the bedlam life led by the margrave of Durlach; he is completely mad. I fear that he has turned into a complete imbecile; [his life style] has never been crazier, and I have never heard of anything like it, except for a painter in Paris named Santerre; he did not have apprentice boys or helpers who served him, but only young girls who dressed and undressed him; he was, however, not married [unlike the margrave of Durlach]. (13 September 1719)

Der gelehrte von Hall[e] gewindt gewiß eine staffel im himmel, ursach zu sein, daß der margraff von Durlach sein scandalleus leben verlest undt seinen serail abgeschafft . . .

The [unidentified] man of letters from Hall[e] will surely be given a leading position in heaven if he can persuade the margrave of Durlach to abandon his scandalous life and shut down his seraglio . . . (4 June 1722)[13]

Consequently, Carl Wilhelm's courtly life style has conjured up visions of harems reminiscent of the *Arabian Nights* to this very day and tempted historians over the course of the past three centuries either to omit this topic intentionally or misuse it as a means through which to project their own fantasies.[14]

---

[13] Cited in Wilhelm Ludwig Holland, ed., *Elisabeth Charlotte Herzogin von Orléans: Briefe aus den Jahren 1676–1722*, 6 vols. (Stuttgart and Tübingen, 1867–81; repr. Hildesheim: Olms, 1988), III: 474, IV: 239, VI: 407; see also VI: 67 (letter of 3 April 1721).

[14] Liselotte von der Pfalz had already given this impression in her letters (see ibid.). In the nineteenth century, among others, it was Carl Eduard Vehse who portrayed Carl Wilhelm's court as an oriental miniature in his multi-volume publication, *Geschichte der deutschen Höfe seit der Reformation* (1851–60; see particularly *Die Höfe zu Baden*, selected, revised, and ed. by Wolfgang Schneider (Leipzig and Weimar: Kiepenheuer, 1992), 69–72). Such insinuations are still to be found in Zollner, '. . . *der sich in Carolsruh ein Eden hat erbaut*', 29–30, when he writes of the young Carl Wilhelm: 'Vor allem schwärmte der Erbprinz für die bunten holländischen Tulpen, und verguckte sich . . . schon recht frühreif in schöne Mädchen und Frauen. Alles in allem vereinte dieser blendend aussehende, vitale und charmante Prinz in seinem Naturell kräftige Männlichkeit und eine Sinnlichkeit, die sich gleichermaßen ins Ästhetische, ins Kreative und ins Erotische erstreckte' (Above all, the hereditary prince was passionate about colourful Dutch tulips and, as a precocious male, turned his attention . . . to beautiful girls and women very early. All in all, the disposition of this extremely attractive, vigorous, and charming prince combined a strong masculinity and a sensuality which extended equally

An eyewitness account of Carl Wilhelm's court was provided by Baron Karl Ludwig von Pöllnitz in 1730:

Mitten inne [im Fasanengarten] ist ein grosses Bassin, welches jederzeit voler wilder Enten, um dasselbige aber stehen 4. Pavillons, in Form von Türckischen Zelten gemacht, davon zwey vor Vogel-Häuser dienen, die andere beyde aber sind Cabineter, vorne mit grünen Vorhängen von grünem Tuch zugemacht, und liegen gewisse Polster nach der Morgenländischen Weise daarinnen. An diesem angenehmen Ruhe-Platz hält sich täglich der Marggraff etliche Stunden auf, und hat er ordinaire einige von den Mädgens bey sich, welche, gleichwie er sie in der Music hat unterrichten lassen, also machen sie dahier die angenehmsten Concerten. . . . Zu Mittag speiset er ordinair nur in einer Gesellschaft von vier Personen, und haben die Weibsleute, so er an seinem Hofe hält, die Aufwartung dabey. Es sind deren an der Zahl 60. doch haben ihrer täglich nicht mehr als 8. die Auffwartung. Wann der Marggraff ausfähret, folgen ihm selbige als Hussaren gekleidet zu Pferde nach. Der mehreste Theil von ihnen verstehet nebst der Music auch das Tantzen, und wird die Opera auf dem Hoff-Teatro von ihnen gespielet, sonsten auch die Kirchen-Music durch sie versehen, und logieren sie allesamt bey Hoff.

In the middle [of the pheasant garden] stands a great basin, which is always filled with wild ducks; positioned around it, however, are four pavilions modelled on Turkish tents. Two of these serve as aviaries, while the other two are private rooms with entrances covered with green curtains made of green cloth, wherein can be found certain cushions set out according to oriental custom. The margrave spends several hours a day in this agreeable resting place, and usually has some of the girls with him, who – since he has had them trained in music – perform the most delightful concerts in this venue. . . . Ordinarily, for his midday meal he dines in the company of no more than four people, with the women he maintains at his court waiting upon them. The latter number sixty in total, yet no more than eight attend upon him daily. When the margrave goes for a ride [in his carriage], these same [females] follow him on horseback, dressed as hussars. The majority of them are not only competent musicians, but also dancers, and they perform in operas at the court theatre as well as providing church music; moreover, they all live at court.[15]

into aesthetic, creative, and erotic matters). Zollner also notes (p. 32) that 'als Heiducken oder Husaren kostümierten Mädchen . . . sogar die Dienste von Kammerdienern bei ihm versehen haben sollen' (girls, wearing costumes of heyducks or hussars . . . are supposed to have served as his chamber valets); naturally, they would not have lived in the same residence as the margravine, 'die verständlicherweise mit den Amouren ihres Gatten nicht einverstanden war' (who, understandably, did not approve of her husband's amours). Schiedermair had already tried to correct this one-dimensional perspective; see 'Die Oper an den badischen Höfen', 370–71.

[15] Karl Ludwig von Pöllnitz, *Des Freyherrn von Pöllnitz Neue Nachrichten, welche seine Lebens-Geschichte und eine ausführliche Beschreibung von seinen ersten Reisen in sich enthalten: Wie sie nach der neuesten Auflage aus dem Frantzösischen in das Hoch-Deutsche übersetzt*

The margrave was clearly a connoisseur of females and also of flowers.[16] It should be noted, however, that the employment of these *Hofsängerinnen* was in no way a by-product of an excessive interest in the keeping of mistresses, a common practice at courts around this time. In 1992, Olivia Hochstrasser re-examined the social and reception history of this institution, using primary sources rather than literary reports, and arrived at the same conclusion.[17] She traced the fates of individuals as far as possible and, while conceding that there had been sexual contacts between the margrave and individual *Sängerinnen*, emphasizes that the young women's respectable duties were their primary focus and that the label 'seraglio' was exaggerated.[18] Indeed, the staff of *Hofsängerinnen* could be seen to have contributed to the court's image in a very special manner, and to have been established primarily for musical and economic reasons. The Venetian *ospedali* appear to have served the margrave as a model. Originally orphanages for girls, these institutions became musical centres providing girls and young women with a comprehensive musical education, which presented concerts that were also recommended as an attraction for tourists.[19] In fact, for eighteenth-century travellers, a visit to the Venetian *ospedali* with their all-female choirs and orchestras was mandatory.[20] Antonio Vivaldi served (albeit intermittently) as a music master at the largest one, the Ospedale della Pietà. He had been reappointed in 1711, and since the margrave of Baden may have visited this particular *ospedale* in 1712, it is possible that he made personal contact with Vivaldi.

In view of the fact that engaging vocalists, above all Italians, was always an expensive undertaking, the court saved money by training locals. Furthermore, most of the Italians – vocalists and instrumentalists – left Durlach and Karlsruhe soon after their arrival; only the bass singer Bettinardo stayed until 1729. The group of *Hofsängerinnen* at the court remained until 1733, despite a slight reduction in the number of positions over time. While at first glance, the number given by Pöllnitz – sixty women – seems implausible, it is nevertheless confirmed by information contained in numerous primary sources.[21] In total, during the period between

*worden* (Frankfurt am Main, 1739), 15 February 1730, as cited in Klaus Häfner, *Der badische Hofkapellmeister Johann Melchior Molter (1696–1765) in seiner Zeit: Dokumente und Bilder zu Leben und Werk* (with a chapter by Rainer Fürst), exhibition catalogue (Karlsruhe: Badische Landesbibliothek, 1996), 22–4.

[16] The margrave was an avid gardener and in particular an enthusiast for tulips (which were extremely precious items at the time). See the excerpt from the manuscript 'KS Nische C 13' published as Gerhard Stamm, *Karlsruher Tulpenbuch: Eine Handschrift der Badischen Landesbibliothek*, unrevised edn (Karlsruhe: Badische Bibliotheksgesellschaft, 1984).

[17] Olivia Hochstrasser, 'Hof, Stadt, Dörfle: Karlsruher Frauen in der vorbürgerlichen Gesellschaft (1715–1806)', in *Karlsruher Frauen 1715–1945: Eine Stadtgeschichte*, ed. Stadt Karlsruhe: Stadtarchiv, Veröffentlichungen des Karlsruher Stadtarchivs, 15 (Karlsruhe: Badenia, 1992), 19–101, at 23–40.

[18] Ibid., 34–5. Numerous primary sources are extant in D-KAg, 47/787–90.

[19] Berthold Over, *Per la Gloria di Dio: Solistische Kirchenmusik an den venezianischen Ospedali im 18. Jahrhundert*, Orpheus-Schriftenreihe zu Grundfragen der Musik, 91 (Bonn: Orpheus, 1998), 22–6.

[20] See ibid., 22 n. 3, for a list of relevant travel reports and related sources.

[21] See Hochstrasser, 'Hof, Stadt, Dörfle', 30–31, who occasionally provides numbers, which

1714 and 1733, approximately 160 females are documented as having served as *Hof-sängerinnen*.[22] The number peaked in 1717, with eighty-eight names listed in the accounts for the first quarter of that year.[23]

The *Hofsängerinnen* were a separate category of employees to the actual *Hof-musik* and reported to the *Hofmarschallamt* (court chamberlain's office). Along-side the singers themselves, the group comprised maids, nannies, and occasionally female teachers and other servants as well; they were taught by members of the *Hofkapelle*. At least some of the *Hofsängerinnen* were provided with lodgings in the *Schloßturm* (palace tower); and, from 1718, the margrave also sold ten adjacent houses in the Draisgasse (today Herrenstraße) to *Hofsängerinnen*.[24] Above all, the *Hofsängerinnen* participated in opera productions: they performed the leading roles, as well as singing in the chorus and dancing.[25] According to Pöllnitz, they also provided musical entertainment for the margrave and took part in perfor-mances of church music.

Let us now turn to the *Hofkapelle* in general terms. During the year 1715, the ensemble was still in a state of upheaval, with only the outlines of a perma-nent structure beginning to emerge. An inventory of the *Hofmusik* dating from 1716 documents the number of employees at the time of the foundation of the Karlsruhe residence (see Table 13.1, pp. 382–7 below).[26] In total, thirty-four posi-tions are listed, including an 'Opernschneider' (costume maker for the opera) and a dancing master, as well as the seven member band of 'Bayreuther Hautboisten' who had been recommended to the Baden court by the Bayreuth *Geheimrat* (privy councillor) von Stein in 1715.[27] The Venetian Giuseppe Boniventi had served as *Kapellmeister* since 1712, and in about 1715 a number of additional musicians were appointed to key roles.

Of prime significance here is Johann Philipp Käfer (1672–1728 or 1735), for-mer *Kapellmeister* at the court of Saxony-Hildburghausen.[28] According to his

have been revised downward. The collection of archival documents comprises the following: financial statements pertaining to the instructors ('Praeceptores') who rehearsed the young women in operatic roles between 1714 and 1716 (D-KAg, 47/787); a 'Besoldungstabelle' (salary table) for the first quarter of 1717 (D-KAg, 47/788); and complete 'Besoldungsbücher' (salary registers) for 1722–33 (D-KAg, 47/789–90), each of which covers twelve months from *Georgi* (St George's Day, 23 April) forward (D-KAg, 47/789). The last register was set up to accom-modate entries until 1734, but indicates that the last quarterly payments were made in July 1733.

[22] The exact number is very difficult to determine, as the use of fluctuating first names with the same surname means it is sometimes unclear whether one or two people are being referred to.

[23] D-KAg, 47/788.

[24] Hochstrasser, 'Hof, Stadt, Dörfle', 38–9.

[25] See Schiedermair, 'Die Oper an den badischen Höfen', 375–6. Numerous entries in these primary sources specify the roles learnt by these women: the most detailed is the 'Specification Sambtl. hierinnen vermelter Preceptorum welche die Fürstl. Singerin[n]en denen Operen vom Jahrgang 1714 biß georgy [sic] 1716 Informiret' (D-KAg, 47/787), in which a table lists both teachers and singers, plus the corresponding works.

[26] Schiedermair, 'Die Oper an den badischen Höfen', 374.

[27] Ibid., 371.

[28] Ingward Ullrich, *Hildburghäuser Musiker: Ein Beitrag zur Geschichte der Stadt*

appointment decree from 26 August 1715, he was appointed 'Componist bei der Hoff-Music' (composer with the *Hofmusik*) and promoted to *Vicekapellmeister* on 29 March 1716.[29] When Boniventi left Karlsruhe in 1718, Käfer succeeded him as *Kapellmeister*. The previously mentioned Enoch Blinzig was *Vicekapellmeister* at the Durlach court in 1715 (and most likely until 1717).[30] Jean Charles Petit seems to have served as concertmaster. His surname is listed in extant primary sources, but without reference to a specific position; however, a publication entitled *Apologie de l'exellence de la musique* (London, 1740) identifies the author, 'J. C. Petit', as former 'Maître de Musique & Directeur de la Chapelle' of the duke of Saxony-Eisenach, as well as the concertmaster ('Maître de Concerts') and 'Premier Musicien de la Chambre' of the margrave of Baden-Durlach.[31]

The exact position in the *Hofkapelle's* hierarchy held by the composer Casimir (or Caspar) Schweizelsperg(er) (1668–after 1722) is difficult to determine, despite the existence of a draft 'Instruction', or set of regulations relating specifically to his employment.[32] Dating from March 1714, this comprises four points, of which the first three address general matters pertaining to obedience, discipline, and loyalty. Only the last item refers to Schweizelsperg's responsibilities and salary. His actual function, however, is described in rather vague terms:

> weilen 4.) nicht thunlich [ist] all und jedes so in ein: oder des anderen func-
> tion lauffet, zu beschreiben als behalten wir Uns das weiters zu verordnen,
> crafft dieses je und allwegen bevor.

> because (4) it is not feasible to describe each and every thing associated with
> one or the other position, we therefore reserve the right to continue to pre-
> scribe this, by virtue of this order.

Schweizelsperg was, however, explicitly required to provide the *Hofkapelle* with new compositions, both works of his own and by other composers. For this task he was tentatively promised an additional honorarium. Schweizelsperg obviously attended to these tasks immediately, for his opera *Romanische Lucretia* was performed in 1715.[33] Other court musicians, and not only those in leading positions, also expanded the repertoire of the *Hofkapelle* with their own compositions. Of

*Hildburghausen*, Schriften zur Geschichte der Stadt Hildburghausen, 4 (Hildburghausen: Frankenschwelle, 2003), 31–3.

[29] D-KAg, 56/973; Schiedermair, 'Die Oper an den badischen Höfen', 373–4.

[30] See D-KAg 56/965, which contains student test papers that Blinzig signed as *Kapellmeister* in 1715, despite the fact he was listed as *Vicekapellmeister* in the 1715/16 salary roll; cf. Schiedermair, 'Die Oper an den badischen Höfen', 374, 377.

[31] Schiedermair, 'Die Oper an den badischen Höfen', 373. I am grateful to Armin Brinzing for providing me with information regarding Petit's *Apologie de l'exellence de la musique*.

[32] D-KAg, 56/967.

[33] This is the only surviving opera from the Karlsruhe repertoire of the first half of the eighteenth century; see also Günther Haaß, 'Theater am markgräflichen Hof in Durlach, 1666–1719', in *Karlsruher Theatergeschichte*, ed. Badischen Staatstheater Karlsruhe and the Generallandesarchiv Karlsruhe (Karlsruhe: G. Braun, 1982), 9–16.

these, Johann Matthäus Trost (fl. 1714–26) deserves special mention, since four of his operas were performed at the court between 1714 and 1718.[34]

The 1716 inventory of the *Hofmusik* personnel does not include *Kapellknaben*, even though there had been at least six in 1715. It is unclear to what extent the various *Kapellmeister* were responsible for their musical education. A unique testament to the training of these young musicians are the surviving test papers completed by *Kapellknaben* at the house of concertmaster Blinzig on 11 September 1715.[35] The students were tested on their knowledge of copying text and music as well as in arithmetic. *Kapellmeister* Johann Melchior Molter's role with regards to the training of the *Kapellknaben* from 1722 onwards is unclear.[36]

Cantatas were regularly presented on Sundays in the palace chapel (consecrated in 1717), including two complete cycles composed by *Kapellmeister* Käfer of which only the librettos have survived.[37] Large-scale works of the oratorio type were also given. In Holy Week 1719, for example, the performances included Käfer's monumental passion setting, *Der leydende und sterbende Jesus* on Monday, 3 April, followed by Georg Philipp Telemann's *Brockes-Passion* (TWV 5:1) on Wednesday, 5 April; it had been premiered in Frankfurt in 1716.[38] Instrumental compositions by Telemann also belonged to the *Hofkapelle*'s repertoire, including the Concerto in E major for transverse flute, oboe d'amore, viola d'amore and strings (TWV 53:E1), and the Concerto grosso in D major (TWV 53:D1).[39]

On 13 January 1719, the theatre in the east wing of the new palace was inaugurated with the 'musicalisches Divertissement' *Celindo*[:] *Hoch-gepriesene Gärtner-Treue*; once again, the librettist and the composer are unknown.[40] The tradition of opera performances which had begun in Durlach was continued in Karlsruhe and remained an important part of court's musical life. This is evident from the

---

[34] Schiedermair, 'Die Oper an den badischen Höfen', 387–8, 391–423; see also Renate Brockpähler, *Handbuch zur Geschichte der Barockoper in Deutschland* (Emsdetten/Westfalen: Lechte, 1964), 155–7. The following works have been attributed to Trost: *Die bestürzte Königin in Schottland Maria Stuart* (between 1714 and 1716), *Die enthauptete Königin in Schottland Maria Stuart* (between 1714 and 1716), *Rhea Sylvia* (1716), and *Ademarus* (1718).

[35] D-KAg, 56/965.

[36] See Häfner, *Der badische Hofkapellmeister Johann Melchior Molter*, 95.

[37] The texts of the works performed during that week were gathered together in a volume published in Durlach in 1719: *Die grosse Wochen der Carlsruhisch-Fürstlichen Hof-Capelle, das ist: Verschiedene geistreiche Andachten . . . bey denen öffentlichen Gottesdiensten sich deß leydenden Jesu erinnert wird.* A copy is held in D-KA, Sign. O52 A 51. See Klaus Häfner, 'Georg Philipp Telemann, Johann Melchior Molter und der baden-durlachische Hof in Karlsruhe', *Telemann-Beiträge: Abhandlungen und Berichte*, 3 (1997), 7–27, at 12; as well as Häfner, 'Karlsruher Musikleben im 18. Jahrhundert', in *Leben in der Fächerstadt: Vortragsreihe des Forums für Stadtgeschichte und Kultur zur Gründung der Stadt Karlsruhe vor 275 Jahren*, ed. Stadt Karlsruhe, Karlsruher Beiträge, 6 (Karlsruhe: G. Braun, 1991), 77–93, at 77–8.

[38] Häfner, 'Georg Philipp Telemann, Johann Melchior Molter', 12.

[39] Both works are included in the inventory that Häfner ('Georg Philipp Telemann, Johann Melchior Molter', 16) believes dates from 1740 (D-KA, Mus. Hs. Inventare, pp. 17–26).

[40] This piece had already been performed in Durlach in 1713; see Günther Haaß, 'Theater am markgräflichen und kurfürstlichen Hof in Carolsruhe, 1719–1806', in *Karlsruher Theatergeschichte*, 17–27, at 17–19; see also Schiedermair, 'Die Oper an den badischen Höfen', 394.

extensive performance schedules for the years up until 1732 listed by Schiedermair, who examined a total of thirty-seven librettos (many of which were performed multiple times).[41]

## 1730: THE BEGINNING OF A DECLINE

Fifteen years after the founding of Karlsruhe little had changed with regard to the fundamental structure of the court's musical life. In addition to the actual *Hofkapelle*, both the *Hofsängerinnen* and the 'Bayreuther Hautboisten' continued to be involved in musical performances (see Table 13.1). The majority of the Italian musicians, however, had only stayed in Baden-Durlach for a short period of time; last to be dismissed was the bass vocalist Natale Bettinardo in 1729. Otherwise, the personnel had remained virtually unchanged. As was common practice at most small and medium-sized courts, two musicians were now in charge of the *Hofmusik*. Johann Melchior Molter (1696–1765) had been appointed *Hofkapellmeister* in 1722, and ranked among the most important composers in south-western Germany around this time.[42] When he took over as *Kapellmeister*, a shift in artistic priorities occurred, as Molter was above all a prolific composer of instrumental music.[43] In contrast, by 1730, the number of newly staged operas had considerably decreased: Renate Brockpähler could confirm only four new titles between 1723 and 1732.[44] In 1728, the violinist Sebastian Bodinus (*c.*1700–1759) became concert-master in Karlsruhe; he was a member of the *Hofkapelle* from 1718 to 1752, albeit intermittently.[45]

The year 1733 marked a turning point for life at court. With the outbreak of the War of the Polish Succession and related troop movements in Baden, the court was forced into exile in Basel. Music at the court was brought almost to a standstill, when the majority of the musicians, including *Kapellmeister* Molter, had their positions 'downsized'; in other words, they were dismissed. The margrave returned to his residence only in 1736, but after the end of the war there was little time for Carl Wilhelm to re-establish his *Hofmusik*, since he died on 12 May 1738. The number of court musicians had declined notably. A salary register from 1738 specifies only eight musicians, listed under the rubric 'Hoff Music Bediente' (those serving with the *Hofmusik*). In addition to concertmaster Bodinus, *Cammerdiener* and *Musicus* Schmelzer, *Cammerdiener* Dill, Eberhardt (no title provided), *Hofmusicus* and bass vocalist Thill, and *Hofmusici* Hengel, Gebhardt, and Mensinger, four trum-

---

[41] Schiedermair, 'Die Oper an den badischen Höfen', 387–8, 391–423; Brockpähler, *Handbuch zur Geschichte der Barockoper*, 150–57.

[42] On Molter's life and works, see Häfner, *Der badische Hofkapellmeister Johann Melchior Molter*.

[43] Häfner, 'Karlsruher Musikleben im 18. Jahrhundert', 87.

[44] Schiedermair, 'Die Oper an den badischen Höfen', 388; Brockpähler, *Handbuch zur Geschichte der Barockoper*, 157: *Amore e Amore* (1724), *Orpheus* (1728), *Curtius*, and *Sieg der Schönheit* (both 1730). The composers of these works are unknown.

[45] Klaus Häfner, 'Bodinus', *MGG 2*, Personenteil, III: 191–3.

peters and one kettledrum player are also listed. A number of lackeys were used for musical performances at court as well, but listed in a different category and identified as lackeys and *Hautboisten*, with one even designated *Hoforganist* and lackey.[46]

In the place of Carl Wilhelm's successor and grandson, Carl Friedrich (1728–1811, r. from 1746) — who was still a child at the time of Carl Wilhelm's death — the dowager margravine Magdalena Wilhelmina ruled together with her nephew Carl August (1712–1786). When she passed away in 1742, Carl August became the new regent of Baden-Durlach, supported by his younger brother, Wilhelm Eugen (1713–1783). Archival documentation is sparse for the decade between Carl Wilhelm's death in 1738 and the beginning of Carl Friedrich's reign in 1746, with musical life at court probably being restricted to occasional festive works and chamber music. The margravine in particular appears to have possessed little appreciation of music, or at least there is no evidence of her ever having promoted musical performances at court. Carl August, on the other hand, reappointed Molter as *Kapellmeister* in February 1743, despite the fact that the *Hofkapelle* had shrunk to a small ensemble by this time and was not immediately expanded.[47]

Fortunately, two inventories survive from the mid-eighteenth century that detail the instrumental works available at the time. According to Klaus Häfner, the first inventory dates from 1740 and was prepared by the court musician Johann Georg Thill (c.1685–1758).[48] It contains exclusively works for one or more transverse flutes in various combinations with other instruments (including solo, trio, and quadro sonatas as well as concertos and sinfonias). The inventory, entitled 'Catalogus', lists a total of 119 consecutively numbered compositions. In addition to Karlsruhe musicians such as Molter and Bodinus, and the already mentioned Telemann, the composers named include Antoine Mahaut, Johann Joachim Quantz, Johann Adolf Hasse, Johann Friedrich Fasch, Fortunato Chelleri ('Kelleri'), Giovanni Battista Sammartini ('Martino'), and (Johann) Stamitz ('Steinmetz').

### 1747: A NEWLY REGULATED BEGINNING UNDER JOHANN MELCHIOR MOLTER

In 1746, the eighteen-year-old Margrave Carl Friedrich assumed power. He developed into an enlightened ruler, for whom his grandfather's sense of opulence and a love for opera were foreign concepts. The new margrave introduced a series of socio-political reforms, including the reorganization of his administration and the abolishment of both torture and serfdom in 1767 and 1783 respectively. He also turned his attention to rebuilding the parts of the Karlsruhe palace that by the mid-eighteenth century were in a state of disrepair, owing to the extensive use of wood during the initial building phase in 1715; renovations began in 1752 and

---

[46] D-KAg 74/1804; see also Schiedermair, 'Die Oper an den badischen Höfen', 390.

[47] Häfner, *Der badische Hofkapellmeister Johann Melchior Molter*, 60.

[48] D-KA, Mus. Hs. Inventar 1; see Häfner, 'Georg Philipp Telemann, Johann Melchior Molter', 16.

continued until 1775. In 1751, Carl Friedrich married Caroline Luise of Hesse-Darmstadt (1723–1783), a connoisseur of the fine arts who excelled as a painter and collector. The reigning couple also appreciated music: Carl Friedrich played the transverse flute, his wife the harpsichord; however, they both refrained from any ostentatious displays of splendour.[49]

Carl Friedrich's austere attitude, shaped by his own limited means, common sense, and the economic situation, is also evident in the reorganization of the *Hofmusik*. In January 1747, Molter was asked by the young margrave to prepare a plan 'von einer zwar nicht allzu großen, jedoch wohl eingerichteten Capelle' (for a not too large, but nevertheless well-appointed *Kapelle*).[50] Molter envisioned an ensemble of forty-five individuals, comprising a *Kapellmeister*, five (later reduced to four) vocal soloists, and sixteen choral singers (all pupils at the local *Gymnasium*, four per part), plus twenty instrumentalists, as well as a music copyist and a *Calcant*. He also specified the names of the musicians, together with their respective salaries. Molter's is the first list of Karlsruhe musicians in which the players are differentiated by their instruments. For each part Molter identified a soloist (made clear by the use of the term 'concert'), whereas the ripienists did not have to be specialists on a particular instrument. According to this plan, the annual costs for the *Kapelle* would amount to a total of 6,000 *Gulden*.

At the same time Molter also formulated a set of disciplinary regulations ('Leges') which were presented to the musicians by the court chamberlain's office on the margrave's behalf.[51] The first rule demanded that the musicians accept their respective salaries willingly and refrain from inundating their 'Gnädigste Herrschaft' (Most Gracious Ruler) with petitions. Second, they were to comply fully with the orders given by the *Kapellmeister* or else risk 'Ser[enissi]mi Höchste Ungnad' (His Serene Highness's utmost disfavour) and even dismissal. In the other rules the court musicians were urged to be disciplined. Specifically, they had to practise diligently at home, and no one was permitted to be absent from work or go on leave without prior approval from the *Kapellmeister*. Moreover, conflicts among musicians would be handled by the *Kapellmeister*.[52]

On 9 March 1747, the margrave approved Molter's plans in principle, but corrected a number of details. For instance, he considered the music copyist specified by Molter to be unnecessary, for 'es könnten die Musici ihre Musicalia selbst

---

[49] Carl Friedrich's flute playing is documented in, among other places, a personal diary that he kept for a few short months, from December 1752 to March 1753 (D-KAg, Familienarchiv 5.46.1). In 1736, Caroline Luise had studied with Johann Samuel Endler (1694–1762) in Darmstadt, and her harpsichord playing was praised; cf. Jan Lauts, *Karoline Luise von Baden: Ein Lebensbild aus der Zeit der Aufklärung*, 2nd rev. edn (Karlsruhe: C. F. Müller, 1990), 13–14, 116; Joanna Cobb Biermann, *Die Sinfonien des Darmstädter Kapellmeisters Johann Samuel Endler, 1694–1762*, Beiträge zur mittelrheinischen Musikgeschichte, 33 (Mainz: Schott, 1996), 45.

[50] The corresponding archival materials are extant (D-KAg, 47/792, 'Die Einrichtung einer Hofmusik') and have been published by Häfner, *Der badische Hofkapellmeister Johann Melchior Molter*, 169–77.

[51] Ibid., 170–71.

[52] D-KAg, 47/792, 'Die Einrichtung einer Hofmusik'; cf. Häfner, *Der badische Hofkapellmeister Johann Melchior Molter*, 169–77.

schreiben' (the musicians were capable of copying their parts themselves).[53] After Molter's death, most of these rules remained in effect.[54] Concrete information regarding musical life at the court after 1747 is, however, sorely lacking. And since the theatre built by Carl Wilhelm was not among those sections of the palace being renovated, operatic performances recommenced only during the last quarter of the eighteenth century.[55] Accordingly, the *Hofkapelle*'s focal point during the 1750s was probably concerts at the palace, featuring primarily instrumental music and occasionally cantatas as well. Molter undoubtedly composed the majority of his more than one hundred sinfonias and concertos as well as chamber music for these performances.[56] The works of Giovanni Battista Sammartini (1700/1701–1775) also appear to have been particularly valued in Karlsruhe around the year 1750. Carl Friedrich ordered music in Milan in person, with the composer himself sending six 'Concertini' to Karlsruhe.[57] An accompanying letter from just such a shipment, dated 23 November 1750, remains extant.[58]

## 1760: 'EINE NICHT ALLZU GROSSE JEDOCH WOHL EINGERICHTETE CAPELLE'

An overview of salaries – prepared almost fifteen years to the day after the approval of Molter's plan – shows that his reforms were indeed implemented in principle. A surviving list of 'Hoff Music Bediente' from 2 April 1762 itemizes a total of twenty musicians, among them Molter, four trumpeters, and a kettledrum player (see Table 13.1).[59] The position of concertmaster had remained vacant ever since Bodinus had escaped ('entwichen') in 1752, later dying in the 'Tollhaus' (lunatic asylum) at Pforzheim in 1758.[60] The violinist Giacynto (Hiacintho) Schiatti (d. 1776), who had come from Ferrara to Karlsruhe in 1754, was included in the 1762 list, but was only officially appointed concertmaster in 1765. Since his salary of 560 *Gulden* (which comprised both cash and payments in kind) was only slightly less than that of *Kapellmeister* Molter (who received 589 *Gulden*), Schiatti had

---

[53] D-KAg, 47/792, cited ibid., 175.

[54] For example, the draft set of instructions prepared for concertmaster Schiatti in 1765 is clearly based on Molter's 'Leges'; see D-KAg 56/973.

[55] Joseph Aloys Schmittbauer, for example, had apparently prepared a German version of Pierre-Alexandre Monsigny's *opéra comique Le Déserteur*; see Schmittbauer's letter to the *Oberhofmarschallamt* (court chamberlain's office) dated 17 November 1773, D-KAg, 56/974. And on 15 July 1774, his serenata *Endymione* (libretto by Pietro Metastasio) was performed on the occasion of the marriage of Hereditary Prince Carl Ludwig and Princess Amalie Friderike of Hesse-Darmstadt (libretto: D-FRu, E 749).

[56] Häfner, 'Karlsruher Musikleben im 18. Jahrhundert', 90.

[57] Sammartini's letter is reproduced in Häfner, *Der badische Hofkapellmeister Johann Melchior Molter*, 362–3.

[58] D-KAg, Großherzogliches Familienarchiv 5, Corr. vol. 38,66, facsimile and transcription ibid.

[59] D-KAg, 56/1095.

[60] Cf. Häfner, 'Bodinus'.

probably already served in that position prior to 1765.[61] Only two of the original vocal positions were filled, neither of them permanently. Consequently, the ensemble which Molter had at his disposal during his second term as *Kapellmeister* was a relatively small, albeit flexible group. An increase in the number of vocalists occurred only when the ensemble was amalgamated with the Rastatt *Hofkapelle* in 1772.[62]

An extant draft of instructions prepared for concertmaster Schiatti after Molter's death in 1765, sheds light on the duties assigned to the court musicians:

1.) Solle derselbe in verfolg derer Bereits aufhabenden Pflichten Sr. Hochfürstl: Durchlt: und Dero fürstl: Hauße getreü hold gehorsam und gewärtig seÿn, dero Nutzen so viel an ihm ist, fördern, Schaden aber abwenden, und sich überhaupt so verhalten, wie es einem ehrliebenden getreüen Diener gebühret, und wohl anstehet, auch sich gegen seine Vorgesezte mit schuldigem Egard und Gehorsam betragen, und alles sorgfältig vermeÿden, so gegen ihn gegründete Klagen oder Beschwerden veranlaßen könnten.

2.do) hat der Concert Meister, bis zu Wieder Besetzung der gegenwärtig erledigten Capell Meisters Stelle, oder auch in Abwesenheit eines jeweiligen CapellMeisters beÿ Hofe an bestimten Cour oder anderen Tägen angestellt werdende Musique zu dirigiren, die Hof-Musicos dabeÿ in gutter Ordnung und fleißiger Versehung ihres dienstes zu halten, und nicht zu gestatten, daß sie ohne erhaltene Erlaubnus und erhebliche Ursache solchen versäumen. wie dann

3.) die Hof Musicos anzuhalten, damit dieselbe zu Hauße fleißig sich zu üben, und sich zum fürstln: Vergnügen geschickt zu machen, angelegen seÿn laßen. Anneben hat derselbe

4.to) sich gegen die Hof Musicos nicht allein selbst bescheiden zu betragen, sondern auch dieselbe zu einer bescheidenen begegnung unter sich und Vermeÿdung alles ohnnöthigen Gezänks anzuweÿßen, und die allenfalls entstehende den Dienßt berührende Streitigkeiten ohnparteyisch abzuthun, die von wichtigem Belange aber an das fürstl: Hof Marschall Amt zu verweißen. Wornach sich dann derselbe zu achten, und beÿ Wieder bestellung eines Capell Meisters sich deßen Anordnungen ebenfalls gemäß zu Bezeügen hat.

1. So shall the same [concertmaster Schiatti], in attending to his current duties for His Most Princely Highness [the margrave] and His Princely House, be faithful, obedient, and prepared to undertake whatever is required of him, avert calamities and, in general, always behave in a manner proper for an honourable [and] faithful servant, and as is befitting to him,

[61] Cf. Häfner, *Der badische Hofkapellmeister Johann Melchior Molter*, 72.
[62] Cf. the list of musicians included in the *Hochfürstlich-Markgräflich-Badischer Hof- und Staats-Kalender auf das Jahr 1773* (Karlsruhe, 1773; a copy is extant in D-HEu, A 2665), which details the membership of the *Hofkapelle* in autumn 1772.

[and] also show the necessary regard and obedience to his superiors, and carefully avoid anything that could cause someone to file a grievance or lodge a complaint against him.

2. Until such a time as the post of *Kapellmeister*, which is currently vacant, has been filled, or also in the case that the appointed *Kapellmeister* is absent, the concertmaster has to direct the music at court on certain court or other days, ensuring that the *Hofmusici* behave properly and undertake their service diligently, and not allowing them to be absent without prior approval and for good reason. Moreover,

3. [he must] concern himself with encouraging the *Hofmusici* to practise diligently at home, and thus bring pleasure to prince through their skill. In addition, that the same [concertmaster]

4. must not only act in a modest way when dealing with the *Hofmusici*, but also ensure that they behave modestly when working together and avoid any unnecessary quarrels, and should conflicts arise and cause their working relationship to suffer, [the concertmaster must] mediate in an impartial manner; important issues, however, must be brought to the attention of the court chamberlain's office. [The concertmaster] must follow the latter's orders, as well as those given by the *Kapellmeister*, once that post has been filled.[63]

The difficult conditions under which Schiatti and his musicians had to work are documented in a letter to the margrave, dated 30 January 1766:

Euer Hochfürstlichen Durchlaucht wird hinlänglich bekandt seÿn, wie daß die Haus-Zinse hier von Tag zu Tag höher steigen, welches ich dermalen gleichfalls sehr empfindlich spühren mus, indem ich nicht mehr als 2. Zimer, welche doch so nöthig als das liebe brod habe, und gleichwohl 100. f: jährl: Hauß-Zins geben mus. Da es mir also ohnmöglich beÿ dem so schweren Haus-Zins beide Zimer zu wärmen, und gleichwohl des einen, so wohl zum componiren[,] als [auch] exerciren sehr benötiget wäre, auch nach Eu: Hochfürstl: Durchlaucht höchst-gnädigstem Befehl, daß ich nemlich alles durch den Copisten in meinem Haus solle schreiben lassen, gleichfalls nicht wüßte, wie solches in dem einzigen Zimer, allwo doch meine gantze Familie sich aufhalten mus, geschehen könte.

Your Most Princely Highness must surely be aware that the house taxes seem to increase daily, which has had negative consequences for me, because [my house] has only two rooms which, I believe, are as necessary as my daily bread, and nevertheless, I have to pay 100 *Gulden* annually in house taxes. Due to such high house taxes, it is impossible for me to heat both rooms at the same time, of which one is, nevertheless, much needed for both composition and practising. However, after [receiving] Your Most Princely Highness's most gracious order that the copyist should come to my house to do all

63 D-KAg, 56/973.

of his writing, I am not sure how this is to be accomplished in the other room — after all, my entire family must stay there.[64]

The repertoire of the *Hofkapelle* is further documented by a second inventory of music, prepared by Molter himself in around 1755.[65] The *Kapellmeister* recorded a total of 213 works in four categories with works by the following composers (in addition to anonymous works):

> Sinfonie e Qvatri — Sammartini, Enderle, Lebrecht Schultz, Hasse, Besozzi, and Le Messier.
> Sonate a 3 — Schiatti, Besozzi, Le Messier, L.[ebrecht?] Schultz, Bizzarini, Köhler, Mahaut, Hasse, Neumann, Santo Lapis, Tusco, Sammartini, and Schaffrath.
> Duetti Senza Basso — Mahaut.
> Concerti e Qvatri concertanti — Sammartini, Stamitz, Neumann, Mahaut, Schiatti, Hasse, Le Messier, Lampugnani, San Angelo, Quantz, Fischer, Woditzka, Wendling, Coraucci, Quintinori, Bernasconi, Caputti, Blavet, Le Chevalier, Silliti, Piarello, Benneger, Köhler, Holzbauer, Schultz, Albertini, and Torti.[66]

According to Häfner, most of the music listed here is still held by the Badische Landesbibliothek.[67] The forthcoming catalogue of their music manuscripts, which has been prepared as part of the RISM cataloguing project, is bound to provide answers to this and many other questions concerning the repertoire of the Karlsruhe *Hofkapelle*.[68]


### POSTLUDE

Johann Melchior Molter died on 12 January 1765, but his position as *Kapellmeister* was not immediately filled. The court calendar for 1766 details the members of the *Hofkapelle* following his death.[69] In addition to concertmaster Schiatti, the *Hofmusik* comprised two violinists, a *Waldhornist*, two flautists, one cellist, one 'Clavicinist' who also served as court organist, a bassoonist, and an oboist — a total of ten musicians. These were joined by a *Kapelldiener* and a *Calcant*, four trumpeters and a kettledrum player, as well as three servants who were not listed under the rubric 'Hofmusic'. Instead, they were identified as lackeys, listed with the additional remarks 'auch bei der Music' (also with the music) or 'Hautboist'. The Karlsruhe *Hofmusik* had now reached a new low and presumably not only with

---

[64] D-KAg, 56/973, 'Jeweilige Anstellung der Kapellmeister bei dem Hoforchester'.
[65] D-KA, Mus. Hs. Inventar 3.
[66] Häfner, *Der badische Hofkapellmeister Johann Melchior Molter*, 200–201, 242, 367.
[67] Ibid., 200–201.
[68] Brinzing, *Badische Landesbibliothek Karlsruhe*, forthcoming.
[69] *Markgräflich Baden-Durlachischer Staats- und Adresse-Calender auf das Jahr 1766* (Karlsruhe, 1766), 29–30, 32. In general, the court calendars represent the state of affairs immediately prior to their publication, that is, during the late autumn of the previous year.

regard to the number of musicians employed. The following year, in 1767, Schiatti was appointed *Kapellmeister*, and the violinist Carl August Pfeiffer succeeded him as concertmaster. The number of personnel, however, remained virtually the same; only the number of trumpeters decreased slightly. It was not until 1769 that a moderate increase in the number of positions in the musical establishment is seen in the court calendars.[70]

In 1771, August Georg, the last margrave of the Catholic line of the house of Baden, died without legal issue. According to the stipulations of a contract drawn up beforehand, the two territories were then reunited. Many of the Rastatt court musicians were accepted into the Karlsruhe *Kapelle* either immediately or when permanent positions became vacant, resulting in a considerable expansion of the ensemble. The reunification of the two margraviates of Baden thus resulted in significant growth for the Karlsruhe musical establishment in terms of both quality and quantity. The court calendar for 1773, for example, indicates that the number of court musicians had already risen to twenty-four under the category 'Hof-Music' alone.[71] Furthermore, for the first time in many years vocalists were once more given permanent appointments within the *Hofkapelle*, specifically the soprano Martin Lorenz (d. 1799) and the tenor Ignaz Thau (d. 1794 or 1795). They were joined by eight new musicians: three violinists and five woodwind players.

The *Kapelle* also gained an excellent concertmaster and composer through the appointment of Joseph Aloys Schmittbaur (1718–1809), who had served previously as *Kapellmeister* and concertmaster in Rastatt. He, however, was unhappy with his subordinate position, and instead accepted a two-year appointment as *Kapellmeister* of Cologne Cathedral. After Schiatti's death, Schmittbaur returned to the Baden residence in 1777 and led the court musical establishment until his own death in 1809. He was instrumental in transforming the *Hofkapelle* into a modern orchestra, one better able to meet the expectations of the times. Under his direction the ensemble playing of the court musicians became more precise, the instrumentalists increasingly came to specialize on a single instrument, and the 'Accessisten' system – in which individuals played with the orchestra either for free or for a nominal fee until a permanent position became available – gained acceptance.

During the 1780s, the Karlsruhe *Hofmusik* prospered, and numerous visiting musicians made guest appearances at the court. At the end of the eighteenth century, however, the French Revolutionary Wars resulted in a restriction of the court's musical life once again, with the margravial family absent from the town between 1795 and 1797.[72] By this time, only one of Molter's reforms from 1747 remained in place: in the fifty years until 1800, the annual budget of the *Hofmusik* only marginally exceeded his estimate of 6,000 *Gulden*.

---

[70] See the listings for musicians in *Markgräflich Baden-Durlachischer Hof- und Staats-Kalender auf das Jahr 1770, nebst einer mercantilischen Abhandlung über die Markgräfl. Baden-Durlachischen Lande* (Karlsruhe, 1770).

[71] *Hochfürstlich-Markgräflich-Badischer Hof- und Staats-Kalender auf das Jahr 1773*.

[72] See Wagner, 'Von der Stadtgründung', 181–7.

TABLE 13.1. Membership of the Baden-Durlach Court Music Establishment in 1715, 1730, 1747, and 1762

| Year | 1715 | 1730 | 1747 | 1762 |
|---|---|---|---|---|
| Ruler | Margrave Carl Wilhelm (r. 1709–38) | | Margrave Carl Friedrich (r. 1746–1811) | |
| Numeric Overview | 1 *Kapellmeister*<br>1 *Vicekapellmeister*[a]<br>27 instrumentalists<br>2 trumpeters & 1 kettledrummer<br>7 'Bayreuther Hautboisten'<br>4 vocalists and 68 *Hofsingerinnen*<br>10 unspecified musicians | 1 *Kapellmeister*<br>1 concertmaster<br>12 instrumentalists<br>2 trumpeters & 1 kettledrummer<br>7 'Bayreuther Hautboisten'<br>2 vocalists and 60 *Hofsingerinnen*<br>6 unspecified musicians | 1 *Kapellmeister*<br>1 concertmaster<br>14 instrumentalists<br>5 trumpeters & 1 kettledrummer<br>2 vocalists (1 doubling as instrumentalist)<br>1 additional person | 1 *Kapellmeister*<br>14 instrumentalists<br>4 trumpeters & 1 kettledrummer |
| *Kapellmeister* | Giuseppe Boniventi | Johann Melchior Molter | Johann Melchior Molter | Johann Melchior Molter |
| *Vicekapellmeister* | Enoch Blinzig | | | |
| Concertmaster | Jean Charles Petit? | Sebastian Bodinus | Sebastian Bodinus, 'Principal Violino' | |
| 'Componist bei der Hoff-Music' | Johann Philipp Käfer | | | |
| Instrumentalists | | | | |
| Violin | | Johann Jacob Hengel | Johann Jacob Hengel<br>Johann Heinrich Klepper<br>Georg Melchior Cramer<br>Wenzel Großbach | Giacynto Schiatti<br>Johann Heinrich Klepper<br>Carl August Pfeiffer<br>Ludwig Kauz |

| | | | |
|---|---|---|---|
| Viola | See Organ and Hautboisten | Anton Mocker (also hn) | Anton Mocker (probably also hn) / See Organ |
| Violoncello | Dominico Amadeo Moranti | Neumann[b] (vn 2) | |
| Contrabass | | See Hoftrompeter / Georg Fritz | |
| Oboe | See Duties not specified | See Bass and Hoftrompeter / Johann Gottlieb Benndorf / Johann Philipp Trost / Johann Reusch | Johann Gottlieb Benndorf / Johann Reusch |
| Bassoon | | Johann Wolfgang Dill / Christ[ian? Christoph?] Friedrich Graßold / Johann Jacob Nollda | Johann Philipp Müller |
| Waldhorn | See Duties not specified | See Violin | Bernhard Pompeati / Maximilian Friedrich Nast, 'Jagd Waldhornist' / Andreas Ehrenfried Forstmeyer, 'Jagd Waldhornist' / See Violin |
| Organ | Johann Georg Cramer (also va and copyist) | Johann Georg Eberhardt | Georg Melchior Cramer (also vn?) / Neumann |
| Hautboisten | Georg Fritz (also va?) | | |

| Year | 1715 | 1730 | 1747 | 1762 |
|---|---|---|---|---|
| Hautboisten (cont.) | Lorenz Engelhardt | Johann Georg Rittershoffer | | |
| | Georg Conrad Ohrt | Johann Thomas Kühndorff | | |
| | | Georg Michael Wegelin | | |
| | Jeremias Schmelzer | | | |
| | Johann Christian Schmidt | | | |
| | Hieronymus Schmidt | | | |
| | Theodor Schwarzkopf | | | |
| | Hieronymus Buchriß | | | |
| Kapellknaben[c] | Johannes Minsinger | | | |
| | Frantz Weber | | | |
| | Lorentz Ölser | | | |
| | Martin Gotthold Beck | | | |
| | Johann Philipp Eisen | | | |
| | Johann Ferdinand Rößle | | | |
| | Seuffert | | | |
| Hoftrompeter | Christoph Oßwald | Johann Zacharias Beswillibald | Carl Pfeiffer ('concertirt Trompet') | Carl Pfeiffer |
| | Johann Burckhard Oßwald | Johann Hartmann (or Heinrich) Oßwald | Johann Burckhardt Pfeiffer (sen.) (also va) | Friedrich Ludwig Pfeiffer (jun.) |
| | | | Friedrich Ludwig Pfeiffer (jun.) | Johann Hartmann Oßwald |
| | | | Matthäus Eyring (also va) | Matthäus Eyring |

| Position | | | | |
|---|---|---|---|---|
| *Hofpaucker* | Carl Ludwig | Johann Hartmann Oßwald (also vn); Abraham Bitsche | Abraham Bitsche | Abraham Bitsche |
| *'Bayreuther Hautboisten'* | | | Johann Georg Dietrich Bob; Johann Reusch; Johann Georg Rimmler; Christ[ian? or Christoph?] Friedrich Graßold; Johann Friedrich Gretsch; Johann Heinrich Kern; Johann Matthias Vogelsteller | Sigmund Böhringer; Johann Stefan Gobmüller; Johann Heinrich Klepper; Johann Erhard Spörl; Johann Zechgruber; Johann Brandt; Johann Georg Maltzer |
| *Vocalists* | | | | |
| Soprano | | Elisabeth Hengel | | Maria Maddalena Frigieri |
| Alto | | | | |
| Tenor | | Johann Wilhelm Thill (also va) | Johann Georg Thill | Natale Bettinardo (Bettinardi) |
| Bass | | | Johann Matthias Quintana | Charlotte Michler |
| Range not specified | | | | Dominica Frigieri Schweizelsperg(er) |
| | | | 68 | 60 |
| *'Hofsingerinnen'* | | | | |

| Year | 1715 | 1730 | 1747 | 1762 |
|---|---|---|---|---|
| Duties not specified | Casimir Schweizelsperg(er), 'Componist' | Jeremias Schmelzer | | Renner, 'Hof Tantz Meister und Hof Musicus' |
| | Heinrich Christian Döll (lackey and musician) | Hieronymus Schmidt | | |
| | Johann Georg Eberhardt (also *Cammerdiener*) | Johann Georg Eberhardt | | |
| | Sturm | Christian Andres Gebhardt | | |
| | Johann Matthäus Trost | Freyburg | | |
| | Albrecht Andreas Fischer | Fritz Benda | | |
| | Christian Andres Gebhardt | | | |
| | Ortmann | | | |
| | Johann Wolfgang Dill (bn?) | | | |
| | Hartmann Huber (hn?) | | | |
| **Additional Personnel** | | | | |
| Copyist | | *See* Organ | | |
| Calcant | | | Grübel | |
| *Tanzmeister* | | | | *See* Duties not specified |

*Sources*

1715: Based on primary sources examined by Schiedermair, 'Die Oper an den badischen Höfen', 374.
1730: The overview of personnel was reconstructed from various source documents in D-KAg, Bestand 56, 'Generalintendanz der Civilliste'.

1747: The year 1747, rather than 1745, was chosen in view of *Kapellmeister* Molter's 1747 'plan for a not too large, but nevertheless well-appointed *Kapelle*'. See D-KAg, 47/79, 'Tabell Über die Capell-Musicos und Ihre Besoldungen', 9 March 1747.

1762: See D-KAg, 56/1095, 'Summarische Besoldungs Tabell Über Die Hoff Music Bediente', 2 April 1762.

[a] In 1715, the labels *Vicekapellmeister* and concertmaster were used synonymously, and their areas of responsibilities were not as clear-cut as in later years.

[b] Musicians listed simply by surname cannot be identified further at this time.

[c] It is impossible to determine the exact duties of *Kapellknaben* in 1715 – it is probable that they played instruments, but they may also have sung. Around 1720, they appear to have been musicians in training who were also taught basic writing and arithmetic skills.

# 14

# The Court of Brandenburg-Culmbach-Bayreuth

## *Rashid-S. Pegah*

LTHOUGH STATE ARCHIVES — most importantly those in Bamberg
and Berlin — continue to house a vast number of archival documents
relating to the Bayreuth court, scholars who focus on the Franconian Hohenzollern residence struggle with the loss, if not the destruction, of a great many
fundamental primary sources after 1801, including payments and employment
records.[1] In addition to documentation kept in Bamberg and Berlin, records are
dispersed amongst civic archives and university libraries in Bayreuth and Erlangen.
Of special significance are manuscripts and archival documents held by the Historischer Verein für Oberfranken, whose founding members were able to obtain
significant archival sources at Plassenburg Castle in Kulmbach before the dissolution of the house archive of both Franconian Hohenzollern lines. In addition,
consideration must be given to individual documents associated with related noble
families that remain extant in archives and libraries in Aurich, Dresden, Harburg
(Swabia), and Stuttgart.

Today, the music of the Upper Franconian town of Bayreuth is primarily associated with Richard Wagner, in particular his legendary *Festspielhaus* on the
'Grüner Hügel' and, of course, the Bayreuth *Festspiele*. Otherwise, Wilhelmine,
the older sister of the Prussian crown prince, Friedrich (later Friedrich II, king of
Prussia, sometimes called 'Frederick the Great'; 1712–1786), who referred to her
as his 'Lieblingsschwester' (favourite sister), comes to mind. But Bayreuth had
been an important site of courtly musical life ever since the arrival of the Berlin
Hohenzollern family in 1604. Municipal music benefited as well, with court musicians performing in town and civic musicians at court.[2] Indeed, when the young
Margrave Christian of Brandenburg (1581–1655, r. from 1603), eldest son of the

---

[1] This is also the case with archival documents relating to the court of Ansbach. Moreover,
in 1943 the partial holdings of the Brandenburg-Preußisches Hausarchiv (in D-Bga) pertaining
to Ansbach suffered losses.

[2] On the history of music in Bayreuth, see the following seminal works: Ludwig Schiedermair, *Bayreuther Festspiele im Zeitalter des Absolutismus: Studien zur Geschichte der deutschen
Oper* (Leipzig: Kahnt, 1908); Karl Hartmann, 'Musikpflege in Alt-Bayreuth', *Archiv für Geschichte und Altertumskunde von Oberfranken*, 33/1 (1936), 1–66; Hans-Joachim Bauer, *Barockoper in Bayreuth*, Thurnauer Schriften zum Musiktheater, 7 (Laaber: Laaber-Verlag, 1982).

Elector Johann Georg (1525–1598, resident in Berlin), moved the margravial residence from Plassenburg Castle to Bayreuth a year after taking office, the small town began to flourish and continued to do so for over 160 years; its various phases were shaped by the ambitions of the respective reigning members of the younger line of the Franconian Hohenzollern family.[3]

The most significant event in the history of music at the Bayreuth court during Margrave Christian's reign was the dedication of a new organ in the Lutheran *Stadtkirche* (civic church) in 1619; its predecessor had been destroyed in a town fire. Several important contemporary musicians made special trips to Bayreuth to examine the instrument, including Heinrich Schütz from Dresden, Michael Praetorius (1571–1621), court *Kapellmeister* in Wolfenbüttel, Samuel Scheidt (1587–1621), court organist in Halle, and Johann Staden (1581–1634), organist at St Sebaldus in Nuremberg from 1618, who had held the post of margravial court organist in Bayreuth and Kulmbach between 1604 and 1610. Scheidt later recalled that court musicians had participated in the event – at least in the *Tafelmusik* that accompanied the meal following the dedication of the organ.[4]

Although Margrave Christian was able, for the most part, to prevent the destruction of his residential town during the Thirty Years' War, his personal participation in the conflict undoubtedly prevented any noteworthy activities on the part of his court musicians. However, as documented by letters first brought to the attention of the public by Irene Hegen in 1998, Melchior Franck (c.1580–1639), *Hofkapellmeister* in Coburg since 1603, composed for the court of Bayreuth; in addition, a musician from Altenburg named Eduardo von Leech sent music to Margrave Christian in February 1625.[5]

The early development of the Bayreuth *Hofkapelle* was interrupted by the margrave's death in 1655. At this time, his grandson and successor Christian Ernst (1644–1712; r. alone from 1661) was still underage and, furthermore, out of the country. During the regency of his uncle, Margrave Georg Albrecht of Brandenburg-Culmbach (1619–1666), music appears to have been restricted for the most part to the usual civic musical activities. Only with Christian Ernst's return to Bayreuth in 1661 and his formal accession to the title of margrave (with its accompanying responsibilities) was the course set for the evolution of a court culture that met the requirements and the needs of a baroque prince.

In November 1662, the arrival (*Heimführung*) of the margrave's first bride, Princess Erdmuthe Sophia of Saxony (1644–1670), was marked by a number of

---

[3] Karl Hartmann, *Geschichte der Stadt Bayreuth in der Markgrafenzeit* (Bayreuth: Steeger, 1949), 107–61; Karl Müssel, *Bayreuth in acht Jahrhunderten: Geschichte der Stadt* (Bindlach: Gondrom, 1993), 60–116; Rainer Trübsbach, *Geschichte der Stadt Bayreuth, 1194–1994* (Bayreuth: Druckhaus Bayreuth, 1993), 85–149.

[4] In the preface to his *Pars prima concertuum sacrorum* (Hamburg, 1622); see Hartmann, 'Musikpflege in Alt-Bayreuth', 34 n. 69.

[5] Irene Hegen, *Neue Materialien zur Bayreuther Hofmusik: Katalog zur Ausstellung 1998 im Steingraeber-Haus Bayreuth* ([Bayreuth: private imprint], 1998), 15; D-Bga, Brandenburg-Preußisches Hausarchiv, Rep. 43 I Markgraf Christian, F, No. 2, letter of Eduardo von Leech to Margrave Christian, February 1625.

musical performances. The *Ballet der Natur* and *Sophia*, an allegorical *Singspiel*, provided the first glimpses of the future activities of the court musicians.[6] Giovanni Andrea Angelini Bontempi (*c.*1624–1704), castrato and *Vicekapellmeister* at the Saxon court of Dresden, apparently directed the musicians during the festivities. As part of the wedding celebrations held in Dresden, he had premiered his opera *Il Paride* on 3 November 1662.[7] Bontempi also seems to have directed the court musicians at the Upper Franconian residence on the occasion of the second marriage of Margrave Christian Ernst, to Princess Sophie Louise of Württemberg-Teck (1642–1702), for whose *Heimführung* in May 1671 the margrave had ordered the performance of a ballet entitled *Sudetische Frülingslust*. In the previous year, following the death of his first wife, he had invited David Pohle (1624–1695) to Bayreuth to compose the funeral music and direct its performance.[8] Pohle also composed a work of homage ('Huldigung') for the Bayreuth musicians to perform on the occasion of the Württemberg princess's *Heimführung*.[9] The nominal director of music at the court was Martin Coler (1620–1703/4); however, since Bontempi and Pohle were engaged for these prestigious occasions, it appears that the margrave may not have been fully satisfied with Coler's skills.

As was also the case during the reigns that followed (as outlined below), Margrave Christian Ernst consistently appointed additional musicians for important occasions. Among those playing a part in the court's music-making in 1671 was the young Johann Philipp Krieger (1649–1725, later Weißenfels court *Kapellmeister*), who distinguished himself enough to be appointed as margravial chamber organist. Within two or three years he had advanced to the position of director of the

[6] Joachim Heinrich Hagen, *Hochfürstliche Ehren-Burg und daran gepflanzter Palmen-Hayn*: *Der Stamm- und Vermählung-Verwandtschaft beyder chur- und hochfürstlichen Häuser Sachsen und Brandenburg* (Bayreuth, 1669), 6; Sigmund von Birken, *Hochfürstlicher brandenburgischer Ulysses*, 2nd edn (Bayreuth, 1676), 562–3; Birken, *Teutsche Rede-Bind und Dicht-Kunst, oder Kurze Anweisung zur teutschen Poesy mit geistlichen Exempeln* (Nuremberg, 1679; facs. edn Hildesheim and New York: Georg Olms, 1973), 315–17. See also Gertrud Rudloff-Hille, 'Die Bayreuther Hofbühne im 17. und 18. Jahrhundert', *Archiv für Geschichte und Altertumskunde von Oberfranken*, 33/1 (1936), 67–138, at 74–80; Joachim Kröll, 'Der Dichter Sigmund von Birken in seinen Beziehungen zu Creußen und Bayreuth', *Archiv für Geschichte von Oberfranken*, 47 (1967), 179–276, at 224–5, 247–58; Kröll, 'Bayreuther Barock und frühe Aufklärung I: Markgräfin Erdmuthe Sophie (1644–1670) und ihre Bedeutung für Bayreuth', *Archiv für Geschichte von Oberfranken*, 55 (1975), 55–175, at 75–9; Kröll, 'Bayreuther Barock und frühe Aufklärung II: Die Briefe des Bayreuther Generalsuperintendenten Caspar von Lilien an Sigmund von Birken', *Archiv für Geschichte von Oberfranken*, 56 (1976), 121–234, at 123; as well as Karl-Bernhard Silber, *Die dramatischen Werke Sigmund von Birkens (1626–1681)*, Mannheimer Beiträge zur Sprach- und Literaturwissenschaft, 44 (Tübingen: Narr, 2000; Diss., Universität Passau, 1998), 347–419. Adam Krieger (1634–1666), electoral chamber organist, had also come to Bayreuth as part of the electoral princess's entourage.

[7] Moritz Fürstenau, *Zur Geschichte der Musik und des Theaters am Hofe der Kurfürsten von Sachsen und Könige von Polen*, 2 vols. (Dresden, 1861–2; repr. with commentary and indexes by Wolfgang Reich, Leipzig: Peters, 1971), I: 206–14.

[8] Hans Mersmann, *Christian Ludwig Boxberg und seine Oper 'Sardanapalus', Ansbach 1698*, mit Beiträgen zur Ansbacher Musikgeschichte, Beiträge zur Ansbacher Musikgeschichte (Leipzig: Breitkopf & Härtel, 1916; Diss., Friedrich-Wilhelms-Universität Berlin, 1916), 21 n. 3.

[9] D-Sha, G119, Büschel 4, David Pohle, *Musicalisches Vivat*, unfoliated.

Bayreuth court musical establishment and procured a post as organist there for his younger brother, Johann Krieger (1652–1735). It seems that the appointment of Italian, in particular Venetian, vocalists can be traced back to the influence of Margravine Sophie Louise. They received considerably higher salaries than their German colleagues, and consequently came into bitter conflicts with them. This situation resulted in some musicians, including the Krieger brothers, eventually leaving the Bayreuth court.[10]

Johann Philipp Krieger's successor as margravial *Kapellmeister* from 1678 appears to have been the Venetian bass singer and viola player Ruggiero Fedeli (1651/2?–1722). He carried out the role of *Kapellmeister* until 1712, despite accepting a post in Kassel in 1701 and undertaking short-term engagements that took him away from Bayreuth to Dresden (1686–8), Hanover (1689–96), Berlin (1694–6, 1701, 1703, 1705, and 1708), and Wolfenbüttel (1702, 1704, and 1707).[11] Fedeli's tenure marked the beginning of the first important period of Italian operatic performance at the court. This lasted over three decades and yielded compositions by Fedeli himself, as well as by Agostino Steffani (1654–1728), Carlo Francesco Polaroli (*c.*1653–1723), and Giovanni Bononcini (1670–1747), which were presented in Bayreuth and at the secondary residence in Erlangen (Christian-Erlang).[12]

The instrumental ensemble at Fedeli's disposal at the Bayreuth court consisted primarily of German musicians, together with a number of so-called *Cammertürken* (chamber turks) and *Cammermohren* (chamber moors).[13] The singers were partly German – including the well-known vocalist Pauline Kellner (d. 1736), the *Hofkantor* Pancratius Tröger (d. 1719), and Fedeli's future wife, Maria Barbara Hopf (1661–1715) – and partly Italian – such as Gianetta Bernardi and the castra-

---

[10] D-BHa, Archiv des Historischen Vereins für Oberfranken, Hist. 2509, 'Dienerbesoldung', 1674, unfoliated: Martin Lorentz Anßfelder (bass vocalist), 140 *Gulden* plus payments in kind; Samuel Peter von Sidon (*Cammermusicus*, violinist), 120 *Gulden* plus payments in kind and an additional 60 *Gulden* from the margrave's privy purse; Hanß Georg Loßnizer (violinist), 120 *Gulden* plus payments in kind; Johann Philipp Krieger (*Hoforganist*), 180 *Gulden* plus payments in kind; Georg Carl Lockel (violinist), 50 *Gulden* plus payments in kind; Georg Dämel (*Stadtorganist*), 30 *Gulden* plus grain and beer; an unidentified *Calcant*, 10 *Gulden* plus grain; three Italian 'Musici' (castratos), 1,640 *Gulden* from the margrave's privy purse plus payments in kind (wine, wood, bread rolls, beer, and feed for three horses). See also Johann Mattheson, *Grundlage einer Ehren-Pforte* (Hamburg, 1740, repr. ed. by Max Schneider, Berlin: Liepmannssohn, 1910), 151.

[11] Hartmut Broszinski and Rashid-Sascha Pegah, 'Fedeli [Fidel], Ruggiero, [Rudcher, Rüdiger],' in *Die Musik in Geschichte und Gegenwart: allgemeine Enzyklopädie der Musik*, 2nd rev. edn (Kassel: Bärenreiter, 1994–2008), Personenteil, VI: 864.

[12] Two arias from Agostino Steffani's *I trionfi del fato, ò Le glorie d'Enea* (Hanover, 1695; libretto: Bartolomeo Hortensio Mauro) were included in the opera *Cloco* (Bayreuth, 1697; libretto: Pietro d'Averara). Carlo Francesco Polaroli's *Amage, regina de' Sarmati* (Venice, 1693/4; libretto: Giulio Cesare Corradi) was performed in Bayreuth in 1699. Giovanni Bononcini's *Galatea* (Lietzenburg [now Charlottenburg], 1702; libretto: Attilio Ariosti) was presented in Elisabethenburg (Christian-Erlang) in 1706, while *L'Etearco* (Vienna, 1707; libretto: Silvio Stampiglia) was performed in Bayreuth two years later, in 1708.

[13] D-BAa, Geheimes Archiv Bayreuth, No. 4766, Collectanea Ellrodt, 'Verschiedene Suppliken', unfoliated.

tos Riccardini and Marenghi, as well as Fedeli himself.[14] Additional musicians were occasionally also brought in from Dresden, Stuttgart, Kassel, and Weißenfels.[15] The most important students of Fedeli in Bayreuth were Johann Christian Rau (1654/5?–1721) and Georg Heinrich Bümler (1669–1745). Both would later work in Ansbach, as *Director Musices* and *Hofkapellmeister* respectively. Bümler also distinguished himself by making a significant contribution to the musical life later enjoyed by Margrave Christian Ernst's son and daughter-in-law.

### COURT MUSIC AT BAYREUTH
### UNDER MARGRAVE GEORG WILHELM (1712–26)

Following the death of Margrave Christian Ernst in May 1712, his son Georg Wilhelm (1678–1726) succeeded to the title. Initially, his participation in the final military actions of the War of the Spanish Succession, together with lengthy disputes with his stepmother Elisabeth Sophie (1674–1748, Christian Ernst's third wife) regarding her widowhood and inheritance, prevented representative displays of courtly splendour in Bayreuth and at the margravial secondary residences. Indeed, shortly after his accession, Georg Wilhelm introduced a series of retrenchments to his household, including the release of several court musicians. Within two years, however, these dismissals appear to have been reversed, and additional musicians, both male and female, were also hired.

For this reason, the revival of activities on the part of the court musicians can only be confirmed from 1714. Margravine Sophia Wilhelmine (1684–1752), originally princess of Saxony-Weißenfels, was probably the principal champion of German-language operas at the court. This approach distinguished the performance traditions of the new reigning couple from the Italian musical dramas that had been initiated in Bayreuth by Margravine Sophie Louise and Margrave Christian Ernst. There had been a long tradition of German-language opera being performed at the princess's home in Weißenfels, and it was apparently upon her initiative that this was now emulated at her new home in Upper Franconia. At least, the first evidence of musico-dramatic productions in German dates from after her arrival in Bayreuth in 1700.[16] With the death of Margrave Georg Wilhelm in 1726, the period of approximately two and a half decades during which Bayreuth distinguished itself as an important centre of German opera in the south of modern-day Germany came to an end.

---

[14] Pietro Torri (*c.*1650/65–1737) had substituted as *Hofkapellmeister* in Bayreuth in 1687/8, before accepting a position for the remainder of his career at the Bavarian electoral court.

[15] Schiedermair, *Bayreuther Festspiele*, 15–16.

[16] Johann Christoph Gottsched, *Nöthiger Vorrath zur Geschichte der deutschen dramatischen Dichtkunst* (Leipzig, 1757; repr. Hildesheim and New York: Georg Olms, 1970), 270, 272; Friedrich Wilhelm Marpurg, *Historisch-kritische Beyträge zur Aufnahme der Musik* (Berlin, 1754–78, repr. Hildesheim and New York: Georg Olms, 1970), v, 'Viertes Stück' (1762), 311–12.

The Bayreuth court musicians initially performed both Italian and German operas, as on the occasion of the opening of Georg Wilhelm's opera house (located at the foot of the margravial palace) in November 1714, as well as during Carnival season in 1715. However, the serenatas and operas that followed up until 1726 were (with two exceptions[17]) all in German. At that time the *Hofkapelle* was directed by the alto castrato Philippo (Filippo) Antonio Scandalibene (d. 1735) who left the Bayreuth court in either October or November 1715 and was employed as a *Cammermusicus* in Stuttgart, as a music director in Durlach-Karlsruhe (where he also worked as an architect), and finally in Trier.[18] The tenor and falsettist Johann (Jean) Ernst Michel (1678–1727) became Scandalibene's successor in Bayreuth, and probably composed the music for the majority of the German-language operas performed at the court.[19] Whether or not Scandalibene was also responsible for providing music is unclear.

The *dramma per musica* entitled *Il trionfo della virtù* performed to celebrate the birthday of the Bayreuth ruler in 1714 was an adaptation of *La Statira*, a work performed in Venice in 1705/6. The text booklet printed for the performance in the Upper Franconian residence clearly deviates from the original libretto, written by Pietro Pariati (1665–1733) and Apostolo Zeno (1668–1750). In particular, the many aria texts that were substituted in Bayreuth imply that the original music by Francesco Gasparini (1661–1727) was used side by side with newly-composed music by Scandalibene, or previously-existing music taken from other contexts. A comparison between a libretto written by Pietro Antonio Bernardoni (1672–1714) for the opera *L'amor tra nemici* – originally given at the Viennese imperial court in 1708 – with the text booklet printed for the Bayreuth Carnival performance in 1715 shows that they are virtually identical. It may be assumed then, that this was a repeat performance of the composition by the Bolognese musician, active in Berlin, Vienna, and London, Attilio Ariosti (1666–1729).[20]

The first German-language opera premiered after Georg Wilhelm's accession in mid-November 1714 was *Der glückliche Wechsel unbeständiger Liebe*. The libretto of this musical *Schäferspiel* (pastorale) can be attributed to Johann Wolfgang Kipping (1695–1747), son of the court bookbinder and a literary talent discovered and mentored by the margrave.[21] There is, however, no indication that Kipping was in-

---

[17] *Hercules* (Bayreuth, 1716) and *Die triumphirende Tugend* (St Georgen am See, 1720).

[18] See also Walther Pfeilsticker, *Neues Württembergisches Dienerbuch*, I (Stuttgart: Cotta, 1957), §908; Norbert Dubowy, 'Italienische Instrumentalisten in deutschen Hofkapellen', in *The Eighteenth-Century Diaspora of Italian Music and Musicians*, ed. Reinhard Strohm, Speculum Musicae, 8 (Turnhout: Brepols, 2001), 61–120, at 89.

[19] Schiedermair, *Bayreuther Festspiele*, 30.

[20] Ibid., 45–6.

[21] D-BAa, Markgrafschaft Bayreuth, Hofkammer Bayreuth, No. 497, 'Taffel und Tisch Ordnung. Beym HochFürstl[ichen]: Brandenburg[ischen]: Hoff-Stadt Zu Bayreuth', 4 December 1714, unpaginated; Georg Wolfgang Augustin Fikenscher, ed., 'Kipping, Johann Wolfgang', in *Gelehrtes Fürstenthum Baireut, oder Biographische und literarische Nachrichten von allen Schriftstellern, welche in dem Fürstenthum Baireut geboren sind und in oder außer demselben gelebet haben und noch leben . . .*, v (Erlangen, 1803), 69–74.

volved with any further musical activities. Most likely, it was Johann Ernst Michel who set to music the 'musicalischen Opern' *Die Durchlauchtigste Statira* and *Alba Cornelia*, first performed in February and March 1715, respectively, using librettos by Kipping.[22]

In addition to Carnival season and the birthday of Margrave Georg Wilhelm, both his name day and the birthday of the margravine provided further important occasions when serenatas and operas were performed.[23] The premiere of the musical 'Schäfer-Gedicht' (pastoral poem) *Die siegende Treu* took place in early August 'auf dem Theatro zu Christian-Erlang', as part of Sophia Wilhelmine's birthday celebrations. Three months later, in mid-November 1715, the margravine herself participated in a performance of a 'tragicomedia' entitled *Die unglückliche Regierung der durchlauchtigsten Antonia* at the Bayreuth opera house on the occasion of Margrave Georg Wilhelm's birthday.[24] She praised her husband in song during the prologue in the role of Aurora, goddess of the dawn (alongside other persons of rank who appeared as goddesses), and also took the play's title role. Between the five acts were short sung scenes, which were almost certainly performed by members of the *Hofkapelle*.

The extant court records from the first few years of Margrave Georg Wilhelm's reign contain insufficient information to identify the other participants in these performances. At most, only those individuals who were paid chiefly for their musical services were included under the rubric 'musicians'. Additional court musicians were listed under their (frequently unknown) secondary functions (for example, as clerks and secretaries) or as lackeys.[25] Therefore, in light of this difficult situation, it is at best only possible to approximate the constitution of the Bayreuth *Hofkapelle* in 1715.

Fortunately, other primary source evidence provides information on at least three musicians from related courts who visited Bayreuth at the request of Margrave Georg Wilhelm. For example, for the two operas premiered at the opening of the new opera and playhouse on the occasion of the margrave's birthday in mid-November 1714, Georg Wilhelm asked his cousin Prince Albrecht Ernst II of Oettingen-Oettingen (1669–1731; r. alone from 1688) to send the vocalist 'Mademoiselle Degin', daughter of a court trumpeter in Oettingen.[26] She also participated in the three premieres that took place during the Bayreuth Carnival season early the following year. For these specific performances Georg Wilhelm

[22] The text of *Alba Cornelia* is based on the 1714 Vienna version of the libretto with the same title by Silvio Stampiglia (1664–1725), set to music by Francesco Bartolomeo Conti (1682–1732), imperial court composer and theorbo player.

[23] Bauer, *Barockoper in Bayreuth*, 194–202.

[24] Schiedermair, *Bayreuther Festspiele*, 48 n. 2; Bauer, *Barockoper in Bayreuth*, 62.

[25] Johann Heinrich Feetz, 'Secretarius' and bass vocalist; Grimmer, lackey and *Hofmusicus*; Leonhard Andreas Denner, 'Kanzellist' (clerk), chamber valet, and vocalist; and Andreas Belling, chamber valet and *Hautboist*.

[26] D-Bga, Brandenburg-Preußisches Hausarchiv, Rep. 43 III Markgraf Georg Wilhelm, J.O., No. 2, fols. 1r, 3v, 2r: draft of a letter of Margrave Georg Wilhelm to Prince Albrecht Ernst II of Oettingen-Oettingen, 9 December 1714, and letter of Prince Albrecht Ernst II to Margrave Georg Wilhelm, 27 December 1714.

requested that another cousin, Margrave Wilhelm Friedrich of Brandenburg-Ansbach (1686–1723; r. from 1703/04), allow him to make use of 'Capell-Director' Georg Heinrich Bümler as well as the falsettist Georg Jacob Bösewillebald.[27] Judging from the important role which Bümler appears to have played in the musical life of Georg Wilhelm's court (as revealed, for example, in Johann Friedrich Fasch's autobiography), it is entirely possible that the musical director and later court *Kapellmeister* of Ansbach may also have composed for the Bayreuth opera house.[28]

In addition to performing in operas, the full-time *Hofmusici*, along with other musicians employed on a casual basis, provided *Tafelmusik*, dance music for balls, and background music for masquerades and *Redouten* (which included dancing, gaming, and feasting alongside other forms of entertainment). That court musicians occasionally also performed at the weddings of high-ranking officials at court is evident from at least one source that dates from 1726.[29] The same document also sheds light on the question of which individual musical ensembles constituted the *Hofmusik* during Margrave Georg Wilhelm's lifetime. In addition to *Cammermusici* and *Hofmusici* (the latter also known as 'Capell-Musici'), we find references to *Hautboisten* (who played several instruments), musicians of the 'Jägerey' or 'bey der Jagt' (with the hunt), and the 'Bocks-Music'.[30] Overall, the instrumentalists made up an ensemble consisting of sixteen to twenty individuals, plus court trumpeters and kettledrummers (see Table 14.1, pp. 408–12 below).

Thanks to Michael Maul's publication of an inventory of music from the Gera court of the counts of Reuß that appears to date from 1719/20, we are now able to gain an impression of the instrumental repertoire in Bayreuth.[31] According to this document, the musicians had at their disposal concertos by Johann Christoph Pepusch (1667–1752), intradas and sonatas by Casimir Schweizelsperg(er) (1668–after 1722), and ouverture suites by Georg Philipp Telemann, alongside many other works.[32] Their repertoire of vocal chamber music probably included single arias from operas and cantatas performed at the Bayreuth court.[33]

[27] D-Bga, Brandenburg-Preußisches Hausarchiv, Rep. 43 III Markgraf Georg Wilhelm, J.A., No. 6, fol. 33[r-v]: [draft] letter of Margrave Georg Wilhelm to Margrave Wilhelm Friedrich of Brandenburg-Ansbach, 22 December 1714.

[28] For Johann Friedrich Fasch's autobiography, see 'Lebenslauf des Hochfürstl. Anhalt-Zerbstischen Capellmeisters, Johann Friedrich Fasch' (addendum to Johann Gottfried Walther, *Musicalisches Lexicon* (Leipzig, 1732), 240), in Marpurg, *Historisch-kritische Beyträge*, III, 'Erstes Stück' (1757), 124–9, at 127; Lorenz Christoph Mizler von Kolof, 'VI. Denkmal dreyer verstorbenen Mitglieder der Societät der musikalischen Wissenschafften', 'A. ... Georg Heinrich Bümler', in *Neu eröffnete musikalische Bibliothek, oder Gründliche Nachricht nebst unpartheyischem Urtheil von musikalischen Schriften und Büchern*, 4 vols. (Leipzig, 1739–54), IV/I: 135–40, at 136 (the whole 'Denkmal' is on 129–76).

[29] D-BHa, No. 601, 'Den hiesigen Stadt-Thurmer betr.', unfoliated.

[30] On the latter, see Chapter 2, 'The Court of Saxony-Dresden', pp. 20–21 above.

[31] Michael Maul, 'Johann Sebastian Bachs Besuche in der Residenzstadt Gera', *Bach-Jahrbuch*, 90 (2004), 101–19, at 110–11, 114–19.

[32] See ibid., 119–20.

[33] See ibid., 119: '2 *Italiani*sche *Arien* aus der Bareuthischen *Opera* mit *Instr*. Welche Ochse von Bareuth mit bracht' (two Italian arias from the Bayreuth Opera with instr[umental accompaniment]. Which Ochse brought with him from Bayreuth). Arias from Gottfried Heinrich

Information regarding sacred music is scarce: the printed collection *Gottgeheiligte Sing-Stunde* (Rudolstadt, 1704) by Philipp Heinrich Erlebach (1657–1714), *Hofkapellmeister* of the Prince of Schwarzburg-Rudolstadt, was bought by the *Kantor* Johann Bartholomaeus Zabitzer for the Ordenskirche in nearby St Georgen am See (a small town founded in 1702, now part of Bayreuth) in either April or May 1715.[34] Moreover, in 1717 Gottfried Heinrich Stölzel (1690–1749) composed a sacred work for Reformation Day specifically for the Bayreuth court.[35] It is also likely that in 1725/6 Telemann's sacred cantata cycle with chamber scoring, the *Harmonischer Gottes-Dienst*, was purchased as well.[36]

Stölzel was not the only well-known musical guest at the Bayreuth court: Johann Baptist Kuch, who was Fasch's predecessor as *Kapellmeister* at Anhalt-Zerbst, visited in 1714/15.[37] Then, in 1716, two Dresden musicians, the violinist (and later concertmaster at the Saxon court) Johann Georg Pisendel (1687–1755) and the oboist Johann Christian Richter (d. 1744), came to Bayreuth; Johann Friedrich Fasch (1688–1758) visited as well.[38] Mattheson recorded that in 1726, Conrad Friedrich Hurlebusch (1691–1765) performed at Bayreuth.[39] Moreover, on 11 June 1716, Margrave Georg Wilhelm's sister, Electress Christiane Eberhardine of Saxony (1671–1727), recommended six boys and their mentor, Johann Gottfriedt Rauchfus, a chamber and court musician from Zerbst.[40]

Stölzel's *Diomedes* (Bayreuth, 1718) also survive as part of extant cantatas; see D-B, Mus. ms. 30176.

34 D-BHa, R 10693, 'Belege zur Gotteshauß-Rechnung zu St: Georgen *ad annum* 1715', No. 15, unfoliated; R 10694, 'Gotteshauß-Rechnung über Einnahm und Außgab ab Geldt, Bey der Sophien, *Ordens-* und Pfarr-Kirche zur Stadt St: Georgen am See. Angefangen Vom *Quatember Luciæ Anno* 1714. biß wiederum dahin des 1715.ten Christ-Jahrs.', fols. 18ʳ, 29ʳ⁻ᵛ.

35 The title of the work is not known; see Mattheson, *Grundlage einer Ehren-Pforte*, 346. See also Mizler, 'VI. Denkmal dreyer verstorbenen Mitglieder', 'B. . . . Gottfried Heinrich Stölzel', 143–54, at 151.

36 See Stefanie Gansera-Söffing, *Die Schlösser des Markgrafen Georg Wilhelm von Brandenburg-Bayreuth: Bauherr – Künstler – Schloßanlagen – Divertissements*, Bayreuther Arbeiten zur Landesgeschichte und Heimatkunde, 10 (Bayreuth: Rabenstein, 1992), 172.

37 D-Dla, Geheimer Rat (Geheimes Archiv), Loc. 8590/2, fol. 134ʳ: Johann Baptist Kuch 'Jst nacher Bayreuth *recommendi*ret worden den 8. Sept[embris]: 1714' (Was afterwards recommended to Bayreuth on 8 September [*recte* November] 1714). See Bernhard Engelke, 'Einige Bemerkungen zu Ludwig Schiedermairs "Bayreuther Festspiele im Zeitalter des Absolutismus"', *Zeitschrift der Internationalen Musikgesellschaft*, 10 (1908–9), 14–16, at 15; Engelke dates the recommendation to Bayreuth to the summer of 1713.

38 [Johann Friedrich Agricola], 'Nachricht von den Lebensumständen des letzt verstorbenen berühmten Königl[ichen] Concertmeisters, H[er]rn Joh[ann] George Pisendels', *Dreßdnische Gelehrte Anzeigen auf das Jahr 1756*, 'XVIII. Stück', 299–304, at 302; Johann Adam Hiller, ed., 'Lebenslauf: Des ehemaligen Königl[ichen] Pohlnischen und Churfürstl[ichen] Sächsischen Concertmeisters: Herrn Johann George Pisendel', *Wöchentliche Nachrichten und Anmerkungen die Musik betreffend* (Leipzig, 1766–70, repr. Hildesheim and New York: Georg Olms, 1970), 'Eilftes Stück' (3 March 1767), 277–81, at 281; 'Lebenslauf des Hochfürstl. Anhalt-Zerbstischen Capellmeisters, Johann Friedrich Fasch', 127.

39 Mattheson, *Grundlage einer Ehren-Pforte*, 123.

40 D-Bga, Brandenburg-Preußisches Hausarchiv, Rep. 43 II Markgraf Christian Ernst, WI, No. 51, letter of Electress Christiane Eberhardine of Saxony to her brother Margrave Georg

As noted above, during the reign of Georg Wilhelm the direction of the Bayreuth *Hofmusik* was initially in the hands of two vocalists who were labelled 'Musicdirectoren': the castrato Scandalibene and, later, the falsettist and tenor Michel.[41] In 1721, following his return from a study trip to Venice, Sigmund Martin Gajarek (1689–1723), who served as court organist from 1716, was appointed to the position of *Hofkapellmeister* by the margrave. His untimely death two years later motivated Georg Wilhelm to transfer the title 'Capell-Meister von Hause aus' (*Kapellmeister* by proxy) to the renowned Hamburg music director Georg Philipp Telemann. The label 'von Hause aus' described a contractual arrangement in which the employee in question was not required to maintain a (permanent) presence at the prince's court. Telemann was allowed to keep the title at least until the death of Georg Wilhelm's successor. When Margrave Georg Wilhelm passed away in December 1726, southern Germany lost an eminent patron and promoter of German-language opera.

## MUSIC AT THE COURT OF BAYREUTH
### UNDER MARGRAVE GEORG FRIEDRICH CARL (1727–35)

Margrave Georg Wilhelm died without a male heir. His widow, Margravine Sophia Wilhelmine, left Bayreuth and lived at her dowager residence in Erlangen until 1734. Thus, with the main branch of the ruling family having died out after four generations, the Margraviate of Brandenburg-Culmbach together with its seat of power, the town of Bayreuth, passed to the subsidiary line of Brandenburg-Culmbach-Weferlingen. During the spring of 1727 the new margrave, Georg Friedrich Carl (1688–1735), accepted the pledge of allegiance from his subjects. For this occasion the *Kantor* Johann Bartholomaeus Zabitzer performed a sacred cantata in Bayreuth on Saturday 17 May 1727.[42]

Following his formal accession to the title, Margrave Georg Friedrich Carl introduced significant changes to the organization of his new court. As a strict Pietist, he placed less value on courtly representation than his cousin and predecessor, who had been a great lover of displays of splendour. Consequently, the court of Bayreuth changed to a 'hausväterlich', economy-oriented seat of government.[43] Georg Friedrich Carl closed the theatres built by Georg Wilhelm in Bayreuth, St Georgen am See, and Erlangen and dismissed the majority of the court musicians,

Wilhelm, 11 June 1715, unfoliated. See also Chapter 9, 'The Court of Anhalt-Zerbst', p. 261 above.

[41] D-Bga, Brandenburg-Preußisches Hausarchiv, Rep. 43 III Markgraf Georg Wilhelm, J.b. 26, letter of Francesco Antonio Bonporti to Margrave Georg Wilhelm, 18 December 1714, fol. 1ʳ; Schiedermair, *Bayreuther Festspiele*, 30.

[42] D-BHu, Bibliothek des Historischen Vereins für Oberfranken, MS 29, 'Mein Erdman[n] Johan[n] Creta Stad- Schul- und Rechen-Meisters zu Bayreuth, Kurtz- und nach Möglichkeit zusammen getragene Lebens- und Reiß-Beschreibung' [Bayreuth, 1715–22], p. 781.

[43] For a definition of a 'hausväterlicher Hof', see Chapter 1, 'An Introduction to German *Hofkapellen*', p. 2 n. 3 above.

but above all the virtuosos employed at the opera house, the actors, and the dancers. Moreover, he sold off the remarkable collection of costumes accumulated by his predecessor.[44]

Instead of maintaining a regular *Hofkapelle*, the frugal margrave engaged vocalists for short periods only. Visits made by Georg Friedrich Carl's high-ranking relatives were occasions upon which the skills of his court musical establishment – specially enlarged for several weeks at a time – could be showcased. Thus, the programme presented during the visit of the crown prince of Denmark and his bride, a younger sister of the margrave, as well as the prince of Ostfriesland (East Frisia) with his wife, included evening *Tafelmusiken* (as, for example, on 23 July 1728), in which both male and female vocalists participated. A special offering was the performance of a serenata, *Die Freude des Fürstenthums Brandenburg-Bayreuth*, on Monday, 5 July 1728, with text and music composed expressly for the occasion. Moreover, as had been the case during the reign of Georg Friedrich Carl's predecessor, dance music was played at the balls held at court.[45] Following the departure of his guests, the margrave travelled to take the waters at Karlsbad (Karlovy Vary).

Soon after his return to Bayreuth, Georg Friedrich Carl dismissed most of the court personnel who had been hired specifically to make his court appear more magnificent during the visit of his relatives, an action that enabled him to achieve his higher purpose – frugality.[46] Among those released were a number of musicians. That the margrave nevertheless maintained a permanent music ensemble after 1730 was probably due to the demands and interests of the younger generation. While staying in Paris for several months as part of his *Kavaliersreise*, Hereditary Prince Friedrich (1711–1763; r. as margrave from 1735) had taken lessons on the transverse flute with the famous virtuoso Michel Blavet (1700–1768).[47] Approximately two years later the prince married a daughter of the king in Prussia (Friedrich Wilhelm I), the highly cultivated and music-loving Princess Friderique Sophie Wilhelmine (1709–1758). During his stay at the Berlin court Friedrich met Johann Joachim Quantz (1697–1773), who rounded off the young man's instruction on the transverse flute. Until 1741 Quantz was a frequent guest at the Upper Franconian residence, as, for example, in 1736.[48] Upon her arrival in 1732, the new

[44]  D-BAa, Geheimes Archiv Bayreuth, No. 750, fols. 81ʳ⁻ᵛ, 61ᵛ, 60ʳ⁻ᵛ, 9ʳ; Johann Christoph Silchmüller, *Continuatio I. Diarii Baruthini Anno 1727. Die XIII. Nov*[embris]: a copy is extant at D-HAf, AFSt/H A 116, p. 961; see also K. Weiske, 'Johann Christoph Silchmüller's Bayreuther Tagebuch, eine neue Quelle für die Erforschung der Geschichte des Pietismus in Bayreuth, veröffentlicht aus einer Handschrift der Waisenhausbibliothek in Halle/Saale', *Archiv für Geschichte und Altertumskunde von Oberfranken*, 29/2 (1925), 17–100, at 37–8.

[45]  D-BHu, 'Mein Erdman[n] Johan[n] Creta', pp. 805, 807.

[46]  Ibid., p. 808.

[47]  D-BAa, Markgrafschaft Bayreuth, Hofkammer Bayreuth, No. 505, 'Berechnung Uber Einnahme und Ausgabe, auf der von des Herrn Erb–Printzens HochFürstl[ichen]: Durchl[aucht] glücklich vollbrachten Reiße durch Franckreich, Flandern, Brabant und Holland . . . vom 19.ᵗᵉⁿ Octobr[is] anno 1730. biß den 17.ᵗᵉⁿ Mai[i] anno 1731', pp. 83, 121, 138.

[48]  Sabine Henze-Döhring, 'Wilhelmine Markgräfin von Bayreuth und die preußische Hofmusik: Musik- und Musikeraustausch zwischen Ruppin/Rheinsberg und Bayreuth; Neue Quellen zur Bayreuther Hofkapelle in den Jahren 1732 bis 1740 unter besonderer Berücksichtigung des Solokonzerts und der Autorschaft des Markgräfin Wilhelmine zugeschriebenen

hereditary princess was greeted in the company of both her husband and father-in-law with the performance of a cantata at the town's main church.[49]

Little by little, during the final three years of Margrave Georg Friedrich Carl's life, the Bayreuth court's image gradually began to change. From 1732 musicians were again appointed on a permanent basis, and by 1734 their number had risen to nine or ten. Among them were the lutenist Adam Falckenhagen (1697–1754) and his wife Johanna Aemilia, a capable singer, who performed a cantata on New Year's Day in homage to Margrave Georg Friedrich Carl.[50] In charge of the musicians as temporary *Kapellmeister* was Andreas Belling, who had initially served in Bayreuth as 'Premier Hautboist' and chamber valet. However, it seems probable that Johann Pfeiffer (1697–1761), a much admired violin virtuoso who had already been in the employ of Margrave Georg Friedrich Carl, may have taken over from Belling as director shortly afterwards.[51]

Based on the overview provided in 1936 by Karl Hartmann (drawing upon primary sources that no longer appear to exist), around 1734 the *Kapelle* comprised a *Kapellmeister* (who, as an *Hautboist*, presumably played the oboe together with a selection of other instruments), a concertmaster (a violinist), a lutenist, four additional violinists (one of whom may also have been an organist), a viola player, and two *Waldhornisten* (see Table 14.1).[52] They were joined by the vocalist Johanna Aemilia Falckenhagen.[53] Moreover, it is likely that the young hereditary princess occasionally performed on the harpsichord and lute, while her husband played the transverse flute to the accompaniment of court musicians. To please his daughter-in-law, Margrave Georg Friedrich Carl also provided the musicians with frequent opportunities to perform at balls and smaller festivities or *divertissements*.[54]

With the exception of the above-mentioned printed and handwritten cantata texts, important sources regarding the repertoire of the margravial musical establishment during the five years prior to the arrival of Hereditary Princess Wilhelmine in Bayreuth in 1732 are no longer extant. Georg Philipp Telemann may occasionally have sent compositions to Upper Franconia until about 1735; on the title page of his *Musique de table* (Hamburg, 1733) he continued to refer to himself

Cembalokonzerts in g-Moll', in *Wilhelmine von Bayreuth heute: Das kulturelle Erbe der Markgräfin; Referate des Bayreuther Symposiums 'Wilhelmine von Bayreuth heute: Das kulturelle Erbe der Markgräfin', gehalten im Landrätesaal der Regierung von Oberfranken vom 26. bis 28. Juni 2008*, ed. Günter Berger, Archiv für Geschichte von Oberfranken, 'Sonderband' [special volume] (Bayreuth: Ellwanger, 2009), 207–30.

[49] D-BAa, Geheimes Archiv Bayreuth, No. 4889, Collectanea Sauerwein; music now lost.

[50] The handwritten text is extant in the Handschriftenabteilung of D-ERu, MS 1423; music now lost.

[51] Hartmann, 'Musikpflege in Alt-Bayreuth', 55.

[52] Ibid., 55–6.

[53] Johann Heinrich Feetz (d. 1740), a 'Secretarius' and renowned bass singer, had already left for Stuttgart by 1731. Pfeilsticker, *Neues Württembergisches Dienerbuch*, I, §918.

[54] It is also possible that some of the pupils from the orphanage founded in 1732 by Margrave Georg Friedrich Carl assisted with music at court; after all, they were specifically instructed in music. See Johann Christoph Silchmüller, *Neue Spuren der gütigen Vorsorge Gottes* (Bayreuth, 1736), 46–7.

as 'Maitre de Chapelle de S[on]. A[ltesse]. S[érénissime]. le Margrave de Bayreuth'. Subscribers to this publication included the Dowager Margravine Sophia Wilhelmine in Erlangen, and Margrave Friedrich Ernst of Brandenburg-Culmbach-Weferlingen (1703–1762), the younger brother of Margrave Georg Friedrich Carl and Danish governor in Schleswig-Holstein.[55] In addition to Telemann's works, music composed by members of the *Kapelle* was probably performed, including works by the lutenist Falckenhagen, the violinist (possibly *Kapellmeister*) Pfeiffer, and the concertmaster Frantz. Following the arrival of Princess Wilhelmine in 1732, cantatas and opera arias by Johann Adolf Hasse (1699–1783) and Carl Heinrich Graun (1703/4–1759), as well as instrumental music by Quantz, Johann Gottlieb Graun (1702/3–1771), Christoph Schaffrath (*c.*1709/10–1763), and the Prussian Crown Prince Friedrich were presented.[56]

This shift in repertoire clearly indicates Bayreuth's promising future as it increasingly modelled itself on the leading *Hofkapellen* in the Holy Roman Empire: Dresden, Rheinsberg, and, from 1740, Berlin, when Crown Prince Friedrich became king in Prussia. That the musical ambitions of the hereditary princess and prince were to lead to entirely different duties for the members of the Bayreuth *Hofkapelle* became evident soon after the death of the economically frugal Margrave Georg Friedrich Carl in 1735.

### THE BAYREUTH *HOFKAPELLE* UNDER MARGRAVINE FRIDERIQUE SOPHIE WILHELMINE AND MARGRAVE FRIEDRICH (1735–58)

Even today, the 'Markgräfliches Opernhaus' in Bayreuth has an international reputation. Its inauguration, which coincided with the festivities celebrating the wedding in 1748 of the margravine's daughter Elisabeth Friderique Sophie (1732–1780) with Duke Carl Eugen of Württemberg (1728–1793; r. alone from 1744), must have been a wish long cherished by Margravine Friderique Sophie Wilhelmine and Margrave Friedrich. As early as 1736, the year after their accession, an 'operetta' was performed at the Bayreuth court during the visit of Friedrich Carl von Schönborn (1674–1746), bishop of Bamberg and Würzburg and a renowned music lover.[57] One year later, in 1737, a pastorale (probably *Tirsi*) by Giuseppe Antonio Paganelli (*c.*1710–after 1775) was performed for the occasion of the margrave's birthday. After an initial renovation of the theatre in the secondary margravial residence

[55] Georg Philipp Telemann, *Tafelmusik I–III*, ed. Johann Philipp Hinnenthal, Georg Philipp Telemann: Musikalische Werke, 12–14 (Kassel: Bärenreiter, 1959–63). In 1739, Margrave Friedrich Ernst of Brandenburg-Culmbach-Weferlingen employed the composer and writer Johann Adolph Scheibe (1708–1776) as his *Kapellmeister*; see Mattheson, *Grundlage einer Ehren-Pforte*, 346.

[56] Henze-Döhring, 'Wilhelmine Markgräfin von Bayreuth', 207–30.

[57] Dieter J. Weiß, 'Fürstenbegegnungen in Franken: Bamberg und Bayreuth im 18. Jahrhundert', *Archiv für Geschichte von Oberfranken*, 83 (2003), 363–78, at 365. See also Chapter 11, 'The Court of Würzburg', p. 312 ff.

of Christian-Erlang (Erlangen), the margrave's birthday was again celebrated on 5 May 1738 with a large-scale opera, *Didone abbandonata*, also composed by Paganelli to a libretto by Metastasio.[58] Italian opera was once again central to the *Hofkapelle*'s duties in Bayreuth and Erlangen, as it had been during the reign of Margrave Christian Ernst.

The performances in May 1738 warranted the temporary engagement of musicians from Stuttgart, Dresden, and Berlin – a standard practice under previous margraves.[59] Since Paganelli himself performed on stage in Christian-Erlang as a singer, Margravine Friderique Sophie Wilhelmine specifically asked the duke of Saxony-Eisenach for his 'Premier' violinist Johann Wolfgang Kleinknecht (1715–1786) to direct the *Hofkapelle* in these performances in Erlangen. Afterwards Kleinknecht spent further time at the Bayreuth court before returning to Eisenach. Following the death of Duke Wilhelm Heinrich of Saxony-Eisenach in 1741, Kleinknecht eventually accepted the post of margravial concertmaster in Bayreuth.[60]

The changing artistic priorities of the *Hofkapelle* are also evident in the lists of the members of the Bayreuth court musical establishment in the *Brandenburg-Culmbachischen Addreß-Kalender* published from 1738 onwards.[61] In contrast to the margravial court records dating from the first two decades of the eighteenth century in which hardly any string (or other) players can be found, these address calendars categorize vocalists and instrumentalists according to their voice type or instrument(s) played. A considerable increase in the number of string players – up to a dozen instrumentalists – is also evident (see Table 14.1).

Following a phase of transition, this expansion of the court musical establishment, translated into an ever-increasing workload for the musicians. Moreover, in addition to the two operas by Paganelli mentioned above, two smaller serenatas were performed, including *Sacrificio devotissimo*, which had been requested by Margravine Wilhelmine on the occasion of her husband's birthday in 1739.[62] In the following year, the musical offering for Margrave Friedrich's birthday – the 'tragedia' *L'Argenore*, composed by the margravine herself – required additional forces.[63]

[58] Erich Schenk, *Giuseppe Antonio Paganelli: Sein Leben und seine Werke, nebst Beiträgen zur Musikgeschichte Bayreuths* (Vienna and Salzburg: Waldheim-Eberle, 1928; Diss., Ludwig-Maximilians-Universität, Munich, 1927), 26, 35–6, 39.

[59] Erich Schenk, 'Zur Musikgeschichte Bayreuths', *Archiv für Geschichte und Altertumskunde von Oberfranken*, 30/1 (1927), 59–67.

[60] [M.] Degen, 'Einige Nachrichten von dem im Febr[uar] 1786 verstorbenen Hochfürstl[ichen] Anspachischen Konzertmeister Johann Wolfgang Kleinknecht', in *Miscellaneen artistischen Innhalts*, ed. Johann Georg Meusel, xxx (Erfurt, 1787), 340–52, at 344–6.

[61] Cf. Schiedermair, *Bayreuther Festspiele*, 110–11, 131–3.

[62] D-BAa, Geheimes Archiv Bayreuth, No. 4889. The other serenata, *Gioia universa*, was performed in 1738.

[63] Libretto (text by Giovanni Andrea Galletti) in D-ERu, 8° Rar. A 17/1; autograph score in D-AN, VI g 44. For a facsimile of the latter, see Hans-Joachim Bauer, *Rokoko-Oper in Bayreuth: Argenore der Markgräfin Wilhelmine*, Thurnauer Schriften zum Musiktheater, 8 (Laaber: Laaber-Verlag, 1983); see also Wilhelmine von Bayreuth, *Argenore (1740): Oper in drei Akten*, Das Erbe deutscher Musik, 121 (Abteilung 4: Oper und Sologesang, 13), ed. Wolfgang Hirschmann (Mainz: Schott, 1996).

Otherwise, only one of Wilhelmine's compositions remains, a sonata for transverse flute.[64] The performance of *L'Argenore* by the members of the margravial *Hofka-pelle*, together with select German and Italian virtuosos, marked the inauguration of a new performance venue close to the old opera theatre built during the reign of Georg Wilhelm and Sophia. From this point until 1756, large-scale musical works for the stage were produced almost annually.

In addition to the margrave's birthday, the court musicians were also given opportunities to perform operas for the margravine as well as during Carnival season. For example, the musico-theatrical works *La clemenza di Tito* and *Sirace* with librettos by Metastasio and Giovanni Andrea Galletti (*c.*1710?–1784) were premiered in 1744 during Carnival to mark the opening of the opera house in Christian-Erlang, which had been remodelled by Giovanni Paolo Gaspari (1712–1775). No similar performances seem to have been given in 1745, but further operatic offerings can be confirmed for 1746.[65] The text for *Sirace*, a *dramma per musica*, had been penned by Galletti, a baritone who also wrote the libretto for the margravine's *L'Argenore* (probably to her own template), and for *Lucidoro*, a *pastorale per musica* (1743).[66] It is not clear when Galletti left Bayreuth. A concert announcement in Frankfurt am Main, dated 7 September 1749, documents that 'Mons[ieur] und Madame Galetti, . . . gegen 6 Jahr am Bayreuthischen Hoff als Italiänische Sänger gestanden' (Monsieur and Madame Galletti, . . . were employed for approximately six years at the court of Bayreuth as Italian vocalists).[67]

Among the Italian vocal virtuosos at the Bayreuth court, the two castratos Giacomo Zaghini (fl. 1738–58) and Stefano ('Stefanino') Leonardi (fl. 1742–63) particularly stand out. They also belong to the exclusive number of margravial musicians for whom portraits survive, thus providing an impression of their physical appearance.[68] Leonardi had come to Bayreuth from Berlin, where he had performed the role of Cesare in the premiere of the opera *Cleopatra e Cesare* on 5 December 1742, a setting by the royal Prussian *Hofkapellmeister* Carl Heinrich Graun to a libretto by Giovanni Gualberto Bottarelli (d. 1779). As late as 1754 Friedrich II in Prussia used Leonardi's Italian connections to engage new musicians, specifically vocalists.

[64] On the margravine's sonata for transverse flute and basso continuo, see Nikolaus Delius, 'Eine Sonate für Bruder Friedrich? Der Anonymus Herdringen Fü 3595a', *Tibia*, 28/4 (2003), 571–7.

[65] Bauer, *Barockoper in Bayreuth*, 208–11.

[66] From 1750 onward Galletti and his wife were employed at the court of Gotha, where he wrote librettos for works directed by the court *Kapellmeister* Georg Anton (Jiří Antonín) Benda (1722–1795), including intermezzos (among them *Il buon marito*, 1766) and one opera, *Xindo riconosciuto* (1765). Galletti also penned a libretto for the court of Saxony-Hildburghausen; see Hiller, ed., *Wöchentliche Nachrichten*, 'Neuntes Stück' (25 August 1766), 65–6.

[67] Carl Israël, 'Frankfurter Concert-Chronik von 1713–80', *Neujahrsblatt des Vereins für Geschichte und Altertumskunde zu Frankfurt am Main für das Jahr 1876*, 36.

[68] The portraits of one female musician, Maddalena Gerardini ('la Sellarina'), two male musicians (Leonardi and Zaghini), and some unidentified musicians, as well as those of male and female dancers and actors are on permanent display in the Neues Schloß in Bayreuth; see Erich Bachmann, 'Die "Comödiantenbildnisse" der Markgräfin Wilhelmine von Bayreuth', in *Im Glanz des Rokoko – Markgräfin Wilhelmine von Bayreuth: Gedenken zu ihrem 200. Todestag*, ed. Wilhelm Müller, Archiv für Geschichte von Oberfranken, 38 (Bayreuth: Historischer Verein für Oberfranken, 1958), 186–93.

As was the case at the courts of Stuttgart, Dresden, and Berlin, the vocalists who sang the main operatic parts in Bayreuth were Italian; members of the ballet company were primarily French; and the instrumentalists of the *Hofkapelle* were almost all German. However, Norbert Dubowy – drawing on research carried out by Ludwig Schiedermair published in 1908 – has drawn attention to several Italian instrumentalists at the Bayreuth court.[69] During the 1750s and early 1760s these included Italian violinists as well as the oboist Vittorino Colombazzo (d. after 1768). Following the dismissal of several Italian musicians by Margrave Friedrich's successor, Colombazzo accepted employment with the Württemberg *Hofkapelle*.[70]

Court musicians also accompanied Margravine Wilhelmine and Margrave Friedrich when they occasionally stayed at the small *Lustschloß* Kaiserhammer during the hunting season. For example, in September 1744 the margravial hunting party included the concertmaster Kleinknecht, the castrato Leonardi, the chamber flautist Christian Friedrich Döbbert (c.1700–1770), the bassoonist Johann Gotthelf Liebeskind (d. after 1769), and the flautist Johann Stephan Kleinknecht (1731–after 1806), a younger brother of the concertmaster. According to a biographical essay on the flautist Georg Gotthelf Liebeskind (b. 1732), chamber concerts took place at Kaiserhammer that occasionally featured travelling virtuosos.[71]

The repertoire of the court musicians must have been similar to that performed following Wilhelmine's arrival in Bayreuth in 1732 (see above). In addition, we can draw upon extant manuscripts and printed editions for information regarding the church music performed in Bayreuth during Wilhelmine and Friedrich's reign. On 18 October 1735, civic *Kantor* Zabitzer performed the obligatory (probably specially composed) *Erbhuldigung* cantata for the new margravial couple, surely with the participation of the court musicians.[72] It is also likely that the *Hofmusici* took part in the performance of a German-language cantata, *Wieviel euer gekaufft sind*, with which the new *Stadtkantor* Kieffhaber celebrated the baptism of a converted Jew on 27 August 1741 (13th Sunday after Trinity). On 16 April 1746 (Misericordia Domini Sunday), the *Hofkapelle* dedicated a cantata entitled *Schuldiges Dankopffer* to Princess Elisabeth Friderique Sophie, who had recently recovered from a grave illness. And at the end of March 1748, about six months before her wedding to the

[69] See Dubowy, 'Italienische Instrumentalisten in deutschen Hofkapellen', 61–120, esp. 104, 116–17; Schiedermair, *Bayreuther Festspiele*, 131–2.

[70] Pfeilsticker, *Neues Württembergisches Dienerbuch*, I, §891.

[71] D-BAa, Markgrafschaft Bayreuth, Hofkammer Bayreuth, 1672, fol. 11^r-v, '*Fourier* Zettel Zu der bevorstehenden Reiße nacher Kayserham[m]er den 23. *September* 1744'. See M. Degen, 'Nachricht von dem berühmten Flötenisten Liebeskind in Anspach', in *Miscellaneen artistischen Innhalts*, ed. Johann Georg Meusel, IX (Erfurt, 1781), 151–61, at 153–4. See also Karl Müssel, 'Bauten, Jagden und Feste der Bayreuther Markgrafen in Kaiserhammer: Ein vergessenes Kapitel aus der Zeit des Absolutismus im Fichtelgebirge', *Archiv für Geschichte von Oberfranken*, 41 (1961), 271–344, at 308.

[72] [Editors' note: The *Erbhuldigung* was a ceremony of homage, in which a new sovereign was officially acknowledged by his subjects.]

duke of Württemberg and on the occasion of the princess's first Holy Communion, chamber musicians sang a Latin cantata, *Instruis coram mensam*.[73] In a letter addressed to her brother in Berlin, Margravine Wilhelmine herself referred to the funeral music composed by *Hofkapellmeister* Johann Pfeiffer and performed for the burial of a Catholic court employee, probably in July 1754.[74] On 26 August 1758, following a devastating fire, the inauguration of the restored palace chapel was marked with a Latin cantata (*Deus est nostrum refugium*), composed by Pfeiffer and sung by margravial chamber musicians.[75] These predominantly Italian male and female vocalists distinguished themselves in operatic performances at the court, resulting in their being exceptionally well paid. The wages of several other members of the highly renowned Bayreuth *Hofkapelle*, however, were not in proportion to the demands made upon them. It was for this reason, to name but one example, that the bassoonist and composer Friedrich Beringer (d. 1760) left the court of Bayreuth in the dead of night and procured a better post with the equally renowned landgravial *Hofkapelle* in Darmstadt.[76]

## THE BAYREUTH *HOFKAPELLE* UNDER MARGRAVE FRIEDRICH AND MARGRAVINE SOPHIE CAROLINE MARIE (1759–62)

In October 1758 Margravine Wilhelmine died. Although the widowed margrave appeared to be inconsolable, in order to ensure the succession he was compelled to marry again. Little less than one year later, on 8 October 1759, the court musicians, dancers, and several members of the French theatrical troupe performed a *ballèt héroïque* entitled *Aristée* (which featured both dancing and singing) in a small theatre in the margravial stables.[77] This theatrical production marked both the *Heimführung* and the birthday of the new margravine of Bayreuth, Sophie Caroline Marie (1737–1817), a princess of Braunschweig-Lüneburg-Wolfenbüttel and niece of the late Wilhelmine. According to the libretto, the vocal as well as the instrumental transitional music in *Aristée* was composed primarily by the violinist

[73] D-BAa, Geheimes Archiv Bayreuth, No. 4887, [Johann Stephan Sauerwein], 'Beschreibung der Pfarr- und Stadt-Kirche in Bayreuth', unfoliated.

[74] D-Bga, Brandenburg-Preußisches Hausarchiv, Rep. 46 König Friedrich Wilhelm I., W., No. 17, ad vol. I, letter of Margravine Friderique Sophie Wilhelmine to her brother, King Friedrich II in Prussia, undated (July? 1754), unfoliated.

[75] [Sauerwein], 'Beschreibung der Pfarr- und Stadt-Kirche in Bayreuth'.

[76] D-DSsa, D8 Konv. 15 Fasc. 6 Hofmusikpersonal 1700/40[–1754], unfoliated copy of an appointment decree made by Landgrave Ludwig VIII of Hesse-Darmstadt (1710–1768, r. from 1739) for the bassoonist Friedrich Beringer from Bayreuth, 3 November 1753; his salary was backdated to October 1753; D8, Konv. 15, Fasc. 7, fols. 694ʳ–697ᵛ, 700ʳ–701ʳ, 704ʳ–707ʳ, 710ʳ–ᵛ; also D-Bga, Brandenburg-Preußisches Hausarchiv, Rep. 43 v Markgraf Friedrich, J. Lit. H, No. 8, letter of Landgrave Ludwig VIII to Margrave Friedrich, 14 May 1754, unfoliated. See also Wilibald Nagel, 'Zur Geschichte der Musik am Hofe von Darmstadt (Fortsetzung)', *Monatshefte für Musikgeschichte*, 32/4 (1900), 58–74, at 67–9; Elisabeth Noack, *Musikgeschichte Darmstadts vom Mittelalter bis zur Goethezeit* (Mainz: Schott, 1967), 234–5; Chapter 12, 'The Court of Hesse-Darmstadt', pp. 333–63 above.

[77] Hegen, *Neue Materialien zur Bayreuther Hofmusik*, 29.

Giovanni Piantanida, while court *Kapellmeister* Pfeiffer contributed the dance music.

One month earlier, on Sunday, 9 September 1759, civic *Kantor* Johann Dörffler had supervised the performance of a cantata in the *Stadtkirche* to celebrate the *Heimführung* of the young bride. The music was composed by the margravial chamber musician Johann Balthasar Kehl (1725–1778).[78] After the death of Johann Pfeiffer in 1761 the *Hofkapelle* was directed by concertmaster Johann Wolfgang Kleinknecht, who may have been assisted by his brother Jacob Friedrich Kleinknecht (1722–1794) as 'Cammer *Compositeur*'.[79] Moreover, the harpsichordist Christian Ludwig Hien possibly co-directed the *Kapelle* at times. On which occasions the Italian singer Marciani performed in Bayreuth is unknown, but in November 1759 he was recommended by the margrave to the French envoy extraordinary at the Munich court.[80] It is likely that a daughter of the court architect Joseph Saint-Pierre (*c*.1709–1754), who designed the plans for the façade of the opera house, participated as a vocalist in performances of the *Hofkapelle* before being recommended to Kassel in May 1760.[81]

Together with other members of the *Hofkapelle* (see Table 14.1), male and female vocalists may also have been involved in a concert held 'in der Fr[au] Marggrävin ihren Cabinet' (in the margravine's cabinet) on the evening of 10 October 1761; this is detailed in a confidential letter from Bayreuth written by a Franconian aristocrat.[82] It was at concerts of this kind or those held at the Academie der Künste (founded in 1756), that works composed by the margrave himself may have been heard, including, at the very least, a concerto for lute 'a 4', according to the lexicographer Ernst Ludwig Gerber (1746–1819).[83] That even in his favourite *Lustschloß* Kaiserhammer the margrave could not bear to do without dramatic productions – possibly involving the *Hofkapelle*? – is evident from the repeated references to a newly-built theatre nearby.[84] To mark the twenty-fifth birthday of his new wife Sophie Caroline Marie, a *pastorale per musica* – a setting of the libretto *Angelica* by Metastasio – was performed in Bayreuth, at the margrave's command. Afterwards, members of the French ballet company danced a pantomime representing the

[78] D-BAa, Geheimes Archiv Bayreuth, No. 4889, fols. 63ʳ–64ᵛ.

[79] Hiller, ed., *Wöchentliche Nachrichten*, 'Vier und zwanzigstes Stück' (9 December 1766), 183–7, at 183–4; the article includes only the initials of authors: 'D. G. D. L. v. D. G.' and is dated 'T. den 30. Octbr. 1766.'

[80] D-BAa, Geheimes Archiv Bayreuth, No. 846, letter of Hubert de Folard (1709–1799?) to Margrave Friedrich, 22 January 1760, unfoliated.

[81] D-MGs, Bestand 4 f, Brandenburg (fränkisch), No. 288, letter of Margrave Friedrich to Landgrave Friedrich II of Hesse-Kassel (1720–1785, r. from 1760), 17 May 1760, unfoliated.

[82] Letter of Christoph Joachim Freiherr Haller von Hallerstein (1723–1792) to his wife, 11 October 1761, cited by Karl Müssel, 'Hofleben, Feste und Gäste der Herzogin Elisabeth Friederike Sophie auf Schloß Fantaisie und in Bayreuth (1763–80)', *Archiv für Geschichte von Oberfranken*, 79 (1999), 225–324, at 226, 228, 314 n. 6.

[83] Ernst Ludwig Gerber, *Historisch-Biographisches Lexicon der Tonkünstler*, part 1 (Leipzig, 1790), 445.

[84] D-BAa, Markgrafschaft Bayreuth, Hofkammer Bayreuth, 1684, fols. 335ʳ, 285ʳ. See also Müssel, 'Bauten, Jagden und Feste der Bayreuther Markgrafen', 291–2.

contest between the river god Acheloos and the demigod Hercules over the love of Princess Dejanira. This event marked the last performance of an opera in margravial Bayreuth during the eighteenth century.[85]

## THE END OF THE BAYREUTH *HOFKAPELLE* (1763–69)

In February 1763, Margrave Friedrich died from pneumonia, leaving no male heirs. He was succeeded by his uncle Friedrich Christian (1708–1769), who was to be the last margrave residing in Bayreuth. Despite also being a lover of music, Friedrich Christian relinquished the Italian musicians, releasing them from service.[86] He did, however, continue to use the *Hofkapelle* for chamber concerts until his death. At his disposal were more than thirty musicians (not including trumpeters and kettledrummers).[87] When he died in 1769 the margraviate was amalgamated with the margraviate of Brandenburg-Ansbach and ruled from Ansbach in central Franconia. The musicians were either absorbed by the Ansbach *Hofkapelle*, remained in Bayreuth, or were dismissed. Among those who were redeployed to the new residence were the brothers Kleinknecht, Bernhard Joachim Hagen (violinist and lutenist), Johann Balthasar Kehl (violoncellist, organist, and composer), Georg Gotthelf Liebeskind (flautist), and his father.[88]

The dissolution of the Bayreuth court in 1769 brought to a close the history of the margravial *Hofkapelle*, just as the abdication of the last margrave, Carl Friedrich Alexander, in 1791 marked the end of the cultivation of music and the arts by the Franconian members of the house of Hohenzollern. In its development and its various stages of rise and decline, music at the court mirrored the specific interests of each reigning couple. Indeed, seen in retrospect, courtly musical life in Bayreuth reached its zenith following the death of the frugal Pietist Georg Friedrich Carl in 1735, when Margrave Friedrich and Margravine Friderique Sophie Wilhelmine came into power. Both were composers in their own right and facilitated Bayreuth's rise in status as highly-regarded venue for performances of Italian operas, the legacy of which can still be seen today in the form of Bayreuth's 'Markgräfliches Opernhaus', one of Europe's most celebrated baroque theatres.

[85] The libretto is extant at D-Sl, Fr. D. qt. K. 49. It includes a book-plate of Duchess Elisabeth Friderique Sophie of Württemberg.

[86] Hiller, ed., *Wöchentliche Nachrichten*, 'Vier und zwanzigstes Stück' (9 December 1766), 182–7, at 183.

[87] Ibid., 183–4.

[88] Günther Schmidt, *Die Musik am Hofe der Markgrafen von Brandenburg-Ansbach vom ausgehenden Mittelalter bis 1806* (Kassel and Basel: Bärenreiter, 1956), 84–5, 87–9.

TABLE 14. Membership of the Brandenburg-Culmbach-Bayreuth Court Music Establishment in c.1732–6, 1745/6, and 1760/61

| Year | c.1732–6 | 1745/6 | 1760/61 |
|---|---|---|---|
| Ruler | Margrave Georg Friedrich Carl (r. 1727–35) | Margrave Friedrich (r. 1735–63) | |
| Numeric Overview | 1 *Kapellmeister* / 1 concertmaster / 9 instrumentalists / 1 vocalist | 1 *Kapellmeister* / 1 concertmaster / 11 instrumentalists / 5 trumpeters & 1 kettledrummer / 4 vocalists / 1 additional person | 1 *Kapellmeister* / 2 concertmasters / 31 instrumentalists / 6 vocalists / 2 additional personnel (at least) |
| *Ober-Director* | | Count Albrecht Carl von Schönburg | Count Louis Alexandre de Riquetti von Mirabeau |
| *Kapellmeister* | Andreas Belling (also ob; *Cammerdiener*) | Johann Pfeiffer | Johann Pfeiffer |
| Concertmaster | Bartholomaeus Frantz (vn) | Johann Wolfgang Kleinknecht | Johann Wolfgang Kleinknecht |
| Vice-concertmaster | | | Jacob Friedrich Kleinknecht, *Cammermusicus* |
| Instrumentalists | | | |
| *Cammermusici* | Samuel(?) Hofmann (org; also vn)[a] / Johann Adam Falckenhagen (lute) / Johann Michael Köhler (possibly va) / Johann Künzel (vn) | Christian Friedrich Döbbert (fl) / Johann Gottlieb Richter (vn) | *See* Vice-concertmaster |

*Hofmusici* ('Hofcapell-Music')

| | | | |
|---|---|---|---|
| Violin | [Caspar?] König<br>*See* Concertmaster *and* Cammermusici | Caspar König<br>Johann Daniel Leuthardt (sen.)<br>Bernhard Joachim Hagen (also lute)<br>Heinrich Kürbiz<br>Christian Benjamin Köhler<br>Johann Lorenz Steinhäuser<br>*See Cammermusici*<br>*See Hoforganist* | Johann Gottlieb Richter<br>Johann Daniel Leuthardt (sen.)<br>Johann Michael Glaser<br>Johann Christoph Hofmann (sen.)<br>Giovanni Piantanida (sen.)<br>Caspar König<br>Bernhard Joachim Hagen (also lute)<br>Georg Heinrich Thomas<br>'N. Dressel'<br>Gottfried Wilhelm Morus<br>Johann August Hofmann (jun.)<br>Friedrich Carl Schemer<br>*See Hoforganist* |
| Viola | *See Cammermusici* | | Johann Lorenz Steinhäuser<br>Samuel Friedrich Leuthardt (jun.)<br>Johann Siegmund Weidemann |
| Violoncello | *See Waldhorn* | Andreas Stöhr | Johann Heinrich Constantin Zabitzer<br>Peter Buchta<br>Giorgio Piantanida (jun.) |

| Year | c.1732–6 | 1745/6 | 1760/61 |
|---|---|---|---|
| Violoncello (*cont.*) | | | Johann Balthasar Kehl |
| | | | Johann Lorenz Englert |
| Contrabass ('Contraviolinisten') | | | |
| Flute | | | Johann Nicolaus Kohl |
| | | | Johann Georg Vitus Halmb |
| | | | Christian Friedrich Döbbert |
| | | | Christian Ferdinand Wunderlich |
| | | | Johann Stephan Kleinknecht |
| | | | Georg Gotthelf Liebeskind (jun.) (also bn) |
| Oboe | *See Kapellmeister* | Johann Gotthelf Liebeskind (sen.) | Johann Gotthelf Liebeskind (sen.) |
| Bassoon | | | *See Flute* |
| Waldhorn | [Johann Georg?] Vogel | | Johann Georg Vogel |
| | Creuzberg (?) | | Johann Friedrich Heinel |
| | Johann Sieger | | |
| | Johann Caspar Rönnig (also vc) | | |
| Lute | *See Cammermusici* | *See Violin* | *See Violin* |
| Hoforganist | *See Cammermusici* | Christian Samuel Hoffmann (also vn/va) | Christian Samuel Hoffmann (also vn) |
| Hautboisten | | Peter Buchta | Johann Conrad Tiefert |
| Hoftrompeter | | Wenzel Anton Straub | |

| | c.1732–6 | 1745/6 |
|---|---|---|
| *Hofpaucker* | Johann Eucharius Zahr; Johann August Hoffmann; Johann Friedrich Huck; Georg Simon Zaubzker | |
| **Vocalists[b]** | | |
| Soprano | Giustina Eberharde; Maddalena Gerardini ('La Sellarina'); Giacomo Zachini | Maria ('Mia') Giustina Turcotti; Nicolina Rosa |
| Alto | Stefano ('Stefanino') Leonardi | Stefano ('Stefanino') Leonardi |
| Tenor | | Leopoldo Burgioni; Andrea Grassi; Ernst Christoph Dreßler |
| Range not specified | Johanna Aemilia Falckenhagen [soprano] | |
| **Additional Personnel** | | |
| Copyist | | Christ[ian? Christoph?] Erdmann Ludwig Andreae |
| *Kapelldiener* (servant) | Christoph Steininger | Christoph Steininger's surviving dependents |

*Sources*

No documentation is extant for the year 1715.

c.1732–6: Cf. Hartmann, 'Musikpflege in Alt-Bayreuth', 55–6; there were two sources used by Hartmann: one covering the years 1732–34 and 1736, the second relating only to 1734; neither is extant.

1745/6: *Hochfürstlich-Brandenburgisch-Culmbachischer [...] Address- und Schreib-Calender Auf das Jahr nach der Geburt Jesu Christi 1746*, pp. 100–1.

1760/61: *Hoch Fürstlich Brandenburgisch Culmbachischer Address- und Schreib-Calender auf das Jahr nach der Geburth Jesu Christi 1761*, pp. 43–4.

a  It is unclear whether *Cammermusicus* Hofmann was the same person as Christian Samuel Hofmann (*Hoforganist* and violinist/viola player).

b  The are no references made to bass singers in the primary sources consulted for this table.

# 15

# 'Die vornehmste Hof-Tugend': German Musicians' Reflections on Eighteenth-Century Court Life

*Steven Zohn*

A S MUCH AS THE EXTANT RECORDS of German *Hofkapellen* tell us about courtly musical life during the eighteenth century, they tend to provide only the official view of musicians' experiences: a decree is handed down, a violinist hired or dismissed, a grievance filed, a judgement rendered, and so on. That we know comparatively little about how court musicians regarded their duties, colleagues, and surroundings should not be surprising, given that most were understandably hesitant to speak candidly about the environment in which they earned their living, and thereby risk offending an aristocratic, noble, or royal employer. Yet a variety of their writings — including personal letters, autobiographies, theoretical treatises, and even novels — offer valuable, if fleeting, glimpses of *Hofkapelle* life as seen from the musician's perspective. The following survey focuses on six noteworthy court musicians active between the last quarter of the seventeenth century and the third quarter of the eighteenth: Wolfgang Caspar Printz (1641–1717), Johann Beer (1655–1700), Johann Kuhnau (1660–1722), Georg Philipp Telemann (1681–1767), Johann Georg Pisendel (1687–1755), and Johann Joachim Quantz (1697–1773). Printz, Beer, and Kuhnau all penned novels that are either about musicians or contain scenes featuring them; Printz, Beer, Telemann, and Quantz left us exceptionally informative autobiographies; and Pisendel provided unusually frank assessments of the Dresden *Hofkapelle* in his surviving correspondence with Telemann. It is worth observing at the outset that not all of these writings can be taken at face value, for autobiographies often contain a strong element of self-promotion, and fictional characters and situations in novels, no matter how realistic they appear to be, do not necessarily reflect the personal viewpoints of their authors.[1]

---

[1] For an overview of musical references in the novels of Beer, Kuhnau, Printz, and Daniel Speer, see Stephen Rose, 'Musician-Novels of the German Baroque', in *The Worlds of Johann Sebastian Bach*, ed. Raymond Erickson (New York: Amadeus Press, 2009), 175–90. On Beer's

Printz, who served as *Kantor* and director of music at the court of Count Balthasar Erdmann von Promnitz at Sorau (now Żary) in Upper Silesia, offers perhaps the most jaded view of *Hofkapelle* culture. In the chapter entitled 'Hof-Leben' (Court Life) of his novel *Musicus magnanimus, oder Pancalus*, the eponymous hero joins the newly formed *Hofkapelle* of Marquis Pomponio in Naples as a viola da gamba player. Having achieved such high status and low pay, he likens his situation to the village cowherd who climbs the professional ladder to become a town cowherd for only a modest increase in salary; he has, in effect, gained nothing but a fancy title. Once he settles into his new 'Füchse Paradeiß' (fox's paradise) and 'einfältigen Hölle' (simple-minded hell), Pancalus quickly discovers that 'das *Simuli*ren ist die vornehmste Hof-Tugend, und eines Hof-Schrantzen gröste Kunst ist, wohl an sich halten, und anderst scheinen, als er ist' (dissembling is the foremost courtly virtue, and a fawning courtier's greatest art is surely to behave and appear completely different than he is).[2] Moreover, the most common activity at court is flattery, and accordingly one tells a master and his favoured servants whatever they wish to hear. As part of their initiation, Pancalus and his musician colleagues receive some valuable advice from the Italian castrato serving as *Kapellmeister*:

> 'Ihr Herren, ihr könnt euch nicht recht in das Hof-Leben schicken. Wenn ihr wollet fortkommen, so müsst ihr die *Politic* lernen, und euch in die Welt schicken.' 'Herr Capell-Meister', fragte ich, 'was ist dann ein *Politicus*?' 'Ein *Politicus*', antwortete er, 'ist ein solcher Mensch, der Gott also dienet, daß er den Teufel nicht *offendi*re: Er ist ein Mann, der sich in alle Höfe, in alle Städte, zu allen Leuten, und in alle Zeiten zu schicken weiß; der zugleich ein Fuchs und Haaß ist; lincks und rechts: der predigen kan, wenn er gleich nicht drauff studiret hat: der mahlen kan ohne wahrhafftige Farben: der gegen jederman freundlich, gegen niemand auffrichtig ist.'

> 'You gentlemen don't know how to behave at court. If you want to get ahead, you must learn politics and reconcile yourselves to the ways of the world.'

novels in particular, see Hellmut Thomke, 'Musikerfiguren und musikantisches Erzählen in Johann Beers Romanen', in *Johann Beer: Schriftsteller, Komponist und Hofbeamter, 1655–1700; Beiträge zum Internationalen Beer-Symposion in Weißenfels, Oktober 2000*, ed. Ferdinand van Ingen and Hans-Gert Roloff (Bern: Peter Lang, 2000), 235–54. Printz's literary references to civic and lower-class musicians are considered by Eckhard Roch, 'Von Kunstpfeifern, Bierfiedlern und anderen Bernheutern. Zur sozialen Charakteristik des Musikers bei Wolfgang Caspar Printz', in *Professionalismus in der Musik: Arbeitstagung in Verbindung mit dem Heinrich-Schütz-Haus Bad Köstritz vom 22. bis 25. August 1996*, ed. Christian Kaden and Volker Kalisch (Essen: Die Blaue Eule, 1999), 145–55. Thoughtful reflections on the close relationship between autobiography and novel in early-eighteenth-century Germany are provided by Bernhard Jahn, 'Autobiographie und Roman: Zu den literarischen Elementen der Autobiographie in der Zeit Telemanns am Beispiel einiger Musikerautobiographien', in *Biographie und Kunst als historiographisches Problem: Bericht über die Internationale Wissenschaftliche Konferenz anläßlich der 16. Magdeburger Telemann-Festtage, Magdeburg, 13. bis 15. März 2002*, ed. Joachim Kremer, Wolf Hobohm, and Wolfgang Ruf (Hildesheim: Georg Olms, 2004), 121–9.

2 Wolfgang Caspar Printz, *Musicus magnanimus, oder Pancalus* (Freiberg, 1690), 198–9. Edited in *Wolfgang Caspar Printz: Ausgewählte Werke*, I: *Die Musikerromane*, ed. Helmut K. Krausse (Berlin: de Gruyter, 1974), 267–8.

'Herr *Kapellmeister*,' I asked, 'what is a politician?' 'A politician,' he answered, 'is someone who serves God in such a way that he doesn't offend the devil: he is a man who knows how to act properly at all courts, in all towns, with all people, and at all times; who is at once a fox and a hare; left and right; who can give a sermon without having studied at all; who can paint without true colours; who is friendly to everyone, sincere to no one.'[3]

To the extent that the views of Pancalus and his *Kapellmeister* reflect those of Printz himself, such disillusionment with court life may have resulted in part from the author's own complex relationships with colleagues and superiors at Sorau. In his colourful autobiography for Johann Mattheson's *Grundlage einer Ehren-Pforte*, Printz writes of having a 'heimlichen Feind' (secret enemy) at court, being denied gratuities given to his colleagues, being called a drunken and slovenly musician, and even being poisoned at a friend's home. On another occasion, he was the target of a prank designed to make him look foolish at festivities held in honour of a visiting prince, during which

wurden wir Musikanten in Schäffer-Kleider eingekleidet, und bekam jeder von uns einen Schäffer-Stab, auf welchem solch Nahmen geschrieben waren, deren Anfangs-Buchstaben den Nahmen des Hertzogs in sich hielten. Mir wurde der erste von dem Herrn Grafen selbst gegeben: allein der Vornehmste von denen Musikanten, welcher mehr, als ich, seyn wollte, unangesehen er von der Composition nichts verstund, und nur ein *merè practicus instrumentalis* war, ließ mir denselben entwenden, und einen andern an dessen Stelle legen. Als ich merckte, daß dieses zu meiner Unterdrückung angesehen wäre, klagte ich solches dem Herrn Grafen, welcher alsobald befahl, daß mir mein Stab wieder gegeben werden muste.

we musicians were decked out in shepherd's clothes, and each of us received a shepherd's staff on which names were written that began with letters spelling out the duke's [count's?] name. I received the first staff from the count himself. But the most refined among the other musicians, who wanted to outdo me, regardless of the fact that he understood nothing about composition and was simply an instrumentalist, had arranged for my staff to be stolen and replaced with another. When I realized that this was intended to undermine me, I complained to the count, who immediately commanded that my staff be returned.[4]

Whether or not Printz somehow encouraged the surprising amount of disrespect he was shown at Sorau, his difficulties with musician colleagues brings to mind a passage in Mattheson's biography of the composer and violinist Johann Fischer (1646–*c*.1716/17), who apparently ruffled more than a few feathers at the Mecklenburg-Schwerin court in 1701–4: 'Man sagt, er sey mit den Hofmusikanten

[3] Printz, *Pancalus*, 201–2; *Ausgewählte Werke*, I: 269–70.
[4] Johann Mattheson, *Grundlage einer Ehren-Pforte* (Hamburg, 1740; repr. with original pagination, Kassel: Bärenreiter, 1969), 268–9.

daselbst offt in Streit gerathen: darüber er sich zuletzt mit Verdruß wegbegeben habe; ohne daß man wisse, ob der selbst, oder die andern, Schuld daran gewesen sind. Ohne Ursach hat er wohl seinen Abschied weder hie[r], noch anderswo, genommen' (It is said that he was often in conflict with the court musicians, which finally caused him to depart in frustration; it is not known whether he or the others were at fault. It was surely not without reason that he took his leave hither and thither).[5]

Georg Philipp Telemann's first court appointment was at Sorau (1705–8), where, as he recalled in his autobiography published in 1740, he engaged Printz in apparently heated discussions about melody.[6] Yet he tired of court life after less than a decade. In his autobiography of 1718, Telemann recalled his youthful desire to become a court musician while still a student at the University of Leipzig:

> Ist etwas in der Welt, wodurch der Geist des Menschen aufgemuntert wird, sich in dem, was er gelernet, immer geschickter zu machen, so wird es wohl der Hoff seyn. Man suchet die Gnade derer Grossen, die Höfflichkeit derer Edlen, und die Liebe nebst der Hochachtung derer übrigen Bedienten zu erlangen, und läßt sich keine Mühe verdriessen, seinen Zweck zu erreichen, zumahl wenn man noch bey denen Jahren ist, die zu solchen Unternehmungen das benöhtigte Feuer haben.

> If there is anything in the world to encourage a person's spirit, to make him ever more skilful at what he has learned, then it is surely the court. One seeks to gain the grace of great lords, the courtesy of nobles, and the love and deep respect of other servants, sparing no effort to reach one's goal, especially when one is still young enough to have the necessary fire for such undertakings.[7]

Telemann's court appointments afforded him a number of valuable privileges and experiences.[8] While at Sorau, he famously encountered the Polish traditional music that would greatly enrich his compositional idiom.[9] His experience at tav-

---

[5] Mattheson, *Grundlage einer Ehren-Pforte*, 63.

[6] Ibid., 361. In these discussions, Telemann noted that he played the role of Democritus (known as the 'laughing philosopher') and Printz that of Heraclitus (the 'weeping philosopher'): the older composer 'beweinte bitterlich die Ausschweiffungen der itzigen melodischen Setzer; wie ich die unmelodischen Künsteleien der Alten belachte' (wailed bitterly about the melodic excesses of contemporary composers, while I laughed at the unmelodic artificiality of the old composers). Telemann added that Printz hoped his younger colleague 'würde aus dem Babel der ersten heraus gehen' (would be the first to depart Babel [that is, Sorau]).

[7] Georg Philipp Telemann, 'Lebens-Lauff mein Georg Philipp Telemanns: Entworffen In Frankfurth am Mayn d. 10.[–14.] Sept. A. 1718', in Johann Mattheson, *Grosse General-Baß-Schule, oder Der exemplarischen Organisten-Probe* (Hamburg, 1731; repr. Hildesheim: Georg Olms, 1968), 174.

[8] For Telemann's recollections of his years as a court musician, see ibid., 174–7, and Mattheson, *Grundlage einer Ehren-Pforte*, 360–63.

[9] See the discussion of Telemann and Polish music in Steven Zohn, *Music for a Mixed Taste: Style, Genre, and Meaning in Telemann's Instrumental Works* (Oxford and New York: Oxford University Press, 2008), chap. 9.

erns in the Polish countryside and at Cracow must have contrasted sharply with the presumably more stylized rustic music of Poles, Turks, and miners offered at the courts of Bayreuth, Dresden, Stuttgart, Weißenfels, and Zeitz by ensembles called 'Bock-Pfeiffer', 'Bockmusic', 'Janitscharen-Musicanten', 'Bergsänger', 'Berg Musicanten', and the like. Removed from its original context and perhaps played by court, rather than folk, musicians, such music was heard both indoors and outdoors, during hunts and meals, and as exotic entertainment during festivals. Johann Beer's encounter with 'Turkish' music in connection with a visit by King August II of Poland to Leipzig may be taken as typical. As the king dined at a house on the market square, he was entertained by a company of 150 janissaries, 'welche eine recht Barbarische Music auf kleinen Schallmeien, kupffernen Tellern, kleinen Pauken, und großen Trummeln bey sich führten' (who made a positively barbaric music on the small shawms, copper plates, small kettle drums, and large bass drums they wielded).[10]

At Sorau, Telemann also solidified his grasp of the French style while exploring instrumental genres more fully than before. He was apparently highly valued by the count, and he made a point of noting that 'Der Hof wurde zu zweienmahlen grossen Theils abgedanckt, und selbst Günstlinge wurden mit fortgerissen; ich aber blieb' (On two occasions the court was largely discharged, and even the favourites were swept away with it; I, however, remained).[11] This was no small achievement, for court musicians were not only regularly dismissed when a new ruler assumed power, but also when pressures brought on by wartime expenditures or careless handling of finances forced a 'downsizing' of personnel. While serving at the Eisenach court (1708–12), Telemann met and married his first wife, experienced a religious reawakening, wrote large quantities of vocal music (especially church cantatas), composed his first concertos, and took on a secondary position as court secretary, which allowed him to dine at the marshals' table (an honour also extended to him at Sorau). His secondary employment in a non-musical capacity was something he had in common with his brother-in-law Johann Michael Böhm (wind player and secretary at Stuttgart) and with many other musicians at smaller German courts.

Despite the many positive aspects of his positions at Sorau and Eisenach, by 1711 Telemann was already contemplating a career as a municipal musician, though not without a certain amount of trepidation:

> Aber wie gerathe ich zu denen HHnn. Republicanern? bey welchen, wie man glaubet, die Wissenschafften wenig gelten. . . . Ich vermeynte, es würde die an einer Reichs-Stadt zu hoffende Ruhe zur Verlängerung meines Lebens zuträglich seyn; Und, ob schon nicht bey allen Höfen eintrifft,
>
> > Qu'au matin l'air pour nous est tranquille & serein,
> > Mais sombre vers le soir & de nuages plein;

[10] Johann Beer, *Sein Leben, von Ihm Selbst Erzählt*, ed. Adolf Schmiedecke (Göttingen: Vandenhoeck & Ruprecht, 1965), 83 (entry of 7 October 1699).
[11] Mattheson, *Grundlage einer Ehren-Pforte*, 360.

Am allerwenigsten aber in Eisenach zu vermuthen war, so ließ mir doch endlich den Rath gefallen: Ich möchte die Wahrheit dieses Spruchs nicht in eigener Erfahrung erwarten.

But how did I find these republicans, among whom, it is said, the sciences count for little? . . . I considered the hoped-for calm of a[n Imperial] Free City conducive to the prolongation of my life; and although it is not true of all courts

      That for us the morning air is tranquil and serene,
      But sombre toward evening and filled with clouds,

least of all at Eisenach, I finally took the advice that I shouldn't look for the truth of this saying in my own experience.[12]

In his autobiography of 1740, Telemann also referred (more obliquely) to the instability of court life: 'Ich weiß nicht, was mich bewog, einen so auserlesenen Hof, als der eisenachische war, zu verlassen; das aber weiß ich, damahls gehört zu haben: Wer Zeit Lebens fest sitzen wolle, müsse sich in einer Republick niederlassen' (I don't know what induced me to leave such a choice court as the one at Eisenach; but I do know that I heard it said at the time: Whoever wishes to have lifelong security must settle in a republic).[13]

At Frankfurt, Telemann seems to have let down his guard about what it was that prompted his renunciation of court life. In his letter of application for the position of 'Directoris Musices', submitted sometime between 10 December 1711 and 9 February 1712, he stated cryptically that he had for various reasons decided 'das Hofleben zu Quittiren und in ein ruhigers zu begeben' (to quit court life and take up a quieter one). But much more revealing is an entry for 18 March 1712 in the private chronicle kept by Johann Georg Ochs, member of a prominent Frankfurt family. Ochs reported that Telemann accepted the Frankfurt post 'uneracht d[aß der] Hertzog Ihn ungern gelassen, ja von d[em] König in Pohlen 600 thl. Salarium versprochen, allein Er soll zu verstehen gegeben haben, bey Hoff würde mann zu starck mit genommen, die Herrn wären nicht alle Libhaber d[er] Music, und könte sonst leicht in ungenaden kommen' (despite the duke's reluctance to let him go and a promise from the king of Poland [Elector Friedrich August I of Saxony, also King August II of Poland] of a salary of 600 *Reichsthaler*, he gave me to understand that at court one is worked too hard, the masters are not all music lovers, and one can all too easily fall into disfavour).[14] Telemann's wishes to escape the demands of courtly employment, to find an audience more appreciative of his music, and to avoid the sort of courtly intrigues that might end up in dismissal must have been strong indeed, for he had turned down a lucrative position in the celebrated Dresden *Hofkapelle* to come to Frankfurt.

[12] Telemann, 'Lebens-Lauff', 177.
[13] Mattheson, *Grundlage einer Ehren-Pforte*, 363.
[14] Both documents are transcribed in Roman Fischer, *Frankfurter Telemann-Dokumente*, ed. Brit Reipsch and Wolf Hobohm, Magdeburger Telemann-Studien, 16 (Hildesheim: Georg Olms, 1999), 178, 197.

As the desire of both Christoph Graupner and Johann Sebastian Bach to leave courtly *Kapellmeister* positions for the job of 'Cantor zu St. Thomae et Director Musices' at Leipzig demonstrates, Telemann was not alone among court musicians in being attracted to a municipal career. In 1690, Johann Beer, who served at the Weißenfels court from 1676 until his death in 1700 (as concertmaster starting in 1685), reflected on four advantages cities have over courts in retaining good musicians. The first concerns stability and remuneration: because princely servants may be dismissed as a result of the smallest disruption,

> sehnen sich viel Fürstliche *Musici* nach denen Städten, würden auch, im Fall die Städte so starck als der Hof, bezahleten, sich dort bald einfinden. Denn was mag wol vortrefflicher in einer Sache seyn, als der Bestand? . . . Ich sage: Die beständige Armuth könne glückseeliger geheissen warden, als ein unbeständiger Reichsthum. . . . Es ist weit besser, keines Menschen Gunst jemals haben, als dieselbe ohne Bestand geniessen. Ist also dieses ein Haubt-*Principium*, warum die Städt gute *Musik*en halten könten. Wann sie nur kräfftig bezahleten.

> many court musicians yearn for the cities, and would go there immediately if the cities paid as well as the court. For what is more splendid in anything than constancy? . . . I say: constant poverty could be considered more blissful than fleeting riches. . . . It is far better never to enjoy patronage than to have it without constancy. This is one main reason why cities can retain good musicians. If only they paid well.[15]

Beer also criticized the restless nature of court life, the limited opportunities for professional advancement, and the lack of benefits for musicians' children:

> Heute muß man mit dem Hof da-, morgen dorthin. Tag und Nacht leiden da keinen Unterschied. Sturmwind, Regen und Sonnenschein, gilt da eines wie das andere. Heute muß man in die Kirche, morgen zu der Tafel, übermorgen aufs *Theatrum*. . . . Je *excellenter* er ist, je mehr wird er eben bey der *station*, darzu er einmal angenommen, zu bleiben genöthiget, und ihme alle Federn aus denen Flügeln gerupfft, damit er sich nicht höher aufschwingen möge. . . . Hat man in denen *Republiqu*en (welches ein grosses ist) vor seine Kinder *stipendia* zu hoffen, bey Hofe nicht, oder gar selten.

> Today one must go there with the court, tomorrow somewhere else. Day or night, heavy gale, rain, or sunshine, it makes no difference. Today one must be at church, tomorrow at the table, the day after in the theatre. . . . The more excellent [a musician] is, the more he will be obliged to remain at the same rank at which he was hired, all the feathers plucked from his wings so that

---

[15] Johann Beer, *Musicalische Discurse* (Nuremberg, 1719), 18. Edited in *Johann Beer: Sämtliche Werke*, XII/1, ed. Ferdinand van Ingen and Hans-Gert Roloff (Bern: Peter Lang, 2005), 305. In his autobiography (Beer, *Sein Leben*, 31), Beer recorded that he wrote the *Musicalische Discurse* in November 1690.

he cannot rise any higher. . . . One can hope for stipends for one's children in
republics (which is a great thing), but very seldom, if ever, at courts.[16]

Numerous entries in Beer's autobiography, conceived as part diary and part collection of anecdotes, bear witness to the hectic schedule of trips he took with the
court.[17] The issue of musicians' compensation surfaced again during Beer's dispute
over music's morality with the Gotha Fürstenschule (*Gymnasium illustre*) principal, Gottfried Vockerodt. Just as the squeaks of a cart are remedied with grease,
Beer observed, 'je mehr man die Hoff-*Capelle* bezahlt und schmiert, je mehr und
besser *musici*rt sie' (the more one pays and lubricates the *Hofkapelle,* the more and
better it performs).[18]

Elsewhere Beer is more sanguine about court life, as in his 1683 novel *Die
kurtzweiligen Sommer-Täge* (Summer Tales), where a comfortable meal at court is
contrasted with the inferior food and entertainment featured at the typical town
wedding.[19] In his autobiography, he proudly records the honour of sitting at his
master's table during such courtly repasts. On the other hand, an entry for 17 January 1698 wryly notes that Carnival characters are being painted on the walls of the
knight's room at the palace: 'Man darff die Narren nicht an die Wand mahlen, sie
kommen von sich selbsten wohl nach Hoff' (One needn't paint fools on the wall,
for they will surely come to court by themselves).[20] There is, moreover, a strongly
parodistic element in the portrayal of court musicians in Beer's first novel, *Der
Simplicianische Welt-Kucker, oder Abentheuerliche Jan Rebhu* (The Simplician Observer of the World, or The Adventurous Jan Rebhu). Towards the novel's beginning, the young soprano Jan Rebhu finds himself at a gathering of foreign court
musicians held at the *Kapellmeister*'s home. The group consists mostly of Italian
singers, but also present are unnamed stock types such as 'Der Frantzösische Vi-
oldegamist' (the French viola da gamba player) and 'Der teutsche Lautenist' (the
German lutenist). In the course of a long grievance session that begins with the musicians discussing their colleagues' talent, the highly compensated castrato Signor
Vitali casually observes that

> Ich lernete 20. Wochen singen, gab 20. Ducaten Lehr-geld, und gewinne biß
> auf diesen Tag damit schon in die Tausend Reichsthaler. Jene geben Hundert
> Thaler Lehrgeld, und gewinnen nicht Tausend Pfennig damit, dennoch bil-
> den sie sich ein , daß sie Magister *in omnibus* seyn, da doch die armen *alumni*
> über wenige Zeit sie alle überstiegen und die Narren dazu auslachen.

> I took twenty weeks of voice lessons, paid 20 ducats for them, and as a result
> have earned close to 1,000 *Reichsthaler* to date. Others pay 100 *Thaler* for les-
> sons and earn not even 1,000 *Pfennig* for it, yet fancy themselves as universal

---

[16]  Beer, *Musicalische Discurse*, 18–19; *Sämtliche Werke*, XII/1: 305–6.

[17]  Beer, *Sein Leben,* 21–94.

[18]  Johann Beer, *Ursus vulpinatur: List wieder List, oder Musicalische Fuchs-Jagd* (Weißenfels, 1698), 42. Edited in *Johann Beer: Sämtliche Werke*, XII/1: 70.

[19]  See Thomke, 'Musikerfiguren', 236; Rose, 'Musician-Novels', 184.

[20]  Beer, *Sein Leben,* 66.

masters, even though they are surpassed by the poor students in no time and laughed at by fools.[21]

The ridiculous ease with which this Italian settled into a lucrative career seems intended as a commentary on the often great disparities in pay between local and foreign musicians at German courts. Understandably, such disparities – along with the inevitable cultural and religious differences – could easily engender tension between colleagues, as was the case at the Bayreuth court, where a 'grosse Uneinigkeit' (great disagreement) arising between German musicians and three Italian castratos led Johann Philipp Krieger to seek his release from service around 1677.[22] Difficulties arose at the Württemberg-Stuttgart court when some of the French and Italian Catholic members of the *Hofkapelle* skipped Lutheran church services at which they were to perform, and a dispute between Reinhard Keiser and Giuseppe Antonio Brescianello over the vacant post of *Oberkapellmeister* during the period 1719–21 caused a rift between German and Italian musicians.[23] At the Dresden court, as at Darmstadt, Bayreuth, Berlin, Stuttgart, and Würzburg, most of the principal singers during the early eighteenth century were Italians. Increasing numbers of their countrymen in the orchestra and in positions of authority eventually led to considerable friction with the court's German concertmaster, Johann Georg Pisendel. In a 1749 letter to his good friend Telemann, Pisendel complained that Italians are by nature untrustworthy, malicious, false, cowardly, and self-interested, as witnessed by their dissembling and flattery: 'Die Prob seh ich hier alle Tag, u[nd] kan der Wind nicht so oft sich endern als deren ihre Freundschafft unter sich' (I see proof every day here, and the wind doesn't change as often as do [the Italians'] friendships amongst themselves).[24] In subsequent letters, the violinist criticized the new *Kapellmeister* Nicola Porpora (1686–1768) – 'viel Geschrey[,] wenig Wolle, er ist und thut hier gar nichts, und hat doch jährlich 1200 Thl. Besoldung' (all talk and no action; he is and does nothing at all here, and receives an annual salary of 1,200 *Reichsthaler*) – and related how he clashed with the Dresden *Oberkapellmeister* Johann Adolf Hasse, a German who had spent most of his career in Italy, and whom Pisendel derisively referred to as 'Herr Haß' (Mr Hatred), over Italian instrumentalists in the orchestra. When Pisendel asked Hasse not to hire any more such players because they lacked technical polish and good orchestral discipline, the *Oberkapellmeister* 'nahm es aber heimlich übel auf und verhezte wider mich fast alle Italiäner' (secretly took offence at this and turned almost all the Italians against me).[25]

---

[21] Johann Beer, *Der Simplicianische Welt-Kucker, oder Abentheuerliche Jan Rebhu* (Halle, 1677–9), 44. Edited in *Johann Beer: Sämtliche Werke*, 1, ed. Ferdinand van Ingen and Hans-Gert Roloff (Bern: Peter Lang, 1981), 32.

[22] Mattheson, *Grundlage einer Ehren-Pforte*, 151. See also Chapter 14, 'The Court of Brandenburg-Culmbach-Bayreuth', p. 392 above.

[23] See Chapter 6, 'The Court of Württemberg-Stuttgart', pp. 172–3 above.

[24] Georg Philipp Telemann, *Briefwechsel: Sämtliche erreichbare Briefe von und an Telemann*, ed. Hans Grosse and Hans Rudolf Jung (Leipzig: VEB Deutscher Verlag für Musik, 1972), 349, No. 117 (letter of 16 April 1749).

[25] Telemann, *Briefwechsel*, 355, No. 118 (undated letter of 1750); 361–2, No. 120 (letter of 3 June 1752).

One aspect of musical life at court that has received comparatively little attention before this volume is the use of supplementary musicians — whether drawn
from among the ranks of lackeys, valets, clerks, secretaries, *Hautboisten*, trumpeters, and other court employees; from local students and *Stadtpfeifer*; from
travelling musicians; or from other *Hofkapellen*. Related to this phenomenon is
the employment of musicians who could both play and sing or perform compe-
tently on several instruments. As is clear from the preceding chapters, all but the
largest *Hofkapellen* relied on supplementary musicians to varying degrees. An additional case in point is the Eisenach *Hofkapelle* under Telemann and Pantaleon
Hebenstreit, an ensemble that officially included a total of sixteen musicians. Yet
on Easter Sunday 1709, the *Kantor* Johann Conrad Geisthirt led a performance
that included twenty-three 'Chorschüler' (choral students) along with Telemann,
Hebenstreit, Johann Friedrich Helbig, Johann Christian Koch, six trumpeters
and drummers, six *Hautboisten*, and seven *Stadtpfeifer*.[26] Johann Joachim Quantz
recalled that as an apprentice *Kunstpfeifer* between August 1708 and December
1713, he was hired to supplement the Merseburg *Hofkapelle* during church services
and for *Tafelmusik*, an experience made all the more valuable because musicians
from other courts were often present as well.[27] But the widespread practice of hiring amateur, municipal, and itinerant musicians at court was decried by Johann
Mattheson and presumably many others as well.[28] Surely the talents of many 'extra'
court musicians would have left much to be desired — in contrast to the 18-year-old
Bach, who as a lackey-musician at the Weimar court of Duke Johann Ernst in 1703,
must have been as skilled as servants with the more impressive titles of *Hofmusicus*
and *Cammermusicus*.

To judge from extant lists of court musicians, many of which are summarized in
the tables found throughout this volume, the use of musicians capable of performing on a variety of instruments or singing at German courts seems to have peaked
during the first quarter of the eighteenth century. Thus Johann Christoph Pez could
observe in 1714 that instrumentalists at the Württemberg-Stuttgart court were all
proficient on three to five different instruments.[29] Upon being hired at Eisenach in
1708, Telemann both performed on violin and sang solo church cantatas. He was
soon asked to reorganize the *Hofkapelle* by hiring additional singers who could also
play the violin; yet his subsequent promotion to the position of *Kapellmeister* did
not release him from his previous duties.[30] Quantz's early experiences were in many
respects typical of such court musicians. During his apprenticeship, he specialized
on the violin, oboe, and trumpet, but also learned the cornetto, trombone, hunting

[26] Claus Oefner, *Telemann in Eisenach: Die Eisenacher Musikpflege im frühen 18. Jahrhundert* (Eisenach: Kreiskommission zur Erforschung der Geschichte, 1980), 12, 48.

[27] Johann Joachim Quantz, 'Herrn Johann Joachim Quantzens Lebenslauf, von ihm selbst
entworfen', in Friedrich Wilhelm Marpurg, *Historisch-kritische Beyträge zur Aufnahme der
Musik*, 5 vols. (Berlin, 1754–78), I, 'Drittes Stück' (1755), 201.

[28] For Mattheson's denunciation of such practices, see Chapter 1, 'An Introduction to German *Hofkapellen*', p. 4 above.

[29] See Chapter 6, 'The Court of Württemberg-Stuttgart', p. 168 above.

[30] Mattheson, *Grundlage einer Ehren-Pforte*, 361.

horn, recorder, bassoon, German bass violin, cello, viola da gamba, 'und wer weis wie vielerley noch mehr, auf welchen allein ein rechter *Kunstpfeifer* muß spielen können, blieb ich auch nicht verschonet. Es ist wahr, daß man wegen der Menge so verschiedener Instrumente, welche man unter die Hände bekömmt, auf jedem insbesondere ein Stümper bleibt' (and who knows how many more, all of which the real *Kunstpfeifer* must be able to play. It is true that because of the great variety of instruments that come into one's hands, one remains a bungler on each one in particular).[31] When Quantz joined the Polish *Kapelle* of King August II in 1718, he switched from his principal instrument, the violin, to the oboe:

> Auf beyden Instrumenten aber, wurde ich, durch meine Cameraden, welche länger in Diensten waren, gehindert, mich hervor zu thun: welches mir doch sehr am Herzen lag. Der Verdruß hierüber veranlassete mich, die Flöte traversiere, worauf ich mich bishero für mich selbst geübet hatte, mit Ernst zur Hand zu nehmen. . . . Ich bediente mich, etwan vier Monate lang, der Unterweisung des berühmten Flötenspielers Buffardin; um die rechte Eigenschaften dieses Instruments kennen zu lernen.

> However, I was prevented by my colleagues, who had been in service longer, from excelling on either instrument, which I very much wanted to do. My chagrin over this caused me to take up seriously the transverse flute, which until then I had practised only for my own pleasure. . . . For about four months I took instruction from the famous flautist Buffardin in order to learn the peculiarities of this instrument.[32]

Given his success at Dresden, one suspects that Quantz was either reasonably proficient on the flute by 1718, or that his formal studies with Buffardin lasted more than four months. In any case, he was far from unique in being required to learn a new instrument upon joining a *Hofkapelle*. At Gotha, for example, the *Kapellknabe* and vocalist Gottfried Diestel was ordered to learn the lute in 1743, and in 1747 Georg Christoph Stubenrauch stated that he was willing to learn how to play the violin, flute, and oboe when applying for an *Hautboist* position at the court.[33]

The pervasive use of multi-talented musicians at German courts was satirized by Johann Kuhnau in his 1700 novel, *Der musicalische Quack-Salber* (The Musical Charlatan). Halfway through his misadventures, Caraffa, an incompetent German musician posing as an Italian virtuoso, attempts to impress noble patrons through his versatility as an instrumentalist:

> Damit er sich nun in der Music bey dem Edelmanne und der Dame immer mehr *Gloire* erwerben möchte, so ließ er sich bey einer jeden Gasterey mit einem andern *Instrumente* hören: Einmahl geigte er auff der *Violino*, das andermahl auff der *Viola da Gamba*, das dritte gar auff der Baß-Geige, und

---

[31] Quantz, 'Lebenslauf', 200. Trans. in Paul Nettl, *Forgotten Musicians* (New York: Greenwood Press, 1969), 282.

[32] Quantz, 'Lebenslauf', 209. Trans. adapted from Nettl, *Forgotten Musicians*, 289.

[33] See Chapter 7, 'The Court of Saxony-Gotha-Altenburg', p. 209 above.

sange drein: Bald nahm er die Laute, bald die *Angelique*, bald die *Chitarre*, bald die Harffe, bald das *Clavier*, und was nur etwa vor *Instrumente* zu bekommen und zu borgen waren, (denn er hatte nichts mehr, wie oben gedacht worden, als eine *Chitarre* bey sich.). . . . Daß er aber auff iedweden was machen konte, solches war um so viel weniger zu verwundern, weil er doch die ersten *Elementa* von der Composition verstande. . . . Allein, wen man eines, es sey auch das geringste, mit guter *Manier* und *en Maître tractiren* soll, dazu gehöret fast eines Mannes Alter, und ein tägliches *Studium*. Ja es wird manchmahl eine geringe *Subtilität* und *Manier* an *Accentuationibus* und andern schlechten Dingen, welche der Zuhörer fast nicht mercket, öffters kaum in 1. 2. Biß 3. Jahren recht erlernet, wie es denn in allen Künsten und Wissenschafften, zum Exempel in der Mahlerey und Bildhauer-Kunst, also herzugehen pfleget. Drum konte auch freylich unser *Caraffa* auff keinem *Instrumente*, wegen der Vielheit derselben, den Nahmen eines *Virtuosen* verdienen.

Because he wanted to win more glory in music from the nobleman and the lady, he performed on a different instrument at each festivity. Once he fiddled on the violin, the next time on the viola da gamba, the third even on the bass violin while he sang along. Now he took up the lute, now the angélique [a two-headed lute], now the guitar, now the harp, now the keyboard, and whatever instruments could be located and borrowed (for, as was said, he had only his guitar with him). . . . That he could do something on each of them, however, was all the less astonishing because he did know the basic elements of composition. . . . But if a person is to play one, even the most insignificant, with good ornaments and masterfully, that requires almost a generation and daily study. Indeed, sometimes a slight subtlety, ornament, accentuation, and other minor things the listener scarcely notices can hardly be learned in one to three years, as tends to be the case in all arts and sciences, for example, in painting and sculpture. Therefore, to be sure, our Caraffa could deserve to be called a virtuoso on no instrument because there were so many of them.[34]

Encouraged by receiving a ducat each time he performed on a new instrument, Caraffa subsequently goes so far as to hire an organ-grinder, bagpiper, and horn player to provide serenades that he subsequently claims to have played himself. He may be a true bungler (to quote Quantz) on every instrument he touches, but he knows that at court a jack-of-all-trades may be more highly prized than a virtuoso specializing on a single instrument. And like many real-life musicians of the time, Caraffa manages, for the moment at least, to take advantage of the professional

---

[34] Johann Kuhnau, *Der musicalische Quack-Salber* (Dresden, 1700), 249–52. Edited as *Der Musicalische Quack-Salber von Johann Kuhnau (1700),* ed. Kurt Benndorf (Berlin: B. Behr's Verlag (E. Bock), 1900), 120–21. Trans. adapted from John R. Russell, *The Musical Charlatan* (Columbus, S.C.: Camden House, 1997), 76. See also Nos. 30–34 of the sixty-four maxims entitled 'Der wahre *Virtuose* und glückselige *Musicus*' (The True Virtuoso and Happy Musician) in the novel's penultimate chapter.

opportunities offered by court employment while embodying the foremost courtly virtue of dissembling.

The picture of court life that emerges from this admittedly small sample of first-person accounts, philosophical reflections, and satirical commentaries is of an environment that, under the best circumstances, offered young musicians the opportunity to develop their talents and realize their professional ambitions in relatively comfortable surroundings; by doing and saying the right things, one might quickly climb the ladder of success. Yet, all too often, membership in a *Hofkapelle* came at the price of inadequate pay for demanding work, complex and potentially treacherous social codes, lean periods brought on by financial or artistic retrenchment, and employers with little understanding or appreciation of music. Additionally, one's professional advancement could be stalled by an overly rigid hierarchy or derailed through the politics of envy. Certainly there was much to find fault with in the culture of eighteenth-century German *Hofkapellen*. But when assessing the critical views of Beer, Pisendel, Printz, Telemann, and others, we must not forget that such institutions nurtured their artistic gifts in ways that were scarcely possible elsewhere at the time.

# Index

Page numbers in *italic* type refer to tables and their endnotes. *Cf.* indicates that two names may refer to a single individual, but this is not certain.

Christian Ludwig, margrave of Brandenburg-
    Schwedt (*cont.*):
    *Hofkapelle* of  81, 88, 108–9, *129–30*
Christian Wilhelm I, prince of Schwarzburg-
    Sondershausen  291, 296, *300*
Christiana of Schleswig-Holstein-
    Sonderburg-Glücksburg, duchess
    of Saxony-Merseburg  236, 238
Christiane Eberhardine of Brandenburg-
    Bayreuth, electress of Saxony and
    queen of Poland  261, 397
Christiani (instrumentalist)  84, 88, *119, 125
    n. b*
Christiani, Georg Gustav  88
Christine of Baden-Durlach, duchess of
    Saxony-Gotha-Altenburg  199
Christlieb, Franz Adolph  21, *44, 45,* 72
Christoph Franz von Hutten, prince-bishop
    of Würzburg  311
church music; *see* sacred music
churches and chapels:
    cathedrals  81, *116,* 227, 237, 239, 241,
        310–11, 381
    civic  *183,* 273, 273 n. 89, 288, 298, 321,
        349, 390, 406
    court  3, 232
        Anhalt-Zerbst  261, 262, 264, 272,
            278, *285*
        Brandenburg-Prussia  82, 95
        Hesse-Darmstadt  340
        the Palatinate  134, 146, 146 n. 64
        Saxony-Dresden  20–23 *passim,* 25,
            26, 31, 34, 36, 37, 37 n. 108, 105
        Saxony-Gotha-Altenburg  197
        Saxony-Weißenfels  228
        Saxony-Zeitz  243
        Sondershausen  288, 289
        Warsaw  72
        Württemberg-Stuttgart  *193*
churching of women, music for  34
civic musicians  178, 198, 229, 240, 260, 275,
        307, 389, 390, 417, 419
    apprentice  422–3
    *Kunstpfeifer*  4, 4 n. 11, 58, 423
    *Stadtpfeifer*  236, 239, 263, 282, 422
    tower musicians  272, *326, 361*
Clam-Gallas, Count Christian Philipp von
    212
clarinets  211, 353
clarinettists, at the court of:
    Hesse-Darmstadt  *358*
    the Palatinate  135, 137, 139, 151 n. 86, *158*
    Saxony-Dresden  139 n. 35

Saxony-Merseburg  24
Württemberg-Stuttgart  139 n. 35, 167,
        *186, 193*
Würzburg  319, 320 n. 53, *326*
clarino; *see under* trumpeters
Clausius, David  264 n. 30, *283*
clavichords  340
Clemens August I of Bavaria, coadjutor
        archbishop of Cologne and prince-
        bishop of Münster  *161*
Clemens Franz, duke of Bavaria  133
Cleves  154
Clezenne (costume maker)  *125*
*Cloco*  392 n. 12
Cobb Biermann, Joanna  348
Coburg, court of  229, 390
colascione  56
Coler, Martin  391
collegia musica  247, 265, 290, 337
Collegium Germanicum  309, 312
Collizzi, Agatha  *123, 126 n. l*
Cologne  154
    cathedral of  381
Cologne, electoral-archbishopric of:
    court of (Bonn)  136
    *Hofkapelle* of  5–8
Colombazzo, Vittorino  404
Coltrolini, Giovanni Antonio  152 n. 89
Comati; *see* Camal
*comédie-ballet*  58
Comédie Française  23
Comédie Italienne  23
*comédie-lyrique*  58
comedies; *see under* plays
*comici italiani*  52, 55–62 *passim,* 65, 66, 68
*commedia dell'arte*  23, 55, 65, 68, 73
commemorations, music for  228, 278
Commerell, Adam Friedrich  *188*
*componimenti per musica*  65 n. 66, *161*
composers, official court  109, 395 n. 22
    at the court of:
        Baden-Durlach  372, *382, 386*
        Brandenburg-Culmbach-Bayreuth  85,
            406
        Brandenburg-Prussia  11, 94, 100, *118,
            119*
        Saxony-Dresden  11, 19, 25, 33, *38, 41–3
            passim, 45, 48 n. b, 49 n. f,* 60, 65–6
        Saxony-Weißenfels  234
        Saxony-Zeitz  247
        Würzburg  *327*
    ballet  *42, 49 n. f,* 66, 101
    chamber  *38, 41, 45, 48 n. b, 118*

'moors' *194 n. k*, 392
Moranti, Dominico Amadeo *383*
Morasch, Carl 34, *44, 45*, 61, 63, 64, 75
Mordaxt, Baron Johann Siegmund von *41*
Morgenstern, Johann Gottlieb 34, *42, 43*
Mori, Alessandro *159*
Moritz, duke of Saxony-Zeitz 223, 236, 242, *250*
Moritz, Jacob *115*
Moritz, Johann George *115*
Moritz, Johann Jacob *115*
Moritz Wilhelm, duke of Saxony-Merseburg 239, 241, 242, *250*
Moritz Wilhelm, duke of Saxony-Zeitz 242, 246, 247, *250*, 366 n. 6
Moritzburg, Schloß (near Dresden) 22, 57, 58
Moritzburg, Schloß (Zeitz) 242, 247
Morus, Gottfried Wilhelm *409*
Morzin, Count Wenzel 265
Moscow 32, 62, 296 n. 41
motets 26, 26 n. 46, 144, 244, 245, 315; *see also* sacred concertos
Mouchy, Louise de (née Dimanche) 60
mourning, music during periods of 260
Mozart, Leopold 140, 181
Mozart, Wolfgang Amadeus 140, 182
Muffat, Friedrich *156*
Mühlhausen 202
Müller, Adolf 342 n. 42
Müller, George Elias 74
Müller, Johann *285*
Müller, Johann Georg 76
Müller, Johann Philipp *383*
Mulley (instrumentalist) 101
Munich 33, 154, 155, 166, 167, 172, 306, 318, 322 n. 61; *see also* court of *under* Bavaria, electorate of
Münter, Balthasar: *Cantaten über die Sonn- und Festtäglichen Evangelia* 213 n. 71
musettes and musette players 353, *358*
music:
    acquisition of 390
        by exchange 11, 12, 18, 85, 101, 176, 248, 266–7, 271
        by the nobility while abroad 367, 367 n. 8, 377
        reimbursement for shipping costs for 266
        through purchase 11, 35, 57, 263 n. 25, 274
    disputes regarding ownership of 333 n. 2
    dissemination of beyond court 11, 91

musicians accused of stealing 347
    reworked by other composers 19, 36–7, *49 n. b*, 213
    stationery for, supply of 57
music collections:
    court 11 n. 40, 18, 31, 34, 51, 80, 109, 176, 176 n. 50, 266, 287
    destruction of 148
    inventories of 11, 18, 18 n. 4, 34, 35, 35 n. 95, 37 n. 108, 60, 99, 147 n. 67, 176, 232, 241, 269–70, 272, 277, 315, 367, 375, 380, 396
    nationalities represented in 315
    of court musicians 11–12, 27, 35, 347
music lessons; *see* musical education
music stands 109, 263 n. 24
music theory 59
musical education:
    court musicians providing music lessons 5, 19, 86 n. 25, 81, 91, 94, 98, 103–4, 107, 139, 151, 179, 240, 261, 263, 268, 274, 274 n. 93, 295, 307, 308, 322, *326*, 340, 344, 348, 352, 371, 393
    for court musicians:
        ongoing professional training 12, 26, 63, 141, 210, 269, 277, 310, 322
        prior to appointment 238, 243, 272, 274, 274 n. 93, 422–3
        sent away to study 27, 88, 166, 292, 310, 314, 318, 322, 335, 338, 398
        *see also under specific types of musicians*
    for members of the nobility 79, 81, 83, 90, 104, *117 n. b*, 134, 167, 176, 179, 238, 262, 275, 334, 352, 352 n. 87, 376 n. 49, 399
    for other court employees 313
    for school pupils and orphans 289, 307, 321
    payment for tuition 5, 103, 106, 141 n. 44, 151, 210 n. 62, 261, 322 n. 59, 348, 420
    tuition in composition 20, 104, 167, 176, 243, 265, 266, 269, 295, 322 n. 58, 334, 340, 352
Mylius, Wolfgang Michael 199–202 *passim*, 205
    *Rudimenta musices* 202

Naffziger, Johann Rudolff *115*
name days, music to celebrate 7, 35, 57, 65, 66, 133, 138, 145–7 *passim*, *161*, 173, 174, 228, 395